DAY-BY-DAY TRIVIA ALMANAC

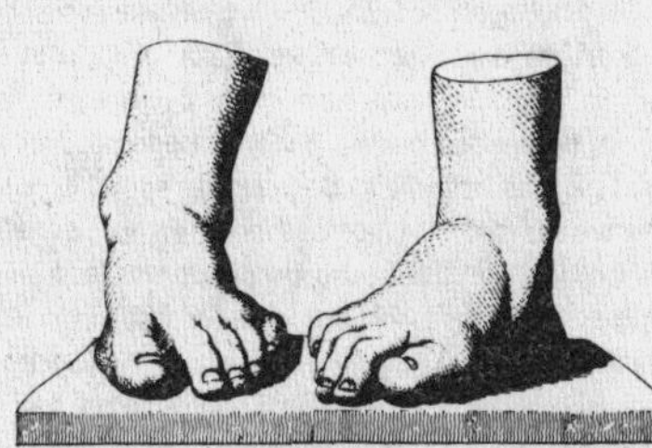

BY GUS McLEAVY

BELL PUBLISHING COMPANY
New York

For Laura,
and, of course, for Mom,
and for Stillman Hobbs and Burtis Vaughan,
two teachers who mattered,
and for all the wonderful people I've met along the way,
especially those at the libraries of Swarthmore and Bowdoin Colleges, without whose willingness to suffer a fool gladly, this would never have been completed; and with special thanks to Susan Milius and Martin Natvig; and last, but by no means least, to my editors, Judy Hendra and Cornelia Guest, and to Harry Chester and his associates.

A Disclaimer

The famous American journalist H.L. Mencken was unhappy with the war-related material for his column during the Christmas holidays of 1917, and so he decided to make up something more in keeping with the spirit of the season. He chose a fictitious, tongue-in-cheek piece on the history of the bathtub in America, which was originally published in the *New York Evening Mail* on December 28, and has since become the most tenacious fabrication-as-fact story in United States publishing history.

According to Mencken, the first bathtub in this country was displayed by Adam Thompson in Cincinnati, on December 10, 1842. Supposedly, Thompson had been inspired by the Englishman Lord John Russell's lead-lined mahogany cabinet for bathing, and felt this appliance would indeed be a boon to mankind. He introduced his version at a stag party — to the great enjoyment of his guests who spent all night trying it out.

As the bathtub spread, Mencken continued, it encountered opposition from all over the country. Physicians claimed it would become a menace to public health, Virginia imposed a $30-per-tub tax, and it was indeed completely banned in Boston. It wasn't until Millard Fillmore took the first presidential bath ten years later that the bathtub began to gain any acceptance whatsoever.

What Mencken had intended as a humorous story quickly spread and was treated totally as fact. He was amused for a time to see his brainchild celebrated so widely, but the situation eventually got out of hand. In a column he wrote for the *Boston Herald* in 1926, entitled, "The American Public Will Swallow Anything," he recounted how a little "harmless fun in war days" had in less than a decade been accepted as legitimate fact. The story of the bathtub had reached the floor of Congress, had traveled to Europe, and had even been included in a number of reference books. It was time to stop all this, he said, and he was hoping to do just that with the column.

Three weeks later, the *Herald* itself reprinted Mencken's original column on the bathtub as straight, factual news.

Despite Mencken's refutation, over fifty reprints of the journalist's "history" appeared in major American newspapers and magazines in the next twelve years. Even today it shows up annually in publications that really should know better.

So don't believe everything you read, especially not here. No doubt somewhere I have been bathtubbed myself, and I'm not above tubbing you.

Gracious acknowledgment is given for permission to reprint the following:

Excerpt from *The Book of Strange Facts and Useless Information* by Scot Morris. Copyright © 1979 by Scot Morris. Reprinted by permission of Doubleday & Company, Inc.

Maps reprinted courtesy of the American Automobile Association. Copyright © AAA—Reprinted by Permission.

Roger Williams' photograph reprinted by permission of *The Providence Journal-Bulletin.*

Quote and list of Geoffrey Handley-Taylor from *The Annotated® Mother Goose.* Copyright © 1962 by William S. Baring-Gould and Ceil. Baring-Gould, Bramhall Books, New York. Reprinted through the kindness of Clarkson N. Potter, Inc.

Excerpts reproduced by permission of the American Folklore Society from *Urban Folklore from the Paperwork Empire,* American Folklore Society Memoir Series, Volume 62, pp. 54, 55, 70, 71, 72, 84, 85, 140 and 141. Copyright © 1975 by the American Folklore Society.

Riddles from *1,800 Riddles, Enigmas and Conundrums* by Darwin A. Hindman. Copyright © 1963 by Darwin A. Hindman. Reprinted by permission of Dover Publications, Inc.

Designed by Harry Chester Associates

This 1985 edition is published by Bell Publishing Company, distributed by Crown Publishers, Inc. by arrangement with Frederick Fell Publishers, Inc.

Manufactured in the United States of America

Library of Congress Cataloging in Publication Data
Main entry under title:

Day-by-day trivia almanac.

1. Curiosities and wonders. I. Bell Publishing Company.
AG243.D39 1985 031'.02 84-24596
ISBN: 0-517-467879

h g f e d c b a

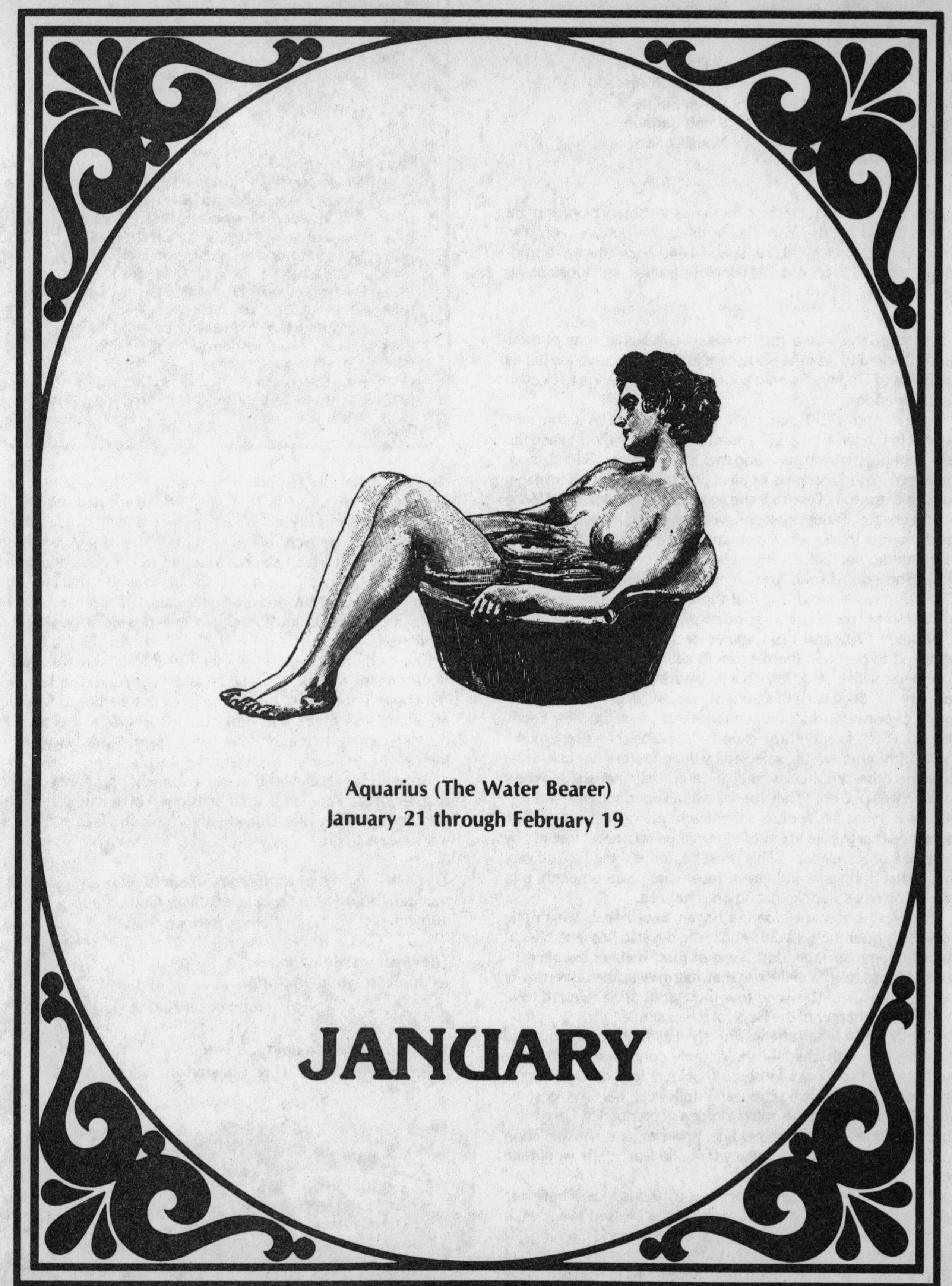

Aquarius (The Water Bearer)
January 21 through February 19

JANUARY

JANUARY 1

Question: By what names are these people better known?

Walter Palanuik
Dorothy Rothschild
Lester Polfus
Sarah Cannon
Maria Cartas

Notable Births

1449	Lorenzo de Medici	1879	William Fox
1730	Edmund Burke	1889	Charles Bickford
1735	Paul Revere	1895	J. Edgar Hoover
1745	Mad Anthony Wayne	1900	Xavier Cugat
1752	Betsy Ross	1909	Barry Goldwater
1864	Edmund Rostand	1909	Dana Andrews
1879	E.M. Forster	1919	J.D. Salinger

Notable Events

1353	An earthquake in Modina killed 2,000 people
1776	Norfolk, Virginia, burned by Lord Dunmore
1801	First asteroid discovered by Piazzi (Ceres)
1801	Union of Great Britain and Ireland official
1808	Slave trade abolished in United States
1821	First Bachelor's Tax in effect in Missouri
1837	Earthquake in Syria claimed at least 3,500 victims
1863	Emancipation Proclamation effective
1901	Commonwealth of Australia formed
1939	First flea laboratory opened in California
1941	ASCAP strike kept most music off radio
1959	Fidel Castro assumed power in Cuba
1975	Haldeman, Ehrlichman, and Dean found guilty on Watergate charges

Otis Thompson holds the dubious distinction of being the first man arrested in New York City in three consecutive years. On New Year's Day in 1938, 1939, and 1940 respectively, Thompson was pulled in for assault, felonious assault, and for stabbing his wife.

⚜

Although she was a most unlikely cult leader, tens of thousands flocked to Joanna Southcote in the 1790s, revering her as the Bride of God who would vouchsafe their passage to Heaven at Armageddon.

Born in April 1750, Joanna Southcote worked as a domestic servant in Exeter, England. Around the year 1790, she joined the new Methodist movement, and met a man named Saunderson, for whom Methodism was a cult of prophecy. Under his tutelage, Joanna came to believe that she was the woman described in the twelfth chapter of the Book of Revelation ("And there appeared a great wonder in Heaven, a woman clothed with the sun, and the moon under her feet, and upon her head a crown of twelve stars . . ."). She soon broke from Methodism, announced that the Millenium was at hand, and that she would save all the souls she could. Her personal cult was underway.

Between 1792 and 1794, she wrote down prophecies as they occurred to her, had them carefully sealed and stored away in envelopes, with instructions that they were not to be opened until January 1, 1803. With this aura of mystery, Joanna drew thousands of converts during the intervening years. On New Year's Day, in 1803, twenty-three experts "appointed by divine command" (in other words, selected by Joanna from her followers) examined the prophecies and declared that, indeed, Joanna's "calling was of God." That Joanna was illiterate and her "writing" merely a series of illegible scribbles made no difference. She explained that the illegibility of her writings was in fact foretold by the Book of Revelation: "This must be, to fulfill the Bible. Every vision that John saw in heaven must take place on earth; and here is the sealed book, that no one can read."

Later in the decade, Joanna began to sell seals which she personally guaranteed would entitle the buyer to heavenly bliss at the imminent Armageddon. Tens of thousands of people purchased these tokens, believing that Joanna was the dispenser of the "hundred and forty and four thousand" seals referred to in the seventh chapter of the Book of Revelations.

In early 1814, when she was nearly sixty-four, she announced that she was with child — the divinely conceived Shiloh. She predicted the baby would be born at midnight on October 19 that year. Her hundred-thousand followers became ecstatic when she developed the outward signs of pregnancy. Carrying a child was no easy thing at her age, however, and she was soon confined to bed, in such misery that she feared she would die before coming to term.

She didn't. On the night of October 18, thousands of believers gathered outside her quarters to await the blessed event. Midnight came and went with no signal of the Second Coming. By late afternoon it was necessary to dispense the restless crowd through the false information that Joanna was in a trance. Days passed, and still there was no child. By now Joanna's physical condition had improved, but she was angered by the non-delivery of her divine child. For a time she felt she had been deceived by an evil spirit. Then she decided she had misread the heavenly message. She realized she would first have to die and her soul go to Heaven, where God would make her conception legitimate, after which she could return to her body and deliver the Shiloh. With this in mind, she proclaimed that her body should be kept warm for four days after her death so that her reoccupation of it, and the child's eventual delivery, would be facilitated.

She died on December 27. Her instructions were duly carried out for nearly a week by her lieutenants. They cared for her body, but she did not return. Finally the body putrified beyond endurance and was made ready for burial. Joanna's movement disbanded rapidly thereafter except for a few stalwarts who kept the faith alive into the mid-nineteenth century.

An autopsy disclosed that her corpulant pregnancy was the result of flatulance and bile, occasioned by a slothlike lifestyle and an unhealthy diet. But when you're a cult leader, there are worse ways to go.

There are scores of thousands of sects who are ready at a moment's notice to reveal the will of God on every possible subject. George Bernard Shaw

The best qualification of a prophet is to have a good memory.
Marquis of Halifax

If a thing is worth doing, it is worth doing badly. G.K. Chesterton

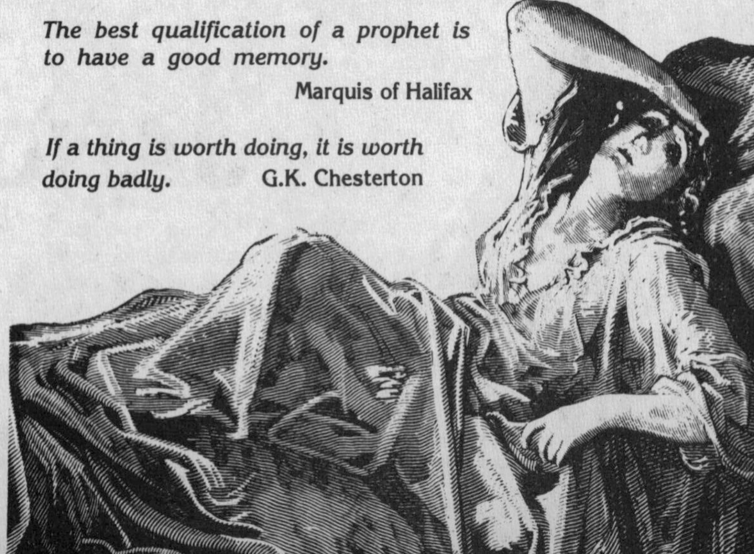

Answer: Jack Palance, Dorothy Parker, Les Paul, Minnie Pearl, Isabel Peron.

JANUARY 2

Notable Births

1727	General James Wolfe	1894	Robert Nathan
1752	Philip Freneau	1920	Isaac Asimov
1877	George Chappell	1930	Julius La Rosa

Notable Events

1602	Spaniards surrendered at Kinsdale
1716	King James III went to Scotland
1757	Lord Clive took Calcutta
1776	First flag of Continental Army hoisted
1777	First U.S. Army officer killed in action
1788	Georgia ratified Constitution
1921	First religious radio broadcast made, Pittsburgh
1931	Eight U.S. Marines killed in Nicaragua ambush
1935	Lindbergh baby trial opened
1942	Allies agreed to no separate peaces
1946	King Zog of Albania deposed

On this date in 1872, the seventy-one-year-old leader of the Mormon Church, Brigham Young, was arrested by Federal officials on a charge of bigamy, or polygamy or something — he then had twenty-five wives.

It is as absurd to say that a man can't love one woman all the time as it is to say a violinist needs several violins to play the same piece of music.

Honoré de Balzac

During the American Revolution the white population of the United States was about two-and-a-half million people: half a million of them sided with the British, twenty thousand fought for the British, and sixty thousand fled to Canada or back to Europe. At the beginning of the conflict, fewer than twenty-five thousand people had heard of George Washington or were in favor of the war.

The best way to win an argument is to begin by being right.

Jill Ruckleshaus

All the historical books that contain no lies are extremely tedious. Anatole France

Question: These are the nicknames of some U.S. states. What are the real names?
Heart of Dixie
First State, Diamond State
Land of Lincoln, Inland Empire State
Sunflower State

Praying mantises are among the most ferocious of all insects. They'll eat anything they can capture, and have been known to devour bees, garter snakes, mice, and hummingbirds. In season, a male mantis gets in a terrible quandary. He wants to mate, but something tells him he'll regret it if he does. The sex urge usually propels him into the proximity of a female, after which she solves the problem for him: she bites his head off. His body then mounts her, and intercourse begins. The act can sometimes last six hours, the female lazily nibbling on her mate . . . who ends up as just an appendage of twitching nerves. A female has been known to mate with and consume seven males in a session, whether her eggs need fertilization or not.

Radio-control — body perform work while brain detached.

Charlie Chan

It is not true that life is one damn thing after another — it's one damn thing over and over.

Edna St. Vincent Millay

Raghunat Singh wanted to break his father's record of heading the Indian state of Jargawan for seventy-five years, but in 1850 he was killed on the battlefield, aged ninety-two, after ruling for only seventy-two years.

The word "alligator" comes from the Spanish *el ligarto*, meaning "the lizard," the name given to these creatures by the early Spanish explorers. Coincidentally, the English word "crocodile" derives from the Greek *krokodeilos*, the name given by the ancient Greeks to the beasts they discovered when they first visited Egypt. It also means "the lizard."

Indian crocodiles usually take a bite out of their victim's bum before they attack.

In January 1950, during a recess in the French Senate, Victor Biaka-Boda, the representative of the Ivory Coast to that legislative body, toured the rural areas of his country to find out the natives' concerns. Food, apparently, was one of them. His constituents ate him.

Is it progress if a cannibal uses a knife and fork?

Stanislaus Lec

Answer: Alabama, Delaware, Illinois, Kansas.

JANUARY 3

Question: What is it that by losing an eye has nothing left but a nose?

On January 3, 1947, a handyman named Al Herrin died in a shack near Trenton, New Jersey, at the age of ninety-two. One curious aspect of Herrin's little home was that it contained no bed. This was hardly surprising, as Herrin had never, he said, slept a wink in his entire life. A team of doctors documented that he did go for several months without sleeping, and agreed that if he went that long, then indeed he could have been awake his whole life.

Men who are unhappy, like men who sleep badly, are always proud of the fact.

Bertrand Russell

Back in 1852, an Englishman named Simpson and a French couple named Poitevin were found innocent of cruelty to a horse because of conflicting evidence presented at their trial. It seems that the cruelty charge stemmed from their having given a horse a balloon flight.

They were not chastised by this close call, however. The three balloonists were convicted on a similar charge later that year when they ascended with a cow bearing Madame Poitevin as Europa on her back.

Gary Cooper gave a great performance in *Pride of the Yankees*, you might remember, even though Cooper was right-handed and Gehrig was in reality a southpaw. The actor's facility as a batter and fielder was the result of a brainstorm on the part of

the film director. He reversed the logos and numbers on the Iron Horse's uniform; and shot him at third base instead of first, batting right instead of left, and running from home to third. When the film was edited, these scenes were simply spliced in backward.

Notable Births

107 B.C.	Cicero	1898	Zasu Pitts
1797	Lucretia Mott	1903	Ray Milland
1803	Douglas Jerrold	1907	Anna May Wong
1841	Father Damien	1909	Victor Borge
1879	Mrs. Calvin Coolidge	1916	Betty Furness
1883	Clement Attlee	1918	Maxine Andrews
1892	J.R.R. Tolkien	1939	Bobby Hull

Notable Events

1777	Battle of Princeton fought
1871	Oleomargarine patented by H.W. Bradley
1921	United States bought its first leper hospital, Carville, Louisiana
1940	FDR asked Congress for wartime powers
1944	FDR gave Hyde Park home to nation
1946	William Joyce, "Lord Haw-Haw," pro-Nazi broadcaster, hanged for treason
1955	Panamanian President Remon assasinated at race track
1961	United States severed relations with Cuba
1961	Three killed in Idaho Falls nuclear plant explosion
1964	Goldwater announced his presidential candidacy
1967	Jack Ruby died

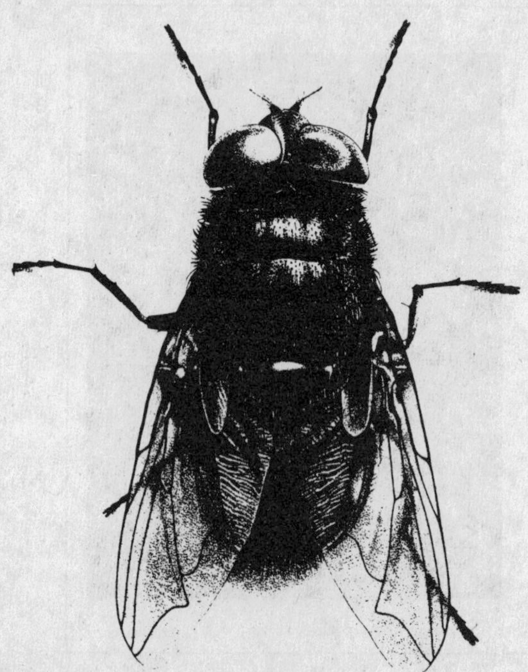

Aphids are one thing (see June 2), flies are another. If a pair of flies were able to breed unmolested, its progeny at the end of one summer season would total about 335 trillion new flies. Piled on top of one another, those flies would manage to cover a country the size of West Germany to a depth of about forty-seven feet.

Certain porpoises have been trained to throw a football in excess of sixty feet. That's not such a big deal, except that they throw perfect spirals.

A contemporary criticism of Charles II was that he encouraged his many spaniel bitches to give birth to and nurse their litters in his bedroom. After a time it became practically uninhabitable by anyone not accustomed to the smell.

Answer: A noise.

JANUARY 4

Notable Births

1580	Archbishop James Ussher	1920	William Colby
1643	Isaac Newton	1927	Barbara Rush
1785	Jacob Grimm	1930	Don MacMahon
1809	Louis Braille	1930	Don Shula
1906	William Bendix	1935	Floyd Patterson
1914	Jane Wyman	1937	Dyan Cannon

Notable Events

1493	Columbus left New World on return from first voyage
1717	Triple Alliance formed
1887	First round-the-world bicycle trip completed, San Francisco
1896	Utah admitted to the Union
1908	Fire in Rhoads Theater, Boyertown, Pa., killed 170 people
1915	Moses Alexander, first elected full-time Jewish governor, sworn in, Idaho
1922	Conference of Cannes opened
1932	Gandhi arrested
1937	Italy landed 10,000 troops in Spain
1958	Sputnik I disintegrated
1964	Paul VI became first pope to fly in plane

In 1725 a tax collector, Signor di Corte, dunned a poor Corsican farmer named Cardone for the half cent he still owed the city of Genoa, which then ruled Corsica. The Corsicans promptly took up arms in support of their countryman. Subsequently, Genoa landed an army on the island and began a war that lasted forty-four years, eventually involving Spain, Germany, France, and Savoy, and taking eighty thousand lives.

When I was young I thought that money was the most important thing in life; now that I am old I know it is.

Oscar Wilde

In 1862, to cure the problem of babies crying during performances, a Salt Lake City theater that charged 35 cents admission for adults raised its price for infants to $10.

When money talks, few are deaf.

Charlie Chan

If we can believe the Reverend William Stukeley, who was a close friend of Isaac Newton, that story about the apple is not a myth. The Reverend Stukeley described the incident in a monograph dated 1752, and identified the apple as a rather granular one, without much meat or taste to it, called a "Flower of Kent." A single tree of this species, supposedly descended from Newton's tree, grows on the campus of Babson Institute in Wellesley, Massachusetts.

All the really good ideas I ever had came to me while I was milking a cow.

Grant Wood

Four-fifths of the human race uses some kind of drug daily. The remainder use "the headier and infinitely more dangerous drugs of indignation, ambition, and absolutism," according to Bergen Evans.

There is perhaps no phenomenon which contains so much destructive feeling as moral indignation, which permits envy or hate to be acted out under the guise of virtue.

Erich Fromm

Questions: How long is an inch in South Africa?

What's a Catty in Indonesia?

On this date in 1838 was born Charles S. Stratton, the first known American to sit on the lap of an English queen (he's better known as General Tom Thumb). P.T. Barnum engineered the occasion to promote Stratton's English tour (see also July 5). Victoria, reportedly, *was* amused. Despite his diminutive size, Tom Thumb was anything but cute. He had a miserable temper and drank so heavily that Barnum had to lock him up under guard to keep him sober. To ensure that Thumb didn't escape or have liquor sneaked in to him the guards had no key to his room.

But the clever General would bribe the guards to bring a bottle and a pipe to the door, and he'd use the pipe stem as a straw to suck the alcohol through the keyhole.

Round about the year 1750, a young boy from Carlisle, England, named J. Strong hid in a cathedral so he could examine the church organ in private, and try to find out how it was made. From this single investigation he made an instrument for his own use and sold several others before he turned twenty. Strong, incidentally, was born blind.

The word bicycle is an unscholarly combination of a Latin and a Greek root, *bis* being Latin for "twice"; and *kylos* Greek for "circle."

Answers: 1.033 U.S. inches, 1.3616 pounds.

JANUARY 5

Question: By what names are these people better known?

Aristocles
Taffy Paul
Paula Ragusa
Jerome Rabinowitz
Emanuel Goldenberg

Notable Births

1745	Benjamin Rush	1918	Jeane Dixon
1779	Zebulon Pike	1926	W.D. Snodgrass
1779	Stephen Decatur	1928	Walter Mondale
1876	Konrad Adenauer	1947	Mercury Morris

Notable Events

1800	First Swedenborgian service in United States held in Baltimore
1840	Emperor of China declared all British outlaws
1919	Nazi party formed in Germany
1925	N.T. Ross became first woman governor, Wyoming
1950	Great Britain recognized Communist China
1961	King Deva of Nepal announced failure of attempt at democratic government
1964	Paul VI met Athenagoras, Eastern Order Patriarch, first east-west meeting in 500 years

When Mrs. Calvin Coolidge went to Europe after her husband's death on January 5, 1933, she was afraid that a lot of fuss would be made over her as a former First Lady. Her traveling companion assured her that the places they'd be visiting were small and somewhat naive about world events. "They won't know one President from another," the friend said.

And so it was. At first they attracted no undue attention. Then word leaked out and a little Italian town mustered as much pomp and ceremony as it could for Mrs. Coolidge's arrival. When she reached her hotel, the manager bowed deeply and said, "We are extremely honored to welcome the wife of the great President of the United States. Won't you please register, Mrs. Lincoln?"

Early European visitors to China often came back with incredible stories of the Chinese mania for gambling. In the 1850s, a Frenchman, E. R. Huc, wrote that a man would not infrequently wager away his possessions, clothing, and even his wife if he ran out of other negotiables. On several occasions in the winter he had seen naked men running through the streets of northern provincial towns who had lost their clothes at cards or dice and were looking for a warm chimney corner. Rather than lend a coat to an unfortunate loser, Huc said the winners would follow and taunt the poor creature until he fell dead of exposure, then nonchalantly return to their game.

An Arab commentator told of an equally extreme Chinese measure taken for the love of chance. When all exchangeable goods had been lost by a gambler, he was sometimes allowed to play for his fingers. A small hatchet and a pot of hot vegetable oil would be supplied by the house for this contingency. If the loser did not win the first "hand" his victor would chop off one of his fingers. The stump would then be placed in the oil to cauterize the wound. This writer had also seen armless Chinese, whose limbs had been amputated on the roll of a die or the turn of a card.

Better for Oriental to lose life than to lose face.

Charlie Chan

In England, the poor people were customarily interred farther away from the altar of their church than were the rich people, whether the church was large enough to contain crypts within it, or whether all the parishioners were buried in the churchyard. Elizabeth Ireland died in 1779 and was buried in Ashburton Church, with this inscription on her tombstone:

> Here I lie at the chancel door,
> Here I lie because I'm poor.
> The farther in, the more you pay;
> Here I lie as warm as they.

Worcestershire sauce must mature for months before it is palatable. In 1835, Lea and Perrins, two English chemists, were commissioned to try to duplicate a garnish recipe that Lord Sandys had brought back with him from India. The results of their first attempts were so dreadful that they abandoned the project. A few months later out of curiousity, they sampled the sauce, which had been abandoned in their basement. To their surprise, it had aged by this time and was delicious. Lea and Perrins got permission from Lord Sandys to market the sauce commercially and named it Worcestershire, after the county where they lived in England.

Answer: Plato, Stephanie Powers, Paula Prentiss, Jerome Robbins, Edward G. Robinson.

Question: What occupation do the men below have in common?

Jack Lousma
Owen Garriott
Harrison Schmidt

Notable Births

1410	Joan of Arc	1914	Danny Thomas
1854	Sherlock Holmes	1915	Alan Watts
1878	Carl Sandburg	1920	Reverend Sun Myung Moon
1880	Tom Mix	1920	Early Wynn
1882	Sam Rayburn	1921	Cary Middlecoff
1883	Kahlil Gibran	1931	E.L. Doctorow
1913	Loretta Young	1957	Nancy Lopez-Melton

Notable Events

1540	Henry VIII married Anne of Cleves
1892	Mining disaster in Krebs, Oklahoma, killed 100
1896	Start of first six-day bicycle race for women, New York City
1912	New Mexico joined the Union
1927	U.S. Marines sent to Nicaragua
1936	Agricultural Adjustment Administration declared unconstitutional
1967	Two buses carrying Catholic pilgrims plunged into ravine in Philippines, 84 killed

George Washington and Martha Dandridge Custis were married on this day in 1759. He was twenty-seven, she was twenty-eight, with four children by her late husband.

On January 6, 1868, hundreds of seamen lost their lives in Broughton Bay, Wales, in a tidal wave occasioned by an earthquake in South America, five thousand miles away.

One day in January 1935, the firebell rang at the Peoria, Illinois, station, and Joe Turner rushed to the pole. As he slid down it, friction ignited some matches he had in his pocket. In his astonishment at finding himself on fire, Turner let go of the pole and dropped to the floor, breaking both his legs.

It proved to be a false alarm.

Somehow, the sixth of January came to be a day of celebration for the aristocracy in Medieval England. Papier-mâché castles were built, which the nobility would proceed to bombard from similarly constructed toy ships complete with cannon. Wine flowed (liberally) from pasteboard stags' heads, and celebrants would also hurl eggshells filled with rosewater at one another. The high point was the attempted consumption of pies in which live frogs had been baked.

On this date it was also traditional for the peasants to run madly through the winter fields with torches to frighten off witches, demons, and other enemies of the coming year's crops.

Some rules that governed Henry VIII's household:

None of His Majesty's attendants to steal any locks, or keys, tables, forms, cupboards, or other furniture, out of noblemen's, or gentlemen's, houses where he goes to visit.

No herald, minstrel, falconer, or other, to bring to the Court any boy or rascal; nor to keep lads or rascals in Court to do their business for them.

Master cooks not to employ such scullions as shall go about naked, or lie all night on the ground before the kitchen fire. Dinner to be at ten, and supper at four.

The Knight Marshall to take care that all such unthrifty and common women as follow the Court be banished.

The proper officers are, between six and seven o'clock every morning, to make the fire in and straw his Highness' Privy Chamber. Officers of his Highness' Privy Chamber to keep secret everything said or done, leaving harkening or inquiring where the King is or goes, be it early or late, without grudging, mumbling, or talking of the King's past time, late or early going to bed, or any other matter.

Coal only allowed to the King's, Queen's, and Lady Mary's Chambers. The Queen's Maids of Honor to have a chet loaf, a manchet, a gallon of ale, and a chine of beef, for their breakfasts.

Among the fishes for the table is a porpoise, and if it is too big for a horse-load, a further allowance is made for it to the purveyor.

Answer: They're all astronauts.

JANUARY 7

Questions: What's the cheapest plastic surgery operation you can have performed, and how much is it?

How can you tell that your nose and chin dislike each other?

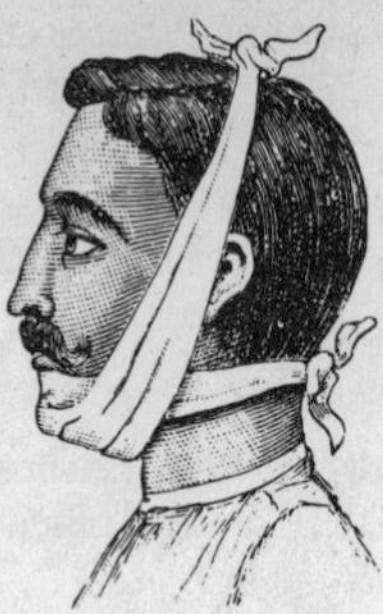

Notable Births

1800	Millard Fillmore	1922	Alvin Dark
1873	Adolph Zukor	1929	Terry Moore
1912	Charles Addams	1948	Kenny Loggins

Notable Events

1617	Lord Bacon appointed chancellor
1785	First balloon crossing of English Channel
1789	First national U.S. election held
1911	First airplane bombing demonstrated, San Francisco
1914	First ship passed through Panama Canal
1929	Tarzan comics began
1934	New Deal oil control ruled unconstitutional
1939	Tom Mooney pardoned
1949	Dean Acheson named secretary of State by Truman
1953	Winston Churchill visited mother's home in Brooklyn
1964	Major General Ton That Dinh took over in South Vietnam

The exalted title of chancellor had a humble origin. In Rome, a chancellor was a petty official stationed behind bars or lattice work who introduced arrivals at the court or refused entrance to certain people. The Emporer Carinus, exemplifying the Roman spoils system, made the chancellor a prefect of Rome, a position of importance and power. Later, in the Eastern Empire, a chancellor was first a secretary who worked within a cage. He gradually became responsible for some judicial matters, and eventually supervised all the other ministers of the Empire. The office of Lord High Chancellor in England and its equivalent in other countries evolved from these traditions.

During the rehearsals for an American opera company's production of Verdi's *Otello*, the tenor who was playing Otello received a curious stage command from the director. During a short pause in Otello's aria, while the chorus was singing, he had to move quickly upstage and then back to center stage. The tenor protested that there was very little time to make that move and, anyway, what was the point? The director insisted, explaining that the action had been created by the great Tamagno himself, and was now traditional. So it was done that way.

Some months later, the tenor was traveling in Italy and called on the aging Tamagno. After chatting for a while, the American singer asked the master about the significance of Otello's upstage march.

Tamagno couldn't remember immediately and went to the score of the opera. "Yes, it is very simple," he explained. "You remember that in the final passage Otello must sing a high B-flat. So while the chorus was singing, I went upstage to spit."

There are more infants under a year old in China than there are Australians, or Greeks, or Saudi Arabians, or Ugandans, or Danes, or Dutch, or Cubans, or Belgians, or Bulgarians, or Swiss, or Swedes, or Hungarians, or Venezuelans, or Rhodesians, or Iraqis.

The first motion picture film to be copyrighted was entitled *Fred Ott's Sneeze*, and it was registered on January 7, 1894. It starred Fred Ott, sneezing.

Two men were accosted on the street by a gang of young toughs, who wanted their credit cards, money, and watches. The men had perforce to agree. But before giving his wallet to the gang leader, one man took out a bill and handed it to his friend. "Here, Tom. This is the ten dollars I owe you."

Pravda, ever alert to clues to normal American life, interpreted the celebrated "Batman and Robin" this way: "[They're] representative of the broad mass of American billionaires who kill their enemies beautifully, effectively, and with taste, so that shoulder blades crack loudly and scalps break like cantaloupes."

Pierre Blanchard and his paying passenger, Dr. John Jeffries, completed the first crossing of the English Channel by balloon on January 7, 1785, but it was a *very* close call. The wind died and their bag cooled too quickly. The aeronauts were forced to jettison everything — including their clothes — to stay out of the sea. After landing safely in France, the naked heroes reported that they'd even urinated into the Channel in order to reduce weight.

Answers: Your nostrils are two for a cent.

There are always words between them.

Notable Births

1824	Wilkie Collins	1909	José Ferrer
1892	Charles Ruggles	1926	Soupy Sales
1902	Georgi Malenkov	1935	Elvis Presley
1904	Peter Arno	1941	Yvette Mimieux

Notable Events

1815 Battle of New Orleans fought
1856 Borax discovered at Tuscan Springs, California
1918 Wilson delivered "Fourteen Points" speech
1959 De Gaulle inaugurated as French president
1969 Two FBI agents killed by bank robber
1976 Death of Chou En-lai

The history teachers tell us that the Battle of New Orleans, in which Andrew Jackson defeated the British, was an unnecessary encounter, because the Treaty of Ghent, which ended the War of 1812, had already been signed. True, the treaty had been signed and news of its signing was en route to the United States when Ol' Hickory took New Orleans, but the war was not over. A clause in the treaty stipulated that it would not become effective until each country had ratified it, and the U.S. Senate at the time had not even heard of it. Jackson's victory was by no means phyrric, for it gave the United States clear title to the Louisiana Territory, which the British had not acknowledged after the purchase of the region from France a decade before.

No Englishman is ever fairly beaten.

George Bernard Shaw

During the invasion of Nanking, China, in January 1938, the Japanese military command felt obliged to file an official protest about "unsportsmanlike conduct" on the part of the Chinese. The protest stated, that "... the Chinese are insincere in this war and do not show a proper respect for the Japanese."

It seems the Chinese had constructed cardboard tanks to divert their enemies and make them waste precious ammunition.

William Gohl was furious! Between 1909 and 1912 alone, forty-one bodies, mostly merchant seamen, had been found floating in Gray's Harbor. In the decade he'd been the Aberdeen, Washington, representative for the Sailors' Union of the Pacific, there'd been many others, and Aberdeen had become known as the "Port of Missing Men." He demanded action!

Spurred on by Gohl and the threat of losing the port's trade, the police investigated ... and found out that the first thing a sailor did when he got into port was to call for mail at Bill Gohl's office, and maybe leave his valuables for safe-keeping. Gohl would check to see whether anyone was nearby, then shoot the sailer in the head, dump his body down a trapdoor, through a chute, and directly into the swift current of the river below. Several days later, the body would float to the surface out in the harbor.

Gohl was lucky. The State of Washington had eliminated capital punishment just before his trial got underway, and he only got life imprisonment, although he may well have murdered one hundred men. He died in prison in 1928.

A cynic is a person searching for an honest man, with a stolen lantern.

Edgar A. Shoaff

Questions: What's the difference between a loaf of bread and an elephant?

What goes up but never comes down?

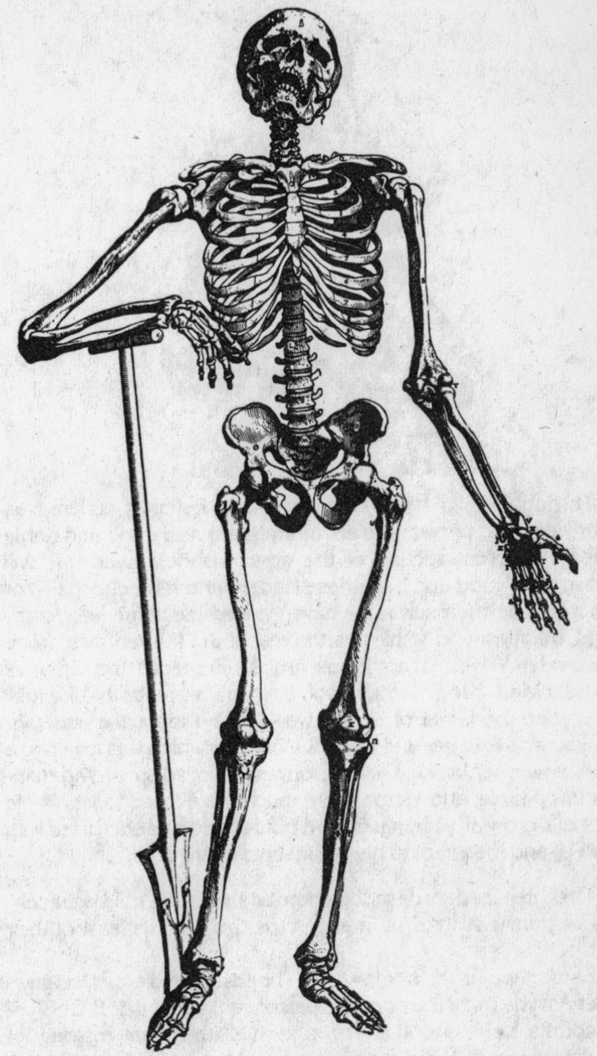

In the late seventeenth century, Alex, a French mathematician and inventor from Provençal, discovered the sympathy of sound and pitch with guitars. As a joke, he made a skeleton with working fingers, sat it at a window, and placed a guitar in its lap. From behind he played an exactly tuned guitar. People below, seeing the skeleton and hearing the music, denounced Alex as a sorcerer. The French Parliament condemned both Alex and his skeleton to be burned alive.

When swallows fly high it is an indication of fair weather. The birds feed on gnats and flies, which are found farther from the ground when warm air is rising. The rising air is generally a sign of good weather.

An investigation conducted by two fellows named Guttmacher and Weihofen found that, among criminals incarcerated for the twenty-seven most common crimes, sex offenders were the least likely recidivists. Rapists ranked twenty-third, and miscellaneous sex offenders ranked twenty-sixth.

Answers: Guess I won't send you for a loaf of bread!
Your age.

JANUARY 9

Question: By what names are these people better known?
William Dukenfield
William Shields
Marilyn Louis
Margaret Hookum
Gwyllyn Ford

Notable Births

1890	Karel Capek	1913	Richard Nixon
1902	Rudolf Bing	1934	Bart Starr
1904	George Balanchine	1941	Joan Baez
1908	Simone de Beauvoir	1941	Susannah York

Notable Events

1788	Connecticut ratified Constitution
1793	François Blanchard completed first American balloon flight
1861	Mississippi seceded
1873	Napoleon III died at Chiselhurst, England
1878	King Victor Emmanuel I of Italy died
1932	Germany announced it could not pay war reparations
1964	Panama severed diplomatic relations with United States
1964	Mandy-Rice Davies began night club act
1964	Ghana declared war on capitalism

Throughout its history, mankind has certainly suffered as many evil and perverse rulers as it has enjoyed good and noble ones. Any cross-section of the world's leaders over time will prove that, good and bad, those leaders whom we choose — or who choose themselves — have evinced the same shortcomings, oddities, and foibles as the rest of the human race. Pope Alexander VI was a notorious orgiast; Frederick the Great of Prussia and King James I of England were both bisexual; Catherine the Great of Russia was a nymphomaniac and zoophiliac who met her end when the harness which was lowering a horse over her broke; Oliver Cromwell enjoyed spreading manure on people; and Victor Emmanuel of Italy used to let his big toenails grow all year, have them gold-plated and encrusted with jewels, and then sent to his two favorite courtesans.

The three leaders described here all shared the mild debauchery of transvestism, but in each case this was the least of their subjects' woes.

Sardanapalus, also known as Thonos Connolerous, reigned over Assyria (now the northern part of Iraq) about 822 B.C.. By all accounts he was entirely heterosexual (the great majority of transvestites are), but his people resented his prancing in women's garb among his concubines, and rebelled against him. (That he was an inept ruler did not disturb his subjects nearly as much.) Sardanapalus was beseiged by his armies for two years at Ninevah, and finally ended it all by burning the city himself. He, his wives, his concubines, and children all perished in the conflagration.

Rome's Nero (37-68 A.D.) was a profligate deviant. A fat, beady-eyed, double-chinned, thick-necked, big-bellied, thin-legged creature, he was, ironically, a narcissist, and had a 120-foot-tall painting of himself on display in Rome. He would often join a play in progress while dressed in women's clothes, and commit sodomy in public. He kept a young boy, Sporus, as a wife, and forced him also to wear women's clothing. He would sometimes clothe himself in animal skins, sexually abuse men and women he had had tied to posts, and then have himself sodomized by his slave Doryphorus.

But these aberrations paled before his nonsexual brutality. He had his wife Olivia killed, and he himself kicked to death another of his wives, Poppaea. He also arranged his mother's murder, and afterward her corpse was stripped naked and brought to the square. There he gave a public accounting of each part of his mother's anatomy, detailing the good parts and the bad. Nero's most renowned transgression was the execution of thousands of Christians after he had wrongfully blamed them for the burning of Rome in 64 A.D.

A more recent and less heinous decadent was Edward Hyde, third Earl of Clarendon, who as Viscount Cornbury served as the governor of colonial New York and New Jersey from 1701 to 1708. In 1702, he opened the New York Assembly in high drag, carrying a fan, wearing a hooped skirt, and flouting an exaggerated coiffure. When a member criticised his inappropriate splendor, he replied, "You are very stupid not to see the propriety of it. In this place and particularly in this occasion I represent a woman [Queen Anne] and ought in all respects to present her as faithfully as I can."

The viscount has also been described as a "a spendthrift, a grafter, a bigotted oppressor, and a drunken, vain fool." When he employed milliners and a cobbler on the government payroll to make his clothes and slippers, and sat for his official portrait in drag, his hopelessly corrupt administration was finally brought down. In 1708, he was convicted of bribery and misuse of public funds, removed from office, and imprisoned in England for indebtedness — until 1711, when he was made a member of the English Privy Council.

Virtue would not go nearly so far if vanity did not keep her company.

La Rochefoucauld

Men are men, but Man is a woman.

G.K. Chesterton

I have heard with admiring submission the experience of the lady who declared that the sense of being well-dressed gives a feeling of inward tranquility, which religion is powerless to bestow.

Ralph Waldo Emerson

All women become like their mothers. That is their tragedy. No man does. That is his.

Oscar Wilde

Answer: W. C. Fields, Barry Fitzgerald, Rhonda Fleming, Margot Fonteyn, Glenn Ford.

Notable Births

1737	Ethan Allen	1927	Gisele MacKenzie
1814	Aubrey de Vere	1927	Johnnie Ray
1883	Francis X. Bushman	1938	Willie McCovey
1883	Florence Reed	1939	Bill Toomey
1887	Robinson Jeffers	1939	Sal Mineo
1904	Ray Bolger	1949	George Foreman

Notable Events

1429 Order of the Golden Fleece established by Philip, Duke of Burgundy
1645 Archbishop Laud executed
1815 Great Britain declared war on king of Kandy, Ceylon
1840 Penny postage began in Britain
1861 Florida seceded
1911 First aerial photograph taken, San Diego
1920 League of Nations began
1934 Marinas van de Lubbe executed for Reichstag fire in Germany
1946 First meeting of UN General Assembly
1961 Sinhala replaced English as official language of Sri Lanka

About 1640, an English barrister named William Prynne published a nearly indecipherable treatise called *Histriomatrix* that devoted most of its thousands of pages to diatribes against plays, music, dancing, hunting, Christmas, maypoles, festivals, and bonfires. These fulminations accorded well with the religious temper of the time (just before the advent of Cromwell), except that Archbishop Laud, arch-foe of all things Puritanical, decided it specifically attacked ceremonies he had introduced into the English church service. He hauled Prynne into court for libel and made sure the jury favored the prosecution. Prynne was ordered to be disbarred, pilloried, fined £5,000; to have his ears cut off, and be imprisoned for life. The sentence was duly carried out, but Prynne continued writing from his prison cell. He was tried a second time and nobly defended his right to speak the truth about such an impious man as Laud. The judge passed sentence, and ordered that the remnants of his ears be cut off, that he be heavily fined, and that he be physically branded as a schismatic and libeller. Prynne bore these humiliations proudly. But before long the tables were turned. With the triumph of the Parliament over Charles I, Prynne was freed, a hero; Laud was imprisoned for treason, and executed on January 10, 1645.

Nothing has an uglier look to us than reason, when it is not on our side.

Marquis of Halifax

Question: About how long do the following animals live?
Chimpanzee
Opossum
White rhinoceros
Domestic sheep

King Yasalalak a Tissa of Ceylon had a double in the person of Subha, an unskilled laborer. Whenever the affairs of state exhausted the king, he'd summon Subha to take his place for a few hours, and then go out in commoner's clothes. Finally Subha decided to play the game for keeps. One day, he summoned the real king before him, accused him of treason, and had him executed. Subha ruled six years until his trick was discovered, and he was slain in the wars that ensued.

Whoever has flattered his friend successfully, must at once think himself a knave, and his friend a fool.

Alexander Pope

The destination of Jason and the Argonauts in their search for the Golden Fleece was probably the ancient town of Colchis, on the Black Sea. Legend has it that the people of this area (which is now Georgia) used to stretch the skins of slaughtered sheep beneath the many waterfalls that rained down the slopes of the Caucasus Mountains in order to catch the heavy gold flakes as they swept over the falls. The gold was then picked out from the sheepskins.

⚜

On the average, the human body has twenty square feet of skin, nine thousand taste buds, five million hairs, and thirteen billion nerve cells.

Answer: 20 years; 1 year; 20 years; 12 years.

JANUARY 11

Questions: Why does a man's hair turn grey before his mustache does?

Why don't women go bald as often as men?

On January 11, 1841, an American, whom today we would call a stuntman, was performing a miraculous escape from roped bondage before plunging into London's icy River Thames . . . when he managed, unmiraculously, to hang himself.

The Count Dracula (*Draculaea*, incidentally, is Rumanian for "Son of the Devil") of Europe may have been much more common than the single fictional character in Bram Stoker's 1897 novel. Medical researchers have discovered that, because of prolonged inbreeding, the European nobility has had a far greater incidence than commoners of a rare disease called *erythropoietic protoporphyria*. This disease causes the body to manufacture too much porphyrin, a basic ingredient of red blood cells. Symptoms of the affliction include redness of the eyes, skin, and gums, and a receding upper lip. Cracks in the skin, lips, and gums that bleed when exposed to light are also common.

Today, those afflicted with the disease are given drugs that readily control its symptoms. But in the nineteenth century, victims were locked up in dark rooms during the day, and given blood to drink at night.

The real-life model for Stoker's Dracula was one Vlad V, who ruled Wallachia between 1456 and 1462. He was known as "The Impaler," because of his macabre habit of impaling people on long stakes and pikestaves. Vlad reputedly had forty thousand people murdered in this fashion during the six years of his reign. Oddly enough he struck indiscriminately. Friends and nobles were as likely to be run through as enemies and peasants.

Notable Births

1757	Alexander Hamilton	1903	Alan Paton
1821	Feodor Dostoevsky	1915	William Proxmire
1842	William James	1930	Rod Taylor

Notable Events

1693	Earthquake killed 60,000 people in Catania, Italy
1770	First American rhubarb exported to England
1830	William Banks executed at Horsemonger Lane for burglary
1861	Alabama seceded
1919	Romania annexed Transylvania
1923	Ruhr occupied by France and Belgium
1938	F.E. Moulton became first American woman bank president, Limerick, Maine
1943	FDR called for $100 billion for war effort
1974	Rosenkowitz quintuplets born, South Africa
1975	Floods in Thailand claimed 131 lives

In 1611, a Hungarian countess named Erzsebet Bathory was tried for murder — not unreasonably. In her lifetime, Bathory murdered some 600 young girls, in a variety of grisly ways. She would lock up the young woman in a narrow iron cage that impaled the victim when the door was closed. She then hoisted the cage to the ceiling, and, while listening to the girl's dying shrieks, would sit beneath and revel in the rain of warm blood. Or the unfortunate girl would be embraced by a special mechanical man that locked around her and shot spikes into her body. A trough carried the blood to a vat that was then heated for m'lady's blood bath, which she believed would keep her youthful.

Her occultist accomplices, not being of noble birth, were either beheaded or burned, but out of deference to her position, Madame Bathory was simply walled up alive in her castle in the Minor Carpathians — so carelessly walled up, in fact, that her servants were able to provide her with drink and scraps of food that kept her alive for four years.

Whether women are better than men I cannot say — but I can say they are certainly no worse. **Golda Meir**

Answers: Because it's usually about twenty years older.

Because they wear their hair longer.

Notable Births

1578	John Winthrop	1856	John Singer Sargent
1628	Charles Perrault	1860	Anton Chekhov
1729	Edmund Burke	1876	Jack London
1737	John Hancock	1893	Hermann Goering

Notable Events

1853 Willamette University incorporated, first college on Pacific Coast
1879 British-Zulu war began
1915 U.S. House of Representatives defeated women's suffrage proposal
1932 Oliver Wendell Homes retired from Supreme Court, aged ninety
1960 Dolph Schayes scored 15,000th point
1964 Rebellion in Zanzibar began
1968 Soviets sentenced four dissidents for anti-Soviet activities
1970 Biafra surrendered after Nigerian civil war lasting 32 months

A novel way of delivering the mail was described in an English newspaper of January in 1821. The ninety-seven-year-old postmaster of the town of Lismore, Scotland, a fellow named Huddy, put on a red stocking cap and set out for Fermoy to deliver the mail. His vehicle was an oyster tub pulled by two cats, a hedgehog, a goose, a badger and a pig. To spur his team on he drove them with a pigherd's whip and blasted at them through a cow's horn.

Reportedly he did this on a wager, and the mail got through.

Question: Within 10 years, when were the following invented?
electric stove
micrometer
geiger counter
evaporated milk

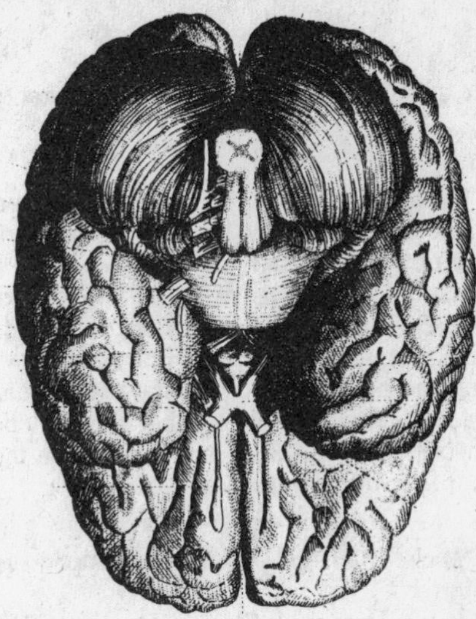

The brain of the average human is almost four times as large as that of a chimpanzee. The brain of the average dolphin is over five times as large as a chimp's.

The youngest grandmother on record was a young girl named Mum-Zi of Calabar, Nigeria, who became one at the age of sixteen.

Sexual enlightenment is justified insofar as girls cannot learn too soon how children do not come into this world.
Kraus

Osa G. Candler, Jr., son of the Coca-Cola magnate, inaugurated "Candler's Floating School" in 1923. It was a prep school on board an ocean-going ship that would therefore offer few distractions for its students, who for various reasons had not done well in regular schools. Candler explained it as "... a school for the children of the unfortunate rich" who couldn't "buckle down as poor folks do."

Candler's son was in the first class.

We owe many of our familiar children's stories to a Frenchman, Charles Perrault, who was born on this date in 1628. He was the first folklorist to set down such traditional tales as "Puss and Boots," "Little Red Riding Hood," and "Cinderella."

That Cinderella's foot fits a glass slipper in the modern English version of the story was the result of a translator's error. The tale was well known in England at the time but it was not written down, and it originally involved a fur-lined slipper, a more sensible luxury than a glass one, considering the stone-cold castle floors of the time. When an English writer mistranslated the French word "*vair*" as "glass" (*verre*) instead of "fur," the English adopted it, and their story became unique among the many versions of "Cinderella."

Answer: 1896; 1636; 1913; 1880.

JANUARY 13

Question: By what names are these people better known?
John Sanford
Jacques Thibault
Anthony Papalco
Arlene Kazanjian
Concetta Franconero

Notable Births

1808	Salmon P. Chase	1901	A.B. Guthrie, Jr.
1834	Horatio Alger, Jr.	1919	Robert Stack
1899	Kay Francis	1925	Gwen Verdon

Notable Events

1874 Conscription introduced in Russia
1903 Tuomato Archipelago earthquake killed 1,000 people
1912 Record low temperature recorded at Oakland, Maryland: minus 40°F
1915 Estimated 29,970 people lost their lives in Avezzano, Italy, earthquake
1953 Gimbel's became first department store to sell apartments
1960 Bathysphere *Trieste* explored deepest part of Marianas Trench
1977 Palestine Liberation Organization seated at UN
1978 Brueghel the Elder painting brought record price, $560,000, for Old Master still life

On this date in 1932, bright pink snow fell in Durango, Colorado.

Before the British got to them, the Dyaks of Borneo were a people with curious pastimes. With their teeth blackened from chewing beetle-nut, and brass rings adorning their arms and ears, they spent much of their leisure time talking to, feeding, and petting their heads — the ones that formerly belonged to other Dyak tribesmen, but which now hung from their new owners' ceilings, or dangled on strings from their waists. Status among the Dyaks was solely based on the number of other tribesmen's heads a man owned. This, of course, was before the British introduced money to the island.

The name "Mickey Finn" originated with the potion's popularizer, Mickey Finn.

Finn was a tavern-keeper on Chicago's rugged Whiskey Row in the 1890s, the owner of the Lone Star Saloon and Palm Garden. It was a real dive, frequented by toughs, bums, and men looking for inexpensive women. But, compared to his neighbors, Finn was a respectable businessman, seldom doing more than some pimping or occasionally rolling a drunk.

In 1898, he bought the recipe for a secret formula from a self-styled black voodoo witch doctor. When a few drops of this concoction were put into raw booze it became the "Mickey Finn Special." The girls who worked for him were encouraged to push it to unaccompanied male customers, especially if they looked well-heeled. After imbibing the potion, a customer would first become very loquacious, then he would become hysterical, and then he would fall into a stupor.

It was during the third stage that Mickey and his wife went to work. In a back room, Finn would don a bowler hat and a clean apron, and then strip the unconscious individual to the skin to search for any valuables he had concealed in his clothes. After the victim had been picked clean, he'd be redressed (in rags, if Finn felt his clothes were worth anything) and then removed to some out-of-the-way alley. The hapless victims seldom remembered a thing.

When the Chicago police finally caught on to Mickey and got his license revoked, they unknowingly did the country a great disservice. Unable to earn a living at his trade, Finn sold his special formula to other barkeepers and to sundry other people who certainly had no honest use for it.

Answer: Redd Foxx, Anatole France, Tony Franciosa, Arlene Francis, Connie Francis.

JANUARY 14

Notable Births

1741	Benedict Arnold	1896	John Dos Passos
1850	Pierre Loti	1901	Bebe Daniels
1875	Albert Schweitzer	1925	Yukio Mishima
1882	Hendrik van Loon	1926	Thomas Tryon
1886	Hugh Lofting	1940	Julian Bond
1888	Sophie Tucker	1941	Faye Dunaway

Notable Events

1797 Napoleon defeated Austrians at Rivoli
1814 Treaty of Kiel ceded Norway to Sweden
1907 Jamaican earthquake — 1,400 people killed
1929 First international dog-sled mail delivery, Montreal
1943 Casablanca Conference opened
1964 Castro visited Russia
1977 Claudine Longet found guilty of negligent homicide, Aspen, Colorado

Chief Justice Kirby Benedict, Lincoln's appointee to the New Mexico Territory Supreme Court, never was behindhand when it came to telling defendents just what he thought of them, whether or not it might prejudice an appeal. (Of course, in those legally benighted days, the average defense lawyer was less technically sophisticated than his counterpart today.) While passing sentence on a Mexican murderer, he observed:

"José Maria Martin, you have been indicted, tried, and convicted by a jury of your countrymen of the crime of murder, and the Court is now about to pass on you the dread sentence of the law. As a usual thing, José Maria Martin, it is a painful duty of a judge of a court of justice to pronounce upon a human being the sentence of death. There is something horrible about it, and the mind of a court naturally revolts from the performance of such a duty. Happily, however, your case is relieved of all such unpleasantness, and the court takes positive delight in sentencing you to death."

He who cannot love must learn to flatter.

Goethe

Although "Old Nick" is now a slang name for the devil, the term originally referred to the Scandinavian sea god Nicor.

Dogs and other animals suffering from rabies do not foam at the mouth. In the last stage of the disease, when infected animals are supposedly rushing about madly and salivating profusely, the creatures are actually so paralyzed by the disease that they cannot stand. They drop to the ground, their jaws open, and the saliva drips out.

❦

Answer: They were all the Speaker of the United States House of Representatives.

Question: What occupation do the following men have in common?

Frederick Muhlenberg
Samuel Randall
William Bankhead
Howell Cobb
Galusha Groa

Mary Russell Mitford, aged ten, dreamed of the number seven on three consecutive nights. She thought it a good omen, so she multiplied seven by three and bought a lottery ticket with the same number. The winning number was twenty-two — which is exactly what Mary Mitford's faulty arithmetic had given her. She won $100,000.

The world is neither wise nor just, but makes up for all its folly and injustice by being damnably sentimental.

T.H. Huxley

Give your decisions, never your reasons; your decisions may be right, your reasons are sure to be wrong.

Earl of Mansfield

The "Little Red Schoolhouse" was often that color because red was the cheapest kind of paint to buy.

In 1939, Pearl and Benjamin Mason, a Philadelphia couple on welfare, won $150,000 in the Irish Sweepstakes. As any other big winners might, they immediately went out and bought a new home, new furniture, and a car. Uncle Sam then took his $57,000 share. After that, the Masons repaid the City Relief Board the $2,133.90 that they'd received in welfare payments at various times. With the remaining $80,000, the Masons bought and rehabilitated a block of dilapidated tenements into a modern housing development for poor families.

It is the mark of a good action that it appears inevitable in retrospect.

Robert Louis Stevenson

Make the most of the day, by determining to spend it on two sorts of acquaintances — those by whom something may be got, and those from whom something may be learned.

Colton

JANUARY 15

Questions: When is a rope like a child in school?

When is a pie like a poet?

Our word "easel" is almost identical to the Dutch and German words (*ezel* and *esel*) for the same thing, but in those languages the words mean "little donkey," because an easel, too, bears a burden.

An Austrian named Rudolf Schmied, aka "Rayo," had strange ways of making a living. He once had himself buried alive for nine days. On three different occasions, he nailed his tongue to a board for periods of from twenty-four to ninety days. For a 1952 tour of Europe he had himself welded into a glass bottle measuring seven-and-a-half feet tall, vowing to remain inside it for a year, subsisting only on dextrose, glucose, vitamins, and four ounces of either coffee or fruit juice a day. At night his six assistants would tip the 840-pound glass cage over, and Rayo would sleep on an air mattress. For entertainment he would often play chess with spectators, or pet his two four-foot poisonous snakes (they shared his captivity the whole time).

Back in the seventeenth century, an English soldier named Tommy Atkins was caught with a deck of cards in church and brought before the mayor for punishment. Atkins admitted his guilt, but explained:

"You see, your Honour, this pack is my Bible, my prayerbook, and my almanac. The ace reminds me that there is but one God; the deuce of the Father and Son, the three of the Holy Trinity; the four makes me think of the great evangelists Matthew, Mark, Luke, and John, and the five of the five wise men and the five foolish virgins. The six stands for the six days in which the world was made, and the seventh for the Sabbath. Eight brings to mind the eight good members of Noah's family who were saved from the Flood; and the nine reminds me of the lepers whom the Lord cleansed. Ten is the Ten Commandments which the Lord gave to Moses on Mount Sinai."

At this point he put aside the knave, and continued. "The queen puts me in mind of the Queen of Sheba, and therefore the wisdom of Solomon, and the King is the Creator, the King of all, and likewise His Majesty, King George, and reminds me to pray for him. The days of the year are represented by the number of spots in the deck, and the weeks by the number of cards. So you see, it is my Bible, prayer book, and almanac."

"And what is the knave for?" asked the mayor when Atkins had finished.

"Why, your Honour, the knave is for the constable what brought me here, the greatest knave of all!"

Notable Births

1622	Jean Baptiste Molière	1909	Gene Krupa
1791	Franz Grillparzer	1915	Lloyd Bridges
1870	Pierre S. DuPont	1926	Maria Schell
1906	Aristotle Onassis	1929	Martin Luther King, Jr.
1908	Edward Teller	1937	Margaret O'Brien

Notable Events

1777	Vermont declared independence as New Connecticut
1870	First use of donkey to represent Democratic party in cartoon
1935	Saar voted for union with Germany
1940	FBI arrested 18 in plot to overthrow government
1964	Teamsters negotiated first national labor contract
1965	Russia detonated world's largest underground nuclear bomb

The mayor good-naturedly cuffed Atkins on his ear, dismissed the case, and gave him several pounds for his wit.

Sharp wit sometimes better than deadly weapon.

Charlie Chan

Answers: When it is taut.
When it is Browning.

JANUARY 16

Notable Births

1874	Robert Service	1930	Norman Podhoretz
1909	Ethel Merman	1933	Susan Sontag
1911	Dizzy Dean	1935	A.J. Foyt

Notable Events

1772 Danish Queen Caroline arrested for adultery, banished by king
1778 France recognized U.S. independence
1878 U.S. signed treaty of friendship with Samoa
1919 Ratification by Nebraska passed Prohibition amendment
1942 Plane crash killed Carole Lombard while on war-bond drive
1968 Britain ended 150 years of military activity east of Suez

In 1964, writer-thinker Susan Sontag published in *The Partisan Review* what has become the definitive article on the cult of Camp. The following is Ms. Sontag's list of "Random examples of items which are part of the canon of Camp."

Tiffany lamps
Scopitone films
The Brown Derby restaurant on Sunset Boulevard in Los Angeles
The Enquirer, headlines and stories
Aubrey Beardsley drawings
Swan Lake
Bellini's operas
Visconti's direction of *Salome* and *'Tis Pity She's a Whore*
certain turn-of-the-century picture postcards
Schoedsack's *King Kong*
the Cuban pop singer La Lupe
Lynn Ward's novel in woodcuts, *God's Man*
women's clothes of the twenties (feather boas, fringed and beaded dresses, etc.)
the novels of Ronald Firbank and Ivy Compton-Burnett
stag movies seen without lust

In the first year of the Volstead Act, 44 percent of the budget of the United States District Attorneys' Office went for Prohibition-related matters.

The cost of living has gone up another dollar a quart.
W.C. Fields

Yukon Travesty — 1901
The Last Poem of Robert Service

©1976 G. McLeavy

A dark afternoon in December saw a dog team speed over the land,
A dozen or more miles from Whitehorse, urged on by a man, whip in hand.
Gloves and a coat made of Dall sheep, and an icicled mustache he wore.
Viciously he whipped and he cursed the dogs, as over the powder they tore.
"Mush on, oh mush on, you Huskies! Mush on much faster, I say!
"Mush much much faster, you husky Huskies, we must reach Whitehorse by end of day."

The voice that rang over the barking was the cry of the famous Mountie,
The father of law in the Yukon, Sergeant Preston, R.C.M.P.
With his noble dog King in lead harness, through the snow and the spruce trees they bore
Hour upon hour, without rest, all frozen of lung and footsore.

"Mush on you beasts!" cried the Sergeant. "We've got to reach Whitehorse tonight,
"Before loving Lorna can marry that murderous blackguard Sam Wright."

Yes, that was the reason that Preston was whipping his dogs with such will:
His dear, loving, buxom Lorna Mae Doone had been won in a game of skill.
He chided the team, for their slowness, for their so lethargic footfalls.
He whipped them again and again and again, and he pelted them hard with snowballs.
"Mush on, oh mush on, you Huskies! Mush on much faster, you creeps!
"Mush much much faster, you husky Huskies, (and miles to go, tra la, before I sleep)."

One by one the dogs began falling, having given their all and their last;
And mindlessly Preston pressed onwards, as the seconds and minutes flew past.
And soon all 'twas left of the sled team was Sergeant Preston and King.
The others lie scattered at trailside, all coughing up blood and dying.
"Mush on, oh mush on, you Husky! Mush on much faster, old King!
"Mush much much faster, you husky Husky! And cut out your damned whimpering!"

The lights of old Whitehorse were glowing, so deep by the river below,
When a heart on the trail stopped beating, and a body fell dead in the snow.
"King! King!" were the words that he cried out, when the Sergeant fell off of the sled.
"Go save my dear, loving Lorna Mae Doone from that villainous Sam Wright," he said.

King leapt through the snow, oh so proudly, with but loyalty giving him strength.
He sprung over fallen spruce timbers, and finally, finally, at length,
He reached the dear Lorna's cabin, and flung himself in through the door.
And there, not two feet before him, all crumpled and dead on the floor—
(He'd said "Mush on, oh mush on, you Huskies. Mush on much faster, I say.
"Mush much much faster, you husky Huskies, for the love of my dear Lorna Mae.")
— Lay the villain his master had hated, the murderous blackguard Sam Wright.
Then Lorna spoke out from the corner, "He died of starvation last night.
"There's been no food for a month now, and half of the people have died.
"But good King, your coming has saved me," she said, and she slit open the noble dog's hide,
And sang, "I'll make a mush of you, Husky. I'll cut out steaks of your flesh.
"You'll keep me alive through the winter, and I've always found dog delicious."

She stoked up her fire, oh so warmly, and the skin from the dog she undressed.
She cut out his entrails so deftly, and she readied her sausage press.
Strange things are done in the Midnight Sun, but the strangest of all in my log
Is the night that the dear, loving Lorna Mae Doone made a King-sized, Husky hot dog,
And a breakfast of mush of the Husky. She ate him from haunches to eyes;
And so from the peak of her cache's roof the noble dog's tail now flies.

Question: Can you name the five biggest-selling magazines in America?

Answer: *TV Guide; Reader's Digest; National Geographic; Family Circle; Woman's Day.*

JANUARY 17

Question: By what names are these people better known?

Betty Goldstein
Greta Gustafsson
Lucy Johnson
Jules Garfinkle
Frances Gumm

Notable Births

1706	Benjamin Franklin	1899	Nevil Shute
1863	Konstantin Stanislavski	1931	James Earl Jones
1863	David Lloyd George	1934	Shari Lewis
1886	Ronald Firbank	1944	Joe Frazier

Notable Events

1712 Walpole imprisoned in the Tower of London
1733 Polar bears exhibited in Boston
1786 Encke's Comet discovered
1905 Punchboards patented
1945 Russians took Warsaw
1950 Brink's robbery in Boston
1961 Patrice Lumumba died under mysterious circumstances
1978 Gary Gilmore executed

An Englishman named John Curtis liked thunderstorms, preferred wet weather to dry, walked an average of twenty miles a day, and was never seen in a wheeled vehicle. But, of course, the English *are* eccentric. What set Curtis apart from his countrymen was his fondness for English courts and prisons. For decades, he attended almost every trial held at New Court and took down in shorthand the complete testimony in each case. Only an execution kept him out of court. He attended close to a thousand in or near London over a period of twenty-five years. He would also join the condemned man in his cell and share his last night on earth. Over one hundred felons were so treated by John Curtis.

Although Benjamin Franklin wrote numerous epigrams on the wisdom of careful money management, and his birthday celebration always begins National Thrift Week, he was apparently not financially prudent himself. When the records of the Bank of North America were turned over to the Historical Society of Pennsylvania, it was discovered that Franklin was overdrawn on his account an average of three days a week for years.

Benjamin Franklin Epitaph:

The body of
B. Franklin,
Printer,
Like the cover of an old book
its contents torn out
and stripped of its lettering and gilding,
lies here, food for worms.
But the work shall not be wholly lost;
for it will, as he believed, appear once more,
in a new and more perfect edition,
corrected and amended
by the Author.
He was born Jan. 6, 1706
Died ____________ 17__.

(Franklin wrote this for himself before he died, leaving the dates blank. His birthdate is Julian calendar; his Gregorian calendar birthdate is January 17.)

Answer: Betty Friedan, Greta Garbo, Ava Gardner, John Garfield, Judy Garland.

Notable Births

1689	Montesquieu	1892	Oliver Hardy
1782	Daniel Webster	1904	Cary Grant
1880	D.W. Griffith	1913	Danny Kaye
1882	A.A. Milne	1942	Muhammad Ali

Notable Events

1792 Prussia gained Ansbach and Bayreuth by escheat, under Treaty of Teschen
1871 William I proclaimed German Emperor at Versailles
1919 Versailles Peace Conference began in Paris
1944 First Chinese (E.B. Kan) granted naturalized American citizenship
1964 Plans for World Trade Center, NYC, announced
1967 Brazilian flood claimed 900 victims

Although the teacher had repeatedly chastised the little boy for his dirtiness, day after day he appeared, looking as if he'd slept in a pig sty. Finally, she could stand it no longer, and told him if he ever again came like that to school, she'd whip him.

A few days later, she noticed that his face was smudged, so she called him forward to inspect his hands. On the way, the youngster spit quickly into one hand and wiped it on his pants. It didn't help much, but the teacher gave him a chance. "If you can show me another hand in this class that's dirtier than that one, I won't whip you."

Daniel Webster promptly lifted his other hand.

Daniel Webster used to tell a story of New England hospitality. He had been out hunting some distance from his home in New Hampshire and, coming out of the woods at dusk, realized he was quite far from the nearest inn. After a long walk, he reached a farmhouse, and pounded on the door. A second-floor window was raised and an old farmer stuck his head out. "What do you want?" he demanded.

"I'd like to spend the night here," said Webster from below.

"All right, then," replied the farmer. "Stay there!"

Questions: What's big and red and eats rocks?

What's white on the outside, green on the inside, and hops?

ST. PETER'S AND THE VATICAN, ROME

In 1913, the world's largest structure was the Building of Manual and Liberal Arts, erected for the 1902 Buffalo World's Fair. At 1,687 feet long and 787 feet wide, it could have comfortably contained the world's second-largest building, Saint Peter's in Rome. The cost of construction was about $1,750,000, which wouldn't begin to build a mile of road today.

The word "pagoda" is not of Chinese origin. It comes from the Persian *but-kadah*, meaning "idol-temple," and was introduced to China by Portuguese traders.

Back in January 1938, forty-inch-tall Olive Brasno had her heart broken by forty-four-inch-tall Billy Curtis. They'd been engaged, but instead, Curtis married the seventy-five-inch-tall (that's six-feet, three inches) Lois de Fee, a former nightclub bouncer.

Every Maybe has a wife. Wife called Maybe-Not.

Charlie Chan

A century ago, leech farming was a boom industry in Europe. In 1882, 57,500,000 of the little suckers were imported into France alone.

The phrase "lick into shape," often associated with military training camps and the like, comes from the medieval notion that bear cubs were born shapeless and the she-bear licked her young into their proper shape as she was cleaning up their birthsacks.

Answers: A big red rockeater.

A live frog sandwich.

JANUARY 19

Questions: When is a schoolboy like a postage stamp?

Why is a blindfolded woman like a poor schoolteacher?

Notable Births

1736	James Watt	1916	Victor Mature
1798	Auguste Comte	1919	J.D. Salinger
1807	Robert E. Lee	1923	Jean Stapleton
1809	Edgar Allan Poe	1923	Judy Garland
1839	Paul Cezanne	1946	Dolly Parton

Notable Events

1764	Wilkes expelled from House of Commons
1861	Georgia seceded
1871	First Black Freemason Lodge warranted, New Jersey
1915	Electric neon sign patented
1919	German National Assembly elected
1931	Round Table discussions on India closed, London
1933	Soviets exiled 45,000 Cossacks to Siberia
1941	Nazis agreed to greater participation in Mediterranean with Mussolini

In 1780, Charles Cornwall was elected Speaker of the House of Commons. That august body soon realized it could have chosen better. Although Cornwall had a commanding figure and a booming voice, he also had a fondness for liquor, and he kept a full tankard of spirits on the Speaker's dais. He often drank himself into a stupor, which, according to one account, "... considerably detracted from the dignity of his office and personal demeanor." Occasionally he also drank himself to sleep, which "... caused considerable inconvenience to the House."

Thanks to medical technology, major breakthroughs in psychiatric care, I'm no longer a woman obsessed with an unnatural craving. Just another normal ... very socially acceptable ... alcoholic.

Lily Tomlin

Robert E. Lee's mother had been pronounced dead fifteen months before he was born.

The silkworm is an amazing little creature. A single one of its eggs weighs only about 1/100,000 of an ounce, but in the first four weeks of its life, the worm increases its birth weight 9,500 times. Then for the next month, before its transformation into a silk moth, the worm eats nothing. About ten pounds of mulberry leaves are needed for the silkworm to manufacture a pound of cocoons, and a single pound of cocoons can be spun into a silk thread over 100 miles long.

Epitaph from Nettlebed, Oxfordshire, England:

Here lies Father & Mother, & Sister and I,
Wee all died within the short space of one short Year.
They be all Buried at *Wimble* except I,
And I be buried here.

In 1937, the United States had two million domestic refrigerators. Great Britain had three thousand.

The lee, or sheltered quarter of a ship, was a landlubber term from the Anglo-Saxon *hleow*. This referred to the side of a shed or hedge that was out of the wind, where a laborer would take his lunch.

An elephant's trunk has about forty thousand muscles.

Answers: When he is licked and put in the corner to make him stick to his letter.

Because her pupils are kept in the dark.

Notable Births

1734	Robert Morris	1910	Joy Adamson
1876	Josef Hoffmann	1920	Federico Fellini
1880	Ruth St. Denis	1926	Patricia Neal
1891	Mischa Elman	1930	Edwin Aldrin
1896	George Burns	1937	Dorothy Provine

Notable Events

1841 Hong Kong ceded to Britain at end of Opium War
1885 Roller-coaster patent granted to L.A. Thompson of Coney Island
1892 First basketball game played, Springfield, Massachusetts
1935 King George V died
1936 Howard Hughes set transcontinental air record: 7 hours, 30 minutes
1944 Seige of Leningrad ended
1948 Gandhi assassinated
1961 Mao Tse Tung ordered China's Great Leap Forward slowed
1964 Max Feinberg arrested in Philadelphia for selling Sterno to winos, caused 31 deaths
1977 President Ford pardoned Tokyo Rose

The first full-length talking picture to be filmed outdoors was entitled *In Old Arizona*, and was released on this date in 1921. Nine-tenths of the footage was shot in California and Utah.

Question: Within 10 years, when were the following invented?
ballpoint pen
electroplating
carpet sweeper
elevator brake

Today is also Grandmother's Day in Bulgaria, when it is customary to dunk young boys and girls under water to ensure their healthy futures.

On this date in 1795 the French general, Charles Pichegru, led his cavalry troops against the entire Dutch Navy — and won. An exceptionally cold winter had frozen the fleet in Amsterdam Harbor, so Pichegru ordered his horsemen to charge across the ice and take the ships. They had an easy time of it, and the defeat led directly to the surrender of the Netherlands.

Impossible to prepare defense until direction of attack is known.

Charlie Chan

Answer: 1880; 1805; 1876; 1852.

JANUARY 21

Question: By what names are these people better known?
Brenda Webb
Francesca von Gerber
Roberta Streeter
Marion Levy
Samuel Goldfish

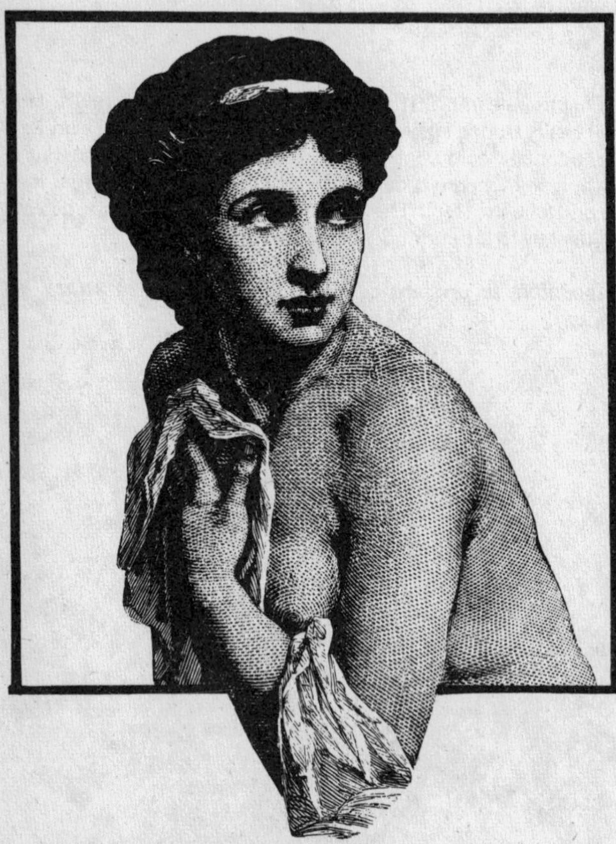

In fifteenth-century Venice, a law was passed requiring prostitutes to lean from their windows in such a way that their breasts would be completely exposed. This was to ensure that young men would be deterred from the "unnatural aberration" of homosexuality.

In January 1955, sixty-nine-year-old Fanny Ennis brought suit against seventy-three-year-old John Purser in Ockley, England, for breach of promise. She claimed he'd promised to marry her in 1908 and still hadn't.

In January 1956, nine-year-old James Darnell of Woolwich, Maine, who was recuperating from a broken leg, wrote a note, stuck it in a bottle, and asked his mother to cast it adrift in Hockomock Bay. The bottle was retrieved a year later four miles off the coast of Spain by a Spanish fisherman with a broken leg.

Answer: Crystal Gayle, Mitzi Gaynor, Bobbie Gentry, Paulette Goddard, Samuel Goldwyn.

Notable Births

1824	Stonewall Jackson	1922	Paul Scofield
1900	J. Carroll Naish	1924	Telly Savalas
1919	Jinx Falkenburg	1940	Jack Nicklaus

Notable Events

604 B.C. Nebuchadnezzar became sovereign of Babylonia
1793 Louis XVI beheaded
1865 First oil well drilled by torpedo
1924 Nikolai Lenin died
1954 Mamie Eisenhower christened nuclear sub *Nautilus*, Groton, Connecticut
1964 Carl Rowan succeeded Edward R. Murrow as head of USIA

The twenty-first day of the month was an important one throughout the life of Louis XVI of France. On April 21, 1770, he was married. On January 21, 1782, 1,500 people were trampled to death at the celebration of the birth of the dauphin, Louis's first son. On June 21, 1791, he fled to Varennes after escaping from the revolutionaries. On September 21, 1792, the crown was officially abolished in France, and on January 21, 1793, Louis was beheaded.

Louis XVI conducted himself in a less than kingly fashion at his execution. Prior to being brought to the guillotine, he violently resisted having his hair cut above his neck and fought having his hands tied behind him. At the scene, he refused to step from the coach and had to be pulled out bodily. On the platform he yelled and fought with his jailers, and finally burst into tears, crying "I die innocent! I ever desired the good of my people."

When a man is all wrapped up in himself, he makes a pretty small package.

John Ruskin

They who do not know how to live must make a merit of dying.

George Bernard Shaw

I am not a crook.

Richard Nixon

In January 1935, a collie managed to maroon herself on a chunk of ice in Lake Michigan. Police and firemen tried to coax her to swim ashore — to no avail. She merely went on howling. Finally, the lure of some pork chops did the trick. The dog swam ashore, gobbled up the chops — and immediately swam back to her icy roost.

The greatest pleasure of a dog is that you may make a fool of yourself with him, and not only will he not scold you, but he will make a fool of himself, too.

Samuel Butler

Mahogany wood does not always come from a mahogany tree. Contemporary standards may have changed, but "mahogany" formerly referred to sixty-seven different kinds of wood that shared similar characteristics and so could be sold in the United States under the name "mahogany."

JANUARY 22

Notable Births

1561	Francis Bacon	1909	U Thant
1729	Gotthold Lessing	1909	Ann Sothern
1747	Timothy Dexter	1917	Yehudi Menuhin
1775	Andre Ampere	1932	Piper Laurie
1788	Lord Byron	1934	Bill Bixby
1849	Auguste Strindberg	1937	Joseph Wambaugh

Notable Events

1814 First Freemason encampment held, New York City
1901 Death of Queen Victoria
1930 Five Power Naval Conference opened in London by George V
1937 Floods in Mississippi and Ohio Valleys killed 250 people
1944 Anzio beachhead established
1949 Nationalist Chinese surrendered Shanghai to Mao Tse Tung
1961 Portuguese cruise ship *Santa Maria* seized in Caribbean in attempted coup to overthrow Salazar
1973 Supreme Court overturned state laws concerning first-trimester abortions
1973 Boeing 707 crashed in Nigeria, 176 deaths

Questions: What's a Mud in the Netherlands?

What's a Pond in Surinam?

An aspiring young poet brought one of his poems to the Harvard professor William Dean Howells, and asked him for his opinion. Howells read it, and was mightily impressed. "This is a magnificent poem. Did you write it unaided?"

The young man assured him that it was completely his own work.

Howells then replied, "I'm very glad to meet you, Lord Byron. I was under the impression you had died at Missolonghi a good many years ago."

Lord Byron is widely — and erroneously — believed to have had a club foot. His left leg was an inch-and-a-half shorter than his right and had a slightly deformed ankle, but both his feet were exceptionally thin and narrow, exactly the opposite of a club-foot.

The Fifty-third Congress of the United States (1893-95) included among its members George Washington Smith of Illinois; George Washington Fithian of Illinois; George Washington Ray of New York; George Washington Houck of Ohio; George Washington Hulick of Ohio; George Washington Wilson of Ohio; George Washington Shell of South Carolina; and George Washington Murray of South Carolina.

According to the 1783 Treaty of Paris, which ended the Revolutionary War, part of the northeastern border of the United States was to follow the upper Saint John River between Canada and Maine. That agreement worked well for many years; in that part of the world there were so few people that no one bothered much about national distinctions. However, the Webster-Ashburton Treaty of 1840 called for the border to be surveyed, to avoid any problems in the future.

Accordingly, the surveyors arrived in northern Maine, and were warmly greeted by the residents. Very warmly welcomed; *spiritously* welcomed, in fact. By the time the group and their local guides reached the confluence of the Saint John and Saint Francis Rivers, a region of many channels and islands that make the separate rivers almost indistinguishable, they were quite drunk. The locals proceeded to shuttle the surveyors up the Saint Francis, and had them all the way to Estcourt before they sobered up enough to realize their mistake. Rather than complicate matters by retracing their steps and starting over, they simply drew a line to the Saint John from Estcourt and called the whole thing fair and square. The little mistake cost Canada several hundred square miles of territory, worth many million dollars today.

In 1949, housewives in Niteroi, Brazil, began to complain of tadpoles in their milk. When questioned, the milkman confessed that, although he normally watered the milk down from the hydrant, because of the water shortage he had been forced to use the nearby creek.

On January 22, 1937, in a newspaper feature called "Today Is the Day," it was reported that, "An earthworm can grow a new tail or hand in place of one cut off."

I've never seen an earthworm with a tail, have you?

Answers: 2.471 acres.
1.102 pounds.

JANUARY 23

Questions: If a woman were to change her sex, why could she no longer be a Christian?

What kind of men are most likely to worship their Maker?

Notable Births

1632	Samuel Pepys	1903	Randolph Scott
1783	Stendhal	1907	Dan Duryea
1832	Edouard Manet	1919	Ernie Kovacs
1861	Katharine Tynan	1928	Jeanne Moreau
1899	Humphrey Bogart	1936	Jerry Kramer

Notable Events

1793	Russia and Prussia agreed on second partitioning of Poland
1891	First United States integrated hospital incorporated, Chicago
1942	Battle of Macassar Straits began
1942	Congress appropriated 12.5 billion for 33,000 planes
1968	North Koreans seized U.S.S. *Pueblo*
1978	North Carolina governor reduced terms for 9 of Wilmington Ten

Very often, the popularizer of a catchy phrase has a larger audience than its originator, so the authorship of that saying is attributed to its promulgator rather than to its creator. Look at the following examples:

"Everybody talks about the weather, but nobody does anything about it." This remark was originally made by Charles Dudley Warner, not by Mark Twain.

"Go west, young man, go west." The Ohio newspaperman John L. Soule said it first; Horace Greeley merely repeated it in the *New York Tribune*, which had a much greater circulation. Therefore, the dictum is attributed to Greeley.

"*L'état, c'est moi*." There's no record that Louis XIV ever said it, though he no doubt wished it were true. The credit probably belongs to Voltaire.

"I disapprove of what you say, but I will defend unto death your right to say it." This comes from S. C. Tallentyne, not Voltaire, although several phrases in the French writer's works come close to it.

"Let them eat cake!" This is Rousseau's phrase, not Marie Antoinette's.

"Britain is a nation of shopkeepers." Napoleon didn't coin this; the British economist Adam Smith did.

"God is always on the side of the biggest battalions." It's a Napoleonic statement, but Voltaire is more likely responsible for it. Frederick the Great came up with a similar statement, and the Roman Tacitus, 1,600 years earlier, had said essentially the same thing.

The phrase, "Peace in our time," comes from the Anglican *Book of Common Prayer*; Neville Chamberlain merely echoed it.

Winston Churchill is generally credited with the phrase "blood, sweat, and tears." But John Donne used it in a slightly different form 300 years earlier, and Byron used a form similar to Donne's nearly 150 years ahead of Churchill.

Face-patching was a popular custom during the late Roman Empire, but after its fall the habit was not practiced for over a thousand years.

The use of patches was reborn under Louis XV in France about 1640. Initially, women stuck bits of black taffeta on their faces simulating strategically placed moles or beauty marks. After the Restoration, this practice was widely adopted in England, where it was considerably embellished. English women in the late seventeenth century often appeared at social events covered with patches in the shapes of planet signs, stars, and crescents. More daring ladies might wear silhouettes of a coach-and-six or a cavalry rider pasted on their cheeks and foreheads.

Men didn't find the patches attractive, at least at first. Samuel Pepys complained once in his diary that he had reprimanded his wife for patching herself, only to record less than a month later that at the previous evening's ball, his wife wore two patches and looked "far handsomer than Princess Henrietta."

The English eventually developed an etiquette for patches; Whig wives patched on the right side of their faces, Tory wives on the left; the politically neutral wives patched both and would present their left or right profile according to their company's political persuasion. Also, patches, although generally black, were taboo during periods of mourning.

The cosmetic use of patches reached its height in the mid-seventeenth century; one commentator lamented that women's faces were becoming "one big patch." The custom died out by the end of the century.

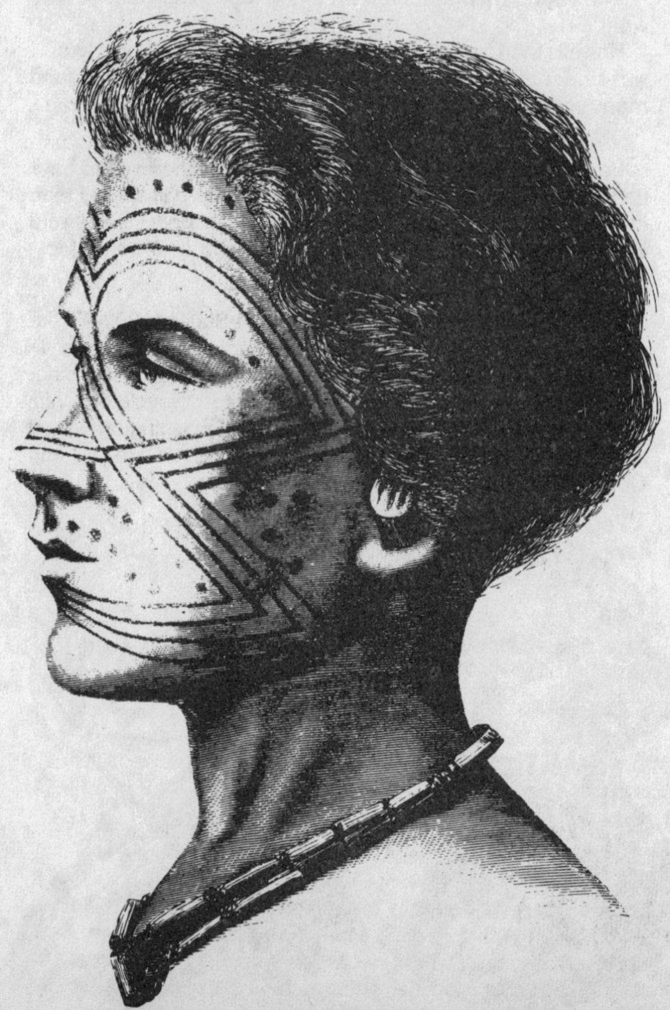

Answers: Because she would be a he-then.

Self-made men.

Notable Births

1712	Frederick the Great	1894	Vicki Baum
1732	Pierre de Beaumarchais	1917	Ernest Borgnine
1834	Charles H. Webb	1918	Oral Roberts
1862	Edith Wharton	1925	Maria Tallchief

Notable Events

661	Caliph Ali murdered
1556	Earthquake in Shensi Province, China, took 890,000 lives
1848	John Sutter and James Marshall discovered gold in California
1868	Impeachment of Andrew Johnson
1908	First Boy Scout troop organized in England
1922	Eskimo Pie patented
1935	Canned beer first distributed, Richmond, Virginia
1939	Chilean earthquake killed 30,000
1945	New York Yankees sold for $3 million to McPhail and Topping
1952	Alger Hiss appealed for third trial, accused Chambers of forgery
1964	Hayes Jones won 50th straight race, broke world hurdle record
1966	Boeing 707 crashed into Mont Blanc, killed 117 people

Polar bears use only their front legs for swimming, yet they have been spotted eighty miles away from any ice floe or land.

The igloo is an invention of the white man. Half of all Eskimos have never seen one.

On January 24, 1794, in the Solway Firth, Scotland, there raged a vicious storm that eventually resulted in the bodies of forty-five dogs, 180 rabbits, 1,840 sheep, nine cattle (all black), and three people washing ashore in the area.

Wasps can and do get drunk, and they are more likely to sting you than sober ones. When grapes, certain kinds of plums, and other similar fruits start to decay, their sugars ferment. Wasps, which feed on these fruits, take in the alchoholic juices and the effect is immediate. Though it usually means just a few hours of staggering around on the ground, the insects do occasionally OD on the stuff.

Question: Five numbers are in a row. The second number is twice the fourth. The third is twice the fifth. The fourth is twice the third. Twice the first equals the first. What's the number?

Epitaph of John Randall, on a stone in Warwickshire, England:

"Here old John Randall lies, who counting by his tale,
Lived three score years and ten, such virtue was in ale;
Ale was his meat, ale was his drink, ale did his heart revive,
And could he still have drunk his ale, he still had been alive."

According to Edward Batzner, a Milwaukee exterminator, mice aren't particularly fond of cheese. He's found the best bait is a lemon gumdrop. He believes they're attracted by the color, and thinks that the stickiness of the jelly is an asset when the bar springs in the trap. Cotton, which the mice use for nests, is also a good bait, Batzner claims.

Always very hard winter when honorable cheese runs after mouse.

Charlie Chan

What happens to the hole when the cheese is gone?

Bertolt Brecht

If you walked around ancient Greece with the udder of a hyena tied to your left arm, women were sure to fall madly in love with you. It was reputed to be one of the strongest of all aphrodisiacs.

Death rates around the world are lowest at the temperature of sixty-four degrees, and a relative humidity of 80 percent. A rise in temperature of ten degrees increases the death rate by about 17 percent.

Answer: 08241.

JANUARY 25

Question: Name their vice-presidents:
T. Roosevelt
William Taft
George Washington
John Adams

Notable Births

1759	Robert Burns	1919	Edwin Newman
1874	Somerset Maugham	1924	Lou Groza
1882	Virginia Woolf	1935	Dean Jones
1886	Wilhelm Furtwangler	1937	Don Maynard

Notable Events

1533 Henry VIII married Anne Boleyn
1904 179 people killed in Cheswick, Pennsylvania, mining disaster
1938 Chilean earthquake took 80,000 lives
1940 First Social Security checks mailed
1945 Grand Rapids, Michigan, became first community to fluoridate water
1946 John Lewis and UMW joined AF of L
1950 Alger Hiss found guilty of perjury
1959 John XXIII called first Vatican Council since 1870

On this date in 1904, the English Parliament passed a law which required that a commoner be licensed to shoot a long bow. Lords were exempt from this provision.

A bar in Grand Rapids, Michigan, was ordered not too long ago to install a ramp up to the stage — to accommodate handicapped strippers.

Even though legend has endowed Anne Boleyn, the young woman for whom Henry VIII managed to get England excommunicated, with surpassing beauty, one of her contemporaries commented acidly on her dark, unattractive complexion, the ugly growth on her neck, and her sixth finger.

The devil hath power to assume a pleasing shape.
Shakespeare

Answer: Charles Fairbanks; James Sherman; John Adams; Thomas Jefferson.

Some words in English that used to begin with the letter *n* now begin with a vowel, and others that used to begin with vowels now begin with *n*. Why? It's due to the back-and-forth transference in speech of the *n* from the articles "a" and "an," and the first syllable of the following word. Some examples:

original	transferred form
an ewt	a newt
an ekename	a nickname
a nadder	an adder
a napron	an apron
a norange	an orange
a nompair	an umpire

Eke is an Anglo-Saxon word meaning also. Umpire comes from the French words *non par*, or "not equal," referring to a third, disinterested party who settles disputes between two involved individuals.

A rogue's tombstone from Witchingham, England, 1650:

Thomas Alleyn and His Two Wives.

Death here hath advantage of life, I spy,
One husband with two wives may lie.

Waterspouts at sea are generally composed of fresh water, which comes from accompanying clouds and rain. Very little sea water is involved, and that only near the base of the ocean tornado.

Sir John Dalyell of Binns, England had a sea anenome for a pet. It lived sixty-six years. He called it Grannie.

How much is a part per million?
It's:

An ounce in 31.25 tons
An inch in sixteen miles
A needle in a two-thousand-pound haystack
A penny in $10,000
A minute in 1.9 years
A snowball's chance in hell (roughly).

Notable Births

1831	Mary Mapes Dodge	1925	Joan Leslie
1871	Warner Fabian	1928	Eartha Kitt
1880	Douglas MacArthur	1928	Roger Vadim
1925	Paul Newman	1929	Jules Feiffer

Notable Events

1531	Lisbon, Portugal, earthquake claimed 30,000 lives
1695	First Workman's Compensation agreement in America made
1861	Louisiana seceded
1870	Virginia readmitted to the Union
1930	De Rivera quit in Spain
1931	Gandhi released from prison in general amnesty, Poona, India
1934	Germany and Poland signed 10-year non-aggression pact
1950	First babysitter's insurance policy issued, St. Louis
1965	Hindi became official language of India
1971	Charles Manson and three followers found guilty of seven murders, Los Angeles

Fritz Haarmon worked as a food smuggler between 1919 and 1924 in his native Germany, where food was often scarce. Sometimes, when demand was overwhelming, Haarmon would attempt to improve the situation. This latter-day Sweeney Todd killed at least twenty-eight and possibly as many as fifty teenagers, ground them up, and sold their spiced flesh as sausage.

Culture is what your butcher would have if he were a surgeon.

Mary Poole

Bait only good if fish bite on same.

Charlie Chan

The town of Shirhatti in Sangli, India, has been owned by the Desai family for over 370 years. This came about in an odd way. One night in 1607, its former owner, a wealthy man named Anushkar, was playing chess with his wife when his lamp began to sputter. Afraid he would be unable to finish the game, he allowed that he would trade the whole town for a cup of lamp oil. A woman from the Desai family overheard the remark, provided a cup of melted butter, and took title to the town.

Questions: If the Devil lost his tail, where would he get it replaced?

Why is the Devil always a gentleman?

In 1955, a Londoner, Norman White, had five jobs in three weeks. It wasn't that he was a lazy or unskilled worker; quite simply, he would get himself hired, then call his new employer anonymously and tell him, "White is a homicidal maniac." He'd be fired, pick up a week's severance pay, and go on unemployment compensation. The court admired his ingenuity, but not his honesty, and sent him to prison for eight months.

Labor disgraces no man; unfortunately, you occasionally find men disgrace labor.

Ulysses S. Grant

If you don't want to work you have to work to earn enough money so that you won't have to work.

Ogden Nash

Water in the form of steam is invisible. The whitish cloud that forms above a boiling pan of water or comes from the spout of a teakettle is simply that — a cloud of condensed water vapor, cooled down steam. If you look just above a boiling vessel's liquid surface, where the steam is above 212 degrees, you'll notice that it is indeed invisible.

It's not that sheep are stupid, it's just that they merely suffer from what is known as a regressive instinct. If you hold a stick horizontally before the leading ram of a flock of sheep, the ram will, if coaxed, jump over it. If you then direct the rest of the sheep along the same path, each will jump where the ram jumped, even if you remove the stick or place it in a different position. The instinct has come down from the time before sheep were domesticated, and it was a valuable asset when herds of wild sheep faced dangerous mountainsides and the threats of predators.

Answers: At a liquor store, where bad spirits are re-tailed.

As the Imp o' Darkness, he can never be Imp-o-lite.

JANUARY 27

Question: Give me your huddled masses . . .
Can you name the five countries that sent the most immigrants to the United States in 1978?

Notable Births

1756	Wolfgang Mozart	1908	William R. Hearst, Jr.
1832	Lewis Carroll	1918	Skitch Henderson
1850	Samuel Gompers	1921	Donna Reed
1872	Learned Hand	1937	Troy Donahue
1885	Jerome Kern	1948	Mikhail Baryshnikov

Notable Events

1891	Mine cave-in in Mount Pleasant, Pennsylvania, killed 109 people
1931	Laval became French premier
1941	Willkie and Churchill conferred
1943	First all-American air raids over Germany
1964	Margaret Chase Smith announced her candidacy for presidency
1973	End of the draft announced by Defense Secretary Laird
1977	Vatican reaffirmed its exclusion of women from the priesthood

The Catholic Church has made saints of some remarkable individuals. Saint Frances (or Francesca) was one. She was beatified in 1608 for being an aesthetic flagellatrix. Throughout her life she ate nothing but peas, beans, and herbs, and drank nothing but water. Her habit, day and night, was an iron girdle next to her skin, a woolen chemise, and a hair cloth. According to Nicholas Vignier, ". . . this Roman matron was ranked among the saints by the pope, because she used to check the stimulations of the flesh by dropping scalding bacon on her pudenda."

No one has ever loved anyone the way everyone wants to be loved.

Mignon McLaughlin

Fanaticism consists in redoubling your efforts when you have forgotten your aim.

George Santayana

Do not do unto others as you would that they should do unto you. Their taste may not be the same.

George Bernard Shaw

In 1960, 1.7 million Americans died. The money spent on their funerals was more than the entire country spent on dentistry, police protection, or fire protection that year. It was also more than the money spent on room, board, tuition, and books of the nation's 3.6 million college students. Between 1948 and 1960, the cost of living rose 26 percent, while the cost of dying rose 49 percent.

A man must swallow a toad every morning if he wishes to be sure of finding nothing still more disgusting before the day is over.

Chamfort

Answer: Mexico, Vietnam, Philippines, British West Indies, Korea.

JANUARY 28

Notable Births

814	Charlemagne	1873	Colette
1596	Sir Francis Drake	1884	Auguste Piccard
1775	Peter the Great	1887	Artur Rubenstein
1833	Sabine Baring-Gould	1936	Alan Alda

Notable Events

1547 Death of Henry VIII
1878 First commercial telephone exchange began operation, Hartford, Connecticut
1881 British defeated at Laing's Neck
1934 First rope ski tow commenced operation, Woodstock, Vermont
1938 FDR asked for a two-ocean navy
1941 U.S. troops landed in Northern Ireland
1960 United States bounced first photographs off the moon
1961 Rebels proclaimed Ruandan independence
1964 U.S. T-39 jet trainer shot down over Germany

The phrase "Mad as a Hatter" doesn't come from the Mad Hatter of *Alice in Wonderland* — although hatters in England *were* prone to insanity because the chemicals they used in tanning leather tended to damage their brain cells after many years' exposure. The term is actually a Cockney corruption of "mad as an adder"; in other words, venomous as a viper.

On January 27 and 28, 1939, many of the more astute residents of the Long Island community of Stony Brook decided to go fishing. No one used any fishing tackle, and yet they brought home over ten tons of fish.

How? Using saws and pickaxes. An exceptionally high tide, followed by a record cold snap, had carried some five thousand bass into a coastal lagoon and frozen them *in situ*. People simply chopped out the three-to-fourteen pounders, which were, naturally, already frozen and salted.

Question: Can you name the five most popular breeds of dogs in the United States?

President Rutherford B. Hayes's wife was a teetotaller, or so she thought, and an ardent supporter of Prohibition. Under pressure from her, Hayes proscribed the serving of liquor at White House dinners. However, the Chief Executive's chef was a rather insubordinate fellow, and at the very first dinner of the administration he served up a sorbet liberally laced with hootch. Mrs. Hayes sampled the punch, thought it delightful, and instructed that it be prepared for every White House function thereafter. Diplomats came to refer to the punch bowl table as the "life-saving station."

Horace Cole, an Englishman, bet several thousand pounds with some friends in 1910 that he could lie on his back for half an hour in the busiest intersection in Paris, and walk away unscathed.

During the rush hour on the appointed day the shrewd Cole calmly drove his truck into the intersection, stopped it, crawled underneath, and monkeyed with its underpinnings for thirty minutes. He then emerged, apologized for the enormous traffic snarl he'd created, and went to collect his winnings.

What is moral is what you feel good after.

Ernest Hemingway

Answer: Poodle, Doberman Pincher, Cocker Spaniel, German Shepherd, Labrador Retriever.

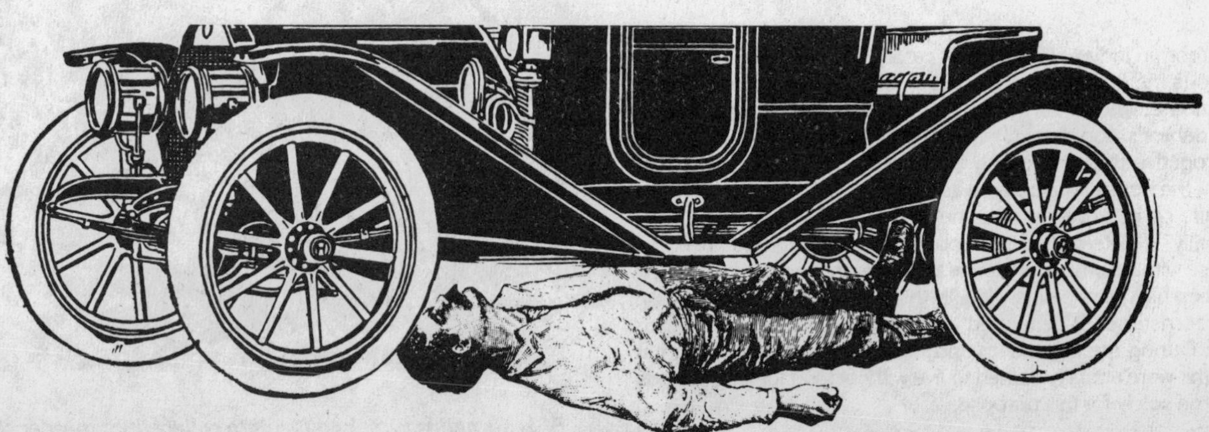

JANUARY 29

Question: Do you know what Ty Pickup, Doc Bass, Allie Watt, Red Lutz, Tige Stone, Heinie Odom, and Curly Onis have in common and are famous for?

Notable Births

1688	Emanuel Swedenborg	1918	John Forsythe
1737	Thomas Paine	1923	Paddy Chayevsky
1843	William McKinley	1925	Robert Crichton
1874	John D. Rockefeller, Jr.	1939	Germaine Greer
1915	Anita Louise	1943	Katharine Ross
1918	Bill Rigney	1945	Donna Caponi

Notable Events

1900	Baseball's American League organized
1916	First Zeppelin raid on Paris
1921	Germany agreed to pay $57 million in war reparations, Paris
1924	Ice-cream cone rolling machine patented
1931	United States apologized to Italy for General Butler's slur of Mussolini
1932	Japanese invaded Shanghai
1934	Senate rejected United States membership in World Court
1964	Major General Nguyen Van Thieu took over in South Vietnam

Two sets of Murphy's Laws:

MURPHY'S LAWS

1. In any field of scientific endeavor, anything that can go wrong, will go wrong;
2. Left to themselves, things will always go from bad to worse;
3. If there is a possibility of several things going wrong, the one that will go wrong is the one that will do the most damage;
4. Nature always sides with the hidden flaw;
5. Mother Nature is a Bitch;
6. If everything seems to be going well, you have obviously overlooked something.

MURPHY'S LAWS

A set of maxims that seems to fill the gaps between all the laws, rules, and regulations governing and explaining human behavior:

If anything can go wrong, it will.
Nothing is as simple as it seems.
Everything takes longer than you expect.
If you fool around with something long enough, it will eventually break.
If you try to please everybody, somebody is not going to like it.
It is a fundamental law of nature that nothing ever quite works out.
Whatever you want to do, you have to do something else first.
It's easier to get into a thing than to get out of it.
If you explain something so clearly that no one can misunderstand, someone will.

from *Urban Folklore from the Paperwork Empire*

The saying "to eat humble pie" stems from an ancient French word *ombles*, the entrails of animals. A thousand years ago, if a household servant had meat at all it was probably a meat pie made from the intestines of animals. To eat "humble pie" is therefore to lower oneself to a servile level. The word entered England with the Normans in 1066, and gradually evolved to the cockneyish "humble."

Brahmin Indians (the highest caste) had, until fairly recently, a curious method of collecting debts. When one was owed money by another who would not pay, the creditor would sit "dhurna" on the debtor's doorstep. Once there, he fasted and assumed the prerogative of allowing only those people he chose to enter or leave the house. The object was to starve the debtor out, or make his life so inconvenient that he paid the bill in question. Occasionally, a determined bill collector would enter the debtor's house with a number of friends and surround the deadbeat's bed to keep him from eating. Usually the bills were paid fairly quickly, but sometimes it depended on who succumbed to starvation first. During the eighteenth and nineteenth centuries, Brahmin youths were actually trained to live without food for long periods of time solely for this purpose.

Bills sometimes more difficult to collect than murder clues.
Charlie Chan

Answer: All have major league lifetime batting averages of 1,000.

Notable Births

1775	Walter Savage Landor	1928	Hal Prince
1866	Gelett Burgess	1931	Gene Hackman
1882	Franklin D. Roosevelt	1933	Richard Brautigan
1912	Barbara Tuchman	1934	Tammy Grimes
1914	David Wayne	1937	Boris Spassky
1925	Dorothy Malone	1937	Vanessa Redgrave

Notable Events

1649	Charles I beheaded by Cromwell
1798	House of Representatives brawl, Philadelphia
1835	First attempted assassination of a U.S. president, (Jackson)
1884	First meeting of anti-vivisectionist society, Philadelphia
1889	Suicide of Crown Prince Archduke Rudolf of Austria at Mayerling
1933	Hitler appointed German chancellor
1958	First moving sidewalk began operation, Dallas

Questions: Why is a sermon like a stalk of asparagus?

Why is Westminster Abbey like a fireplace?

When Franklin Delano Roosevelt was a young attorney in New York City, one of his first cases was a particularly complicated one, and his opponent was an extremely distinguished and successful lawyer. Both sides knew that the effectiveness of each lawyer's concluding arguments would probably swing the verdict. Roosevelt's opponent gave an impassioned but overlong statement that did not, however, appear to sway the jury. When Roosevelt's turn to speak finally came, he addressed himself to the jury and said simply, "You have heard the evidence. You have also listened to my distinguished colleague, a brilliant orator. If you believe him, and disbelieve the evidence, you will have to decide in his favor. That's all I have to say."

The jury debated for exactly five minutes. Roosevelt won the case.

Until late in the nineteenth century, the people of the Quilacare region of southern India had their own curious version of the two-term limit. No king could rule for more than twelve years; he was then required to commit ritual suicide.

After a huge feast, the outgoing king would bathe, pray to an idol, and ascend a scaffold draped with silken cloths. Armed with a sharp knife, he would cut off his nose, ears, lips, penis and testicles, and as much of his flesh as loss of blood would allow. When he felt himself getting faint, he cut his throat. Aspirants to the kingship had to attend this ceremony to learn the occupational hazards of leadership.

The purification of politics is an iridescent dream.

John James Ingalls

Education is what you get from reading the small print. Experience is what you get from not reading it.

Carl Albert

Forty years ago, the Philadelphia Zoo took an inventory of their animals and found that two of the anacondas were of a species previously unknown to herpitologists. The snakes had already been at the zoo for eleven years when the discovery was made.

Must turn up many stones to find hiding place of snake.

Charlie Chan

A motorist was bogged down in the mucky clay of a thoroughfare in Georgia's Tobacco Road region. A cracker came along with a team of mules and offered to pull the man out for $10 — a steep price — but the man had no choice.

"I guess you folks must be pulling people out of this mud day and night," said the tourist as he started on his way.

"Nope," said the Georgian. "At night we gotta bring in the water to make the mud."

The motor seems to slow down as it passes by.

Harvey E. White

On January 30, 1937, Charlie Johns married Eunice Winnstead in Sneedville, Tennessee. That Eunice was thirteen years her husband's junior would have raised few eyebrows, except that Charles was only twenty-two. Actually, in 1900, the legal age for marriage in nearly half the states was fourteen for males, twelve for females.

Only the young die good.

Oliver Herford

The youngest mother on record was a Chilean girl who gave birth via Caesarian section when she was five years old.

Only a mother would think her daughter has been a good girl when she returns from a date with a Gideon Bible in her handbag.

Laurence J. Peter

Answers: Because most people enjoy the end the most.

Because it contains the ashes of the great.

JANUARY 31

Question: Can you name the world's five largest lakes?

Thrift can be a misfortune. An Englishman named John Little was too parsimonius and suspicious for his own good. Once when Little was ill, a physician prescribed some wine as a medicine. Little protested the expense, but finally agreed to try it. Still, he wouldn't trust any of his servants to enter the wine cellar, so he was carried from his warm bed into the chilly cellar several times a day to fetch the wine. This thoroughly chilled him and led to complications that soon brought about his death. He left a fortune equivalent to about $200,000, in a day when a decent bottle of wine cost roughly a dime.

We're all born brave, trusting, and greedy, and most of us remain greedy.

Mignon McLaughlin

After spending some money in his sleep, Hermon the miser was so mad he hanged himself.

Lucilius

In Amsterdam on the last day of January 1790, a thick fog caused about 250 people to wander into the frigid canals of that city and drown.

Falstaff is one of Shakespeare's most beloved characters, and the role is not entirely without an historical basis. Sir John Falstaff was a real and endearingly ingenious fifteenth-century gentleman. A hero of sorts, as well. On this date in 1429, the French cavalry was moving rapidly on the English forces at Orléans. Falstafff succeeded in "repelling" his enemies by piling up some 400 carts of rapidly spoiling herring, meant as supplies for the English forces he feared he could not reach. The wall, though not impenetrable, was sufficiently unpleasant to hold the French at bay.

Many women in the Caucasus Mountains of Russia wear leather underwear.

The administration of law in the West was occasionally eccentric, but there were men who were basically honest. A judge in Nevada Territory was about to try a mining claim suit. He opened the proceedings in this fashion:

"Gentlemen, this court has received from the plaintiff in this case a check for $10,000. He has received from the defendant a check for $15,000. The court has returned $5,000 to the defendant and will now try the case on its merits."

There are a lot of mediocre judges and people and lawyers, and they are entitled to a little representation.

Senator Roman Hruska

Mind like parachute, only function when open.

Charlie Chan

Notable Births

1797	Franz Schubert	1915	Thomas Merton
1885	Anna Pavlova	1919	Jackie Robinson
1892	Eddie Cantor	1920	Stewart Udall
1903	Tallulah Bankhead	1920	Barbara Walters
1905	John O'Hara	1923	Carol Channing
1914	Jersey Joe Walcott	1923	Norman Mailer

Notable Events

1917	Germany resumed unrestricted submarine warfare on high seas
1920	First Ukranian daily newspaper published, New York City
1934	U.S. dollar devalued to 59.6 cents
1943	German Sixth Army surrendered at Stalingrad, turning point of World War II
1950	Harry Truman authorized Atomic Energy Commission to produce H-bomb
1958	First U.S. satellite *Explorer I*, launched

Lawyers today get a lot of bad press, much of it unjustified. Still, it's not quite as bad as it was 600 years ago. On January 31, 1381, Jack Cade and his supporters were so aggravated by the abuses of English barristers that they stormed the English Court of Chancery, destroyed all its records, and then proceeded to behead every lawyer they could find within reach.

You can as easily open an oyster without a knife as a lawyer's mouth without a fee.

Proverb

A research team at an American university planted a single shaft of winter wheat and let it grow for four months. They then carefully removed the dirt from the root system — and counted fourteen million distinct roots, totalling 378 miles. According to their estimates, there were fourteen *billion* root hairs, in a single cubic inch of dirt, and the total length of the root hairs approached 6,000 miles.

Answer: Caspian Sea, Lake Superior, Lake Victoria (Africa), Aral Sea, Lake Huron.

Pisces (The Fish)
February 20 through March 20

FEBRUARY

FEBRUARY 1

Question: By what names are these people better known?
Thomas Stevens
Annie Mae Bullock
Leslie Hornby
Ann Myrtle Swoyer
McKinley Morganfield

Notable Births

1859	Victor Herbert	1902	Langston Hughes
1887	Charles Nordhoff	1904	S.J. Perelman
1895	John Ford	1918	Muriel Spark
1895	Conn Smythe	1929	Stuart Whitman
1901	Clark Gable	1933	Stansfield Turner

Notable Events

1790	First sitting of U.S. Supreme Court, John Jay presiding
1861	Texas seceded
1896	X-rays discovered by Roentgen
1906	Leavenworth Prison completed
1908	King Carlos and the Crown Prince of Portugal murdered, Lisbon
1914	First motion picture censorship board, appointed, Pennsylvania
1935	Boulder/Hoover Dam began operation
1956	Blizzard in western Europe claimed 1,000 lives
1960	Woolworth lunch counter sit-ins began, Greensboro, North Carolina
1964	Johnson rejected de Gaulle's Vietnam peace proposals
1974	Sao Paolo, Brazil, bank building fire killed 189 people

Elizabeth Woodcock was unfortunately caught in a snowstorm near Cambridge, England, in 1779 and lost consciousness. Later she woke up under two feet of snow, but hadn't the strength to extricate herself; she did, however, manage to thrust a twig with her handkerchief tied to it through the snow. Eight days later she heard a voice ask, "Are you there , Elizabeth Woodcock?" Weakly she replied, "Dear John Stittle, I know your voice. For God's sake, help me out!"

He did, and she recovered. It would have been pleasant to report that the couple married and lived happily ever after, but it was not to be. Elizabeth's toes had been frostbitten; they became gangrenous, and caused her death several months later.

The virtuoso violinists Jascha Heifetz and Mischa Elman were dining at a restaurant one evening when a waiter approached their table with an envelope. The note was addressed simply: "To the World's Greatest Violinist." Politely, Elman pointed out that it must be for Heifetz, while Jascha insisted it had to be for Mischa. Finally, one of them opened it.

The salutation read: "Dear Mr. Kreisler."

I'll play it first and tell you what it is later.

Miles Davis

In 1870, Frank Damek of Chicago began to collect playing cards that he found on the street. By 1880, he needed fifteen cards to complete a full deck, and considered himself lucky to find eleven of those during the next three years. A further year passed before he found number forty-nine. Soon after, he was overjoyed to see what he thought was a full deck of cards on a Dearborn street sidewalk. This gave him fifty and fifty-one, but there were a half-dozen cards missing from the deck, including the last card he needed, the two of diamonds. He spent five-and-a-half years looking for that final card, and found it — at last — on a suburban commuter-train floor in 1890.

A yarborough is a hand of thirteen cards, in which no card is higher than a nine. The Duke of Yarborough used to wager odds of a thousand to one against any given individual being dealt such a hand — hence its name. The wily duke's odds were nearly two to one in his favor, as the mathematical chance of a deal of this kind is one in 1,860.

On February 1, 1936, Niagara Falls stopped falling, its flow of water blocked by a huge ice jam.

Charles Henri, a French professor, discovered in 1923 that when he placed new wine in a 60-100K electrostatic field for several minutes, it came out tasting exactly like vintage wine.

Humbly suggest not to judge wine by barrel it is in.

Charlie Chan

Answer: Terry-Thomas, Tina Turner, Twiggy, Nancy Walker, Muddy Waters.

Notable Births

1811	Delia Bacon	1905	Ayn Rand
1859	Havelock Ellis	1915	Lorne Greene
1875	Fritz Kreisler	1923	James Dickey
1882	James Joyce	1923	Red Schoendeinst
1886	William Rose Benet	1928	Stan Getz
1895	George Halas	1928	Elaine Stritch
1901	Jascha Heifetz	1937	Tom Smothers

Notable Events

1703 Earthquake in Japan killed 200,000 people
1779 Anti-popery riots began in Edinburgh, Scotland
1802 First leopard in the United States exhibited in Boston
1848 Treaty of Guadeloupe-Hidalgo ended Mexican War
1860 Jefferson Davis introduced slave trade resolutions to Congress
1863 First use of the pseudonym "Mark Twain" by Samuel Clemens
1876 National League formed
1912 First jump by a stuntman from Statue of Liberty
1953 Eisenhower declared he wouldn't hold Chiang Kai-shek back from Mainland China
1962 John Uelses became the first 16-foot indoor pole vaulter

James S. Moran was a press agent in the 1930s who delighted in controverting old sayings and traditional beliefs. He sold an ice box to an Eskimo, and found a needle in a haystack. He recorded the yowls of a female orangutan and sent the disc to Sumatra to be used as bait for a male orangutan. He trained a canary to sing "Yankee Doodle," and he sold advertising space on the ceilings of barbershops. In 1939, in collaboration with Fred Waring, the director of the famous singing group, the Pennsylvanians, he led a prize bull into a Fifth Avenue china shop. "Royalist Dandy Victor" didn't break a penny's worth of the $50,000 inventory.

We are not satisfied to be right, unless we can prove others to be quite wrong.

William Hazlitt

Between 1919 and 1967, the city of Chicago recorded over one thousand "gangland" slayings. Fully thirteen of these murders have been solved.

Very little is known of Pope John VIII, who wore St. Peter's ring from A.D. 855-857. The prelate was probably raised in Mentz, Germany, and was possibly the child of an English priest (Roman Catholic clergy were allowed to marry at the time). John was educated in Athens and Rome, and there was no one so well respected or so expert in matters of the church as this saintly priest. On the death of Pope Leo IV, John was elected to the papacy by the College of Cardinals.

John's reign was a short one, however. During a procession near Saint Clements Church in Rome, less than two-and-a-half years after ascending the throne, the pope collapsed and died—while giving birth. From her adolescent years, when she followed her lover-tutor to Athens, the pope had affected male garb and manner in order to pursue a life of scholarship ordinarily closed to women, and she had carefully concealed her sex from all but her lovers. No one knows who got her with child, but the culprit may have been anyone from a cardinal to a servant, according to contemporaries. And the story of "Pope Joan" may not be true at all — except that at least sixty-five papal historians have taken it seriously, and the Papal Curia, soon after her death, built two chairs with holes in their seats "... to feel under whether the newe-chosen Pope were furnished of all his ware," according to one commentator.

Question: What's the state shown here?

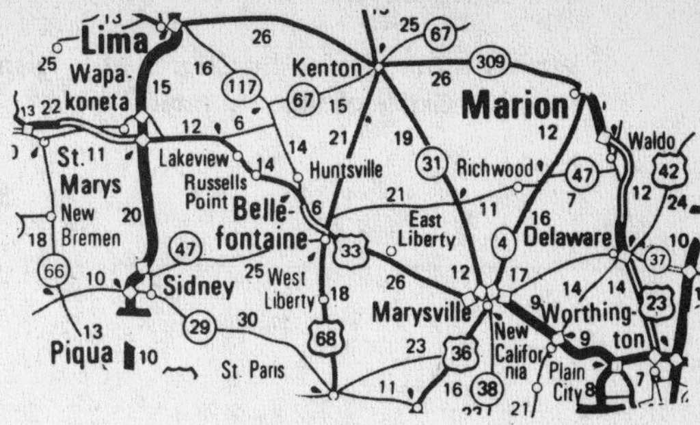

Answer: Ohio.

FEBRUARY 3

Questions: Why does a minister have an easier time than a doctor or a lawyer?

Why is a minister of the Church of England the most unreliable of all sermonizers?

Considering the clarity of his handwriting, Horace Greeley might have done better to have been a doctor instead of a newspaperman. In response to a request that he speak to a group in Illinois, he wrote this letter:

> Dear Sir: I am overworked and growing old. I shall be 60 on next February 3rd. On the whole, it seems I must decline to lecture henceforth except in the immediate vicinity. If I go at all, I cannot promise to visit Illinois on that errand, certainly not now.
>
> Yours truly,
> Horace Greeley

Several days later, Mr. Greeley received this reply in the mail:

> Dear Sir: Your acceptance to lecture before our association next winter came to hand this morning. Your penmanship not being the plainest, it took some time to translate it; but we succeeded and would say your time, February 3rd, and the terms, $60, are entirely satisfactory. As you suggest, we may be able to get you other engagements.
>
> Respectfully,
> H. M. Castle

Answers: Because it is easier to preach than practice.
Because he is never long a-ccurate if he can help it.

Notable Births

1809	Felix Mendelssohn	1894	Norman Rockwell
1811	Horace Greeley	1907	James Michener
1821	Elizabeth Blackwell	1926	Shelley Berman
1826	Walter Bagehot	1926	Art Arfons
1842	Sidney Lanier	1940	Fran Tarkenton
1874	Gertrude Stein	1941	Carol Mann
1890	Charles Correll (Andy)	1945	Bob Griese

Notable Events

1647 Scots army sold Charles I to Parliament for £400,000
1789 William Pitt introduced Regency Bill to strip insane George III of monarchical powers
1862 First U.S. newspaper printed on a train, at Port Huron, Michigan
1945 Yalta Conference began
1945 United States troops entered Manila
1959 Buddy Holly, Richie Valens, and The Big Bopper killed in plane crash
1960 Macmillan gave "Winds of Change" speech at Cape Town, South Africa

This is Gertrude Stein's favorite cryptogram. Can you figure it out?

stand	take	to	taking
we	you	throw	our

We understand you undertake to overthrow our undertaking.

It was hard, but not impossible, to get the best of Teddy Roosevelt. Once, while he was giving a speech during one of his campaigns, he was heckled by a man who kept shouting, "I'm a Democrat! I'm a Democrat!"

After some time, Roosevelt paused, smiled benevolently, and asked the man why.

He was told, "My grandfather was a Democrat, my father was a Democrat, and I am a Democrat!"

So Roosevelt asked him: "Suppose your father and grandfather were both jackasses. What would you be then?"

Without hesitation the man shot back, "A Republican!"

It makes no difference who you vote for — the two parties are really only one party representing four percent of the people.
Gore Vidal

A study of 1,600 intersections in Wilmington, Delaware, over a five-year period showed that death rates were eight times higher at intersections with traffic lights than at those without. Of course, the signals were generally installed at busier or more dangerous crossroads, but the experts also found that the lights tended to "tempt the reckless, and disarm the prudent."

Our national flower is the concrete cloverleaf.
Lewis Mumford

Notable Births

1895	Nigel Bruce	1905	Eddie Foy
1897	Ludwig Erhard	1918	Ida Lupino
1902	Charles Lindbergh	1921	Betty Friedan
1904	MacKinlay Kantor	1931	Isabel Peron

Notable Events

1169 Earthquake in Sicily killed 15,000 people
1555 Queen Mary began to burn and persecute Protestants
1783 Earthquake in Calabria, Italy, took 50,000 lives
1797 41,000 victims in Ecuadorian earthquake
1853 Louis Napoleon freed 4,300 political prisoners in honor of his marriage to Empress Eugenie
1861 Secessionist convention met in Montgomery, Alabama
1899 12,000 Filipinos began guerrilla war for independence
1974 Patty Hearst kidnapped
1976 $22 million in pay-offs by Lockheed to foreign officials disclosed

In February 1935, a sports dealer in Sturgeon, Michigan, lent an amateur hunter his best bird dog. When the man returned from his trip, the businessman asked him how things went.

"Not so good at first," he was told. "Your dog would sniff around, then seem to freeze up and stand stiff. But I booted him a couple or three times and he got over that habit!"

As bad a shape as the American Merchant Marine was in at the turn of the twentieth century, it might not have managed as well as it did if it hadn't been for the exploits of Shanghai Kelly. This notorious character was active in the San Francisco Bay area, and he was very successful in supplying men for crew-starved ships. It's been estimated that he secured as many as ten thousand men during his career.

His greatest achievement came when he got a triple-rush order for ninety bodies when three vessels needed to sail almost immediately. Shanghai was more than equal to the task. He rented a broken-down steamboat, contracted some lady friends, and ordered a couple of barrels of drugged whiskey. Then he sold tickets around the docks at a very attractive price for what he promised would be a three-day sex excursion.

As soon as the steamer got out into the harbor, the whiskey kegs were tapped, and in due course all of the male passengers were unconscious. The ladies were ferried back to shore, the stupified soon-to-be sailors were put aboard the contracting vessels, and Kelly collected both on the supine deckhands and on the tickets to the non-orgy. When the shanghaied sailors woke up, they were far out to sea.

Answer: *d,c,b,a*

Question: Can you put these events in order from the earliest to the most recent?

a Leonardo da Vinci paints the Mona Lisa.
b Gutenberg prints his first Bible.
c Chaucer finishes *Canterbury Tales.*
d Marco Polo writes *Travels* about visiting China.

In February 1952, Friedrich Bauer was sentenced in Alzey, Germany, to ten weeks in jail for buffing the fuzz from gooseberries and selling them as grapes.

In Turkey in the early eighteenth century it was the prerogative of the pasha to eat free at the home of any peasant family he cared to visit. That was bad enough but, in addition, at the completion of a meal he was allowed to charge his hosts a "tooth tax" for the wear and tear on the royal teeth occasioned by the dinner.

On February 4, 1874, Garnet Wolseley burned Kamasi, the capital city of what is now the Ashanti province of Ghana. A week later, the Ashanti War was officially concluded by the Treaty of Fommenah. King Koffee of the Ashanti tribe promised the British free trade, an open road to Kamasi, and a war indemnity. As a part of the treaty, he was also forced to agree to try to stop his tribe's practice of human sacrifice.

There never was a good war or a bad peace.
Benjamin Franklin

If there be a God, I think he would like me to paint Africa British-red as possible.
Cecil Rhodes

FEBRUARY 5

Question: By what names are these people better known?
Marion Morrison
Webb Hollenbeck
Jerome Silberman
Bessie Warfield
Shirley Schrift

Notable Births

1848	Belle Starr	1919	Red Buttons
1848	J.K. Huysmans	1926	Arthur Sulzberger
1906	John Carradine	1934	Hank Aaron
1914	William S. Burroughs	1942	Roger Staubach

Notable Events

1626 Peace of Rochelle ended Huguenot revolt
1631 Roger Williams arrived in America
1644 First branding legislation in United States enacted, Connecticut
1782 British forces lost Majorca
1792 British defeated Tippoo at Seringapatum
1811 George III declared insane again; Prince Regent given power for a year
1861 Moving-picture peep show patented
1901 Loop-the-loop centrifugal railway patented
1904 Russo-Japanese War began
1937 Roosevelt's "court-packing" proposal revealed
1947 Bierut became president of Poland

Until the influence of British colonialization took root, the women belonging to the warriors of certain Australian aborigine tribes generally went to war with their menfolk — but not to fight. They were used in peace negotiations before conflicts ever got started. When one band of warriors met another, it was the custom for one tribe to send its women over to the other side. If the receiving part wanted to continue good relations, they would have intercourse with the women, and no fighting would take place. If they wanted to go to war, they would send the women back untouched.

Playwright William Saroyan and Ross Bagdasarian, of "Alvin and the Chipmunks" fame, were cousins.

It's been said that only about 10 percent of American women can whistle.

The Englishman James Puckle introduced the first working machine gun in 1718. It was a flintlock, capable of firing sixty-three rounds in seven minutes. One of its notable features was that it had interchangeable barrels, one set of which could be used to fire square bullets when the British were warring against infidels. (The use of square bullets was an efficient and unpleasant method of tearing an enemy apart.)

Whenever science makes a discovery, the devil grabs it while the angels are debating the best way to use it.

Alan Valentine

Until the end of the Middle Ages, people convicted of drunkenness in England had the shape of a bottle or the letter *D* branded into their foreheads. Habitual offenders were cured permanently by being forced to drink molten lead or boiling urine.

On subject of drink, I am one-round prize fighter. Second round always knockout.

Charlie Chan

Scientists at the University of California have discovered that, if male birds are scarce, female seagulls will set up lesbian relationships with each other, with one bird taking the traditional male role and the other the female. They perform mating rituals and sex acts, lay sterile eggs and attempt to hatch them, guard their nests, and otherwise act as a normal male and female.

Answer: John Wayne, Clifton Webb, Gene Wilder, Duchess of Windsor, Shelley Winters.

Notable Births

1756	Aaron Burr	1923	Zsa Zsa Gabor
1895	Babe Ruth	1932	François Truffaut
1911	Ronald Reagan	1943	Fabian Forte

Notable Events

1715 Peace of Madrid ended Spanish-Portuguese hostilities
1788 Constitution ratified by Massachusetts
1936 K.E. Ohi became first Japanese woman to receive Doctor of Laws degree in United States
1948 First demonstration of radio-controlled aircraft
1952 George VI died
1956 First circular school building opened, Kankakee, Illinois
1964 Cuba cut water supply to Guantanemo Naval Base

Brian G. Hughes was a businessman in New York at the turn of the century who delighted in making other people look foolish. On one occasion, he snuck up to the door of the Metropolitan Museum of Art at night, and deposited several empty picture frames and some burglary tools. Then he waited for all hell to break loose. It did, much to the amusement of Hughes and his friends. For another joke, he scattered a bag of counterfeit jewels in front of Tiffany's during the busiest part of the day, and delightedly watched customers and passersby scramble for the jewels.

One of Hughes's favorite running gags was the phony invitation. He would make up elaborate engraved invitations to nonexistant social functions, and distribute them to business and community leaders whom Hughes felt were particularly in need of having their egos deflated. On one occasion, he himself was feted by the city's Board of Aldermen in appreciation of his gift of some land in Brooklyn, which he had given to the city to be turned into a park. The lot he had so generously given turned out to be sixteen square feet of useless property. Once again, Hughes was left laughing at official pomposity.

Two of Hughes's best stunts involved animals. He bought a mangy alley cat for a dime, fed him, nursed him, cleaned him up for a few weeks, and the put him in a prestigious New York cat show. The feline was entered as a Dublin Brindle breed named Nicodemus, by Broomstick, out of Dustpan by Sweeper. The cat took a first prize.

Hughes pulled a similar trick with a broken-down horse he bought for $11.50 when the horse-drawn trolleys of New York City were being replaced by electric ones. According to papers that were filed by Hughes before the horse show, Orphan Puldeca was sired by Metropolitan, and his dam was called Electricity. These names led someone who knew Hughes and his reputation to become suspicious. When it was discovered that Orphan's rider, the young Miss Clara Hughes, had to ring a bell before the horse would move, suspicions were pretty much confirmed. Hughes owned up to the hoax before the contest got underway, but insisted that he thought "Often Pulled a Car" could have won it.

Question: By what other names are these ladies known?
Claudia Taylor
Thelma Ryan
Elizabeth Bloomer
Eleanor Smith

Who knows what he is told, must know a lot of things that are not so.

Arthur Guiterman

The word "pedigree" was derived from the resemblance of an ancestral family tree to a bird's foot. Tables of pedigree are made up by drawing lines from a common ancestor to each one of his or her descendants. On some charts the radiating lines resemble the foot of a large bird, and so the French named them *pied-de-grue* — or "foot of the crane."

Q: What is seventeen inches at the neck, forty-two inches at the waist, and sixty inches at the hips?
A: Babe Ruth's 1935 baseball uniform.

Answer: Lady Bird Johnson, Pat Nixon, Betty Ford, Rosalynn Carter.

FEBRUARY 7

Questions: How is the house of a tidy woman like a motion to adjourn?

Why is an empty matchbox better than any other kind?

It has been reliably estimated that during the Victorian era, 10 to 15 percent of the female population of London engaged in prostitution at least occasionally. That figure represents about one adult woman in four.

If you cannot get rid of the family skeleton, you may as well make it dance.

George Bernard Shaw

Sir Thomas More in his book *Utopia* lambasted the follies and foolishnesses of the Catholic Church, contemporary European states, and the leaders of church and state, and offered rational, scientific ideas to construct a just and efficient social system. He hoped, by writing *Utopia*, to stimulate the imagination of his contemporaries. *Utopia* was clearly written about a fictitious island, and More was devastated when, immediately after its publication, many of the most intelligent men in Europe, especially members of the clergy, wanted to know the location of Utopia so they could bring it *up* to European standards.

Idealism increases in direct proportion to one's distance from the problem.

John Galsworthy

Be virtuous and you will be eccentric.

Mark Twain

Charles Dickens could only sleep if his head was at the north end of the bed.

Notable Births

1478	Thomas More	1883	Eubie Blake
1812	Charles Dickens	1885	Sinclair Lewis
1834	Dimitri Mendeliev	1901	B.A. Botkin
1835	Samuel Butler	1908	Buster Crabbe
1867	Laura Ingalls Wilder	1920	Eddie Bracken

Notable Events

1792	Austro-Prussian alliance formed against France
1898	Trial of Emile Zola began
1933	Dutch sailors mutinied on battleship in Dutch West Indies
1936	Flag of the vice-president of the United States established
1964	Sargent Shriver named to direct War on Poverty
1964	Beatles arrived in United States
1978	Russian flu at Air Force Academy disabled 65 percent of student body

James Dickens was a careless thief. He was picked up by the Denver police in the fall of 1954 shortly after he'd been released from the prison where he had been serving time for two robberies. During the first theft, he had left his Air Force I.D. tags behind him. In the second one, he left his wallet. And in Denver, it was his three-day-old parole papers that Dickens forgot.

Biggest mistake in history made by people who didn't think.

Charlie Chan

In 1977, a baggage clerk at Union Station in Washington, D.C., began a frustrating ordeal, perhaps similar to many the computer has in store for all of us sooner or later. Wanda Marie Johnson received a bill for some medical attention she had not received; was ordered to drive with her glasses on (though she'd never owned a pair); and was taken to court for non-payment of a bill for furniture she had never bought.

The problem? It wasn't entirely the computer's fault. She was born on the same day, in the same district as another person whose married name had just become Wanda Marie Johnson. Both had two children, drove the same model car, had lived in Grenada, and had eight of the same digits on their Social Security cards. The State of Maryland assigns driver's licenses by a computer using standardized information, so their licenses were identical.

An eye test administered four times finally showed up the difference in the women's eyesight, and when newspapers picked up the story, the rest of the problems were worked out. The second W.M. Johnson now uses her former name in legal situations.

Sinclair Lewis, the first American to win the Nobel Prize for Literature, was once fired from his job because his boss felt he was an incompetent writer.

Every bird seeks its own tree — never tree, the bird.

Charlie Chan

Answers: Because both are always in order.
Because it is matchless.

Notable Births

1819	John Ruskin	1895	King Vidor
1820	William Tecumseh Sherman	1911	Elizabeth Bishop
1828	Jules Verne	1920	Lana Turner
1878	Martin Buber	1925	Jack Lemmon
		1931	James Dean

Notable Events

1587 Execution of Mary Queen of Scots at Fotheringay Castle
1622 James I dissolved Parliament
1872 Viceroy of India, Lord Mayo, assassinated
1910 Boy Scouts of America incorporated
1923 Dawson, New Mexico, mining disaster killed 120 people
1924 First execution using gas, Carson City, Nevada
1955 Malenkov ousted as premier of Russia

Question: Which city is farther from New York (by air)?
Moscow or Rio de Janeiro
Rome or Honolulu
Caracas (Venezuela) or San Francisco

In the late 1940s, when a number of the southern states were still officially "dry," a state representative in Louisiana provided an alternative to the moonshiner for hundreds of thousands of satisfied customers. It was a tonic called Hadacol, a mixture of minerals, vitamins, honey, water — and a healthy 12 percent alcohol.

Dudley J. LeBlanc was a super salesman and an entrepreneur of the first order. Born in 1894 in a wooden shack in Cajun Louisiana, in high school he began to sell burial insurance, patent medicine, and tobacco to help support his family. He was so successful he was able to put himself and four of his brothers through college. After a tour of duty with the army he began his own burial insurance company, which numbered two hundred thousand customers within a few years. He branched out in the late thirties with a preparation called Happy Day Headache Powder and made another bundle before the Food and Drug Administration made him close shop because of the unsubstantiated miracles he claimed on the label.

LeBlanc, now a state senator, began to experiment with vitamin B formulas for his own rheumatism in 1943 (or so he said). In short order he had concocted a mixture of various vitamin chemicals, booze, iron, manganese, liquor, calcium, phosphorus, honey and hootch, which seemed to do the trick for him.

As far as "Couzin Dud" and the Hadacol label were concerned, the stuff was good for "anemia, arthritis, asthma, diabetes, eczema, epilepsy, gallstones, hay fever, heart trouble, high and low blood pressure, rheumatism, cancer, paralytic strokes, pellagra, pneumonia, tuberculosis, and ulcers." And the price was right: $1.25 for the half pint, $3.50 for the twenty-four-ounce family size.

Actually, Hadacol had been developed by a company called Wonder Medicine, Inc. Quietly introduced on the market, and poorly promoted, its sales were disappointing before pitchman LeBlanc put his expertise behind it. Taking over the advertising in late 1947, a year in which the medicine accounted for a paltry $75,000 in retail sales, by 1949 he'd built it up to several million dollars.

Then LeBlanc pulled out all the stops. He advertised Hadacol on a thousand billboards, every available barnside, over 819 radio stations, and in 4,500 newspapers and scores of magazines. He even advertised for a parrot who could say "Polly wants Hadacol," and formed Captain Hadacol Clubs for the kiddies.

His greatest achievement was the Hadacol Good Will Caravan, which hit the road in late 1950. This procession traveled 3,800 miles through eighteen southern states that winter. On all or on portions of the tour were Mickey ("Andy Hardy Uses Hadacol") Rooney, Carmen Miranda, Chico Marx, George Burns and Gracie Allen, Roy Acuff, Jack Dempsey, Jimmy Durante, Bob Hope, and Hank Williams. Admission wasn't quite free — you needed a Hadacol boxtop to get in — and it cost Couzin Dud $400,000 to stage. But over three million bottles of the tonic were sold on the caravan alone, and demand for it grew greater than LeBlanc's manufacturing capabilities. Black market Hadacol went for two dollars a bottle. Sales totalled $24 million in 1950, and LeBlanc's projection of $75 million for 1951 seemed within reach.

Then LeBlanc's old nemesis, the federal government, stepped in. Despite glowing testimonials from satisfied users ("I was too disabled to get over a fence. After I took eight bottles of Hadacol . . . I felt like jumping over a six-foot fence and am getting very sassy"), the Federal Trade Commission sampled the elixir and found it wanting. Not wishing to stir up a controversy in the midst of his second campaign for the governorship, LeBlanc toned down the advertising. That satisfied the FTC, but by this time both the State of Louisiana and the Internal Revenue Service were interested in Hadacol and Couzin Dud's tax payments, or lack of them. Admittedly, LeBlanc compounded his problems. On a 1951 $75,000 Hadacol radio special (which featured Judy Garland) when Groucho Marx asked him what Hadacol was good for, he replied, "It was good for five-and-a-half million dollars for me last year." That raised some IRS eyebrows. That LeBlanc often bragged he was so rich he turned in his Cadillacs when the ashtrays got full couldn't have helped, either.

In any event, LeBlanc's empire disintegrated rapidly. Tax payments and legal expenses took away a good deal of his operating capital, and a lot of his customers began to suspect they'd been boondoggled. The company filed for bankruptcy in October, 1951, and Couzin Dud faded away into the background while legal proceedings dragged on for nine years. Not until there was only enough money left to pay the lawyers was the case concluded.

The reason crime doesn't pay is that when it does it is called by a more respectable name.

Laurence J. Peter

Advertising is the rattling of a stick inside a swill bucket.

George Orwell

Answer: Rio, Honolulu, San Francisco, in that order.

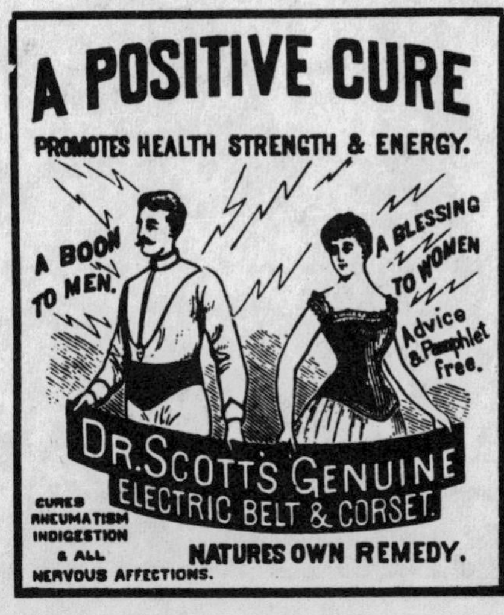

FEBRUARY 9

Question: By what names are these people better known?
Steveland Judkins
Isaiah Leopold
Golda Mabovitz
Helen Mitchell
Lebrecht Hommel

Notable Births

1773	William Henry Harrison	1914	Gypsy Rose Lee
1874	Amy Lowell	1914	Carmen Miranda
1886	George Ade	1923	Brendan Behan
1891	Ronald Colman	1923	Kathryn Grayson
1903	Brian Donleavy	1928	Roger Mudd
1909	Dean Rusk	1941	Carole King
1914	Bill Veeck	1946	Mia Farrow

Notable Events

1795	France and Tuscany concluded peace treaty
1801	Peace of Luneuille made between Austria and France
1861	Jefferson Davis elected president of the Confederacy
1918	Ukraine concluded peace with Central Powers
1941	Germany occupied Bulgaria
1943	Japanese evacuated Guadacanal
1955	AF of L and CIO agreed to merge

Manna, the mysterious food that fed the Israelites during their forty years in the wilderness, is, in a way, related to the word "kangaroo." When Captain James Cook landed in Australia in the eighteenth century, he was intrigued by the animal we call a kangaroo, and he asked the aborigines what the name of the creature was. They answered, "Kangaroo," not understanding a word of the captain's question. In their tongue, kangaroo meant, "What did you say?"

The word "manna" is a similar one. It is a corruption of the Hebrew *man-hu*, which means, "What is this?" When the Jews first found this food, they did not know what it was, and could give it no name. So they simply repeated the phrase *man-hu, man-hu*. The "What-is-this-from-Heaven" sustained them through four decades.

A peace activist in Northern Ireland named Elizabeth McClelland finally got so fed up with the situation in Belfast that she immigrated to New Zealand. There, at a peace rally in Christchurch a few years ago, she was killed when a demonstrator's sign struck her in the head.

One of the movie moguls the Marx Brothers had to deal with was Irving Thalberg of MGM. Purposefully or not, Thalberg had the annoying habit of making people wait outside his office for extended periods of time. One time he kept *les frères Marx* longer than they liked. When he finally got aroung to seeing them, he discovered they were stark naked outside his doorway, roasting potatoes in the lobby's fireplace.

It was the last time he kept them waiting.

Answer: Stevie Wonder, Ed Wynn, Golda Meir, Nellie Melba, Lauritz Melchior.

Question: How would a mathematician describe a pair of dice?

a 2 hexahedrons
b 2 tetrahedrons
c 2 icosahedrons

Notable Births

1670	William Congreve	1898	Bertolt Brecht
1775	Charles Lamb	1898	Dame Judith Anderson
1868	William Allen White	1914	Larry Adler
1879	W.C. Fields	1927	Leontyne Price
1890	Boris Pasternak	1930	Robert Wagner
1893	Jimmy Durante	1940	Roberta Flack
1894	Harold Macmillan	1950	Mark Spitz

Notable Events

754 Council at Constantinople proclaimed against image worship
1763 Treaty of Paris ended Seven Years' War, with Canada ceded to the British
1899 Spanish-American War treaty signed
1931 Nazis walked out of the Reichstag
1933 Singing telegram introduced, New York City
1933 League of Nations demanded that Japan return Chinese territory
1944 Income-tax withholding introduced
1953 General Naguib declared himself dictator of Egypt
1964 Nossenko of KGB defected
1964 House passed Civil Rights Bill
1964 Frank Sinatra, Jr., kidnapping case opened in Los Angeles

Back in 1940, Raymond C.C. Thatcher, a banker from Pueblo, Colorado, complained to the State of Colorado that he had been overcharged a total of $375 in taxes due on money and property he had recently inherited. State tax officials agreed to look into the matter. They found that the legacy had indeed been misclassified — and promptly charged Thatcher an additional $116,188 in taxes.

Anybody has a right to evade taxes if he can get away with it.
J. P. Morgan

If Patrick Henry thought that taxation without representation was bad, he should see how bad it is with representation.
The Old Farmer's Almanac

A Pasadena, California, horseplayer named Johnny Bowler was arrested in February 1953 for stealing a tube of toothpaste worth 71 cents. He had $14,690 in his wallet at the time.

My idea of the ideal jury is twelve Irish unionists deciding the case of my client, Patrick O'Brien, a union bricklayer, who was run over by Chauncy Marlborough's Rolls-Royce while Marlborough was on the way to deposit $50,000 in the bank.
Melvin Belli

The origin of the name of the country of Canada is unclear, but it is probably from one of three sources, two of which are from Indian languages. *Kannata* is the Iriquois word for a collection of huts; while *kan ada* comes from a neighboring tribe and means "a river mouth," which refers to the eastern Saint Lawrence region.

The third source, the least flattering, but also the least likely, is Portuguese. Captain Gaspar Cortereal was one of the first to explore the Saint Lawrence in the hope that it was the much-sought-after Northwest Passage to the Pacific Ocean. When he and his men realized that the Saint Lawrence was only a river, they cried out in disgust, "*Ca nada! Ca nada!*" — "Here, nothing!" According to the story, the natives remembered the words they'd heard the sailors shout to one another, and when later European explorers visited the region, they repeated the phrase to the new white men, fully expecting that the strangers would know what they were saying.

Kangaroo!

When you get there, there isn't any there there.
Gertrude Stein

I don't even know what street Canada is on.
Al Capone

Canada is the only country in the world that knows how to live without an identity.
Marshall McLuhan

Perhaps the most striking thing about Canada is that it is not part of the United States.
J. Bartlett Brebner

W.C. Fields had the reputation of being a crusty old buzzard who disliked children (and animals, too) but that was hardly the case. On one occasion, when Fields was dining at an Italian restaurant in New York City, the proprietor's son, a boy of about ten, came up to Fields's table and said, "Hello, Big-nose!"

"Hi," said Fields.

A waiter overheard the conversation and told the boy's father, who appeared immediately and removed his son to the kitchen for a caning. Fields was upset by this overreaction and sorry that the boy had been punished on his account, so when the snuffling lad returned a few moments later to apologize fo the remark, Fields gave him a private, twenty-minute show of juggling and magic tricks.

Answer: a.(Hexahedrons have 6 equal sides; icosahedrons have 20; and tetrahedrons have 4.)

FEBRUARY 11

Questions: Why is a pretty girl like a well-made mirror?

What is the difference between an auction and seasickness?

Notable Births

1657	Bernard de Fontanelle	1925	Kim Stanley
1847	Thomas Alva Edison	1925	Eva Gabor
1909	Max Baer	1925	Virginia Johnson
1917	Sidney Sheldon	1934	Mary Quant
1920	Farouk I	1936	Burt Reynolds

Notable Events

1889 Japanese constitution granted
1929 Treaty of the Lateran created Vatican City
1929 Young War Reparations Committee met
1943 Eisenhower selected to command allied armies in Europe
1945 Yalta agreement signed
1953 Russia broke relations with Israel after Russian embassy bombed
1958 R.C. Taylor became first black airline stewardess

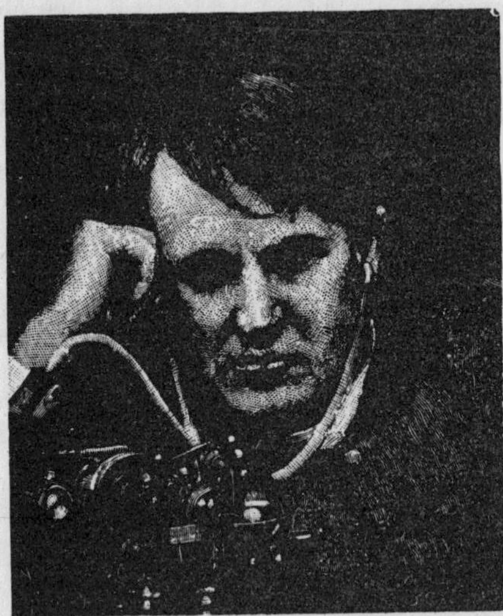

Thomas Edison had a peculiar yardstick for measuring the value of his creations, and he was perhaps at heart more a businessman than an inventor. After seeing a newspaper article that referred to him as a scientist, he commented:

"That's wrong. I am not a scientist. I am an inventor. Faraday was a scientist. He didn't work for money, he said he hadn't time. But I do. I measure everything I do by the size of a silver dollar. If it won't come up to that standard, then I know it's no good."

Some additional evidence of Edison's priorities can be seen in a story related by a friend, Alfred O. Tate. The two men were riding through central New Jersey one day, when Edison said to Tate, "See that valley?"

"It's a beautiful valley," Tate said.

"Well, I'm going to make it more beautiful," Edison went on. "I'm going to dot it with factories."

Nor was Edison a man who would let any available resource go unutilized. He used to have a great many visitors at his summer residence, and he would always show them the grounds, of which he was very proud. As they returned to the house from the tour, the guests discovered that they had to pass through a turnstile that led to the main path. It took a lot of effort to move it. Eventually one friend asked Edison what it was there for. She thought that, considering all the other wonderful inventions he had on the estate, such a heavy turnstile was most certainly out of place.

"Not at all," he replied with a smile. "Everyone who pushes that turnstile around pumps eight gallons of water into the tank on my roof."

But for all his inventiveness and genius in practical matters, Edision was not very knowledgeable in a number of areas. Once, a British firm wired him and offered "thirty thousand" for one of his patents. A friend of Edison's told him that this offer was too small, but Edison said it actually wasn't worth half that. He was finally convinced by his friend to accept the offer as stated. Several weeks later, Edison received a draft from the company for $150,000. He thought it was a mistake, but after consulting with his friend, he realized that the British firm had made its offer in pounds, not dollars.

At another, earlier time, the Western Union company offered him $100,000 for an invention of his, but Edison did not understand the advantages of a lump sum. He wrote back, "Safer with you. Give me six thousand a year for seventeen years." This method of payment, considering inflation and the interest rates of the time, in effect cost Edison over $100,000.

Do you realize if it weren't for Edison we'd be watching TV by candlelight?

Al Boliska

Every man of genius is considerably helped by being dead.

Robert S. Lynd

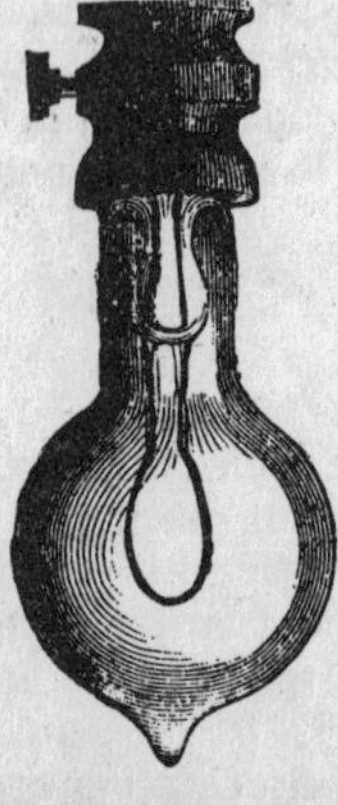

Answers: Because she is a good lookin-glass.

One is the sale of effects, the other the effects of a sail.

FEBRUARY 12

Notable Births

1663	Cotton Mather	1895	R. Buckminster Fuller
1775	Mrs. John Q. Adams	1912	R.F. Delderfield
1809	Charles Darwin	1916	Joseph Alioto
1809	Abraham Lincoln	1926	Charles Van Doren
1828	George Meredith	1926	Joe Garagiola
1880	John L. Lewis	1934	Bill Russell
1893	Omar Bradley	1944	Charles Pasarell

Notable Events

1542	Execution of Catherine Howard, wife of Henry VIII
1733	James Oglethorpe landed in Georgia
1794	Mahdoji Sindhia, ruler of central India, died
1878	Baseball catcher's mask patented
1880	National Croquet Team organized in Philadelphia
1953	Britain and Egypt made agreement on Sudan
1934	Civil War broke out in Austria
1953	Earthquake killed 530 people in Iran
1960	Russia launched Venus probe
1964	Five thousand students protested OSU coed's jay-walking arrest

Abraham Lincoln's coffin was opened in 1887 and 1901 to make sure he was still in it. He was.

A man named Samuel Schofield of East Weymouth, Massachusetts, bought sixty-four bars of army surplus soap in 1946. When he unwrapped the bars, he found that each was inscribed, "Save Soap to Win the War, (signed) Commander-in-Chief, Abraham Lincoln."

We have it on good authority that Abe Lincoln always moved his lips when he read to himself.

Question: Give the nicknames of the following states:
Arkansas
Georgia
Louisiana
Michigan

Abraham Lincoln had no love for patronage seekers, especially when they took his time away from the duties of the presidency during the Civil War. On one occasion, he gathered together a number of would-be office holders and told them this story:

"There was once a King who wished to go out hunting, so he asked his minister if it was going to rain. The minister assured him that it would not. On the way to the woods, the King passed a farmer who was working the land with his donkey. The farmer warned the King that it would rain soon, but the King just laughed and continued on. A few minutes later it was pouring, and the King and his retinue were soaked to their skins. Upon his return to the castle, the King dismissed his minister and sent for the farmer. He asked the man how he knew it was going to rain.

"'It was not me, your Majesty. It was my donkey. He always droops one ear when it is going to rain.'

"So the King bought the donkey from the farmer and gave him the position of minister at court. That was where the King made his mistake."

"How was that?" asked several people in the audience.

"Because ever since then," Lincoln continued, "every jackass wants an office. Gentlemen, leave your credentials and when the war is over you'll hear from me."

George Hardinge, a poetic judge who died in England in 1816, took the letter of the law seriously. Three hours before his death, he wrote these lines to a creditor who had been dunning him for payment of some long-overdue bills. The firm's letter was addressed to the judge "if living, or his executors," so he replied:

Dear Messrs. Tippens, what is fear'd by you,
Alas! the melancholy circumstance is true,
That I am dead, and more afflicting still,
My legal assets *cannot pay your bill.*
To think of this, I am almost broken-hearted,
Insolvent I, this earthly life departed;
Dear Messrs. T., I am yours without a farthing,
For executors and self,

George Hardinge

Louis Lichtman of Westville, New Jersey, was one of this century's great innovators in the science of hog farming. He found his four thousand pigs loved music, and fattened up much faster when he played it in the pig sheds. They were especially fond of Guy Lombardo and Bing Crosby, Lichtman asserted.

Ancient adage say — music soothe savage beast.

Charlie Chan

Answer: Land of Opportunity; Peach State; Pelican State; Great Lake State or Wolverine State.

FEBRUARY 13

Question: By what names are these people better known?
Ethel Zimmerman
David Margulois
Vera Ralston
Reginald Truscott-Jones
Lucy Collier

Notable Births

1754	Talleyrand	1920	Eileen Farrell
1885	Bess Truman	1922	R.P. Tristram Coffin
1892	Grant Wood	1933	Kim Novak
1903	Georges Simenon	1936	George Segal
1919	Tennessee Ernie Ford	1942	Carol Lynley

Notable Events

1601	First voyage of British East India Company began
1933	Hoover urged return to Gold Standard
1935	Hauptmann found guilty in Lindbergh kidnapping case
1939	Judge Louis Brandeis retired
1945	Russians took Budapest after 49-day seige
1974	Alexander Solzhenitsyn deported to West Germany

In 1934, February 13 and 14, an eclipse occurred before it even began. Because of the path of the shadow on the earth, the eclipse started on the fourteenth, some 200 miles east of the Malay Archipelago, and ended on the thirteenth off the coast of Alaska, across the International Date Line.

Until the end of the eighteenth century, the most common contract between a creditor and a debtor was the tally-stick. These short pieces of willow or hazel were notched and cut with various marks signifying the amount of the debt, and then split down the middle, with one half going to the creditor as his receipt, and the other to a government office as an official record.

The system of tallying was not abolished until the reign of George III, and it was not until the 1830s that the old tally records were destroyed. The accumulated pile of sticks — now very dry with age — was burned in a stove in the House of Lords. The stove overheated, the panelling near it caught fire, and the chambers of both the Houses of Parliament were destroyed.

The British who visited Java in the early nineteenth century thought the native populations were, at worst, a bunch of savages, and at best, simply lazy. They were therefore amazed when, in the spring of 1814, there appeared, almost overnight, a beautifully constructed road, twenty feet wide and sixty miles long, which stretched up to the top of Mount Sumberg, one of the island's highest peaks.

The force behind this remarkable road was the dream of an old woman. The formidable lady, who had the reputation of being a witch, dreamt that a god would soon be descending from heaven via the mountain, and this god would be very unhappy if there was no good road down to the valley. Five or six thousand natives worked day and night for two months to complete the road, which, strangely — but according to the woman's instructions — crossed no water. During the construction, the old woman distributed palm fronds with secret symbols on them to ward off sickness and accidents among the builders. Oddly enough, it was reported that none of the workers was ever ill or hurt in an accident.

According to one British commentator, when the road was finished no one waited for the god, there were no festivals, and nothing further happened. The Javans went home calmly and returned to their indolent (to the British) existences.

A perpetual holiday is a good working definition of hell.
George Bernard Shaw

The word "score," meaning "twenty," comes from two sources. As a unit of measurement, it is certainly pre-Biblical, and probably developed as a name for one full count of the human fingers and toes. The English word itself comes from the Anglo-Saxon verb, *sceran*, "to cut," which was used when people wanted to refer to the cut made on a tally stick when a unit of twenty was recorded in a business transaction.

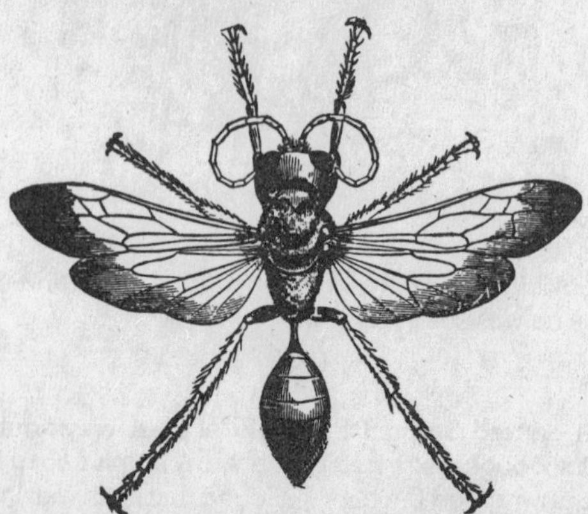

Some varieties of wasps are parasitic to the fifth order. That is, they feed on creatures that are parasites of other creatures, who, in turn, are parasites of other parasites. In fact, parasitic insects comprise 10 percent of all our known species.

Answer: Ethel Merman, David Merrick, Vera Miles, Ray Milland, Ann Miller.

FEBRUARY 14

Notable Births

1766	Thomas Malthus	1913	Mel Allen
1817	Frederick Douglass	1913	Bishop James Pike
1856	Frank Harris	1921	Hugh Downs
1882	George Jean Nathan	1931	Boom Boom Geoffrion
1894	Jack Benny	1934	Florence Henderson
1905	Thelma Ritter	1935	Mickey Wright
1913	Jimmy Hoffa	1944	Carl Bernstein

Notable Events

1876	Telephone patented by Bell
1929	Seven gangsters gunned down in Chicago's St. Valentine's Day Massacre
1940	First porpoise born in captivity, in Marineland, San Diego
1956	20th Congress of Soviet Communist Party denounced Stalin
1964	Castro visited USSR
1966	Soviet writers Sinyavsky and Daniel sentenced to hard labor
1969	Vito Genovese, New York underworld head, died in prison, age 71

Question: Name the five most populous states.

Have you ever wondered who in Hell is in charge? — of Hell, that is. Johannas Wierus did. Studying all the manuscripts he could find, he compiled a definitive chart of the hierarchy of Hades, and published it in his sixteenth-century book, *Pseudomonarchia Daemonum*. Beelzebub, who had at some time previously overthrown the original emperor, Satan, headed the list. Beelzebub had been worshiped by the Canaanites in the form of a fly, and this cult gave rise to the Order of the Fly, the underworld's only fraternity. The rest of the hierarchy, with their specialties, assignments, and honors, are given in this comprehensive list.

Princes

Eurynome	Prince of Death, grand-cross of the Order of the Fly
Moloch	Prince of the Country of Tears, grand-cross of the Order of the Fly, member of the Council of State
Pluto	Prince of Fire, superintendent of infernal punishment
Leonard	Grandmaster of the Sabbaths, inspector general of magic and sorcery, knight of the Order of the Fly
Baalberith	Master of the Alliances, secretary general, keeper of the archives of Hades
Proserpine	Archduchess of Hades, sovereign princess of evil spirits

Ministers

Adramelee	Grand chancellor, grand-cross of the Order of the Fly
Astaroth	Grand treasurer
Nergal	Chief of the secret police
Baal	General-in-chief of the armies, grand-cross of the Order of the Fly
Leviathan	Grand admiral, knight of the Order of the Fly

Ambassadors

Belphegor	To France — an unclean demon, often appeared as a young woman, giver of inventions, discoveries, riches
Mammon	To England — an avaricious demon, inventor of metal mining
Belial	To Turkey — an exceptionally vicious demon
Rimmon	To Russia — chief court physician
Thammuz	To Spain — inventor of artillery
Hutgin	To Italy — a friendly demon, who obliged people
Martinet	To Switzerland — a magician demon, who often helped travelers

Other officers

Lucifer	Minister of Justice
Alastor	Executioner
Verdelet	Master of ceremonies, conveyed witches to Sabbaths
Succor Benoth	Chief eunuch, demon of jealousy
Chamos	Grand chamberlain, demon of flattery, knight of the Order of the Fly
Melchom	Treasurer, paymaster
Nisroch	Chief of the kitchen
Behemoth	Grand cup-bearer
Dagon	Master of the pantry
Mullin	principle valet-de-chambre

Officers of the Privy Purse

Kobal	Director of theaters, patron of comedians in upper world
Asmodeus	Superintendent of gambling houses
Nybbas	Grand-parodist, manager of dreams and visions
Antichrist	Juggler and necromancer of shades

In case you're wondering how many souls this bureaucracy served, Wierus informs us that there were 6,666 legions of 6,666 souls each — a total population of 44,435,556.

If I owned Texas and Hell, I'd rent out Texas and live in Hell.
General Philip Sheridan

Molière's remains lie in an unmarked grave, and no one knows quite where the grave is. He could not be given a Christian burial in seventeenth-century France because he was an actor.

Answer: California, New York, Texas, Pennsylvania, Illinois.

FEBRUARY 15

Questions: Why should you never tell a man to take a back seat to anyone?

Why is a shipboard lecture like a young lady's necklace?

Notable Births

1564	Galileo	1882	John Barrymore
1748	Jeremy Bentham	1886	Sax Rohmer
1809	Cyrus McCormack	1907	Cesar Romero
1814	Ernest Shackleton	1927	Harvey Korman
1820	Susan B. Anthony	1929	James Schlesinger
1845	Elihu Root	1931	Claire Bloom
1861	Alfred North Whitehead	1940	John Hadl

Notable Events

1898	Battleship *Maine* blown up in Havana Harbor
1933	Attempted assassination of FDR in Miami killed Chicago's Mayor Cermak
1935	Saar voted for union with Germany
1940	FBI captured 18 suspects in government seizure plan
1942	British surrendered Singapore
1957	Andrei Gromyko became Russian foreign minister
1958	Blizzard in Northeast killed 171 people
1964	Teamsters negotiated first national labor contract
1970	DC-9 from Santo Domingo crashed, 102 people killed
1978	Accord reached on Rhodesian majority rule

Good old Doctor Gustav Jaegar! Not only did this zoologist introduce the work of Charles Darwin to Germany, he also gave the world Jaegar's Sanitary Woolens and the concept of "duft."

In his book *The Discovery of the Soul*, Jaegar wrote that the soul was actually an odorous emanation of the skin, mouth, nose, and brain. This was the way to sense a person's essence. Good odors (fragrances) were "duft," the light of a person's being; bad odors (ordures) were evil.

What, then, was the best way to retain fragrances while passing off ordures? After much research, Jaegar determined that animal wool was the only material that did this effectively. So, an eager public soon enjoyed the benefits of Jaegar's Sanitary Woolens, advertised in a way that would have done Dr. Bronner's Soap proud.

> Women should wear all underclothes, stockings, even corsets, made of pure wool. A dress of pure wool, closing well around the throat and having a double woolen lining at the chest and downwards, should be the winter and summer dress of women . . .

Later experiments led him to the conclusion that, of the various parts of the human body, the hair was the choicest depository of the odor-soul.

> If you smell the hair of a flapper, you will find the odor somewhat insipid and flat, or, as one of my women observers put it, the odor was like that of a "rubber stopper" — not a bad observation.

This discovery eventually resulted in Jaegar's classification of "sympathetic" odors, which were often inherited within families. These could be very beneficial if utilized correctly. For example, in one self-conducted experiment, he found his normal reaction time to a certain stimulus was .76 seconds. After smelling his wife's hairnet it dropped to .68 seconds. He achieved similar results by savoring the hair of his daughter and her husband. And the benefits of hair smelling did not decrease with time. Jaegar related how, when he was twenty-seven years old, his wife had cut a lock of her hair and put it away as a keepsake. When he unwrapped it he was fifty-two years old, but he soon felt the "strong soul" of his youth surge through his body once more.

That a person's hair could transfer ability was something else he found from his researches. Jaegar once took the hair from the head of an eighteen-year-old woman who was a professional singer, put it in a glass of beer, and drank the beer. He claimed that it later made his own voice purer, clearer, and freer, and that he was able to hit a higher note than he had ever reached before.

If your girlfriend is a classical scholar, don't tell her she has satiny hair — all you're saying is that her hair is hairy. The word "satin" is derived from the Latin *seta*, meaning "hair." While the Latin adjective *setinus* means "shiny like hair," even then the best literal translation of satiny is "shiny like hair hair."

Answers: Because if you do he's likely to take afront.

Both are deck-orations.

Notable Births

1838	Henry Adams	1903	Edgar Bergen
1876	G.M. Trevelyan	1920	Patricia Andrews
1886	Van Wyck Brooks	1926	Vera Ellen
1898	Kate McClintic	1935	Sonny Bono
1901	Chester Morris	1959	John McEnroe

Notable Events

1723	Louis XV of France reached majority
1868	BPOE organized
1905	First Esperanto club in America established
1933	Attempted assassination of Roosevelt in Miami; Chicago's Mayor Cermak killed
1940	Congress voted against fortifying Guam
1942	British surrendered Singapore
1945	Russians occupied Warsaw
1949	Chaim Weizmann inaugurated first president of Israel
1958	Fidel Castro became Cuban premier
1964	International Longshoreman's Union refused to load wheat bound for Russia

On February 16, 1812, Jeremiah James Colbath was born near Farmington, New Hampshire. You might never have heard of him, except that he was the first American vice-president to be elected under an assumed name — Henry Wilson.

What, you still haven't heard of him?

The vice-presidency of the United States isn't worth a pitcher of warm spit.

John Nance Garner

Robins migrating northward average about fifty miles a day; southward, only about thirty.

Questions: What's a Batman in Iran?

What's a Candy in Burma?

William Miller, the doorkeeper of the House of Representatives for three decades, recounts in his book, *Fishbait*, how Representative Torbett MacDonald of Massachusetts once claimed that it was against the law in his state to make clam chowder using tomatoes. This isn't true, but it set off an odd competition in the House as other congressmen followed suit and contributed their own favorite odd laws. Some of these may not be true, but they are amusing:

Corn flakes can't be sold in Columbus, Ohio, on Sunday.

In Houston, it's illegal to buy Limburger cheese on Sunday; but if you do buy it, you cannot take it from the store.

In Gary, Indiana, it's illegal to go into a theater or ride a trolley within four hours of eating garlic.

In Hampton, New Hampshire, you cannot kiss your wife while riding on horseback on Sunday.

Corvallis, Oregon, has a law that prohibits young girls from drinking coffee after six in the evening.

In a town in New York State there is an ordinance against eating peanuts and walking backwards outside a concert hall while a performance is in progress.

In Detroit, throwing banana peels on the street is forbidden in case a horse should have an accident.

In Waterloo, Nebraska, barbers may not eat onions during working hours.

Marion, Ohio, forbids cream puffs within the city limits.

During World War II, a New York state court ruled that it was legal to serve pickles as a substitute for butter. In Connecticut, a state court ruled that the proper way to measure the freshness of a pickle was to see whether it bounced when it was dropped from a height of one foot. A bouncing pickle was a fresh pickle.

New Jersey doesn't allow the slurping of soup in public.

And in Lexington, Kentucky, you may not carry ice-cream cones in your pockets.

The highest virtue is always against the law.

Ralph Waldo Emerson

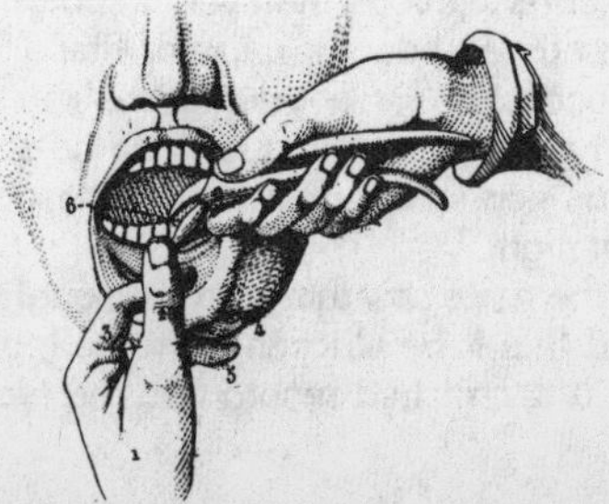

There are more than fifty miles of canals in the human tooth.

Answers: 6.546 pounds.

9 tons.

FEBRUARY 17

Question: By what names are these people better known?
Maria daCunha
Roberta Anderson
Muni Weisenfreund
Appolina Chapulez
Peggy Lou Snyder

Notable Births

1856	Frederick Ives	1925	Hal Holbrook
1877	Andre Maginot	1929	Chaim Potok
1894	Andrés Segovia	1934	Alan Bates
1902	Marian Anderson	1936	Jimmy Brown
1914	Arthur Kennedy	1942	Huey Newton
1924	Margaret Truman	1952	Guillermo Vilas

Notable Events

1673	Molière died while rehearsing his play *Le Malade Imaginaire*
1720	Peace concluded between Quadruple Alliance and Spain
1800	Napoleon completed full centralization of French administration
1867	First ship passed through Suez Canal
1936	Supreme Court ruled FDR's TVA was legal
1961	Burnice Geiger sentenced to 15 years for embezzling $2,126,850.10 from her father's bank
1962	Floods on the German coast killed 343 people
1964	Lee Harvey Oswald's mother announced her son was a CIA agent

Only 4 or 5 percent of rattlesnake bites are preceded by a rattle. If they are left untreated, rattlesnake bites are only fatal for about 10 percent of adults who are attacked.

A little boy whose father was a tradesman came home one day and asked his father about business ethics. His class had been talking about this subject at school.

"Well," said the shopkeeper, "business ethics is when a man comes in to my store and makes a purchase, and pays for it with a five-dollar bill. I give him his change, but then as he's leaving, I notice it's actually two five-dollar bills he's given me, stuck together. Now business ethics is, do I tell my partner?"

When two men in a business always agree, one of them is unnecessary.

William Wrigley, Jr.

When I see a merchant overpolite to his customer, begging him to take a little brandy, and throwing his goods on the counter, thinks I, that man has an axe to grind.

Benjamin Franklin

The captain of a merchant freighter was known for his fair but strict application of shipboard regulations. On one voyage, a very able and conscientious man was on board as first mate, sailing for the first time under the captain. After a few days at sea, there was an occasion for a celebration, and the mate, who was off-duty, had a bit more liquor than he should have had. The meticulous skipper duly entered into the log, "The first mate was drunk last night."

When the mate saw this entry, he sought out the captain and requested that it be stricken from the log. He pointed out his previous unblemished record and the fact that his overindulgence was harmless under the circumstances, and solemnly promised not to drink in the future while on board. The captain would have none of it, however, insisting that a fact was a fact, and the entry remained in the log.

The next morning, the mate drew the second watch, and he attended to it scrupulously — to the extant that when the captain read the log later in the day, he found in it a fact he could not refute: "The captain was sober last night."

I know no method to secure the repeal of bad or obnoxious laws so effective as their stringent execution.

Ulysses S. Grant

Did you know that the majority of America's ninety-million gamblers are women? And that about ten thousand women make all or part of their livings as bookies?

Answer: Carmen Miranda, Joni Mitchell, Paul Muni, Pola Negri, Harriet Nelson.

Notable Births

1745	Alexander Volta	1909	Wallace Stegner
1784	Nicolo Paganini	1915	Dane Clark
1795	George Peabody	1920	Bill Cullen
1859	Sholom Aleichem	1920	Jack Palance
1890	Adolph Menjou	1922	Helen Gurley Brown
1892	Wendell Willkie	1929	Len Deighton

Notable Events

1688	First anti-slavery protest in the United States staged, Germantown, Pennsylvania
1861	Jefferson Davis inaugurated as Confederate president
1867	Hungarian Constitution of 1848 restored
1930	First recorded flight of a cow in an airplane
1943	Madame Chiang Kai-shek addressed joint session of Congress; first woman so honored
1953	First 3-D movie shown, *Bwana Devil*
1964	President Mbu of Gabon ousted
1970	Chicago Seven found innocent of all major charges in Chicago

Attention conservationists! The Emperor Francis, the Princess Charlotte of Lorraine, and twenty-two other notables went on an eighteen-day hunting spree in Bohemia some time ago. There were 116,209 shots fired (including 9,798 by the emperor and 9,010 by the princess) to bag a total kill of 47,950 head of game, itemised as follows: nineteen stags, seventy-seven roebucks, ten foxes, 18,243 hares, 19,545 partridges, 9,499 pheasants, 114 larks, 353 quail, and 454 other birds. This happened in 1755, and is one of the reasons why there is considerably less game than there used to be in Europe.

Questions: How many miles long is the Great Wall of China?

a 500
b 8,000
c 1,200
d 1,400

There is an old wives' tale that if a boy and a girl are born as twins, the girl will be sterile. The belief comes from observing cattle, and it is true in that case, but it is not so for people. Both male and female cattle are held in one amniotic sac during pregnancy, and because of this, the male's hormones sterilize the female fetus. But human fraternal twins are carried in two separate birth sacs, and there is little or no hormone transfer. One seventeenth-century writer thought this two-sac arrangement was ". . . an admirable provision to inspire man from the germ with the laws and rules of chastity."

Sir John Paxton died on February 18, 1466. His body was taken for burial to the Bromholm Priory, which was in the village of Barton on the northeast coast of England. His funeral feast was one of the grand events of the fifteenth century. Better than forty barrels of ale and beer, and fifteen gallons of fine red wine, were consumed in the festivities, and fifteen coombs of malt had to be instantly brewed when the original supplies ran dry. Forty-one pigs, forty calves, ten cows, thirty gallons of milk, eight gallons of cream, and 1,300 eggs were consumed. One man was employed for three long days to slaughter the animals, and a barber worked for five days to neaten up the guests' hair in preparation for the feast.

Answer: *d.*

FEBRUARY 19

Questions: What makes the best eavesdropper?

Why is a loquacious young boy like a small pig?

Notable Births

1473	Copernicus	1912	Stan Kenton
1893	Sir Cedric Hardwicke	1916	Eddie Arcaro
1896	Andre Breton	1917	Carson McCullers
1911	Merle Oberon	1924	Lee Marvin

Notable Events

842	Council of Constantinople declared itself against iconoclasts
1614	Civil war began in France
1789	King George III officially returned to sanity
1864	Knights of Pythias founded in Washington, D.C.
1884	Phonograph patented
1916	Albert Smith set nonstop flight record, 8 hours, 42 minutes
1945	Marines landed at Iwo Jima
1964	Zanzibar severed relations with United States and Britain

John Ward may not be *the* most unpleasant Englishman who has ever lived, but he's definitely one of them. Not much is known about his early life, except that he was employed for a time making cloth. From that point on, no one knows how he amassed a fortune of £200,000 by the time he was middle aged, but all the existing evidence points to his use of forgery, blackmail, and other crimes.

But, before his honesty became suspect, he was respected for his intelligence and energy (if disliked for his personality), and was even elected to the House of Commons.

He sat in Parliament for only a short time, however. In 1727, the Duchess of Buckingham prosecuted Ward for forging a deed to some of her property. As Ward put it, he had "made a mistake with respect to a name in a deed," that was all. Of course, no malice was intended. The courts saw his actions rather differently, and he was convicted, kicked out of the Commons, and made to stand in the pillory. Shortly after this humiliation, it was revealed that Ward had been the beneficiary of £50,000 in an embezzlement scheme involving the South Sea Company. Although he vehemently denied it, the company sued successfully, and Ward was instructed to repay the money together with damages. This he refused to do, so the South Sea Company attached all his assets it could find.

The total value of the confiscated merchandise came nowhere near to equalling the settlement, however, since Ward had had the foresight to hide most of his fortune. He was arrested and ordered to pay the difference or be hanged, and he again refused to pay the money. He was then imprisoned to await his execution (even petty theft legally earned the death sentence in England at this time). While Ward was in custody, this unpleasant man passed his time poisoning the dogs and cats which roamed about the jail. On the day before he was to die, Ward finally relented and settled up with the company, after living several months at public expense. He was always proud of that fact.

Few remember John Ward's story anymore, but something he wrote has survived as a literary curiousity. It is known as "The Miser's Prayer," and although it is now highly amusing in its presumption, Ward wrote it as a serious entreaty to his Maker:

> O Lord, Thou knowest that I have nine estates in the City of London, and likewise that I have lately purchased one estate in fee simple in the county of Essex; I beseech Thee to preserve the two counties of Middlesex and Essex from fire and earthquakes; and as I have a mortgage in Hertfordshire, I beg of Thee likewise to have an eye of compassion on that county; and for the rest of the counties Thou mayst deal with them as Thou art pleased. O Lord, enable the Bank to answer their bills, and make all my debtors good men. Give a prosperous voyage and return to the *Mermaid* sloop, because I have insured it; and as Thou has said the days of the wicked are but short, I trust in Thee that Thou wilt not forget Thy promise, as I have purchased an estate in reversion, which will be mine on the death of that profligate young man, Sir J.L. Keep my friends from sinking, and preserve me from thieves and housebreakers, and make all my servants so honest and faithful that they may attend to my interests, and never cheat me out of my property, night or day.

The worst cliques are those which consist of one man.

George Bernard Shaw

When men grow virtuous in their old age, they are merely making a sacrifice to God of the Devil's leavings.

Jonathan Swift

The word "idiot" comes from the Greek, and was used originally only to distinguish a private citizen from one who held public office. It is odd that its meaning is now exactly the opposite of the original one.

When you find three young cads and idiots going about together and getting drunk together everyday, you generally find that one of the three cads and idiots is (for some extraordinary reason) not a cad and not an idiot.

G. K. Chesterton

Answers: An icicle.

Because both are likely to become great bores.

FEBRUARY 20

Notable Births

1694	Voltaire	1924	Sidney Poitier
1890	Sam Rice	1934	Bobby Unser
1904	Alexei Kosygin	1937	Nancy Wilson
1914	John Daly	1942	Buffy Sainte-Marie
1920	Robert Altman	1949	Jennifer O'Neill

Notable Events

1725	First recorded instance of scalping by whites, attacking New Hampshire Indians
1811	Austria declared bankruptcy
1905	Mining disaster in Virginia City, Alabama, took 112 lives
1917	United States purchased Danish West Indies
1919	Ameer of Afghanistan murdered
1930	Byrd left Antartica after year's stay
1952	Emmet Ashford became first black major league umpire
1962	John Glenn became first American to orbit earth

Back in February 1948, Daniel Griskus was offered the job of supervisor for the garbage disposal department of the city of Waterbury, Connecticut. Griskus said he would accept the job on one condition: that the city officially change his title to superintendant of used food collection.

Waterbury agreed.

In 1720, rumors spread throughout England about the incredible profits of the South Sea Company and inspired dozens of imitators and thousands of fools — who in many cases were soon parted from their money. One project was advertised as, "A company for carrying on an undertaking of great advantage, but nobody to know what it is." So rife was people's greed that this speculative company took in a thousand deposits of £2 each in six hours.

Two liars are company, three are a crowd, and four or more a chamber of commerce.

Laurence J. Peter

Advertising may be described as the science of arresting the human intelligence long enough to get money from it.

Stephen Leacock

The wages earned by John Kreusi, an assistant of Thomas Edison, for building the first phonograph (from T.E.'s specifications), totalled $18.60. The machine was patented on February 19, 1884.

Question: By what names are these people better known?
Michael Peschkowsky
Estelle Thompson
Hugh Krampe
Maureen FitzSimmons
Clara Fowler

Alexander the Great insisted that his soldiers be clean-shaven and crop-headed, because he felt an enemy soldier could easily hold on to a man's long hair or a beard and kill him. Nineteenth-century American Indians were more willing to gamble with their lives. Warriors from many tribes let a "chivalrous lock" grow on the tops of their heads, just to give a victorious enemy something to grab onto while a scalping took place.

Scalping, it must be pointed out, was an invention of the white man. An Indian's scalp was taken as proof of his murder and used to claim a bounty payment in the same way as a bobcat's ears were. The earliest recorded payment was on February 20, 1725, when a party of men returned to Dover, New Hampshire, with ten Indian scalps. They were paid 100 pounds per scalp from general revenue funds in Boston for the unprovoked murder of the Indians.

There is no man so friendless but what he can find a friend sincere enough to tell him disagreeable truths.

Edward Bulwer-Lytton

Voltaire might have been just another starving author had he not had a little mathematical ability. It seems that the French government, as usual during that era, was in need of money, and a national lottery was therefore announced, with an enormous sum offered to the lucky winner. Voltaire did some quick calculations on the likelihood of his chances, and quickly put together a syndicate to buy up all the *billets*. The prize money totalled far more than the money the syndicate put out, and the author's share made him independently wealthy.

Copernicus was a famous astronomer, but also the mayor, military governor, physician, registrar, tax collector, vicar-general, bailiff, and chief magistrate of his home town — simultaneously.

Man is designed to be a comprehensivist.

Buckminster Fuller

He not only overflowed with learning, but stood in the slop.

Sydney Smith

Answer: Mike Nichols, Merle Oberon, Hugh O'Brian, Maureen O'Hara, Patti Page.

FEBRUARY 21

Question: Which of the following plants are most closely related botanically?
artichoke
asparagus
Brussels sprouts
sunflower

Around the year 200 B.C., a gentleman named Citesibus developed a piston-operated apparatus that used compressed air to shoot arrows. Don't laugh. It was reported that an arrow fired from this machine would travel clear through a bull at a range of a thousand yards. For a modern rifle to be able to do that with a bullet would be exceptional.

The current in the lower part of the Mississippi River runs at an average of 2.26 miles per hour, but it can vary almost a full mile an hour, depending on whether the water level is high or low. The elevation of the river drops an average of 2.18 inches per mile for the last 400 miles of its length.

One of the more eccentric clergymen ever to live in England was Isaac Vossius, a Dutch scholar whom Charles II made a canon of Windsor on the misguided belief in his intelligence (while Vossius spoke a dozen languages, he knew them all incorrectly) rather than his piety. The prelate treated all religious matters contemptuously, and maintained that the divine origin of Christianity was hogwash. The King once said of him, "This learned divine is a strange man; he will believe anything except the Bible." When he did attend church, Vossius usually read from Ovid's *Ars Amandi* (The Art of Love) during the service. One of his notable eccentricities was the delight he took in having his hair combed rhythmically, and he would often call for a favorite meter — a poetic iamb, perhaps, or a lively jig — when his valet combed out his hair. On his deathbed he received the sacrament only with the onlookers' understanding that he took it to save his brethren embarrassment, and that it was not a religious action on his part.

There were only ten men, including George Washington, who was made a general by the Continental Congress in 1775, who achieved that rank in the United States military during the 160 years after Washington's appointment.

I'd hate to tell you how many generals there are today in the United States Army.

Answer: The sunflower and the artichoke; they are both in the composite family. Asparagus is in the lily family, and Brussels sprouts are in the mustard family.

Notable Births

1795	Santa Anna	1925	Sam Peckinpah
1801	John Henry, Cardinal Newman	1927	Erma Bombeck
1903	Anais Nin	1933	Nina Simone
1907	W.H. Auden	1936	Barbara Jordan
		1946	Tricia Nixon

Notable Events

1903	Cornerstone of U.S. Army War College laid
1919	Kurt Eisner, Bavarian premier, assassinated in Munich
1940	Lowell Thomas delivered his first TV newscast
1965	Malcolm X assassinated, New York City
1971	Tornado in Mississippi Delta region took 110 lives
1972	Richard Nixon arrived in Peking

The sixteenth-century gentleman Sir Henry Wotton instructed that his tombstone be inscribed thus (the words have been translated from the original Latin epitaph):

Here lies the first author of this sentence:
"The Itch of Disputation will prove the Scab of the Church."
Inquire his name elsewhere.

More padded bras are sold in the United States than in all the rest of the world combined.

Of a horse, a cow, and a mule, only a mule will leave a burning barn of its own volition. A cow will go if she's prodded by a few slaps on her behind to get her moving — but a horse must usually be blindfolded and led out. Horses are said, in fact, to be the highest-strung of all domestic animals.

Notable Births

1732	George Washington	1907	Robert Young
1788	Arthur Schopenhauer	1917	Sheldon Leonard
1810	Frederic Chopin	1918	Charles O. Finley
1819	James Russell Lowell	1923	Edward Gorey
1857	Lord Robert Baden-Powell	1932	Edward M. Kennedy
1892	Edna St. Vincent Millay	1934	Sparky Anderson
1900	Luis Buñuel	1950	Julius Erving

Notable Events

1630	Indians introduced English colonists to popcorn
1711	Administrative Senate formed in Russia
1819	Florida ceded to United States by Spain
1879	F.W. Woolworth opened first store, Utica, New York
1885	Washington Monument dedicated
1909	Great White Fleet completed world cruise of 46,000 miles
1920	Mechanical rabbit first used at dog track, Emeryville, California
1923	First U.S. chinchilla farm started, Los Angeles
1931	Death of Nellie Melba

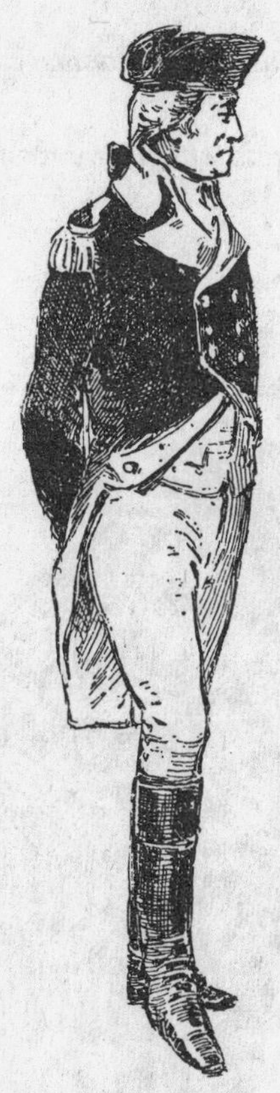

During the Revolutionary War, horses where one of the scarcest commodities for the Continental Army. On one occasion, an officer in Virginia was ordered to scour the countryside and confiscate all the horses he could find.

After riding around for a while, he came to a large farmhouse and noticed a pair of horses attached to a plow in a field below the house. He rang the bell, and was greeted by a dignified old woman who showed him into the drawing room.

"Madam, I have come to claim your horses in the name of the government," he said.

"I'm sorry, sir, but you cannot have them. I need them for spring plowing," she told him.

"But ma'am, those are the orders of my chief," the officer protested.

Question: By what names are these people better known?

Betty Thornburg
Phyllis Isley
Irwin Kniberg
Icle Ivanhoe
Abdullah Khan

"And who is your chief?" the woman asked archly.

"General George Washington, Commander-in-Chief of the Continental Army."

"Then go back and tell George his mother says he can't have her horses."

And he didn't get them.

One set of George Washington's dentures was made from rhinoceros ivory.

Little Washington College (later Washington and Lee University) of Virginia contributed a company of 150 men to the Fourth Virginia Infantry early in the Civil War. By the time the hostilities had ended, the collegians had experienced 100 casualties, and forty-six of the remaining fifty men had been taken prisoner.

A year into the Civil War, for every forty-one men in Union blue there was one military musician, and the Union Army boasted a total of 618 complete bands in July 1862. Strategists believed their men fought better to music.

In the South the picture was somewhat different. Poorly supplied Confederate troops often found the most effective way of obtaining nourishment was to have their own much-smaller bands (they were sometimes only trios) serenade the most prosperous-looking house in the neighborhood, in hopes of a handout.

It stands to reason that the Roman Rat Race was a very different one from the contemporary Rat Race. It was. The Roman Rat Race involved a pack of rats chasing a hunk of sausage, and a bunch of Romans standing around placing bets.

In February 1957, Clayborne J. Allmond was sentenced in Cleveland to four years' imprisonment for breaking his parole of the previous year. It seems that, since he left prison, he'd been involved with forgery, had committed several thefts, had a bigamy charge levied against him, and had skipped town. He'd gone to San Francisco, where he'd been employed as a probation officer.

The strength of a man's virtue should not be measured by his special exertions, but by his habitual acts.

Blaise Pascal

Answer: Betty Hutton, Jennifer Jones, Alan King, Burl Ives, Robert Joffrey.

FEBRUARY 23

Question: Which of the following is *not* a tropical fruit?

Sweetsop
Mangosteen
Froude
Ceriman

The first criminal to be executed by a drop-door gallows was Earl Ferrers. Before his execution in 1760, condemned people stood on a cart beneath a gallows or tree, and the cart was then driven away.

A unique non-hanging occurred on February 23, 1898, that of John "Babbacombe" Lee, a young Englishman who was convicted of killing his elderly employer bacause she had cut his salary by a shilling a week. When he went to the gallows, the drop door, although it had been checked earlier and found to be in perfect mechanical order, failed to work when Lee stood on it with a noose around his neck. Three times Lee was moved on the trap, and each time it failed, although it was checked and rechecked between each attempt.

After the third try, Lee was removed to his cell and the scaffold dismantled. Lee did not realize it at the time, but there was an English law that prohibited a prisoner from facing the drop more than three times. His sentence was commuted to life imprisonment, but he was pardoned after serving twenty years.

Law is whatever is boldly asserted and plausibly maintained.

Aaron Burr

I don't like to be an iconoclast, but most of what you know about Davy Crockett ought to be spread on next summer's cornfield.

Crockett was an illiterate juvenile delinquent who ran away from home as a teenager to escape a beating he richly deserved from his father. He ended up in Baltimore, where he became virtually a bum. The only education he ever received came when he was eighteen and enamored of a girl of some breeding. To impress her, he enrolled in school and learned some basic writing and arithmetic, but this education ended in six months when the affair soured. He later married a woman kindly said to be "unintelligent," and set out to be a farmer. An acquaintance described him as "poor . . . indolent and shiftless," and after he had sired a brood of children, he deserted his family and took off for the woods.

Here he lived off his hunting, but his claim to have killed 105 bears in a nine-month period is almost certainly fraudulent — a contemporary of Crockett's was certain he couldn't count nearly that high. And, although some accounts give Crockett a hero's role in the Creek Indian War, he never even participated. When his militia unit was called up, Crockett hired a substitute. In addition, the literary works attributed to him, notably *The Autobiography of Davy Crockett*, are doubtless ghostwritten — Crockett had trouble writing anything more complicated than his name and address. Finally, as a legislator, Crockett did best when he was drunk.

So much for the king of the Wild Frontier.

The major fact about history is that in large part it appears criminal.

W. E. Arnold

Notable Births

1633	Samuel Pepys	1904	William Shirer
1635	George F. Handel	1929	Elston Howard
1868	W.E.B. DuBois	1939	Peter Fonda

Notable Events

1807	Forty spectators crushed to death in crowd at hanging in London
1836	Siege of the Alamo began
1870	Mississippi readmitted to Union
1847	Battle of Buena Vista began
1937	Italians executed 1,400 Ethiopians for attacking General Graziani
1942	Japanese submarine shelled Elwood, California, oil refinery
1945	American flag raised on Mount Suribachi, Iwo Jima

God cannot alter the past, but historians can.

Samuel Butler

A clear conscience begins with a clear memory.

Laurence J. Peter

Answer: Froude was an English biographer and historian (1818-1894).

Notable Births

1786	Wilhelm Grimm	1909	August Derleth
1836	Winslow Homer	1914	Zachary Scott
1874	Honus Wagner	1938	James Farentino
1890	Marjorie Main	1940	Jimmy Ellis

Notable Events

1495 Columbus sent first boatload of slaves to Spain
1848 Louis Philippe abdicated as French emporer
1868 First float parade held, Mobile, Alabama
1931 Supreme Court upheld legality of Prohibition amendment
1938 Nylon bristle toothbrushes first manufactured
1943 Churchill refused to liberate Gandhi
1946 Juan Peron elected president of Argentina
1954 Nasser overthrew Naguib in Egypt
1966 Kwame Nkrumah ousted in Ghana

Question: By what names are these people better known?
Reginald Dwight
Thomas Woodward
William Pratt
Irving Lahrheim
Frank LoVecchio

People who achieve fame in any field are often allowed a few eccentricities, but Henry Cavendish, the great eighteenth-century English scientist, was more than usually strange in his behavior.

Cavendish was born in 1731, and boarded at school most of his young life. He was exceptionally shy, even as a boy. If he was surprised by a greeting from a stranger, he would let out a scream and run away. If he had to attend a social gathering, he would remain alone on a terrace whenever he possibly could. If he was somehow cornered and forced into meeting someone, he would stare at his feet, trembling all over, and take the first opportunity to escape. He hardly ever spoke, and when he did it was with great difficulty. He stammered terribly.

His all-consuming passion was science, and when a bequest from an uncle made him a rich man in 1773, he was free to pursue his work without any social or business interruptions whatsoever. He did, however, condescend to see his nephew and heir once a year for an audience of half an hour.

Although he was rich, he cared nothing for money or its management, except that he took care not to spend it foolishly. On the infrequent occasions when he had other scientists to his house (and he often didn't sit with them), the only food ever to be found on his table was a leg of mutton. Once, when his servant informed that one leg of mutton could not possibly make a meal for the five people who were to be at dinner, he snapped, "Well, then, get two!" On another occasion, the bankers who handled his estate discovered that Cavendish had allowed a balance of £80,000 to accumulate in a stagnant account and a messenger was sent to ask the gentleman how he wished to invest it. When the messenger arrived, Cavendish was greatly agitated that he had been disturbed.

"What did you come here for? What do you want with me?"

"Sir, I thought it proper to wait on you, as we have a very large balance in hand of yours, and we wish to receive your orders respecting it."

"If it is any trouble to you, I will take it out of your hands. Do not come here to plague me!"

"Not the least trouble to us, sir, not the least; but we thought you might like some of it to be invested."

"Well, well. What do you want to do?"

"Perhaps you would like £40,000 invested."

"Do so, do so! and don't come here to trouble me, or I'll remove it."

Cavendish was terrified of women. He passed instructions to his head housekeeper by note, and if any other female servant happened to see him by chance, she was immediately fired. He was not entirely a recluse, however, and always took a daily walk. For many years he traveled exactly the same way, but on one occasion he noticed three people looking at him, and he never went on that particular walk again.

When Cavendish died on February 24, 1810, he was the largest proprietor of bank stock in England, yet he didn't own a coat that was less than thirty or forty years old.

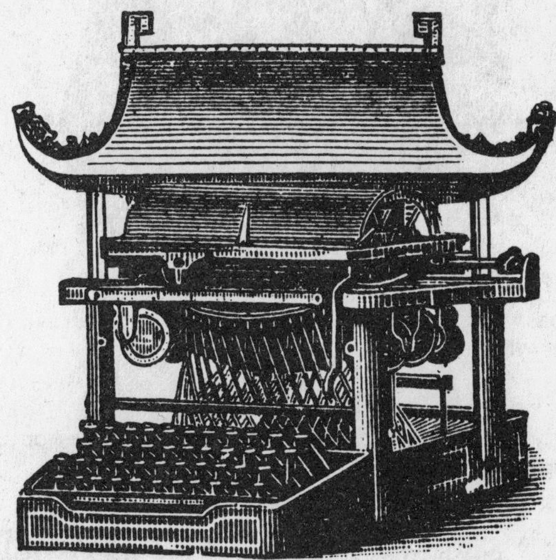

The Chinese typewriter was invented by Lin Yutang.

During the reign of Charles II of England, a law was passed that required all coffins to be lined with flannel. This was to help revive the sagging British woolen trade.

In addition to being one of the top theatrical producers of all time, showman Billy Rose was the amateur shorthand champion of New York in 1916, and once served as Bernard Baruch's stenographer.

Back when they were all listed in *Who's Who*, three sons of Franklin Roosevelt identified themselves as the children of the thirty-first president. The fourth son, FDR Junior, listed himself as the son of the thirty-second president.

Eleanor Roosevelt's love life has been the subject of some controversy of late, but say it ain't so, Mr. Truman!

Answer: Elton John, Tom Jones, Boris Karloff, Bert Lahr, Frankie Lane.

FEBRUARY 25

Questions: Why is a lie like a wig?

When must a man keep his word?

Dubash Meghji of Zanzibar ate a page of the Koran every day for thirty years.

Thirty-five thousand French prostitutes pay taxes on their earnings.

In 1917, only two beauty parlors in the United States paid any income tax. A decade later, 18,000 did.

When Victor Hugo found writing was difficult, and he felt like taking a walk to avoid the problems facing him, he would strip naked and instruct his servant to take his clothes and hide them. Incapable of moving out of the house, he could then find the remaining discipline needed to sit down and write.

Back in 1705, the French and English were, once again, at war with each other. Wartime propaganda warned the residents of both countries to be on the watch for spies, and cautioned them that spies were often masters of disguise.

A vessel was wrecked that year off the coast of West Hartlepool, England, and all hands were lost except the ship's pet, a monkey. He was picked up from a piece of the wreckage by local fishermen and brought to the village. The people had never seen anything like him, but they took the monkey's jabberings to be French, and they hanged the beast as a spy.

How good bad music and bad reason sound when we march against an enemy. **Friedrich Nietzsche**

Answers: Both are false-hoods. When no one else will take it.

Notable Births

1707	Carlo Goldoni	1901	Zeppo Marx
1778	José de San Martin	1904	Adelle Davis
1802	Victor Hugo	1908	Frank Slaughter
1841	Auguste Rodin	1913	Jim Backus
1846	Buffalo Bill Cody	1917	Anthony Burgess
1873	Enrico Caruso	1937	Tom Courtenay

Notable Events

1885	Germany annexed Tanganyika and Zanzibar
1908	Hudson River Tunnel opened, New York City to New Jersey
1913	Income Tax Amendment became law
1931	Al Capone arrested in Chicago for contempt of court
1936	Military rule began in Japan
1955	Chiang ordered last-ditch effort in defense of Quemoy-Matsu
1964	Clay (Ali) retained heavyweight title against Liston in Lewiston, Maine
1974	Herbert Kalmbach, Nixon lawyer, found guilty of illegally offering ambassadorships

HANDBILL FROM PECKHAM FAIR IN 1726

Our ancestors just 133 years ago had but limited opportunities for gratifying a taste for Natural History if we may judge from the supply of animals deemed sufficient to attract attention in 1726.

To the lovers of living curiosities. To be seen during the time of *Peckham Fair*, a Grand Collection of Living Wild Beasts and Birds, lately arrived from the remotest parts of the World.

1. The *Pellican* that suckles her young with her heart's blood, from Egypt.

2. The Noble *Vultur Cock*, bought from *Archangell*, having the finest tallons of any bird that seeks his prey; the fore part of his head is covered with hair, the second part resembles the wool of a Black; below that is a white ring, having a Ruff, that he cloaks his head with at night.

3. An *Eagle of the Sun*, that takes the loftiest flight of any bird that flies. There is no bird but this that can fly to the face of the Sun with a naked eye.

4. A curious Beast, bred from a *Lioness*, like a foreign *Wild Cat*.

5. The *He-Panther*, from Turkey, allowed by the curious to be one of the greatest rarities ever seen in *England*, on which are thousands of spots, and not two of a likeness.

6 & 7. The two fierce and surprising *Hyenas*, Male and Female, from the River *Gambia*. These Creatures imitate the human voice, and so decoy the Negroes out of their huts and plantations to devour them. They have a mane like a horse, and two joints in their hinder leg more than any other creature. It is remarkable that all other beasts are to be tamed, but *Hyenas* they are not.

8. An *Ethiopian Toho Savage*, having all the actions of the human species, which (when at its full growth) will be upwards of five feet high.

Also several other surprising Creatures of different sorts. To be seen from 9 in the morning till 9 at night, till they are sold. Also, all manner of curiosities of different sorts, are bought and sold at the above place by John Bennett.

FEBRUARY 26

Notable Births

1808	Honoré Daumier	1922	Margaret Leighton
1887	William Frawley	1924	Tony Randall
1914	Robert Alda	1928	Fats Domino
1916	Jackie Gleason	1932	Johnny Cash
1921	Betty Hutton	1933	Godfrey Cambridge

Notable Events

1796	Earthquake in Asia Minor killed 1,500 people
1815	Napoleon escaped from Elba
1848	French Republic proclaimed
1871	Preliminary treaty signed to end Franco-Prussian war
1921	Near East Conference of Allies closed in London
1941	Britain captured Somaliland, East Africa
1971	Flooding in Brazil took 130 lives

A sentry from an army camp on Long Island was on patrol one evening when he was bitten by a dog from a nearby estate. He reacted instinctively and ran the attacking dog through with his bayonet. The animal was a show dog, and its owners sued the soldier for several hundred dollars. At the hearing, the judge asked the man why he hadn't hit the dog with the butt end of his rifle instead of stabbing the animal.

"Why didn't the dog bite me with his tail?" was the reply, and the soldier won the case.

Questions: Which of the following movies did *not* win an Oscar for best picture?

West Side Story
My Fair Lady
Oliver
Cabaret

Tippoo Sahib, the Sultan of Mysore, who ran the British in India ragged for many years, was an avowed avisodomist (look it up).

In February 1943, Mrs. Belle Bearison of Newark, New Jersey, lost her purse with $25 in it. Several days later it was anonymously returned to her with $17 and a note explaining that its finder had once lost a purse with $8 and was "just making up the difference."

Some eighty years after the death of France's Louis XIV in 1715, the eccentric Very Reverend William Buckland, Dean of Westminster, somehow came into possession of the embalmed heart of the king.

He ate it.

This advertisement appeared in a Cheboygan, Michigan, newspaper in February 1952: "*For Sale*: Police dog. Will eat anything. Very fond of children."

John Ward (see February 19) was probably Britain's most miserly miser, but the United States had a gentleman who could have given him a run for his money. John G. Wendel controlled a million-dollar inheritance left to himself and his six sisters, and was very careful to ensure that none of the money be squandered foolishly. He remained a bachelor all his life, and persuaded his sisters to remain single, too, by practically keeping them prisoners for fifty years in their family home.

Wendel's parsimonious ways apparently paid off, for even after his death in 1915 his sisters continued to live frugally. When the last one died in 1931, it was discovered that she had never owned a car, nor did she have a phone or electricity in her home. Her one extravagance was her "wardrobe," which consisted of one dress she had made for herself in 1906 and worn every day since that time. All of this was despite the fact that she was a millionairess.

Answer: *Cabaret.*

FEBRUARY 27

Questions: What can you break with a whisper more easily than with a hammer?

What asks no questions, but receives many answers?

Since the early days of Christianity, holy relics have been in great demand, and fortunes have been made by men peddling the supposed relics of Jesus and his Apostles. At one time during the late Middle Ages, the remains of a dozen foreskins existed in Europe, and a each one was supposed to have been Christ's.

The most sought-after relic in Medieval Europe was a piece of the True Cross, which, according to tradition, had been unearthed by Constantine's mother, Helen, in 326 A.D. Although most scholars believe that, by the middle of the twelfth century, the greater part of the wood she found had been lost or destroyed in various conflicts in Asia Minor, there are still enough "real" pieces of it preserved in monasteries and churches to build a large house. Obviously, not all of these fragments are genuine, even if Helen did find the cross that once stood upon Calvary.

Other greatly valued relics were the tears of Christ, and the blood of Christ and the Martyrs. Mary's milk was also a precious commodity, and so were the hair and toenails of the Apostles. For some unexplained reason, Saint Peter's toenails, particularly, are to be found all throughout Europe.

Of course, other religions have their own precious objects, and sometimes plain souvenirs have been raised to the level of relics. The boots of an honest magistrate have long been esteemed in China, and bullets and uniform buttons from the Battle of Waterloo were immensely popular and quite expensive throughout Europe during the nineteenth century.

Notable Births

288	Constantine the Great	1910	Peter de Vries
1807	Henry W. Longfellow	1912	Lawrence Durrell
1888	Arthur Schlesinger, Jr.	1913	Irwin Shaw
1902	John Steinbeck	1930	Joanne Woodward
1903	Reginald Gardner	1932	Elizabeth Taylor
1904	James T. Farrell	1934	Ralph Nader
1910	Joan Bennett	1937	Jay Sylvester

Notable Events

1617	Peace of Stolbova ended Russian-Swedish hostilities
1883	Oscar Hammerstein I patented first cigar-rolling machine
1932	Discovery of the neutron announced
1933	Nazis burned Reichstag, blamed fire on Communists
1939	Fascist government of Franco recognized by France and England
1968	House of Commons voted overwhelmingly to restrict immigration of nonwhites to England
1973	American Indian movement members seized Wounded Knee, South Dakota

There's an American by the name of Sam Brooks who *loves* to see his name in print. About all he does anymore (he's a retired mail carrier) is travel around the country by bus, stopping in towns where there's a newspaper or magazine being published, and trying to talk an editor into mentioning his name. As of a few years ago, he'd succeeded 150 times, and he could prove it to you — he always carried a copy of each clipping with him.

The largest piece of ambergris ever found was discovered inside a whale by Captain John Earle of New Bedford, Massachusetts. It weighed 780 pounds and was worth about $100,000.

A tuning fork vibrating between 250 and 500 cycles per second will drive the species of mosquitos that carry yellow fever and malaria crazy with lust.

The expression "get into a scrape" comes from Scotland, golf, and rabbits. Centuries ago in the northern part of Scotland, golf was played on the downs near the sea where there was usually an abundance of rabbits. When a MacDuffer hit his shot, he always hoped that it wouldn't end up in a "scrape," the area dug out of the sward by a rabbit digging its burrow. Getting into a scrape wasn't that bad, though, since it was a free drop to come out of one.

Answers: A confidence.
A door or a telephone.

Notable Births

1533	Michel Montaigne	1907	Milt Caniff
1797	Mary Lyon	1909	Stephen Spender
1890	Waslaw Nijinsky	1913	Vincente Minnelli
1895	Guiomar Novaes	1915	Zero Mostel
1901	Linus Pauling	1917	John Connally
1904	Jimmy Dorsey	1940	Mario Andretti

Notable Events

1704	Deerfield, Massachusetts scene of Indian massacre
1772	Boston Assembly threatened secession unless rights were restored
1843	Great Comet of 1843 discovered
1854	Republican Party founded, Ripon, Wisconsin
1871	Yellowstone created as first national park
1876	Charles VII fled Spain
1934	Henry Pu-yi crowned emperor of Manchuria
1959	Storm in Bahrain killed 300 people
1966	Astronauts See and Bassett killed when jet trainer crashed into building where their capsule was built

A pelican's skeleton is pretty light. In a twenty-five-pound bird, the bones weigh less than one-and-a-half pounds.

They say figures lie and liars figure. The truth of this maxim can be seen in statistics computed to show the relative safety of car and airplane travel. Death rates for each are calculated solely by passenger miles, and no allowance is made for the amount of time spent in either conveyance in relation to the distance traveled. That a commercial jet might jeopardize a passenger for an hour in traveling 500 miles, while a car puts him in a risk position for ten hours, is certainly an important consideration, though always overlooked. In terms of sheer miles traveled against number of fatalities, the safest way to get anywhere would be on board a United States spaceship. America has yet to register a death of one of its astronauts *on* a space flight, despite the many millions of miles travelled.

Still, I'd rather fly over the New Jersey Turnpike than drive on it.

He uses statistics as a drunken man uses lamp posts — for support rather than for illumination.

Andrew Lang

Get your facts first, and then you can distort 'em as you please.

Mark Twain

Flatworms (*Planaria*) can regenerate themselves from any severed part, and often a flatworm cut in two will become two identical flatworms, either of which will happily devour its former self if given half a chance.

You can't catch a whale in Oklahoma. There's a law against it.

You can't catch a whale in North Dakota, either. No law, just no whales.

The chess term "checkmate" comes from Persia, together with the game itself. It evolved from the Persian words *shah mat*, which meant, "The king is dead."

Answer: Betsy Ross and the Marquis de Sade.

Question: If traveling had been easy, which two of the following people could have met?

Copernicus
Betsy Ross
Marquis de Sade
Pocahontas

The following bill was presented in 1527 to the officials of Kingston-upon-Thames, England, for the construction of a cucking-stool:

	£	s	d
The making of a cucking-stool	0	8	0
Ironwork for the same	0	3	0
Timberwork for the same	0	7	6
Three brasses and three wheels	0	4	10
Total	1	3	4

Judging from the money subsequently paid out for repairs of the cucking-stool, Kingston-upon-Thames must have been a lawless place. Shrews and scolds throughout England were commonly punished by immersion in the village pond, and the *d*ucking stool was used for this during this period. The cucking-stool was different. Its occupant was not ducked in water. Instead, the cucking-stool exposed her private parts to the townspeople. The victim was more often a prostitute than a shrew or scold.

A century later, both of these punishments had given way in favor of the brank, a bridle that was locked on a culprit's head in such a way that it was excruciatingly painful for the unfortunate wearer to move his or her mouth.

I love the English; they are so *civilized*.

If you know what to look for, you can tell the sex of a box turtle by the color of its eyes.

FEBRUARY 29

Question: By what names are these people better known?

Hedwig Kiesler
Dorothy Kaumeyer
Michael Orowitz
Emily LeBreton
Alfred Cocozza

Notable Births
1712 Louis Montcalm
1736 Ann Lee
1908 Victor Wolfgang von Hagen

Notable Events
1720 Queen Ulrika Eleanor of Sweden abdicated

The record is 79 feet 8½ inches, and Frank Rugani set it on February 29, 1964. Can you guess what it is?

It's the longest recorded drive of a badminton shuttlecock.

If a woman proposes to a man in Whitesville, Delaware, she can be charged with disorderly conduct.

William Beckford is know primarily as the author of *Vathek*, the book that began the passion for Gothic romance that existed during the last decades of the eighteenth century. But Beckford was also responsible for one of England's most famous architectural follies, Fonthill Abbey.

Beckford's father died when he was ten, and as his father's only legitimate heir, William inherited over a million pounds in cash and an income of a half-a-million pounds annually from the family's Jamaican plantations. This extensive fortune allowed Beckford to do anything he wished, at any time, and in any place. In 1798, he decided to create an estate for himself.

It was no mean undertaking. First, Beckford hired 500 artisans and built a whole town to house them. Then, the men worked day and night in shifts, seven days a week, to build a twelve-foot-high, seven-mile-long wall around his property. Then came the house itself — it was huge, with dozens of rooms and a myriad of secret passages.

But the highlight of the estate was the Tower. Whether or not he had some kind of phallic obsession is hard to judge, but Beckford decided he had to have a tower, a big one. The first one his men erected was 400 feet tall, and made of wood, just so Beckford could see how a permanent tower would look. It proved to be exactly what he wanted. Engineers told him that his projected wooden frame structure for the tower would never support the weight of the mortar, but Beckford would not listen. He went ahead with his plans, and the tower collapsed before it was completed. He ordered it rebuilt with bricks and mortar. The engineers told him that the foundation (the tower was built on an old summer house site) would not support that much weight if it were not reinforced, but Beckford was impatient and adamant. The tower was built immediately, and hurriedly, by workers who were almost completely drunk from the rum and ale Beckford supplied (to boost their morale and make them strong, he thought). Within a few days of its completion it, too, toppled.

Beckford had only a little more success with his magnificent house. One day in November he announced that he was determined to have his Christmas feast cooked in Fonthill Abbey's kitchen, whether the house was finished or not; so it had damned well better be ready! The kitchen turned out to be quite ready enough to have the holiday goose cooked there, but the mortar hadn't had enough time to settle and season properly. The heat of the cooking in the kitchen . . . well, you can guess the rest.

Finally, after years of work, Fonthill Abbey was completed with a tower that stood, to Beckford's satisfaction, and he enjoyed several years of reclusive bliss. But in 1822, after deciding he needed a change, he bought property in Bath and put Fonthill Abbey up for auction. (He needed the money as much as the change: the Court of Chancery had just deprived him of two of his Jamaican plantations with their huge workforces of 1,500 slaves.) It brought £350,000 from a speculator who'd made his money in India, a Mr. Farquhar. It seems that Mr. Farquhar had a thing about towers, too . . . and he was very upset when Beckford's only successful tower crumbled to the ground within two years of his purchase.

Rich is just a way of wantin' bigger.

Lily Tomlin

Those who do not complain are never pitied.

Jane Austen

Kitchen stove most excellent weapon — good for cooking goose.

Charlie Chan

'Look on my works, ye mighty, and despair.'
Nothing beside remains. Round the decay
Of that colossal wreck, boundless and bare
The lone and level sands stretch far away.

Percy Bysshe Shelley

Did you know the state of Ohio boasts the nation's two largest producers of Chinese food?

Answer: Hedy Lamarr, Dorothy Lamour, Michael Landon, Lily Langtree, Mario Lanza.

Aries
(The Ram)
March 21
through April 20
MARCH

MARCH 1

Question: What's the state shown here?

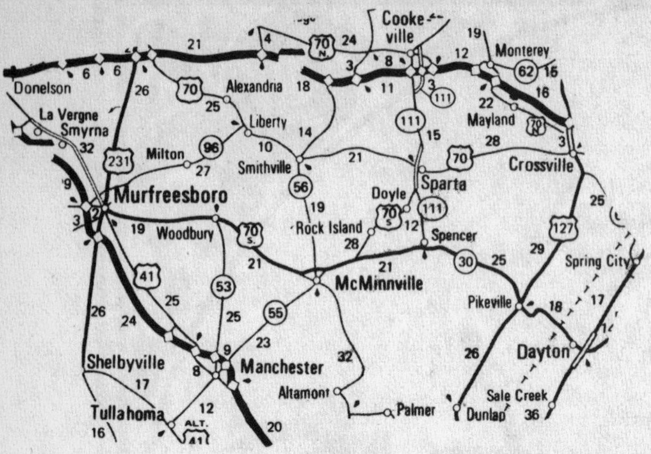

Deiotarus I, King of Galatia, had a favorite son whom he wanted to make sure would succeed him as king, so he had his other six sons put to death.

Like cotton-wool — filial devotion softens weight of parental crown.

Charlie Chan

Notable Births

1837	William Dean Howells	1914	Ralph Ellison
1848	Augustus Saint-Gaudens	1917	Dinah Shore
1883	George Lytton Strachey	1917	Robert Lowell
1886	Oskar Kokoschka	1920	Howard Nemerov
1900	Kurt Weill	1921	Richard Wilbur
1904	Glenn Miller	1926	Pete Rozelle
1910	David Niven	1927	Harry Belafonte

Notable Events

1074 Pope Gregory announced First Crusade
1815 Napoleon returned to France from exile
1847 Michigan abolished the death penalty
1863 Rebecca Lee became first black woman doctor in United States
1883 National Women's Christian Temperance Union organized, Cleveland
1912 First parachute jump from an airplane, Albert Berry, Missouri
1936 U.S. Steel raised workers' wages to $5 a day
1941 Bulgaria joined the Axis Powers
1942 Japan invaded Java
1954 H-bomb tested at Bikini Atoll
1954 Radical Puerto Ricans shot up House of Representatives
1960 Earthquake in Morocco killed 12,000 people
1961 Peace Corps established
1961 Sukarno forebade Rotarians, Freemasons, and Rosicrucians in Indonesia
1966 Adam Clayton Powell denied House seat

Famous Eagles

Teddy Roosevelt
Warren G. Harding
Franklin D. Roosevelt
Harry S. Truman
John F. Kennedy
Father Flanagan
Senator Robert Wagner
Jack Dempsey
Stan Musial
Earl Warren

Famous Shriners

Harold Lloyd
Barry Goldwater
Red Skelton
Irving Berlin
Arthur Godfrey
Earl Warren

Famous Masons

George Washington
James Monroe
Andrew Jackson
James K. Polk
Andrew Johnson
James A. Garfield
William McKinley
Teddy Roosevelt
William H. Taft
Warren G. Harding
Franklin D. Roosevelt
Harry S. Truman
Lyndon B. Johnson
John Jacob Astor
Irving Berlin
Luther Burbank
Henry Clay
Henry Ford
Thomas Dewey
Barry Goldwater
Samuel Gompers
J. Edgar Hoover
Charles Lindbergh
Douglas MacArthur
Andrew Mellon
John J. Pershing
Will Rogers
Sigmund Romberg
John Philip Sousa
Earl Warren

Giraffes clean their ears with their tongues.

Because the earth's path of orbit around the sun is elliptical and not circular, the sun's gravitational attraction to the earth is not constant, and so the planet moves at different speeds at different times of the year. Beginning at the spring equinox, the periods of time the earth takes to reach each successive season are about ninety-three, ninety-four, eighty-nine, and eighty-nine days, respectively; spring and summer actually being nine days longer than winter and fall in the Northern Hemisphere, while in the Southern Hemisphere the reverse is true.

Early inoculations against disease often did not meet with the same enthusiasm that the polio vaccine received in the mid-fifties. Of Edward Jenner's "success" against smallpox, using a vaccine derived from the blood of cow-pox infected cattle, a Doctor Smyth wrote in 1796:

> Among the numerous shocking cases of cow-pox which I have heard is a child at Peckham, who, after being inoculated with cow-pox, had his former natural dispositon absolutely changed to the brutal; so that *it* ran upon all fours, bellowing like a cow, and butting with *its* head like a bull.

In the same vein, a satiric poet wrote:

> There, nibbling at thistles, stand Jem, Joe and Mary;
> On their foreheads, oh horrible! crumpled horns bud;
> Here, Tom with a tail, and poor William all hairy,
> Reclined in a corner, are chewing their cud.

Answer: Tennessee.

MARCH 2

Notable Births

1769	DeWitt Clinton	1904	Dr. Seuss
1793	Sam Houston	1913	Marjorie Weaver
1824	Friedrich Smetana	1917	Desi Arnaz
1858	Samuel Untermeyer	1919	Jennifer Jones
1876	Pope Pius XII	1931	Tom Wolfe

Notable Events

1825 Earthquake in Algeria took 7,000 lives
1836 Texas declared its independence from Mexico
1915 Layland, West Virginia, mining accident killed 112 men
1956 France recognized independence of Morocco
1962 Wilt Chamberlain scored 100 points in a game against the Knicks
1978 Charlie Chaplin's body stolen in Switzerland

Some strange things used to happen in the Chase family burial vault near Christ Church, in the Barbados.

The tomb was built by a family named Goddard, and two family members of the Goddard clan, an infant and her grandmother, were interred in it before the Chases took it over in 1808. In that year, a Chase daughter was buried, and a year or so later her father was laid to rest beside her.

But in 1812, when the crypt was opened for another of the Chase daughters, pallbearers found the vault in a shambles. The father's lead-sheathed coffin, which was so heavy that eight men had carried it at the funeral, had been moved to the end of the chamber and upended, and the daughter's coffin lay on the floor, off its bier. Immediately the authorities suspected grave robbers, but there were no signs that the crypt had been broken into, and except for the two coffins, everything inside was in perfect order. The boxes containing the Goddard burials had been left undisturbed.

In 1816, the tomb was opened to receive another Chase. The identical situation was found. There was no evidence of a break-in, no sign of theft, but all the Chase coffins were strewn about. Once more, the Goddards' remains were unmolested. This time, the family hired armed guards to watch the tomb day and night, and they ordered the door sealed so it would be easy to see if someone opened it forceably or not.

Three years later, the crypt was opened again, and once more the Chases' coffins were tossed about; while the Goddards' remained on their biers.

This time Lord Combermere, the governor of the Barbados, intervened and personally supervised the sealing of the crypt. He proclaimed that the dead have a right to lie in peace and he also ordered fine sand be spread on the floor of the vault, to show up any footprints. Armed guards continued to be stationed at the tomb.

One year later, in 1820, Combermere ordered the Chase vault opened for investigation. The guards had reported no trespassers, the seal had not been broken, and there were no footprints in the sand — but the Chase coffins were scattered helter-skelter throughout the tomb. The governor ordered the crypt to be locked up securely and never opened again. Which it never has — but the people of the Barbados certainly know what they'd find if it were.

I can understand anyone's allowing himself to be bullied by the living, but not, if he can help it, by the dead.

Samuel Butler

Pity is for the living, envy is for the dead.

Mark Twain

Questions: What character in Shakespeare kills the most chickens and geese?

Why is a Greek fable like a garret?

The word "manure" is a contracted form of the French word *manoeuvrer*, which means to work with the hands or till the soil. Gradually, this came to mean the use of dung to improve the soil.

The term "quarantine" comes from the early days of the sea-going traders. When a vessel arrived at a harbor from an area known to be infected with contagious disease, it was forbidden all intercourse with the shore for a certain period to insure against epidemics. The length of time was often forty days, and the word comes from the Latin *quadraginta*, which means "forty."

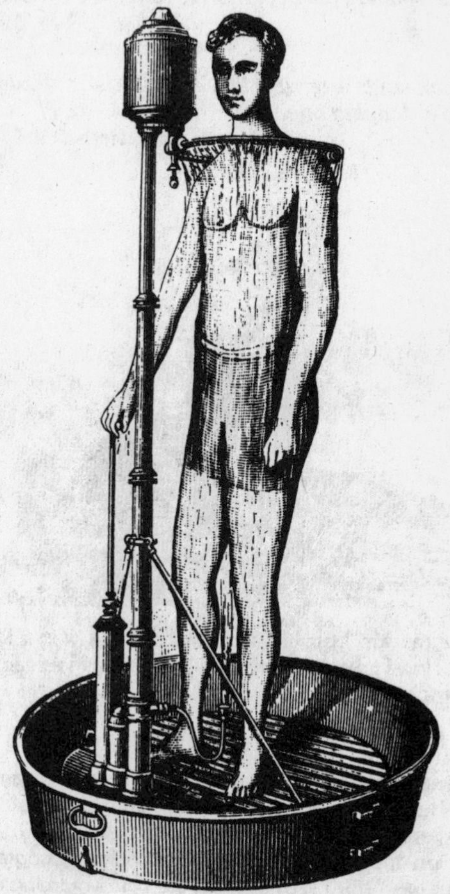

Men generally sound better singing in the shower than do women, and more men than women do so. One of the reasons for this is that most bathroom tiles are made of materials that resonate best to lower pitches, so men's voices are enhanced more.

Answers: Hamlet's uncle — he did "murder most foul."
Because it's an attic story.

MARCH 3

Question: What do the following athletes have in common?
Gene Conley
Dave DeBusschere
Ron Reed

Al Smith, while he was governor of New York, went to Sing Sing Prison to speak to the inmates there. He began his speech as he always did with, "My fellow citizens," but then he hesitated, realizing the inmates had been stripped of their privileges of citizenship. Then he said, "My fellow convicts," but knew immediately that that was wrong. He fumbled for a moment, and finally just blurted out: "Well, in any case, I'm glad to see how many of you are here."

Life is like playing a violin solo in public and learning the instrument as one goes on.
Samuel Butler

Tongue often hang man quicker than rope.
Charlie Chan

Speech is a faculty given to man to conceal his thoughts.
Talleyrand

A politician leads a terrible life. When he isn't straddling an issue, he is dodging one.
Herbert V. Prochnow

One of the top pop hits in China in 1974 was a little ditty entitled, "How I Love to Carry Fertilizer Up the Mountainside for the Commune."

Time magazine for fifty years bore the indelible stamp of its founder, Henry Luce, a man who was known to hold strong and rigid opinions. In Volume 1, Number 1 (March 3, 1923), *Time* reported on the new Immigration Bill before Congress, and noted that the "1890 Provision" in the bill "would increase the influx of hardy, industrious northern Europeans" allowed into the country, to the delight, Luce went on to say, of both labor and business.

Our word "admiral" comes from the Arabic phrase *Amir a'ali*, a man in high authority. The French picked it up from the Genoese while they were on crusade in 1249, and soon after that it entered the English language.

Notable Births

1756	William Godwin	1904	Red Ruffing
1842	Alexander Graham Bell	1911	Jean Harlow
1853	Vincent Van Gogh	1920	Julius Boros
1895	Matthew Ridgway	1920	Ronald Searle

Notable Events

1801	David Emanuel of Georgia became country's first Jewish governor
1815	United States declared war on Algeria
1820	Missouri Compromise agreed on
1861	Russian serfs emancipated
1875	Desert Homestead Act became law
1899	Dewey made an admiral at Manila Bay
1903	Sing Sing prison took first fingerprints
1916	Royal commission announced 10 percent of Britons had VD
1974	Turkish DC-10 crashed near Paris, 346 lost lives

Roscoe Penn was arrested in March 1935 for car theft, but he insisted to the Atlanta police that he was innocent. He told them he'd been walking for a long time and had grown fatigued, so he decided to stop and sit in a car to rest. He said his foot struck the floorboard starter and off he went — but he was so tired he didn't have the energy to stop.

Elaborate excuse seldom truth.
Charlie Chan

The American slang term "riffraff" comes from two Old French words *rifler*, "to rifle or ransack"; and *rafler*, "to snatch up." By the time the shortened word "riffraff" appeared in Middle English, it had come to denote refuse and rubble, and was applied to the dregs of humanity.

The profligate fourth Earl of Sandwich once became embroiled in a heated argument with the reformer John Wilkes. "I am convinced, Mr. Wilkes," he said, "that you will die either of a pox or on the gallows."

To which Wilkes quickly replied, "That depends, my lord, on whether I embrace your mistress or your principles."

In 1924, a horse sold for a penny in some parts of Australia.

Answer: All three played both pro basketball and major league baseball.

MARCH 4

Notable Births

1678	Antonio Vivaldi	1894	Dazzy Vance
1748	Casimir Pulaski	1901	Charles Goren
1881	T.S. Stribling	1912	John Garfield
1888	Knute Rockne	1932	Miriam Makeba

Notable Events

1789 U.S. Constitution became effective
1797 Matthew Lyon became first ex-convict elected to Congress
1868 House indicted President Johnson on 11 counts
1881 James Garfield became first president to live in the White House with his mother
1908 Fire in a Collingwood, Ohio, school killed 108 children
1928 Pyle's "Bunion Derby" began
1944 First raid of U.S. planes on Berlin
1952 Chinese accused United States of using germ warfare in Korea
1958 Submarine *Nautilus* reached North Pole
1962 Crash of DC-7C in Cameroons killed 111 people
1969 Jimmy Hoffa convicted of jury tampering in Chattanooga

The first treaty between the United States and Canada was ratified by the Senate on March 4, 1923. It regulated halibut fishing by each nation.

How many times has someone mentioned in conversation that there was a man who was president of the United States for one day, but no one in the group knows who he was?

Missouri's David R. Atchison, as president pro tem of the Senate, served as acting president from the expiration of James K. Polk's term at noon, Sunday, March 4, 1849, until the new president, Zachary Taylor, was sworn in shortly after noon on Monday.

Now you know.

An elected official is one who gets 51 percent of the vote cast by 40 percent of the 60 percent of voters who registered.

Dan Bennett

Randall Harmon, a tool engineer for the Delco Battery Company in Muncie, Indiana, was elected to Congress in 1958 as a Democrat, after he had been defeated on the four previous occasions he ran as a Republican. He bragged that his victorious campaign had cost him only $162. Once in office, he discovered a provision that allowed representatives $1,200 a year to maintain an office in their home districts — so he enclosed his front porch and, in effect, rented it to the government for $100 a month.

He was not reelected.

To be a chemist you must study chemistry; to be a lawyer or a physician you must study law or medicine; but to be a politician you need only to study your own interests.

Max O'Rell

Experience enables you to recognize a mistake when you make it again.

Franklin P. Jones

Answer: Roy Rogers, Mickey Rooney, Romy Schneider, Lizabeth Scott, Omar Sharif.

Question: By what names are these people better known?

Leonard Slye
Joe Yule, Jr.
Rose-Marie Albach
Emma Matzo
Michael Shalhoub

Philemon Herbert, a native of Pine Apple, Alabama, served as a representative from California to the Thirty-fourth Congress, which met between 1855 and 1856. One day while he was having lunch at the exclusive Willard Hotel in Washington, the honorable Mr. Herbert decided the service was not fast enough for his liking. He summoned the waiter over to his table and shot him dead.

The rainfall throughout the world averages 960 million tons of water a minute.

In March 1957, a court in Genoa, Italy, decided that Mario Mattioli had lied about his length of service, and had stayed in the navy an extra year. He was convicted of defrauding the government of 730 meals, 1,125 cups of coffee, 2,190 cigarettes, two uniforms, two caps, two pairs of shoes, three pairs of socks, three sets of underwear, seven handkerchiefs, and the equivalent in cash of $31.

Any fool can tell the truth, but it requires a man of some sense to know how to lie well.

Samuel Butler

The word "arena" comes to us from the Latin *arena*, which means "sand." The floors of the Coliseum and the other gladiatorial sites were strewn with sand to absorb the blood of the contestants and the beasts slaughtered in the exhibitions.

MARCH 5

Question: Which of the following is not a language in Ghana?
Paw
Twi
Fanti
Ga
Dagbani

Notable Births

1512	Gerard Mercator	1927	Jack Cassidy
1853	Howard Pyle	1936	Dean Stockwell
1870	Frank Norris	1945	Randy Matson
1908	Rex Harrison	1950	Eugene Fodor

Notable Events

1496 Henry VIII presented John Cabot with his commission for an American voyage
1623 Virginia passed first temperance order in America
1770 Boston Massacre occurred
1836 Alamo siege ended
1912 *Principe de Asturias*, Spanish steamer, foundered, 500 dead
1924 Frank Caruana, Buffalo, New York, became first man to bowl two 300 games
1927 U.S. Marines landed in China
1933 FDR ordered bank holiday
1934 Dillinger escaped from prison using a wooden pistol
1963 Patsy Cline killed in air crash
1966 Boeing 707 crashed into Mount Fuji, killed 124 people

At a temperance lecture in the Midwest, sometime before the advent of Prohibition, an impassioned speaker ran through the familiar diatribes against drink, and displayed the old "worm in the whiskey" demonstration for emphasis. By the time the worm's agonized death throes were over, most of the audience had been won. To dispell any lingering doubts, the speaker then tried to show that even the dumbest of creatures would not dare tread where some supposedly intelligent men rushed in. "If I put a pail of water and a pail of whiskey in front of a donkey, which would he drink?" he asked.

"The water!" cried a loud voice from the back of the audience.

"That's right!" cried the speaker. "And why would he drink the water instead of the whiskey?"

"Because he's a *jackass*!" the same voice replied.

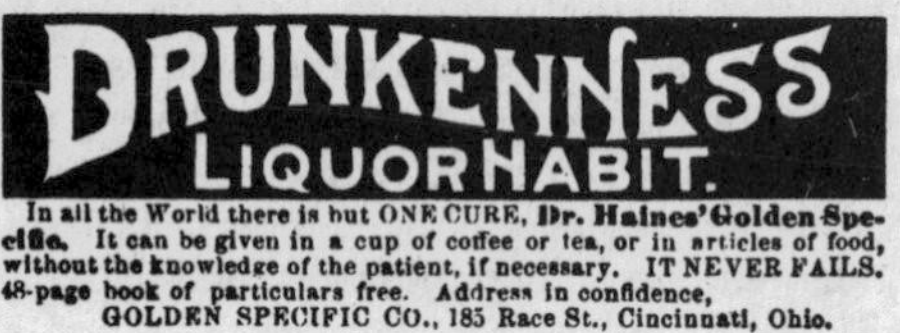

The great Italian painter Correggio died young, thanks to the meanness of the church fathers of Parma. They commissioned him to paint *The Assumption of the Virgin Mary* on the ceiling of their new cathedral and Correggio spent many months in the work. When he had completed it, the churchmen not only refused to pay him the agreed upon price, but made him take the 500 crowns they did hand over in copper instead of silver. It was a scorchingly hot day when Correggio carried this money home to his poverty-stricken family some distance from Parma, and he labored greatly under the weight of coins. When he stopped at a spring to quench his thirst, the combination of the heat, his heavy burden, and the icy water gave him a heart attack, which killed him.

Buy Old Masters. They fetch a much better price than old mistresses.

Lord Beaverbrook

In 1952, it was reported that forty Soviet Georgians had been selected for their physiological resemblance to Joseph Stalin and were being tested with some new life-prolonging serums in a Russian laboratory. The Kremlin hoped that a medicine could be developed that would keep the Russian dictator in good health for many years to come. An article about these experiments, entitled "Why Stalin May Live to Be 100" appeared in the April 1953, issue of *Science Digest*. Coincidentally, that issue of magazine hit the newsstands on the day of Stalin's death, March 5, 1953. He was seventy-three.

There cannot be a God because, if there were one, I would not believe that I were not He.

Friedrich Nietzsche

Our word "whiskey" comes from the Gaelic *wisge*, which itself was a contraction of *uisge-beatha*, meaning "water of life."

You can get the death penalty in Arkansas for putting salt on a railroad track.

One tricky way to load dice is to let a straight pair rest in a little mineral oil in a saucer for several weeks. Primitive doctored cubes have been found by archaelogists digging in the ruins of Pompeii.

For all the patriotic fervor that has come to be associated with the defense of the Alamo, the battle was as serious a blunder as Americans have made in their long military history, and the defenders of the fort were solely to blame. To begin with, the Alamo itself was "indefensible and strategically dubious . . ." according to Sam Houston, and, on January 17, 1836, he ordered the fortress to be abandoned and destroyed. The men at the Alamo ignored these orders, and generally did a poor job otherwise of preparing for their defense against the Mexicans. Scouting patrols were not sent out, nor was any information collected on the Mexican Army's movements or its strength; in fact, when intelligence was volunteered by travelers, it was ignored. There were no supply channels, and no stockpiles of ammunition and food, although they were both in bountiful supply nearby. There was plenty of whiskey at the fort, however; some of the gallant defenders traded their rifles for a large quantity before the seige began. Many of the 187 "Heroes of the Alamo" died drunk; among them probably both Jim Bowie and Davy Crockett.

Opposition may become sweet to a man, when he has christened it persecution.

George Eliot

Perfect case like donut — has hole.

Charlie Chan

Answer: Paw is a cat's foot, not a language.

MARCH 6

Notable Births

1475	Michelangelo	1900	Lefty Grove
1619	Cyrano de Bergerac	1908	Lou Costello
1806	Elizabeth Barrett Browning	1923	Ed McMahon
1834	George du Maurier	1940	Willie Stargell
1885	Ring Lardner	1947	Dick Fosbury

Notable Events

1775	First black Mason inaugurated, Boston
1930	Communists gassed at White House demonstration
1935	Government announced 22 million people on relief in United States
1946	Churchill delivered "Iron Curtain" speech, Fulton, Missouri
1957	Gold Coast independent, renamed Ghana

Questions: What is the difference between a blacksmith and a steady steed?

What is the difference between a chess player and a gambler?

There were seventy-two people in California jails in 1925 who were imprisoned under that state's Syndicalism Act. Mere membership in a forbidden organization called for incarceration, and sentences as long as fourteen years were routinely imposed.

War was going on long before anybody dreamed up communism. It's just the latest excuse for self-righteousness.

Joan Baez

In a dictatorship, suppression is nine points of the law.

Laurence J. Peter

One of "those" (waiters and waitresses will know who I mean) customers sat down one morning at a diner, and ordered breakfast. "I would like ham and eggs, and I want the eggs eliminated," he said archly, to the waitress.

The waitress was a feisty woman, and that morning particularly she didn't need this kind of customer. When the order was ready, she came from the kitchen with a slice of ham and two eggs, sunny side up.

"I told you I wanted the eggs eliminated," the man said.

"I know that, sir, but our damn-fool cook dropped the eliminator and busted it all apart. You'll have to have these. Here's your check."

Can't a critic give his opinion of an omelette without being asked to lay an egg?

Clayton Rawson

In the yard of the New Church in Amsterdam, there is a memorial inscribed simply "Effen Uyt," which boasts a sculptured pair of slippers on its top. "Effen uyt" is Flemish for "exactly." The monument belongs to a man who decided that he would die at a certain time and, quite systematically, spent his assets so that he would have nothing left at his death. When all he possessed was a pair of slippers, he died.

Punctuality is the thief of time.

Oscar Wilde

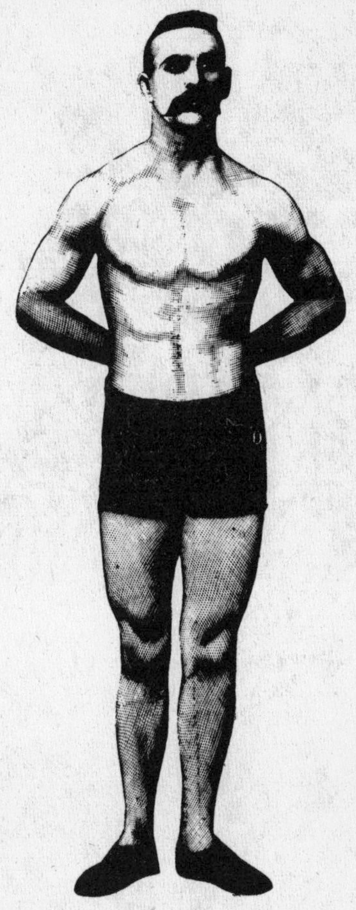

In March 1892, in a small Arkansan town, heavyweight champion John L. Sullivan was staging a "spar with the champ" exhibition, which was all in good fun. But one of his opponents didn't take kindly to the force of one of John L.'s blows and, forgetting the nature of competition, let go with a roundhouse punch. It knocked Sullivan cold.

Miss Hessie Wanner Donahue, then aged eighteen, is the only person, male or female, ever to knock big John L. out.

Good dose of land only effective medicine.

Charlie Chan

The prolonged slavery of women is the darkest page in human history.

Elizabeth Cady Stanton

A gentleman is a man who never strikes a woman without provocation.

H. L. Mencken

A science career for women is now almost as acceptable as being cheerleader.

Myra Barker

Answers: One is horseshoer, the other a sure horse.

One watches the pawn, the other pawns the watch.

MARCH 7

Question: By what names are these people better known?

Ehrich Weiss
Leslie Stainer
Roy Scherer, Jr.
Janet Cole
Arthur Gelien

Notable Births

1792	John Herschel	1912	Elizabeth Taylor
1849	Luther Burbank	1930	Anthony Armstrong-Jones
1875	Maurice Ravel	1950	Franco Harris

Notable Events

1080	Pope Gregory VII excommunicated Henry IV of England
1857	Dred Scott decision
1911	Coin-vended locker patented
1930	Byrd Antarctic expedition reached Dunedin, New Zealand
1931	Catholic bishops in Germany forbade Catholics from becoming Nazis
1932	3,000 workers rioted for jobs at Ford Motor Company, Detroit
1935	Sir Malcolm Campbell set land speed record of 276.8 mph
1940	Queen Mary docked at New York for duration of war
1951	Shah Ali Razmara of Iran assassinated

Do you remember those brightly colored, plastic, stick-on flowers that were found all over cars, especially Volkswagens, a few years back? The world's largest flower resembles them, but it's so large that a single bloom would just about cover a Beetle's roof.

Its botanical name is *Rafflesia arnoldi*, and it was discovered on the island of Sumatra in 1818 by an expedition under the leadership of an English gentleman, Sir Stamford Raffles. This remarkable plant is often more than three feet in diameter, and has dark, flesh-colored petals an inch thick. Its nectary is large enough to hold up to six quarts of water. From the basin of the nectary grow the reproductive parts of the flower, which are so big that they look like railroad spikes driven into a huge pincushion. For all this luxurious growth, the plant has no vegetative parts, and is parasitical, anchoring itself to a vine and deriving its nourishment from it. Large specimens weighing as much as fifteen pounds have been found locked onto a root only an inch in diameter. Many of the first blooms to be discovered had large amounts of elephant dung scattered on and around them, and this gave rise a century ago to the theory that this was their method of pollination.

Rafflesia's neighbor on Sumatra is another flower of monstrous size, *Amorphophallus titanum*, discovered by the Italian botanist, Odoardo Beccari, in 1878. *Rafflesia* is dwarfed by this amazing plant, which can easily weigh more than a hundred pounds. But *Amorphophallus* does not qualify for the title of world's largest flower because it is actually thousands of flowers masquerading as one. When this plant is in bloom it resembles the traditional Howard Johnson's ice-cream cone balanced upside down. Where the ice cream would be are thousands of male and hundreds of female flowers, which surround a towering influorescence (the cone part) often six to eight feet tall.*

A specimen in the New York Botanical Garden drew international attention in 1937 when it was announced that it was just about to bloom. Newspapers, wire services, and movie companies from all over the world sent reporters to cover the event, and a twenty-four-hour vigil was kept beginning on May 26. It turned out to be a most unpleasant assignment, as the plant needed a constant temperature of ninety-six degrees and sweltering humidity. Also, as the important day drew nearer, the more intense did the plant's peculiar odor become. It was described by one onlooker as a smell combined of "rotten fish and burnt sugar." As the days passed, many newspapermen and writers decided the event wasn't so important that they would have to be present at the precise moment the flower bloomed.

Finally, on June 7, the *Amorphophallus titanum* unravelled itself from its 8-foot, 5-inch influorescence and flowered into the upside-down, ice-cream-cone shape, four feet across and thirteen feet in circumference. It bloomed for four days, and thousands of people flocked to see it. It was *the* media and social event of the season in New York City.

In a week it was dead and rotten — which may or may not contain a moral.

There's nothing fishy about this story . . .

In March 1941, a Fort Wayne, Indiana, man named Artemus Knuckles, sued for the return of one of his wandering swine, which had been confiscated by a neighbor. His lawyer, David Hogg, cited as a legal precedent in the case a decision made by a circuit judge named Martin Pigg.

* If you don't remember the Howard Johnson pointy-topped ice-cream cone, dig out your Latin dictionary and take a look at the scientific name again.

Answer: Houdini, Leslie Howard, Rock Hudson, Kim Hunter, Tab Hunter.

MARCH 8

Notable Births

1841	Oliver Wendell Holmes	1923	Cyd Charisse
1859	Kenneth Grahame	1939	Jim Bouton
1898	Sam Jaffe	1942	Richie Allen
1912	Claire Trevor	1943	Lynn Redgrave

Notable Events

1765	Stamp Act passed by Parliament
1855	Niagara Falls suspension bridge opened to public
1936	Italian-Ethiopian peace talks began
1949	France recognized Vietnamese independence
1951	Iranian assembly voted to nationalize oil industry
1958	USS *Wisconsin* became last battleship to enter mothball fleet
1965	United States landed 3,500 marines in South Vietnam

The first-known recorded sighting of a UFO in America occurred on March 8, 1639, at Muddy River, just outside Boston. There, James Everell and his two companions, all claiming sobriety, watched a mysterious light for several hours. They said it was about three yards square and took the shape of a pig when it darted about.

Most elephants weigh less than the tongue of a blue whale.

The dingo, or Australian dog, is the only mammal native to the continent which is not a marsupial. The dingo itself may not be native, either. It may be an ancient import.

Question: By what names are these people better known?

Joyce Botterill
Carol Johnson
Gabriel Bonheur
Tula Finklea
Ray Robinson
Debs Garms

Three barrels of spilled oil will create a two-square mile slick on the ocean.

Attention, dog lovers! How big was the world's largest collection of china dogs in 1937? (Answers may be rounded out to the nearest hundred.)

400,230 (400,130 to 400,330 accepted), all owned by a school teacher in Milton, Massachusetts.

According to the British medical journal *Lancet*, of the 237 portrayals of doctors in 428 movies made in 1950, only twenty-five of the roles depicted medical men whose conduct was less than admirable, and only two of them showed a doctor who was humorous.

We have not lost faith, but we have transferred it from God to the medical profession.

George Bernard Shaw

The practice of medicine is so specialized today that each doctor is a healer of one disease and no more. The country is full of physicians, some for the eye, some of the teeth, some of the stomach, some of the hidden diseases.

Herodotus *circa* 430 B.C.

I got the bill for my surgery. Now I know what those doctors were wearing masks for.

James H. Boren

The man we call a specialist today was formerly called a man with a one-track mind.

Endre Balogh

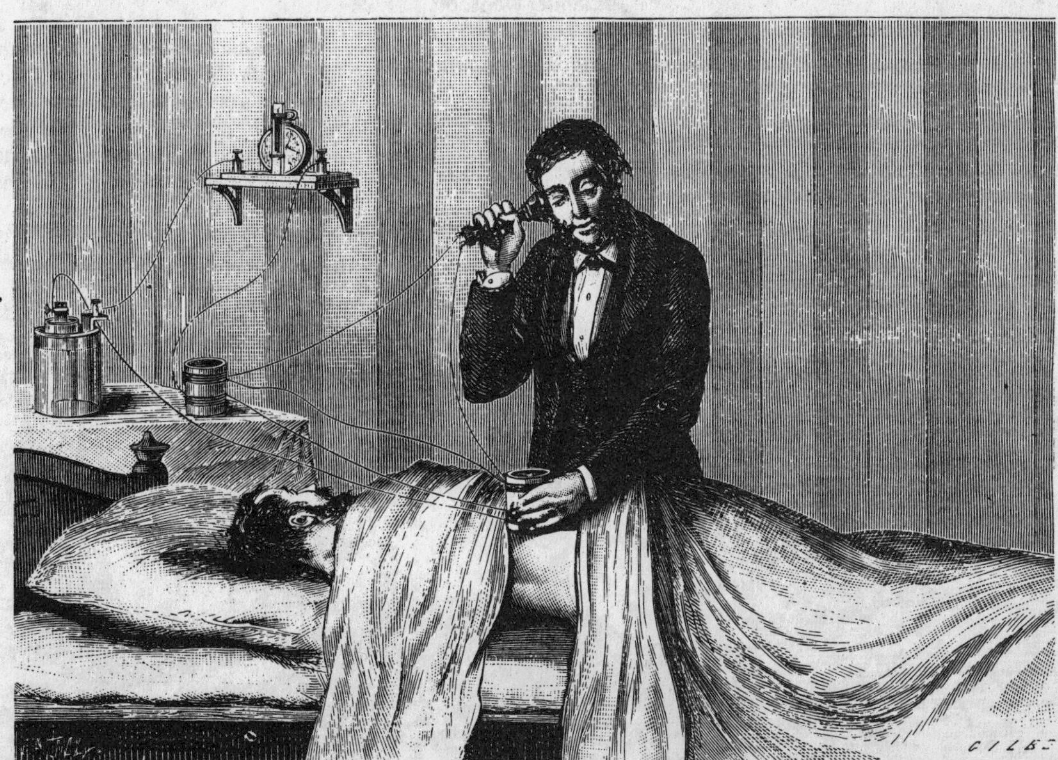

Answer: Judy Garne, Diahann Carroll, Coco Chanel, Cyd Charisse, Ray Charles, Debs Garms.

MARCH 9

Question: Uncle Henry was three times as old as Elsa when he told her she was too young to understand rock music. Twelve years later, he is only twice as old as she is, and he says they are both now too old to understand. How old is Uncle Henry?

The slogan of the *New York Times* is, "All the news that's fit to print." A French corollary during Napoleon's march from his exile on Elba to Paris might have been, "Fit the news to what you dare to print." This is how the headlines read in the government-censored newspapers as Napoleon fled from Elba and made his way to the French capital in 1815.

March 9	The Cannibal has escaped from his den
March 10	The Corsican ogre has just landed at Cape Juan
March 11	The Tiger has arrived at Gap
March 12	The Monster has passed the night at Grenoble
March 13	The Tyrant has crossed Lyons
March 14	The Usurper is directing his course towards Dijon, but the brave and loyal Burgundians have risen in a body, and they surround him on all sides
March 18	Bonaparte is sixty leagues from the capital; he has had skill enough to escape from the hands of his pursuers
March 19	Bonaparte advances rapidly, but he will never enter Paris
March 20	Tomorrow Bonaparte will be under our ramparts
March 21	The Emperor is at Fontainebleau
March 22	His Imperial and Royal Majesty last evening made his entrance into his Palace of the Tuileries, amidst the joyous acclamations of an adoring and faithful people

***The people of Germany are just as responsible for Hitler as the people of Chicago are for* The Chicago Tribune.**

Alexander Woollcott

I fear three newspapers more than a hundred thousand bayonets.

Napoleon

A free press is one that prints a dictator's speech but doesn't have to.

Laurence J. Peter

Notable Births

1451	Amerigo Vespucci	1918	Mickey Spillane
1809	Edwin Forrest	1918	George Lincoln Rockwell
1890	Vyacheslav Molotov	1924	Herbert Gold
1914	Fred Clark	1934	Yuri Gagarin

Notable Events

1798	France annexed left bank of Rhine
1860	Battle of the *Monitor* and the *Merrimack*
1919	Supreme Court upheld Debs's conviction under the Espionage Act
1932	Eamon de Valera elected president of Irish Free State
1961	Dalai Lama appealed to United Nations to restore Tibet's autonomy

The idea of socialism as a political system was introduced by early Germanic immigrants into the United States. Of the seventeen socialist newspapers published in the United States in 1876, thirteen were founded by Germans, three by Bohemians, and another by a Swede.

The hyphenated American always hoists the American flag undermost.

Teddy Roosevelt

In 1213, the Turks captured King Ferrand of Portugal and held him for ransom. He remained their captive for thirteen years, because the queen refused to send payment. Her refusal wasn't so much out of principle as the result of the grudge she bore the monarch. Just before he was taken hostage she had beaten him in a game of chess, and Ferrand had promptly blackened her eyes. The queen was not by nature a forgiving woman.

The battle between the *Monitor* and the *Merrimack* off Hampton Roads, Virginia, on March 9, 1862, was the first engagement between iron-clad warships in United States naval history; that much is irrefutable. But did you know the *Merrimack*'s real name at the time of the encounter was the *Virginia*? The *Merrimack* was a wooden frigate that had been scuttled and burned by her Northern crew when she was caught in a Southern port at the outset of the Civil War. The Confederates raised her, rebuilt her, clad her with iron, and renamed her the *Viriginia*.

Answer: Uncle Henry is forty-eight.

Notable Births

1772	Friedrich von Schlegel	1870	Wilbur Glenn Voliva
1839	Joaquin Miller	1888	Barry Fitzgerald
1863	Gaekwar of Baroda	1943	Bobby Fischer

Notable Events

1797	Albany made capital of New York
1880	First member of Salvation Army landed in America
1930	Wickersham Committee reported on breakdown of Prohibition
1933	Earthquake in Long Beach, California, killed 127 people
1934	FDR ordered airmail returned to civilian carriers, after ten army casualties in twenty days
1935	Hitler ordered conscription in Germany
1945	B-29s began incendiary bomb raids in Tokyo
1955	Death of Matthew Henson

Questions: Why is it a good idea for every king or leader to have several court jesters?

Why are two Germanic kings sometimes like three miles?

Not that Johnny Walker would have been much better for the Indians, but early in this century much of the liquor sold on Indian reservations contained such additives as strychnine (to give the booze a kick), red peppers (for bite), and soap (to give a glass of beer a frothy head). Many merchants cut their Indian hootch with plugs of tobacco because, they said, their customers felt that any alcohol that didn't make them sick had to be weak.

The first blindfolded, multi-game chess player was the extraordinary Louis Paulsen. He came to the United States in 1854 and settled in Dubuque, Iowa, to make a living as a tobacconist. In France he had won his town's chess championship at age seven, but played only infrequently during his teens. In the United States he started to enter tournaments again, and in 1857 amazed onlookers by simultaneously playing four games while he was blindfolded in a New York competition. In Chicago the following spring, he matched himself against ten strong opponents in a similar exhibition, and won nine of the games, drawing the tenth. The *Illustrated News* called it "perhaps the most astounding feat of memory the world has ever heard of."

A century later in San Francisco, the Belgian master, Koltanovski, easily surpassed Paulsen. In a 1960 exhibition he played fifty-six games simultaneously while blindfolded, winning fifty games and drawing the rest.

I don't think we did wrong in taking this great country away from them. There were great numbers of people who needed new land, and the Indians were selfishly trying to keep it for themselves.

John Wayne

The only good Indian is a dead Indian.

General Philip Sheridan

Answers: That way he can always keep his wits about him.

They always make a league.

MARCH 11

Question: We speak of a litter of kittens, a school of fish, and a troop of kangaroos. Give the group terms for:
crows
goats
parrots
peacocks

Although most laymen, and probably most mucisians, think of the symbol C after the clef sign denoting common time (4/4), it originally meant something very different. Years ago, "perfect" time was 3/4, because the three beats to the measure embodied the three persons of the Christian Trinity. It was represented by a complete circle. When 4/4 time was used, it was considered imperfect, and was represented by an incomplete circle. From the incomplete circle came our C, which is now popularly thought of as common time.

I've never heard such corny lyrics, such simpering sentimentality, such repetitious, uninspired melody. Man, we've got a hit on our hands.

Brad Anderson

The term "swan song" refers to the final performance of an entertainer. The phrase is derived from the mistaken belief that swans do not utter a sound throughout their lives, but commence to sing sweetly shortly before they die.

In 1736, Mr. Samuel Baldwin died in Hampshire, England. By his own request, his body was thrown into the ocean instead of receiving conventional burial. The reason for this was domestic strife; his shrewish wife had promised to dance on his grave if she outlived him.

A man in love is incomplete until he has married. Then he is finished.

Zsa Zsa Gabor

The richest one-twentieth of the people in America own five-sixths of its corporate stock.

Issac Antrobus was the notorious parson of Egremond in England. He resisted removal from his living for several years, despite a concerted effort by the townspeople to get rid of him. They finally managed to have him removed by bringing these charges against him in court:

He'd baptized a cock and named him Peter—
He'd committed adultery with a woman *and* her daughter—
He'd allowed himself to be led around naked by a woman who'd attached a leash to his privates—
He was always drunk—
He never preached.

Antrobus denied all the charges at first, but after the prosecution produced its evidence, admitted they were all true.

I know what I meant.

Richard Nixon

Notable Births

1754	Juan Valdes	1903	Lawrence Welk
1885	Sir Malcolm Campbell	1916	Harold Wilson
1892	Ferde Grofe	1926	Ralph Abernathy

Notable Events

537	Goths laid siege to Rome
1862	McClellan relieved of command of Union Army
1882	Intercollegiate Lacrosse Association founded, Princeton, New Jersey
1888	Great Blizzard of '88 began in Northeast, 400 eventually died
1930	Babe Ruth signed two-year contract for $80,000
1938	Hitler invaded Austria
1941	FDR signed Lend-Lease Act

A striped billiard ball takes about twice as long to bake as a cue ball does — fifteen as against seven days.

The lady who starred in *The Devil in Miss Jones* wasn't really named Georgina Spelvin. George (and its variations) Spelvin has been a stage name with a lucky reputation for hundreds of actors since 1907, when a cast member of *Brewster's Millions* used it. Since then there has been a Georgette Spelvin, a young dramatist called George Spelvin, Jr., and even the Russian Gregor Spelvanovich (in 1922).

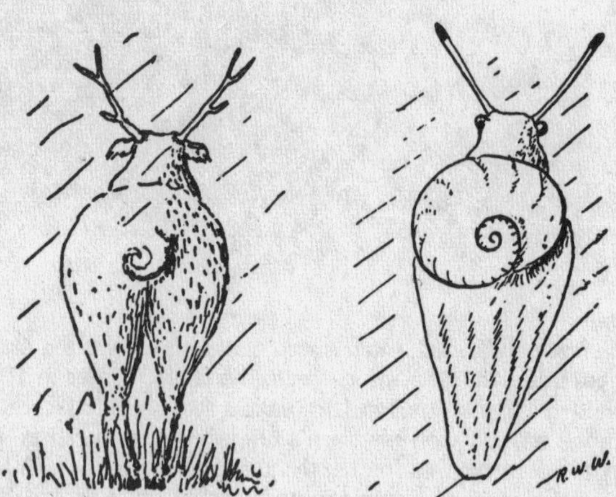

Elk-Whelk

A roar of welkome through the welkin
Is certain proof you'll find the Elk in;
But if you listen to the shell,
In which the Whelk is said to dwell,
And hear a roar, beyond a doubt
It indicates the Whelk is out.

Robert Williams Wood

Answer: A murder, a trip, a company, a muster.

MARCH 12

Notable Births

1626	John Aubrey	1928	Edward Albee
1863	Gabriele D'Annunzio	1941	Barbara Feldon
1922	Andrew Young	1946	Liza Minnelli
1922	Jack Kerouac	1948	James Taylor

Notable Events

1789 U.S. Post Office established
1912 Girl Scouts organized by Juliette Low, Savannah, Georgia
1932 Ivar Kreuger, Swedish match king, committed suicide
1933 FDR delivered first fireside chat
1938 Nazis took Austria
1940 Finland signed treaty of peace with Russia
1952 Kefauver defeated Truman in New Hampshire primary election
1964 Kitty Genovese murdered
1974 "Wonder Woman" TV series began

Question: By what names are these people better known?
Richard Jenkins
Aaron Chwatt
Maria Calogerpoulos
Mario Moreno
Edward Iskowitz

There was a year, almost a thousand years ago, when Europe collapsed. All construction and repair of buildings and roads ceased, and what educational systems there were fell into complete disarray. Even taxes went uncollected. Any thunderstorm or shooting star occurring anywhere during that time caused widespread panic, and tens of thousands of people fled from Europe and crowded into the Middle East.

Apparently everyone believed that the Millennium was at hand, and that Armageddon was due at any time.

Well, the world didn't end, but it took the West a generation to recover from the fear and destruction, and centuries for ecclesiastics to decide why the prophesies were incorrect.

Here are some other dates that have been variously predicted to be the Last Day:

Oct. 13, 1736	Predicted by Whiston, a "respected" English prophet
April 5, 1761	By an Englishman named Bell, who was soon after committed to a mental hospital
Oct. 22, 1844	By the Millerite movement
March 12, 1903	By Michael Baxter, an Englishman doing missionary work in Canada

Persistent prophecy is a familiar way of assuring the event.
George Gissing

To destroy false prophet must first unmask him before eyes of believer.
Charlie Chan

Fred Small had grown tired of his wife, but he didn't dare divorce her. He stood to inherit a small fortune if she died before he did. But it did seem that Fred would have to encourage her journey to a better world, because she was healthy as a horse.

So he beat her over the head with an iron pipe, strangled her with a rope, and shot her, in that order.

Of course, Fred knew that a body looking as this one did would never pass as an accidental death, so he had a plan to erase the evidence completely. Using a timer and some thermite, a substance used in blast furnaces to create great heat in a short time, Small decided to burn his cottage in Lake Ossipee, New Hampshire, while he was in Boston that afternoon. The intense heat of the thermite with which he had pasted his wife's corpse would not only complete destroy her body, but also melt the lead of the bullet he had shot her with. So he arranged everything, called a cab, and was soon on the train to Massachusetts. Once in Boston, he visited practically everyone he knew to establish his alibi.

When he returned later that evening, the police were at the site of his burnt-out home, as he had expected. What he did not expect was that he was immediately placed under arrest for the murder of his wife.

The fire had destroyed his house, all right — but early in the blaze the floor of the cottage had collapsed, sending Mrs. Small and the remains of the timer into the basement. It had been extremely wet in central New Hampshire that summer, and the cellar was partially flooded. The body, the bullet, and the timer were quite enough to convict Fred Small, and he was hanged in 1918.

Regret such alibis have habit of disappearing, like cheese in vicinity of mouse.
Charlie Chan

"Necessity is the mother of invention" is a silly proverb. "Necessity is the mother of futile dodges" is much nearer the truth.
Alfred North Whitehead

She made a ravishing corpse.
Ronald Firbank

Answer: Richard Burton, Red Buttons, Maria Callas, Cantinflas, Eddie Cantor.

MARCH 13

Question: Which of these animals would win a quarter-mile race?
chicken
pig
black mamba snake
squirrel

Notable Births

1733	Joseph Priestly	1884	Hugh Walpole
1781	Johann Wyss	1910	Sammy Kaye

Notable Events

1519	Cortez landed in Mexico
1852	First newspaper cartoon depicting Uncle Sam appeared, New York City
1884	Standard Time established in United States
1887	Chester Greenwood, Farmington, Maine, patented earmuffs
1917	Wilson announced arming of U.S. merchant vessels
1928	Saint Francis Dam collapsed, Santa Paula, California
1930	Discovery of planet Pluto announced
1933	Roosevelt asked for immediate legalization of beer
1961	Elizabeth Flynn chosen national chairman, U.S. Communist party

A few years ago, the Cheshire, England, Baptist Association decided to construct a tableau of the ideal Bible family to be displayed at a local fair. As the fair was a sunrise to sunset affair, human players were ruled out, and a call was made to a nearby wax museum for assistance.

The exhibit proved to be very popular, but not because of the piety of the fair-goers. The father in the Ideal Bible Family was represented by the wax figure of a notorious murderer; his wife was a composite of the body of Queen Elizabeth I and the face of an Olympic ice skating champion; the daughter was the waxwork's model of Snow White; and the minister guiding their studies was a currently celebrated swindler.

The Domicile Erected by John

Behold the mansion reared by daedal Jack.

See the malt stored in many a plethoric sack,
In the proud cirque of Ivan's bivouac.

Mark how the Rat's felonious fangs invade
The golden stores in John's pavilion laid.

Anon, with velvet foot and Tarquin strides,
Subtle Grimalkin to his quarry glides —
Grimalkin grim, that slew the fierce *rodent*
Whose tooth insidious Johann's sackcloth rent.

Lo! now the deep-mouthed canine foe's assault,
That vexed the avenger of the stolen malt,
Stored in the hallowed precincts of that hall
That rose complete at Jack's creative call.

Here stalks the impetuous Cow with crumpled horn,
Whereon the exacerbating hound was torn,
Who bayed the feline slaughter-beast that slew
The Rat predacious, whose keen fangs ran through
The textile fibers that involved the grain
Which lay in Han's inviolate domain.

Here walks forlorn the damsel crowned with rue,
Lactiferous spoils from vaccine dugs, who drew,
Of the corniculate beast whose tortuous horn
Tossed to the clouds, in fierce vindictive scorn,
The harrowing hound, whose braggart bark and stir
Arched the lithe spine and reared the indignant fur
Of Puss, that with vermicidal claw
Struck the weird rat in whose insatiate maw
Lay reeking malt that erst in Juan's courts we saw,
Robed in senescent garb that seems in sooth
Too long a prey to Chronos' iron tooth.

Behold the man whose amorous lips incline,
Full with young Eros' osculative sign,
To the lorn maiden whose lact-albic hands
Drew albu-lactic wealth from lacteal glands
Of that immortal bovine, by whose horn
Distort, to realm ethereal was borne
The beast catulean, vexer of that sly
Ulysses quadrupedal, who made die
The old mordacious Rat that dared devour
Antecedaneous Ale in John's domestic bower.

Lo, here, with hirsute honors doffed, succinct
Of saponaceous locks, the Priest who linked
In Hymen's golden bands the torn unthrift,
Whose means exiguous stared from many a rift,
Even as he kissed the virgin all forlorn,
Who milked the cow with the implicated horn,
Who in fine wrath the canine torturer skied,
That dared to vex the insidious muricide,
Who let auroral effluence through the pelt
Of the sly Rat that robbed the palace Jack had built.

The loud cantankerous Shanghae comes at last,
Whose shouts arouse the shorn ecclesiast,
Who sealed the vows of Hymen's sacrament,
To him who, robed in garments indigent,
Exosculates the damsel lachrymose,
The emulgator of that horned brute morose,
That tossed the dog, that worried the cat, that kilt
The rat, that ate the malt, that lay in the house that Jack built.

Translated from the *Vulgate*

Answer: The black mamba snake.

Notable Births

1691	George P. Telemann	1879	Albert Einstein
1820	Victor Emmanuel II	1933	Michael Caine
1868	Maxim Gorky	1933	Quincy Jones

Notable Events

479 B.C.	Eclipse of the sun scared Xerxes' army
1493	Columbus dispatched first letter about discoveries
1794	Cotton gin patented
1900	Gold Standard in effect in United States
1925	First transatlantic radio broadcast made
1932	George Eastman, of Eastman-Kodak, committed suicide
1945	Iwo Jima fell to U.S. troops
1948	Ahmad became leader of Yemen
1964	Jack Ruby found guilty of murdering Lee Harvey Oswald
1972	Danish airliner crashed in Dubai, 112 people killed

Questions: What is the difference between Congress and progress?

Why are many politicians like lobsters?

There really was a Casey Jones, and "The Ballad of Casey Jones" was loosely based on the train accident that cost the engineer his life.

John Luther Jones was born in southeastern Missouri on March 14, 1864, and moved to Caycee, Kentucky, as a teenager. Because of the confusion his name sometimes created, he adopted the name of his new home to distinguish himself from other John Joneses when he began working for the Illinois Central Railroad. His diligence, skill, and intelligence served him well, and by the time he was twenty-six, Jones was an engineer, one of the youngest the Illinois Central had.

For fifteen more years Casey Jones compiled an outstanding record of punctuality and safety in an era when there was no sense in being careful if the rig didn't come in on time. "Make time, or come into the office and get your time," was railroading's favorite slogan. Casey Jones, as the song says, was a "brave engineer."

On April 30, 1906, Casey was in Engine 382 on his passenger run from Memphis, Tennessee, to Canton, Mississippi. As he neared Canton he was running a bit late, but Casey calculated that in the dozen or so miles from Vaughn he could make up that time and coast in ahead of schedule.

But just before Vaughn, there was a double-S curve in the track. Riding in the engine cab on the inside of the curve, Sim Webb, Casy's fireman, saw — too late — the red lights of a stopped freight train, Casey, on the outside of the curve, could not see them at all. When Sim saw the other train, he hollered to Casey to stop, but a collision by this time was unavoidable. Jones ordered Webb to jump for his life while he stayed on board to apply the brakes and cut the boiler pressure. When his body was found in the wreckage, there was an iron bolt through Casey's neck.

History has it that, as he wiped Casey's blood from the wreckage of the locomotive, Wallace Saunders, a black man who worked in the Canton roundhouse, was humming a railroad song he'd heard shortly before in Kansas City. He made some name changes and added some appropriate lyrics, and so composed the famous ballad even as Casey's blood remained on Number 382.

Answers: Pro and con.

They change their colors when they get in hot water.

MARCH 15

Question: Which of these are *not* geographic entities?

Benin
Comoros
Oerter
Djibouti
Danek
Kiribati

There aren't too many bank cashiers who have songs written about them, but Abraham Newland was not an average cashier. Beginning in 1748, his career with the Bank of England lasted nearly sixty years. After 1782, when he was made chief cashier, he slept every night inside the bank itself for twenty-five years and became as much a symbol of England as John Bull. A favorite fighting and drinking song of British soldiers of the period went:

We'll make their ears ring in defense of our king,
Our country, and Abraham Newland,
Oh, Abraham Newland, Darling Abraham Newland—
No tricolor, elf, nor the Devil himself
Shall e'er rob us of Abraham Newland.

His epitaph, which it is believed he wrote himself, is ironic, given his countrymen's admiration for him.

Beneath this stone old Abraham lies;
Nobody laughs and nobody cries,
Where he's gone, and how he fares,
No one knows, and no one cares.

You should know who to love and who to hate and who to just plain like, and it's important to know the difference.

Jane Fonda

The word "schooner" is of very recent American origin. These ships got their name from the pastime of skipping rocks across the water, which was called scooning in England. When New Englanders began to construct their clean-lined, swift trading vessels, they adopted the name from the game of scooning because both the rocks and the ships traveled so quickly and lightly over the water.

Notable Births

1767	Andrew Jackson	1915	MacDonald Carey
1875	Wallace Irwin	1916	Harry James
1876	Harold Ickes	1918	Richard Ellmann
1904	George Brent	1924	Sabu

Notable Events

44 B.C.	Julius Caesar assassinated
1493	Columbus reached Spain on return from first voyage
1607	Charles IX crowned King of Sweden
1767	Andrew Jackson born posthumously; became first president so born
1812	Russians established settlement at Cazadero, California
1820	Maine became a state
1849	Cholera epidemic began in New York City
1897	Nation's first indoor flycasting tournament held, New York City
1917	Prohibition effective in Washington, D.C.
1934	Samuel Insull fled Athens in drag to escape prosecution
1964	Burton and Taylor secretly married in Montreal

The average American works about 230 days a year, gets two-weeks vacation, ten or so holidays, and there are as many as twenty million people in the United States who are undernourished because they can't afford to pay for decent food. Nineteen centuries ago, the average Roman worked only about 205 days a year, and there was government-subsidized grain for everyone. Of the remaining days in the Roman year, about ninety were holidays devoted to athletic competitions, feasts, and dramatic festivals.

Of course, even the most prosperous Romans didn't have recreational vehicles.

The word "trivial" comes from a particular place in Rome where the minor matters of the day were discussed. Serious topics in Julius Caesar's time were dealt with at the marketplace and the Forum, while the citizenry bantered gossip at the intersection of three roads nearby; the "Tri-Via." The geographic location soon came to be applied to the kind of conversations that took place there.

This is the epitaph on Ira Prentice's tomb. He died in 1819 in Burlington, Maine.

He died of the cholera morbus
caused by eating green fruit,
In the hope of a blessed immortality.
Reader go thou and do likewise.

In ancient Rome, a man could get a meal with a pint of wine, hay for his horse, and a room with a girl for eight cents.

Answer: Oerter and Danek are Olympic discus-throwing champions.

MARCH 16

Notable Births

1751	James Madison	1903	Mike Mansfield
1787	G.S. Ohm	1912	Pat Nixon
1839	M.P. Moussorgsky	1926	Jerry Lewis

Notable Events

1749 Royal Charter given to Ohio Company
1802 West Point established
1871 Delaware enacted first state fertilizer law
1961 Tanganyika declared independence
1964 Hornung and Karris reinstated after year's suspension for betting
1968 My Lai massacre
1969 DC-9 crashed on takeoff in Venezuela, 155 dead

In 1627 a law was passed by Parliament requiring Englishmen to keep the dung and urine from their farm animals for collection by King Charles I's "Saltpeter Men." Britain, as usual, had been involved in a series of wars that necessitated great quantities of nitre for gunpowder, which could be cheaply extracted from animal effluents. For nearly thirty years, these collectors were empowered to rip apart homes, stables, and cellars without the permission of the owners or any repayment to them, and those who used dung for fertilizer, or resisted the collection of manure and urine, were often fined or imprisoned.

Self-sacrifice enables us to sacrifice others without blushing.

George Bernard Shaw

Nationalism is a silly cock crowing on his own dunghill.

Richard Aldington

The flush toilet is the basis of Western Civilization.

Alan Coult

In March 1951, the City Council of Southport, England, voted to dock James Clarkson, aged thirty-five, the equivalent of fifty-five cents for the hour and a half he'd been away from work. Clarkson had missed some part of his duties at the city wharves because he was engaged in saving the life of a man who had been trapped in a sandbank.

A law passed in Nebraska in 1912 really set down some hard rules of the road. Drivers in the country at night were required to stop every 150 yards, send up a skyrocket, then wait eight minutes for the road to clear before proceeding *cautiously*, all the while blowing their horn and shooting off flares.

Average heights and weights of some European males *circa* 1855:

Country	Height	Weight
England	5 feet 9½ inches	151 pounds
France	5 feet 4 inches	137 pounds
Belgium	5 feet 6¼ inches	140 pounds

Question: By what names are these people better known?

Oliver Williams
Melvin Kaminsky
Taidje Khan
Nathan Birnbaum
Edna Gillooly

On March 16, 1802, Congress authorized the creation of the United States Military Academy, but neglected to appropriate any money for it, and the academy's first class of 156 cadets was admitted to an institution with no buildings or instructors. Congress later rectified this oversight by voting the funds for buildings and a token stipend for the cadets. Well, almost rectified it: Congress again forgot that schools require teachers, and as late as 1812 the academy had no faculty because the government had not appropriated any money to hire one.

There's no trick to being a humorist when you have the whole government working for you.

Will Rogers

The first official American war was declared in the spring of 1637 by the General Court of Connecticut against the Pequot Indian tribe. Destroying everything in their path, and killing Indian men, women, and children indiscriminately, the good Christians of New London drove the Indians far enough west to satisfy them and then returned to do what all postwar heroes do. Legislators raised taxes to pay for the conflict; generals wrote their memoirs; soldiers demanded bonuses; and everyone quarrelled over who should have the most glory for the famous victory.

To delight in war is a merit in soldier, a dangerous quality in a captain, and a positive crime in a statesman.

George Santayana

Riley Bubier was a tough old dude. When he was eighty-eight years old, he managed to cut and stack three full cords of wood for Vance Oakes up in Rangeley, Maine, in a single day.

He got home and fell down dead.

Answer: Oliver Cromwell, Mel Brooks, Yul Brynner, George Burns, Ellen Burstyn.

MARCH 17

Question: Three little pigs went to market and each bought groceries. The first little pig spent 57 cents less than the average little-pig grocery bill that day; the second little pig spent 58 cents more, and the third spent $7.00. What was the average bill?

A Michigan clergyman delivered a diatribe on a Sunday in 1906 directed at a creature he said was "destroying all the instincts of motherhood and leading our nation to race suicide." The target of his sermon was the newly popular teddy bear.

Appearances sometimes deceiving — like wolf in lamb's clothing.

Charlie Chan

The textile and other manufacturing mills of Lowell, Massachusetts, attracted thousands of unskilled immigrants during the days of America's "open door" policy, and the city's construction of new houses couldn't come close to meeting the rate of population growth. At the height of the population pressure, an average of 119 people per *acre* lived in Lowell's four-story downtown tenements. That is equivalent to 76,000 people per square mile. By contrast, the city of New York today has about 26,300 inhabitants per square mile, Boston has about 14,000, and Los Angeles about 6,100.

I am weary of seeing our laboring classes wretchedly housed, fed, and clothed, while thousands of dollars are wasted every year over unsightly statues. If these great man must have their outdoor memorials let them be in the form of handsome blocks of buildings for the poor.

Elizabeth Cady Stanton

The aristocracy created by business rarely settles in the midst of the manufacturing population which it directs; the object is not to govern that population, but to use it.

Alexis de Tocqueville

The tumultuous populace of large cities are ever to be avoided.

George Washington

In 1927, Ellsworth Huntington and Leon Whitney attempted to prove that distinguished people *are* different. They searched the biographies of *Who's Who* to find out what kind of homes the "Who's" came from. Using 1870 as their base year, they discovered that one of every seven families headed by a Unitarian minister had produced an individual who was recorded in *Who's Who*. Their other figures included:

Employment of Family Head	Number of Families per Listing
Unskilled laborers	48,000
Trade/craftsmen	1,600
Farmers	690
Doctors	104
Businessmen	80
Lawyers	52
Sea captains	42
Clergymen	20

Answer: $6.99.

Notable Births

1777	Roger B. Taney	1914	Sammy Baugh
1804	Jim Bridger	1918	Mercedes McCambridge
1846	Kate Greenaway	1919	Nat King Cole
1894	Frank Buck	1938	Rudolf Nureyev
1902	Bobby Jones	1944	John Sebastian

Notable Events

1776	British evacuated Boston
1856	Earthquake in Moluccan Islands killed 2,900 people
1860	Second Maori War began, New Zealand
1864	Grant assumed control of Union army
1884	J.J. Montgomery made first U.S. glider flight, Otay, California
1912	Camp Fire Girls organized, Sebago Lake, Maine
1936	Flooding of midwestern U.S. rivers killed 171 people
1940	"Murder, Incorporated" uncovered in Brooklyn
1959	Dalai Lama fled Tibet
1966	Missing H-bomb found in waters off Spain
1969	218 dead in British floods

In 1948, Parisian Alfredo Bindi tried to commit suicide in a most unusual manner: he ate his suspenders. It didn't work.

A fellow named Samuel Jessup died in Heckington, England, on May 17,1817. A year previously, Jessup had been taken to court by a druggist for the payment of what must have been a substantial bill. In testimony before the court, it was revealed that Jessup in the past two decades had consumed at least 226,934 pills and 40,000 bottles of various *aqua vitae*.

Although the harshness of the Russian winter is greatly overrated as the main reason for Napoleon's failure to conquer all of Europe 150 years ago, the weather was *the* determining factor in Edward III's inability to take France in the fourteenth century. While besieging Paris in 1360, the English forces were routed by a hailstorm on April 30 that killed one thousand of their men and six thousand of their horses. The hour-long freak storm was the deciding factor of the war.

Back in 1778, the citizens of Boston gave a banquet in honor of the French admiral, D'Estainge, who had recently arrived in New England to help the Americans in their war effort. The chef, hearing that the French considered frog a delicacy, went out and defrogged every pond in the city. He served them in a specially prepared cold soup — live.

I also avoid green vegetables. They're grossly overrated.

Noel Coward

MARCH 18

Notable Births

1721	Tobias Smollett	1905	Robert Donat
1782	John Calhoun	1918	Irving Wallace
1837	Grover Cleveland	1926	Peter Graves
1842	Stéphane Mallarmé	1927	George Plimpton
1844	Nickolai Rimsky-Korsakov	1932	John Updike
1858	Rudolf Diesel	1938	Charlie Pride
1886	Edward Everett Horton	1956	Ingemar Stenmark

Notable Events

1734	First magician's advertisement appeared, New York City
1865	Argentinian-Paraguayan war began
1871	Smith College established
1922	First intercollegiate polo championships held, Princeton, New Jersey
1922	Gandhi sentenced to 6 years imprisonment for civil disobediance
1925	Tornadoes killed 689 people and injured 15,000 in Midwest
1937	Explosion in New London, Texas, school killed 413 children
1937	Amelia Earhart began solo attempt to circle the world
1938	Mexico nationalized foreign oil company holdings
1949	NATO treaty adopted by United States
1965	First space walk made by Alexei Leonov

During the early 1950s, only 6 percent of the people listed in *Who's Who* were women. Of these notable women, only 60 percent were married, and half of those who were married were childless.

John Calhoun resigned the vice-presidency to serve in the Senate in 1832.

Saint Francis of Assisi, the founder of the Franciscan order, was not named Francis at all. His real name was Giovanni. He was called Francis because he spoke French so well.

Members of Calvinist Churches are certainly better known for their "puritanical" attitudes towards sex than for their encouragement of it, but there's a religious group in the Netherlands where some very peculiar things happen. This is the Reformed Association Church, centered in the town of Staphorst, about fifty miles northeast of Amsterdam. The church prohibits dancing and card playing, and frowns upon such worldly things as newspapers, electricity, and indoor plumbing.

But when it comes to marriage, the Reformed Association Church has an odd custom: a girl cannot be married unless she is pregnant. It's traditional on Friday nights for papa to hang a copper plate on his front door to show he had a daughter who is "receiving visitors," and the girl leaves her bedroom window open for that purpose. When the young lady gets pregnant, everyone gets together for a traditional wedding, and hopes she has married the baby's real father.

That's the only "free love" in the church's practices, though. Upon conviction, adulterers are commonly paraded through town in a dung cart, and the townspeople hurl all sorts of things at them, including epithets. Transgressors are afterwards banished from the community for life.

Questions: Why is a lawyer like a devoted rabbi?

What's the difference between a duck?

For some unknown reason, if you enter a turkey pen and yell out, "Where's Francis?," the turkeys will greet you with a cacophony of gobbling.

Try it if you don't believe me.

Next time you visit your local shopping mall, think what a wonderful place it would be to stage a field hockey game. The word "mall" comes from the Italian *maglio*, which means both a mace or a mallet and also a place for playing games with mallets and balls.

In 1938, there was one automobile for every 5 people in the United States, one for every 22 in France and Britain, one for every 109 in Italy, and one for every 1,284 in Poland.

Today, in Communist China, there is one car for every 14,500 Chinese.

Here's a cheerful little epitaph from Michaelchurch, in Hertfordshire, England:

John Prosser is my name, & England is my nation,
Bowchurch is my dwelling place, & Christ is my salvation.
Now I am dead, & in my grave, & all my bones are rotten,
As you pass by, *remember* me, when I am quite *forgotten*.

Female chemists have a suicide rate about two-and-a-half times greater than their male counterparts.

The term "hallmark" originated in London in about 1300. At that time, an assay office was established called Goldsmith's Hall, where metalsmiths could go to have the purity of their materials tested. There, one of a variety of die-impressions would be stamped into an ingot according to its quality, hence "Hallmark."

Answer: The rabbi studies the Law and Prophets, while the lawyer studies the law and profits.

One of its feet is both the same.

MARCH 19

Question: Name a president born in:
Iowa
Missouri
New Jersey
Nebraska

Notable Births

1800	Frederic Curie	1883	Joseph Stilwell
1809	Nikolai Gogol	1891	Earl Warren
1813	David Livingston	1904	John Sirica
1821	Sir Richard Burton	1933	Philip Roth
1860	William Jennings Bryan	1938	Ursula Andress

Notable Events

592	Solar eclipse recorded in Greece
1687	LaSalle murdered by his own men in what is now Texas
1775	Prussia and Poland signed commercial treaty
1782	Lord North resigned as British prime minister
1831	First bank robbery in United States occurred, New York City
1952	Stassen defeated Eisenhower in New Hampshire Republican primary
1967	Fire in Rio de Janeiro took 436 lives

On this date in 1927, the first episode of "Amos and Andy" was broadcast. Up until a few minutes before air time, the show and the two principles were to have been called "Jim and Charlie," but Freeman Gosden, who played Amos, didn't think the title was catchy enough, and he hurriedly consulted a dictionary of names. He never got to the *B*s.

Three things I'll never forget about America are the Rocky Mountains, Niagara Falls, and "Amos and Andy."

George Bernard Shaw

Usually the swallows show up every year at Capistrano March 19, but in 1935, storms delayed their arrival for three days.

I just thought you might like to know.

Letting a horse walk away with a wagon-load of stolen gold seems extraordinarily stupid, but it's nothing compared to the way the law-enforcement officials of New Hampshire handled the thieves who let this happen.

One night, the Larned brothers pulled a nice clean bank job in Charlestown, New Hampshire, a small community on the Vermont border. The year was 1859. The gold they stole from the bank would have set them up comfortably for life, except for one thing: the horse pulling the loot-filled wagon walked away.

The Larneds, who were natives of Oxford, Massachusetts, had a long history of criminal activity and occasional imprisonment throughout New England, as well as a reputation (*generally*) for ingenuity. Since he had some inside information on the Charlestown bank, Abijah Larned decided it was worth the trouble to travel the 100 miles from their home to rob it. His brother dressed in women's clothes to avoid suspicion, and they traveled together as an innocent young couple. The robbery was simple and successful, and they were able to begin their southward escape at about midnight.

Eleven miles south of Charlestown they reached Hatch Hill, a long, fairly steep incline, and both men got off the cart to lighten the load for the horse. Abijah, an energetic man, strode up the hill ahead of the wagon, while his brother fell behind it.

It was a fatal mistake. When the brothers met at the crest of the hill there was no sign of the horse or wagon. Abijah was sure the horse had not overtaken him; his brother was equally positive he had not passed the horse. They searched for a while, but to no avail. Wary of capture, the two split up. Abijah went to Keene; his brother disappeared.

It turned out that halfway up the hill the horse had discovered a gently sloping logging road going off from the main thoroughfare and simply took the path of least resistance. At dawn he was discovered by Horace Gee of Marlow, who was returning home after sitting up with a sick friend overnight. Gee led the horse to his farm and tied him up next to the road, expecting his owner would soon be by.

Later that morning, Gee heard of the robbery and the $500 reward the bank had offered for the return of the gold and/or the thieves. He searched the wagon, found the gold, the women's clothing, and a buffalo robe with the name S. Barton sewn into it. The bank directors, annoyed that Gee seemed to have had so little trouble in earning the bounty, reduced the award to $400, even though they came into possession of the stolen money and several-hundred-dollars worth of horse and wagon.

The authorities found S. Barton in Oxford, Massachusetts. He had no connection with the Larneds, but was able to provide law officers with enough information to issue a warrant for the brothers' arrest.

A New Hampshire deputy caught up with Abijah Larned in Utica, New York, in December, and took him into custody. This was the last sensible action by a law-enforcement official, judge, or bank director in this strange case. Apparently, Abijah had just pulled off an extremely successful robery in Utica, and so went quite willingly with the deputy back to New Hampshire, without the formality of an extradition procedure, which would certainly have made him a suspect in the Utica break. Once in New Hampshire, he was the model of a prisoner. He approached the officials of the Charlestown bank, and offered to pay all their expenses in the affair, a damage settlement as well, and the extra $100 properly owing to Horace Gee. The bankers agreed. He then volunteered to pay the state for the cost of his own capture. This exemplary behavior sat well with the county judge, who promised to release Larned on $2,500 bail if he could find some person of good character to post the bond for him. That was easy. Larned simply offered $2,750 of his own stolen money to a local gentleman, and his generosity was accepted in short order. Then he went back to the bank directors and audaciously insisted that they return his burglar's tools. At first they refused, but soon agreed when Larned threatened to sue. All that Abijah then had to do was jump bail.

Several years later Abijah Larned was convicted of a holdup in Cooperstown, New York, and was sentenced to a long imprisonment. He died incarcerated. His brother was never heard of after the Charlestown robbery.

Birds never divide worm until safe in nest.

Charlie Chan

A study in China some years ago revealed that there were nearly twice as many bacteria on each fly from the slums as there were on flies from better neighborhoods.

Answer: Hoover; Truman; Cleveland; Ford.

MARCH 20

Notable Births

1804	Neal Dow	1908	Michael Redgrave
1828	Henrik Ibsen	1914	Wendell Corey
1869	Neville Chamberlain	1922	Ray Goulding
1890	Benjamin Gigli	1922	Carl Reiner
1890	Lauritz Melchior	1925	John Ehrlichman
1904	B.F. Skinner	1931	Hal Linden
1906	Abraham Beame	1948	Bobby Orr

Notable Events

1602	Dutch East India Company founded
1784	Holland ceded Negapatam to Britain
1804	Duke of Enghien executed
1933	Zangara executed
1956	France recognized Tunisian independence
1965	National Guard called up to protect Alabama Freedom Marchers
1976	Patty Hearst convicted of bank robbery

When he was arrested for drunkenness in Albequerque, New Mexico, in 1956, Emanuel Welch confessed to the police that he sometimes used an alias. The police didn't believe the name Welch gave then, until he spelled Sebastian Bogankinzenellenriinzinskiyork for them the same way three times in a row.

A supervisor for a moving company was going over the inventory for a load of goods that had been packed that afternoon. It was a large load, but the inventory looked accurate and complete. Reaching the heading "Miscellaneous," he read the item, "One quart whiskey, full," and noted that his employee had been exceptionally thorough. A dozen entries later, he found, "One bottle whiskey, partially full," but didn't think it out of the ordinary. The last two items on the list were, "One whisky botle, emtpy," and, "2 revolving orientil ruggs."

On this date in 1549, Sir Thomas Seymour, the forty-one-year-old Lord High Admiral of the English navy, was executed for proposing marriage to the wrong girl. The girl in question was Princess (later Queen) Elizabeth. Seymour was so persistent in his protestations of love that the government had him charged with treason and beheaded.

Were it not for imagination, sir, a man would be as happy in the arms of a chambermaid as of a duchess.

Samuel Johnson

According to a survey by the United Nations, proportionately fewer dogs bite mailmen in England than in any country on earth.

March is usually kind of slow in Ohio, but if you happen to be in that state on or about March 20, go check out the town of Hinckley's Buzzard Sunday. Good weather brings out crowds approaching thirty thousand, and the buzzards'll love ya for it.

Answer: Dorothy Collins, Mike Connors, Joseph Conrad, Alice Cooper, Howard Cosell.

Question: By what names are these people better known?
Marjorie Chandler
Krekor Ohanian
Teodor Korzeniowski
Vincent Furnier
Howard Cohen

Although the right ear is normally more acute, people who don't know much about music usually hear it better in the left ear.

The term "smack" has several different meanings, and at least three distinct sources. "Smacking" a child, either with a kiss or a spank, is an onomatopeic word (it imitates the sound). If something "smacks" of a certain flavor, its origin is the Anglo-Saxon *smoec*, to taste. When a fleet of fishing "smacks" goes out to the banks, the word comes from the Danish *snakke*, which referred to the snakelike movement the Danes' long, narrow boats made in the water.

Coward comes from the Old French *couard*, which in turn derived from the Latin *cauda*, or "tail." This is derived from the observation that an animal that drops its tail between its legs is scared; so when it runs away, it "turns tail."

MARCH 21

Question: The Pyrenees Mountains lie between France and Spain. Where else are there mountains called the Pyrenees?

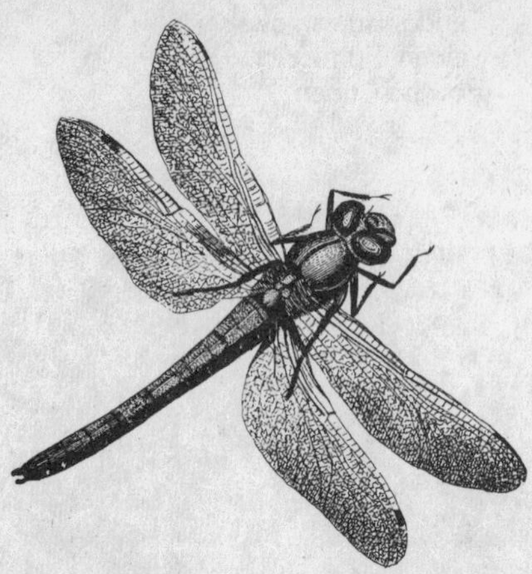

Notable Births

1274	Robert Bruce	1905	Phyllis McGinley
1685	J.S. Bach	1906	John D. Rockefeller III
1763	Jean-Paul Richter	1926	John Fowles
1903	Edgar Buchanan	1929	James Coco

Notable Events

1556 Archbishop of Canterbury burned at stake by Queen Mary
1621 Governor Carver signed treaty with Massasoit
1886 Geronimo captured
1931 Austro-German customs union announced
1932 Tornadoes in Alabama left 268 dead
1933 FDR announced plans for Civilian Conservation Corps, 250,000 jobs
1960 Massacre of Bantus by South African police
1961 Goldwater went on record against Federal aid to public schools

Philip Calvert, a professor at the University of Pennsylvania for most of his academic career, published over 750 books and articles on one topic during his ninety years of life: dragonflies.

During the reign of Li Hsui, one of the Manchu emperors, every Pekingese dog at court had its own human wet nurse and a personal eunuch to protect it against other dogs. Certain favorite canines had private palaces equipped with large staffs of human servants.

From a tombstone in Holyoke, Massachusetts:

In Memory of
Mr. Nath. Parks,
AEt. 19, who on
21st March 1794
Being out hunt-
ing and conceal'd
in a Ditch was
casually shot by
Mr. Luther
Frink.

The epitaph of Ellen Shannon, aged twenty-six, Girard, Pennsylvania:

Who was fatally burned
March 21, 1870
by the explosion of a lamp
filled with R. E. Danforth's
Non-Explosive
Burning Fluid.

Let advertisers spend the same amount of money improving their product that they do on advertising and they wouldn't have to advertise it.

Will Rogers

Here's what you'd have paid to go between here and there in 1927 and the time it would have taken you (the fares are in dollars and the times in hours and minutes):

	By Air		By Train	
	Fare	Time	Fare	Time
Chicago - San Francisco	200.00	22.40	79.84	68.00
New York - Boston	30.00	3.50	8.24	5.00
Portland (Oregon) - Los Angeles	113.50	11.15	40.88	39.30
Salt Lake City - Los Angeles	60.00	7.15	28.05	30.00
Chicago - Minneapolis	40.00	5.50	14.66	12.00
Cheyenne - Pueblo (Colorado)	25.00	3.00	8.16	8.00
Detroit - Grand Rapids	18.00	1.45	5.49	4.00
San Diego - Los Angeles	17.50	1.10	4.55	3.30

Answer: On the moon.

Notable Births

1599	Anthony Van Dyck	1923	Marcel Marceau
1891	Chico Marx	1930	Stephen Sondheim
1914	Karl Malden	1931	William Shatner
1920	Werner Klemperer	1936	May Britt

Notable Events

1622 First American Indian massacre occurred at Jamestown, Virginia
1765 Stamp Act became law
1777 Oldenburg made dukedom under Frederick Augustus of Holstein Gottorp
1816 Columbus became capital of Ohio
1874 Young Men's Hebrew Association formed in New York City
1961 Brazil established diplomatic relations with Hungary, Bulgaria, and Romania
1972 Equal Rights Amendment approved by Senate, 84-8
1978 Four thousand UN troops moved into south Lebanon

Questions: Why should a fat man always wear a plaid vest?

If you were in a room with only a bed and a calendar, could you live? How?

Until the middle of the eighteenth century, all animals in continental Europe were considered to be subject to local civil and ecclesiastical laws. Domestic animals were tried in municipal courts, while wild animals, as God's creatures, were tried in church courts. Both courts could impose the death penalty, but the church could also prescribe banishment, exorcism, and excommunication. Biblical authority for trying animals was found in Exodus ("When an ox gores a man or a woman to death, the ox shall be stoned, and its flesh shall not be eaten; but the owner of the ox shall be clear ....") and in several other places in the Old Testament. All the formalities of justice were observed, from the opening of the trial proceedings to the passing of the sentences, and each animal had the right to an advocate on its behalf. In France there were at least ninety trials during the Middle Ages and the Renaissance. The last one was in 1740, when a cow was tried and executed.

Weighty arguments were raised regarding the propriety of legal action against animals, especially in the ecclesiastical courts. Some theologians felt that because God had blessed the lower animals, and because they were man's elders on earth, the church should have no dominion over them. The church insisted that, as God's representative on earth, it was incumbent upon it to exorcise, anathematize, and excommunicate all living or inanimate things if they, too, sinned. Still others challenged the church on the grounds that it could not pronounce an anathema against something that was not baptized. The church held to its position, however, and went on exorcising and excommunicating transgressing beasts, birds, and insects. (Actually, the church avoided exorcism if at all possible. Most animals did not respond to exorcism, and it was embarrassing when an exorcised creature did not, in fact, "wither off the face of the earth.")

Executing the law against animals was often anything but easy. The residents of the commune of Saint Julien brought suit in 1445 against a golden beetle (*Eynchitus aureus*) for what was then the legal equivalent of harassment. After years of legal argument, the people proposed that a certain part of their land be given in perpetuity for the use of the beetles. The insects' lawyer agreed to this on behalf of his clients, and it looked as if the case was closed, until a farmer with a right of way through the property insisted on his legal use of it. The court decided this would disturb the insects and declared the original compromise void. The case dragged on for a total of forty-two years, but no one knows its outcome: the documents are too deteriorated to be legible.

Several other remarkable cases also occurred in France at about this time. The residents of Autun had papers served on their rats to appear in court. So there would be no mistake, the rodents in question were carefully defined as ". . . dirty animals in the form of rats, of a grayish color, living in holes." Counsel for the rats was Bartholomew Chassanee, who was to become one of France's greatest lawyers.

When the rats didn't appear in court, Chassanee argued that the initial summons, although certainly read at a place frequented by rats, was of too local a character. Since all the rats in the area were interested parties in the case, each one should be summoned. The court could not simply assume that all the rats had heard of the case. The court accepted this explanation, and the curate of each parish in the district was instructed to inform every rat under his jurisdiction when and where to appear in court. When no rats came the second time, the lawyer explained that, since all the rats had been summoned, young and old, sick and well alike, many preparations were necessary, and more time was needed. The court agreed, and set a third date.

When no rats appeared this time, Chassanee argued that the court's paperwork was faulty. Although a summons was supposed to guarantee the rats' safe conduct, adequate protection had not been provided for his clients from the townspeoples' rat-hungry cats, which lined the rats' passageway to the courthouse. The rats were most desirous of obeying the court's order, Chassanee said, but until the plaintiffs could post a bond against the conduct of their cats, the rats did not dare attend. The court admitted the legitimacy of this argument, but the plaintiffs refused to be bound over for the conduct of their cats, and Chassanee won his case by default.

In 1451, in Lausanne, a number of leeches were brought into court to hear a *monitoire* (admonishment) of their conduct. They were directed to leave the district within three days. When they did not do so, they were formally exorcised by the church. It was reported that after the exorcism the leeches began to die, and soon disappeared entirely — a notable success for the local clergy.

On the same day that a man named Henry Ford was arrested for driving without a license in Long Beach, California, police in that city also arrested a fellow named I.W. Harper for drunkenness. This was in March 1955.

The French national anthem, "La Marseillaise," derived its title from the enthusiasm of the men of Marseilles, who sang it when they marched into Paris at the outset of the French Revolution. Rouget de l'Isle, its composer, was an artillery officer stationed at Strasbourg. According to his account, he fell asleep at a harpsichord and dreamt the words and the music. Upon waking, he remembered the entire piece from his dream and immediately wrote it down.

Answers: To keep a check on his stomach.

Yes. You could drink water from the springs of the bed and eat the dates from the calendar.

MARCH 23

Question: Can you think of a word to rhyme with the following?

a smooth
b dunce
c baby
d tenet
e devious

Notable Births

1699	John Bartram	1908	Joan Crawford
1857	Fannie Farmer	1912	Werner von Braun
1900	Erich Fromm	1929	Roger Bannister

Notable Events

1208	Pope Innocent III put England under Papal Interdict
1775	Patrick Henry delivered "Liberty or Death" speech
1918	Lithuania declared independence
1925	Evolution law enacted in Tennessee; led to Scopes Monkey Trial
1933	Hitler given dictatorial powers for 4 years
1945	Patton's Third Army crossed Rhine River
1949	Armistice declared between Israel and Lebanon
1973	Letter of James McCord opened up Watergate scandal

Being a lion tamer isn't as dangerous as some other jobs in the circus. Bears are reputed to be significantly more dangerous to work with, and so are fully grown chimpanzees, which can be really nasty if their tempers are roused.

Carrie Nation, the hatchet-swinging lady (she stood a good six feet) who made a name for herself busting up saloons at the turn of the century, insisted she was not interested in unwarranted publicity — but what a coincidence it was that the first bar she attacked was owned by heavyweight champion John L. Sullivan!

Among a number of American Indian tribes it was the custom for a small child to be given a temporary name, and to receive a new one in his teens when he became a full brave. The famous Crazy Horse was first given the name Curly, and Jumping Badger became Sitting Bull. Incidentally, Geronimo was calle *Goyathlay* by the members of his own tribe. In their tongue the name meant "one who yawns."

The left leg of a chicken is generally more tender than the right, and the proper etiquette for a dinner party where chicken is served dictates that the guest of honor be served the left leg. The reason is that a chicken sleeps on her right leg, which then develops tougher tendons and muscles.

A berry that is often eaten by many of the beasts in southern Africa is the *maroela*. One rather unpleasant side effect of its consumption is drunkenness, because at certain stages of ripeness the berry will ferment in the animal's stomach before it can be passed through and out of the body. Drunk lions tend to act like kittens, it is said, but baboons (which are reported to eat the berries so they *will* become intoxicated) become malicious. Drunken elephants make an astonishing sight. The huge beasts lean against trees because they're too unsteady to be able to walk.

Answer: *a* soothe, *b* once, *c* maybe, *d* senate, *e* previous.

Notable Births

1834	William Morris	1904	Malcolm Muggeridge
1834	John Wesley Powell	1914	Richard Conte
1855	Andrew Mellon	1919	Lawrence Ferlinghetti
1867	Arturo Toscanini	1930	Steve McQueen
1897	Wilhelm Reich	1944	Denny McLain
1902	Thomas Dewey	1947	Elton John

Notable Events

1603	Crowns of England and Scotland joined
1783	Spain recognized U.S. independence
1792	Ministry of Girondists began in France
1834	Bank of Maryland failed
1882	Koch announced discovery of tuberculosis germ, Berlin
1900	Last sighting of a wild passenger pigeon
1934	FDR signed Philippine Independence Bill
1962	Benny Paret knocked out by Emile Griffith; later died

The reason that passenger pigeons became extinct was the discovery in the middle of the last century that they tasted delicious. The birds, unaccustomed to natural predation, fell an easy prey to nets, and even clubs; and, because they flew or roosted in such enormous flocks, dozens could be killed with a single shotgun blast (an unofficial record for one cartridge is 130 pigeons). In fact, passenger pigeons were such easy targets (sitting ducks?) that a trio of men working near Traverse City, Michigan, around 1850, supplied a food processor with five million birds in just three weeks.

The last wild sighting of a passenger pigeon was on March 24, 1900, and the last pigeon in captivity died at the Cincinnati Zoo on September 1, 1914.

The sun, the moon, and the stars would have disappeared long ago, had they happened to be within reach of predatory human hands.

Havelock Ellis

Mrs. Ivy Cannon was a cleaning lady in the British War Ministry during World War II, and an inveterate home canner. Of course, everything was scarce in Great Britain during the war, even paper, so Mrs. Cannon used to take home scraps to use in labeling her preserves.

Odd as it seems, this brought her to the attention of her superiors as a possible spy. She was cleared of espionage charges, but ended up serving two years in prison in addition to being fined £500 for pinching government supplies in time of war.

One of the theories about the shark's uncanny ability to sense prey from far away is that the shark has extremely sensitive electronic receptors in the skin of its snout, which are capable of detecting minute changes in the sea's electric fields. According to the Wood's Hole Oceanographic Institute in Massachusetts, a shark could theoretically detect a charge produced by a flashlight battery a thousand miles away if the battery circuit were to be connected by wires close to him.

Question: By what names are these people more commonly known?

Julius Ullman
Ann Leppert
Baldemar Huerta
Maude Kiskadden
Judith Tuvim

The word "king" does not necessarily specify a male ruler. It is a term signifying a leader or head of state of either sex. A "queen" who ascends the throne through lineal inheritance is a king, while a queen consort, or one who would rule through marriage, is not. Anne, Victoria, and both Elizabeths are rightfully English kings as well as queens.

A single magpie in the spring heralds bad weather. When the forecast is good, magpies generally travel in pairs.

During the period of the later Middle Ages, shoes were made with long toes that tied to the wearer's knees. In England the law allowed for different toe lengths according to the wearer's position in the hierarchy. Knights were allowed eighteen inches, barons twenty-four inches, and princes thirty inches. Presumably, the king could wear any length he wished.

At various times in its legislative history, the State of New York has outlawed the cha-cha, the mambo, the rhumba, and the tango, presumably because of the lascivious nature of those dances. In a somewhat similar vein, it's against the law in Norfolk, Virginia, for a girl to dance unless she's wearing a corset.

Answer: Douglas Fairbanks, Alice Faye, Freddie Fender, Maud Adams, Judy Holliday.

MARCH 25

Question: Which of the following words are misspelled?
Missisippi
Massachussetts
concieve
fluoresent

Notable Births

1820	Anne Bronte	1929	Howard Cosell
1881	Bela Bartok	1934	Gloria Steinem
1921	Simone Signoret	1940	Anita Bryant
1925	Flannery O'Connor	1942	Aretha Franklin

Notable Events

1306	Robert Bruce crowned King of Scotland
1682	William Penn's charter granted by Duke of York
1822	Christians massacred at Constantinople
1827	Greece declared independence from Turkey
1900	Socialist Party founded in America, Indianapolis
1911	Triangle Factory fire killed 145 people in New York City
1937	First perfumed page of advertising appeared in a newspaper, *Washington Daily News*
1947	Mine explosion in Centralia, Illinois, killed 111 people
1975	Saudi Arabian King Faisal killed by nephew; nephew beheaded June 18

A fellow named Gerard Gasson was driving his 1936 Citroën auto in the French countryside one day in March, 1976, when the car stalled on some railroad tracks. Needless to say, he could not get it off before the oncoming train reached him. The train, led by a locomotive worth $800,000, crashed into his car and then derailed; smashed the supports to the nearby Marne-Rhine Canal bridge; tore up 100 yards of track; and ended up (or at least the locomotive and twenty-five of the cars did) in the river. Barge canal traffic was blocked for ten days, and it was nine days before the bridge was fixed (this required local traffic to make a 150-mile detour). The goods on forty barges spoiled, as did much of the beer and soup that the train had been carrying. In all, the damage from the accident totalled over $5 million.

Monsieur Gasson's insurance premium was raised from $33 to $38 as a result of the accident.

Perhaps the only man who never laid eyes on a woman was a fellow named Mihailo Tolotos. His mother died when he was born, and the next day he was taken to the "Monk's Republic" on Mount Athos, a peninsula which is part of Greece but which is governed by a committee of representatives from twenty Greek Orthodox monasteries. Under a consitution dating from 1045 A.D., no females of any species are allowed in the domain, although hens and female cats have been allowed in recent years. Tolotos grew up there, tooks orders there, and died there in 1938, never having seen a human female.

In Medieval Europe, sweet basil was thought by some to have bizarre effects on people. An Italian gentleman named Hilarius once swore that a scorpion had been bred in the brain of one of his friends who inhaled the herb. Another prevailing belief was that sweet basil was mutable, and often changed into wild thyme.

In 1965, Mike Nichols, the actor and director, praised Gloria Steinem, the future founder of *Ms.* magazine, in these words: "She's the smartest, funniest, and most serious person I know, and she looks great."

What's the matter, kid? Afraid there's no hope for you? Well, Albert Einstein did so badly in school both academically and physically that for many years his own father was convinced the boy was retarded. While he was teaching at Princeton, Einstein frequently forgot where he lived and had to ask passersby how to get home. He was also completely oblivious to what was going on around him, and once managed to walk into an open manhole. He never wore socks to class, and never could learn how to drive a car.

The word perfume comes from two Latin words, *per*, meaning "through"; and *fumus*, meaning "smoke." It thus denotes a smell which permeates the air like smoke.

In Barnet, England, in 1949, Albert Fitzherbeit brough suit against Mrs. Julian Hewitt for keeping a noisy dog. Fitzherbeit testified he'd clocked the dog at sixty-five barks per minute. Mrs. Hewitt was fined two pounds.

Answer: All of them. They should be Mississippi, Massachusetts, conceive, and fluorescent.

MARCH 26

Notable Births

1850	Edward Bellamy	1916	Sterling Hayden
1859	A.E. Housman	1930	Gregory Corso
1874	Robert Frost	1934	Alan Arkin
1875	Syngman Rhee	1939	James Caan
1886	Al Jolson	1942	Erica Jong
1914	William Westmoreland	1943	Bob Woodward
1914	Tennessee Williams	1944	Diana Ross

Notable Events

1676 Providence, Rhode Island, partially burned in Indian attack
1793 Britain declared war on France
1845 Corrugated lifeboat patented
1931 Treaty of friendship signed between Iraq and Trans-jordan
1934 Driving tests instituted in Great Britain
1950 McCarthy called Owen Lattimore top Red spy in United States
1959 Storms in Madagascar killed 305 people
1962 Supreme Court decision curbed rural domination of state legislatures

Questions: What is the longest-lasting kind of dress?

Why should a person be careful to avoid the services of a drunken tailor?

In 205 B.C., a law was passed in Rome that prohibited women from driving chariots. In Memphis, Tennessee, a woman driving a car legally must have a man walking in front of her, waving a red flag.

The weight of the earth is about 6.6×10^{21} tons. There are about the same number of molecules in a drop of water.

The ancient Romans believed that if a person ate the fruit of a tree touched by a salamander, he would die of a terrible coldness. Medieval Europeans thought that a salamander was so cold that it could put out a fire and not be burned itself.

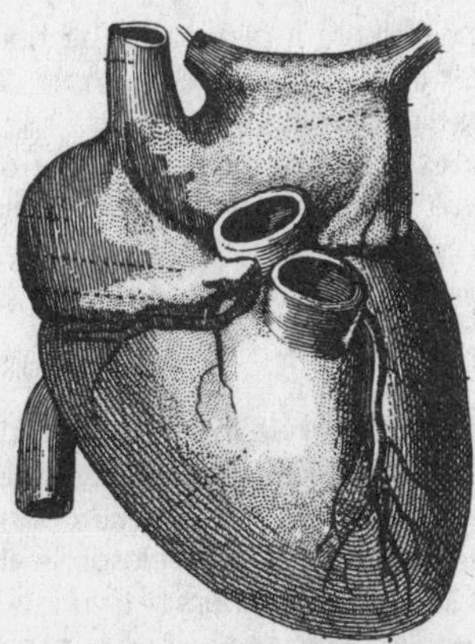

In the womb, a girl's heart usually beats faster than a boy's. At maturity, a man's heart usually has five to ten more heartbeats a minute than a woman's does.

On March 26, 1649, the town fathers of Newcastle, England, decided to get rid of the witches they believed infested the town. They appropriated money and sent out a party to procure a good witch hunter. A Scotsman was then hired, who agreed to divine witches at the cost of twenty shillings for every witch. That summer he came to Newcastle, and stuck pins into the thirty local people who had been denounced by their neighbors as evil ones. Twenty-seven individuals were found to be witches after this test, and sixteen of these unfortunate people were eventually hanged.

Later that year, the witch hunter was denounced as a fraud and was apprehended and brought to trial in Scotland. He confessed he knew absolutely nothing about witches one way or the other, and that he's pursued his career only to make an honest living (his fees varied from twelve shillings to three pounds per witch, plus expenses). He also admitted that in his time he had been responsible for the hangings of at least 220 supposed witches.

Expedience and justice frequently are not even on speaking terms.

Arthur H. Vandenburg

"Know thyself?" If I knew myself, I'd run away.

Goethe

Answers: A housedress — it's never worn out.
To make sure he doesn't get bad habits.

MARCH 27

Question: What's the state shown here?

Saheb was the leader and greatest scholar of Persia during most of the tenth century. His library contained 117,000 volumes. Whenever he traveled, for either military of diplomatic reasons, the library went with him, loaded onto 400 camels that were specially trained to line up alphabetically according to the books they carried.

Books . . . are the curse of the human race.

Benjamin Disraeli

An English aristocrat named Jack Mytton came to be known as the Mad Squire of Halston early in the nineteenth century. Among other things, he regularly drank a gallon of port for breakfast, and kept sixty cats and 2,000 dogs, all of which he fed on steak and champagne. He'd also occasionally ride a bear to dinner parties, and it was not uncommon for him to bring his horse into the parlor to share a bottle of wine with him after a hard day's hunting.

Mytton was a rather impatient fellow, too. One day, bothered by a case of the hiccups, he decided to get rid of them by giving himself a fright. To do that he set fire to his shirt.

"Well, my hiccups are gone, thank God," were his last words.

Notable Births

1813	Nathaniel Currier	1917	Cyrus Vance
1845	William Roentgen	1924	Sarah Vaughan
1899	Gloria Swanson	1930	David Janssen
1914	Budd Schulberg	1942	Michael York

Notable Events

1482 Queen Mary of Burgandy died after falling from a horse
1625 Charles I crowned in England
1836 First Mormon Temple dedicated, Kirtland, Ohio
1847 Vera Cruz captured
1855 Congress appropriated $30,000 for camel importation for army in Texas
1860 Corkscrew patented by M.L. Bryn
1931 Charlie Chaplin received France's Legion of Honor decoration
1933 Federal pay cut 15 percent
1955 First mobile Jewish synagogue dedicated
1964 Good Friday earthquake in Alaska left 114 dead; strongest ever in United States
1978 KLM 747 and Pan Am 747 in runway collision, Canary Islands, 581 dead, worst aircraft disaster in history

Thomas J. Owens of Boston got three months for theft in March 1957. He'd aroused suspicion by trying to sell a trumpet worth $300. First he called it a clarinet; realized that was wrong, and so tried to market it as a trombone.

The name "backgammon" comes from the way the pieces are arranged in the game. The little markers (originally knuckle bones or lumps of clay) are often arranged in the course of play so they touch one another like the vertebrae of the spine. Hence the Anglo-Saxon *baec* ("back"); and *gamen* ("game").

A fellow named Muhammad Bikhtani was brought to trial for the theft from Isfahan University in Iran of 195 tables, 340 typewriters, 959 desks, 1,069 chairs, and 27,056 (yes, the exact number!) paper clips. Bikhtani plead that he had no criminal intent in the matter, that the thefts were simply part of an academic exercise he had undertaken.

The nature of the exercise remains unclear, but shortly after this trial, Bikhtani was named professor of Criminology at the University.

Perhaps the one fib that has had the longest-lasting effect was the lie Amerigo Vespucci told Martin Waldseemuller in a letter at the beginning of the sixteenth century. Although it has been proved that Vespucci was in the Spanish city of Seville at the time, he wrote to his friend about the wonders of the New World, which he claimed to have seen on a voyage he had commanded. When the cartographers were drawing up maps of the continent, Waldseemuller suggested they name it after Vespucci the great explorer, who, according to *only* himself, had made four trips there.

A really accomplished imposter is the most wretched of geniuses; he is a Napoleon on a desert island.

G. K. Chesterton

Answer: Vermont.

Notable Births

1868	Maxim Gorky	1918	Pearl Bailey
1878	Herbert Lehman	1921	Dirk Bogarde
1895	Christian Herter	1924	Freddie Bartholomew
1909	Nelson Algren	1928	Zbigniew Brzezinski
1914	Edmund Muskie	1944	Rick Barry

Notable Events

1715 Lord Bolingbroke fled to France
1784 Christian VII declared insane; succeeded by son
1834 Jackson censured for removing deposits of National Bank
1915 Emma Goldman fined $100 for speaking to U.S. audience about contraceptives
1921 First lethal gas execution authorized, Nebraska
1939 Madrid surrendered to Franco; Spanish Civil War over
1964 King Saud of Saudi Arabia succeeded by son Faisal
1970 Earthquake in west Turkey took 100 lives

Question: By what names are these people better known?
Edward Heimberger
Alphonso d'Abruzzo
John F. Sullivan
Melvin Israel
Allen S. Konigsberg

Our word "berserk" comes from an old Norse word meaning "clad in bearskin." It originated a thousand years ago when Viking raiders were plundering much of northern and western Europe. Their attacks were as intimidating as they were ferocious, for the Norsemen would customarily attack a village in a mad rage — screaming, biting their shields, and killing everything in their path. From this behavior and its association with the Vikings' traditional garments, the word "berserk" was derived.

This advertisement appeared in the March 28, 1716, edition of the *Stamford Mercury*: "Whereas the majority of Apothecaries in Boston have agreed to pull down the price of Bleeding to sixpence, let those certifie that Mr. Richard Clarke, Apothecary, will bleed any body at his shop, gratis."

The Catholic Church has at various times limited the occasions when a man and wife could have sexual intercourse. Initially, it forbade Sundays, Wednesdays, and Fridays — a mere 42 percent of the year. Later on, the forty-day periods before Christmas and Easter were proscribed. For a time, sex was forbidden for the three days before an individual received communion, and the period from conception to forty days after the birth was proscribed as well. Alternate Tuesdays in leap-year Februaries were days when sexual intercourse was usually allowed.

Trouble rain over many already wet.

Charlie Chan

Synthetic pearls were manufactured in Greece as early as 1000 B.C.

In 1669, the ground beneath Runswick, England, gave way and the entire town slipped into the sea. No one was hurt. All the townspeople had gone to a nearby village for a funeral when their town drowned.

Despite the belief of many people to the contrary, someone's life does not pass before his or her eyes shortly before death, even in those cases where death is sudden, or accidental.

The pigeon is the only bird that sips water, using its bill as a straw. Most birds gather water in their bills then toss their heads back to swallow. The hummingbird laps its liquid, though.

Answer: Eddie Albert, Robert Alda, Fred Allen, Mel Allen, Woody Allen.

MARCH 29

Question: Can you think of the foreign phrases, which are commonly used in English, that mean the following?

the common people
know-how, or poise
all together
a mistake

Notable Births

1674	Jethro Tull	1908	Arthur O'Connell
1738	Joseph Guillotine	1916	Eugene McCarthy
1790	John Tyler	1917	Man o' War
1867	Cy Young	1919	Eileen Heckart
1875	Mrs. Herbert Hoover	1937	Billy Carter

Notable Events

1792	Swedish King Gustavus III assassinated
1809	Gustavus IV abdicated
1844	U.P. Levy became first Jewish U.S. Navy captain
1936	Hitler got 98.79 percent of vote in Germany
1942	Britain's offer of dominion status after war rejected by India
1947	Madagascar began war of independence against French
1951	Rosenbergs found guilty of spying
1952	Harry Truman announced his non-candidacy
1955	President Guizado of Panama implicated in assassination of President Remon, sentenced to six years
1971	William Calley found guilty of My Lai massacre, sentenced to life
1974	Tubaro, Brazil, flood claimed 1,000 lives

One of the more curious topics of discussion among naturalists 150 years ago was the fabulous Upas tree of Java. This tree, according to *Foersch's Description of Java*, gave off such a poisonous effluvient that all living creatures around it for a distance of ten to twelve miles immediately died. Birds flying over the desolate circle dropped from the air, according to reports.

The Javanese government was even said to use it as the state instrument of capital punishment. A condemned man was given the choice of the executioner or the Upas tree. If he chose the Upas, he was required to undergo the ordeal of retrieving the poison gum of the tree from beneath its bark. If he succeeded in returning with the poison, he was freed by the court and given a small stipend. The poison was then used to dip the tips of arrows, spears, and darts. One official who lived near the perimeter of the poisoned area, and who advised prisoners about journeying to the tree, recounted that of the 700 men in thirty years who had undertaken to fetch the sap, fewer than 70 had returned.

Many naturalists were incredulous, but respected magazines printed the story, and even Charles Darwin credited its authenticity. There was an understandable scandal, therefore, when the Horticultural Society of Chiswick, England, announced it had a Upas tree growing in its garden. How big, people speculated, did the Upas have to get before it began to kill everything around it?

This was yet another success for George Steevens, master hoaxer, who was called the "Puck of Commentators" by his contemporaries. Steevens made a career of pulling the eminent legs of "experts" by writing scandalous but apparently authentic stories of great English writers, such as Milton and Shakespeare, and then trapping various authorities into foolish conclusions. Then he widened his field by embracing horticulture. The Upas tree did indeed secrete a poison, a strychninelike chemical, and Javanese criminals were executed with it — but from the tip of a dart shot into their bodies, not from fetching the poison itself. That was Steevens's personal embellishment to the Upas story.

Another trick involved antiquities. In order to settle a grudge against Gough, the preeminent archaeologist of the day, Steevens took a piece of chimney slate and scratched out in old Anglo-Saxon letters:

("Here, Hardicanute drank a wine horn dry, stared about him, and died.") He arranged to have it placed casually but conspicuously in an antiquarian's shop that Gough was known to frequent, with instructions to the proprietor to mention, if Gough inquired about the tablet, that it had been discovered by a farmer in Kennington Lane, where Hardicanute supposedly had died.

Gough fell for it, totally. He bought the piece and immediately brought it to the attention of the Society of Antiquaries. One of the luminaries of that organization, the Reverend Pegge, wrote a paper on the find, and the society's draftsman engraved a copy of the slate for *Gentleman's Magazine*. Although the secret was leaked before the publication of the issue, it was nevertheless a great triumph for Steevens, and one which Gough never lived down.

Roots of tree lead in many directions.

Charlie Chan

Many ancient mariners believed that if they pierced an ear and wore a ring in it, this would improve their eyesight. Everyone else said that was crazy — except the Chinese, who for many, many centuries had been using that very spot in their acupuncture treatments to improve eyesight.

The rings in the ears of Scottish sailors were always of gold, and were there to pay for a Christian burial should a sailor lose his life at sea and be washed ashore in a foreign land.

Virginians Patrick Henry and James Monroe both opposed their state's ratification of the Constitution.

People keep pointing out that the bald eagle is not really bald, it just looks that way.

I'll give anyone a dollar for each hair he can find on one on its head, or anywhere else.

Answer: hoi polloi, savior faire, en masse, faux pas.

Notable Births

1135	Moses Maimonides	1913	Richard Helms
1820	Anna Sewell	1925	Art Buchwald
1746	Francisco Goya	1937	Warren Beatty

Notable Events

1282 "Sicilian Vespers" massacre of thousands of French at Palermo
1858 H.L. Lipman patented first pencil with attached eraser
1867 Alaska purchased from Russia for 2 cents an acre
1870 Texas readmitted to Union
1923 First dance marathon began, New York City
1933 Nazis began Jewish boycott
1937 Supreme Court upheld minimum wage law
1941 United States seized 41 Axis ships in U.S. harbors
1945 Russians took Danzig
1964 Riots between Mods and Rockers, England

Questions: What is always at the head of fashion, and yet always out of date?

When is a pair of old socks like a very sick person?

Fairbanks' "Yukon Howard," who claims to be one of the only people in the world to experience a tidal wave 500 miles from the ocean (on that occasion an earthquake dislodged a huge mass of rock from a cliff above the Yukon River, and Howard was inundated by a five-foot wall of water created by the avalanche), told me this story about his closest encounter with a bear.

"I was out on the river one day," said Howard, "when I got stiff from sitting in the kayak, and decided I'd go ashore and walk around a bit. So I beached her and went off looking for some berries for a snack. I hadn't gone too far when all of a sudden I spotted a couple of cubs playing in the bushes. I didn't see their mama with them, so I started looking around — you know how mad a she-bear gets when you're between her and her cubs. Well, just as I'd feared, there she was, fifty yards behind me, and reared up sniffin'. She caught a whiff of me and down she came, headed right for me. I looked around quick and the only thing I could see was this dead birch tree, thirty-five, forty yards to my left. I tell you, I feared for my life right then — them bear'll travel at forty miles an hour, and even if I made it to the tree before she got me, there was only one branch on it, and it had to be a *good* eighteen, twenty feet in the air. Anyway, I lit out for it, and just as I was about to jump I could feel her breath coming clear through my pants. I leapt up — and sure enough I missed that limb!

"But I caught it on the way down."

If you're into Meerschaums, briars, or Holmeses, you might do well to avoid the Clyster pipe, unless you're a collector. Back in the seventeenth century, the enema was deemed to be a panacea of disease if properly chosen and administered. The Clyster pipe was the name of the device used for giving tobacco smoke enemas. James I of England declared it was the only way to take a pipe.

The word "meerschaum" comes from the German and means "sea foam." The fine white clay from which the pipes are made was once thought to be the petrified foam of the ocean.

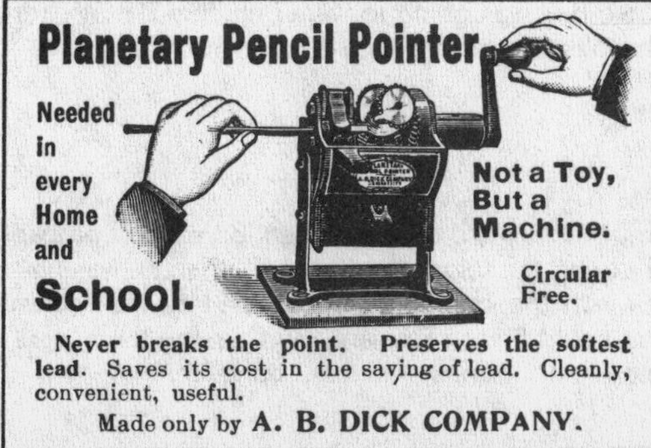

The term, "boycott," is only a century old. During the agrarian troubles in Ireland in 1880, Lord Erne instructed his land agent in Mayo, a Captain Boycott, not to accept the field rents at the reduced rates his lessees had offered. The farmers banded together and refused to work for or have any commerce with Boycott during the harvest. Eventually, Erne's crops were brought in by fifty scab laborers, but they had to be protected by 900 militiamen, so great was the animosity of the tenant farmers.

The word "pencil" comes from the double-diminutive *penecillus*, a Latin word meaning "a very little tail."

Answers: The letter F.
When they're on their last legs.

MARCH 31

Question: How many times does the figure *V* appear on the face of the average grandfather clock?

Dear Sir:

We have the distinction of being members of a committee to raise $50,000,000 to be used for placing a statue of Lyndon B. Johnson in the Hall of Fame in Washington, D.C.

The committee was in a quandary about selecting the proper location for the statue. It was thought unwise to place it beside that of George Washington, who never told a lie, or beside that of Franklin D. Roosevelt, who never told the truth, since Lyndon Johnson could never tell the difference.

After careful consideration, we think it should be placed next to the statue of Christopher Columbus, the greatest "New Dealer" of them all, in that he started out not knowing where he was going, and in arriving, did not know where he was, and in returning did not know where he had been, and managed to do it all on borrowed money.

The inscription on the statue will read: "I pledge allegiance to Lyndon B. Johnson and to the national debt for which he stands, one man, expendable, with graft and corruption for all."

Five thousand years ago, Moses said to the children of Israel, "Pick up your shovels, mount your asses and camels, and I will lead you to the Promised Land." Nearly five thousand years later Franklin D. Roosevelt said, "Lay down your shovels, sit on your asses, and light up a Camel, this is the Promised Land." Now Lyndon B. Johnson is stealing the shovels, kicking our asses, raising the price of Camels, and taking over the Promised Land.

If you are one of the few who has any money left after paying taxes, we will expect a generous contribution from you toward this noteworthy project.

Yours sincerely,

National Committee on
the Johnson Bust

from *Urban Folklore from the Paperwork Empire*

Both the words "bullet" and "bulletin" come from the papacy. When an edict was issued by a pope, a drop of lead was used to seal and make the document official. *Bulla* is Latin for "seal," and "bulletin" is the diminutive of it; in other words, it was a small announcement. "Bullet" came later, and of course referred to the drop of lead itself.

Answer: Four times. A French king changed it by fiat from IV to IIII centuries ago, and clockmakers didn't argue.

Notable Births

1519	Henry II	1926	John Fowles
1596	Rene Descartes	1926	Sydney Chaplin
1621	Andrew Marvell	1927	Cesar Chavez
1732	Franz Joseph Haydn	1928	Gordie Howe
1809	Edward Fitzgerald	1934	Shirley Jones
1844	Andrew Lang	1935	Herb Alpert
1915	Henry Morgan	1935	Richard Chamberlain

Notable Events

1900	First national auto advertisement appeared, *Saturday Evening Post*
1917	United States received Virgin Islands from Denmark
1931	Knute Rockne killed in plane crash
1931	Earthquake in Nicaragua killed 1,000 people
1936	Japan invaded Mongolia
1939	Britain and France pledged aid to Poland if Hitler attacked
1968	Lyndon Johnson announced he would not run for reelection
1976	New Jersey Supreme Court ruled Karen Ann Quinlan's respirator could be turned off

Most people believe that a flounder (or a similar fish such as a halibut, a sole, a plaice, or a turbot) has its camouflaging coloring and eyes on its top half. Not so. These fish are born with eyes on either side of their heads, and the camouflaging ability develops on a lateral side, not the top half. One eye actually migrates to the other side of the head as the fish grows. The top and bottom of a flounder are really its two sides.

In August 1956, Paul Bell from Chicago placed a bet with a fellow he thought was a bookie. He turned out to be a detective. The horse Bell was going to wager on, "So Bet Me," dropped dead that afternoon in the race.

"Bonfire" is a word of fairly recent origin, and probably was coined during the reign on Henry VIII, when he was having his troubles with the church. Henry burned all the ecclesiastical relics he could find in England, and among them were many supposed saints' bones — hence, "bone fire."

One third of the telephone numbers in Los Angeles are unlisted.

Taurus
(The Bull)
April 21
through May 21
APRIL

APRIL 1

Question: By what names are these people better known?
Florence Graham
Eunice Quedens
Lucille Langhanke
Frederick Austerlitz
Betty Joan Perske

Notable Births

1578	William Harvey	1889	Wallace Beery
1697	Abbé Prévost	1909	Eddy Duchin
1815	Otto von Bismarck	1922	William Manchester
1868	Edmund Rostand	1929	Jane Powell
1873	Sergei Rachmaninov	1932	Debbie Reynolds
1875	Edgar Wallace	1944	Rusty Staub

Notable Events

1793	Japanese earthquake claimed 53,000 victims
1843	First magazine for mental patients, *The Illuminator*, published
1860	Lion-washing hoax perpetrated
1935	Scottsboro defendents granted new trial
1939	United States recognized Franco's government in Spain
1948	Berlin blockade begun by Russia
1954	Air force academy authorized
1959	Oklahoma repealed Prohibition
1964	Belgian doctors and dentists went on strike

Louis Mortison never meant to fool anyone with his stories about Lester Green, but the stories were so good and the public so easily fooled that it was sometimes inevitable that he did deceive people. Mortison used to write a column for two Waterbury, Connecticut, papers. Whenever he had a tidbit of information about someone he knew in his home town of Prospect, he'd substitute the name "Lester Green" for the real name. Pretty soon, there was a whole family of Greens doing amusing, dumb, or embarrassing things, often helped by Mortison's imagination.

One time, Lester's chimney caught fire, so he quickly hopped up on his roof with a bucket of sand to put the flames out. Almost immediately, his wife also noticed the fire in the kitchen stove. Mistaking a box of washing soda for salt, she threw it into the stove's firebox to put the flames out at her end. The sand and soda hit the the heat at the same time, and when the stove cooled down, Lester investigated and found it was filled with a solid chunk of glass. A cute story, but close enough to the truth so that two chemical engineers from a large Massachusetts corporation drove down to Prospect to check out the glass-filled stove.

Mortison once reported that Lester flooded a meadow one fall to ensure he'd have a good crop of ice the following summer. When he was cutting it in February, he discovered a hen's nest with several eggs in it, frozen in a block of ice. He took the eggs home, thawed them from the ice, and then incubated them near the famous stove. In a few days, out popped several little chicks, all covered with fur instead of feathers. A Canadian poultryman wrote Mortison to see if he could purchase the fur-coated fowl, but the writer had Lester reply "personally" that he was sorry, but as soon as the weather had started to get warm the chickens had sweltered to death in their fur coats.

The imaginary Lester once managed to extract and duplicate the oil that makes pigs' tails curl, and reported that his wife and daughter had gotten beautiful permanent waves by using it. The "Greens" received hundreds of letters from people asking for the formula.

Lester also invented a machine to shake milkweed plants so they secreted butter from their leaves, and once made a new shell out of concrete for a snapping turtle that had crawled out of his old one. The snapper showed his gratitude by hanging around Lester's barn and keeping the property free of rodents.

Perhaps the height of Mortison's success came in 1935, when the February 9 issue of *Newsweek* ran this item as straight news, obviously to make fun of a quaint old country character:

> Lester Green of Prospect, Connecticut, puts two setting hens on his auto motor cold nights. "A setting hen's temperature is 102," Green explained, "and consequently two hens is 204. With that heat the engine is sure to start the first time it kicks over."

Obviously, the yolk was on *Newsweek*.

The difference between journalism and literature is that journalism is unreadable and literature is not read.
Oscar Wilde

Answer: Elizabeth Arden, Eve Arden, Mary Astor, Fred Astaire, Lauren Bacall.

"Bloomers" got their name from their creator, Amelia Bloomer, of Seneca Falls, New York, a very unfrivolous woman (despite the connotation of the word "bloomers" today), who edited the temperance journal *The Lily*. On July 19, 1848, she introduced her outfit at a women's rights convention in Seneca Falls. It consisted of a calf-length skirt, more tailored than the current fashions demanded, and full trousers reaching to the ankle. In winter, the elasticized cuff could be raised to the boot top. Mrs. Bloomer pointed out that this was a superior mode of dressing because the garments wouldn't become soiled in the street, and were durable, cheap, and required little care.

Notable Births

742	Charlemagne	1914	Alec Guinness
1725	Casanova	1920	Jack Webb
1805	Hans Christian Andersen	1927	Kenneth Tynan
1840	Emile Zola	1928	Rita Gam
1875	Walter Chrysler	1941	Leon Russell

Notable Events

1512 Ponce de Leon discovered Florida
1792 U.S. Mint established
1801 Lord Nelson bombarded Copenhagen
1877 First Easter-egg roll held on White House lawn
1907 Goethals became head engineer, Panama Canal
1936 Tornadoes in southern United States killed 400 people

Many people have an all-consuming passion in their lives. Sometimes the obsession is immortalized in a will, as was the case with Mrs. Margaret Thompson, a Londoner who died on April 2, 1776. Her passion was snuff. The following is an extract from her final testament:

> In the name of God, Amen. I, Margaret Thompson, being of sound mind, &c, do desire that when my soul is departed from this wicked world, my body and effects may be disposed of in the following manner: I desire that all my handkerchiefs that I may have unwashed at the time of my decease, after they have been got together by my old and trusty servant, Sarah Stuart, be put by her, and by her alone, at the bottom of my coffin, which I desire may be made large enough for that purpose, together with such a quantity of the best Scotch snuff (in which she knoweth I always had the greatest delight) as will cover my deceased body; and this I desire the more especially as it is usual to put flowers into the coffins of departed friends, and nothing can be so fragrant and refreshing to me as that precious powder. But I strictly charge that no man be suffered to approach my body till the coffin is closed, and it is necessary to carry me to me burial, which I order in the manner following:
>
> Six men to be my bearers, who are known to be the greatest snuff-takers in the parish of St. James, Westminster; instead of mourning, each to wear a snuff-coloured beaver hat, which I desire may be bought for that purpose, and given to them. Six maidens of my old acquaintance . . . . to bear my pall, each to bear a proper hood, and to carry a box filled with the best Scotch snuff for their refreshment as they go along. Before my corpse, I desire the minister may be invited to walk and to take a certain quantity of the said snuff, not exceeding one pound, to whom I bequeath five guineas on the condition of his so doing. And I also desire my old and faithful servant, Sarah Stuart, to walk before the corpse, to distribute every twenty yards a large handful of Scotch snuff to the ground and upon the crowd who may possibly follow me to the burial-place; on which condition I bequeath her 20£. And I also desire that at least two bushels of the said snuff may be distributed at the door of my house in Boyle Street. . . .

Mrs. Thompson continued to itemize her legacies in the rest of the will, which in every case included a pound of her favorite snuff.

Question: Can you translate this cryptogram?

ESTIMATE YOUR comings
DO Ø

Human life, by its very nature, has to be dedicated to something.

José Ortega y Gasset

The Scotswoman Elizabeth Gray died on April 2, 1856, at Edinburgh, at the reputed age of 108. If she was indeed that old, she'd outlived her half-brother by 128 years.

Here is more from the "It's always been that way in Massachusetts" department: Pennies minted by the Commonwealth of Massachusetts in 1787 and 1788 cost two cents each to produce.

In April 1951, in Santa Fe, New Mexico, a public accountant, Charles Churchill of the State Bureau of Revenue, who had been hired by a Democratic administration, was fired when it was discovered he was a registered Republican. He was hired two days later by the incoming Republican administration, and then fired again later that week, when it was found out that he had changed his party registration to Democratic.

All politics is applesauce.

Will Rogers

It is impossible for a man to be cheated by anyone but himself.

R. W. Emerson

Answer: Do not underestimate your shortcomings.

APRIL 3

Questions: What one thing can give a cold, cure a cold, and pay the doctor?

What common term could you use to describe a man who didn't have all of his fingers on one of his hands?

Notable Births

1593	George Herbert	1924	Doris Day
1783	Washington Irving	1924	Marlon Brando
1822	Edward Everett Hale	1934	Jane Goodall
1898	George Jessel	1942	Wayne Newton
1898	Henry Luce	1942	Marsha Mason
1923	Jan Sterling	1945	Bernie Parent

Notable Events

1721	Robert Walpole became England's chancellor of the exchequer
1860	First ride of the Pony Express
1882	Jesse James killed by Robert Ford, Saint Joseph, Missouri
1936	Hauptmann executed
1946	General Homma, leader of Bataan death march, executed
1964	Diplomatic relations restored between United States and Panama
1974	Tornadoes in the South killed 350 people

J. Edgar Hoover frequently declared that the solution to juvenile delinquency was for young people to attend church. That statement is at odds with almost every study on criminology. A far higher percentage of incarcerated criminals of all ages claim a strong religious belief or a church affiliation than does the general public. Of six thousand juvenile delinquents interviewed in Detroit some years ago, 72 percent said they attended church regularly, about twice the number of non-delinquents. Similar figures have been recorded in England, the Netherlands, Australia, and even in Islamic countries. One of the most famous juvenile delinquents of all time didn't smoke, drink, gamble, or run around with loose women. He was extremely devout, and read his Bible daily. His name was Jesse James.

Good families are generally worse than any others.
Hope

Jesse James shot children but only in fact, not in folklore.
John Greenway

The term "hooligan" came into existence only ninety years ago, in a neighborhood of southern London. There resided a bawdy Irish family named Houlihan, notorious for its members' behavior. As stories about them spread, both their name and its spelling were modified in the retelling.

The electric eel is not — an eel, that is. It's a carp.

Someone once asked Edward Everett Hale when he was chaplain of the Senate if he ever prayed for the lawmakers.

"No," said Hale. "I look at the Senators and I pray for the country."

One cried "God bless us!" and "Amen the other . . ."
Shakespeare

Here are some sure ways *not* to get into *Who's Who*:

Offer a $5,000 bribe.
Send in a blank check.
Send in two cubic feet of material about yourself.
Insist you should be included because the same doctor who delivered your grandmother delivered Queen Victoria.

These have all been tried, to no avail.

In 1923, *Time* magazine reported that Cubism and other similar art forms were in decline, and speculated that T.S. Eliot's immortal poem *The Waste Land* was nothing more than a hoax.

Pigs never sleep on their left side.

When a stage version of Harriet Beecher Stowe's *Uncle Tom's Cabin* first played in the USSR, the Soviets found it necessary to change the ending to conform with atheistic Marxist doctrine. Instead of Little Eva dying and going to heaven, the Russian version showed her recovering and going to work in a cement factory.

When I want your opinion I'll give it to you.
Laurence J. Peter

John Wilson, who died in 1782 in Worlingworth, England, at the supposed age of 116, ate nothing but roasted turnips for supper for over forty years.

Every man desires to live long; but no man would be old.
Jonathan Swift

Answers: A draft.

Normal — normal people have half their fingers on each hand.

APRIL 4

Notable Births

1802	Dorothea Dix	1907	Nathan Pusey
1875	Pierre Monteux	1908	Edward R. Murrow
1883	Tris Speaker	1913	Oleg Cassini
1895	Arthur Murray	1915	Muddy Waters
1896	Robert Sherwood	1927	Don Adams

Notable Events

1611 Denmark declared war on Sweden
1704 First newspaper in America founded, *Boston News-letter*
1818 Present rules adopted for modification of U.S. flag
1932 Vitamin C isolated
1968 Martin Luther King assassinated
1975 Air force Galaxy C-58 crashed on take off with Vietnamese orphans aboard, 172 dead

Until fairly recently, "arranged" marriages were fairly common among the British upper classes, but more recent marriages were not as open about the arrangement as the old-fashioned marriages were. On April 4, 1528, Sir William Sturton entered into an agreement with Sir William Hungerford, a squire to the king. By it, Sir William's eldest son, Charles, was to have the hand of one of Hungerford's three daughters, according to Sir William's own choice. His second son, Andrew, was to marry the girl his father selected out of the remaining two daughters. In order to ensure that the marriages were made, Hungerford was to have custody of Charles or, in the event of his death, Andrew. In return, Hungerford had to pay £800 in installments upon receipt of Charles into his home.

If you collect baseball cards, look out for a Topps 1969 issue of the California Angels player, Aurelio Rodriguez. A notorious practical joker, Rodriguez had the Pittsburgh Pirate's batboy dressed up in his own uniform for that year's photo session. Several thousand cards were printed and distributed before the Topps company realized it had been duped. Of all recent baseball cards, this one promises to become one of the most valuable.

Question: You are writing to the following dignitaries. What form of address do you use instead of Dear Mr./Mrs.?

the Queen of England
an archdeacon
a foreign representative to the United Nations
the Pope

From a churchyard in La Pointe, Wisconsin:

To the Memory of Abraham Beaulieu
Born 15 September 1822
Accidentally shot
4th April 1844
As a mark of Affection
from his brother

A railroad worker named Morris Barieult was arrested in April 1951, for assaulting three of his coworkers with an iron poker while they slept. When the police asked him why he had done it, Barieult explained he thought the three were plotting against him by snoring in Morse Code.

Walnuts have nothing to do with walls, though the shell of the nut is a thick and complicated one. Walnut trees are native to Iran, and were introduced to Britain by the Romans. The Anglo-Saxon word *wealh*, simply means foreign, and walnuts at first were called "foreign nuts."

For hundreds of years in Italy, it was believed that walnut trees harbored evil spirits, and could incite people to hostile and obscene behavior. However, it was also believed that if a walnut were dropped on the lap of a witch, he or she would be unable to rise.

Answer: Madam *or* May it Please Your Majesty
Venerable Sir
Excellency *or* Dear Mr./Mrs. Ambassador
Your Holiness *or* Most Holy Father

When potatoes were first introduced to Spain in 1534, they were thought to be an aphrodisiac, and fetched as much as $1,250 a pound.

APRIL 5

Question: By what names are these people better known?
Dianne Belmont
Catherine Balotta
Annemarie Itliano
Walter Lanier
Theodosia Goodman

One night, a black man was walking from Grand Central Station to a hotel, carrying a heavy suitcase and a heavier valise. A young man walked up behind him, set his hand on the valise, and said kindly, "Pretty heavy, brother! Suppose you let me take one. I'm headed your way."

The first man hesitated, but the younger man insisted. They walked to the hotel, chatting amiably. When they reached the entrance, they said good-bye to each other and shook hands.

"And that was the first time I ever met Theodore Roosevelt," related Booker T. Washington years later.

The eccentric and paranoid American recluse Langley Collier met his untimely end in 1947. While he was bringing food to his equally odd brother Homer, who lived as a total hermit, he tripped on a wire to one of his own booby traps and was crushed beneath a suitcase filled with metal, a sewing machine, three breadboxes, and several bundles of newspapers. Homer starved to death, and their bodies were undiscovered for three weeks.

There are 228 muscles in an ordinary caterpillar's head. The entire human body has only about three times this many.

Beneath this stone, and not above it,
Lie the remains of Anna Lovett;
Be pleased good reader not to shove it
Lest she come again above it.
For twixt you and I, no one does covet
To see again this Anna Lovett.

Answer: Lucille Ball, Kaye Ballard, Anne Bancroft, Red Barber, Theda Bara.

Notable Births

1588	Thomas Hobbes	1904	Richard Eberhart
1649	Elihu Yale	1908	Bette Davis
1834	Frank Stockton	1908	Mary Hemingway
1837	Algernon Swinburne	1916	Gregory Peck
1856	Booker T. Washington	1920	Arthur Hailey
1900	Spencer Tracy	1923	Nguyen Van Thieu
1901	Melvyn Douglas	1941	Michael Moriarty

Notable Events

1794	Danton and his followers executed
1936	Tornado in Mississippi left 216 dead
1944	Wendell Willkie withdrew from presidential race
1955	Churchill resigned as prime minister
1976	Howard Hughes died

A knowledge of runic characters, the early writing of a number of northern European peoples, was kept to a small, select group of individuals who were deemed responsible enough to be entrusted with powerful magic created by writing. In this sense, tribal elders in Scandinavia and the British Isles were much like the shamans and witch doctors of Amerindian and African peoples. The word "runes" itself comes from the Anglo-Saxon *run*, meaning a mystery or a secret.

Fifty or sixty years ago, arsenic was used to color wallpaper green. A square foot of such paper often contained five to twenty times as much arsenic as it would take to kill a person.

On April 5, 1614, John Rolfe married the young Indian maid Pocahontas. John Smith, therefore, made her a bigamist.

APRIL 6

Notable Births

1670	Jean Baptiste Rousseau	1892	Lowell Thomas
1866	Lincoln Steffens	1893	Millard Tydings
1866	Butch Cassidy	1929	Andre Previn
1874	Harry Houdini	1937	Merle Haggard
1884	Walter Huston	1953	Janet Lynn

Notable Events

1453	Constantinople seized by Turks
1712	Slave revolt in New York City
1814	Napoleon abdicated
1830	Mormon Church organized by Joseph Smith
1862	Battle of Shiloh began
1909	Peary reached North Pole
1917	United States declared war on Germany
1927	Massachusetts Supreme Court overruled Sacco and Vanzetti's right of appeal
1936	Tornado in Georgia left 203 dead
1956	First circular office building dedicated, Los Angeles

One of the appointments made for the first time by Queen Elizabeth I of England was that of Official Uncorker of Bottles. During her reign, British warships occasionally sent messages in bottles, and on one occasion a fisherman off Dover Beach retrieved a message describing how the Dutch had taken over an island previously owned by the Russians.

For the fisherman to know that was a breach of national security, of course, so an official uncorker was appointed, and the appointment continued to be made for 230 years.

On this date in the year 1199, King Richard the Lionhearted lost his life by an arrow in France, after a dispute with a petty nobleman over a debt of a few pounds. Knowing Richard, he probably deserved it. Certainly the French seemed to think so, for they dismembered his body, burned his heart at Rouen, sent his entrails to Chalun, and disposed of the rest of the corpse at Fontevrault.

Now I know what a statesman is; he's a dead politician. We need more statesmen.

Bob Edwards

Answer: 1/7, 1/8, 2/7, 3/8.

Question: What fractions do these decimal equivalents represent?

.1429
.1250
.2857
.3750

The kaleidoscope was invented in the sixteenth century by a man named Baptiste Porta, but it wasn't perfected until 1817, when Sir David Brewster did so. In the first two months that Brewster marketed his model, he sold two hundred thousand kaleidoscopes in London and Paris alone. The name is taken from three Greek words that together mean, "Beautiful appearance I behold."

The term "flak" is a rough acronym of the German name for the air defense gun, Flieger Abwehr Kanone, which produced it.

A Russian general named Tamax once received a proposal from a Frenchman who desired to join the Russian Army. Tamax was impressed by the man, and offered him a lieutenant's rank, but the man insisted he be commissioned as no less than a major, so their negotiations broke off.

The man in question was Napoleon.

The chickens have come home to roast.

Jane Ace

History is the record of an encounter between character and circumstance.

Donald Creighton

Don't open an umbrella in the presence of a horse in New York City. You can be arrested.

What Houdini is to escape artists, Enrico Rastelli is to jugglers and acrobats. Born to a circus family in Samara, Russia, in 1896, he showed his great potential at an early age. By the time he was twelve, his tricks included juggling four lit torches with one hand while doing a handstand on his father's head. He could juggle two balls with one foot while the other foot held an eight-foot flagpole complete with flag — all this while he was performing a handstand on a lamp balancing on a table. He could also juggle six two-foot-long sticks while balancing a seventh on his head; or eight plates. He is also the only man ever known to have succeeded in juggling ten balls at one time.

APRIL 7

Questions: Why is a doctor less likely than another to make an ocean voyage "by rail?"

What was the greatest surgical operation in medical history?

The world's first slot machine was invented by Hero of Alexandria at about the time of Christ. You put your money or your token in, and out came holy water.

Elinor Glyn's official Hollywood "It" list for 1927 included Douglas Fairbanks, John Gilbert, Gloria Swanson, Vilma Banky, and Rex the Wonder Horse. Clara Bow, the "It" girl, was added later. Weekly salaries of selected actors and actresses were reported as follows: Thomas Meighan, $7,500; Pola Negri, $6,000; Clara, $6,000; Adolphe Menjou, $5,000; Lon Chaney, $3,500; and Wallace Beery, $2,800.

A few more can't do's:

Can't slap an old friend on the back in Georgia;
Can't fall asleep under a hair dryer in Florida;
Can't play hopscotch on Sunday afternoons in Missouri;
Can't eat rattlesnake in public in Kansas; and
Florida *housewives* are also prohibited by law from breaking more than three plates a day.

We've been citing a number of strange laws to be found in America — but did you know it's illegal in Sweden to teach a seal to balance a ball on his nose?

Notable Births

1770	William Wordsworth	1915	Billie Holiday
1772	M.C. Fourier	1920	Ravi Shankar
1780	William Ellery Channing	1928	James Garner
1893	Allen Dulles	1931	Donald Barthelme
1897	Walter Winchell	1938	Jerry Brown
1908	Percy Faith	1939	David Frost
1908	Frank Fitzsimmons	1939	Francis Ford Coppola

Notable Events

30	Catholic Church's official date for Christ's crucifixion
1864	First American camel race held, Sacramento, California
1917	Cuba declared war on Germany
1926	First attempted assassination of Mussolini
1932	FDR delivered "Forgotten Man" speech
1933	3.2 proof beer became legal again
1939	Italian army invaded Albania, King Zog fled

At Carlisle, England, on April 7, 1832, Joseph Thomson, a farmer, sold his wife of several years in the belief that auctioning a wife was as legally binding as a divorce. In his sales pitch he admitted that his wife, Mary Anne, had been his "tormentor, a domestic curse, a night invasion, and a daily devil," but then added, tongue-in-cheek, that she did have some positive qualities: "She can read novels and milk cows ... She can make butter and scold the maid ... she cannot make rum, gin or whiskey, but she is a good judge of the quality from long experience in tasting them."

He offered her at fifty shillings, but ended up settling for twenty shillings and a Newfoundland dog from a man named Henry Meárs.

A contemporary wrote of the event, "It can only be considered as a proof of the besotted ignorance and brutal feelings of a portion of our rural population."

In every well-governed state wealth is a sacred thing; in democracies it is the only sacred thing.

Anatole France

Answers: Because he is accustomed to see-sickness.

Lansing, Michigan.

APRIL 8

Notable Births

1460	Ponce de Leon	1918	Betty Ford
1893	Mary Pickford	1929	Jacques Brel
1908	Ilke Chase	1935	James Gavin
1913	Sonja Henie	1940	John Havlicek

Notable Events

1513 Ponce de Leon landed near Saint Augustine
1826 Clay-Randolph duel
1873 Oleomargarine patented
1911 Mine disaster near Littleton, Alabama, took 128 lives
1952 Truman ordered seizure of steel mills
1953 Jomo Kenyatta got 10 years for engineering Mau Mau uprisings
1974 Hank Aaron hit 715th homer off Al Downing

John Randolph was a Virginian who served fourteen terms as a representative, and was for a time a senator, and the United States minister to Russia. He was also an opium eater, and was well known for his imaginative diatribes while intoxicated. Of Henry Clay he once said, "Like rotten mackeral in the moonlight, he shines and he stinks." This remark occasioned a duel between the two men, who were both senators at the time. The duel was fought on April 8, 1826, but neither man was hurt.

What really flatters a man is that you think him worth flattering.

G. B. Shaw

If a man could not say nothing against a character but what he could prove, history could not be written.

Dr. Johnson

In 217 A.D., Antonius Caracalla, Roman emperor for the previous six years, took a straw vote to see how he would do in the upcoming election. That April 8, the results passed through the hands of one Macrinus, prefect of the Praetorian Guard. Macrinus discovered that he himself was quite popular, second to Antonius, in fact. To save the populace from the bother of a proper election, Macrinus immediately went to Antonius — and killed him.

Always mistrust a subordinate who never finds fault with his superior.

Collins

Greater love hath no man than this, that he lay down his friends for his political life.

Jeremy Thorpe

Question: Arrange these buildings in order from the tallest to the shortest:

a Sears Tower in Chicago
b General Motors Building in New York
c Empire State Building in New York
d Peachtree Plaza in Atlanta
e John Hancock Tower in Boston

The elegy on the tombstone of John Dale in Bakewell Churchyard, England, reads:

Know, Posterity, that on the 8th of April, 1757, the rambling remains of John Dale were in the 86th year of his Pilgrimage, laid upon Two Wives.

This Thing in Life will raise some Jealousy;
Here all three lie together lovingly;
But from embraces here no Pleasure flows,
Alike are here all human joys and woes,
Were Sarah's chiding John no longer hears.
And old John's rambling Sarah no more fears:
A period comes to all their toilsome Lives,
The Good Man's quiet; still are both his Wives.

The Roman emperor, Elagabulus, who ruled from 218 to 222 A.D., was an obnoxious practical joker. At dinner parties he would serve his guests glass, marble, and ivory, which had been fashioned to look like food, and etiquette required that the guests eat every bit of "food" that was put on their plates. When the emperor served real food, as often as not it contained a large proportion of animal dung and insects. Anyone who fell asleep during these dinners (or was rendered unconscious by the fare) could expect to wake up in a roomful of leopards, lions, and bears. As a measure of his affection for various ladies who attended his court, Elagabulus would send special gifts, such as scorpions and poisonous snakes; although on one occasion he is known to have showered some favorites with rose petals — to such an extent that they were smothered to death under the flowers. He often arrived at state functions in a chariot pulled by women — naked women.

The Roman Empire could only endure so much of this, and he was finally murdered on the orders of his grandmother. He was eighteen.

What is exhilarating in bad taste is the aristocratic pleasure of giving offense.

Baudelaire

Life is a maze in which we take the wrong turn before we have learned to walk.

Cyril Connolly

Answer: a, c, e, d, b.

APRIL 9

Question: By what names are these people better known?

Ethyl Blythe
Dallas Burrows
David Green
Benjamin Kubelsky
Bernard Schwartz

This incident was reported by the *American Weekly* in 1874, and later confirmed by Gould and Pyle in their *Anomalies and Curiosities of Medicine.*

In one Civil War battle, a bullet shot off one of the testicles of a young soldier, carried into a house behind him, and wounded a young lady in the stomach. Both the man and woman survived. Nine months and eight days later, the girl gave birth to an eight-pound boy, although she insisted she had never been with a man. The pieces of the story were put together, and the soldier was sent for. He was skeptical, but the child certainly did have his features. Happily, he ended up falling in love with the young lady, and they were married.

Why shouldn't truth be stranger than fiction? Fiction, after all, has to make sense.

Mark Twain

The only recorded murder of an ostrich in the United States happened on the night of April 9, 1926. A Bostonian called Mr. Nemo found himself locked out of what he thought was the back door of his house. Actually, as the inebriated gentleman learned the next morning, it was the door of the ostrich pen at the Franklin Park Zoo. He succeeded in breaking into the pen, which scared the daylights out of "George Washington," a 250-pound feathered occupant. The bird attacked him, and Nemo responded by strangling it to death.

When in danger, or in doubt, run in circles, yell and shout.

Laurence J. Peter

A museum caretaker named Ernest Ebbitson of Hertfordshire, England, has spent the last thirty years trying to develop a transparent frog, which he expects will have an orangish hue. His humanitarian reason for the experiment is that the lives of millions of frogs would be saved if anatomy and biology students could simply see inside frogs and therefore wouldn't have to kill them.

Answer: Ethel Barrymore, Orson Bean, David Ben-Gurian, Jack Benny, Tony Curtis.

Notable Births

1821	Charles Baudelaire	1905	William Fulbright
1870	Vladimir Lenin	1910	Abraham Ribicoff
1888	Sol Hurok	1926	Hugh Hefner
1889	Efrem Zimbalist	1933	Jean-Paul Belmondo
1898	Paul Robeson	1942	Brandon de Wilde

Notable Events

1691	La Salle reached Mississippi River
1833	First free library in America opened, Peterborough, New Hampshire
1865	Lee surrendered to Grant at Appomattox
1867	Purchase of Alaska ratified by Senate
1918	Latvia declared independence
1931	Soviets accused Hoover of plotting overthrow of USSR
1933	Scottsboro defendants' appeal failed
1940	Germany invaded Denmark and Norway
1942	United States forces on Bataan surrendered
1961	Death of King Zog
1963	Winston Churchill made honorary citizen of United States

Francis Bacon, whose name is still occasionally cited as the man who really wrote Shakespeare's plays, died on April 9, 1626, after trying to anticipate Clarence Birdseye. While experimenting to determine whether stuffing a chicken with ice delayed the decaying process, he caught cold. This developed into bronchitis, which killed him.

Notable Births

1778	William Hazlitt	1903	Claire Booth Luce
1794	Matthew Perry	1921	Chuck Connors
1827	Lew Wallace	1929	Max von Sydow
1829	William Booth	1932	Omar Sharif
1847	Joseph Pulitzer	1934	David Halberstam
1885	Bernard Gimbel	1941	Paul Theroux

Notable Events

1603	James VI proclaimed king of England as James I
1866	ASPCA chartered
1877	Catamaran patented
1932	Hindenburg barred SS troops from Reichstag
1963	U.S. submarine *Thresher* lost
1972	Iranian earthquake left over 5,000 dead
1973	British Vanguard turboprop crashed in Alps, killed 104 passengers

On April 10, 1927, the first performance of George Anteil's modernistic *Ballet Mechanique* was a real test for the audience, which was largely unfamiliar with and unappreciative of the new style of music. They sat politely at first as the car horns, sirens, an airplane propeller, six xylophones, and ten grand pianos attacked their ears, but became very uncomfortable as the performance continued. Soon many of the audience were in obvious pain. Finally, a man in the front tied a handkerchief to his cane, waved it in the air, and brought down the house.

Applause is the spur of noble minds, the end and aim of weak ones.

Colton

In the spring of 1941, a lawyer in Atlanta, Georgia, cleverly used an 1864 statute to win his client a divorce from her husband. The law provided grounds for divorce if the spouse was in "the military service of the United States." The law had been enacted during the Civil War when Georgia was part of the Confederacy, and service in the Union Army was tantamount to treason.

I don't want a lawyer to tell me what I cannot do; I hire him to tell me how to do what I want to do.

J. P. Morgan

Here is a late seventeenth-century epitaph from Wolverhampton Church in England,

Here lie the bones
Of Joseph Jones,
Who eat whilst he was able!
But once o'er fed,
He dropt down dead,
And fell beneath the table.
When from the tomb,
To meet his doom,
He rises amidst sinners:
Since he must dwell
In heav'n or hell,
Take him — which gives the best dinners!

Question: Which state is pictured here?

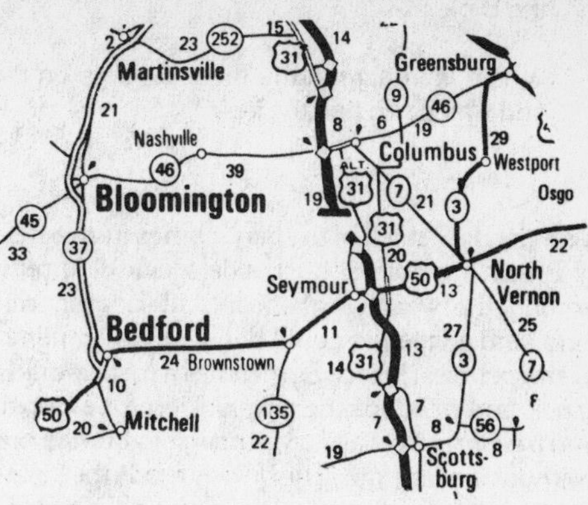

Felix was a cat that belonged to an elderly inhabitant of Saint Kilda, Australia. The old man and the cat were very close, and it was obvious to all who knew them that there was an extraordinary bond between them far greater than the affection that usually exists between the average pet and its owner. When the old man died, his daughter took his cat to live with her family in Melbourne. Although she treated Felix kindly, the cat was morbidly depressed. He lay in front of his master's picture all day and all night, and refused to eat. After a week of this, the woman brought Felix out to the country with the family for a picnic, hoping to cheer him up. Felix ran away, and could not be found. For several days the woman returned to look for him, but there was not a trace of the cat.

Ten days later, with all hope of finding the cat gone, the woman went to visit her father's grave. There was Felix. The cemetery was ten miles from her house, and even farther from the picnic spot, and Felix had never been there before — but there he sat, atop his beloved master's grave. The woman did the only thing she could. She gave the cemetery attendant money to feed and look after the cat, and left him there. Until the day of his own death, Felix never left the graveyard.

Hope is merely disappointment deferred.

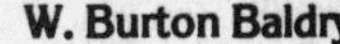
W. Burton Baldry

Answer: Indiana.

APRIL 11

Questions: Who was the best actor among all the characters in the Bible?

Which animal took the most luggage on the Ark, and which two had the least?

Notable Births

1722	Christopher Smart	1862	Charles Evans Hughes
1770	George Canning	1893	Dean Acheson
1794	Edward Everett	1932	Joel Grey

Notable Events

1713	Peace of Utrecht made
1805	Treaty of Saint Petersburg between Russia and England
1947	Jackie Robinson broke major league racial barrier
1951	Truman relieved MacArthur of Far East command
1951	Stone of Scone returned
1965	Tornadoes in Great Lakes states killed 271 people

The phrase "let the cat out of the bag" comes from a nefarious practice by Britain's medieval husbanders. Suckling pig was a delicacy among the wealthy inhabitants of English cities six centuries ago, and a little pig could bring a rural farmer a good price — several pennies, in fact. Sometimes a rustic would plop a cat into a sack and head for the city, looking for a dupe. If the farmer found a victim who was naive enough to buy the contents of the bag without looking into it, he quickly made the transaction and disappeared, leaving the townsmen with an inedible cat. A circumspect buyer would try, before the sale, to let what he suspected was a cat out of the bag.

The next time your kids say "Ugh!" to your spaghetti because it looks like worms, don't slug them. They're simply up on their etymology. The word "vermicelli," a type of spaghetti, means "little worms" in Italian.

In the State of Maine a day of fasting was observed annually for many years, with a proclamation from the governor preceding the day by several weeks. On one occasion, the governor asked his aide to draw up the usual proclamation, expecting he would simply copy one of the announcements from a previous year. Instead, the aide drafted the following:

> Having consulted my Council and learned that none of them has an engagement to dine on that day, and feeling fully assured that I shall receive no invitation to dine until the high school graduating exercises begin and field strawberries get down to eight cents a quart, I do hereby appoint Thursday, the seventeenth day of April, as a day of public humiliation, fasting and prayer. While the scoffers in our sister State (Massachusetts) are holding horse races, playing baseball, and gorging themselves with forbidden food, let us thank our stars that we know when we have enough, and feel grateful for the empty stomach and clear heads we shall have the morning after. Though I am unable to say what the Council will do on that day, for myself I shall attend church if I can find a minister who will stay long enough to preach to me. Given in the Council Chamber, etc. . . .

The aide had it typed up on the governor's stationary and sent it in for his signature. It was signed without being read. The notice was then delivered to the secretary of state to be attested. The secretary began to sign it, but his pen went dry. While he was looking for another, he happened to notice some of the curious wording in the document and so read it through. Calling the aide in, he rebuked him for his frivolity and his trifling with the dignity of the governor's office. The young man then simply pointed to the calendar and said, "April Fool," and all was forgiven.

A blunderer is a man who starts a meat market during Lent.
James Montgomery Bailey

In April 1949, Martha Giles of Newark, New Jersey, filed for divorce from her husband, charging that her husband had attacked her with a live eel. She got the separation.

Hummingbirds are the only birds that can fly backward, but they can't walk.

Answers: Sampson was — he brought down the house.

The elephant had the most, for he took his trunk; the fox and the rooster had the least, for they had only a brush and a comb between them.

Notable Births

1777	Henry Clay	1926	Jane Withers
1827	Johanna Spyri	1940	Herbie Hancock
1919	Ann Miller	1950	David Cassidy

Notable Events

1847	First Chinese students arrived in America
1861	Fort Sumter attacked
1862	Great locomotive chase between the "General" and the "Confederate"
1877	Catcher's mask first used, Lynn, Massachusetts
1908	Chelsea, Massachusetts, destroyed by fire
1945	Tornadoes in Oklahoma took 102 lives
1961	Yuri Gagarin became first man to orbit earth
1964	Chubby Checker married Catherine Lodders, former Miss World

Henry Clay once asked the Riggs Bank for a $250 loan on his personal note. The bank agreed, but mentioned (as a mere formality) that it must have an endorser. When Clay saw Daniel Webster in the bank, he asked him if he would be so kind as to endorse the note. Webster agreed to do so, but as he, too, needed some spending money, he asked Clay to make out a loan for $500 and split it with him. The loan was made, and the two great statesmen walked out with their money.

To this day the loan remains unpaid.

I would rather be right than president.

Henry Clay

Recently, sixteen-year-old Linda Salcedo filed a half-million-dollar damage suit against the directors of the California Teen Pageant, in which she had been a contestant. She charged that they had refused to allow her to perform her chosen act in the talent competition, on the grounds that it was "unladylike." In her talent segment, Linda broke up concrete blocks to music.

May you have a lawsuit in which you know you are in the right.

Gypsy curse

Question: When, approximately within ten years, were the following invented?

air conditioning
electric battery
dictating machine
chronometer

About 1722, the highwaymen outside London were having such bad luck that they posted notices in the city suggesting that travelers should carry at least ten guineas with them when they journeyed from town. Those who had this much or more, the notices went on to say, would simply be robbed; but those who ventured out without that much risked their lives if stopped by the highwaymen.

A man who has never gone to school may steal from a freight car; but if he has a university education, he may steal the whole railroad.

Theodore Roosevelt

For 500 years, from about 700 A.D. onward, there were cricket cults in China. The Chinese housed their favorite insects in elaborate cages, which they hung from their belts and carried everywhere, even to bed. Owners of the crickets would talk to their pets, ask their advice, and so forth, almost as if the insects were people (or plants).

An extensive literature on the rearing and caring of crickets developed. The *Tsu chi king*, or "Book of Crickets," was the Doctor Spock of cricketing. It even prescribed special diets for the various species of crickets or the insects' different occupations. Pet crickets were fed most successfully on cucumbers, lettuce, chopped fish, honey, beans, and chestnuts; while fighting crickets thrived on lotus seeds, mosquitoes, and flower root tonics, according to the book.

Don't laugh. If you paid the equivalent of $10,000 for your fighting cricket you wouldn't want to feed it any old rubbish.

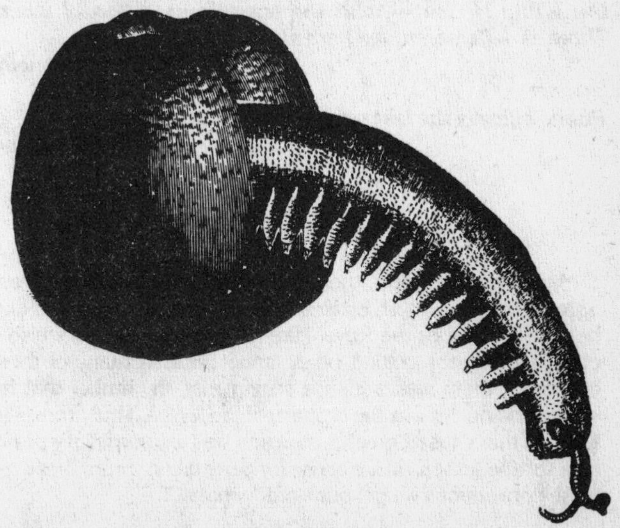

In parts of Zambia, the traditional apples for the teacher are replaced by caterpillars. The teachers are still expected to eat them raw.

Answer: 1911, 1800, 1885, 1735.

APRIL 13

Question: By what names are these people better known?

John Blythe
Joseph Gottleib
Michael Gubitosi
Israel Baline
Thelma Ford

Notable Births

1743	Thomas Jefferson	1906	Samuel Beckett
1852	Frank Woolworth	1907	Harold Stassen
1904	Lily Pons	1909	Eudora Welty

Notable Events

1598	Edict of Nantes proclaimed
1719	Spain began invasion of Scotland
1796	First elephant in America arrived, New York City
1934	4.7 million American families reported on relief
1940	Cornelius Warmerdam broke 15-foot pole-vault barrier
1941	Belgrade fell to Nazis
1961	UN General Assembly condemned apartheid

The inscription on Thomas Jefferson's tomb at Monticello describes him as the author of the Declaration of Independence, founder of the University of Virginia, and father of religious freedom in Virginia; but makes no mention of the fact that he was president of the United States.

I think this is the most extraordinary collection of talent, of human knowledge, that has ever been gathered together at the White House — with the possible exception of when Thomas Jefferson dined here alone.

John F. Kennedy

Public office is the last refuge of the incompetent.

Boies Penrose

Many centuries ago, there was often a clause in the lease agreements of English estates reserving the best pieces of timber for the use of the Royal Navy. There was generally also a charge made for cutting other timber. But, in many of these contracts, there was a clause stating that any timber that fell without being cut was the property of the lessee. Thus, ironically, a storm that caused great destruction was extraordinarily profitable for the lessee, and a cause for celebration. From these old lease conventions we get our word "windfall."

Only 2 percent of reported Rocky Mountain spotted fever cases actually occur in the Rocky Mountains.

The word "boss" comes from the Dutch word *baas*, meaning uncle. The term came into the American language in the New York area during the early days of colonization, when English and Dutch settlers intermingled there. The English, it seems, resented having to call their employers "master," as was the custom in the Old Country, and adopted the friendlier Dutch word.

If a normal child needs glasses by the time he or she is eleven years old, the chances are that the boy or girl is a year or so more advanced intellectually than a non-bespectacled peer.

Answer: John Barrymore, Joey Bishop, Robert Blake, Irving Berlin, Shirley Booth.

APRIL 14

Notable Births

1879	James Branch Cabell	1930	Bradford Dillman
1889	Arnold Toynbee	1932	Loretta Lynn
1897	Lester Pearson	1932	Tony Perkins
1904	John Gielgud	1941	Julie Christie
1909	Papa Doc Duvalier	1942	Pete Rose
1923	Roberto DeVincenzo	1942	Valerie Brumel

Notable Events

1861 Fort Sumter surrendered
1865 Lincoln shot
1894 First peep show opened in New York City
1910 Taft became first president to throw out baseball to open season
1912 *Titanic* sunk on maiden voyage, 1,517 people lost
1912 F.R. Law became first man to jump from Brooklyn Bridge as a stunt
1931 Alphonso XIII of Spain abdicated
1944 Explosion in Bombay Harbor killed 700 people
1956 First public demonstration of videotape
1958 Sputnik II disintegrated

While he was talking over the problems of the country during the Reconstruction Era with some friends, Gil Bates, a sergeant with the Wisconsin Heavy Artillery during the Civil War, made an incredible wager. He bet that he could walk General Sherman's route unarmed, penniless, and carrying an unfurled Union flag, and not be harmed. He intended, he said, to live off Southern hospitality.

His friends immediately took him on. It was decided that he would start from Vicksburg the next January, and that he would have to reach Washington by the Fourth of July to win the wager.

The closest Bates came to being hurt was a single negative editorial, and he reached the capital eleven weeks ahead of schedule, on April 14, 1868.

What they call "heart" is located far lower than the fourth waistcoat button.

George Lichtenberg

A while ago in Massachusetts the inmates in the Berkshire County Jail went on a hunger stike, complaining that their food was inedible and they weren't allowed seconds.

President Taft always had his secretary nudge him whenever the National Anthem was played. He was so tone deaf he could not recognize the tune.

Somebody, presumably a man, made this comparison between women and ships in the mid-nineteenth century:

> A ship is called a she because a man knows not the expense until he gets one — because they are useless without employment — because they look best well-rigged — because their value depends on their age — because they are upright when in stays — because they bring home news from abroad, and carry out news from home.

It's time to button down the hatches, or is it batten down the hedges?

Barbara Straus

Question: Which of these foods has the most calories?

one cup of macaroni and cheese
one cup of roasted peanuts
one 4-inch wedge of lemon meringue pie
one cup of heavy whipping cream

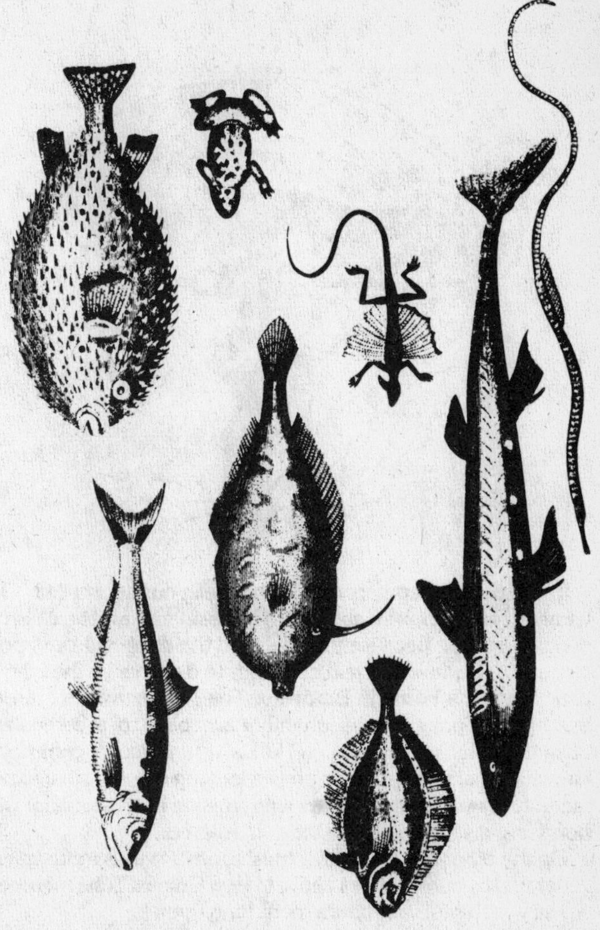

In the past two centuries, there have been over a dozen documented instances in which fish or animals have fallen from the sky like rain. On Easter Sunday, April 14, 1828, three- and four-inch herring fell near Ross in Scotland, some three miles from the ocean, and two years later another fish shower occurred on the Island of Oslay, off Argylshire. Perhaps the most remarkable piscine rainfall happened near Calcutta, India, on September 20, 1839, when three-inch-long fish fell in an eighteen-inch-wide path for a distance of several hundred yards. The chronicler of the event, a British Army officer, noted that the fish that fell in the soft grass were alive, while those that landed on rocks were killed by the impact. Shortly after this storm, several thousand dry, dead herring fell near Allahabad.

Although fish are the most common, they are by no means the only creatures recorded to have rained. Toulouse, France, was inundated by frogs three- and four-deep on the ground in 1804, and on October 17, 1827, Pakroff, Russia, experienced a similar but lighter shower of 1½-inch frogs. A rain of rats was recorded in Norway. Very often, these animal showers were first regarded as divine messages, good and bad, but in every case the rains have been associated with waterspouts and tornadoes occurring in the area at the same time.

Answer: Believe it or not, it's the peanuts.

APRIL 15

Questions: Who is the wickedest man mentioned in the Bible?

Although his name isn't mentioned, who was Jonah's unlikely guardian?

In what way is a good con man like a good Christian?

Notable Births

1452	Leonardo da Vinci	1889	A. Philip Randolph
1843	Henry James	1898	Molly McGee
1861	Bliss Carmen	1933	Roy Clark
1889	Thomas Hart Benton	1933	Elizabeth Montgomery

Notable Events

1817 Connecticut Asylum, country's first school for the deaf, opened
1825 Sacrilege became punishable by death in France
1920 Sacco-Vanzetti payroll robbery
1942 Laval became president of France in German deal
1953 Charlie Chaplin returned his U.S. reentry permit in Geneva, Switzerland
1969 Unarmed U.S. reconaissance plane shot down 100 miles off North Korea

In 1926, the members of a French religious sect called "Our Lady of Tears" took an abbé from his residence and beat him to death. This was because they believed the abbé had been possessed by the devil and had sent birds to defecate on the lawn of their founder's home in Bordeaux. The sect members claimed the bird droppings subsequently gave birth to a particularly objectionable mushroom (*Phallus impudicus*, commonly known as a stinkhorn). This phallic-looking mushroom inflicted the unfortunate cult members who smelled its terrible odor with horrifying diseases — or so the cult believed.

On the other hand, a similar mushroom, *Phallus indusiata*, is venerated by certain tribes native to New Guinea. Tribe members will sit worshipfully for hours meditating upon it.

Religion has done love a great service by making it a sin.

Anatole France

In 1923, the chancellor of the Exchequer calculated the per-capita tax bite in Great Britain as against that of other countries. America's was $26.30, France's $27.00, and England's $85.00.

The income tax had made more liars out of the American people than golf has. Even when you make a tax form out on the level, you don't know when it's through if you are a crook or a martyr.

Will Rogers

At the turn of the century, only 22 percent of all automobiles were powered by internal combustion engines. Battery power accounted for 38 percent, and steam power for 40 percent.

John Hancock was among the most majestic of the many aristocrats who helped create the American Revolution. Though most of the country was undergoing severe hardship at the time (remember the winter at Valley Forge) the *Pennsylvania Ledger* reported in spring, 1778,

> John Hancock of Boston appears in public with all the state and pageantry of an Oriental prince; he rides in an elegant chariot . . . attended by four servants dressed in superb livery, mounted on fine horses richly caparisoned; and escorted by 50 horsemen with drawn sabers, the one half of which precedes and the other follows his carriage.

These comments on British taxation come from the *Edinburgh Review*.

> Taxes upon every article which enters onto the mouth, or covers the back, or is placed upon the feet — taxes upon everything which it is pleasant to see, hear, feel, smell, or taste — taxes upon warmth, light, and locomotion — taxes on everything on earth, and the waters under the earth — on everything that comes from abroad, or is grown at home — taxes on the raw material — taxes upon every fresh value that is added to it by the industry of man — taxes on the sauce which pampers man's appetite, and the drug which restores him to health — on the ermine which decorates the judge, and the rope which hangs the criminal — on the poor man's salt, and on the rich man's spice — on the brass nails of the coffin, and the ribbons of the bride at bed or board, *couchant* or *levant*, we must pay; — the schoolboy whips his taxed top — the beardless youth manages his taxed horse, with a taxed bridle, on a taxed road: — and the dying Englishman, pouring his taxed medicine, which has paid seven per cent., into a spoon that has paid fifteen per cent., flings himself back upon his chintz bed, which has paid twenty-two per cent. — makes his will on an eight-pound stamp, and expires in the arms of an apothecary, who has paid a licence of a hundred pounds for the privilege of putting him to death. His whole property is immediately taxed from two to ten per cent. Besides the probate, large fees are demanded for burying him in the chancel; his virtues are handed down to posterity on taxed marble; and he is then gathered to his fathers — to be taxed no more.

Answers: Moses — he broke all Ten Commandments at once.
The whale — he brought Jonah up.
Because when a stranger comes along he takes him in.

Notable Births

1671	John Law	1904	Clifford Case
1844	Anatole France	1921	Peter Ustinov
1862	Amos Alonzo Stagg	1922	Kingsley Amis
1867	Wilbur Wright	1924	Henry Mancini
1871	John Millington Synge	1929	Edie Adams
1882	Charlie Chaplin	1947	Kareem Abdul-Jabbar

Notable Events

1862 Slavery abolished in Washington, D.C.
1906 Earthquake in Chile killed 1,500 people
1922 B.W. Maynard delivered first sermon from an airplane
1933 British Empire began boycott of Russian goods
1947 French ship *Grandcamp* exploded at Texas City, Texas; 561 victims
1952 Adlai Stevenson declared he was not a candidate for president
1964 General Motors announced first quarter profits of $536,000,000
1975 Cambodian government surrendered to Khmer Rouge

Question: Residents of which of the following states are most likely to die in an accident during a given year?

Alaska
New York
Colorado
Wyoming

Nineteen thirty-five was the year of the chain letter, and Denver, Colorado, was the place of its birth. Chain letters had been used previously to ask people to pray for one another, but when some ingenious person hit on the idea of sending a dime instead of a prayer, Americans went crazy. In a matter of a few days, the volume of mail handled by the Denver Post Office increased from an average of about 170,000 pieces a day to over 400,000. The street in front of the postal building looked like a New York subway at rush hour. Scalpers sold places on chain letters for several dollars, and many business establishments stopped their normal operations to make chain letter forms, which they sold for the inflated price of two for a quarter. One establishment selling these forms made $18,000 in five hours.

The chain letter was, of course, a get-rich-quick scheme which people, in the middle of the Depression, didn't bother to examine closely. In a five-name chain, with each of the five addressees sending a letter to five friends, the initiating individual could hope to receive $1,562.50 if the chain were not broken. This was fine for those few people at the top of the pyramid; they would almost certainly make some money. But for those 15,625 people who sent the first individual in the chain a dime before they could receive the same money themselves, a total of 244,140,625 letters would have to be sent, again assuming that no one broke the chain. That figure is double what the nation's population was at the time.

No matter — for weeks the business boomed, and it spread rapidly to other parts of the country. President Roosevelt received two thousand chain letters, and Governor Al Smith of New York got one thousand. Three chain-letter factories were created overnight in Springfield, Missouri, and "prosperity clubs," which encouraged people to send a dollar, a savings bond, and a bottle of liquor soon followed. Undergraduates in Dallas even began a send-a-pair-of-panties chain.

The fad died in a few months. Few people made any money, but few people lost very much, either. The gullible paid in most cases a reasonable price for their stupidity. The mail service prospered, however. By September, the Denver office alone had over one-hundred thousand chains in its dead-letter vault, and, despite overtime and the hiring of 100 additional clerks, the Denver office made a bundle because of the huge volume.

One happy result of the chain letter hysteria: a Colorado woman who started a chain to try to locate her long-lost husband found him — through a friend of a friend of a friend's friend. With a chain like that, she should have sent a dime.

After I asked him what he meant, he replied that freedom consisted in the unimpeded right to get rich, to use his ability, no matter what the cost to others, to win advancement.

Norman Thomas

A survey conducted in France ten years ago revealed that, since childhood, 57 percent of all French adults had not read a book.

According to an official of the Frankfort, West Germany, Zoo, when the zoo's gorillas were given a TV set to watch, they enjoyed love scenes, auto races, and weight-lifting competitions, in that order of preference.

Answer: Alaska.

APRIL 17

Question: A kindergarten teacher lost control of her class on a trip to the zoo. After an hour of frantic searching, she found a third of the class watching the monkeys, a quarter of them in the reptile house, a twelfth of them rattling cages in the bird wing, and the remaining twelve children wading in a fountain. How many children were in class?

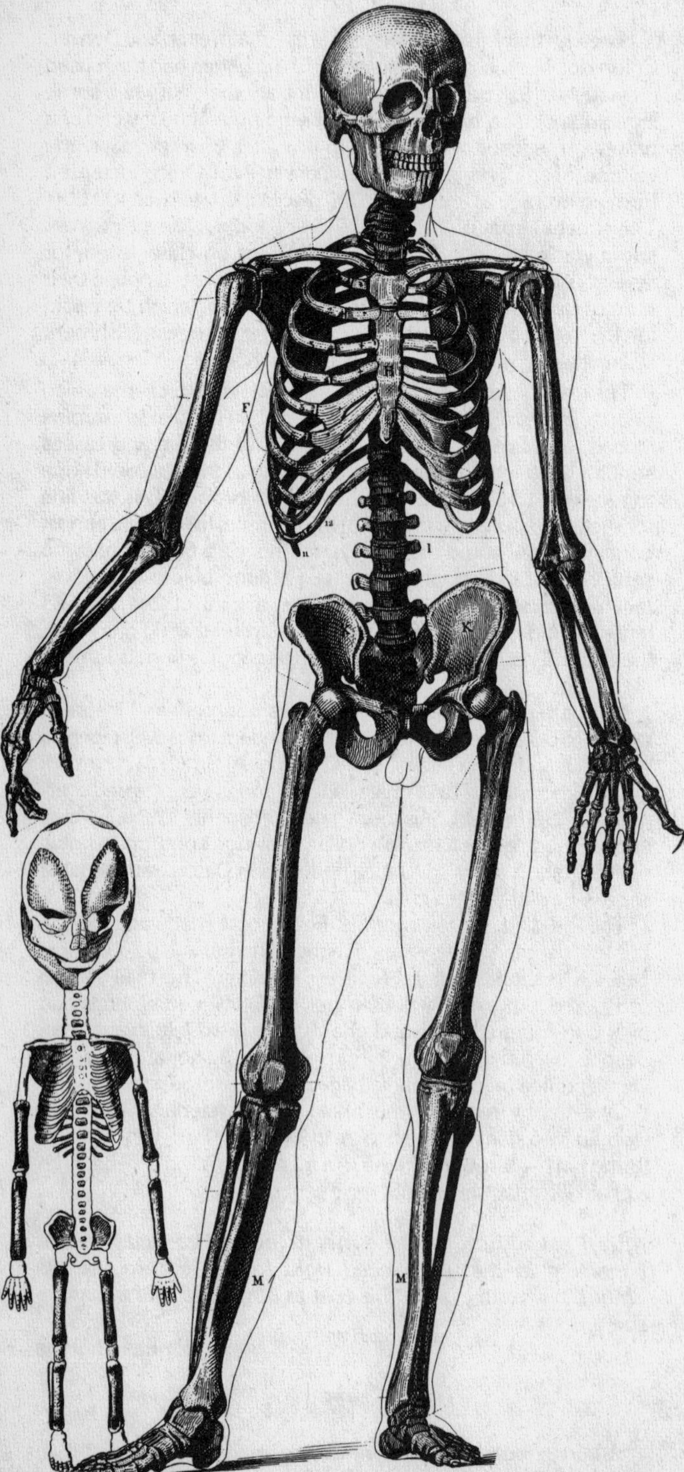

A human being is born with 305 bones, but during childhood a number of them fuse, so that an adult has only about 206.

Notable Births

1741	Samuel Chase	1894	Nikita Khrushchev
1837	J. Pierpont Morgan	1897	Thornton Wilder
1851	Cap Anson	1918	William Holden
1870	Ray Stannard Baker	1923	Harry Reasoner
1885	Isak Dinesen	1930	Genevieve

Notable Events

1521	Martin Luther excommunicated
1782	Netherlands recognized U.S. independence
1810	Pineapple cheese patented
1861	Virginia seceded from Union
1941	Yugoslavia surrendered to Hitler
1961	Bay of Pigs invasion
1965	Student demonstrations against U.S. bombing in Vietnam began, Washington, D.C.
1969	Sirhan Sirhan sentenced to death

On April 17, 1725, John Rudge bequeathed the parish of Trysull, Staffordshire, twenty shillings a year to employ a poor man to keep parishioners awake and dogs quiet during church services.

This may or may not be true, but if it is, it explains a good deal about how J.P. Morgan became a rich man. At a gathering of financiers and bankers in a bar near Wall Street, Morgan summoned a waiter and ordered a beer for himself, and then announced, "When J.P. Morgan drinks, everybody drinks!" Everybody ordered a round. After finishing his beer, Morgan slapped a dime on the table and left, announcing, "When J.P. Morgan pays, everybody pays!"

As a general rule, nobody has money who ought to have it.

Benjamin Disraeli

If you would know what the Lord God thinks of money, you only have to look at those to whom he gives it.

Maurice Baring

Life shouldn't be printed on dollar bills.

Clifford Odets

In April 1941, the citizens of Orfordsville, Wisconsin, voted 121 to 113 against the sale of beer in their town, and 126 to 121 in favor of the sale of hard liquor.

Back in 1939, William S. Wellman of Cleveland entered his homing pigeon in a 100-mile race. The bird was a novice, so Wellman didn't expect it would do particularly well. What he didn't expect was that the bird would finish last, or at least last by such an enormous margin. Every other contestant beat Wellman's bird to its home roost by over nine years.

Canary bird out of cage may fly far.

Charlie Chan

Answer: 36.

Notable Births

1857	Clarence Darrow	1882	Leopold Stokowski
1864	Richard Harding Davis	1911	Huntington Hartford II
1880	Sam Crawford	1922	Barbara Hale
1881	Max Weber	1945	Catfish Hunter

Notable Events

1775	Paul Revere's ride
1850	Hailstorm in Dublin, Ireland, did $150,000 damage
1861	Virginia militia captured Harper's Ferry arsenal
1906	San Francisco earthquake, 452 dead, $300,000,000 damage
1924	First crossword puzzle book published
1942	Doolittle's Shangri-La raid on Japan
1945	Ernie Pyle died on Ie Shima
1946	League of Nations met to abolish itself
1956	E.A. Rommel became first baseball umpire to wear glasses
1974	Sadat cooled relations with Russia

Questions: Can you name three very odd places where you can find fish?

What was the most popular game of the Jews in the Old Testament? Give evidence to support your claim.

Although Lord Byron was in Greece at the time of his death on April 19, 1824, and he had hired mercenaries to fight for Greece's independence from Turkey, it is quite untrue that he died gallantly while leading a force of freedom fighters. Actually, his doctors ("A damned bunch of butchers," as he called them) bled him to death. Feverish and exhausted after a long journey, he was attended by a Dr. Bruno, who felt that Byron could best be helped by bloodletting. Byron would not allow it at first, but as he grew weaker and Bruno's entreaties more desperate, he acquiesced. Bruno, with the help of several other physicians, took four *pounds* of Byron's blood (the average person has six or seven pints, at about a pound per pint) and then purged him with an extremely unpleasant concoction of senna leaves, Epsom salts, and castor oil. The poet was already unconscious by the time the last of his blood had been drained, but leeches were applied to his temples overnight just in case the doctors had still not taken enough. Byron was dead the next day.

A man convinced against his will
Is of the same opinion still.
Butler

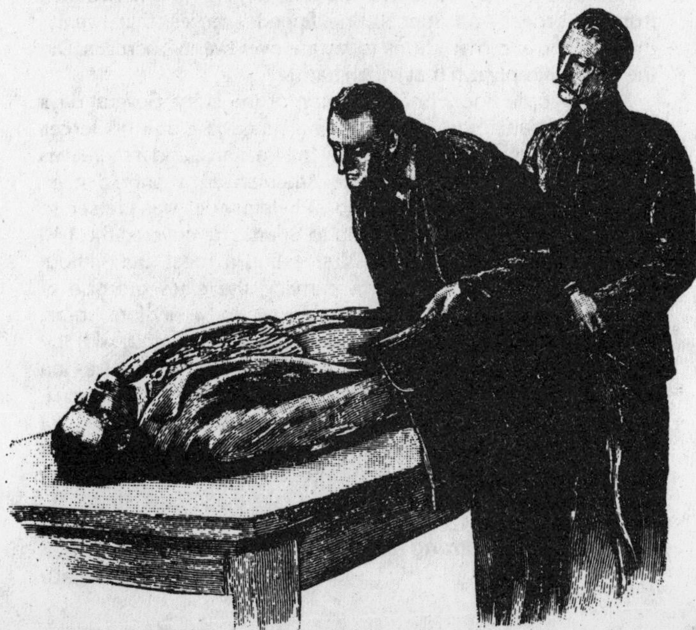

Two nineteenth-century tongue-twisters:

Medical men my mood mistaking,
Most mawkish, monstrous messes making,
Molest me much; more manfully
My mind might meet my malady;
Medicines mere mockery murders me.

I need not your needles;
They're needless to me,
For kneading of needles
Were needless, you see.
But did my neat trousers
But need to be kneed
I should then have need
Of your needles indeed.

Most people are aware that Paul Revere's Ride didn't happen in the way Longfellow's poem celebrates it, and that the actual alarum was sounded, for the most part, by two other rebels, William Dawes and Samuel Prescott. Here are a few more details of the real story.

Revere had arranged for lanterns to be hung in the tower of the Old North Church not for himself, but so others would know in case he was captured before he could get across the river to Charlestown and claim his horse. Revere was quite sure the Redcoats would come by sea. (In fact, they came both by sea and land.) The "muffled oar" that Longfellow mentions was muffled by a woman's petticoat, something the poet was either unaware of or chose not to include. While Revere did rouse the countryside during the part of the ride he completed, his specific purpose was to warn Hancock and Adams at Lexington, so they might escape safely. Having done that, he started for Concord with Dawes and Prescott, but they were waylaid by British scouts. Prescott and Dawes escaped, the former to spread the word to Lincoln and Concord, while the latter returned to Lexington. Revere was captured, but he managed to talk the British into releasing him after a few hours *without* his borrowed horse, Brown Beauty. He, too, returned to Lexington, and busied himself for some time collecting and hiding incriminating correspondence Hancock had left behind when he fled. Thus he missed the Battle of Lexington. Records show he was paid five shillings for his night's work.

The horse does the work and the coachman is tipped.
Anonymous

Answers: You can find a skate in a sporting goods shop, a sole beneath a shoe, and a perch in a birdcage.

Baseball — Genesis refers to the big-inning, Adam stole second, and both he and Eve were put out; Cain made a hit; Noah put the dove out on a fly; King Solomon himself had a diamond; Abraham sacrificed; etc.

APRIL 19

Question: If traveling had always been as easy as it is now, which two of the following people could have met?

Catherine the Great
St. Francis Xavier
Daniel Boone
Oliver Cromwell

Notable Births

1772	David Ricardo	1912	Glenn Seaborg
1900	George O'Brien	1930	Hugh O'Brian
1900	Richard Hughes	1933	Jayne Mansfield

Notable Events

1775 Battles of Lexington and Concord
1794 Treaty of The Hague
1928 Japan occupied Shantung
1931 King Pajadhipok of Siam arrived in North Dakota
1933 United States went off gold standard
1943 First reports of the Holocaust began
1951 MacArthur delivered "Old Soldiers" speech
1964 Phouma overthrown in Thailand by military rightists

The story of Pheidippedes, the Greek runner who carried the news of the defeat of King Darius from the Plain of Marathon to Athens, is well known. As the finest runner in Greece, he was told by his commander to bring the news of the unexpected victory over the Persians to the people of Athens, who were getting ready to evacuate their city. Upon reaching the Athenian marketplace, Pheidippedes shouted "Victory! Victory!" and fell dead.

But, why did the run kill him? Thousands of less-accomplished athletes run marathons in the United States every year, and although they may be exhausted after a race, no one has died from the ordeal. And, after all, Pheidippedes ran less than twenty-three miles, and marathons today are over twenty-six miles. Did the Greek simply run that much harder?

Most people know only a portion of the story. Several days before the battle, the Greek general was aware that his forces would be greatly outnumbered by the Persians, and if there was to be any hope for victory, the Athenian army should need reinforcements of Spartan troops. Pheidippedes was chosen to carry the urgent request for help to Sparta. He covered the 140 miles in a day and a night. After eating a meal, but without sleeping at all, he left Sparta carrying the city's promise of assistance, and ran back to Athens, again in twenty-four hours. Almost immediately, Pheidippedes then had to march with the army to the Plain of Marathon, where he participated as an infantryman in the battle against Darius. When the fight was over, *then* he ran to Athens to spread the news of the victory.

It wasn't the twenty-three miles, it was the lack of sleep, the lack of food, the infantry battle, and over 300 miles of cross-country running in four days that killed him. (Take that, Frank Shorter!)

When you win, nothing hurts.

Joe Namath

Answer: Catherine the Great and Daniel Boone.

APRIL 20

Notable Births

1793	David Laing	1894	Harold Lloyd
1808	Napoleon III	1910	Robert F. Wagner
1889	Adolf Hitler	1914	Lionel Hampton
1893	Joan Miro	1941	Ryan O'Neal

Notable Events

1792	France declared war on Austria
1930	Lindbergh set cross-country flight record, 14 hours, 45 minutes
1943	Warsaw ghetto massacre
1948	Walter Reuther shot in Detroit
1967	Swiss Brittania turboprop crashed on Cyprus, 126 killed
1968	Boeing 707 crashed on take-off in South Africa, took 122 lives
1971	Supreme Court unanimously ruled busing constitutional

Adolf Hitler was both a vegetarian and a teetotaller.

On this date in 1850, the much-maligned President Franklin Pierce vetoed a bill that would have granted ten million acres of land to the insane poor.

This country has come to feel the same when Congress is in session as when the baby gets hold of a hammer.

Will Rogers

Mario Maimone, an Italian-American now in his mid-thirties, once hijacked a Swiss airliner and ordered its pilot to fly to Rome. Maimone claimed he was Jesus Christ and demanded an audience with the pope. He was arrested, and spent eleven months in jail.

In 1978, he was consecrated as a bishop in a Californian sect of the Greek Orthodox church called the Holy Sepulchre Church of Graecia Signe-Sicily. His religious inspiration reportedly stems from the Reverend Sun Myung Moon, who has influenced Maimone because of the money he has made from the Unification Church.

In his first sermon as bishop, Maimone declared that "heathens" should receive a ".38 caliber in the head."

The final test of fame is to have a crazy person imagine he is you.

Anonymous

Everything suffers by translation except a bishop.

Lord Chesterfield

Conventionality is not morality. Self-righteousness is not religion.

Charlotte Bronte

Our word "macaroni" comes fromthe Italian *maccheroni*, meaning a mixture or a medley. European fashion leaders at the end of the eighteenth century were called macaronis (remember "Yankee Doodle"?) because of the eclectic and fanciful costumes they affected, which were often skin-tight. The fashion also dictated wigs topped with an immense knot of artificial hair.

Question: By what names are these people better known?

LaRaine Johnson
Peggy Middleton
Ruby Wallace
Alexandra Zuck
Henry Deutschendorf, Jr.

Greasy Thumb Guzik, who for a time was the head bookkeeper for Al Capone's rackets, was originally brought into the gangster's organization because Capone thought he had a great sense of humor. It turned out that Guzik's sense of humor was a pretty valuable asset as far as business was concerned, too.

Capone's showpiece was an establishment called the Four Deuces, which featured a speakeasy, two floors of gambling rooms, and a luxurious brothel. Down the street was a rival business, the Frolics Cafe. There was plenty of trade for both of them, but when the Frolics began a price war on liquor and women, they offended Capone's sensibilities. It was clear to his aides that Scarface would appreciate their efforts in taming the upstarts at the Frolics.

That's where Guzik's genius for sophisticated comedy came to the fore. One night, a patron was murdered at the Four Deuces. Greasy Thumb knew he had to get rid of the body, and figured it couldn't hurt to have some fun doing it. He had some of Capone's henchmen bundle up the corpse and stuff it down the furnace of the Frolics Cafe. Then he called the police and, pretending he was an irate citizen, complained vehemently that the Frolics was running an unlicensed, illegal crematory on the side. The cops didn't believe him at first, but he challenged them to do see for themselves. The police found the body, and once they'd closed the Frolics and torn it apart looking for more bodies (they found none) the Frolics had vanished forever.

My rackets are run strictly on American lines and they're going to stay that way!

Al Capone

A twenty-four-year-old Frenchman who called himself George Psalmanazar arrived in London in 1703 and became a celebrity overnight. It seems that, despite his Western features, he managed to pass himself off as a native of that far-away island, Formosa. A knowledge of Taiwan or the East in general was not particularly widespread in England at that time, even among the well-educated, and Psalmanazar convinced Oxford University to hire him as a professor. There he taught the language and the history of Formosa, both of which were entirely his own invention. He even wrote a popular book about his homeland, in which he claimed that his pagan countrymen (he was a Christian convert) ate raw meat regularly — and the flesh of executed criminals if they could get it; and each year sacrificed to their gods the hearts of 18,000 boys under the age of nine.

He maintained the hoax for many years, only admitting it on his deathbed in 1763, when, he said, he regretted what he had done.

Man is not incurably drowned — if he still knows he's all wet.

Charlie Chan

One of the first pseudo-unions in America was that of the boardinghouse-keepers in New York City. In 1824 they agreed that, in view of the high costs of living, they would henceforth supply only four prunes with each breakfast they served.

Answer: Laraine Day, Yvonne deCarlo, Ruby Dee, Sandra Dee, John Denver.

APRIL 21

Question: Which of these countries had the highest population density?
Singapore
China
Monaco
Belgium
Japan

Notable Births			
1818	Josh Billings	1909	Rollo May
1821	Charlotte Bronte	1915	Anthony Quinn
1838	John Muir	1926	Queen Elizabeth II

Notable Events

753 B.C.	Traditional date of the founding of Rome
1836	Battle of San Jacinto, Texas
1856	First train crossed Mississippi at Rock Island, Illinois
1857	Bustle patented by Alexander Douglas
1894	Over 136,000 coal miners went on strike in United States
1918	Red Baron shot down by Canadian Roy Brown
1930	Fire at Columbus, Ohio, penitentiary killed 320 men
1971	Death of Papa Doc Duvalier of Haiti

We don't owe the defeat of the Alamo defenders to General Antonio Lopez de Santa Anna as much as to the defenders themselves, but we do owe the invention of modern chewing gum at least partially to him.

Once, when he was in exile during one of Mexico's frequent political turmoils, Santa Anna rented a room on Staten Island. The general had a nervous habit of constantly chewing chicle, and he left his landlord with a large hunk of it when he moved on. The landlord was an inventive man and tried to make a rubber product of the chicle by boiling it and rolling it into sheets, but it didn't work. Falling back on Santa Anna's use of the chicle, he flavored it and cut it into strips instead.

Thus began the Thomas Adams Gum Company.

There is no partriotic art and no patriotic science.

Goethe

Twenty years ago, Mrs. Burl Carter was the proprietor of a family-owned furniture store in Hillisburg, Indiana. It seems that Mrs. Carter occasionally conducted her business transactions in a peculiar manner. For instance, she once accepted an old set of furniture as a down payment for a new set, and later bartered the traded-in pieces for a quart of gooseberries and three frogs' legs.

A typical Babe Ruth post-game snack consisted of six or seven sandwiches washed down with an equal number of beers or sodas. His pregame nourishment often included triple helpings of dinner, a quart of orange juice, and a fifth of gin.

After Queen Anne's death and the end of the Stuart line in 1714, Great Britain didn't have a monarch who was of predominantly English blood until the accession of Queen Elizabeth II in 1952. George I was three-quarters German by ancestry; George III, 31/32; Queen Victoria, 127/128; and Edward VII, 255/256.

England's Queen Anne bore nineteen children, none of whom survived childhood.

The technical manuals for the F-15 fighter bomber were recently revised by the air force. They are now written at a fifth-grade reading level because, officials say, they are likely to be used by Saudi-Arabian technicians.

The navy has not been so clever about its reasons for the simplification of the naval training manuals. They have been changed from a twelfth-grade reading level to eighth- and ninth-grade levels because, the navy freely admits, the average sailor is unable to comprehend anything more complex.

Why should we subsidize intellectual curiosity?

Ronald Reagan

In April 1951, Anna Swick of Pittsburgh was awarded a divorce from her husband. Among the grounds for divorce was Anna's charge that her spouse "was always trying to tattoo me so he could open a circus."

It helps to be somebody. When the wife of the former prime minister of England, Mrs. Stanley Baldwin,was visiting New York, she wanted to see the Futurama pavilion at the World's Fair, but she didn't want to stand in line. So Baldwin called the British Consulate, which called the British Embassy in Washington, which cabled the Foreign Office in London, which got in touch with the United States ambassador, Joseph Kennedy. Kennedy sent a cable directly to the General Motors building at the Fair. A press agent for GM then called Mrs. Baldwin at the Waldorf Hotel and told her to come right over.

I would rather be an opportunist and float than go to the bottom with my principlees around my neck.

Stanley Baldwin

Answer: Monaco.

APRIL 22

Notable Births

1451	Isabella I of Spain	1904	J. Robert Oppenheimer
1707	Henry Fielding	1908	Eddie Albert
1724	Immanuel Kant	1916	Yehudi Menuhin
1766	Mme. de Staël	1937	Jack Nicholson
1876	Ole Rolvaag	1938	Glen Campbell

Notable Events

1769 Madame Du Barry became official mistress of Louis XV
1793 Washington issued neutrality proclamation, then went to the circus — Philadelphia
1794 Capital punishment abolished in Pennsylvania except for first-degree murder
1884 Thomas Stevens left San Francisco on round-the-world bicycle trip
1931 James G. Ray landed autogyro on White House lawn
1953 Joseph O. Bowers became first black Catholic bishop consecrated in United States
1954 Army-McCarthy inquiries began
1964 New York World's Fair opened
1967 First Earth Day celebrations held

Most people believe that Queen Isabella financed Columbus's first voyage of discovery, and that it was an extraordinarily expensive undertaking. This was not so. Most of the money was contributed by Martin and Vincente Pinzon, brothers who supplied as well as captained the *Nina* and the *Pinto*. The *Santa Maria* was leased for the voyage. As chief captain, Columbus's salary was $300 a year, and the Pinzons each made $180. Wages for the crew members averaged $2.50 a month, and the price of feeding each crewman was less than 40 cents a week. The greatest single expense was $3,000 for the ships' cannon, and the total cost of the voyage was about $7,000.

⚜

This genius was less than five feet tall, and weighed less than a hundred pounds. His chest was concave, and he had a deformed shoulder, probably the result of malnutrition during childhood. Although he was brilliant (as a young boy at the University of Konigsberg his mathematics were outstanding), he was horribly dull as a professor. Because of this, it was fifteen years after he had joined Konigsberg's faculty before he was promoted from his lowly position of private lecturer.

He enjoyed company, but only of a certain kind and at a certain time. Morbidly afraid of illness of any sort, he endeavored to walk alone whenever possible, since he would then not have to talk to

Questions: What's the best way to keep fish from smelling?

A skunk, a frog, and a duck all went to the movies, but only two were let in. Which ones, and why? (Admission was a dollar).

anyone. Thus he would avoid breathing through his mouth, which would have invited all manner of coughs, colds, and pulmonary problems. One inside his house, he loved conversation, and he always had people for dinner. Although the guests were generally young men, this should not be misconstrued; it was his belief that robust young men were less likely to be sick than women were, and illness in anyone bothered him greatly.

He had a penchant for punctuality and regularity. He always kept his rooms at a healthful seventy-five degrees, always went to bed at ten, always arose at five, and always went for a walk at precisely three-thirty.

Medicine was a favorite interest of his, and he maintained the Brunonian theory that all disease resulted from either a lack or an abundance of stimuli. He was a contemporary of Jenner, but he had little faith in the doctor's notions of vaccination. He hated beer, and attributed a great many diseases to its use. He was also sure that the stocking garters of the fashionable impeded circulation and caused illnesses too numerous to mention, so he devised his own garters. They resembled a set of suspenders, which attached to his pockets, traveled the length of his legs under this trousers, and hooked to the top of his stockings. They didn't work very well.

He'd always been absent-minded, but as time went on, this condition grew more complicated. He realized that he continually repeated himself in conversations with friends, and so he drew up detailed notes for himself about what to say to whom, and when. Then he would lose the notes.

He began to develop elaborate theories about hows and whys. He believed, and proved to his own satisfaction, that an epidemic then ravaging the cat population of Europe was caused by the sinister evils lurking in electricity. He attributed his headaches to electricity, too.

There were some days when he found he could remember, word for word, lectures on science or poetry he'd heard years earlier. On the same day, he'd often find he couldn't remember what had happened the day before.

He began to doze uncontrollably. One time he woke up with his face in a candle and his nightcap on fire.

Overnight, a retinal hemorrhage took the sight of one eye, and his sight in the other quickly deteriorated. Soon he could recognize his friends only by their voices, and in time, he could not recognize them when they spoke, either — or even remember who they were when he was told their names. But there were days when he could still repeat *verbatim* a lecture on planetary motion he had heard in his youth.

He died a virgin, but this is not all that strange. His early life — sexless and eccentric — was a classic example of the way prodigies and geniuses often live. Nor is it that unusual that he degenerated as he did, for once again it was a classic example of the way prodigies and geniuses often seem to wither away once they reach middle age.

He was nearly 80 when he actually died. His deterioration was, in fact, a common example of cerebral arteriosclerosis (hardening of the arteries in the brain, if you will). That's what killed Immanuel Kant.

Answers: Cut off their noses.

The frog got in because he had a greenback; the duck got in because he had a bill; but the skunk did not, for he had only a scent, and it was a bad one.

APRIL 23

Question: Two chefs usually race to see which can turn out twelve dozen eclairs faster. One day the champion is late to work, and arrives just as his rival finishes eclair number twenty-one. If the champion makes eight eclairs for every six the other chef makes, will the champion still finish first and retain this title?

United States Movie Box Office Champs — 1932 - 1977.

Year	Actor	Actress
1932	Charles Farrell	Marie Dressler
1933	Will Rogers	Marie Dressler
1934	Will Rogers	Janet Gaynor
1935	Will Rogers	Shirley Temple
1936	Clark Gable	Shirley Temple
1937	Clark Gable	Shirley Temple
1938	Clark Gable	Shirley Temple
1939	Mickey Rooney	Shirley Temple
1940	Mickey Rooney	Bette Davis
1941	Mickey Rooney	Bette Davis
1942	Abbott & Costello	Betty Grable
1943	Bob Hope	Betty Grable
1944	Bing Crosby	Betty Grable
1945	Bing Crosby	Greer Garson
1946	Bing Crosby	Ingrid Bergman
1947	Bing Crosby	Betty Grable
1948	Bing Crosby	Betty Grable
1949	Bob Hope	Betty Grable
1950	John Wayne	Betty Grable
1951	John Wayne	Betty Grable
1952	Martin & Lewis	Doris Day
1953	Gary Cooper	Marilyn Monroe
1954	John Wayne	Marilyn Monroe
1955	James Stewart	Grace Kelly
1956	William Holden	Marilyn Monroe
1957	Rock Hudson	(*no actress in top ten stars*)
1958	Glenn Ford	Elizabeth Taylor
1959	Rock Hudson	Doris Day
1960	Rock Hudson	Doris Day
1961	Rock Hudson	Elizabeth Taylor
1962	Rock Hudson	Doris Day
1963	John Wayne	Doris Day
1964	Jack Lemmon	Doris Day
1965	Sean Connery	Doris Day
1966	Sean Connery	Julie Andrews
1967	Lee Marvin	Julie Andrews
1968	Sidney Poitier	Julie Andrews
1969	Paul Newman	Katharine Hepburn
1970	Paul Newman	Barbra Streisand
1971	John Wayne	Ali McGraw
1972	Clint Eastwood	Barbra Streisand
1973	Clint Eastwood	Barbra Streisand
1974	Robert Redford	Barbra Streisand
1975	Robert Redford	Barbra Streisand
1976	Robert Redford	Tatum O'Neal
1977	Sylvester Stallone	Diane Keaton

William Shakespeare drew up his entire will without mentioning his wife, Anne, once. He made provision for this two daughters, his sister, his three nephews, and a number of friends. Later, apparently as an afterthought, he added this bequest: "I give unto my wife my second best bed, with the furniture."

Notable Births

1564	William Shakespeare	1899	Vladimir Nabokov
1775	Joseph Turner	1914	Simone Simon
1791	James Buchanan	1921	Warren Spahn
1813	Stephen Douglas	1921	Janet Blair
1852	Edward Markham	1926	J.P. Donleavy
1891	Serge Prokofiev	1928	Shirley Temple

Notable Events

1896 First showing of a motion picture, New York City
1940 Dance hall fire in Natchez, Mississippi, killed 198 people
1945 Nicholas Murray Butler retired after 44 years at Columbia University
1954 Russia broke relations with Australia over Petrov incident
1954 Hank Aaron hit his first major league homer off Vic Raschi
1961 De Gaulle assumed "special powers" to deal with Algerian situation
1964 Ken Johnson of Houston Colts pitched no-hitter, lost to Reds 1-0

Old Eben Robey left Maine only once, to go to Boston on business. While he was there he decided to see his first movie. In the film there was a scene in which a number of young girls began to undress to go swimming. Before they got too far, however, a train crossed in front of them, and by the time it had passed, they were all in the water.

An usher who had noticed Eben at the matinee was surprised to see the old man still there at the nine o'clock show. He asked Eben why he'd stayed to see the movie six times through.

"Well," Eben drawled, "I figger that soonah or lateh that train is gonna be late."

Hee-ho-hum-Harry, I wish it was Saturday night.

— **Brian McMahon**

Why were colonial homes so often equipped with widow's walks even when they were out of sight of the ocean, or even hundreds of miles inland? The answer is that the so-called widow's walks were developed primarily as a platform from which a chimney fire could be more easily combated.

Answer: Yes.

APRIL 24

Notable Births

1815	Anthony Trollope	1905	Robert Penn Warren
1893	Leslie Howard	1934	Shirley MacLaine
1900	Elizabeth Goudge	1942	Barbra Streisand

Notable Events

1704 First issue of *Boston Newsletter*, first American newspaper
1792 Rouget de l'Isle composed "La Marseillaise," French national anthem
1814 British burned Washington
1833 Soda fountain patented
1888 First Kodak camera marketed
1895 Joshua Slocum completed first solo circumnavigation of earth by ship
1916 Sein Fein rebellion in Dublin
1933 In Chicago 5,000 teachers stormed banks for back pay

In the early eighteenth century, a teacher in Boston was paid about seven cents a day.

They'd been at it for *years*, but finally in 1948, a team of robbers managed to complete a tunnel running right up underneath the vault of the State Bank of Hamilton, in Washington. The only question in their minds was how much loot their extraordinary efforts would be rewarded with.

Not much. The bank had closed its doors in 1944.

Good idea not to accept gold medal until race is won.
Charlie Chan

The 1916 New York Giants set two baseball records that may never be broken. Early in the season they ran up a total of seventeen consecutive victories on the road, and in August and September they amassed twenty-six straight wins at home.

Despite these accomplishments, the team still managed to finish in fourth place.

In April 1948, in Wichita, Kansas, his girlfriend called twenty-year-old Dalton Fanning a coward. He said he wasn't. She told him to prove it, so he shot off the big toe on his right foot.

Question: By what names arethese people better known?

Rose Hovick
Norma Engstrom
Jeannette Morrison
Vivien Hartley
Vladimir Ulyanov

Dear you,

As I have time because I ain't busy, I thought I would write you the up-to-date news about six months old. We are both well as can be expected for the condition we are in. We ain't sick, just don't feel good. I am feeling fine but the neighbor died. Hope you are feeling the same.

I suppose you are anxious to hear about our moving. We never started to move until we left. We never turned off until we came to the crossroad that went there. It didn't take us any longer than from the time we started until we arrived. The trip was the best part of all. If you ever come over here, don't miss that. No one expected to see us until we arrived and most of the people we were acquainted with we know. The people we don't know seem like strangers. We still live in the same place we moved to last, which is beside our nearest neighbors across the road from the other side. Jim thinks we will stay here until we move or go somewhere else.

We are very busy farming three cows. We are going to sell one because we can't milk him. Eggs are a good price. That is the reason they are so high. I sure hope we get a lot of them. We just bought 25 roosters and an old hen. Some of the ground is so poor you can't raise an umbrella on it, but we have a fine crop of potatoes. Some the size of peas and then a lot of little ones. We also have a fine crop of corn. I think we will make about five gallons to the acre. Some worms got in our corn last year, but we fished them out and drank it anyway. Our romance started on a gallon of corn and ended with a full crib.

Our dog died last week. Jim said he swallowed a tape line and died by the inch. Mom said he went up the back alley and died by the yard. Sis said he crawled up under the bed and died by the foot.

My mother-in-law is sick and at death's door. Sure hope the doctor can pull her through. Jane fell off the back porch and bruised her somewhat, and skinned her elsewhere. Alice has the mumps and is having a swell time.

I have a photographic memory for news; I don't think anything will develop.

Every time Jim gets sick, he starts feeling bad; the doctor gave him some medicine and said if he gets better it might help him, and if he didn't get worse he would probably stay the same. I would have sent the $5 I owe you, but I already had this letter sealed before I thought about it. I am sending you an overcoat; I cut the buttons off so it wouldn't be so heavy — you will find them in the left-hand pocket. We are out of jelly, so I am sending Jim downtown for some of that traffic jam.

I am putting your address on the inside of the envelope so it won't rub off. I must close now . . . if you don't get to read this let me know and I will mail it to you. If you can't read my writing, make a copy of it and read your own.

Be sure and write — even if it's nothing but a check.

Love,

Me again

from *Urban Folklore from the Paperwork Empire*

Answer: Gypsy Rose Lee, Peggy Lee, Janet Leigh, Vivian Leigh, Vladimir Lenin.

APRIL 25

Question: Which of these countries do *not* share a boundary with West Germany?

Switzerland
Denmark
Czechoslovakia
Austria
Hungary
Italy

Notable Births

1599	Oliver Cromwell	1891	Ivor Brown
1873	Walter de la Mare	1918	Edward Fitzgerald
1874	Guglielmo Marconi	1940	Al Pacino

Notable Events

1862	New Orleans fell to Union troops
1920	Poland began offensive against Russia
1928	First Seeing Eye dog given to blind person
1945	UN parlay opened in San Francisco
1959	Saint Lawrence Seaway opened
1974	Democracy restored to Portugal in bloodless coup
1978	Supreme Court ruled against higher pension deductions for women

Between 1660 and 1960, the head of Oliver Cromwell was exhibited in various places in England as a tourist attraction. It was finally buried with the Lord Protector's remains three centuries after he died.

Canadian tax authorities received an anonymous letter in 1974 which read, in part: "I haven't been able to sleep since cheating on my income tax. I enclose a check for $50. If I am still unable to sleep, I will send you the balance."

The check, of course, had the man's name on it.

Our word "tragedy" has as its source a Greek word meaning "goat song." Pan, often depicted as half man, half goat, was associated with the theater as well as with goatherds and shepherds. Also, in early Greek theatrical productions, members of the chorus were clad in goatskins.

On April 25, 1769, the wife and daughter of the British ambassador to Turkey peeked out of an embassy window to see an Moslem procession, which was moving through the streets of Constantinople. For a woman to see the parade, especially an infidel woman, ran counter to the best traditions of Islam, and when this was discovered, the embassy was attacked by the Turks. The British managed to hold off the invaders for a time, but eventually they broke in, ransacked the building, and captured the two women. The wife was in the process of being strangled by the time the Turkish police arrived to quell the riot.

The British ambassador filed a heated protest. The Turkish grand vizier, to make amends for the women's ordeal, immediately sent them a rich present of jewels — and a bag containing the heads of the three principle rioters.

A little sincerity is a dangerous thing, and a great deal of it is absolutely fatal.

Oscar Wilde

April 25 is the feast day of Robigus, the Roman god of mildew. Each year on this day, Romans sought to appease him by the sacrifice of a red puppy, lest he hunger for their wheat.

A young Michigan man named Clem Sohn, who was known professionally as the Batman, was a top air-show performer during the 1930s. He developed an early, much smaller version of the present day hang glider, and thrilled international audiences with his amazing daring. At the height of twenty thousand feet, he would step out of an airplane and spread his arms and legs, which had zephyr cloth on a steel frame attached to them, and hurtle the three-and-a-half miles down to earth — banking, soaring, diving, and tumbling. Within a thousand feet from the ground, and only a few seconds away from impact, he'd pull his ripcord and parachute to a gentle landing.

Despite the risks involved and death-defying thrills Sohn's audiences experienced, he maintained he was never scared or even nervous. On April 25, 1937, he was interviewed before an air show in Vincennes, France, and told the reporter, "I feel as safe as you would in your grandmother's kitchen."

But even grandmother's kitchen can be perilous at times. Clem Sohn, an hour after the interview, suffered a failure of both his main and emergency parachutes and crashed to the ground before one hundred thousand horrified spectators. He was twenty-six.

Answer: Hungary and Italy.

Notable Births

1711	David Hume	1893	Anita Loos
1785	John James Audubon	1900	Conrad Richter
1798	Ferdinand Delacroix	1912	A.E. Van Vogt
1812	Alfred Krupp	1914	Bernard Malamud
1834	Artemus Ward	1916	Morris West
1856	Henry Morganthau	1930	Bruce J. Friedman
1890	Edgar Kennedy	1936	Carol Burnett

Notable Events

1865	First Confederate memorial day celebrated
1941	Nazis gained control of Greece
1944	Sewell Avery, president of Montgomery Ward, dragged from office for refusing to show company's books to government. Army seized them.
1959	Cuba invaded Panama
1964	Boston Celtics won 6th straight NBA championship
1964	Tanganyika and Zanzibar merged, became Tanzania
1978	Paul Revere's expense account sold to Malcolm Forbes for $70,000

Questions: How many legs does a horse have, and where are they located?

What would you do if you came home and found a horse in your bathtub?

The following are some guidelines for employees posted by a Boston carriage manufacturing concern in 1872. Although these rules primarily concerned with the office staff, it can be assumed their spirit was to be applied to manual workers as well.

1. Office employees will daily sweep the floors, dust the furniture, shelves, and showcases.
2. Each day fill lamps, clean chimneys, and trim wicks. Wash the windows once a week.
3. Each clerk will bring in a bucket of water and scuttle of coal for the day's business.
4. Make your pens carefully. You may whittle nibs to your individual taste.
5. This office will open at 7:00 A.M. and close at 8:00 P.M. except on the Sabbath, on which day we will remain closed. Each employee is expected to spend the Sabbath by attending church and contributing liberally to the cause of the Lord.
6. Men employees will be given an evening off each week for courting purposes, or two evenings a week if they go regularly to church.
7. After an employee has spent his 13 hours of labor in the office, he should spend the remaining time reading the Bible and other good books.
8. Every employee should lay aside from each pay a goodly sum of his earnings for his benefit during his declining years, so that he will not become a burden on society or his betters.
9. Any employee who smokes Spanish cigars, uses liquor in any form, or frequents pool and public halls, or gets shaved in a barber shop, will give me good reason to suspect his worth, intentions, integrity, and honesty.
10. The employee who has performed his labors faithfully without a fault for five years will be given an increase of five cents per day in his pay, providing profits from the business permit it.

The basketball dribble was first used by Bert Loomis in 1896.

Player sometimes disregard even most expert coaching from sidelines.

Charlie Chan

Answers: Six — forelegs in front, two legs behind.

Pull the plug out.

APRIL 27

Question: By what names are these people better known?

Mladen Seculovich
Dino Crocetti
Walter Matuschanskayasky
Emile Herzog

Ulysses S. Grant was once arrested for driving a spirited team of horses too fast. He is the only president of the United States to be arrested while in office.

A biographer of Edward Gibbon, author of *The Decline and Fall of the Roman Empire*, wrote thus of his peculiar suitability for the pursuit of scholarship: "Gibbon, as is well known, spent his life in celibacy, and was thus the better fitted for undertaking and carrying through a great literary work."

History is little more than the register of the crimes, follies, and misfortunes of mankind.

Edward Gibbon

In April 1951, Wesley Firemoon was arrested for drunk driving in Glascow, Montana. He gave the arresting officer this reason for the accident that led to his being charged, "I dimmed mine, but he didn't dim his." Firemoon had crashed through a roadside railing in broad daylight.

Man who fights law always loses; same as grasshopper is always wrong in argument with chicken.

Charlie Chan

Notable Births

1737	Edward Gibbon	1898	Ludwig Bemelmens
1791	Samuel F.B. Morse	1904	Arthur Burns
1820	Herbert Spencer	1927	Coretta King
1822	Ulysses S. Grant	1934	Anouk Aimée
1896	Rogers Hornsby	1937	Sandy Dennis

Notable Events

1865	Steamer *Sultana*'s boilers exploded on Mississippi River, 1,450 dead
1897	Grant's Tomb dedicated
1917	Mining disaster killed 121 in Hastings, Colorado
1937	Guernica destroyed in Spanish Civil War
1938	Goering required Jews to list assets, empowered himself to use them
1938	King Zog married
1960	Togo independence
1960	South Korean President Rhee resigned in wake of "rigged" election scandal
1974	First International Menstrual Extraction Conference held, San Francisco

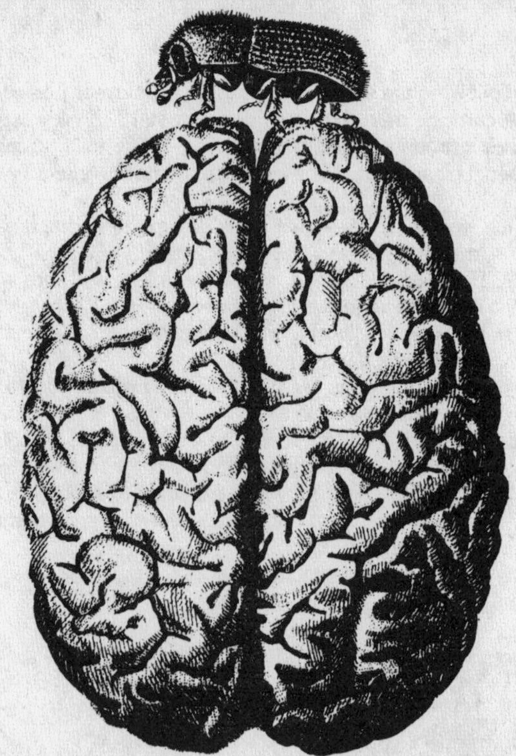

It has been reported that a bug weighing 1½ ounces was found in the brain of the Roman general Titus after his death.

Epitaph on a Tombstone in East Haddam, Connecticut:

Sacred to the Memory
of Amasa Brainard, Jr.
Son of Lieut. Amasa and Mrs.
Jedidah Brainard who
received a mortal wound on his head
by the falling of a weight from the Bell
on Sunday ye 22nd of Apl, 1798
as he was about to enter the Church to attend a divine worship
Who Departed this life
April 27th in ye 20th Year of his Age.

Answer: Karl Malden, Dean Martin, Walter Matthau, André Maurois.

Notable Births

1753	James Monroe	1926	Harper Lee
1874	Sidney Tolar	1933	Carolyn Jones
1878	Lionel Barrymore	1941	Ann-Margret

Notable Events

1772 Danish counts Struensee and Brandt executed for cuckolding Christian VII
1789 Mutiny on the *Bounty*
1862 First U.S. citizen hanged for treason, W.B. Mumford, New Orleans
1914 Mine collapse in Eccles, West Virginia, killed 181 men
1936 Accession of King Farouk
1945 Mussolini executed at Lake Como
1952 War with Japan formally ended
1968 U.S. troops invaded Dominican Republican
1969 De Gaulle resigned as French premier

I was a gangster for Wall Street: I helped make Mexico and especially Tampico safe for American oil interests in 1914; I helped make Haiti and Cuba a decent place for the National City Bank boys to collect revenue in; I helped purify Nicaragua for the international banking house of Brown Bros. in 1909-12; I brought light to the Dominican Republic for American sugar interests in 1916; and I helped make Honduras "right" for American fruit companies in 1903.

General Smedley Butler

We Americans have no commission from God to police the world.

Benjamin Harrison

Hands acrost th' sea and into some man's pocket.

Mr. Dooley (Finely Peter Dunne)

One Gibbon Hedley, of Teesdale, England, upon discovering several years ago that he was being cuckolded, determined he would end his life and that of his wife's lover. He constructed a bomb, attached it to his body, and went out in search of the man who had wronged him. He found him and set off the bomb, but the explosion killed neither man. Undeterred, Hedley crawled over to where his foe lay and strangled him to death.

Of all the tyrants the world affords,
Our own affections are the fiercest lords.

Earl of Sterling

As late as 1960, flogging was still occasionally used as a form of punishment for criminals in England. The transgressor would be put on an apparatus known as the Triangle. His feet would be strapped to the base of the Triangle's rear legs, his torso bent over it, and then his hands secured by straps to the front legs of the machine. He would then be stripped for the flogger, who was screened from the victim's view by a canvas blind. About twelve lashes were inflicted, for which the flogger received two shillings and six pence. A doctor, who was always kept in attendance, would fit a special protective pad on the criminal's buttocks and then return him to his cell. It was usually several days before the floggee could sit down or even wear trousers without pain.

Question: Put a different mathematical symbol between each of the five 8s so their total equals 8.

8 8 8 8 8=8

Can you make another correct equation using only two different mathematical symbols? Can you make yet another correct equation using a different pair of mathematical symbols?

Eric Mackey was despondent in April 1945. *Nothing* in his life was going right, so he decided to end it all. He slashed his wrists. He drank a bottle of disinfectant. He jumped from a seventh-story window.

He lived.

The world gets better every day — then worse again in the evening.

Kin Hubbard

Suicide is belated acquiescence to the opinion of one's wife's relatives.

H. L. Mencken

Failure has gone to his head.

Wilson Mizner

At the Seven Days campaign of the Civil War, the Confederate Army used a balloon to reconnoitre Union positions — a balloon made from the silk petticoats of patriotic southern belles. Unfortunately, when the bag was later being transported on the James River, the boat carrying it ran aground, and was captured by the Union Army. General Longstreet said of the taking of the petticoats by the Northerners, "This capture was the meanest trick of the war and one I have never forgiven."

On April 28, 1772, the first goat known to have circumnavigated the globe twice died. She sailed first on the *Dolphin* under a Captain Willis, and after on the *Endeavour*, under the famous Captain James Cook. Her name has long since been lost.

In 1911, Bobby Leach went over Niagara Falls in a barrel and came out of the roaring surge below with nary a scratch. He died on April 28, 1926, from injuries he received when he slipped on a banana peel.

Answer: 8÷8×8–8+8=8

8–8+8–8+8=8

8÷8×8÷8×8=8

APRIL 29

Questions: Whenever a cat enters a room it will first look to one side, then the other. Do you know why?

Horses are practically unique among animals in the manner in which they eat. Do you know why?

Notable Births

1745	Oliver Ellsworth	1919	Celeste Holm
1863	William Randolph Hearst	1933	Rod McKuen
1879	Sir Thomas Beecham	1934	Luis Aparicio
1899	Duke Ellington	1936	Zubin Mehta
1901	Emperor Hirohito	1947	Johnny Miller

Notable Events

1861	Maryland rejected secession
1879	Alexander of Battenberg elected prince of Bulgaria
1894	Coxey's Army marched on Washington
1918	First victory of air ace Eddie Rickenbacker
1945	Suicide of Hitler
1952	Truman's seizure of steel industry ruled unconstitutional
1978	California Supreme Court ruled host can be responsible for damage done by drunken guests

Until the late nineteenth century, Chinese custom and law prescribed an unusual form of revenge for an individual who felt he had been wronged by another man. He did not take the defendant to court, destroy his property, or harm him physically — he simply killed himself at his adversary's house. Traditionally and legally, the Chinese put the guilt of the death on the man responsible for the wrong, not the suicide himself, and the survivor was arrested preemptorily for murder. Most often an out-of-court settlement would be reached between the accused man and the suicide's family, which not infrequently made a rich family poor and vice versa. The practice finally died out when suicide became an obvious act of greed rather than of honor, and was milking too many wealthy Chinese of too much money.

There are many who dare not kill themselves for fear of what the neighbors will say.

Cyril Connolly

On this date in 4166 B.C., according to fundamentalist British biblical historians, Noah's Ark came to rest upon Mount Ararat.

According to W.W. Chambers, the "million dollar mortician" of Washington, D.C., who became a stool pigeon in a government investigation of funeral practices some three decades ago, a human being could be embalmed with 40 cents-worth of materials, while an elephant would have cost $1.50. The average price of embalming in the United States at the time was about $100.

Visitors to the Ueno Zoo in Tokyo on "be kind to animals" day in 1949 fed a favorite giraffe so much he ate himself to death.

Moles in their tunnels can move about equally quickly forward and backward. Part of this is thanks to the fact that their fur has no grain, and so doesn't lie back as other animals' coats do.

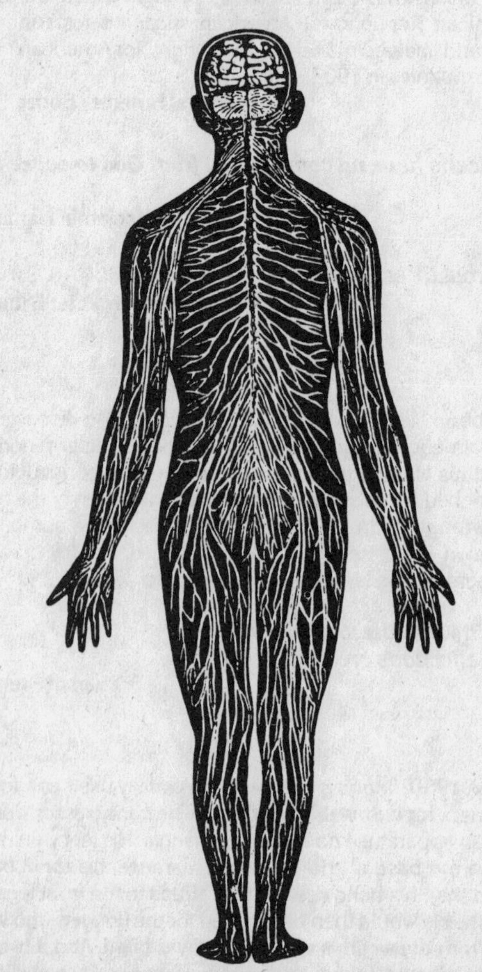

The circulatory system of the human body contains about sixty thousand miles of blood vessels and capillaries, twenty-five billion white blood cells, and twenty-five trillion red cells. The total surface area of the capillaries is about 1½ acres.

Answers: Because a cat can't look in both directions at once.

Horses only eat when they don't have a bit in their mouths.

APRIL 30

Notable Births

1812	Kaspar Hauser	1912	Eve Arden
1877	Alice B. Toklas	1926	Cloris Leachman
1909	Queen Juliana	1946	Don Schollander

Notable Events

1789	Washington inaugurated
1803	Louisiana Purchase made
1936	Selassie vowed Ethiopia would fight to last man against Italy
1937	Franco's flagship sunk by Loyalist plane, 700 drowned
1939	New York World's Fair opened
1947	Boulder Dam's name changed back to Hoover Dam
1973	Nixon insisted aids innocent, but Dean, Haldeman, Ehrlichman left posts
1975	South Vietnam surrendered to North

Question: Given modern travel conditions, which two of the following people could have met?

Lucrezia Borgia
Kublai Khan
Martin Luther
Giovanni Casanova

On May 26, 1828, a bewildered young boy was found wandering in the streets of Nuremburg, Germany. In the 150 years since then, movies, plays, and scores of books have featured him, but no one knows who he was or where he came from.

When the young man was discovered, he had with him a note directing him to the captain of the Sixth Cavalry. The officer read the letter the young man had brought with him and was puzzled by it, but when he questioned the young man, all he replied was "from Regensburg" and, "I don't know." The letter explained that the boy's name was Kaspar Hauser, that he had been born on April 30, 1812, and that his father had been a member of the Sixth Regiment. He had been left on the doorstep of a poor laborer by an unknown woman, with a note requesting he be brought up by the man (despite the fact that he had ten children already). The kind-hearted man had done so, but secretly, and Kaspar had never been out of the house until a few days before he was discovered in Nuremburg. Now, said the note, the boy had been taught to read and write, and had learnt the basic principles of Christianity; and so Kaspar looked forward to becoming a cavalry soldier like his father.

This was all very strange, and the captain called in the authorities. A search for Kaspar's "benefactor" was initiated while the officials investigated his curious history. They discovered that the young boy was ignorant of almost everything he saw around him, and that, contrary to the letter, he could only write his name, could not read at all, and spoke only a few words in an old Bavarian dialect. The condition of his feet showed he had never worn shoes. Except for bread and water, he would eat nothing at all.

The search for his guardians was fruitless, and after a time Kaspar was given over to one Professor Daumer. Kaspar learned quickly at first, but then his intellect dulled. Once he learned to speak he described his life quite differently from the account in the letter. All his life, he said, he had been caged underground in a room so small he could neither stand up nor stretch out straight, and he was often kept in chains. He had never eaten anything but bread and water, which had been brought to his cell while he slept. It had only been several weeks before his discovery in Nuremburg that a man, unseen by him, had taught him to walk, write his name, and say the few words he knew. Except for a small bed of straw, the only items his quarters had contained were two small wooden toy horses, and before Nuremburg, he had never seen another human face. This was all he knew.

Daumer eventually taught the boy enough so he was able to work in an appeals court office, but he could never progress very far.

On December 14, 1833, Hauser received a note from an anonymous stranger claiming he had news from Lord Stanhope, a British nobleman, about the circumstances of Kaspar's birth. Kaspar went to the palace garden to meet the stranger at three that afternoon, but no sooner had he introduced himself than he was stabbed by the unknown assailant. He died three days later.

Kaspar's murderer was never caught, nor was his origin ever explained. It is possible that he was the child of a nun or a priest, or perhaps the illegitimate son of an English nobleman. It is doubtful we'll ever know. During his life, except for some brief storms of publicity following his discovery and death, he was almost a nonbeing; but his claim to be a true child of innocence has inspired hundreds of artists and writers, and is responsible for some of the finest creative achievements of the modern world.

The famous Princeton Tiger Cheer (Tiger! Tiger! Tiger! Sis! Sis! Sis! Boom! Boom! Boom! Ah!) was the invention of an unknown non-student, a soldier. When New York's Seventh Regiment passed through Princeton on April 30, 1861, on its was to the Civil War front, an infantryman, very possibly in his cups, concocted the yell as a marching cadence while his company strode past the campus. Students watching the procession picked it up from the soldiers, and it caught on.

Answer: Lucrezia Borgia and Martin Luther.

Early in 1940, a Cuban postman named Felix Carvajal resolved to win the marathon at the Olympic Games, which were being held at Saint Louis later that year. It was a strange goal. Carvajal had never run in a competitive race, and had never been a long distance runner — and the country of Cuba was not even officially sponsoring an Olympic team. But that was what Carvajal decided, and he followed through on it. He began to train in earnest; and to earn money for his transportation he solicited pledges and contributions as he ran around a square in downtown Havana. He got in shape and finally had the money he needed.

Carvajal boarded a boat for New Orleans, got off, and was promptly robbed. Without friends to pay his passage, no money to buy food, and little English at his command, Carvajal nevertheless started off for Saint Louis, 700 miles away.

He arrived a fortnight later, just as the race was about to get underway, having walked and run all morning. He was wearing heavy shoes, long pants, and a long-sleeved shirt. A pair of scissors was produced, and Felix got a makeshift track suit cut from the clothes on his back, but the street shoes remained.

The gun sounded, and the little Cuban was in his first race — an Olympic marathon, a contest he had already traveled over 700 miles by foot to get to.

And if you've guessed this remarkable man performed a sports miracle and won this, the greatest of all races, unfortunately you're wrong. He finished fourth in a field of thirty-one.

Officially, the United States is still at war with Germany and Japan. An armistice was signed with the two Axis powers; but a formal peace treaty was never made.

Despite all the wonderful names the Puritan settlers of New England came up with for themselves, none of the immigrants on the *Mayflower* had a middle name.

The inside of a cucumber holds heat so well that it is sometimes twenty degrees warmer than the outside temperature. That's cool, for a cucumber!

In the eighteenth century, medical quackery was rampant in England. Though it would seem that "snake-oil" salesmen congregated on every corner, their advertisements often made a point of directing would-be clients very, very carefully to their doors. This advertisement for one such physician appeared in a London newspaper of the 1770s.

> In the Strand, over against the Maypole, on the left Hand coming from Temple-Bar, at the Sign of the Golden Cross, between a Sword Cuttlers and a Milliner's Shop, the Sign of the Sugar Loaf and Barber's Pole, within four Doors of the Mitre Tavern: Where you may see a large Red coloured Lanthorn, with Eleven Candles in it; and a white Sign written upon with red Letters DUTCH DOCTOR, Licensed by his most Excellent Majesty: and a long Entry with a Hatch and a Knocker on it. Where you may come in privately, and speak with him, and need not be ashamed, he having not any in his House but himself and his Family.

As a teenager, Teddy Roosevelt broke an arm, a shoulder, a wrist, a leg, several ribs, and his nose in a series of accidents.

On March 21, 1852, a horse named Black Swan won a nine-mile-long endurance race in Los Angeles. The winner's purse, in addition to $25,000 in gold, included a thousand horses, a thousand cattle, and 500 sheep.

A Paris-to-Madrid auto race in 1903 had to be called off before it was even half over because of the carnage it had already caused. The masses of people who lined the French portion of the route were so excited by the event, and so unfamiliar with automobiles, that they swarmed all over the roads before the oncoming drivers. By the time the lead car had gone but 343 miles of the 870-mile route, 550 people had been killed and thousands injured by the 216 autos in the competition.

Occasionally, one hears about a football player who gets turned around on the field and ends up scoring a touchdown against his own team. Snooks Dowd of Lehigh University did that one better in 1934. Against their traditional rival, Lafayette, Lehigh was within the opponent's ten-yard line when the call went to Dowd. He got the ball, took a hard hit, and was spun around and almost knocked himself out. He took off for the other goal line, both teams in hot pursuit. Dowd "came to" just as he crossed Lehigh's own goal, realized his mistake, and started back upfield. Snooks managed to avoid the stunned Lafayette tacklers and ended up across their goal line — for a TD run of under 10 yards officially, but one that actually covered over 200.

Cleveland Indians pitcher Bob Feller was pretty new to the major leagues in 1939, and his mother had never seen him pitch in the big leagues. As a Mother's Day present that year, the young Feller paid for her transportation from the family farm in Iowa to see him pitch against the Chicago White Sox in the Windy City.

Only a few innings into the game, a Chicago batter fouled one of Feller's pitches behind home plate. Of 45,000 people in the park that day, the ball struck Mrs. Feller. It knocked her unconscious, and she had to be taken to the hospital by ambulance.

Happy Mother's Day!

Gemini (The Twins)
May 22 through June 21

MAY

MAY 1

Question: What language and what day of the week are each of the following?
Dimanche
mercoledi
lunes
Mittwoch

Frogs' legs have been a culinary joke for a long time, and by now everyone knows they taste like chicken. They have enjoyed great popularity, however. In the late 1930s sixty million frogs' legs were consumed annually in New York City restaurants, thirty six million in Chicago eateries, and about sixteen million each in San Francisco, Los Angeles, and New Orleans.

May 1, 1707, was a remarkable day for James, second Duke of Queensbury. Sent by the King of England to Edinburgh several years before to work out a plan of union with Scotland, he was at last successful, and the treaty became official on that day. He took all but two members of his family and household staff to the ceremonies, leaving behind only a small servant boy to turn the roast over the fire, and his eldest son, James, who almost never left his room.

The celebration went as planned, and there was much congratulating and hand-shaking all around. The only bad moment of the day for the duke came when he returned to his house from the festivities to find that the young James had replaced the roast on the spit with the servant boy, cooked the child, and then started to eat him. It certainly explained why the young man was not asked to go along to the party.

Good manners are up of petty sacrifices.
Ralph Waldo Emerson

Answer: French: Sunday
Italian: Wednesday
Spanish: Monday
German: Wednesday

Notable Births

1672	Joseph Addison	1923	Joseph Heller
1825	George Inness	1926	Terry Southern
1847	Henry Ford	1929	Audrey Hepburn
1909	Kate Smith	1939	Judy Collins
1912	Winthrop Rockefeller	1939	Frank Beard
1916	Glenn Ford	1960	Steve Cauthen

Notable Events

305	Roman Emperor Diocletian abdicated
1045	Benedict IX sold papacy to Gregory VI
1695	Britain began to tax births
1751	First American cricket tournament held, New York City
1863	Battle of Chancellorsville began
1872	First U.S. postcard issued
1893	Kapok introduced
1898	Battle of Manila Bay
1931	First American Baha'i Temple opened, Wilmette, Illinois
1960	Francis Gary Powers' U-2 spy plane shot down over Russia
1961	Nkrumah assumed dictatorial powers in Ghana

The song "Tom Dooley," made famous twenty years ago by the Kingston Trio, was written by Dooley himself a few days before he was hanged for murder.

Tom *Dula* grew up in the wild woods of Wilkes County, N.C., an area which was known for its lawlessness and unlicensed sexuality during his time. After the Civil War, Dula returned from his Confederate unit and resumed his ante-bellum occupation, womanizing. For a time he courted Laura Foster, described as being "wild as a buck"; but then he met Anne Melton, chief beauty of the region. Things went well for Tom and Anne until he discovered he'd contracted a venereal disease from Laura. He vowed revenge, and conspired with Anne to murder her.

They dug a shallow grave on a remote mountainside, and Tom lured Laura to it by telling her he was taking her to the next county to be married. Stopping near the gravesite, Tom gave her a drink and then offered to wipe her mouth with his handkerchief. Instead, he jammed it down her throat as Anne rushed from the bushes and stabbed her in the stomach.

When Laura's body was discovered six weeks later, both Dula and Melton were arrested. His trial lasted for two years, and Tom steadfastly refused to admit that Anne had had anything to do with the murder. On the gallows he announced one final time that he alone was responsible for the murder of Laura Foster, but most researchers believe that he was protecting his lover, and that he felt that Anne's neck was "just too pretty to stretch hemp." Some reporters at the time thought the all-male jury at the trial felt the same way.

At 2:17 p.m.,on May Day, 1868, the trap dropped and the career of "Tom Dooley" as a songwriter was over, less than a week after it had begun.

It is hard to believe that a man is telling the truth when you know that you would lie if you were in his place.
H.L. Mencken

At two strokes per second, it would take 91 years to ring the changes on a carillon of twelve bells. To ring them on a fourteen-bell carillon would take 16,575 years, and on one of twenty-four bells, 117,000,000,000,000,000 years.

Notable Births

1551	William Camden	1904	Bing Crosby
1859	Jerome K. Jerome	1922	Satyajat Ray
1902	Brian Aherne	1924	Theodore Bikel
1903	Benjamin Spock	1935	King Hussein

Notable Events

1670 Hudson Bay Company chartered
1733 Eclipse in northern Europe
1829 One foot of hail fell in Tuscaloosa, Alabama
1863 Stonewall Jackson shot by mistake by own men
1865 New York City inaugurated nation's first paid fire department
1939 Lou Gehrig's consecutive games streak ended; replaced by Babe Dahlgrer
1945 Fall of Berlin
1958 Eisenhower proposed demilitarization of Antarctic
1960 Caryl Chessman gassed after 8 stays of execution

Many people, among them the Irish and the Chinese, have dressed small boys as girls in an attempt to deceive evil spirits, believing that the spirits would not be interested in harming a "worthless" female child.

I wish I could change my sex as I change my shirt.

André Breton

The first European settlers brought with them a number of diseases to which the native Americans had no immunity. Smallpox, tuberculosis, viral pneumonia, and measles devastated many tribes. The Puritans felt that God was punishing the Indians for their pagan ways by visiting these plagues upon them.

God had a divine purpose in placing this land between two great oceans to be found by those who had a special love of freedom and courage.

Ronald Reagan

The *coco-de-mer,* or sea coconut, is the product of a certain palm tree that grows in Java and the Seychelle and Maldive Islands. In Europe it was long felt that goblets fashioned from coconuts neutralized any poison that might have been surreptitiously mixed with the goblet's contents. For this reason, and because of their scarcity, they were extremely valuable, especially before the days of extensive sea trade. Whole ships were traded for a single coconut, and as late as 1759 an exceptional specimen weighing nearly fifty pounds was sold for £400 in England. In that same year, Rudolph II of Germany offered a similar price for a coconut he particularly wanted.

In proportion to their numbers, about twice as many American Indians are color-blind as are Eskimos. Blacks are twice as likely to be color-blind as Indians, and whites are twice as likely to suffer from this as blacks are. Some quick math reveals that whites have this infirmity eight times as often as Eskimos.

Question: A man standing next to a shop had only a five-dollar bill, but he needed eight dollars to buy a bus ticket home. He got it. How?

Trials of animals (see March 22) didn't stop after 1740, and they didn't just happen in France. In May 1941, the attorney general of Colorado, Gail Ireland, ruled that a vicious dog was entitled to a jury trial before being condemned to death.

A favored formal greeting in Egypt translated into English as, "How are you sweating?" Understandably, in Egypt's climate, a person who is not sweating well is apt to feel poorly.

In 1778, fashionable Parisian women never went out in blustery weather without a lightning rod attached to their hats.

Answer: The shop was a pawn shop. He pawned the bill for $4, then sold the pawn ticket to a friend for $4.

MAY 3

Question: Can you move only three of the bowling pins and create an equilateral triangle that points straight up?

```
7   8   9   10
  4   5   6
    2   3
      1
```

Notable Births			
1469	Niccolo Machiavelli	1912	May Sarton
1849	Jacob Riis	1913	William Inge
1898	Golda Meir	1919	Pete Seeger
1902	Walter Slezak	1919	Betty Comden
1906	Mary Astor	1920	Sugar Ray Robinson
1907	Earl Wilson	1939	Samantha Eggar

Notable Events	
1654	Nation's first toll bridge opened, Rowley, Massachusetts
1715	Solar eclipse in northern Europe
1765	First medical school in country opened, University of Pennsylvania
1791	Polish constitution adopted
1841	New Zealand formally pronounced a British colony
1911	Lloyd George introduced national health insurance bill in Britain
1937	Wallis Simpson divorced

In 1843, Countess Roza Branicka of Poland went to Germany for medical advice. Doctors there told her she had breast cancer and advised immediate surgery. The countess didn't want to alarm her family, however, and refused the operation. Instead, as she traveled through Europe later that year, the sixty three-year-old woman stopped at several surgical suppliers and bought the equipment necessary for a masectomy. She then locked herself in a hotel room in Paris and performed the operation on herself. The countess successfully removed the tumor and recovered completely, living for nearly twenty years afterwards.

In May 1941, a prostitute filed for workman's compensation for injuries she received while feeding the house dog on the orders of her madame. The claim was made in the tiny (population about eighty) hamlet of Spread Eagle, in northeastern Wisconsin.

My method is basically the same as Masters and Johnson, only they charge thousands of dollars and it's called therapy. I charge fifty dollars and it's called prostitution.

Xaviera Hollander

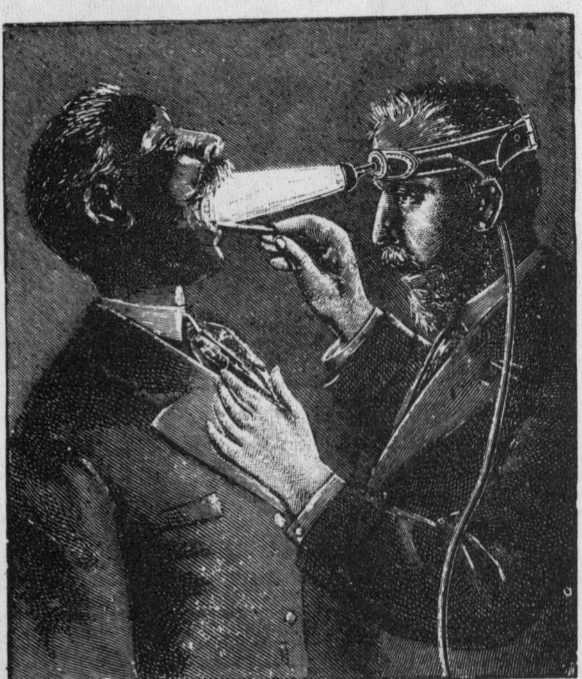

It hasn't always cost sixty dollars an hour for a psychiatrist. The Greek physician Philodotus was called upon to treat his king, who was convinced he was headless. The ancient doctor simply put a lead cap on the monarch's head and directed the king's attention to its weight. The king realized immediately that since he felt the weight on his head, he must indeed have a head, and was cured of his delusion.

A woman in England, who was convinced she had a snake in her stomach, was made to vomit by her doctor. The medical man surreptitiously introduced a serpent into the vomit and the woman immediately stopped being anxious about her digestion.

An Italian named Senes was afraid to urinate for fear he'd drown the whole town. The physician arranged to have the town's fire bell rung and then ordered Senes to make water, lest the town perish. The man did, and believed to his death that he had saved everyone from a terrible conflagration.

An English doctor once had a patient who believed his nose was so long that he would knock down a wall with it if he moved. The doctor gripped the man's nose in a vice of his thumb and forefinger, yanked, and then showed the patient his thumb between the doctor's fisted fingers. The man was convinced, and the size of his nose no longer bothered him.

A physician named Forestus treated a man who believed himself to be dead by having a second man lie next to him and also pretend to dead. Food and drink were then brought to the second man, who rose up and took nourishment. When the patient asked the other man if dead people really ate and drank he was assured they did. He then took some food himself and was cured immediately.

A neurotic is a man who builds a castle in the air. A psychotic is the man who lives in it. A psychiatrist is the man who collects the rent.

Jerome Lawrence

Psychiatrist — a person who pulls habits out of rats.

Douglas Bush

Answer:

```
      1
    8   9
  4   5   6
7   2   3   10
```

MAY 4

Notable Births

1796	W.H. Prescott	1864	Richard Hovey
1796	Horace Mann	1919	Heloise
1825	Thomas H. Huxley	1936	El Cordobes

Notable Events

1776 Rhode Island declared independence
1863 New Maori uprisings began in New Zealand
1886 Haymarket riots in Chicago
1897 Fire at charity bazaar in Paris killed 150 people
1949 Plane crash in Tunisia killed Italian championship soccer team
1961 Stratolab High 5 balloon reached 113,500′; Prather died in ocean recovery attempt

When a dog turns around and around in a circle before lying down, it's an indication that he hasn't lost the instincts of the wild, despite thousands of years of domestication. The dog's ancestral habitat was the grassland, and the turning instinct developed from the desire for a comfortable bed. By circling, the dog flattened the grass and made a soft mattress, at the same time hiding himself from his enemies.

The average surface temperature of the earth is fifty-seven degrees Fahrenheit. About 29 percent of the earth's surface is land, and a quarter of this is used for grazing. The average size of all living things is smaller than a common housefly.

The derogatory term "Frog" is at least a thousand years old. About 1000 A.D., the village of Paris (then called Lutetia) was on low, poorly drained land, only little better than a swamp. Such locations normally harbor frogs, and so the residents of the region were named "Frogs," *grenouilles* in French. Later this was used to characterize all Frenchmen.

As of 1940, Earle W. Graser, radio's Lone Ranger, had never been west of Michigan and had only fired a gun once. On one occasion, he entered a nightclub contest to see who could yell, "Hi ho, Silver!" most like the Lone Ranger. He didn't even place.

Anybody can win — unless there happens to be a second entry.

George Ade

Decades ago, the United States Department of the Interior had an office called the Washington Biological Survey, whose responsibility it was to collect data on the migrations of birds. The agency tagged the birds with metal templates reading "Wash. Biol. Surv," followed by the agency's address.

Apparently, the abbreviation was not as clear as it might have been. One Arkansan wrote to them: "Dear Sirs: I shot one of your crows the other day. My wife followed the cooking instructions on the leg tag, and I want to tell you that bird tasted just terrible!"

By the way, crows are not noted for their culinary virtues, no matter how they're cooked. That's why when you have to swallow your own words you "eat crow."

Question: A soldier on a forced march traveled four miles an hour for eight hours. How many feet did he move?

Some Unique Ordinances from New England

In Boston, Massachusetts, it is illegal to swim within sight of any building; a man cannot escort his family to church without carrying a musket; and a hotel must provide bed and board for a man's horse.

In Quincy, Massachusetts, you may not legally roller skate on any city street; or expose yourself to the sun while bathing.

In Truro, Massachusetts, a man may not marry until he has killed six regular birds or three blackbirds. Throughout Massachusetts, bearded men must pay a goatee tax; it is illegal to eat peanuts in church; and jackasses may not be driven faster than seven mph.

In Coddle, Vermont, a chicken may not appear at a matinee, and all carriage wheels must be made entirely of lampwicks. Throughout Vermont it's illegal to whistle underwater.

In Waterville, Maine, you can go to jail for blowing your nose in public. Throughout Maine it's illegal to walk down a public thoroughfare with your shoes untied.

And in New Hampshire there's a traffic regulation that states quite specifically that when two motorists meet at an intersection, each must remain stationary until the other has gone.

"The law, Sir, is an ass!" So says Mr. Bumble in *Oliver Twist*.

Answer: Two feet — his own.

MAY 5

Question: Margie opened a stand on the boardwalk. During her first week she sold $74.80 of glow-in-the-dark bedroom slippers, taking a 12 percent loss. She also sold $78.40 worth of glow-in-the-dark bedspreads on which she made a 12 percent profit. In total, how much money did she make or lose on these two items?

The following announcement was published in the *North Adams* (Massachusetts) *Transcript*, in May 1941:

> Betsy Earle's parents wish to announce that she is suffering from a severe case of worms, and they urgently urge that, in the interests of her continued good health, the townspeople discontinue the practice of feeding her candy.

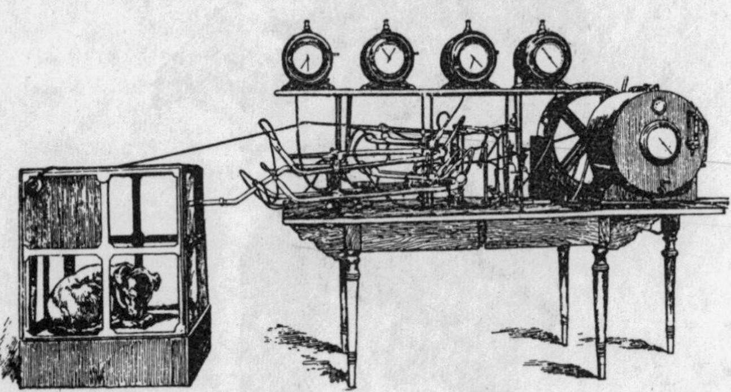

BASIC PRECEPTS OF SCIENCE

MURPHY'S LAW: If anything can go wrong, it will.
PATRICK'S THEOREM: If the experiment works, you must be using the wrong equipment.
SKINNER'S CONSTANT: That quantity which, when multiplied times, divided into, added to, or subtracted from the answer you got, gives the answer you should have gotten.
HORNER'S FIVE THUMB POSTULATE: Experience varies directly with equipment ruined.
FLAGLE'S LAW OF THE PERVERSITY OF INANIMATE OBJECTS: Any inanimate object, regardless of its composition or configuration, may be expected to perform at any time in a totally unexpected manner for reasons that are either totally obscure or completely mysterious.
ALLEN'S AXIOM: When all else fails, read the instructions.
THE SPARE PARTS PRINCIPLE: The accessibility, during recovery, of small parts which fall from the workbench, varies directly with the size of the part . . . and inversely with its importance to the completion of the work underway.
THE COMPENSATION COROLLARY: The experiment may be considered a success if no more than 50 percent of the observed measurements must be discarded to obtain a correspondence with theory.
GUMPERSON'S LAW: The probability of a given event occurring is inversely proportional to its desirability.
THE ORDERING PRINCIPLE: Those supplies necessary for yesterday's experiment must be ordered not later than tomorrow noon.
THE ULTIMATE PRINCIPLE: By definition, when you are investigating the unknown, you do not know what you will find.
THE FUTILITY FACTOR: No expriment is ever a complete failure . . . it can always serve as a bad example.

from *Urban Folklore from the Paperwork Empire*

Notable Births

1813	Soren Kierkegaard	1914	Tyrone Power
1818	Karl Marx	1915	Alice Faye
1899	Freeman Gosden	1934	Don Buddin
1900	Adlai Stevenson	1937	Pat Carroll

Notable Events

840	Eclipse recorded in France
1779	Arnold began treasonable correspondence with Sir Henry Clinton
1864	Battle of the Wilderness began
1936	Screw-top bottle with pourable lip patented
1936	Italians victorious in Ethiopia
1953	Death of Stalin
1955	West Germany became sovereign
1961	Alan Shepard became first American in space
1964	Harold Stassen got 25 percent of vote in Indiana primary

The Reverend Francis Henry Egerton,who was also the Earl of Bridgewater, greatly amused Parisians in the third decade of the nineteenth century. Egerton believed himself to be a man of the utmost breeding, and went out of his way to ensure that every action was a model of decorum. If he lent or borrowed a book, he would always send for or return it in a carriage pulled by two fine horses and attended by four coachmen. He felt it was beneath his dignity to wear a pair of boots more than once, and kept a personal shoemaker. When he had worn a pair of shoes, Egerton would line it up at the end of the day with the rest of his discarded pairs in a special room in his lodgings. There he would estimate how much of the year had passed by looking at the number of boots around him.

Bridgewater's most consuming passion was his collection of pet dogs. He always had at least several of his dogs with him at all times, and they even sat down with him to a formal dinner in the evening. Each night for years, the earl would have places set for a half-dozen of his canine friends, who would be shown ceremoniously to their seats by his servants. The dogs even had special bibs and napkins which the servants tied on for them. If a dog misbehaved or was impolite at the table, it was banished to an anteroom and made to eat in a servant's uniform until the earl forgave it. A contemporary account described such a poor, miserable cur in this way: ". . . he eats in sorrow the bread of shame, and picks the bone of mortification, while his place at table remains vacant till his repentance has merited a general pardon. . . ."

Ladies and gentlemen are permitted to have friends in the kennel, but not in the kitchen.

George Bernard Shaw

Animals are such agreeable friends — they ask no questions, they pass no criticisms.

George Eliot

A rainbow in the morning usually means that bad weather is on the way, not over. Rainbows are generally seen against the clouds opposite the sun, so a rainbow seen in the western sky in the morning portends a storm.

Answer: She lost $1.80.

Notable Births

1856	Robert E. Peary	1914	Randall Jarrell
1856	Sigmund Freud	1915	Orson Welles
1861	Rabindranath Tagore	1915	Theodore White
1895	Rudolph Valentino	1922	Darrin McGavin
1907	Weeb Eubank	1931	Willie Mays

Notable Events

1626 Peter Minuit bought Manhattan
1840 Britain issued world's first postage stamp
1861 Tennessee seceded
1882 Chinese immigration to United States halted
1941 Stalin stripped title of premier from Molotov
1942 Correigador fell
1951 400 people died in El Salvador earthquake
1952 Prison camp of General Dodd seized by inmates, Koje, South Korea
1954 Roger Bannister broke 4-minute-mile barrier
1976 Earthquake in northern Italy claimed 956 lives

Question: A bakery started the day with fifty chocolate chip cookies. The day's sales tallied like this:

sold	had left
20	30
15	15
9	6
6	0
50	51

Where'd the extra cookie come from?

The history books tell us that on May 6, 1626, Peter Minuit bought Manhattan from the Indians for the trifling sum of $24 in cash and trinkets. That was a steal for the Dutch — perhaps. But it wasn't quite as simple as it seemed. Minuit (who was actually a Prussian hired by the Dutch government) bought the island from members of the Canarsee, Montauk, and Rockaway tribes — but those tribes didn't own Manhattan. Later on he had to buy it again from the tribe whose property it actually was.

This kind of thing went on all the time. The clever Raritan Indians sold Staten Island five separate times to various explorers and settlers.

After Minuit had "bought" Manhattan for the $24 worth of trinkets, he was fined by his superiors for "extravagance."

The phrase "a feather in his cap" comes from an old Hungarian military decoration. For centuries, the major preoccupation of the Magyars was the destruction of invading Turks, and for each Turk a Hungarian warrior killed, he was privileged to put a feather into his cap or helmet. The phrase was first recorded in English in a book of travels dated 1598.

Answer: There is no extra cookie. That's just the way this problem works.

MAY 7

Question: What's the state shown here?

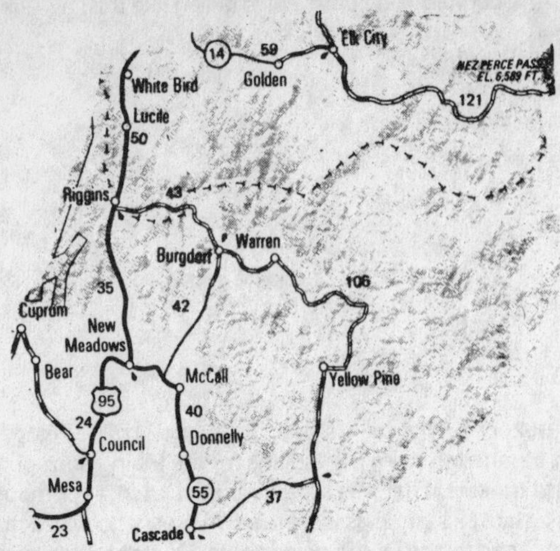

Notable Births

1812	Robert Browning	1901	Gary Cooper
1833	Johannes Brahms	1923	Anne Baxter
1840	Peter Tchaikovsky	1931	Theresa Brewer
1885	Gabby Hayes	1933	John Unitas

Notable Events

1861	Arkansas seceded
1864	Sherman began march to the sea
1915	*Lusitania* sunk, 1198 dead
1931	Toscanini beaten up in Italy for refusing to play Fascist anthem
1932	President Doumier assassinated by Russian fanatic in France
1936	First Catholic mass performed in airship over ocean
1937	*Graf Zeppelin* exploded at Lakehurst, New Jersey
1939	Italy and Germany formed military and political alliance
1940	Churchill given nearly complete control of British war effort
1945	Germany surrendered unconditionally
1954	Fall of Dien Bien Phu

The United States has several architectural monsters to rival Beckford's Fonthill Abbey (see February 29). One of them is the Winchester mansion in San Jose, California. It was begun in 1884 by the wealthy Sara Winchester, who somehow became convinced that she would die if she ever stopped adding on rooms to her house. She managed to keep dozens of workmen busy for thirty-eight years until her natural death at age eighty-five, and spent over five million dollars on the house.

Some of the rooms are royally furnished, with golden chandeliers, stained glass windows, inlaid floors, and satin wallpaper; while some are barely finished. A number of the rooms are huge, high-ceilinged affairs, while others are only a few feet wide and are quite useless. Altogether the house has two thousand doors, ten thousand windows, three elevators, forty-eight fireplaces, nine kitchens, and miles of hallways and secret passages. Its 160 rooms spread over six acres, and it is open today as a museum.

What is the use of a house if you haven't got a tolerable planet to put it on?

Henry David Thoreau

Among all human constructions the only ones that avoid the dissolving sands of time are castles in the air.

De Roberto

The average American brushes his teeth about forty-five thousand times in his lifetime. In his lifetime, Winston Churchill smoked about three hundred thousand cigars.

One day in 1922, Frank Silver felt like having a piece of fruit. He stopped at the cart of a Greek peddler in Lynbrook, Long Island, and asked him if he had any bananas.

"Yes, we have no bananas," the man replied.

So Silver settled for something else and returned to his band's rehearsal at a Bronx hotel. There, he asked his pianist, Irving Cohn, to compose a tune around the phrase, which had caught his fancy, and later on, a man named Lew Brown wrote some lyrics to fit the simple melody.

And so the biggest novelty song of the early twentieth century was created. Two million pieces of sheet music were sold in 1923, a record by far, and it was sung and whistled all over the country for months.

But all was not roses, or bananas, for Silver, Cohn, and Brown. Westman Publishing Company sued the "No Bananas" publisher, Jerome Remick Company, charging that the tune was a note-for-note copy of part of a piece of music Westman had published. Westman demanded damages and a portion of the royalties. The Remick Company denied any plagiarism, but the court found Westman's evidence to be incontrovertable.

So, what piece of music did the melody to "Yes, We Have No Bananas" come from?

Hard to believe, but it's Handel's *Messiah*.

Originality is the art of concealing your source.

Franklin P. Jones

Until the sinking of the *Lusitania*, most Americans were more than happy to let the countries of Europe destroy each other in World War I. There was little real sentiment in the United States for intervention on either side. But when a Geman U-boat sent the supposedly unarmed Cunard liner to the bottom on May 7, 1915, with the loss of over 120 American lives, public opinion in this country was changed dramatically. Media coverage of the war became almost exclusively anti-German, and American involvement on the side of the the Allies was practically inevitable.

There's more to the story than that, however. Although many people believed that the *Lusitania* was an innocent American passenger steamer, she was British, she was armed, and her owners knew the risks of traveling in a declared war zone. She had six-inch guns, and her captain had orders to ram any enemy submarine on sight. Moreover, she was not just a passenger ship. Among the passengers were Canadian fighting troops, and her cargo included four thousand cases of ammunition. In a newspaper advertisement on the day she sailed from New York, the German government specifically warned Americans that it considered the *Lusitania* to be an armed merchant ship carrying war contraband, and, if encountered, she would be attacked. Practically everyone on the ship's manifest laughed at the German warning and went straight on board, even though another legitimate passenger steamer was to leave for England several hours later and had plenty of accommodations. The second vessel reached England unscathed.

Answer: Idaho.

Notable Births

1884	Harry S Truman	1920	Sloan Wilson
1885	Thomas B. Costain	1926	Don Rickles
1895	Fulton Sheen	1930	Gary Snyder
1895	Edmund Wilson	1937	Thomas Pynchon
1906	Roberto Rossellini	1940	Ricky Nelson
1919	Lex Barker	1940	Peter Benchley

Notable Events

1430	Joan of Arc raised siege of Orleans
1878	Paul Hines made baseball's first unassisted triple play, Providence, Rhode Island
1896	Samuel Langley launched "aerodrome" over Potomac River
1902	Eruption of Mount Pelee, 40,000 died on Martinique
1920	Capital punishment abolished in Sweden
1951	Men's Dacron suits introduced
1954	60-foot shot-put barrier broken by Parry O'Brien

The strongest seventeenth-century Englishman was Thomas Topham, who worked as a carpenter before making a living exhibiting his remarkable strength. Topham could throw a horse over a gate, and carry the main beam for a house like a rifle. He could roll up a pewter plate as if it were cardboard and lift two hundred pounds over his head with his little finger. Using his teeth, he could raise a six-foot-long oak table with a fifty-pound weight on the far end of it. On one (unprofessional) occasion, Topham twisted an andiron around the neck of a man who had insulted him and steadfastly refused to remove it until the man had made an apology.

A farmer in Massachusetts once harnessed a squash to a weight-lifting device to see how much pressure the vegetable exerted as it grew. He came up with the subsequently verified figure of over five thousand pounds per square inch.

In 1915, a Saint Louis mortician named August Kron, Jr., embalmed the body of a woman before he found out that her relatives either would not or could not pay for the embalming and funeral. Kron said he'd refuse to bury the corpse until he was paid. He meant it. He kept the body in an open wooden chest in the basement of the mortuary until the police finally intervened in May 1945.

Growing old isn't so bad when you consider the alternative.

Maurice Chevalier

The traditional nuclear family of the Zulu tribe is an interesting one. Number one wife and her husband live in a hut and work together until their finances are such that he can afford another wife. Number two wife then moves into a hut next door. Then the three endeavor jointly to become wealthy enough so the man can marry a third time, and the third wife moves into a hut on the other side of the original one. If the man and the number one wife don't have children, his inheritance passes on to the third wife and her progeny, not to the second.

Answer: Lotte Lenya, Jerry Lewis, Shari Lewis, Mary Livingstone, Carole Lombard.

Question: By what names are these people better known?

Karoline Balmauer
Joseph Levitch
Shari Hurwitz
Sadye Marks
Carol Peters

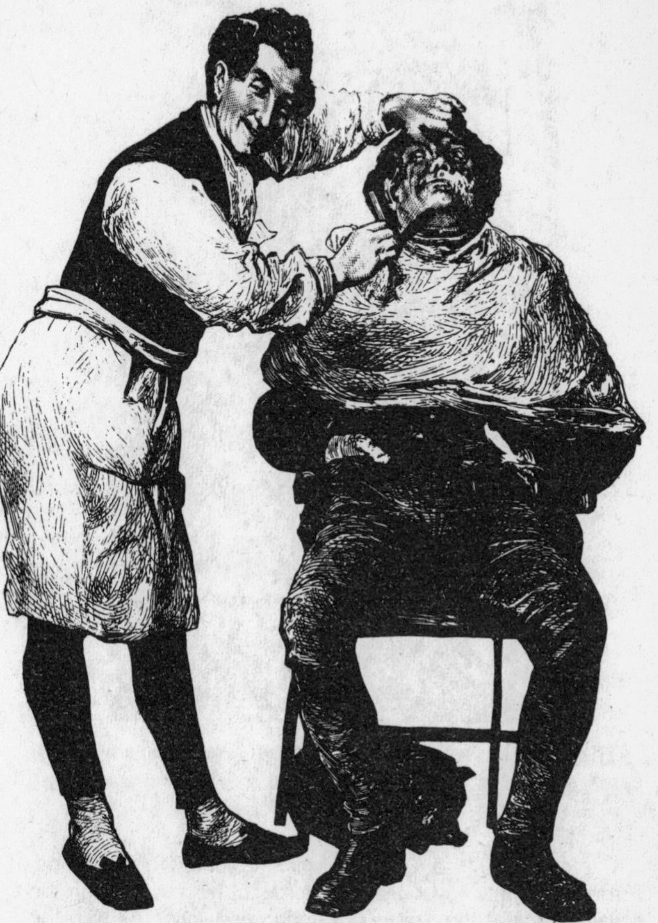

In May 1951, in Quezaltenango, Guatemala, a telegraph operator named Cesa A. Anleu persuaded a barber to give him a shave and a haircut in exchange for a $1 lottery ticket. Reluctantly, the barber agreed, and the next day he won $6,000 with the ticket.

In 1806, two gentlemen from York, England, wagered five shillings that one could outdo the other in creating the most unusual character. The first of them, Thomas Hodgson, papered his waistcoat with one-, five-, and ten-guinea notes, put a purse of gold on his hat, and affixed a sign that read "John Bull" on his back. The other, Samuel Whitehead, dressed half his body as a woman, with slipper, silk stocking, and painted face; and the other half as a black servant, with boot and spur and blackened face. An ostentatious display of wealth being as attractive then as it is now, Hodgson was judged the winner by his townspeople.

An honest politician is one who, when he is bought, will stay bought.

Simon Cameron

The dignity of man lies in his ability to face reality in all its meaninglessness.

Martin Esslin

MAY 9

Question: Do you know the railroad that offers a transcontinental journey clear from the Atlantic to the Pacific for under $10?

The giraffe has fewer bones in its neck (seven) than any bird on earth.

On May 9, 1671, a daring Irishman, Colonel Thomas Blood, armed with only a wooden mallet, fought his way through the royal guards at the Tower of London and made off with the English crown and the other coronation regalia. He was soon captured and brought before King Charles II. Instead of ordering Blood executed, Charles was so impressed by the man's courage and skill that he granted him a full pardon and a large pension.

It is criminal to steal a purse, daring to steal a fortune, a mark of greatness to steal a crown. The blame diminishes as the guilt increases.

Friedrich Schiller

Actually, crime probably does pay . . . In 1951, 97 percent of the burglaries and 91 percent of the robberies committed in Chicago didn't even result in indictments. During the 1930s, the Wickersham and Seabury Commissions on crime and law enforcement both found that, for any given single crime, a criminal was 99 percent sure of *not* going to jail.

The policeman isn't there to create disorder. He's there to preserve disorder.

Richard J. Daley

The tragic lesson of guilty men walking free in this country has not been lost on the criminal community.

Richard Nixon

Notable Births

1800	John Brown	1920	Richard Adams
1860	James Barrie	1926	Pancho Gonzalez
1883	José Ortega y Gasset	1936	Glenda Jackson
1895	Richard Barthelmess	1936	Albert Finney
1918	Mike Wallace	1946	Candice Bergen

Notable Events

1876	Turks began week-long massacre of Bulgarians
1926	Richard Byrd and Floyd Bennett flew over North Pole
1939	Kateri Tekakwitha became first American Indian to be declared a Catholic saint
1942	Battle of the Coral Sea began
1961	Newton Minow delivered "vast wasteland" speech
1964	Khrushchev visited Egypt
1974	Impeachment hearings began for Nixon's removal

English Puritans in the seventeenth century had a habit of giving their children religious names. Sometimes this practice got out of hand. The following are all real Christian names and surnames, and most of them were taken from a 1658 jury list in the county of Sussex, England.

Kill-sin Pimple
Search-the-scriptures Moreton
Joy-from-above Brown
Obediencia Cruttenden
The-gift-of-God Stringer
Be-thankful Playnard
Live-in-peace Hillary
Goodgift Noake
Thunder Goldsmith
Be-of-good-comfort Small
More-tryal Goodwin
Godward Freeman
Faint-not Hewitt
God-reward Smart
Meek Brewer
Be-faithful Joiner
More-fruit Flower
Grace-ful Harding
Seek-widsom Wood
Fight-the-good-fight-of-faith White
The-peace-of-God-Knight
Be-courteous Cole
Make-peace Heaton
Accepted Trevor
Hope-for Bending
Fly-debate Roberts
Weep-not Billing
Called Lower
Stand-Fast-on-High Stringer
Elected Marshall
Repentance Avis
The-work-of-God Farmer

The grand champion was a girl whose first name was "Through-much-tribulation-we-enter-the-kingdom-of-Heaven." For short, people called her "Tribby."

At the Boston Opera House many years ago, the Metropolitan Opera Company tenor Beniamino Gigli was performing *Faust* to an enraptured audience. At one point, Gigli and the bass singing the part of Mephistopheles had to step on a trap door over an elevator that was supposed to convey them to Hell. Something went wrong, and the two men found themselves stuck halfway through the stage. From the rear of the house, an obviously inebriated Irish voice rang out, "Thank God! I'm safe at last. Hell is full!"

Because of the rotation of the earth, an object can be thrown farther if it is thrown west.

Answer: The Panama Canal Railroad.

Notable Births

1850	Thomas Lipton	1908	Carl Albert
1899	Fred Astaire	1910	Eric Berne
1899	Dmitri Tiomkin	1919	Ella Grasso
1902	David O. Selznick	1922	Nancy Walker

Notable Events

1772 Ethan Allen captured Fort Ticonderoga
1863 Stonewall Jackson died
1869 Golden Spike driven, Promontory, Utah
1872 Victoria Woodhull became first woman nominated for president
1908 Mother's Day first celebrated, Philadelphia
1940 Nazis invaded Holland and Belgium
1940 Chamberlain resigned as British prime minister
1950 United States rejected Soviet offer of 2 cents to the dollar on lend-lease
1972 Korean bus plunged into reservoir, 77 people dead

The following strange advertisements have been culled at random from English magazines and newspapers of the mid-eighteenth century. They give us a good idea of the manners and tastes of that period.

> Whereas a tall young Gentleman above the common size, dress'd in a yellow-grounded flowered velvet (supposed to be a Foreigner), with a Solitair round his neck and a glass in his hand, was narrowly observed and much approved of by a certain young lady at the last Ridotto. This is to acquaint the said young Gentleman, if his heart is entirely disengaged, that if he will apply to A. B. at Garaway's Coffee House in Exchange Alley, he may be directed to have an interview with the said young lady, which may prove greatly to his advantage. Strict secresy on the Gentleman's side will be depended on.

> A Lady who had on a Pink-coloured Capuchin, edged with Ermine, a black Patch near her right eye, sat in a front seat in the next Side Box but one to the Stage on Wednesday night at Drury Lane Playhouse; if that Lady is single and willing to treat on terms of honour and generosity of a married state, it would be deemed a favour to receive a line directed to C. D., at Clifford's Inn Old Coffee House, how she may be address'd, being a serious affair.

> To be seen this week, in a large commodious room at the George Inn, in Fenchurch-street, near Aldgate; the Porcupine Man and his Son, which has given such great satisfaction to all that ever saw them: their solid quills being not to be numbered nor credited till seen; but give universal satisfaction to all that ever saw them; the youth being allowed by all to be of a beautiful and fine complexion, and great numbers resort daily to see them.

> A Bullfinch, that pipes "Britons rouse up your great magnanimity," at command, also talks, is to be sold at the Cane Shop facing New Broad Street, Moorfields; likewise to be sold, two Starlings that whistle and talk extremely plain.

Questions: Why is a dog dressed warmer in the summer than winter?

Why is a lame dog like a blotter?

Although enshrined as one of the most critical engagements in American military history, the taking of Fort Ticonderoga was an important but by no means a major battle. Ethan Allen's Green Mountain Boys numbered only eighty-three men, and there were only forty-one British defenders. It has been reliably reported that most of the American forces were just about sober enough to stay on their feet.

By the way, it was Benedict Arnold who planned the whole episode.

The essential matter of history is not what happened but what people thought or said about it.

Frederick Maitland

One bill collector had much success dunning deadbeat clients that no one else could squeeze a penny out of. He attributed this achievement to the simple statement he used on his letters: "Either you *will* pay me, or I'll tell all your other creditors that you *have* paid me."

The Irish are the world's greatest consumers of tea, with about 1,200 cups per capita consumed annually.

Answers: He wears a fur coat in the winter, but in the summer he wears a fur coat, and pants.

A lame dog is a slow pup, a slope up is an inclined plane, and an ink-lined plane is a blotter.

MAY 11

Question: In a new development, gas, water, and electricity must be connected to each of three houses. The utilities and homes are located as follows. Zoning laws won't permit any utility line to cross over another. Can you supply these houses with that in mind?

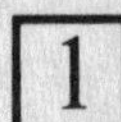
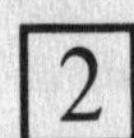

The term "juggernaut" is associated with any extremely powerful force, such as a big battleship or a strong football team, but it is actually one of the thousand names for the Hindu god Vishnu. The god's name became used in this way because of the vehicle the god's image traveled in. It was an enormous, forty-three-foot-high cart with sixteen wheels. During the Car Festival at Puri, India, when Juggernaut and his two associates, Balbhadra and Sabhadra, were brought out in their huge carts, thousands of devotees to Vishnu would hurl themselves beneath the seventy-inch-high wheels to be crushed to death in hope of reincarnation in a higher form.

During the first part of the fifteenth century, the Sawney Beane family, who lived on the coast of Scotland, was personally responsible for keeping the population of their area under control: they managed to do away with over one thousand individuals. Beane, his wife, their fourteen children and thirty-two grandchildren hunted down travelers and locals they found near their home — and ate them. They were finally stopped in 1435.

Necessity is the constant scourge of the lower classes, ennui of the higher ones.

Schopenhauer

I shall not pass this way again.

William Penn

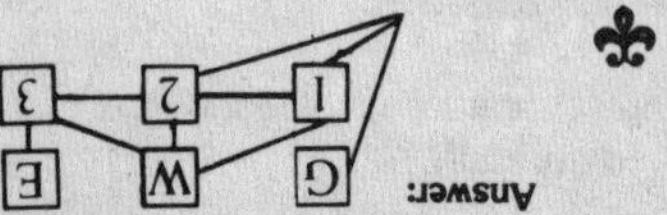

Notable Births

1891	Henry Morgenthau	1903	Salvador Dali
1888	Irving Berlin	1912	Phil Silvers
1894	Martha Graham	1938	Doug McClure

Notable Events

1792	Columbia River discovered by Gray
1866	Black Friday on stock market
1891	Attempted assassination of Czar at Kyoto, Japan
1943	American troops landed on Attu
1949	Siam's name changed to Thailand
1949	Israel voted into United Nations
1953	Tornado in Waco, Texas, killed 114 people
1965	Windstorm in Bangladesh took 17,000 lives

In 1939, Anthoni Przybysz appeared before Judge Joseph Murphy in an effort to legally change his name. The judge agreed that a name like his could probably cause a lot of confusion. Mr. Przybysz said it certainly did, what with some people calling him Tony, some Anthony, and others Anton. He wanted his name changed to Clinton Przybysz.

Names are not always what they seem The common Welsh name Bzjxxllwcp is pronounced Jackson.

Mark Yshirhbbf (Twain)

Hugh Alexander Morris Gene Saul Ralph Giles Gilbert Motoer Marquis Miles Marion Mayo John Charles James Gordon Bennett Adams Christopher Columbus Elijah Green Eversole Bradley Kincaid Robert Jefferson Breckenridge Stallard joined the navy in Louisville, Kentucky, in 1953. The navy averted a crisis by enrolling him as Bennett (no middle initial) Stallard.

Peanut brittle was an accident. Ninety years ago, a woman in New England mistakenly put baking soda into her taffy recipe instead of cream of tartar, and peanut brittle was born.

Basic research is when I'm doing what I don't know what I'm doing.

Werner von Braun

From a tombstone in Montague, Massachusetts:

In Memory of Mr. Elijah Bardwell
who died Janry 26th 1786 in ye 27th
Year of his Age having but a few days
surviv'd ye fatal Night when he was
flung from his Horse & drawn by ye Stirrup
26 rods along ye path as appear'd by ye place
where his hat was found & where he had
Spent ye whole following severe cold night
treading ye Snow in a small circle

Threshold literally means "thrash-wood." It is derived from the Anglo-Saxon words *therscan*, "to thrash"; and *wald*, "wood." When the early Britons entered their huts they stamped their feet on a piece of wood at the door, the thrash-wood.

MAY 12

Notable Births

1812	Edward Lear	1925	Yogi Berra
1820	Florence Nightingale	1925	John Simon
1828	Dante Gabriel Rossetti	1926	Bea Arthur
1902	Philip Wylie	1928	Burt Bacharach
1914	Howard K. Smith	1936	Tom Snyder

Notable Events

1789 Tammany Society founded in New York City
1812 John Langdon declined nomination as vice-president
1868 Russians occupied Samarkand
1873 First-known cancellation of a postcard in the United States
1932 Lindbergh baby found dead
1943 Last Nazis in Africa surrendered at Cape Bon
1964 NcNamara pledged all necessary aid to Vietnam
1975 *Mayaguez* seized by Cambodia
1978 Abortion legalized in Italy

Question: By what names are these people better known?
Sofia Scicolone
Laszlo Loewenstein
Marie LaFleche
Robert Moseley
Mary Krebs

Dietary habits have changed, but the greatest delicacies of the Kamchatka Peninsula of Russia used to be boiled fish eyes, the flesh of fetal reindeer, and the half-digested greens taken from adult reindeer stomachs. Some distance to the southwest of Kamchatka in China, raw monkey brains on the half-skull was the *pièce de resistance*.

Moon rocks are O.K. when everyone is eating.
Goodman Ace

A white dwarf is a star that has nearly exhausted its fuel supply and has fallen in on itself through the force of its own gravity. What remains of the star is so closely compacted that the weight of a white dwarf is over 600 tons per cubic inch. As it continues to burn up its fuel, it collapses further and becomes a neutron star, with a weight of about 20 billion tons per cubic inch.

Bernice Claxton won a divorce from her husband in Los Angeles in 1948. One of the charges she brought against him was that he made her screw and unscrew the light bulbs to save wear and tear on the switches.

... many of us live in a chrome-plated world where the major enemy we face is crab-grass. **John Glenn**

The average adult male eats four pounds of food, sweats sixteen ounces of fluids, and says five thousand words in a day. The average four-year-old says between ten thousand and twelve thousand words daily.

Tammany Hall, the New York City political machine, knew a good thing when it saw one. In the twenty-three days before the 1827 elections, Tammany managed to have an average of 1,147 immigrants a day naturalized, which, of course, gave the newcomers the right to vote.

Answer: Sophia Loren, Peter Lorre, Gisele MacKenzie, Guy Madison, Marjorie Main.

MAY 13

Question: These cities are capitals of which countries?
Tunis
Damascus
Khartoum
Bucharest

Notable Births

1840	Alphonse Daudet	1907	Daphne du Maurier
1842	Arthur Sullivan	1914	Joe Louis
1882	Georges Braque	1950	Stevie Wonder

Notable Events

1607	Jamestown founded
1779	Peace of Teschen between Prussia and Austria
1846	United States declared war on Mexico
1884	Alaska granted civilian government
1940	Churchill delivered "blood, sweat, and tears" speech
1940	Queen Wilhelmina of Netherlands fled to England
1954	Saint Lawrence Seaway authorized
1972	Fire in Osaka, Japan, nightclub took 116 lives

The greatest of baseball poems, "Casey at the Bat," by Ernest Thayer, may very well have been inspired by an actual Casey and a real incident. If so, ironically it was about a *pitcher*, not a renowned slugger.

Dan M. Casey was a twenty-one-year-old pitcher for the Philadelphia club in 1887, and as a pitcher he had a terrific year, winning twenty-eight games and leading the league in shutouts and ERA. As a hitter, however, he was nothing special, tearing the cover off the ball for a mediocre .165 average. But on one fateful day that summer, he smashed a homer — the only one of his career — against the New York club. On his next trip to the plate, with his team trailing and the bases loaded, Mighty Casey did indeed strike out, and his team lost the game.

Thayer wrote the poem the next spring, so Casey probably was its inspiration. "Casey at the Bat" was given its first public reading on Friday, May 13, 1888, by DeWolf Hopper.

In 1860, 13 percent of America's population (31.5 million) was foreign born. In that same year, 86 percent of the paupers in New York City were immigrants.

Dozens of bears are found dead in Alaska and northern Canada every summer, killed by blood lost to the voracious mosquito. The estimated life-expectancy of a naked man on the tundra in summer is about fifteen minutes. In that time, approximately 250,000 mosquitoes would have drawn enough of his blood to kill him.

On May 14, 1650, a law went into effect in England that made adultery a crime punishable by death. It was actually a revival of an old Saxon law, which called for the adultress to be burned alive and a gibbet to be erected over her ashes. The adulterer was then to be hanged from it.

No one was executed under this statute in England, but in the no-nonsense Massachusetts Bay Colony, perhaps a dozen people were put to death this way.

Relations between the sexes are so complicated that the only way you can tell if members of the set are "going together" is if they're married. Then, almost certainly, they are not.

Cleveland Amory

I wonder why murder is considered less immoral than fornication.

George Moore

Answer: Tunisia, Syria, the Sudan, Romania.

MAY 14

Notable Births

1686	Gabriel Fahrenheit	1881	Ed Walsh
1752	Timothy Dwight	1885	Otto Klemperer
1771	Robert Owen	1942	Tony Perez

Notable Events

1609 Henry IV of Navarre assassinated
1787 Constitutional Convention opened in Philadelphia
1804 Lewis and Clark expedition left Saint Louis
1853 Gail Borden applied for condensed milk patent
1856 First importation of camels for commercial purposes, Indianola, Texas
1878 Vaseline trademarked
1913 Rockefeller Foundation chartered
1948 Free State of Israel declared
1955 Warsaw Pact made

Even though you might not have seen them in your *National Geographic* lately, the Cargo Cults of the South Pacific are still going strong. Some aspects of these odd religious sects can be traced to the days of the early Christian missionaries, but their development generally has occurred since the Second World War. The natives were amazed by all the manufactured goods the Allies brought with them during the war and, because they had no concept of industrialization or of factories, the belief came about that the Westerners must have a secret knowledge of the workings of the gods. In only that way could the islanders understand the magical richness of equipment and goods that suddenly appeared with the soldiers. Since then, they have developed elaborate rituals in imitation of the American and Australian soldiers. Now the islanders perform marching rites, worship rusted hulks left after the Allies pulled out, and even pray to quasi-gods named "Joe Navy" and "John Frum," all in the hope they'll discover the soldiers' magic.

In the 1960s, on the island of New Hanover near New Guinea, the locals heard that a fellow named Lyndon Johnson was president of the United States, the strange land from which most of those former blessings had come. Believing that if he came to lead them he would bring the secret of obtaining Cargo, he was unanimously elected to be their chief. When they were told his duties in America would keep him from serving, the natives immediately started collecting money to buy him.

A man named Larry Self, a suspect in a car theft, had his day in court recently in Pensacola, Florida. It seems he didn't take the accusation too well, and it got him a year's sentence for contempt of court. That, too, went poorly with Mr. Self, and by the time he'd cooled down, he had a five-year and then a ten-year sentence for contempt.

But he didn't cool down quite enough. He dared the judge to go all the way, and raise his bail to $50,000 while he was at it. The judge did him one better, and upped the sum to $100,000.

Bet you didn't know this: Evel Knievel's brother John was formerly director of Public Affairs for the Federal Highway Traffic Safety Administration.

Questions: When is a dog's tail not a tail?

When is a red puppy not likely to enter a house?

Most polar bears live their entire life without ever setting foot on land.

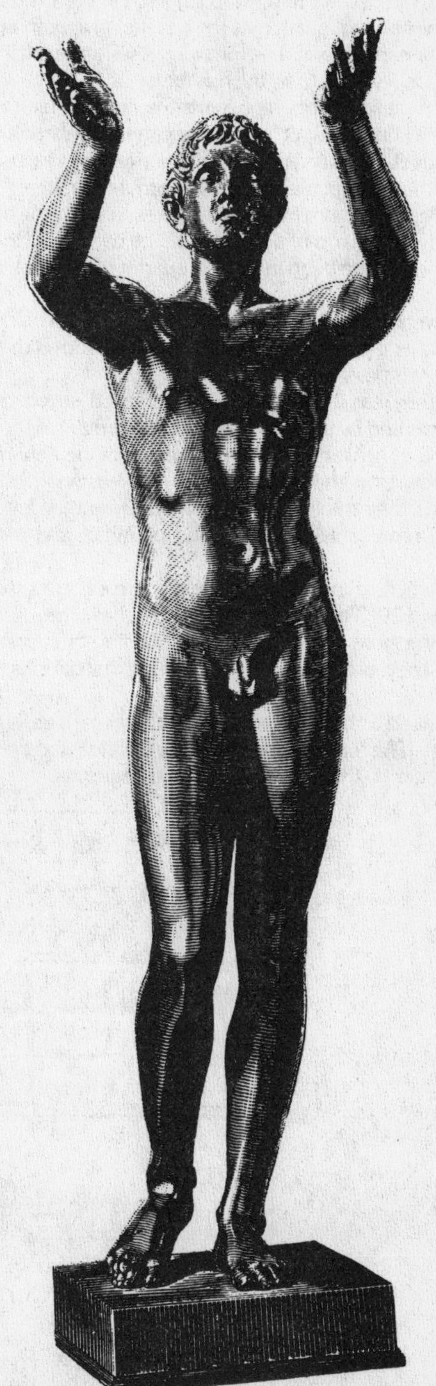

The Greek Thespis was the first actor to emerge from the chorus and play an individual part in a Greek drama. This change in the theater took place about 534 B.C., and we get our word "thespian" from his name.

Answers: When its tail is a-waggin'.
When the door is closed.

MAY 15

Question: Can you, using only two letters and some punctuation, create a headline to describe a minor but statewide epidemic?

Notable Births

1773	Prince Metternich	1909	James Mason
1856	L. Frank Baum	1915	Paul Samuelson
1894	Katherine Anne Porter	1918	Eddy Arnold
1902	Richard Daley	1921	Errol Garner
1904	Clifton Fadiman	1936	Anna Maria Alberghetti
1905	Joseph Cotton	1937	Trini Lopez

Notable Events

1602 Captain Bartholomew Gosnold landed near New Bedford, Massachusetts
1756 England declared war on France
1848 Communist uprising in Paris began
1854 U. S. Inebriate Asylum founded, Binghamton, New York
1902 Portugal declared bankruptcy
1911 Supreme Court ordered dissolution of Standard Oil
1930 Ellen Church became first air stewardess
1932 Japanese Premier Inukai assassinated
1937 Ground broken for Marineland, Florida
1940 Netherlands surrendered to Nazis
1940 First nylon stockings placed on sale
1942 Gas rationing started in United States
1946 Truman seized the railroads
1957 Britain tested its first H-Bomb
1972 George Wallace shot, Laurel, Maryland

NORTH AMERICAN INDIAN WAR DESPATCH

The following is a facsimile of a gazette of a tribe of North American Indians, who assisted the French forces in Canada during the war between France and England in the 1760s.

Here follows an explanation of the gazette, giving an account of one of their expeditions. The following divisions explain those on the plate, as referred to by the numbers:

1. Each of these figures represents the number ten. They all signify, that 18 times 10, or 180 American Indians, took up the hatchet, or declared war, in favor of the French, which is represented by the hatchet placed over the arms of France.

2. They departed from Montreal—represented by the bird just taking wing from the top of a mountain. The moon and the buck show the time to have been in the first quarter of the buck-moon, answering to July.

3. They went by water—signified by the canoe. The number of huts, such as they raise to pass the night in, shows they were 21 days on their passage.

4. Then they came on shore, and travelled seven days by land—represented by the foot and the seven huts.

5. When they arrived near the habitations of their enemies, at sunrise—shown by the sun being to the eastward of them, beginning, as they think, its daily course, there they lay in wait three days—represented by the hand pointing, and the three huts.

6. After which, they surprised their enemies, in number 12 times 10, or 120. The man asleep shows how they surprised them, and the hole in the top of the building is supposed to signify that they broke into some of their habitations in that manner.

7. They killed with the club eleven of their enemies, and took five prisoners. The former represented by the club and the eleven heads, the latter by the figures on the little pedestals.

8. They lost nine of their own men in the action—represented by the nine heads within the bow, which is the emblem of honor among the Americans, but had none taken prisoners—a circumstance they lay great weight on, shown by all the pedestals being empty.

9. The heads of the arrows, pointing opposite ways, represent the battle.

10. The heads of the arrows all pointing the same way, signify the flight of the enemy.

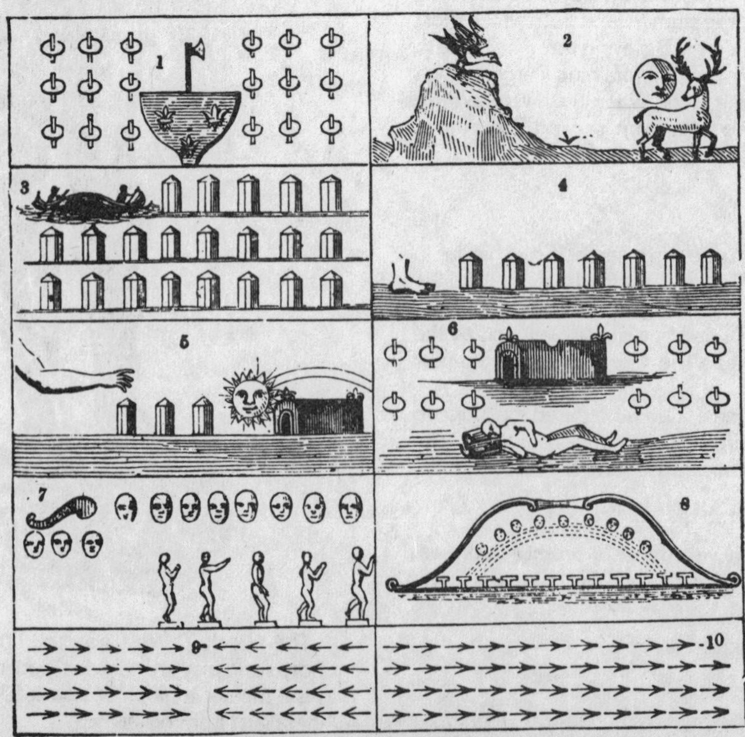

Answer: ILL ILL! ILL.

Notable Births

1905	Henry Fonda	1928	Billy Martin
1912	Studs Terkel	1931	Lowell Weicker
1913	Woody Herman	1955	Olga Korbut

Notable Events

1763 Boswell first met Johnson
1868 Andrew Johnson acquitted in Senate impeachment trial
1875 Venezuelan earthquake claimed 16,000 lives
1920 Joan of Arc canonized
1933 FDR called for worldwide nonaggression pact
1975 Gulf Oil admitted $5 million used to bribe foreign officials

In May 1838, the speaker of the Arkansas House of Assembly was convicted of slaying a fellow congressman on the House floor while Congress was in session. The jury returned a verdict of excusable homicide, and the speaker received a minimum punishment.

In 1973, the town of Kearny, New Jersey, received a revenue-sharing program check for $5,625.27. It disappeared before town officials could cash it, but there was no immediate panic on thier part. After all, even though it was a Treasury Department check and sound as the dollar (ahem), there were only a few people authorized to conduct the town's business, and what bank would cash a check for that amount of money without first ascertaining the official identity of the endorsing individual?

It reappeared a short time later, cashed by a New York City bank, and endorsed by one "Nathan J. Kearny."

Answer: Barbara Eden, Duke Ellington, Mama Cass, Dale Evans, Tom Ewell.

Question: By what names are these people better known?
Barbara Huffman
Edward Kennedy
Ellen Cohen
Frances Butts
Yewell Tompkins

When a new pope celebrates his first mass at Saint Peter's in Rome, he is given a july as payment. The july is a special coin first minted during the papacy of Julius II, and it is only used on this particular occasion.

Two Different Styles of Tombstone

A zealous locksmith died of late,
And did not enter Heaven's gate.
But stood without and would not knock
Because he meant to pick the lock.

Here lies Jane Smith,
Wife of Thomas Smith, Marble Cutter.
This monument was erected by her husband as a tribute to her memory and a specimen of his work.
Monuments of this same style are two hundred and fifty dollars.

During the 1977 uprising in Zaire's Shaba province, the pygmy troops of the Zaire Army, with their poison-tipped arrows, had to be recalled from the front because they were too short to see over the elephant grass in the battlefields.

Let not thy will roar, when thy power can but whisper.
Thomas Fuller

The word "buccaneer" comes from the name the Caribee Indians called the explorers, traders, and pirates of the New World in the sixteenth and seventeenth centuries. *Boucan* was the Indians' word for "smoked meat," and when the sailors copied the Indian way of preserving food, they also received a new name for themselves.

When it's attacked, the petrel, a large bird of the Antarctic, vomits on its assailant.

MAY 17

Questions: What is the easiest-going bird in the world?

Why is a dog's tail like the heart of a tree?

Notable Births

1749	Edward Jenner	1912	Archibald Cox
1766	Isaac D'Israeli	1914	Stewart Alsop
1866	Erik Satie	1919	Merle Miller
1911	Maureen O'Sullivan	1936	Dennis Hopper

Notable Events

603 B.C.	Eclipse recorded in Persia
1814	Norwegian independence declared
1875	Aristides won first Kentucky Derby
1876	Custer left Fort Lincoln on his last patrol
1933	Hitler agreed to FDR's nonaggression pact, insisted on military equality
1954	Supreme Court ruled segregation of schools unconstitutional
1970	Heyerdahl set sail in *Ra II* from Morocco to Barbados
1973	Watergate hearings opened

According to tradition, Aesop was a blind storyteller of the sixth centruy B.C., whose fables were used to illuminate the finer points of behavior and common sense for Greek children. But for all his fame, Aesop is not mentioned in any Greek literature for hundreds of years after his death. It seems his name only became associated with a certain style of proverb-story in the first two centuries before Christ.

Then, a century into the Christian era, a Greek named Babrius collected the fables and put them into verse. It was Babrius' work that a fourteenth-century monk named Maimus Plamides used as a source when he wrote the stories out in prose, and claimed them as his own. Aesop's Fables might more correctly be called Babrius' Fables, as translated by M. Plamides.

Can you guess to what kind of behavior this is a prelude?

First the two individuals slam their heads onto the surface of the water, time after time after time. They they let go with deep, primitive hollers. Subsequently, they blow bubbles for a while and then, taking turns, they ride piggy back on one another. All this time they are blowing water through their noses and laughing, after a fashion. This whole process usually takes a couple of hours.

Give up? Roughly, it's what alligators do before they make love.

In 1895, there were two cars registered in the state of Ohio. They collided.

The city of Saint Louis, Missouri, recently went on a campaign against rape. Part of the program involved the distribution of thousands of cardboard signs that read "Send Help." A fellow named Kevin Foster happened to come by one, and he carelessly threw it onto the back window ledge of his car.

A passing policeman noticed it several days later, and stopped to investigate.

Foster was booked for possession of marijuana.

Answers: The crow, because it never complains without caws.

Because it is farthest from the bark.

Notable Births

1814	Mikhail Bakunin	1904	Jacob Javits
1872	Bertrand Russell	1913	Perry Como
1883	Walter Gropius	1919	Margot Fonteyn
1892	Ezio Pinza	1937	Brooks Robinson
1902	Meredith Willson	1946	Reggie Jackson

Notable Events

1803 Britain declared war on France
1860 Lincoln nominated for president, Chicago, Illinois
1917 First American troops in World War I landed in England
1953 Jacqueline Cochran became first woman to break sound barrier
1974 India became 6th nation with atomic bomb
1978 Belgium and France evacuated 2,500 Europeans from Kolwezi, Zaire

About the only word in English that comes from the Tagalog language of the Philippines is "yo-yo." In Tagalog, a single "yo" means "come." Their yo-yo was originally a weapon.

"Lynching" now means a vigilante action taken illegally, which usually ends in the victim being hanged. This is a disservice to the man who inadvertently gave his name to this kind of punishment. Charles Lynch was an upright justice of the peace in Virginia during the Revolutionary War. When the conflict disrupted the normal channels of the law, Lynch took it upon himself to provide a substitute, with the support of the townspeople in Bedford County. Normally, Lynch's most severe penalties were fines and whippings; only once, in a conspiracy case, did he impose the death penalty. There was nothing vicious about his judicial decisions, and nothing at all to compare with the "lynch mob" activities that took at least five thousand lives between 1882 and 1962, mostly for racial reasons. Nonetheless, these acts bear his name, despite the fact that the Virginia government in 1782 found that all his actions were justifiable, and Lynch was exonerated from any wrongdoing.

One of George Henry Sutton's greater accomplishments, beyond the fact that he was the national billiards champion, was a three thousand-ball run.

Sutton had no arms.

The New York Giants baseball team, now of San Francisco, originally earned their club's name in about 1889, when many of the players were over six feet, six inches, and most of them weighed over 200 pounds.

Answer: Ten.

Question: A bus pulls up to City Hall. The number of people who get on equals the number of people already on the bus. The bus goes six blocks, turns left, and lets off four-fifths of its passengers. There are now six more people on the bus than there were before it stopped at City Hall. How many people boarded at City Hall?

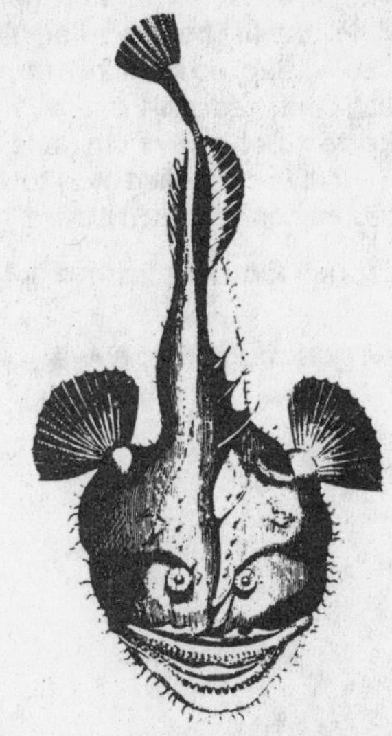

According to the Talmud, there are about seven hundred unclean kinds of fish. Happily, according to recent estimates, there are about forty thousand different varieties of fish.

A train traveling at sixty mph would take 176 years to reach the sun. If it traveled at the speed of sound, it would still take 14 years.

A postscript and an apology: A number of modern experts think that Kaspar Hauser (see April 30) was only an elaborate hoaxer. They believe his fatal wound was self-inflicted, although he only meant to stab himself to the point of injury, not death. Under the circumstances this would have given Kaspar's waning popularity a boost and put him back in the public eye. An investigation by the government determined that the only footprints in the snow where Kaspar was allegedly assaulted were his own.

I'm sorry if I misled you, but it *was* a good story.

A little inaccuracy saves a lot of explanation.

C. E. Ayres

As a matter of fact is an expression that precedes many an expression that isn't.

Laurence J. Peter

A French doctor named Caillet died in 1947, and left behind a strange last will and testament. In it he asked that a prize be given annually to the local citizen who had the best combination of the straightest nose, the smallest wrists, and the largest hands, providing of course that the person also had red hair and black eyebrows.

A judge ruled its limitations made the bequest invalid.

MAY 19

Question: Can you punctuate this to make a witty epigram?
"That that is is that that is not is not is not that so"

Notable Births

1879	Lord Astor	1897	Frank Capra
1861	Nellie Melba	1920	Lorraine Hansberry

Notable Events

1536 Execution of Anne Boleyn
1792 Russia invaded Poland
1796 Britain began taxing dogs
1902 Mine accident at Coal Creek, Tennessee, killed 184 men
1911 First convictions from fingerprints made, New York City
1928 First Calaveras Jumping Frog Jubilee
1928 Disaster at Mather, Pennsylvania, mine claimed 195 lives
1935 Death of Lawrence of Arabia
1941 Italians in Ethiopia surrendered to British
1974 Marianne O'Connor became Notre Dame's first woman valedictorian
1975 Train rammed bus in Poona, India, 66 dead

Anne Boleyn's executioner had a difficult time carrying out his duty. She'd refused to be blindfolded, so he told her to close her eyes. She wouldn't, nor would she turn her gaze from him. The executioner found he couldn't bear to swing his blade while she stared at him, and so he stepped back for a moment, took off his shoes, and quickly conferred with one of his assistants. He instructed the fellow to walk heavily from Anne's blind side as he readied the axe. He did; Anne looked away toward the commotion, and the executioner quickly used his axe.

Man has learned much who has learned how to die.
Charlie Chan

He gave her a look you could have poured on a waffle.
Ring Lardner

In 1941, the New York police instantly solved a murder in an odd way. They had been called to a residence by the victim's wife about midnight, and she told them her husband had been shot by an intruder. The woman said that she and a female houseguest were awakened by the gunshot, but the assailant had fled before they caught sight of him. The other woman corroborated the story, but the cops didn't buy it. The place was such a mess that it was hard to believe a scuffle hadn't occurred that would certainly have awakened one of the women, and the murder weapon had been left behind, wiped clean of fingerprints. Detectives questioned the women all evening, but they couldn't get either one of them to incriminate herself or confess to the murder.

About dawn, groans and noises that sounded like words began to come from the mouth of the corpse. After a few moments the wife became hysterical, believing that the body was accusing her. She admitted she hated her husband and had killed him after a domestic quarrel.

The medical examiner who was present at the time knew what was happening, but didn't say anything, for he knew the possible effects such noises could have on a guilty party. Occasionally, shortly before *rigor mortis* sets into a body, the muscles of the abdomen will contract and force air in the lungs and esophagus of a corpse past the vocal chords, resulting in groans and sounds that sometimes resemble speech—which happened in this case.

In May 1951, a Columbus, Ohio, resident, Thadeus S. Backwood, bequeathed five dollars to his stepson so that he might "buy enough rope with which to hang himself."

In May of 1884, a harness maker sent his six sons out to collect a bill from a traveling circus for which he'd done a significant amount of work. The owners were in dire financial straits, however, and were unable to pay cash. The best the brothers could do was to settle for a partnership in the operation.

A few days later, on May 19, the Reungling Brothers Circus gave its first performance, in Baraboo, Wisconsin.

Answer: That that is, is. That that is not, is not. Is not that so?

MAY 20

Notable Births

1471	Albrecht Durer	1908	Jimmy Stewart
1768	Dolly Madison	1915	Moshe Dayan
1806	John Stuart Mill	1946	Cher

Notable Events

1293 Earthquake in Japan killed 30,000 people
1506 Death of Christopher Columbus
1536 Henry VIII married Jane Seymour
1861 North Carolina seceded
1862 Homestead Act passed
1899 Jacob German became first man arrested for speeding in a car, New York City
1902 United States turned government of Cuba over to Cuban officials
1927 Lindbergh began transatlantic flight from Roosevelt Field, New York
1932 Amelia Earhart began Atlantic solo
1965 Boeing 720-B crashed at Cairo, 121 lives lost
1970 Floods in Romania killed 160

Question: By what names are these people better known?
Elias McDaniel
Maria von Losch
Phyllis Driver
Antoine Domino
Diana Fluck

This is how King Henry VIII's bed had to be made:

Furste, a groome or a page to take a torche, and to goo to the warderobe of the kynges bedd, and bryng theym of the warderobe with the kynges stuff unto the chambr for makyng of the same bedde. Where as aught to be a gentylman-usher, iiii yomen of the chambr for to make the same bedde. The groome to stande at the bedds feete with his torch. They of the warderobe openyng the kinges stuff of hys bedde upon a fayre sheete, bytwen the sayde groome and the bedds fote, iii yeomen, or two at the leste, in every syde of the bedde; the gentylman-usher and parte commaundyng theym what they shall doo. A yoman with a dagger to searche the strawe of the kynges bedde that there be none untreuth therein. And this yoman to caste up the bedde of downe upon that, and oon of theym to tomble over yt for the serche thereof. They they to bete and tufle the sayde bedde, and to laye oon then the bolster without touchyng of the bedd where as it aught to lye. They they of the warderobe to delyver theym a fustyan takyng the saye thereof. All theyr yomen to laye theyr hands teroon at oones, that they touch not the bedd, tyll yt be layed as it sholde be by the comaundement of the ussher. And so the furste sheet in lyke wyse, and then to trusse in both sheets and fustyan rownde about the bedde of downe. The warderopre to delyver the second sheete unto two yomen, they to crosse it over theyr arme, and to stryke the bedde as the ussher shall more playnly shewe unto theym. Then every yoman layeing hande upon the sheete, to laye the same sheete upon the bedde. And so the other fustyan upon or ii with such coverynge as shall content the kynge. Thus doon, the ii yomen next to the bedde to laye down agene the overmore fustyan, the yomen of the warderobe delyverynge theym a pane sheete, the sayde yoman therewythall to cover the sayde bedde. And so then to laye down the overmost sheete from the beddes heed. And then the sayd ii yomen to laye all the ovemost clothes of a quarter of the bedde. Then the warderoper to delyver unto them such pyllowes as shall please the kynge. The sayd yoman to laye theym upon the bolster and the heed sheete with whych the sayde yoman shall cover the sayde pyllowes. And so to trusse the endes of the sayde sheete under every ende of the bolster. An then the sayd warderoper to delyver unto them ii lytle small pyllowes, werwythall the squyres for the bodye or gentylman-ussher shall give the saye to the warderoper, and to the yoman whych have layde on hande upon the sayd bedde. And then the sayd ii yomen to lay upon the sayde bedde toward the bolster as yt was bifore. They makyng a crosse and kissynge yt where there handes were. Then ii yomen next to the feete to make the feers as the ussher shall teche theym. And so then every of them sticke up the aungel about the bedde, and to lette down the corteyns of the sayd bedde, or sparver.

Item, a squyer for the bodye or gentylman-ussher aught to sett the kynges sword at hys beddes heed.

Item, a squyer for the bodye aught to charge a secret groome or page, to have the kepynge of the sayde bedde with a lyght unto the time the kynge be disposed to goo to yt.

Item, a groome or page aught to take a torche, whyle the bedde ys yn makyng, to feche a loof of brede, a pott wyth ale, a pott wyth wine, for them that maketh the bedde, and every man.

Item, the gentlyman-ussher aught to forbede that no manner of man do sett eny dysshe upon the kynge's bedde, for fere of hurtying of the kynge's ryche counterpoynt that lyeth therupon. And that the sayd ussher take goode heede, that noo man wipe or rubbe their handes uppon none arras of the kynges, wherby they myght bee hurted, in the chambr where the kynge ys specially, and in all other.

Fussy bugger, that Henry.

Never learn to do anything: if you don't learn, you'll always find someone else to do it for you.

Mark Twain

Law is merely the expression of the will of the strongest for the time being.

Brooks Adams

Answer: Bo Diddley, Marlene Dietrich, Phyllis Diller, Fats Domino, Diana Dors.

MAY 21

Question: There are five numbers in a row. The second number is twice the fifth. The first number is twice the fourth. The third number multiplied by itself equals itself. The second number times two equals the fourth number. What are the smallest whole numbers that fit this description?

On May 21, 1856, Senator Charles Sumner of Massachusetts verbally assaulted Senator Butler of South Carolina over the latter's views on the admission of Kansas to the Union as a slave state. He picked on the wrong man's uncle. The following day, Butler's nephew, Preston Brooks, a representative from South Carolina, went to Sumner's office and assaulted him physically with a gold-knobbed cane. The beating was almost fatal, and incapacitated Sumner for over three years. He never fully recovered.

Congress, always reluctant to punish its own, placed a formal chastisement in the Congressional Record. It simply informed Brooks that his actions were distasteful, and the representative received no other punishment.

Anger is never without an argument, but seldom with a good one.

Marquis of Halifax

The word "dactyl" is a poetic term used to designate one *foot* of meter which is stressed /∪∪ . Curiously, it derives from a Greek word, which means "finger."

Your feets too big.

Fats Waller

You *can* get blood from a stone! There's a trick to it, though: don't squeeze. Instead, do as a Canadian Red Cross nurse did in Victoria, British Columbia, in 1948, when she treated A. Stone—use a needle.

Another old saw bites the dust!

Answer: 8, 2, 0, 4, 1.

Notable Births

1688	Alexander Pope	1917	Dennis Day
1878	Glenn Curtis	1917	Raymond Burr
1904	Robert Montgomery	1923	Ara Parseghian
1904	Fats Waller	1926	Peggy Cass
1912	Harold Robbins	1926	Robert Creeley

Notable Events

996	Otto III crowned Holy Roman Emperor
1718	John Price, a hangman, hanged for murder, England
1775	Subahdar of Oude ceded Benares to East India Company
1819	First velocipedes used, New York City
1863	General Conference of Seventh Day Adventists organized
1881	American Red Cross organized by Clara Barton
1888	New York State Crematory authorized
1928	Ted Nowak of Boston, New York, walked 148 miles in 29 hours, 29 minutes
1934	Oskaloosa, Iowa, began to fingerprint its citizens
1951	Captain James Jabara of Wichita, Kansas, became first jet ace in history
1968	U.S. nuclear sub *Scorpion* lost at sea

What do the following words have in common : wrimpleplat, sprovit, blort, vit, grundy, vetch?

They're all terms associated with Frisbees, and they were in common Frisbee usage prior to 1957.

When Abigail Adams, this country's second First Lady, arrived in Washington, D.C., in 1800 and moved into the White House, she immediately wrote home to her sister in Massachusetts and complained bitterly of the condition of the mansion.

> Not one room is finished of the whole. . . . It is habitable by fires . . . thirteen of which we are obliged to keep daily, or sleep in wet and damp places . . . We have not the least fenceyard . . . and the great unfinished audience-room I make a drying room of, to hang the clothes in . . . .

Notable Births

1813	Richard Wagner	1924	Charles Aznavour
1859	Arthur Conan Doyle	1934	Peter Nero
1902	Al Simmons	1938	Susan Strasberg
1907	Laurence Olivier	1938	Richard Benjamin
1914	Vance Packard	1940	Michael Sarrazin

Notable Events

1455 Battle of Saint Alban's began War of the Roses
1856 Senator Sumner attacked in chambers by Representative Preston Brooks
1930 Lindbergh baby born
1931 First rattlesnake meat in cans marketed, Arcadia, Florida
1960 Israel announced capture of Adolph Eichmann
1961 South Korean military regime abolished parties, unions, social organizations
1964 Secretary of State Rusk hinted war could be extended to North Vietnam
1967 Department store fire in Brussels killed 322 people

Questions: How can you keep a rooster from crowing at dawn Monday morning?

Why will a bird with one wing always disagree with a two-winged bird?

Since there have been stories already in this book about unsavory characters who were transvestites, it seems only fair to tell the story of one who was more or less a hero. He was the Chevalier d'Eon de Beaumont, a Frenchman whose name has become a synonym for transvestism (eonism).

The first public mention of d'Eon occurred in 1761, when he served as secretary to the Duke de Nivernois in the peace negotiations with England to end the Seven Years' War. D'Eon acquitted himself well with the English court and government, and when a pact had been agreed upon, he was given the honor of carrying the news from George III to Louis XV. Upon his return from England, he was made a knight of the Royal Military Order of Saint Louis. Madame de Pompadour wrote of him in very favorable terms, and de Nivernois was so impressed by his abilities that he successfully petitioned Louis XV to make d'Eon the temporary ambassador to England.

But when Louis appointed the Count de Guercy as the permanent envoy, a position d'Eon expected to get, and relegated him to his former post of secretary, the chevalier refused to submit. He published a paper revealing some of the current secrets around the French court, and specifically indicted de Guercy for certain aspects of his conduct. De Guercy brought a libel action against him, but d'Eon, properly fearful for his life, did not appear at the King's Bench Court in London (where the case was being heard) or make any defense. The case was therefore decided against him. He remained in hiding until the end of 1764, when he himself brought suit against the count for conspiracy to murder him. Instead of simply denying the charges, the ambassador claimed diplomatic immunity, and the case never went to trial.

For the next twelve years, d'Eon laid low, only venturing out occasionally to see fencing matches, a sport in which he was expert. Then, in July 1777, an action was brought at King's Bench concerning a wager, the outcome of which depended on the sex of the chevalier, because apparently d'Eon had for some time been dressing as a woman. D'Eon never settled the score himself, but a memoir was published that claimed the chevalier *was* a woman, born in Burgundy to noble parents. In order to advance their child's position in life, they had, with the "girl's" consent, raised her as a boy. Thus she was able to go to the university, and became a successful doctor of civil and canon law.

The story went on to tell how, about 1754, Louis XV was introduced to d'Eon and made privy to "his" double identity. At that time the king wanted to form an alliance with Russia instead of with Prussia, but some preliminary intrigue was required before he could implement this. D'Eon was selected for the role of spy, and in or about 1755, made two trips to Russia, the first time as a woman, the second as a man. D'Eon succeeded so well that he was rewarded with many valuable gifts from the Empress Elizabeth and a lieutenancy in the dragoons by Louis.

The majority of this memoir is probably false, but there is some reasonable evidence that the story of the spy missions is at least based on fact.

After 1777, d'Eon only returned to France once, as a woman, in 1779. The last thirty years of his life were spent quietly, mostly in England. There is reason to believe that he himself was involved with the wagering about his sex (about £70,000 was involved), but he flatly denied it, and there is no solid evidence either way.

D'Eon died on May 22, 1810, in a London hospital. It was only then revealed that he was a biological male who had confused the majority of his acquaintances for over three decades.

To think that all in me of which my father would have felt a proper pride had I been a man, is deeply mortifying to him because I am a woman.

Elizabeth Cady Stanton

Richard Wagner had a silk fetish. He used to keep a piece of silk around so he could fondle it, and would often ask his wife to put on a silk dress and walk around so that he could listen to its rustling. He said the sound made his mind more fertile.

Wagner's music is better than it sounds.

Mark Twain

Answers: Have him for dinner Sunday.
Because there is always a difference of a-pinion between them.

MAY 23

Question: What's the state pictured here?

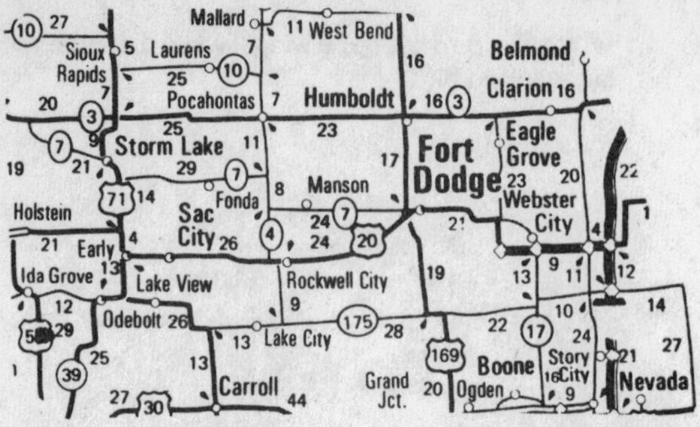

Notable Events

1498	Savanarola burned as a heretic, Florence
1611	Matthias crowned King of Bohemia
1701	Captain Kidd hanged on a trumped-up piracy charge
1785	Benjamin Franklin first described bifocals
1788	South Carolina ratified Constitution
1933	New Yorkers voted 20-1 for repeal of Prohibition
1934	Bonnie and Clyde killed
1937	John D. Rockefeller died
1939	Submarine *Squalis* went down off Portsmouth, New Hampshire, 26 men lost
1944	Icelanders voted to sever ties to Denmark
1945	Suicide of Himmler

There are certain rituals in the Catholic church that must be followed, but justice in certain cases is meted out according to who you are, not what you did. When Henry IV of France was reinstated in the church by Pope Gregory XII, after he had been excommunicated for heresy, church laws required that he must be flagellated as punishment. Henry knew and accepted this, but because he was a king, he was allowed to be whipped by proxy. His substitutes, however, were given heavy coats to wear during the ordeal, and even then, it was far from an ordinary whipping. Out of deference to the station their master occupied, the two whipping boys were hit so lightly it was recorded the punishment was as "if it had been a fly passed over them."

The proxies, men named D'Ossat and Du Perron, were rewarded for their part by being made cardinals of the church.

On top of everything else, Henry VIII was a poor loser. When Sir Nicholas Carew, a former friend of His Royal Highness, beat the king in a bowling match in 1539, Henry had a trumped-up charge of treason levied against him. Carew was promptly imprisoned and eventually beheaded.

Transcendentalism has been defined as the spiritual cognoscence of psychological irrefragibility connected with concutient ademption of incolumnient spirituality and etherialized contention of subsultory concretion. In other words, transcendentalism is two holes in a sandbank. A storm washes away the sandbank without disturbing the holes.

I go to seek a vast perhaps.

Francois Rabelais

Metaphysics is almost always an attempt to prove the incredible by an appeal to the unintelligible.

H. L. Mencken

Studies have shown that the average sex offender is a white, church-going man of average intelligence, who has no drug or alcohol problems.

Perhaps the all-time record for the sheer number of arrests and convictions run up by one person belongs to a man in New Orleans. As of 1975, when he was fifty-three, he'd been taken into custody 820 times and convicted of 421 various offenses, mostly drunkenness.

His name is Alfred L. Vice.

Sir Christopher Hatton (1549-1591) was made Lord High Chancellor of England because he danced so well.

This is the epitaph on a tomb in the County of Essex, England:

Here lies the man Richard
And Mary his wife;
Their surname was Pritchard,
They lived without strife;
And the reason was plain —
They abounded in riches,
They had no care or pain,
And his wife wore the breeches.

Answer: Iowa.

MAY 24

Notable Births

1819	Queen Victoria	1909	Wilbur Mills
1870	Benjamin Cardoza	1940	Joseph Brodsky
1883	Elsa Maxwell	1941	Bob Dylan

Notable Events

1844 First message sent over telegraph, Washington to Baltimore
1856 Massacre at Pottawotomie Creek by John Brown
1883 Brooklyn Bridge opened
1935 First major-league night game played, Cincinnati
1935 Weyerhauser baby kidnapped
1937 Supreme Court ruled Social Security constitutional
1949 Shanghai fell to Red Chinese
1959 First house with built-in bomb shelter shown, Pleasant Hills, Pennsylvania
1964 Three hundred people died in Peruvian soccer riots

Question: By what names are these people better known?
Issur Danielovitch
Melvyn Hesselberg
Michael Dowd, Jr.
Leila Koeber
Robert Zimmerman

All Scotsmen are supposed to be clever with money. One Scotsman named Arthur Furguson was an exceptional salesman as well.

When Furguson was standing in Trafalgar Square one day in the early 1920s, an American from Iowa struck up a conversation about Nelson's Column, the monument honoring Britain's famous admiral that stands in the center of the square. Furguson agreed that it was a beautiful statue — and then he decided to have a little fun. It was a pity, the Scotsman said, that it would so soon be leaving England.

"What?" asked the incredulous American.

Furguson went on to describe how, because of Britain's soaring foreign debt, war costs, and what have you, the government had been forced to put the monument up for sale. Of course, because of the sensitive nature of such a sale, the fact had not been made public; but he, Furguson, knew, since he had been asked to find a buyer.

"How much?" said the American immediately.

Furguson told him the price was £6,000, "including the lions at the column's base." He soon had a draft for the money from the Iowan, and he even recommended a reliable shipping firm. Later that summer, he duped someone into paying £1,000 for Big Ben, and milked another tourist of £2,000 as a down payment on Buckingham Palace, the home of the British royal family.

Furguson was never caught in Britain, and in 1925 he moved to the United States, where he kept making transactions. In that year he leased the White House to a cattle rancher who thought it mighty opulent, and a bargain at the price: $100,000 annually, with the first year of the ninety-nine-year lease payable in advance. He may also have been one of the half dozen or so people in the last hundred years who have managed to sell the Brooklyn Bridge.

It was a sale of an item in Manhattan's other river that led to Furguson's downfall. He'd managed to convince an Australian from Sydney that New York Harbor was being widened, and Bedloe's Island, on which the Statue of Liberty stands, was going to be right in the middle of the new shipping lanes. For a number of reasons it would not be practical to move the statue to another site, so the government had decided to sell it. He was the sales agent. The down payment would be $100,000.

The Australian agreed to the deal, and set off to raise the money from bankers and friends in New York City. When Furguson followed him every step of the way, he began to get suspicious. He arranged to meet Furguson with the money. Then he went to the police and, instead of the down payment, brought a policeman to the meeting place with him. Furguson ended up being convicted of a variety of frauds, but he received only five years in jail, and was released in 1930.

He died eight years later, but lived very well in the meantime on the money he had managed to put away before his capture.

I would rather be the man who bought the Brooklyn Bridge than the man who sold it.

Will Rogers

Answer: Kirk Douglas, Melvyn Douglas, Mike Douglas, Marie Dresser, Bob Dylan.

MAY 25

Question: Theseus went into the Minotaur's maze without string, bread crumbs, or anything, slew the beast, and still managed to find his way out. How?

The Duke of Cumberland once had a less-than-sensible aide-de-camp, one Colonel Disney. Disney was widely noted for his lack of intelligence, and in all probability was mentally subnormal. On one occasion, when the duke was being received by Queen Victoria, Disney decided to investigate the palace while he waited for the duke. He entered Her Majesty's chambers, something prohibited in itself, and proceeded to relieve himself into a conveniently placed golden vase. Needless to say, he himself was relieved of his duties by the duke. To his dying day, Disney never understood why.

A difference in taste in jokes is a great strain on the affections.

George Eliot

In May 1951, the Otis Elevator Company opened its new Washington, D.C., offices in a one-story building.

Notable Births

1803	Ralph Waldo Emerson	1898	Bennett Cerf
1803	Edward Bulwer-Lytton	1898	Gene Tunney
1818	Jacob Burckhardt	1908	Theodore Roethke
1878	Bill Robinson	1926	Miles Davis
1881	Bela Bartok	1929	Beverly Sills
1892	Josef Tito	1943	Leslie Uggams

Notable Events

1482	First book to contain mathematical figures printed
1743	American Philosophical Society founded in Philadelphia by Benjamin Franklin
1887	Fire at Opera Comique killed 200 people in Paris
1935	Babe Ruth hit his last home run
1935	Jesse Owens began streak of 6 world records in two days
1941	The *Bismarck* sunk Britain's largest battleship, the *Hood*
1965	Muhammad Ali beat Sonny Liston in round 1, title defense, Lewiston, Maine

In 1921, sixty-seven businesses founded by people of Czech descent in the United States employed 1,500 people and controlled 75 percent of the world's mother-of-pearl industry.

Notice anything peculiar about these equations?

$78 \times 345 = 26{,}910$
$27 \times 594 = 16{,}038$
$3 \times 5{,}694 = 17{,}082$
$64 \times 915 = 80 + 732$
$2 \times 3{,}485 = 1 \times 6{,}970$

They all contain each digit from 0 through 9 once.

The Swedish scientist Carl Linnaeus once performed an experiment to see if pigs really did eat like pigs. He discovered that they didn't, but that goats and sheep did. These were his findings:

Animal	Foods Eaten	Foods Refused
Cow	276	218
Goat	449	126
Sheep	387	141
Horse	262	212
Pig	72	171

On this date in 1595 was hanged one Troeveetie, of Leyden in the Netherlands. He had been convicted of biting a child's finger, albeit accidentally, and sentenced to death.

If you haven't guessed already, Troeveetie was a dog.

Answer: He simply kept his right (or left) hand along the wall at all times. In that way he'd complete the whole maze and return to the entrance.

Notable Births

673	Venerable Bede	1907	John Wayne
1689	Lady Mary Montagu	1908	Robert Morley
1700	Count von Zinzendorf	1910	Laurance Rockefeller
1894	Paul Lukas	1923	James Arness

Notable Events

1768 Captain James Cook began first round-the-world voyage
1830 Earthquake in Canton, China, killed 7,000 people
1894 Czar Nicholas II crowned
1937 U.S. steelworkers went out on strike
1952 Second World War formally ended with Germany
1956 Nation's first trailer bank opened, Locust Grove, New York
1959 Khrushchev visited Albania
1973 Kiane Nowell became Los Angeles's first female lifeguard

Questions: Why is fresh milk like something that never happened?

When did the greatest drought in the English history take place?

On May 26, 1738, Donald MacKay was hanged in Dornoch, Scotland. The town graciously granted his last request. The condemned man desperately wanted to have a bagpiper play a reel at the gallows, because, MacKay said, he had never danced in his whole life, and could not bear the thought of dying without doing so once.

In Dornoch sixteen years before, Janet Horne was burned as a witch because she mispronounced a word in the Lord's Prayer.

Interesting town, Dornoch.

If you are happy you can always to learn to dance.

Balinese saying

"Don't drink the water!" is the most common warning tourists get from well-wishers before taking a trip abroad. There is good reason for this, of course. Even if the water is disease-free, it may often have a different chemical composition from a traveler's domestic water, and may make him or her quite "uncomfortable."

In 1931, the British novelist Arnold Bennett set out to prove that the warning was an old wives' tale by drinking *l'eau de Paris*. He shouldn't have. He contracted typhoid from it and died.

If everybody contemplates the infinite instead of fixing the drains, many of us will die of cholera.

John Rich

Until a short time ago, Chinese mice would not eat cheese. It was relatively unknown in China until the twentieth century, and the mice never developed a taste for it.

Some of the witch scares of Europe and America may have been the result of people eating poisonous plants. For example, the common Enchanter's Nightshade (*Atropa belladonna*) contains alkaloids that can cause hallucinations, delirium, and even death. It also contains scopolamine, a chemical that often gives someone who ingests it a feeling of flying. Possibly, some people who were poisoned by plants, unknowingly, associated the resulting hallucinations and physical ills with some quite coincidental meeting with a strange or unpleasant neighbor who, they then believed, had used witchcraft against them.

Before mating can take place, a male porcupine must urinate on his partner to soften her quills.

Answers: Because it hasn't a-curd.

1837-1901. There was only one reign in those 64 years.

MAY 27

Question: What's the state shown here?

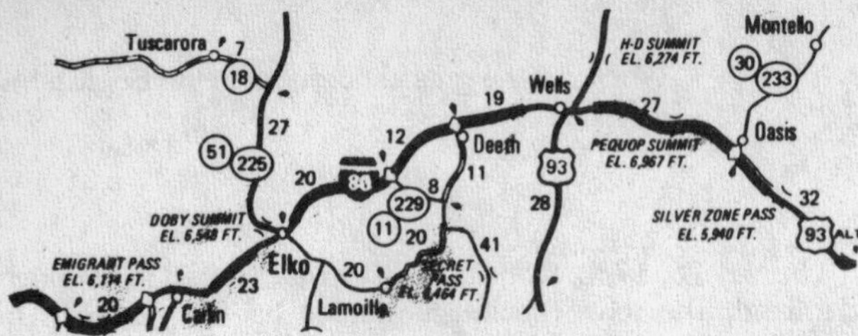

Know ye whom it may concern that I, Norton I . . . have heard serious complaints from our adherents that our wardrobe is a national disgrace. . . . We warn those whose duty it is to attend to these affairs that their scalps are in danger if our said need is unheeded.

Reacting to this imperial fiat, The San Francisco Board of Supervisors voted unanimously to outfit the emperor at public expense.

What kind of man could make a quarter of a million dollars in three years (*1850* dollars!), subsequently proclaim himself emperor of the United States, and end up getting his regal wardrobe on welfare? A real character called Joshua Abraham Norton.

Not much is known about America's only emperor before he arrived in this country at the age of thirty. When he reached San Francisco to take advantage of the Gold Rush, he soon realized that his fortune could be made much more easily in trade than in prospecting. In a year the city had exploded from a hamlet of a few hundred people to a bustling shantytown of over twenty thousand people. He opened an office as a commodity trader and speculated his life's savings and inheritance in various ventures. In less than three years, Joshua Norton had made $250,000.

Then he got involved in rice. The price of this miner's staple varied greatly with supply, from four to thirty-two cents a pound. When he heard that China had placed an embargo on rice going to California, Norton moved as quickly as possible to corner the market, anticipating a shortage and dreaming of a monopoly. The wholesale price was high, but he was so sure of himself that he hazarded every available dollar he had. Then the market collapsed as cheap rice came flooding in. Norton was ruined, and forced to declare bankruptcy.

He moved from his fashionable quarters into a fifty-cent a day boarding house, and for a while worked at odd jobs to support himself. Without a thriving business to keep his mind busy, he began to meditate on the course the country was taking, and he didn't like it. He told his friends that a democracy was too inefficient to get a country through times of stress (the Civil War was imminent), and what America needed was a good dose of monarchy. He repeated this so frequently and fervently that his friends began teasingly to address him as "Emperor" and "Your Gracious Highness." Norton came to take the notion seriously enough to capitalize on it. In September, 1859, he delivered a proclamation to the *San Francisco Bulletin* and declared himself emperor.

Soon thereafter, he appeared regularly, resplendent in a light blue officer's uniform trimmed in gold, and a rose in his lapel. On his head was a general's cap, at his side a saber, and on his feet he wore navy boots cut open along the sides to accommodate his corns. He carried a cane or a colorful umbrella, according to the weather.

And so Emperor Norton I set about making things right with America. Disgusted with the fraud and corruption of Congress, he declared imperially, "We do hereby abolish Congress, and it is hereby abolished." Congress remained in session, of course, and so Norton I dispatched his designated commander of the army, instructing him to "proceed with a suitable force and clear the halls of Congress." A few weeks later he abolished political parties and dissolved the United States itself, suggesting that the governors of the states should maintain order until he could consolidate his power.

To support himself, Norton I issued Bonds of the Empire, which were printed for him for free by a friend to whom he had promised the office of chancellor of the Exchequer. These bonds sold for fifty cents each, and were redeemable in twenty years at 5 percent interest. Norton, however, soon found he could do better by taxing people and businesses directly. Regularly, he would climb on his bicycle and levy anything from a dime to a few dollars on people and businesses. This was duly recorded in Norton's tax roll book, and he would be on his way. The emperor was also known to make appointments with bankers to discuss million-dollar loans for public projects he had in mind, and then leave, quite satisfied with the quarter or fifty cents they gave him instead.

San Franciscans took him to their hearts. He ate for free at the finest restaurants in town. Many of the theaters in the city had an orchestra seat reserved for him, and it was customary for the audience to stand when he paraded down the aisle. The streetcars of the city were free to him, and he had a lifetime pass on the Central Pacific Railroad. Once, Norton was arrested for vagrancy by a policeman who was new to the city. The chief of police heard about it and rushed to the station to release the emperor personally.

Norton took his high office and its responsiblities seriously. He carried on a mostly one-sided correspondence with Lincoln, Davis, Lee, Grant, and Chancellor Bismarck of Germany, and he later annexed the title "Protector of Mexico" to his name to save the poor Mexicans from the avaricious Napoleon III, whom he despised.

In January 1880, Norton died on a San Francisco street, apparently the victim of a heart attack suffered on his way to attend a debate. The headline in the next morning's *Chronicle* read "*Le Roi Est Mort.*" In 1934, his remains were transferred to the Woodlawn Cemetary, with tremendous pomp. At the close of the ceremonies his long-awaited tombstone was unveiled:

NORTON I
EMPEROR OF THE UNITED STATES
AND PROTECTOR OF MEXICO
JOSHUA A. NORTON 1819-1880

A small tribute, really, to the man who was the first to propose the Golden Gate Bridge.

Notable Births

1265	Dante Alighieri	1894	Dashiell Hammett
1794	Cornelius Vanderbilt	1907	Rachel Carson
1818	Amelia Bloomer	1911	Hubert Humphrey
1867	Arnold Bennett	1912	John Cheever
1871	Georges Rouault	1917	Lilli Palmer

Notable Events

1647	Achsah Young executed — first convicted witch in New England
1679	Habeus Corpus Act passed in Britain
1796	Piano patented by J.S. McLean
1896	First intercollegiate bicycle race held, New York City
1905	Russian fleet captured by Japanese
1931	Piccard reached 52,493 feet in a balloon, Austria
1937	Golden Gate Bridge opened
1941	The *Bismarck* was sunk by British ships *Rodney* and *George V*

Answer: Nevada.

MAY 28

Notable Births

1759	William Pitt	1919	May Swenson
1807	Louis Agassiz	1932	Stephen Birmingham
1896	Warren Giles	1935	Carroll Baker
1908	Ian Fleming	1938	Jerry West
1916	Walker Percy	1944	Gladys Knight

Notable Events

584 B.C.	Eclipse in Mediterranean
1864	Maximilian began his reign in Mexico
1919	Armenia declared its independence
1934	Dionne quintuplets born
1935	Supreme Court declared NRA unconstitutional
1940	Dunkirk evacuation began
1959	First animals from a space shot retrieved
1961	South Korea outlawed 90 percent of its newspapers
1961	Members of the American Republic Army blew up 3 A T & T communications towers in Utah and Nevada
1963	Windstorms in Bangladesh claimed 22,000 lives
1977	Southgate, Kentucky, nightclub fire killed 164 people

Probably the greatest collision in the history of the seas happened on May 27, 1945, off Newfoundland, when a lead ship in a convoy of seventy-six vessels struck an iceberg. A quick check by sonar and radar equipment disclosed eight other icebergs in the vicinity, and the ship sounded an iceberg alarm. In the confusion that followed during the next ten minutes, twenty-two ships collided. Miraculously, none of the vessels were lost, and not one sailor lost his life; but since that time ships have not been required to travel in convoy in the North Atlantic Ocean during iceberg season.

Most elephants weigh less than the tongue of the blue whale.

Bostonians have long had the repurations for being rabid sports fans, but perhaps their most notable accomplishment in this field occurred over eighty years ago.

The Boston and the Baltimore baseball clubs were playing a ballgame in May 1894, when the teams' respective third basemen got into a brawl. The benches promptly emptied, and a number of fistfights broke out in the stands. The umpires were just getting everything back in order when someone smelled smoke.

Some fans, for whatever reason, had decided to set fire to the bleachers.

Bleacher fires aren't an uncommon occurrence, but this one went on to destroy 170 buildings and cause a third of a million dollars in property damage. Over two thousand people were left homeless.

That was one of the reasons manager John McGraw wouldn't play his New York Giants, winners of the National League Pennant in 1904, against the Red Sox in the World Series, forcing its cancellation that year. McGraw had been the Baltimore third baseman on that fateful day.

Answer: Maxim Gorky, Lee Grant, Peter Graves, Joel Grey.

Question: By what names are these people better known?
Alexei Peshkov
Lyora Rosenthal
Peter Arness
Joel Katz

Shamyl was a chieftan of the Caucasus who waged war for years against the Russians (1834-59). Once, he even took the czar's uncle prisoner in an ambush. Russian officials went to talk to Shamyl about the possibility of ransom and were instructed to make an offer of one million rubles. But Shamyl drove a hard bargain. He was not going to accept the first offer they made, especially when he didn't really know how much it was. "I won't accept a kopek less than five thousand rubles!" he told them. The officials hedged, but finally agreed to meet his price.

When choosing between two evils, I always like to try the one I've never tried before.

Mae West

MAY 29

Question: A prime number cannot be divided evenly by any whole numbers other than 1 and itself. What are the next 4 prime numbers after 71?

Patrick Henry, of "Give me liberty, or give me death" fame, was a unique politician. During his life he was offered a seat in the Senate, ambassadorships to Spain and France, and the positions of secretary of State and chief justice of the United States Supreme court. He refused them all. He did serve as governor of Virginia for five terms, but declined to run for a sixth, and when he was elected anyway, he refused to take office. Henry was also the first American politician to use the phrase, "My fellow citizens," when referring to his constituents.

You can take all the humility in Washington and fit it into John Wayne's navel and still have room for Carl Albert.

Fishbait Miller

Mohammad II, the sultan of Turkey from 1451 to 1481, loved watermelon, especially for dessert. On one occasion, before he could finish his meal, he was called away by important business, and when he returned, he found his watermelon had disappeared. He questioned the fourteen pages who were in the room, but they all firmly declared that none of them had eaten it. Mohammad didn't believe this, so he sent for his surgeon and ordered him to open up the stomachs of each of the pages. Fourteen operations later, it was evident that none of the pages had had any watermelon.

The sultan said he was sorry.

Blessed is the man who, having nothing to say, abstains from giving wordy evidence of the fact.

George Eliot

We should forgive our enemies, but only after they have been hanged first.

Heinrich Heine

Answer: 73, 79, 83, 89.

Notable Births

1736	Patrick Henry	1898	Bea Lillie
1874	G.K. Chesterton	1903	Bob Hope
1892	Max Brand	1917	John F. Kennedy

Notable Events

1434	Romans revolted against temporal authority of pope
1453	Fall of Constantinople to Turks
1790	Rhode Island ratified Constitution
1914	*Empress of Ireland* sank in Saint Lawrence River; 1,024 people died
1935	Federal drug sanitorium in Lexington, Kentucky, received first patients
1953	Mount Everest conquered by Hillary and Tensing Norkay

It's often been said, and truthfully so, that he who understands, controls. Priests in Medieval Europe were believed to understand the nature of trial by ordeal, and so, of course, they controlled it. And some clerics certainly were not above influencing the outcomes of some of the ordeals. It's known that, in the ordeal of fire, a test reserved for certain of the nobility, priests would on occasion substitute a red-painted rock for the piece of hot lead that was supposed to be used, if they believed in a person's innocence or wished him to be free. In the ordeal of the cross, in which the accused had to choose between two pieces of linen, one wrapped around a stick, the other around a crucifix, it was easy for a priest to ensure that a man made the choice the priest felt was appropriate.

But the clearest instance of the understanding/controlling doctrine was in the case of the ordeal the priests reserved as a test of their own brotherhood. It was called the corsned, the ordeal of bread and cheese. In this, guilt or innocence was determined by whether or not a cleric could eat a piece of bread and a piece of cheese without choking. If he couldn't, he was guilty.

It would seem that a number of these medieval priests have been reincarnated and now sit on the Senate and House Ethics Committees.

Next to knowing when to seize an opportunity, the most important thing in life is when to forgo an advantage.

Benjamin Disraeli

During the summer of 1955, fifty people died in Tokyo from arsenic, which had been inadvertently mixed up in a batch of powdered milk. The product's maker, the Morinaga Milk Company, expressed its "humblest apologies" to their victims and their families.

Here is an epitaph from Maryland:

My father and mother were both insane
I inherited the terrible stain.
My grandfather, grandmother, aunts, and uncles
Were lunatics all, and yet died of carbuncles.

The goosestep is an invention of the British Army.

Notable Births

1672	Peter the Great	1927	Clint Walker
1901	Cornelia Otis Skinner	1936	Keir Dullea
1903	Countee Cullen	1939	Michael J. Pollard
1909	Benny Goodman	1943	Gale Sayers

Notable Events

1431	Joan of Arc supposedly burned at the stake for sorcery
1806	Andrew Jackson fought a duel at Red River, Kentucky
1883	Panic on the Brooklyn Bridge — 12 people trampled to death
1896	First automobile accident in America, New York City
1954	Ms. D. Leather of Birmingham University broke women's 5-minute mile
1962	Bus crash in Ahmadabad, India, killed 69 people

Question: What did the mayonnaise say to the little boy who looked into the ice box?

There seem to be a number of inaccuracies in the traditional story of Joan of Arc.

"Jeanne d'Arc" does mean Joan of Arc in English, but Jeanne d'Arc wasn't the saint's name. She was usually called Jeanne la Pucelle (the Maid), and her family name was in all probability Darc; there was no "Arc" known anywhere near where she grew up, and records in her town list her exclusively as Darc, a common name in that region.

She was born in 1410 in Domremi, on the Meuse River in the province of Champagne. Little is known of her childhood save that she had a reputation as a rather strange young woman, and she was said to be somewhat masculine in appearance.

In 1428, she told her parents that for five years she'd been having visions of Michael the Archangel, and he had introduced her to Saint Catherine and Saint Margaret. He'd also told her that with their guidance, she would become the saviour of France. Later that year, she claimed to have been instructed in a vision to go to Rheims and make sure that the dauphin Charles was crowned king of France. (Charles was thought to be illegitimate, and therefore unable to ascend the throne; and a predictable power struggle among various factions of the French nobility was in progress at the time.) Her parents scoffed at her notions, but an uncle didn't, and he persuaded them to let her go with him to see Charles.

Initially, Charles was no more impressed with the story of Joan than her parents were, but he finally agreed to see her out of curiousity, and because of her growing reputation among the people. They met on February 27, 1429. Joan immediately won his favor by reporting that the Archangel had told her that Charles was indeed the true son of his father and should take the throne. This, and the mysterious discovery of a prophecy of Merlin that foretold that France would be saved by a virgin, were enough for the dauphin. He cleared her of the suspicion of witchcraft, and sent her in soldier's clothes to Orleans, which was being besieged by the British.

Joan's arrival was preceeded by stories of her powers, and when she reached Orleans, the morale of the French force of six thousand soldiers skyrocketed, while that of the English plummeted. To the French she was a holy saviour; to the English a witch. The English raised the seige on May 8 and retreated. Joan and the French Army followed and scored several other victories in May and June.

By this time, however, despite her superb record and leadership, the French nobility at court had turned against Joan. They were jealous of her, and wary of the influence she might hold over Charles after the war was over. They convinced the malleable Charles to order her attack on Paris halted and to bring her to court, where she was in effect kept as their prisoner.

She managed to escape, however, and tried to rally renegade forces of the army to join her in an independent struggle to drive the English out of France completely. Only a small fraction did so. A number of setbacks and portents followed, and public support for Joan fell off rapidly. Finally, after a sortie near Compiegne, the town gate was closed before Joan could reach sanctuary, and she was captured by the British. After some complicated manuevering and an unfair trial, she was convicted of witchcraft and various heresies in Rouen, and was supposedly burned at the stake there on May 30, 1431.

However, the archives of Orleans record the marriage of one Jeanne la Pucelle to a man named d'Armoise after this date, and also list a dozen occasions on which money was paid to one Jeanne la Pucelle or Jeanne d'Armoise. This woman may have been an imposter, but when she visited Orleans it was to see the real Joan's brothers, and these brothers and the other townspeople apparently accepted her as the real Jeanne. Some historians assume that Joan was bought off the stake, or that a woman criminal was substituted for her.

Or, then again, the original story may well be true.

The tyrant dies and his rule is over; the martyr dies and his rule begins.

Soren Kierkegaard

Answer: "Please close the door — I'm dressing."

MAY 31

Question: Which of these countries are *not* on the Equator?

Borneo
Thailand
Brazil
Bolivia
Kenya

Notable Births

1819	Walt Whitman	1912	Henry Jackson
1893	Elizabeth Coatsworth	1923	Prince Rainier
1898	Norman Vincent Peale	1931	Clint Eastwood
1908	Don Ameche	1943	Joe Namath

Notable Events

1770	Louis XVI married Marie Antoinette
1850	Universal suffrage in France abolished
1889	Johnstown Flood took 2,295 lives
1916	Battle of Jutland took place
1919	First wedding performed in an airplane, over Houston, Texas
1929	Reindeer born in Beverly, Massachusetts zoo
1935	Earthquake in Quetta, India, killed 60,000 people
1937	First quadruplets graduated from college, Waco, Texas
1955	Chinese released 4 U.S. airmen charged with espionage
1962	Adolf Eichmann hanged
1964	Longest major league ballgame played, 7 hours, 23 minutes, Mets-Giants
1970	Earthquake in Peru claimed 66,800 victims

On May 31, 1937, an explosion in a Chicago sewer line shot a manhole cover high into the air. It sailed above a five-story building, crashed down through the elevator shaft skylight, and then through the roof of the elevator itself. Three men in the elevator were unharmed, but Alfa C. Day was killed.

Though a good deal is too strange to be believed, nothing is too strange to have happened.

Thomas Hardy

Events explode suddenly, like firecrackers in the face of innocent passerby.

Charlie Chan

After extensive research with mouse deterrants, the Humane Society of Fallstown, Maryland, has found that mice are repelled by tiger urine.

If mankind had continued to be the slave of precedent we should still be living in caves and subsisting on shellfish and wild berries.

Philip Snowden

In baiting a mousetrap with cheese, always leave room for the mouse.

H. H. Munro (Saki)

"Bachelor" originally came from the Low Latin word *baccalarius*, which meant a young man who tended cows. You can see there would be better things to call a bachelor's degree than a sheepskin.

Eighty years ago, when vaudeville was still the movies' elder brother, one immensely popular act featured Jadji Ali, the "Amazing Regurgitator." He could swallow anything and regurgitate it at will — buttons, coins, plugs, you name it.

Not bad, but not great. But as the highlight of his performance, Ali really gave the audiences a fantastic show. First he would down a pint of kerosene and a gallon of water. His assistant then wheeled out a replica of a castle or some such building and lit a match near it. Suddenly, Ali would spew the kerosene up from his stomach in a graceful arc towards the building, which would then immediately burst into a blaze of fire. He'd let it burn for a few moments before extinguishing the inferno by bringing up the water. It seldom failed to result in a standing ovation.

That's entertainment!

Answer: Thailand and Bolivia.

Lots of people have trouble sleeping, but when one hears of the quirks of the high and mighty, there seems to be an extra quality of oddness to them. Cornelius Vanderbilt, for instance, could not sleep unless the legs of his bed were each placed in a saucer and then dusted with salt. It kept the evil spirits away, of course.

If you're a homing pigeon fancier, try this experiment. Take an egg that is about to be hatched and ship it to another location, far from home. Then wait to see if you get a new young bird in a few months. Pigeons hatched under these conditions have often been known to home back to the place where they were laid.

The first official act of King Henry VI of England was the appointment of a royal servant to whip him. This may seem very strange — but when Henry succeeded to the throne in 1422 he was only nine months old. The document, which names "Dame Alice Butler . . . to attend our person with license to chastise us reasonably from time to time" was signed by the child's thumbprint.

The sea cucumber is actually an aquatic animal, although it does look very much like a garden cucumber. The sea cucumber has an odd way of escaping its enemies; it spills its guts out in an explosive burst. Fortunately, it has the capacity to grow a new inside quickly.

For many centuries, females outnumbered males in Mongolia by a goodly number. Among the Urdus, a family avoided the disgrace of having an unmarried daughter at home by developing an ingenious custom — every fifth female child in a family officially married her family's doormat.

JUNE

JUNE 1

Question: By what names are these people better known?

Leonard Hacker
Reginald Carey
Vito Farinola
Mary Frances Penick
Doris von Kappelhoff

If you're a rural Icelandic fisherman, you'd do well to avoid old-fashioned smoked salmon, trout, and mutton. In some areas of Iceland where these foods are consumed heavily, cancer of the stomach accounts for up to 45 percent of all male deaths. The reason seems to lie with the traditional smoking process, which can saturate a kilogram of fish with as much of the known carcinogen 3,4 benzpyrene as is found in two cartons of cigarettes. Many fishermen on long voyages consume daily as much as a kilogram of the suspect foods.

But, rural Icelandic fishermen, take heart! People who eat equivalent amounts of *commercially* smoked fish or meat have rates of stomach cancer of under 5 percent.

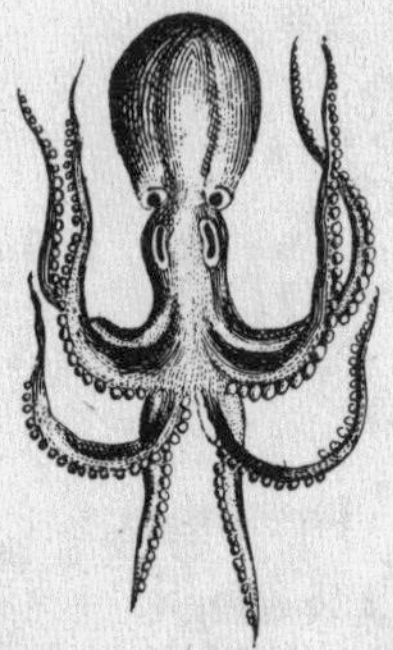

Octopi are smarter than any fish, and are thought by some experts to be as intelligent as cats.

Several years ago, during a gangland war, underworld hitmen Jimmy Gallo and Joe Conigliaro picked up a gentleman who went by the name of Vinnie Ba Ba to take him "for a ride." Vinnie was sandwiched between them in the back seat and they had their guns drawn when the driver of the car suddenly made a sharp turn and sent all the passengers tumbling. The guns discharged, and Gallo and Conigliaro each ended up shot by the other's gun.

Vinnie Ba Ba escaped, and now each year on the anniversary of the bizarre event, he sends Conigliaro, who was permanently paralyzed as a result of his wound, a new set of batteries for his electric wheelchair and a card that reads, "Keep rolling!"

A fellow in Colorado figured it out: In his eighty years, he'd spent six months tying his tie, three months scolding children, and eight days telling dogs to shut up and lie down.

The name "greyhound" has nothing to do with the color of this particular breed. It is a combination of Icelandic and English words, "grey" being the Icelandic word for hound — so greyhound is actually a pleonism, "hound-hound."

Answer: Buddy Hackett, Rex Harrison, Vic Damone, Skeeter Davis, Doris Day.

Notable Births

1637	Jacques Marquette	1926	Andy Griffith
1801	Brigham Young	1926	Marilyn Monroe
1878	John Masefield	1934	Pat Boone

Notable Events

1638	First earthquake in America recorded, Plymouth, Massachusetts
1790	England formed an alliance with Maranthas in India
1813	James Lawrence ordered crew not to give up the *Chesapeake* ("Don't give up the ship!")
1908	John Krohn began walk around nation's perimeter with a wheelbarrow
1939	House defeated Townsend Plan
1941	Crete overrun by Nazis
1957	Don Bowden became America's first under-4 minute miler
1958	De Gaulle became French premier
1958	Fishery limits extended to 12 miles by Iceland
1954	Windstorms in Bangladesh killed 30,000 people

On June 1, 1908, John A. Krohn began the first perimeter walk of the United States by a man pushing a wheelbarrow. He completed his journey 357 days later, after traveling 9,024 miles through 1,209 towns. On the journey he wore out eleven pairs of shoes, 112 pairs of socks, and five wheels, but he never walked on Sundays.

Roundabout way often shortest way to correct destination.
Charlie Chan

In 1939, Walter Nillson undertook one of the greatest stunts of all time. Under the sponsorship of "Ripley's Believe It or Not," he set out to cross the width of America, 3,306 miles, on an 8½-foot-tall unicycle. He completed the journey in 117 days, and was later honored by Ripley's with its "Greatest Feat of the Year" award.

In all of those miles, Nillson never once fell, but the ordeal gave him crippling physical problems for the rest of his life.

JUNE 2

Notable Births

1732	Martha Washington	1899	Edwin Way Teale
1740	Marquis de Sade	1904	Johnny Weissmuller
1803	Mikhail Glinka	1938	Sally Kellerman
1840	Thomas Hardy	1940	King Constantine II
1875	Thomas Mann	1941	Stacy Keach
1890	Hedda Hopper	1944	Marvin Hamlisch

Notable Events

1697 Augustus of Saxony converted to Roman Catholic Church
1793 Fall of Girondists in France
1883 First official night baseball game played, Fort Wayne, Indiana
1932 John D. Rockefeller, Jr., called for repeal of Prohibition
1933 Gift of White House swimming pool accepted by FDR
1946 Italy voted to abolish monarchy
1953 Coronation of Queen Elizabeth II

Martha Washington's bathing suit had weights sewn into the hem at her ankles to ensure modesty.

The wife of Clark Tibbetts, the director of the University of Michigan's Institute for Human Relations, sued him for divorce in June 1948. She claimed he made a note in his little black book every time she burned the toast.

When Mother Nature gets down to reproduction, she doesn't know when to quit. According to the naturalist Edwin Way Teale, if one female aphid and her progeny (aphids are one one-tenth of an inch long) were allowed to breed unmolested for one year, and all the descendants survived to breed themselves, the resulting aphids would, when laid head to tail, cover a distance of 2,500 *light* years.

We hope that, when the insects take over the world, they will remember with gratitude how we took them along on all our picnics.

Bill Vaughn

Evolution loves death more than it loves you or me.

Annie Dillard

Question: Was it more or less expensive to live in each of these cities than to live in New York in 1979?

a Budapest, Hungary
b Damascus, Syria
c Lagos, Nigeria
d Warsaw, Poland

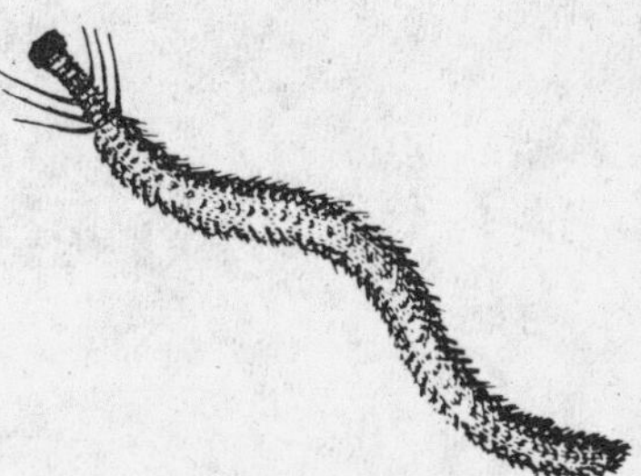

In her Pulitzer Prize-winning book *Pilgrim at Tinker Creek*, Annie Dillard tells the remarkable story of the life-cycle of the horsehair worm. That there are any horsehair worms at all is remarkable enough — they seem to have as much chance of propagating themselves as a gambler does of being dealt two consecutive royal flushes.

The horsehair worm begins by wrapping its eggs around vegetation near the surface of a pond. The eggs hatch and the larvae swim out looking for a host body in which to develop. Some will find a nymph, or a similar host; most won't. The fortunate larvae then feed on their hosts for a time, leave them, and encyst themselves on vegetation near the shore. So far, the horsehair's history isn't radically different from that of many creatures breeding in still waters, but this has been the easy part of the worm's cycle.

Once a larva is encysted, the water level of its home must drop. This has to happen fairly quickly, since the worm has only a limited amount of food in its underwater cocoon on which to sustain itself. *If* the water level drops, then a *suitable* land insect must come to the exposed plant and eat the cyst along with its own dinner of vegetation. (Horsehair worms are particular. Some that will grow in beetles will not grow in grasshoppers, and vice versa.) Assuming all has gone well so far, the cyst bursts to free the horsehair worm, which now measures up to three feet, in the land host's body. The worm then begins to eat its new host. With any luck (and if the horsehair has made it to this point, it's pretty amazing) the worm will either bore out of its host or be excreted by it near enough to a body of water so the worm can reach the water before it dries out — horsehair worms are not agile on land — or so a heavy rain can wash it into the water.

So how long has it been since you went to the casino?

If at first you don't succeed you're running about average.

M. H. Alderson

Ida K. Vartanian from Oakland, California, had a husband who refused to keep their home warm enough to make her pet rat comfortable, and complained all the time that it ate too much. She divorced him in 1948.

No one can have a higher opinion of him than I have — and I think he is a dirty little beast.

W. S. Gilbert

Answer: *a* less, *b* more, *c* more, *d* less.

JUNE 3

Questions: What's the relation of a loaf of bread to a locomotive?

Why is a chicken pie like a gunsmith's shop?

Notable Births

1771	Sydney Smith	1925	Tony Curtis
1780	William Hone	1926	Allen Ginsburg
1808	Jefferson Davis	1926	Colleen Dewhurst
1903	Ellen Corby	1931	Bert Lance
1911	Paulette Goddard	1936	Larry McMurtry

Notable Events

1862	General Lee assumed control of Confederate forces
1893	Anti-saloon League of Ohio formed
1937	Edward VIII and Wallis Simpson married after his abdication
1961	Franco denounced Western policy, democracy, and capitalism
1962	Air France jet crashed on takeoff from Paris, 130 killed
1963	DC-7 crashed in British Columbia, left 101 dead
1963	Pope John XXIII died
1963	Martial law declared in South Korea

There really was a Jethro Tull, and he was alive and gardening in England 250 years ago. Tull was trained as a lawyer, but he discovered this sedentary occupation was bad for his health, and so became an avid and inventive farmer. Through his experiments, he developed his famous techniques for drill sowing and frequent howing. The first saved one-third of the seed usually needed to plant a field and yielded better germination. The second drastically reduced the amount of fertilizer a farmer needed to use on his crops. This simple change in farming methods was one of the greatest advances in agriculture of the eighteenth century. Tull died on June 3, 1740.

In June 1951, Mahmoud Reza Pahlevi, twenty-four, the brother of the late Shah of Iran, got his eighth traffic ticket in two years, this one for speeding sixty miles an hour through the campus of the University of Michigan in his new Cadillac. Mahmoud bolted when he was brought to the police station, but he was soon recaptured and returned to the station house, handcuffed and in tears.

In the summer of 1974, the Polish government, in an effort to reduce the alcohol consumption of its citizens, increased the price of vodka by 23 percent. The strategy worked. Almost immediately there was a drop of 25 percent in vodka sales in Warsaw — there was also a meteoric rise in purchases of sugar and yeast.

A twelve-year study completed in 1977 on six thousand Japanese-Hawaiians determined that those individuals who had a beer or two a day suffered 50 percent fewer heart attacks than those who did not.

Both contain fowl-in-pieces.

Answers: Its mother — bread is a necessity, the locomotive an invention.

Passenger, Stay, Reade, Walk. Here Lyeth,

ANDREW TURNCOAT, WHO WAS NEITHER
SLAVE, NOR SOULDIER, NOR PHYSITIAN
NOR FENCER, NOR COBLER, NOR
FILCHER, NOR LAWYER, NOR USU-
RER, BUT ALL; WHO LIVED NEI-
THER IN CITY, NOR COUNTREY,
NOR AT HOME, NOR ABROAD,
NOR AT SEA, NOR
AT LAND, NOR
HERE, NOR ELSE-
WHERE, BUT EVE-
RY WHERE; WHO
DIED NEITHER OF
HUNGER, NOR POY-
SON, NOR HATCH-
ET, NOR HALTER,
NOR DOGGE, NOR
DISEASE, BUT OF
ALL TOGETHER.
I.I.H. BEING NEI-
THER HIS DEBTOR,
NOR HEIRE, NOR KINSMAN, NOR
FRIEND, NOR NEIGHBOUR, BUT ALL,
IN HIS MEMORY HAVE ERECTED,
THIS NEITHER MONUMENT, NOR
TOMB, NOR SEPULCHER, BUT ALL, WISHING
NEITHER EVIL, NOR WEL, NEITHER TO THEE,
NOR TO ME, NOR HIM, BUT ALL UNTO ALL.

Daniel Lambert was the amiable keeper of the Leicester jail in England during the early part of the eighteenth century. While he was in charge there were few criminals who managed to escape. Even if a prisoner got out of his cell, all Lambert had to do was stand in his way, because he was one of the fattest men who have ever lived. His waist at one time measured 112 inches in circumference. His belly reportedly hung to his knees, and the flesh of his legs nearly buried his feet.

Gluttony is not a secret vice.

Orson Welles

Notable Births

1738	George III	1917	Charles Collingwood
1744	Jeremy Belknap	1919	Robert Merrill
1912	Rosalind Russell	1922	Gene Barry

Notable Events

1674 Horse racing prohibited in Massachusetts
1784 French opera singer Mme. Thible became first woman to ride in balloon
1834 First documented eating of tomatoes in United States
1845 Mexico declared war on United States
1912 Massachusetts enacted nation's first minimum wage law
1944 Allies took Rome
1963 John Profumo resigned in wake of British call-girl/spy scandal
1977 Soviets charged Anatoly Shcharanshy with treason

Question: Give the nicknames of the following states:

Montana
Nebraska
New Jersey
South Dakota

This epitaph comes from Northmavine, Shetland:

M.S.
Donald Robertson
Born 1st of January 1785; died 4th of June 1848
aged 63 years

He was peaceable quiet man, & to all appearance a sincere Christian. His death was very much regretted, which was caused by the stupidity of Laurence Tulloch, of Clotherton, who sold him nitre instead of Epsom salts, by which he was killed in the space of three hours after taking a dose of it.

In the book *The Modern Housewife*, a nineteenth-century cook named Soyer set down the different kinds and amounts of foods a Victorian epicure could be expected to consume in sixty years of good living. The foods listed would have weighed just under thirty-four tons, and were itemized as follows:

30 oxen
200 sheep
200 lambs
100 calves
50 pigs
1,200 chickens
300 turkeys
150 geese
400 ducklings
600 wild ducks
150 haddock
400 herring
5,000 smelt
100,000 whitebait
20 turtles
30,000 oysters
1,500 lobsters and crabs
300,000 shrimp, sardines, etc.
500 lbs. grapes
360 lbs. pineapple
600 peaches
1,400 apricots
240 melons
1,000 lbs. salt and pepper
3,087 gallons wine
584 gallons hard liquor
2,394 gallons coffee and tea
2,736 gallons water
140 salmon
120 turbot
120 cod
260 trout
400 mackerel
300 whiting
800 sole
400 flounder
400 red mullet
263 pigeons
1,400 pheasant and grouse
600 woodcocks
450 plovers
800 quail
500 rabbits
40 deer
120 guinea hens
10 peacocks
400 assorted other birds
5,475 lbs. vegetables
2,435 lbs. butter
684 lbs. cheese
9,000 lbs. bread
4,250 lbs. sugar
1,369 gallons beer
342 gallons liqueurs
304 gallons milk

And several million berries and nuts!

He eats like a horse afire.

Angelina Bicos

Answer: Treasure State, Cornhusker State, Garden State, Coyote Sunshine State.

JUNE 5

Question: How's your movie memory? In what years were these films Academy Award winners?

One Flew Over the Cuckoo's Nest
Mutiny on the Bounty
The Bridge on the River Kwai
Patton

Notable Births

1723	Adam Smith	1920	Cornelius Ryan
1883	John Maynard Keynes	1928	Tony Richardson
1897	Madame Chiang Kai-shek	1934	Bill Moyers
1898	William Boyd	1939	Margaret Drabble
1898	Garcia Lorca	1944	Tommy Smith
1915	Alfred Kazin	1945	John Carlos

Notable Events

1783	Montgolfiers sent up world's first manned balloon
1877	Oleomargarine legislation enacted in New York State
1915	Women got the vote in Denmark
1933	Gold Standard repealed
1967	Six Day War began
1968	Robert Kennedy assassinated
1975	Suez Canal reopened

The following were laws of the land in New Haven during the latter part of the seventeenth century:

Married persons must live together, or be imprisoned.

A man that strikes his wife shall pay a fine of ten pounds.

No priest shall abide in the dominion; he shall be banished, and suffer death of his return. Priests may be seized by any one without a warrant.

A woman that strikes her husband shall be punished as the court directs.

No man shall court a maid in person, or by letter, without first obtaining the consent of her parents: five pounds fine for the first offense, ten pounds for the second; and for the third, imprisonment at the pleasure of the court.

No one shall read common-prayer, keep Christmas or saint-days, make minced pies, dance, play cards, or play on any instrument of music, except the drum, trumpet, and the Jew's harp.

No gospel minister shall join people in marriage; the magistrates only shall join in marriage, as they may do it with less scandal to Christ's church.

No food or lodging shall be afforded to a quaker, adamite, or other heretic.

Every man shall have his hair cut round, using a cap as a guide.

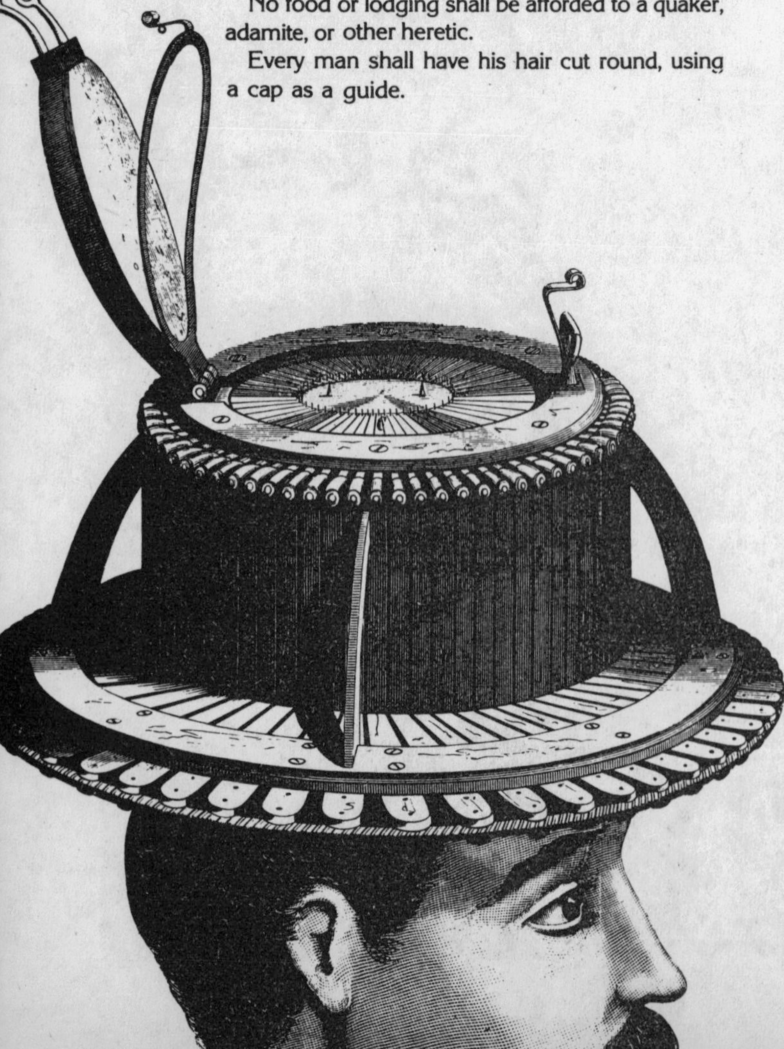

A debtor in prison, swearing he has no estate, shall be let out and sold to make satisfaction.

Whoever sets a fire in the woods, and it burns a house, shall suffer death; and persons suspected of this crime shall be imprisoned without benefit of bail.

Whoever wears clothes trimmed with gold, silver, or bone lace, above two shillings by the yard . . . the selectmen shall tax the offender 300 pounds.

Men-stealers shall suffer death.

No woman shall kiss her child on the sabbath.

No one shall cook victuals, travel, make beds, sweep house, cut hair, or shave on the sabbath-day.

No man shall cross a river without an authorized ferryman.

No one shall run on the sabbath, or walk in his garden, or elsewhere, except reverently to and from meeting.

If any person turns quaker, he shall be banished, and not suffered to return, but upon pain of death.

Commandment number One in any civilized society is this: Let people be different.

David Grayson

Few people now realize it, but Lucille Ball was one of the unsung heroes of the Second World War. Not for her talents as an entertainer with a USO show, but rather as a radio.

Yes, a radio. It seens that whenever Miss Ball traversed a certain section of Hollywood, she'd pick up Japanese radio broadcasts in her fillings. Word of the phenomenon got around, the ever-vigilant government investigated, and an underground spy ring and their broadcasting equipment were flushed out.

Aristotle was a stutterer. The orator Demosthenes couldn't make an *R* sound.

Answer: 1975, 1935, 1957, 1970.

Notable Births

1599	Diego Velasquez	1868	Robert Scott
1606	Pierre Corneille	1886	Paul Dudley White
1755	Nathan Hale	1903	Aram Khachaturian
1756	John Trumbull	1907	Bill Dickey
1799	Alexander Pushkin	1956	Bjorn Borg

Notable Events

346	Eclipse recorded at Nisibis
1665	First Baptist Church in America founded
1797	Ligurian republic established
1833	Jackson became first president to ride on a train
1882	Cyclone and tidal wave killed 100,000 people in Bombay
1897	Samuelson and Harvo began their row across Atlantic in the *Richard K. Fox*
1919	Finland declared war on Russia
1931	Navy decided to drop Guam base; said to have "no military value"
1933	First drive-in movie opened, Camden, New Jersey
1944	D-Day
1966	James Meredith shot from ambush in voting rights march
1967	Israel "accidentally" attacked USS *Liberty*, 34 killed

The Veterans Administration has eight thousand men in its records who are named simply John Smith. That naturally creates a lot of confusion. But one of their biggest headaches concerned a man with the uncommon name of Laughn W. Massey. It seems that Laughn had a twin named Vaughn. Both men went to school together, joined the army together, were in the same training class, traveled to Europe on the same ship in World War II, served in the same unit, were twice promoted to the same rank on the same day, were wounded by the same shell, treated at the same field hospital, and discharged from the same camp on the same day. To compound the problem, both went to work for the same company and used their GI benefits to attend the same business school and take the same classes. It was over three years before everything got straightened out.

This civil rights program about which you have heard so much is a farce and a sham — an effort to set up a police state in the guise of liberty. I am opposed to that program. I fought it in Congress.

Lyndon Johnson

70 percent of America's houses are painted white.

The Muslim Caliph Abdurahman II presided over the tenth century's greatest empire, and is indeed proof of the belief that money, power or fame cannot buy happiness. Despite his power, a yearly income equivalent to hundreds of millions of dollars, and over six thousand wives and 600 children to honor his every wish and to love him, he was a sad, sad man. When his will was read in 962, it was found he had written on his deathbed: "I have counted the days when I enjoyed complete happiness and found them to have numbered but fourteen."

Question: What is the state shown here?

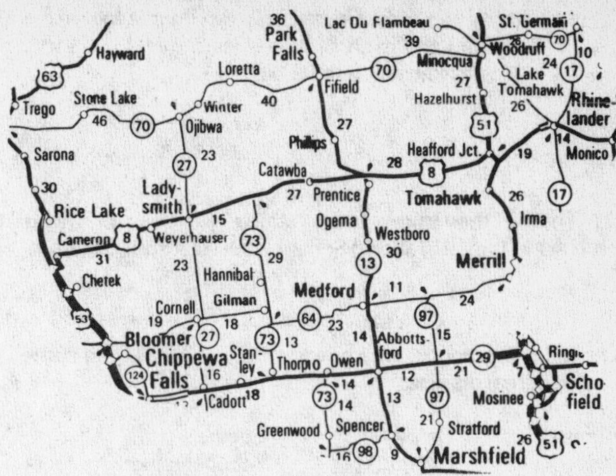

The distribution of a pamphlet entitled "The Races of Mankind," which had been prepared for American servicemen, was delayed in 1944 by a military subcommitee of the House for several interesting reasons. The subcommittee, chaired by a fellow named Durham of North Carolina, found the booklet objectionable in a number of places, among them the depiction of Adam and Eve with navels. Although this wasn't mentioned as a reason for the group's displeasure, a contributing factor in the decision obviously was the pamphlet's reference to blacks. It stated that blacks from several northern states had scored higher on IQ tests than whites from many southern states, and that, in fact, Ohio blacks tested better than whites in eight Dixie states, including North Carolina.

We have rudiments of reverence for the human body, but we consider as nothing the rape of the human mind.

Eric Hoffer

I deplore the fact that throughout the South today subversive elements are attempting to convince the Negro that he should be placed on social equality with white people.

Martin Dies

In 520 B.C. King Darius of Persia laid siege to the city of Babylon. The Babylonians were well-armed and provisioned, however, and weathered the siege for twenty months. Then Zopyros, one of Darius' generals, conceived a desperate strategem. In complete secrecy he cut off both his ears and his nose, and fled to the city asking for sanctuary. He told the Babylonian leader that his disfigurement had been at the hands of the ruthless Darius, and asked to be given a command so he could help the town and exact revenge on his former king. Because of his reputation, experience, and apparent desire for revenge, Zopyros was given supreme authority over Babylon.

He promptly surrendered the town to Darius.

Answer: Wisconsin.

JUNE 7

Question: Monty Python found the Holy Grail in the middle of an island which in turn was surrounded by a moat thirty feet wide. He had only two boards to make a bridge, and each of them was two feet too short. How did he reach the Grail?

Notable Births

1778	Beau Brummel	1909	Peter Rodino
1825	R.D. Blackmore	1933	Jim Nabors
1899	Elizabeth Bowen	1940	Tom Jones
1909	Jessica Tandy	1943	Nikki Giovanni

Notable Events

1509 Henry VIII married Catherine of Aragon, his brother's widow
1692 Jamaican earthquake killed 3,000 people
1755 Earthquake in northern Persia took 40,000 lives
1769 Daniel Boone reached Kentucky
1773 Guatemalan earthquake claimed 25,000 victims
1780 No-popery riots in London
1892 First pinch-hitter used in pro ball game
1948 Benes resigned as Czech prime minister

Jim Thorpe, the famous Indian athlete, was used only as a pinch hitter in the 1917 World Series by the New York Giants.

The following people are known to have suffered from some kind of venereal disease:

Abraham	Henry VIII	Goethe
David	Erasmus	Schopenhauer
Job	Albrecht Durer	John Keats
Caesar	Thomas Wolsey	Franz Schubert
Herod	Ivan the Terrible	Nietzsche
Tiberius	Benvenuto Cellini	Mussolini
Charlemagne	Cardinal Richelieu	Hitler
Pope Alexander VI	John Aubrey	Paul Gauguin
Pope Julius II	Casanova	Auguste Strindberg
Pope Leo X	Boswell	Oscar Wilde

Riddles in the English language go back well over a thousand years. In the early Middle Ages they were told in verse, and were often long and very complex. They had to be: a good riddle meant entertainment for a group of people for a whole evening in those benighted days before television. By the early sixteenth century they had begun to assume the format we're familiar with today, although their subject matter retained much from the old conventions. Here's a sampling of riddles from the year 1511, when they were called "Demands Joyous."

Demand. What bare the best burden that ever was borne?
Response. The ass that carried our Lady, when she fled with our Lord to Egypt.
Dem. What became of that ass?
Res. Adam's mother ate her.
Dem. Who was Adam's mother?
Res. The earth.
Dem. How many calves' tails would it take to reach from the earth to the sky?
Res. No more than one, if it be long enough.
Dem. What is the distance from the surface of the sea to the deepest part thereof?
Res. Only a stone's throw.
Dem. When Antichrist appears in the world, what will be the hardest thing for him to understand?
Res. A hand-barrow, for of that he shall not know which end ought to go foremost.
Dem. What is it that never was and never will be?
Res. A mouse's nest in a cat's ear.
Dem. Why do men make an oven in a town?
Res. Because they cannot make a town in an oven.
Dem. How may a man discern a cow in a flock of sheep?
Res. By his eyesight.
Dem. Why doth a cow lie down?
Res. Because it cannot sit.
Dem. What is it that never freezeth?
Res. Boiling water.
Dem. Which was first, the hen or the egg?
Res. The hen, at the creation.
Dem. How many straws go to a goose's nest?
Res. Not one, for straws not having feet cannot go anywhere.
Dem. Who killed the fourth part of all the people in all the world?
Res. Cain when he killed Abel.
Dem. What is it that a builder, and yet not a man, doeth what no man can do, and yet serveth both God and man?
Res. A bee.
Dem. What man getteth his living backwards?
Res. A ropemaker.
Dem. How would you say two paternosters, when you know God made but one paternoster?
Res. Say one twice over.
Dem. Which are the most profitable saints of the church?
Res. Those painted on the glass windows, for they keep the wind from wasting the candles.
Dem. Who were the persons that made all, and sold all, that bought all and lost all?
Res. A smith made an awl and sold it to a shoemaker, who lost it.
Dem. Why doth a dog turn round three times before he lieth down?
Res. Because he knoweth not his bed's head from the foot thereof.
Dem. What is the worst bestowed charity that one can give?
Res. Alms to a blind man; for he would be glad to see the person hanged that gave it to him.
Dem. What is the age of a field-mouse?
Res. A year. And the age of a hedgehog is three times that of a mouse, and the life of a dog is three times that of a hedge-hog, and the life of a horse is three times that of a dog, and the life of a man is three times that of a horse, and the life of a goose is three times that of a man, and the life of a swan is three times that of a goose, and the life of a swallow three times that of a swan, and the life of an eagle three times that of a swallow, and the life of a serpent three times that of an eagle, and the life of a raven is three times that of a serpent, and the life of a hart is three times that of a raven, and an oak groweth five hundred years, and fadeth five hundred years.

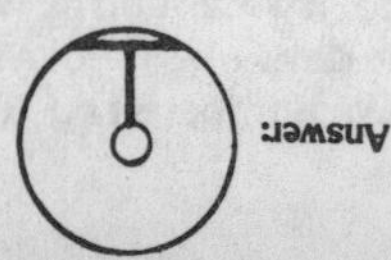

Answer:

JUNE 8

Notable Births

1683	Giuseppe Guarnerius	1921	Alexis Smith
1810	Robert Schumann	1923	Malcolm Boyd
1869	Frank Lloyd Wright	1930	Dana Wynter
1912	Walter Kennedy	1936	James Darren
1918	Robert Preston	1940	Nancy Sinatra

Notable Events

1709 First paper money in America issued, New York City
1786 First ice-cream advertisement appeared
1869 Suction vacuum cleaner patented
1934 First Yoakum, Texas, Tomato Tom Tom Festival held
1953 Michigan tornado killed 116 people
1964 First child of astronauts born, Russia
1965 U.S. troops authorized to fight offensively in Vietnam
1968 James Earl Ray arrested in London
1968 Drysdale's record-setting streak of scoreless innings ended

Door-to-door sales has always been one of the most difficult and frustrating lines of work a man can get into, and life insurance sold door to door is particularly difficult. This is not a recent problem for salespeople. One especially careful life-insurance salesman canvassed a middle-class section of Manchester, England, in about 1850, and kept a complete record of the answers he got from the 1,349 households he visited. His findings are listed below:

471 had heard of life insurance, but didn't understand it.
419 didn't want it.
175 did not answer his knock.
102 houses were empty.
89 said they would consider it, when their finances were worked out.
29 were already insured.
21 refused the circular and his explanation.
19 would take the insurance, if they had the money.
11 had never heard of it.
8 were too old to qualify.
3 had sufficient money not to need it.
2 trusted their families to provide for themselves.
1 was favorable, but feared legal action.
1 preferred a savings bank.
1 swore at him.
1 had been refused insurance, and didn't want to try again.

This unfortunate man did not mention how many policies he actually sold.

Talk about inflation! Back in 1923 the authorized circulation of marks in Germany was 518,000,000,000,000,000,000. Taken another way, the entire German mortgage debt of $8 billion (in old marks) could have been paid off by the newly inflated price of two pieces of bubble gum.

If all the nation's economists were laid end to end, they would point in all directions.

Arthur Motley

Answer: Burma Shave.

Question: Can you add the last line of this almost famous poem?

Listen, birds,
These signs cost
Money.
So roost awhile
But don't get
Funny.

Mischa Elman, the violin virtuoso, was a child prodigy. On one occasion when he was seven, his parents had a party and he was asked to play something for the guests. The little boy chose Beethoven's *Kreutzer Sonata*, a piece in which there are several lengthy rests in the violin part. He related years later that, although he felt he was playing very well, in the middle of one of the rests a matronly woman leaned over to him, patted him on the shoulder, and said, "Play something you know, dear."

The notes I handle no better than many pianists. But the pauses between the notes — ah, that is where the art resides!

Arthur Schnabel

The architect Frank Lloyd Wright once urged that the city of Boston be evacuated and preserved as a museum piece, and that the city of Pittsburgh simply be abandoned.

RIP

Here rests my wife; no pair through life
So equal lived as we did;
Alike we shared perpetual strife,
Nor knew I rest till she did.

Here is my much loved Celia laid,
At rest from all her earthly labors!
Glory to God! peace to the dead!
And to the ears of all her neighbors.

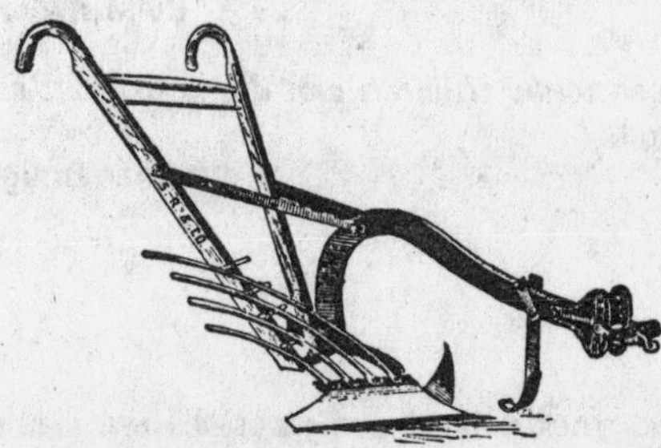

If you're thinking of beating your swords into plowshares, never to learn war anymore, it may be etymologically futile: the word "cutlass" comes from the Latin *culter*, which means a plowshare.

JUNE 9

Question: By what other names are these ladies known?

Florence Kling
Grace Goodhue
Lou Henry
Elizabeth Wallace

Notable Births

1672	Peter the Great	1903	Marcia Davenport
1892	Cole Porter	1910	Robert Cummings
1893	S.N. Behrman	1916	Robert McNamara
1900	Fred Waring	1916	Les Paul

Notable Events

1610	Arabella Stuart imprisoned for marrying William Seymour
1788	Africa Association founded in London
1880	First convention of Greenback Labor party held
1909	Alice Ramsay began first cross-country auto trip by a woman
1956	Eisenhower operated on for ilietis
1972	Rapid City, South Dakota, flood killed 236 people

In March 1935, King Prajadhipok abdicated the throne of Siam, now Thailand, and was succeeded by his nine-year-old nephew, Prince Ananda Mahidol. The young prince publicly expressed his displeasure at the turn of events: "I am not happy to become King of Siam," he said. "I would rather play with locomotives and trains."

His uncle had taken out $40,000-a-year unemployment insurance policy shortly before he left the throne.

Ananda was found dead of a bullet wound, probably self-inflicted, on June 9, 1946.

You know children are growing up when they start asking questions that have answers.

John J. Plomp

If you want to see what children can do, you must stop giving them things.

Norman Douglas

Feel free to tell your next cabbie he might as well be a goatherd for all that his name means. "Cab" is short for "cabriolet," a carriage introduced in Paris in 1823, which was used for hire and was considerably lighter and faster than its predecessor, the hackney. Cabriolet comes from the French *cabriole*, which means a leap or a bound, and which in turn was derived from the Italian *caprio*, a wild goat.

Back in 1930, Charlie Creighton and James Hargis tried to drive from New York to Los Angeles and back without ever stopping their Model A engine. It took them a lengthy forty-two days, but they managed to complete the 7,180-mile journey as they had planned, keeping the motor going every inch of the way — and driving every one of those inches in reverse.

It is not known whether or not at trade-in time they admitted turning back the odometer.

I am an idealist. I don't know where I'm going but I'm on my way.

Carl Sandburg

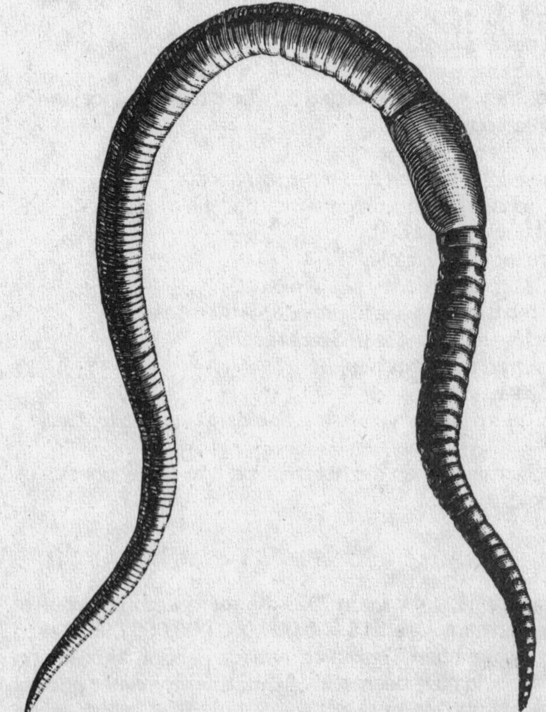

There is a species of earthworm found in Australia that grows to a length of ten feet or more, and is but three fourths of an inch in diameter.

Answer: Mrs. Warren Harding, Mrs. Calvin Coolidge, Mrs. Herbert Hoover, Mrs. Harry Truman.

Notable Births

1840	H.M. Stanley	1915	Saul Bellow
1887	Harry Byrd	1922	Judy Garland
1887	John W. Studebaker	1925	Nat Hentoff
1904	Frederick Loewe	1926	June Haver
1905	Clyde Beatty	1928	Maurice Sendak
1911	Terence Rattigan	1933	F. Lee Bailey

Notable Events

1422	Constantinople seized by Turks
1801	United States declared war on Tripoli
1861	Michael III of Serbia murdered
1903	Alexander I and Queen Draga of Serbia murdered
1905	First forest fire tower occupied, Greenville, Maine
1932	Violet Sharp, Lindbergh's maid, committed suicide
1940	Italy declared war on France and Great Britain
1940	Norway surrendered to Nazis
1941	British and Free French took Damascus
1956	Earthquakes in northern Afghanistan took 2,000 lives

Questions: Why is a pretty woman like a hinge?

Where is it that all women are beautiful?

This is a real case from the Milwaukee police log.

The year: 1940
The month: June
The place: Milwaukee, Wisconsin
The suspects: eight middle-aged, well-known society women
The charge: illegal gambling operation
The specifications: playing gin rummy for pillowcases

Tripoli, in North Africa, has had several curious rulers. In 1629, a twenty-eight-year-old Greek named Giovanni Soffietti was given the choice of being hanged for a murder he'd committed or becoming a Moslem. He chose the latter, took the name Muhammed Abdalla, and joined the army. Two years later, he was elected ruler of the city-state. Once, Abdalla's physician confessed to his master that he'd been offered more than $100,000 to poison him, but had refused. Abdalla thought this was crazy, and had the doctor committed to an asylum for being insanely unselfish.

In 1672, a private in the army was elected pasha, but three hours later his constituents changed their minds and strangled him.

The next year, Ag Mohammed el Haddad was elected because he was the only blond-haired soldier in the army. He ruled for six years and died a natural death.

In 1701, a coffeehouse keeper named Osman was chosen because his coffee was so good. He was supplanted after five months, however, with no mention of whether or not the quality of his coffee had fallen off.

For a man to achieve all that is demanded of him he must regard himself as greater than he is.

Goethe

In 1881, *Scientific American* reported on a paper delivered by Dr. George M. Beard, which was about the "Jumping Frenchmen" of Moosehead Lake, Maine. Beard recounted that certain loggers in that area, all of whom were of French-Canadian descent, had an automatic knee-jerk reaction to authoritative commands. Once, he said, when he came upon a young man cutting a plug of tobacco with a knife, he slapped him on the back and ordered him to, "Throw it!" Immediately, the young man hollered, "Throw it!" and flung his knife into a tree. A few moments later, while the man was filling his pipe, Beard hit him again, saying, "Throw it!" The pipe was hurled thirty feet.

During his investigations, Beard found fourteen cases of the malady in four families, and traced its history back more than fifty years. Most of the men with the condition were also extremely ticklish. Beard reported the reaction was psycho-contagious, and other men picked it up.

Answers: Because she's something to a-dore.
In the dark.

JUNE 11

Question: By what names are these people better known?
Giovanni Montini
Gladys Smith
Robert Meservey
Margie Reed
Mary Frances Reynolds

Notable Births

1572	Ben Johnson	1899	Yasunari Kawabata
1864	Richard Strauss	1910	Jacques Cousteau
1880	Jeanette Rankin	1925	William Styron
1895	Nikolai Bulganin	1935	Gene Wilder

Notable Events

1517 Sir Thomas Pert reached Hudson Bay
1790 Elbridge Gerry began first House filibuster
1927 Lindbergh awarded Distinguished Flying Cross
1928 Britain demanded full reparations payment from Germany
1936 Alf Landon nominated for president
1938 Johnny Van de Meer pitched first of successive no-hitters
1964 Martin Luther King arrested in Saint Augustine restaurant sit-in
1977 Dutch marines rescued hostages from Moluccan-held train

On June 11, 1831, Mr. Moses Alexander, aged 93, married Mrs. Frances Tompkins, aged 103, in Bata, New York. Both were found dead in bed the next morning.

Ancient bones creak with pleasure.

Charlie Chan

Marriage has many pains, but celibacy has few pleasures.

Samuel Johnson

For two people to be able to live together for the rest of their lives is almost unnatural.

Jane Fonda

Reportedly, in the early 1970s, there was a man who, in order to satisfy his sex drive, would frequent the Montreal airport. When he saw a women who appealed to him, he would approach her, and openly ask her if she would like to satisfy his desires (using a much simpler term). He was supposedly successful in one out of every four or five propositions.

Bold and inventive, yes, but he couldn't hold a candle to a West German named Manfred Kah. Kah, using the alias of "Dr. Binder, specialist in virology," would pick out the name of a woman in the phone book, call her up, and explain that he was treating one of her relatives for an unusual viral disease and needed her help. "Help" consisted of scheduling an appointment with her at a hotel for an examination. A hotel room was chosen, he said, to avoid any unnecessary embarrassment on her part.

Once he had lured a cooperative woman to one of his medical trysts, he would tell her that the only way to determine whether she, too, carried the relative's virus was through intercourse. He would suggest, in the interests of professionalism, that the woman wear a blindfold during the procedure. He also told each woman that the validity of the test results could be in jeopardy unless she reached orgasm while the test was being conducted.

Before he was arrested, Kah had seduced at least 160 women in this fashion.

That man that hath a tongue, I say, is no man,
If with his tongue he cannot win a woman.

Shakespeare

Answer: Pope Paul VI, Mary Pickford, Robert Preston, Martha Raye, Debbie Reynolds.

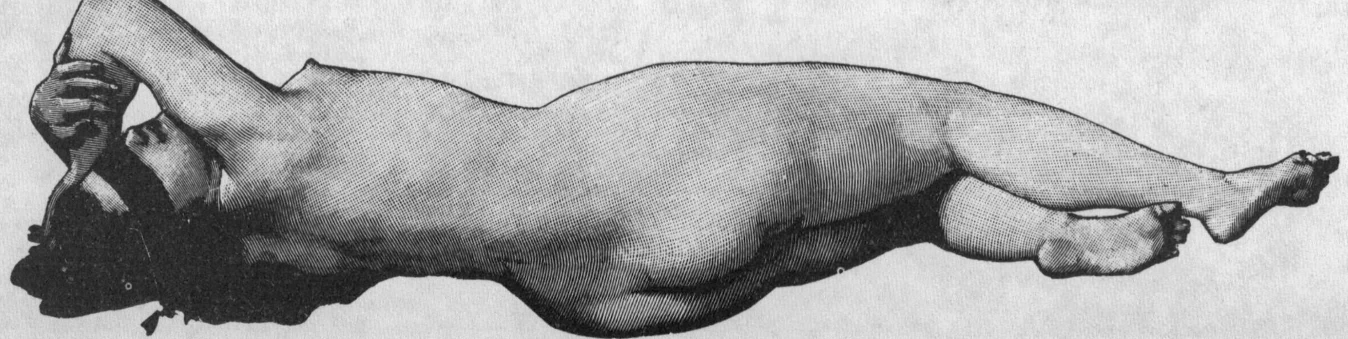

Notable Births

1802	Harriet Martineau	1915	David Rockefeller
1819	Charles Kingsley	1919	Uta Hagen
1892	Djuna Barnes	1928	Vic Damone
1897	Anthony Eden	1929	Anne Frank

Notable Events

1349 Edward II issued archery proclamation
1665 New York City incorporated
1880 Cleopatra's Needle left Egypt for New York
1897 Earthquake in Assam, India, killed 2,000 people
1935 Undeclared Gran Chaco War ended between Paraguay and Bolivia
1942 Japanese seized Attu and Kiska

Questions: What's the first thing that happens to a duckling when it goes into the water for the first time in its life?

What is the only emotion a fireplace can express?

Two guns, two kettles, two coats, two shirts, one barrel of cider, and six bits bought the Bronx in New York, when it was originally purchased by Jacob Bronck in 1639.

According to Victor Marchetti, a CIA employee for over a dozen years, the organization once tried to train a cat to perform undercover intelligence gathering. The cat was wired with a tiny transmitter in the belief that, even if a room were searched high and low for eavesdropping devices, no one would suspect a wandering cat had been equipped with a microphone.

The initial operation to implant the mike was a success, but in early trials the independent feline — a male — had a tendency to drift away and look for food. Veterinarians then implanted two devices in his brain, one to detect hunger and the other to suppress it. That worked well enough, but unfortunately it turned out that the cat got bored listening to military secrets and would wander away to search for a little female company. For some reason the CIA decided against castration (or never even thought of it), and two more gadgets were implanted in his head; one to detect the cat's sex drive, the other to eradicate it.

Finally, after weeks of encouraging results in the laboratory, the cat was ready for his first real assignment. With the CIA monitoring truck following close behind, the cat was put out on a street and ordered to go to a certain location and eavesdrop on a supersecret conversation. The cat, who was a somewhat contrary beast, promptly bounded into the street and was run over by a taxi cab.

Never hunt rabbit with dead dog.

Charlie Chan

The term "gerrymander" has come to be applied to many types of political skullduggery, but it originally meant the redrawing of election boundaries for the benefit of a particular party. Elbridge Gerry, who in 1812 became vice-president, was governor of Massachusetts in the first decade of the nineteenth century. To give his party an edge in an upcoming election, Gerry juggled voting district borders to the detriment of his Republican opponents, but was not exactly subtle in the way he made them up. One observer commented that the lines looked like a salamander had drawn them, to which another critic responded; "A Gerrymander, rather," and the name stuck.

Archery made a big comeback in England during the fourteenth century. On June 12, 1349, Edward III issued a proclamation deploring the falling off of the art during the previous hundred years, and reminded the English people that it was the archers who had saved their country on several occasions. He therefore prohibited some popular pastimes — throwing stones, wood, or iron; playing handball or football, and cockfighting — in favor of archery practice. His sucessor, Edward IV, decreed that every Englishman must own a bow of his own height, and teach his son the art of archery, beginning when a boy turned seven. All those who did not practice on Sundays were fined.

Regular bows at the time were carved out of witchhazel, elm, or ash, and ideally were made to exceed a man's height by the length of his foot. A good war bow was made of imported yew wood, and was an expensive item: at the time of Queen Elizabeth I, a top-quality bow cost about 6s. 8d. — more than a week's pay for many working men. Arrows were customarily twenty-seven to thirty-three inches long, although those used at Agincourt were said to be a full three feet. Grey goose feathers were preferred for the arrow's crown.

I think that people want peace so much that one of these days the government had better get out of their way and let them have it.

Dwight D. Eisenhower

Answers: It gets wet.
Grate-ful-ness.

JUNE 13

Questions: Which of these states joined the Union first? Which was the last to join?

Connecticut
Georgia
New Jersey

Notable Births

1752	Fanny Burney	1893	Dorothy Sayers
1795	Thomas Arnold	1926	Paul Lynde
1865	William Butler Yeats	1951	Richard Thomas

Notable Events

1494 Columbus reached continental America without knowing what it was
1893 One thousand-mile horse race horse began, Chadron, Nebraska
1939 Himmler sent to crush Czech revolt
1940 Germans entered Paris
1953 General Rojas seized power in Columbia
1955 Crash into stands at 24-hour Le Mans race killed 77 people
1971 *New York Times* began publishing the Pentagon Papers

Cats are not necessarily more independent or contrary than other animals — it's more likely that they're stupid. Cats have a brain about the size of a marble. Some animal experts feel they're about as intelligent as the average octopus.

Don't feel too badly if you're a cat owner. The same experts assure us that, except for dolphins and whales, the octopus is the most intelligent creature in the sea.

The Jaycees of Nebraska City, Nebraska, once worked for three months to stage a horse show to benefit charity. When all the receipts were in, they'd grossed $10,435.73.

They dutifully turned over the net profit of 32 cents to worthy causes.

We often do good that we may do harm with impunity.

La Rochefoucauld

A young blacksmith in Bedford, England, called on his girlfriend one evening in 1767. She wasn't home, but her mother let the boy in. Since it was obvious by this time that the smith's courtship was a serious affair, the mother took advantage of her daughter's absence to talk about marriage. Wouldn't it be better for the blacksmith to marry a woman who could provide a dowry of, say, £500, and not her penniless daughter? He admitted it probably would be, and all other things being equal, he'd like to meet such a woman. "I'm the woman," the mother said.

When the daughter arrived home, she found her old boyfriend and her mother on exceptionally good terms, and they were married not long after. She was sixty-four; he was eighteen.

Old enough to know worse.

Oscar Wilde

A bureaucrat attending a conference in Nairobi, Kenya, in 1973, was stopped on the street by two young men who identified themselves as Kenyan detectives. They informed him that, according to Kenyan law, all foreign currencies had to have their serial numbers listed with the proper authorities. The man, an American, took out the $150 he had in his wallet and gave it to the gentlemen. They went into an adjacent office building and were never seen again.

The chump happened to be the American director of the International Monetary Fund.

He should have been carrying American Express Travelers Checks.

Mladen Sekulovich (Karl Malden)

Answers: Connecticut was the first.
New Jersey was the last.

JUNE 14

Notable Births

1811	Harriet Beecher Stowe	1919	Dorothy McGuire
1820	John Bartlett	1925	Pierre Salinger
1906	Margaret Bourke-White	1925	Dennis Weaver
1909	Burl Ives	1933	Jerzy Kosinski

Notable Events

877 Edict of Quieray made fiefs hereditary in France
1623 First breach of promise suit in America brought, Virginia
1777 Stars and Stripes adopted as U.S. flag
1834 Diving suit patented by Leonard Norcross, Dixfield, Maine
1834 Sandpaper patented by Isaac Fischer, Springfield, Vermont
1840 Treaty of Washington set U.S.-Canadian border at 49th parallel
1907 Women's suffrage enacted in Norway
1915 First Protestant church for lepers dedicated, Carville, Louisiana

There's a law on the books in Illinois that makes it a crime for anyone in that state to speak English. At the behest of the Chicago mayor, William Thompson, who hated the English, the legislature passed a law in 1935, which made the *American* language the state's official tongue and penalized those convicted of speaking English.

The word "honeymoon" comes from a custom common to most of northern Europe. Mead, a wine made from honey, was drunk for the period of a lunar cycle after a wedding feast, in celebration of the nuptials.

Questions: Why are writers so funny looking?

What's the difference between a bore and a book?

In 1938, when Rockefeller Center in New York was almost finished, the family commissioned a famous Mexican artist, Diego Rivera, to paint the mural for the main lobby. Rivera set to work diligently, only to be stopped midway through his project. Didn't that bearded fellow in the front look familiar? Yes, Rivera explained, he did. That was Lenin, and the scene around him depicted the masses rising up to overthrow the capitalist system. And the syphilitic in the corner stood for the capitalist system. No, he would not change it.

Young Nelson Rockefeller was in charge of the interior decoration for the center and he ordered that the mural be destroyed, although over $20,000 had already been expended.

Rivera went away feeling his point had been made more effectively than if the artwork been completed.

The French painter Cezanne used to do his still lifes from wax fruit. The master painted so slowly that real fruit rotted before he finished a canvas.

Answers: Because their tales grow right out of their heads.

You can't shut up a bore.

JUNE 15

Question: By what names are these people better known?
James Jordan
Thomas G. Morfit
Don Court
Merle Thompson

Notable Births

1605	Thomas Randolph	1914	Saul Steinberg
1843	Edvard Grieg	1915	Morris Udall
1856	Edward Channing	1916	Marshall Field, Jr.
1901	Mary Ellis	1938	Billy Williams

Notable Events

455	Vandals under Genseric began pillage of Rome
1215	Magna Carta signed
1752	Benjamin Franklin flew his famous kite
1775	Washington appointed commander in chief of colonial forces
1806	Eclipse in North America
1855	Political platform of Know-Nothing party published
1893	Earthquake and tidal wave killed 22,000 people in Japan
1904	Steamer *General Slocum* burned at Hell's Gate, New York, 1,050 perished
1909	Baseball with cork center patented
1934	Finland made final war debt payment to United States, only country to honor debt

The maps that Nazi espionage agents drew up for the German invasion of England were so poorly detailed that they showed Oxford University as a single building; and so out of date that they neglected to plot many of the roads or rail lines constructed since World War I. Better maps could have been purchased at stationery stores.

It is time to turn from quarrels and to build our White ramparts again. The alliance with foreign races means nothing but death for us.

Charles A. Lindbergh, Jr.

"Tycoon" is one of the few words in our language that was originally Japanese. *Taikun*, the Japanese word from which our term comes, arrived in America by courtesy of Commodore Perry's voyages of the 1850s. *Taikun* itself comes from two Chinese words, *ta* meaning great; and *kiun*, for prince. Our spelling is the way Perry anglicized the word when he first heard it.

Out of approximately 80,000 species of flies, about 16,130 are found in the United States.

The word "field" goes back to the Anglo-Saxon *feld*, which meant a place where trees had been cut down (obviously, felled). American pioneers created an equivalent to it with the use of the word "clearing."

Henry Hudson didn't discover the bay, the river, or the straits that have been named for him.

The Christine Keeler-John Profumo call-girl spy scandal was only another chapter in the long British history of sexual chicanery among the upper classes. Back in the Regency period, a woman named Harriette Wilson wrote of her amours with aristocratic customers, and made a fortune by blackmailing them with her threats to publish her memoirs. While the Duke of Wellington retorted by saying, "Publish and be damned!" she did, but was not. In the eighteenth century, the archbishop of York kept a well-known,and very well-frequented harem,while the mistress of George II first caught his eye by appearing at a court ball in a transparent gown. George IV had his wife tried publicly for infidelity. Lord Palmerston in the nineteenth century and Arthur Balfour and David Lloyd George in the twentieth were all prime ministers; *and* adulterers who didn't get caught.

There is something utterly nauseating about a system of society which pays a harlot twenty-five times as much as it pays its prime minister.

Harold Wilson

Answer: Fibber McGee, Garry Moore, Ken Murray, Merle Oberon.

Notable Births

1630	Isaac Barrow	1937	Erich Segal
1895	Stan Laurel	1938	Joyce Carol Oates

Notable Events

1819 Indian earthquake killed 2,000 people
1932 Ban on Storm Troopers lifted in Germany
1940 Russia appropriated Latvia, Estonia, and Lithuania
1941 FDR ordered German consulates closed
1943 Charlie Chaplin married Oona O'Neill; he was 54, she was 18
1955 Juan Peron excommunicated
1959 George Reeves (Superman) committed suicide
1963 Valentine Tereshkova made 48 orbits in *Vostok VI*

The following statements reflected the prevailing beliefs of American high school students in about 1940. These students were of the generation that now runs our business and government.

1. American foreign policy has always been wise and unselfish.
2. All wars in which our country has been engaged were necessary and glorious.
3. The affairs of foreign countries are of little interest to us.
4. Americans are superior to other people, and the United States is a leader in nearly all forms of social and political activity.
5. Freedom of speech has been practiced since the writing of the Constitution.
6. The Constitution is above criticism.
7. Equality of opportunity has been won and is maintained in the United States.
8. The common man may expect to be comfortable and secure in the United States.

Loyalty to petrified opinions never yet broke a chain or freed a human soul in this world — and never will.

Mark Twain

An era can be said to end when its basic illusions are exhausted.

Arthur Miller

The chief object of education is not to learn things but to unlearn them.

G. K. Chesterton

Can't marry your wife's grandmother in Kentucky — just another one of those silly laws.

Questions: Why is a riddle like a coconut?

What's the difference between a Magyar and a starving Indian?

On June 16, 1487, the decisive battle in the War of the Roses was fought. The House of Lancaster won the battle itself, but the House of Tudor eventually ended up with the throne, because Henry VII happened to be the great-grandson of the fourth son of a king who'd ruled Britain 150 years before. Had there been a pretender to the throne with a better claim among the warring factions, Henry VII's son, Henry VIII, would never have ruled.

At first this may all seem rather unimportant, but considering that it was Henry VIII who made England a Protestant country, Henry VII's claim takes on a new light. Four hundred years of religious wars in Europe, the United States as a White Anglo-Saxon Protestant country, and many other enormous changes might not have taken place without it.

Such an apparently insignificant fact as a man's distant relationship to a long-dead ruler altered history so drastically, and cost so many lives.

Man without relatives is man without troubles.

Charlie Chan

About the stongest adhesive in the world is that manufactured by the barnacle to glue itself to rocks. It only takes 3/10,000ths of an inch of the stuff to create a holding power of three tons per square inch. It can be chilled to nearly zero degrees and will not crack, and it is resistant to almost every solvent known to man.

The town fathers of Pulaski, New York, solicited bids for the dredging of the channel between Big Sandy Pond and Lake Ontario in the summer of 1950. The Army Corps of Engineers had estimated the project would cost a minimum of $250,000.

The work was awarded to a local contractor who'd bid $3,500.

Computers will never be perfected until they can compute how much more than the estimate the job will cost.

Laurence J. Peter

A tradesman was having trouble falling asleep, so he went to his doctor to see if he could help his insomnia. The doctor suggested he try counting sheep.

A week later the man was back, his insomnia worse than before. The doctor asked the man if he'd tried counting sheep as he'd advised.

"Yes, doc, yes," he said, "I count for hours. I get to five thousand, ten thousand, twenty thousand sheep. And then I start to figure, twenty thousand sheep is eighty thousand pounds of wool, and eighty thousand pounds of wool is thirty thousand yards of cloth; and thirty thousand yards of cloth is twelve thousand raincoats — and who can sleep with that kind of inventory?

Answers: It's no good until it's cracked.

One is a native of Hungary, the other a hungry native.

JUNE 17

Question: What's the state shown here?

Notable Births

1703	John Wesley	1905	Ralph Bellamy
1818	Charles Gounod	1914	John Hersey
1871	James Weldon Johnson	1917	Dean Martin
1882	Igor Stravinsky	1919	Kingman Brewster

Notable Events

656 Caliph Othman murdered
1775 Battle of Bunker Hill
1778 Congress rejected British peace offer
1843 Maoris revolted against British in New Zealand
1940 Britain offered union to France
1953 Revolt in East Berlin crushed
1960 Maloney and Evans made record walk; San Francisco to New York City, in 66 days
1963 Supreme Court ruled 8 to 1 against classroom prayer
1972 Watergate break-in

In Colorado in 1977, Filbert Maestas stole what he assumed to be several hundred pounds of meat, packed in cardboard boxes. It turned out he'd made off with 1,200 cow rectums. He was apprehended, brought to trial, and convicted, but he appealed on the grounds that the arresting officers had "extorted" a confession by laughing at him. At his appeal hearing he reportedly said, "If I go to jail for stealing beef assholes, I'm really going to be mad."

He must have been really mad.

In times like these, it helps to recall that there have always been times like these.

Paul Harvey

The word "coffee" comes to us from two sources. One is the province of Caffa in Ethiopia, where the bush grows wild and coffee has been drunk since prehistoric times. The drink reached Arabia about 1470 A.D., and its use set off fierce religious debates among the Moslems, some of whom considered it to be an intoxicant, and therefore prohibited by the Koran. This faction gave it the name *kahwah*, which also means wine.

In Atlanta, Georgia, in 1976, Annie Colbath walked into her kitchen and saw a snake on the floor. She screamed. He husband Mort rushed naked from the shower to the kitchen and stepped on the dog, Dudley. Dudley yelped and ran from the room and the offending snake slithered beneath a cabinet. Mort knelt down to look for it.

Dudley, now calmer, came quietly back to the kitchen to investigate. When his cold nose touched Mort's backside, Mort fainted, thinking it was the snake, and Annie called an ambulance. Before it arrived, Mort revived. He told the paramedics he was all right, but the men insisted on him going to the hospital with them, as he might well have suffered a heart attack in all the excitement. Reluctantly Mort agreed, and hopped aboard the stretcher.

While he was being taken out, the slippery serpent slithered out again and scared one of the ambulance attendants, who dropped his end of the stretcher. Mort tumbled out and broke his leg.

(This actually happened, though the names have been changed to protect the embarrassed.)

On June 17, 1871, Mr. and Mrs. Martin Bates were married. He was 7 feet, 2 inches tall; his wife was 7 feet, 5½ inches.

High heels were invented by a woman who had been kissed on the forehead.

Christopher Morley

Answer: Nebraska.

Notable Births

1857	Henry Folger	1913	Sylvia Porter
1905	Kay Kyser	1917	Richard Boone
1907	Jeanette MacDonald	1926	Tom Wicker
1910	E.G. Marshall	1936	Lou Brock
1913	Sammy Cahn	1942	Paul McCartney

Notable Events

1621 First American duel fought at Plymouth
1776 Americans evacuated forces from Canada
1778 British retreated from Philadelphia
1812 United States declared war on England
1815 Napoleon defeated at Waterloo by Wellington
1861 First flycasting tournament held, Utica, New York
1873 Susan B. Anthony arrested for voting, Rochester, New York
1898 Steel pier opened at Atlantic City
1936 First bicycle traffic court held at Racine, Wisconsin
1953 USAF C-124 crashed near Tokyo with 129 aboard
1964 Ted Kennedy broke back in plane crash

One day in 1948, a Philadelphia Traffic Court Judge, Jacob Dogole, heard a real run of botched cases. First, a woman named Elizabeth Morgan, who was charged with lending her motorcycle to an unlicensed driver, proved she didn't own a motorcycle. Next, Helen Porreca, ticketed for illegal parking, showed the court there was no such street as the one where her violation had allegedly occurred. Then Edward Geshen, charged with a similar offense, proved he was out of town with his car when his misdemeanor was said to have happened. Finally, Tim Credan and William Leahan, Jr., both of whom were up for running a red light, were let go because there was no light at the corner where they had supposedly gone through illegally.

After that, Judge Dogole called it a day.

The Lord Chief Justice of England recently said that the greater part of his judicial time was spent investigating collisions between propelled vehicles, each on its own side of the road, each sounding its horn and each stationary.

Philip Guedella

Henry Beebe was arrested in June 1950, in Las Vegas and charged with illegal possession of narcotics paraphernalia, to wit: four cases of morphine syringes. He explained to police that he was selling them to help pay for his tuition at theology school.

Bad alibi like dead fish — cannot stand test of time.

Charlie Chan

Strictly speaking, the word "paraphernalia" denotes the goods a bride brings into a marriage over and above her dowry. This would include her wardrobe, jewelry, and other personal possessions. It comes from the Greek *para*, beyond; and *phemé*, a dowry.

The rich man and his daughter are soon parted.

Kin Hubbard

Question: What's the best disease for a 1950s cheerleader to die from?

In 1786, Marquis Peltier was imprisoned for whistling "disrespectfully" at Marie Antoinette. The tables were turned some during the revolution, when similar abuses of power by the royal family finally resulted in their beheadings, although Peltier was still languishing in jail when Marie lost her life on this day in 1793.

But Peltier was a forgotten man in the turmoil that resulted in the release of unjustly imprisoned people before the revolution fell apart and turned on itself. He was still incarcerated at the time of his death in 1836, fifty years after he'd committed the *faux pas de la bouche*.

It is by the goodness of God that in our country we have those three unspeakably precious thing: freedom of speech, freedom of conscience, and the prudence never to practice either of them.

Mark Twain

The first recorded duel in America took place on June 18, 1621, in Massachusetts. Edward Dotey and Edward Leister fought to a draw, each wounding the other with his pistol. The colonial fathers were not amused or thankful, however; the two duelists were punished by being tied together head and foot, and left outside for twenty-four hours to talk over their differences.

Answer: Dropsy — it's a *swell* disease.

JUNE 19

Question: Although the Bible doesn't specifically say so, modern researchers are sure that Moses wore a toupee. How do they know?

Until the time of James I, an orphaned English heiress was completely at the disposal of the king, and had to marry anyone he chose for her.

In June 1948, an Oklahoma City salesman named Never Fail filed for bankruptcy.

One of the first, if not the first, women to appear on the English stage was Anne, the wife of King James I. Prior to that time, female roles were generally played by boys whose voices had yet to change. Whether or not she was a good actress is hard to judge. After one critic of her performance had his nose and ears cut off, she always received rave reviews.

I love criticism just so long as it's unqualified praise.

Noel Coward

Notable Births

1566	James I	1908	Mildred Natwick
1623	Blaise Pascal	1920	Louis Jourdan
1896	Duchess of Windsor	1932	Pier Angeli
1902	Guy Lombardo	1936	Gena Rowlands
1903	Lou Gehrig	1943	Malcolm McDowell

Notable Events

1867	Emperor Maximilian executed
1897	Japan protested U.S. annexation of Hawaii
1935	Britain and Germany made U-boat parity pact
1939	Atlanta, Georgia, outlawed pinball machines
1953	Rosenbergs executed for espionage
1963	Twin space flights of Tereshkova and Bykovsky ended
1963	Kennedy asked for broad civil rights legislation
1965	Ahmed Ben Bella overthrown in Algeria in bloodless coup

A German officer of the first World War was talking to a member of the British Embassy in Berlin one day in 1933. In the course of the conversation, he mentioned that he felt the British were gentlemen, while the French were not.

"Why do you think that?" asked the diplomat.

"One day in 1920," said the officer, "a delegation from the Military Control Commission came to a barracks I was in charge of, and told me they had reason to believe there was a cache of rifles hidden in the barracks, contrary to the conditions of the treaty. I gave them my word as a German officer that there were no rifles there. The English officer in the group took my word for it like a gentleman, and went away. The French officer did not, and he insisted on searching the barracks anyway — and he found my rifles."

Military intelligence is a contradiction in terms.

Groucho Marx

Great bullpen depth? Not the 1932 Philadelphia Athletics. In a game against the Cleveland Indians on July 10 of that year, veteran Philadephia pitcher Eddie Rommel was called in from the bullpen in the second inning, with the Athletics trailing, three to two. He proceeded to give up fourteen runs on twenty-nine hits during his relief stint — yet the manager wouldn't take him out.

At the end of the game, Rommel walked off the field the winning pitcher in a nineteen-inning, eighteen-to-seventeen Philadelphia victory.

Tony Albano, an unemployed Brooklyn chauffeur, spent twelve days in line outside the Polo Grounds waiting to get the first seats for the Yankees-Giants World Series of 1951. Just before the gates opened, he offered to sell his place in line for $150. There were no takers.

Albano didn't have the money to buy any tickets, anyway.

The finest steel has to go through the hottest fire.

Richard Nixon

Answer: Because he was sometimes seen with Aaron (hair on) and sometimes without Aaron.

Notable Births

1858	Charles Chestnutt	1920	Gail Partick
1907	Lillian Hellman	1924	Audie Murphy
1909	Errol Flynn	1924	Chet Atkins

Notable Events

1714 Corinth captured by Turks
1756 Black Hole of Calcutta
1789 French Revolution began; Louis XVI tried to flee France, captured at Varennes
1825 William Probett hanged for horse theft at Old Bailey
1877 Fire in Saint John, Nebraska, killed 100 people
1919 Fire in Mayaguez, Puerto Rico, theater took 150 lives
1941 Russians opened tomb of Tamerlane in Samarkand
1961 Bechuanaland Legislative Council inaugurated
1964 Jim Bunning pitched perfect game against Mets
1973 Juan Peron returned to Argentina after 20-year exile

Question: By what names are these people better known?
Belle Silverman
Eunice Waymon
H.M. Rowlands
Ruby Stevens
Concetta Ingolia

It would seem that the Black Hole of Calcutta wasn't so black as it was said to be; but the event gave the British a good excuse for doing what they did in India.

First of all, although the Black Hole is generally believed to have been a narrow pit into which 146 men were hurled on top of one another, this is absolutely wrong. The name "Black Hole" had long been a slang term for an English military jail cell, in the same way as the word "brig" is used today in the navy. It was not a tiny cell: accounts vary, but it was probably 250 to 325 square feet in area, and twelve or more feet high.

The confusion about what really happened stems from two accounts written within a year of the incident. One was by an unreliable minor British official who was imprisoned in the Hole; and the other by an army captain who was not an eyewitness, but who had everything to gain by exaggerating the acts of the Indian leaders.

According to the report published by J.Z. Holwell a year after it happened, Suraj-ud-Dowlah, the nawab of Bengal, took Calcutta on June 20, 1756. In the process he rounded up 146 prisoners, the majority of whom were English, and crammed them into the Hole at British military headquarters. Holwell said that many of the wounded were so weak they could not stand, and slumped to the floor, where they were trampled to death. Others who died on their feet remained there, so tightly packed were the bodies in the room. Some prisoners were crushed to death, others suffocated. Twenty-three survived the night. Holwell remained alive, he said, only because he was fortunate enought to get a place next to one of the windows in the cell.

But another account, written by Captain Alexander Grant — who was not there himself — shortly after the incident, gives a vastly different rendition of the facts. Although Holwell estimated there were nearly ninety Englishmen in the cell, Grant said there were only five. He totalled over 180 prisoners, the other men being Portuguese, Dutch, and Indian. Grant also said the disaster happened on the night of June 30, not June 20; that the room was seventy-five-square-feet smaller than Holwell said it was, and that fewer than ten men survived.

Even if these stories are reasonably accurate, the numbers the writers chose don't hold up well. Even if we accept Grant's description of a smaller-sized cell and a greater number of prisoners, the incarcerated men still had more room than a passenger on a New York rush hour subway. Holwell's figures give them 50 percent more space than this, in fact. In either case, there was plenty of room and plenty of air for all of them.

More telling is the fact that no record was made of the incident in the books of the British East India Company, and no other accounts of the nawab's capture of Calcutta record the incident, or accuse him of any kind of cruelty towards the British. Holwell was also known to be a notorious liar, and he had nothing to lose by telling an exaggerated story. This was finally proved without doubt in 1915, when a British historian uncovered evidence showing that Holwell had forged the three documents he had used to prove his story. Grant's rendition was probably a result of the traditional British combination of loyalty and chauvinism. Historically, the British, like other nations, often seemed to find it impossible to admit that a bad show for them could ever be the result of anything but the dirty and underhanded tactics of their enemies. No doubt Grant did not bother to interview the nawab for his version of what happened.

The legend that grew up out of this incident did seem to justify the English presence in India, however. In building her empire, Britain had generally colonized sparsely populated areas, in which the native's cultures were relatively primitive. India was different. There the British conquered a densely populated land with a culture far superior in many ways to their own, subjugated its people, and changed a prosperous, well-established society into a poverty-stricken, broken one. Stories about the infamous Black Hole of Calcutta provided good excuses for British actions.

Many a bum show has been saved by the flag.

George M. Cohan

⚜

Answer: Beverly Sills, Nina Simone, H.M. Stanley, Barbara Stanwyck, Connie Stevens.

JUNE 21

Questions: Why does a spinster always wear cotton gloves?

Why are pianos so noble?

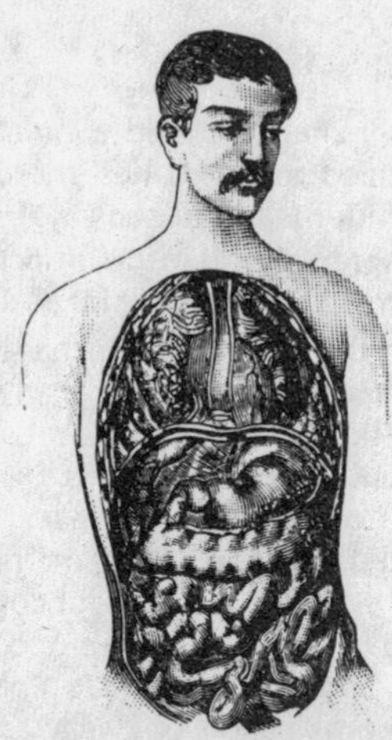

On June 22, 1822, in Michillimackinac, Michigan Territory, a musket accidentally discharged and blew a hole nearly four inches across in the side of eighteen-year-old Alexis St. Martin. Fortunately, Doctor William Beaumont, a surgeon with the United States Army, was nearby and he was able to reach the boy within an hour. Working quickly, he managed to stop the bleeding and sew St. Martin's lung back into his body, but because so much tissue had been blown away, he was unable to close the hole completely. After Beaumont had done all he could, St. Martin was left with a window in his abdomen which looked directly into his stomach.

At first it seemed unlikely that the young French-Canadian would recover. The wound was severe, and he had lost much blood. Because of the location and magnitude of the wound, he could not eat normally, and Beaumont had to feed him through anal injections. Finally, after several critical weeks, the robust young man beat his vicious wound, and began to recover rapidly. Soon, by applying compresses to the hole, he was able to eat through his mouth, and gradually he resumed a more or less normal routine.

For ten months Beaumont tried to induce the wound to heal by exciting inflammation around the borders of the hole, but it refused to congeal. He pleaded with St. Martin to allow him to incise and suture the cavity, but St. Martin would have none of it.

But the young man did agree to allow Dr. Beaumont to use his unique wound for the doctor's experiments in digestive processes, and for eight years thereafter served as the doctor's personal laboratory. In that time, Beaumont gave the medical world more knowledge of the stomach, its juices, and digestion than had been learned since the time of Hippocrates. Many scientists consider Beaumont's work the first important contribution by an American physician to medical science, and it all happened because the doctor's patient wouldn't let him sew him up.

Glory's no compensation for a belly-ache.

Rudyard Kipling

Answers: She hasn't any kids.

Because they're upright, grand, and square.

Notable Births

1639	Increase Mather	1921	Jane Russell
1882	Rockwell Kent	1922	Judy Holliday
1903	Al Hirschfeld	1925	Maureen Stapleton
1905	Jean-Paul Sartre	1927	Carl Stokes
1912	Mary McCarthy	1935	Francoise Sagan

Notable Events

1622	First prohibition officers in America created, Virginia
1788	Constitution became law of land with New Hampshire's ratification
1929	Agreement made between church and state in Mexico
1939	Gehrig's disease announced
1943	Race riots in Detroit; 22 dead, martial law declared
1961	India agreed to let Sikkim expand its 60-man army
1964	Schwerner, Goodman, and Chaney reported missing

Our word for punch, in the sense of an alcoholic drink, actually comes from India. The name, if not the recipe, for a combination of water, sugar, lemon, spice, and spirits was given to England from the Sanskrit *panch*, which means five.

During the New York doctors' strike of 1975, the death rate fell by more than 15 percent.

The term "giddy" comes from the Anglo-Saxon *gyddig*, which meant God-possessed. It was usually not used in a Christian context by the English, but rather denoted one in a high state of intoxication, who acted as if the pagan gods had taken over his body and mind.

The State of Maine not too long ago paid one of its state troopers $5,000 in an out-of-court settlement of a workman's compensation action. A major thrust of the policeman's case was that being on call twenty-four hours a day and never knowing when the phone would ring had left him nervous and irritable, and had ruined his sex life.

JUNE 22

Notable Births

1767	Karl von Humboldt	1906	Anne Morrow Lindbergh
1856	H. Rider Haggard	1921	Gower Champion
1887	Julian Huxley	1921	Joseph Papp
1898	Erich Maria Remarque	1922	Bill Blass
1903	Carl Hubbell	1936	Kris Kristofferson
1906	Billy Wilder	1954	Freddie Prinze

Notable Events

1191	Total solar eclipse in England
1772	Slavery abolished in Great Britain
1930	Lindbergh baby born
1933	Hitler outlawed all political parties except Nazis
1937	Joe Louis took heavyweight crown from Braddock
1939	First international water-skiing championship held, Jones Beach
1941	Hitler invaded Russia
1944	FDR signed GI Bill of Rights
1962	Boeing 707 crashed in storm near Guadaloupe, 113 died

Question: By what names are these people better known?
Laruska Skikne
Edythe Marrener
Margarita Cansina
William Beedle, Jr.

Sixty years ago, the Ku Klux Klan, which had originated as a terrorist organization in the Reconstruction South, experienced a phenomenal rebirth for half a dozen years. Between 1919 and 1925, membership in the secret society climbed from a few thousand to over five million, and before the empire crumbled, the Klan controlled five state legislatures and the governorships of Indiana, Maine, and Colorado.

In 1915, D.W. Griffith's classic movie *The Birth of a Nation* appeared. In it the old Klan was portrayed heroically, fighting against the villainous carpetbaggers and northern federalists who plundered the postwar South. William Joseph Simmons, a former preacher, ladies' garter salesman, and inveterate joiner (he belonged to fifteen fraternal organizations), was inspired by the Klan's cinematic performance, and decided to revive it as a society similar to that of the Masons, with himself as its president. He envisioned a fraternity of Protestant White Americans, vigilant against all the forces that were tearing at the foundation of the country — the non-whites, Catholics, Jews, and southern European immigrants. On one night in 1915, he led fifteen members of his Masonic lodge up Stone Mountain, and by the light of a flaming cross inducted them as knights of the new Invisible Empire.

But Simmons was a poor organizer. He was able to attract only a trickle of new members, until, in 1920, he signed a contract with Edward Young Clark and Mrs. Elizabeth Tyler, directors of the Southern Publicity Association. The SPA had had great success in working different campaigns, but the Klan proved to be their greatest challenge. They developed a clever membership drive in which the individual who brought in a new Klansman received four dollars of the ten-dollar intiation fee. Overnight there were independent salesmen making their livings selling the Klan. Hundreds joined daily. By 1921, the Klan had grown to one hundred thousand members, and by 1924 to over four million.

But in 1922, a cadre led by a fat Texas dentist named Hiram Wesley Evans wrested power from Simmons and changed the direction of the Klan's activities from terrorism (135 lynchings in Georgia in two years) to political action. Simmons was given the powerless office of emperor, and happily spent his time making up names beginning with *K* for the Klan. (A Klan meeting was a Klonvokation, a Klan court a Kloncilium the Klan Bible the Kloran, and offices of Klan Klaverns included the Klaliff, Klokard, Kludd, Kligrapp, Klabee, Klageros, Klexter, and Klokann.) Simmons had found his niche.

Evans moved swiftly to consolidate and then extend his power. He made sure that the most respected and influential people in a community were brought into the Klan, and this guaranteed that other townsfolk joined. "TWK" (Trade With Klan) signs appeared in business establishments and made it almost impossible for non-Klanners to stay in business in many areas. It was an easy next step to get Klansmen into municipal and state offices, even as far as the United States Senate. In 1924, Klan influence kept the Democratic presidental nomination from the "wet" Catholic, Al Smith. For a few years in Indiana, state government *was* the Klan.

Klan members enjoyed their organization because they were a part of a secret fraternity with elaborate rituals, disguises, codes, and camaraderie. The Klan had its own "Kalendar" names for days, weeks, and months, supposedly to ensure that the secrecy of Klonvokations was not compromised. A member who muttered "desolate, woeful, alarming" meant to say that the next meeting would be on Friday of the first week in June. A language of acronyms was also developed. Two men meeting on a street might jabber something like this:

"Ayak?"	(*"Are you a Klansman?"*)
"Akia."	(*"A Klansman I am."*)
"Capowe."	(*"Countersign and password or other written evidence."*)
"Cygnar?"	(*"Can you give me number and realm?"*)
"Nokatga."	(*"Number One Klan, Atlanta, Georgia."*)
"Kigy."	(*"Klansman, I greet you."*)
"Itsub."	(*"In the sacred unfailing bond."*)
"Sanbog."	(*"Strangers are near; be on guard."*)

By 1925, old-time politicians had begun to take a good look at the Klan's success, and the bite it was taking out of their patronage. Also, by then, Mussolini and the Fascists had ruled in Italy for almost four years, and there were striking and frightening similarities between the Klan and the Fascists. In the end, a single event crushed the Klan. In 1925, David C. Stephenson, number-one Klansman in Indiana, was arrested for the mutilation and rape of a young girl on a train. The girl subsequently took poison and died, but not until she had positively identified Stephenson as her assailant. Everyone expected an acquittal, but certain influential people were approached and Stephenson was found guilty of second-degree murder and sentenced to life imprisonment. The myth of the Klan as the defender of law and morality was shattered. Membership plummeted.

When Stephenson didn't get the appeal he was looking for, he turned state's evidence. His testimony eventually convicted and jailed a congressman, the mayor of Indianapolis, a country sheriff, and a number of lesser officials. Only the statute of limitations kept Indiana's governor from a similar fate. Because of the Stephenson affair, between 1925 and 1927 Klan membership dropped from five million to 350,000. It continued to dwindle, and the organization hibernated until the beginning of the Civil Rights movement.

A fanatic is a man who does what he thinks the Lord would do if He knew the facts of the case.

Finley Peter Dunne

Answer: Laurence Harvey, Susan Hayward, Rita Hayworth, William Holden.

JUNE 23

Questions: Why are a woman's kisses like olives in a jar?

Why does a wife hug her husband?

Notable Births

1876	Irvin Cobb	1927	Bob Fosse
1894	George V	1936	Richard Bach
1894	Alfred Kinsey	1940	Wilma Rudolph
1910	Jean Anouilh	1953	Filbert Bayi

Notable Events

1603	Penn signed treaty with the Indians
1606	Peace of Vienna between Hungary and the Hapsburgs; granted religious toleration
1784	First balloon flight in America
1886	Buonaparte and Orleans families banished from France
1926	First American lip-reading tourament held, Philadelphia
1938	German nation put under forced labor
1940	De Gaulle began Free French movement
1945	Okinawa fell to U.S. forces
1964	Henry Cabot Lodge resigned as ambassador to Vietman to help Scranton presidential campaign
1967	"Long Hot Summer" began with race riots in Detroit

On June 23, 1626, a book of religious treatises by the Englishman John Frith was found in the belly of a codfish. Coincidentally, Frith had once been imprisoned in a fish warehouse for his heretical religious views.

In 1948, in the case of *Dittrick* v. *Brown County*, the Minnesota Supreme Court upheld the commitment to a mental institution of a forty-two-year-old father of six as a sexual psychopath. The prosecution claimed he had an "extreme craving" for sexual intercourse with his wife — to wit: three or four times a week.

It is illegal in England to state in print that a wife can and should derive pleasure from intercourse.

Bertrand Russell

Curiously enough, the group of sex offenders with the tallest average height is the voyeurs. They average five feet, ten inches.

WILLIAM III.

An Englishman named John Bernardi died in Newgate Prison in 1736, having spent his last forty years in jail. He was imprisoned for that time without ever having been convicted of a crime. In 1696, he'd been arrested on suspicion of conspiracy to kill King William III, but there was not enough evidence to bring him to trial. Nonethelss, he was kept in prison, and eventually forgotten.

Shirt cuff buttons were originally put on to deter soldiers from wiping their noses on the sleeves of their uniforms. Ever wonder how men's pants came to have cuffs? Fashion, or at least the emulation of a fashionable man.

The story of trouser cuffs goes back only as far as 1896, to England. Edward Prince of Wales was responsible. His horse, Persimmon, was entered in the prestigious English Derby that year, and Edward was at the track to watch the race. Though a long shot, and on a muddy field, Persimmon won the contest under the whip of an American jockey named Johnny Watts. Edward was so overjoyed he leapt from his box and trudged across the sloppy track to congratulate the horse and rider.

On the way his elastic trouser strap broke. To prevent his trousers becoming dirty, the Prince nonchalantly bent over and rolled them up. The next day, trousers were being rolled up all over England.

This sort of fashion phenomenon wasn't seen again until 1934, when Clark Gable ripped off his shirt in the movie *It Happened One Night*. When men in the audiences saw that he wore nothing beneath the shirt, sales of undershirts plummeted.

In 1927, it was announced by a major American meat-packing firm that the perfect zippered hot dog casing had been achieved.

The Syracuse, New York, Zoo was in a sorry state back in '48, according to Mayor Frank Costello. Its leopard had been there for twenty years, and even when he'd first come to the zoo he'd been secondhand. On top of that, the jaguar had bitten the poor old beast's tail off. To make matters worse, the zoo's king of beasts had a bad set of cataracts, and was so blasé about his image that he allowed a pack of rabbits to sleep with him in his den.

Answers: Once you get the first one the rest come easily.

To get around him.

JUNE 24

Notable Births

1450	John Cabot	1895	Jack Dempsey
1813	Henry Ward Beecher	1916	John Ciardi
1842	Ambrose Bierce	1931	Billy Casper
1850	Horatio, Lord Kitchener	1935	Pete Hamill

Notable Events

1497	John Cabot reached Canada
1647	Margaret Brent became first American woman to demand suffrage
1675	King Philip's War began
1793	Second French constitution drawn up
1970	Senate repealed Gulf of Tonkin resolution
1975	Boeing 727 crashed at Kennedy Airport, killed 113 people
1975	Mozambique granted independence, ending 470 years of colonial rule

This news report appeared in papers across the country at the end of June 1896:

> James Romkey, aged 44, shot and killed his wife, and then committed suicide yesterday morning. Unfaithfulness on the part of his wife is said to be the cause. The couple have not been living together for a few weeks, and about 5:30 yesterday morning Romkey jumped through an open window into the room that Mrs. Romkey occupied on the ground floor of a house on West Colt street, and fired at his wife as she was lying in bed. The ball passed through the right temple lodging in the brain. She then rushed into the hall, and Romkey fired three more shots, emptying his revolver, one lodging in the ankle, one in the right arm and one passing through the back, near the left shoulder blade. The woman ran up the stairs and expired as she reached the top. He then returned to his room at the Washington House, on Bank Street, and, reloading the revolver, went into the rear yard and fired a shot through his right temple, which came out through the top of his head. He then placed the revolver directly over his heart, and the second shot was effective.

They don't build 'em like they used to.

The way to fight a woman is with your hat. Grab it and run.
John Barrymore

The lost and found department of American Airlines at LaGuardia Field sent out an APB thirty years ago to try to locate the owners of some lost baggage. Among the unclaimed items were a case of beer, an automatic back scratcher, a straitjacket, and three burlesque show-type G-strings.

In Whistler, Alabama, in 1890, a black man and a white man were convicted of equal guilt in the robbery of a store. The white man was sentenced to five years in prison; the black to 25.

Questions: Why is reciprocated love like gout?

What shape is a kiss?

On Monday, June 28, 1937, Ludovic Vaillancourt of Lewiston, Maine, left his hometown to attend the summer session of the Pius X School of Gregorian Chant in New York City.

The use of cosmetics by women has had its ups and downs for at least the last 600 years in Western Europe. The first documented use of face paints in England occurred during the fourteenth century, and it was common in Shakespeare's time. The vainglorious Queen Elizabeth, in addition to her ten thousand gowns, was said to have powder an inch thick on her face at the time of her death in 1603, not having removed any of it (by washing her face) in over a decade. During the Commonwealth cosmetics were decidedly forbidden — Protector Cromwell decreed that this was the mark of the harlot, and women using cosmetics would be arrested as such. Fifty years later, under Queen Anne, the use of cosmetics flourished once again, and since that time they have been used fairly generally, except during Victoria's long reign. Under her austere rule, the use of make-up was as frowned on as it had been under Cromwell, and the population on the whole agreed with the Queen. As one Victorian wag put it in his prayer, "From beef without mustard, from a servant who overvalues himself, and from a woman who painteth herself, Good Lord, deliver us!"

Answers: Because it's a joint affection.

A-lip-tickle (elliptical).

JUNE 25

Question: Can you figure out what is "different" about this passage?

No, nay! Nat is too bossy, as I say!
"Go! Be off for a fat salami!"
Aloof, at lovers I had named I stare.
Here smegma is food, a kimono is secret sin.
I misled a ticklish sultan at lush silk citadels I minister.
Cession, O Mikado, of Siam Gems ere he rats, I demand!
Ah — is revolt a fool aim?
(A last, a far off foe — bogy as I — says so.)
Boots it any anon?

Notable Births

1903	Anne Revere	1924	Sidney Lumet
1903	George Orwell	1925	June Lockhart
1906	Phil Harris	1942	Willis Reed

Notable Events

1788 Virginia ratified Constitution
1868 North Carolina, Louisiana, Georgia, Florida, and South Carolina readmitted to Union
1872 Jesuits expelled from Germany
1876 Custer's Last Stand
1912 George Lansbury protested to Parliament over force-feeding of imprisoned suffragettes
1925 Gehrig replaced Wally Pipp, began streak of 2,130 straight games
1942 Eisenhower made commander of European operations
1950 North Korea invaded South Korea
1951 First color TV broadcast
1964 Brett Sullivan began attempt to swim Atlantic Ocean

In 1978, Maria Rubio of Lake Arthur, New Mexico, was rolling a burrito for her husband when something caught her eye. The pattern of the skillet burns on the shell looked like Jesus Christ! She showed the thumb-sized replica to her husband and a friend and they both agreed with her. Although the local priest told Mrs. Rubio it was only a coincidence, she would not be dissuaded. She constructed a shrine — a simple wooden frame — for the relic, and placed the burrito in some tufts of cotton batting so it would look as if the burrito Jesus were floating on a cloud.

In six months, over six thousand people came to see it, and Mrs. Rubio had to quit her position as a maid to become the tour guide for the holy burrito.

In America, 40 percent of the wounds inflicted on crime victims by knives and guns are the result of attacks by friends.

Americans consume between four and five tons of aspirin daily.

The directorship of the United Mine Workers decided in 1977 not to include the services of medicine men in its health care package. The request had been made on behalf of some 750 Navajo members, who wished to have the services of a native shaman included. They'd drawn up a list of some two-dozen specific ceremonies they wanted covered by their health plan, which ranged in price from $20 to $750.

A man that should call everything by its right name would hardly pass the streets without being knocked down as a common enemy.

Marquis of Halifax

Studies have shown that women who like literature tend to be better cooks but poorer drivers than women who like math.

Perhaps you've heard that there's a formula for gauging the temperature by the frequency of a cricket's chirps. It's called Dolbear's Law, after its inventor, Professor A.E. Dolbear of Tufts University. In 1897 he figured out that the temperature could be estimated by $T=50 \ \frac{(N-40)}{4}$, in which N represents the number of cricket chirps per minute.

It's a pleasant little recreation if you happen to be listening to a cricket on a summer night when the temperature is within a certain range, and the cricket isn't too excited by the presence of a cricket of the opposite sex, or frightened by the presence of an enemy, or too full of food. Dolbear's Law seldom holds true except under ideal conditions.

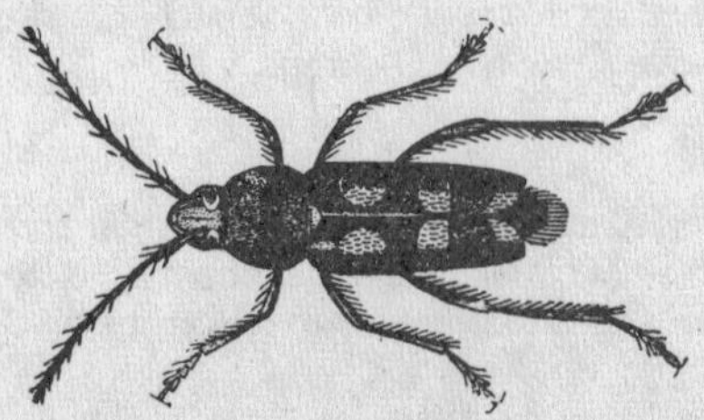

Answer: It's a palindrome, and reads the same backwards and forwards.

Notable Births

1892	Pearl S. Buck	1908	Debs Garms
1901	Stuart Symington	1922	Eleanor Parker
1904	Peter Lorre	1931	Colin Wilson

Notable Events

1721 First smallpox vaccination in America given
1819 Bicycle patented
1858 Treaty of Tientsin ended second Anglo-Chinese war
1917 American expeditonary force arrived in France
1943 Mussolini ousted
1945 United Nation Charter signed in San Fransico
1947 Ken Arnold started UFO scare, sighted 1,200/mph objects in Oregon
1959 Queen Elizabeth opened Saint Lawrence Seaway
1964 Eight hundred vigilantes attacked blacks in Saint Augustine; police freed those arrested
1976 New Guinea earthquake cost 443 lives

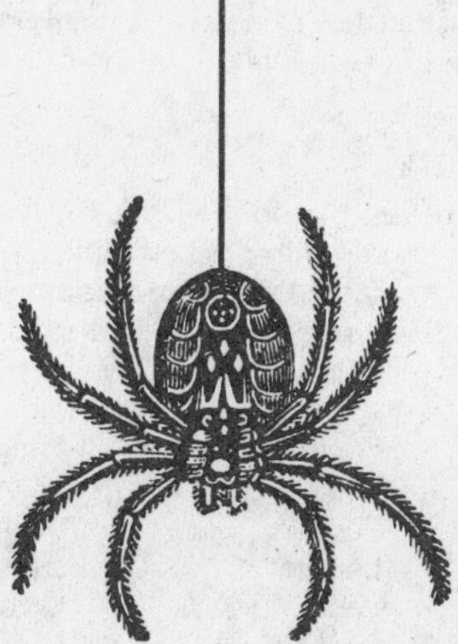

Although the poison of a black widow spider is fifteen times more virulent than that of a prairie rattlesnake, she delivers so little of it that it's unlikely you'd die if she bit you. You'd have severe muscular pain, great difficulty breathing, be subject to recurrent symptoms for months, and your joints would ache in wet weather for the rest of your life, but the chances are 99 out of 100 that it wouldn't kill you.

If you're ever in Cherokee, Alabama, don't miss the National Coon Dog Cemetery.

It was announced early in 1953 that persons suspected of drunkenness in Fitchburg, Massachusetts, would be hauled down to the police station and made to repeat, "Around the rugged rock the ragged rascal ran," as evidence of their sobriety — or intoxication.

Question: In a zoo, all of the following animals are born on the same day. Which one will probably live the longest?

a hippopotamus
a kangaroo
a lion
a wolf

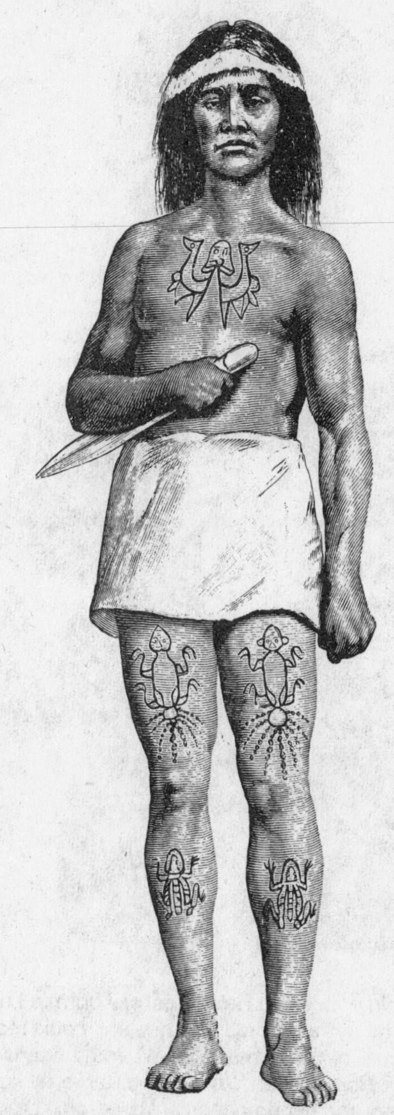

Back in the 1930s, the *Washington Post* once ran a feature on the natives of Papua, which is part of the island of New Guinea. The story reported that the natives tattooed themselves after killing their enemies, and scarred their bodies after completing long sea voyages. On the domestic front, the article described their only piece of clothing — the loin cloth — and how they kept pigs as pets and hung skeletons in their homes as decorations. It went on to imply that the natives couldn't have been too intelligent as their number system only went as far as six.

The noble *Post* called them "Oriental negroes."

Did you know that in the Philippines a dead rooster can be declared the winner in a cock fight if he died while on the offensive? It's true. It took the Philippine Supreme Court months to make this decision.

Answer: A hippopotamus.

JUNE 27

Question: Which of the following cities is not a state capital?
Providence, Rhode Island
Seattle, Washington
Columbia, South Carolina
Madison, Wisconsin

The child prodigy, Christian Heinecker, was born in Lubeck, Germany. When he was a year old, he knew and could recite all the principal events of the Pentateuch. When he was two, he knew all the stories in the Bible. When he was three, he knew as much world history and geography as anyone would ever need to know, and for good measure learned French and Latin as well. When he was four years and four months old, he was dead. It happened on June 27, 1725.

When we are young, we are slavishly employed in producing something whereby we may live comfortably when we grow old; and when we grow old, we perceive it is too late to live as we prospered.

Alexander Pope

I want to know if I can live with what I know, and only that.

Albert Camus

The advantage of a classical education is that it enables you to despise the wealth which it prevents you from achieving.

Russell Green

Notable Births

1682	Charles XIII of Sweden	1913	Willie Mosconi
1872	Paul Lawrence Dunbar	1929	Peter Maas
1880	Helen Keller	1934	Anna Moffo

Notable Events

1743	George II defeated French at Dettingen
1776	First army execution, George Hickey, New York City
1789	Union of Three Estates in France
1834	Cholera epidemic broke out in New York City
1844	Joseph Smith, Mormon Church founder, killed by mob while in Carthage, Illinois, jail
1893	Thousand-mile horse race completed in Chicago
1927	First demonstration of color TV, New York City
1940	Russia seized Bessarabia from Romania
1954	President Arbenz of Guatemala overthrown
1964	Ernest Borgnine and Ethel Merman married; lasted 38 days

In June 1730, Frederick William I of Prussia had a cake made for his army, but the thirty thousand men couldn't eat it. It wasn't a bad cake; it's just that they'd had a huge meal already and didn't have room for the 1,300-square-foot dessert.

In the summer of 1948, London's *Daily Express* ran a contest to see if it could come up with a better name for television than TV, which it thought sounded silly. Here are some of the over-two thousand "sensible" names that were submitted by the paper's readers:

Oculo	Focal	Imagec
Visray	Telio	Vix
Lookies	Peeps	Scan
Vudio	Luksee	Eyeviews
Vizema	Rad-E-Eye	C-U
Look-Hear	Radi-Viz	Gazio
Air-Pic	Opalook	I.C.
Kaladio	Dekko	

TV — chewing-gum for the eyes.

Frank Lloyd Wright

The mockingbird, in English as well as Latin, is well-named. In a space of ten minutes, one bird has been recorded to have imitated the songs of thirty-two other birds. Its scientific name means "many-tongued mimic."

Three founders of modern educational theory — Basedow, Pestalozzi, and Froebel — stated that Jean Jacques Rousseau's story about the education of a young man in his novel *Emile* greatly inspired their thinking. Yet Rousseau himself deposited each of his five children on the doorstep of a foundling home.

Good teaching is one-quarter preparation and three-quarters theater.

Gail Godwin

Answer: Seattle, Washington. Olympia is the state capital.

Notable Births

1491	Henry VIII	1864	Luigi Pirandello
1577	Peter Paul Rubens	1902	Richard Rodgers
1712	Jean Jacques Rousseau	1926	Mel Brooks

Notable Events

1778 Battle of Monmouth, Mary McCauley became Molly Pitcher
1902 United States purchased French rights to build Panama Canal
1914 Assassinations of Archduke Ferdinand and his wife at Sarajevo began World War I
1919 Treaty of Versailles officially ended World War I
1939 Transatlantic passenger service begun by airplane, *Dixie Clipper*
1948 Stalin and Tito broke off relations
1955 State Department dropped charges against Owen Lattimore
1956 Workers' uprising in Posnan, Poland, began

Question: Within 10 years, when were the following invented?
jet engine
iron lung
railroad air brake
bottlemaking machine

If there ever was a real lemon of a car, it was a 1912 Graf and Sift, first owned by Count Franz Harrach of Serbia (now a part of Yugoslavia). This expensive touring car was the finest automobile in the country, but from the beginning neither the count nor his chauffeur cared for it much. The driver claimed that sometimes the steering wheel seemed to have a mind of its own, and that on several occasions he had had narrow escapes because of it. In 1913 the odds caught up with him, and he hit two farmers and a tree in a single accident. The chauffeur was badly injured, but the Graf and Sift was barely scratched.

A few months later, the count lent the car to a friend, reluctantly. Harrach explained that the car was very temperamental, and might be unsafe to drive, but his friend scoffed at the warning, and went on his way. Some time later, the car stalled and the gentleman got out of the car to check the engine. Suddenly the car lunged forward, knocking the man down and running him over, and as a result of the accident, he lost an arm. The count had several mechanics check out the car and they could find nothing wrong with it; but even so, the count had the car locked up.

The following year, the heir to the throne of Austria asked to use the automobile while he was visiting Sarajevo with his wife, and Harrach felt obliged to say yes. During the welcoming parade, a Serbian nationalist burst from the crowd and tossed a bomb onto the car. It was snatched up and thrown from the auto, but four people in the crowd were badly injured when it exploded. Five minutes later, a young man named Gavrilo Pinzip rushed up to the car and assassinated Archduke Francis Ferdinand and his wife. The date was July 28, 1914. Within a week, all of Europe was at war.

Count Harrach pressed the Graf and Sift into service as his staff car. He was soon killed in an Austrian ambush — in the car. General Potiorek of the Austrian Army claimed it as booty, and commandeered it. A few days later, his forces were routed, and soon after, he was relieved of his command. He subsequently went insane. A captain took over the car; nine days later it unaccountably swerved into a tree and the officer was killed.

At he end of the war, the governor of Yugoslavia bought the Graf and Sift. In the four months he owned it, he had four accidents, the last of which crippled him for life. Another government official then bought it, and within a few days he collided with a train. He was killed, but, as usual, the car was only slightly damaged.

By now the car had a widespread and apparently well-deserved reputation. The governor of Yugoslavia ordered it to be destroyed, but a gentleman called Dr. Srkis purchased the car and proceeded to drive it without incident — for six months. Then the undamaged car was found rolled over and atop a fatally injured Dr. Srkis.

After this the car was owned by a jeweler and a race car driver. The jeweler committed suicide shortly after he bought it. The racing driver rebuilt it and souped it up for European competitions. In the first race he used the accursed car he hit a wall on the Orleans racetrack in France and was killed.

As a result of this accident, the auto was battered nearly beyond repair, but a French farmer saved it from the junkyard. He fixed it up and drove it successfully for about two years. Then one day it stalled, and he couldn't start it. As he was getting the tow line hooked up from another car, the G and S suddenly started up again and ran the farmer down, killing him.

The last private owner of this amazing car was a gentleman who was sure he could beat its previous owners' tragic history simply by changing the car's color from black to a cheerful blue. As soon as the paint was dry, he took four friends out for an afternoon drive. Within an hour, the Graf and Sift was in a head-on collision that killed everyone in both automobiles.

Finally, the car was put on display in a Vienna museum, where it was destroyed in a bombing raid during World War II.

Answer: 1937, 1928, 1869, 1903

JUNE 29

Question: What's the state pictured here?

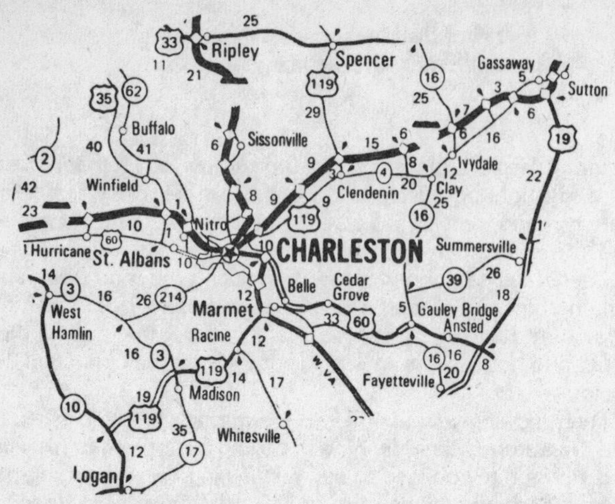

Notable Births

1839	Celia Thaxter	1900	Antoine de St.-Exupery
1841	Henry Stanley	1901	Nelson Eddy
1858	George Washington Goethals	1907	Joan Davis
		1936	Harmon Killebrew

Notable Events

1617 Archduke Ferdinand became King of Bohemia
1848 Croton Aqueduct completed over Harlem River, New York
1868 Michael, King of Serbia, assassinated
1880 France annexed Tahiti
1956 First 7-foot-high jump made, Charles Dumas, Los Angeles
1961 Premier Sukselainen of Finland resigned after influence-peddling conviction
1968 Pope Paul VI rejected all artificial birth control methods for Catholics

On June 29, 1456, Pope Calixtus III issued a papal bull against Halley's Comet, which was then flashing though the sky. He asked all Christendom to pray that God would make it disappear or, failing that, request Him to have it "diverted against the Turks, the foes of the Christian name."

This doctrine of the material efficacy of prayer reduces the Creator to a cosmic bellhop of a not very bright or reliable kind.

Herbert J. Muller

After World War I, the tiny island of Nauru, located near the equator and west of the Gilbert Islands, was mandated to Australia. Appalled by the amount of palm-frond home brew the four thousand natives consumed, the Aussies implemented a total prohibition.

In six months, the infant mortality rate increased sevenfold, to 50 percent. Obstetricians were brought in to investigate, and they found acute vitamin deficiencies among the entire population. They concluded that the palm-frond beer was the only Nauruan foodstuff that normally supplied the islanders with the needed vitamins.

The prohibition was repealed, pregnant women got drunk again, and the infant mortality rate dropped back to 7 percent.

Progress is the mother of problems.

G. K. Chesterton

Marie de Medici, a member of that famous Italian family and a seventeenth-century queen of France, had expensive tastes in clothes. One special dress was outfitted with 39,000 tiny pearls and three thousand diamonds, and cost the equivalent of twenty million dollars at the time it was made in 1606.

She wore it once.

Hector Protector was dressed all in green,
Hector Protector was sent to the Queen.
The Queen did not like him,
No more did the King;
Hector Protector was sent back again.

This is a somewhat obscure nursery rhyme, but another one of those that tells a real story.

During the reign of Henry VIII, Scotland and England were separate kingdoms. Henry wished to see them joined, and one likely way was to bring about the marriage of his young son, who was to become Edward VI, to the young Scottish queen, Mary. Courtship was handled differently in those days, and when the Scottish queen regent turned down the idea of her daughter marrying Edward, the Earl of Hertford was dispatched to woo the princess on Henry's behalf. He did so by sacking Leith and burning everything Scottish between Edinburgh and the border. When he returned, Henry was still not satisfied, and so he was sent back to emphasize the king's feelings. This time he burned seven monasteries, sixteen castles, five large towns, thirteen mills, three hospitals, three abbeys, and 243 villages.

Edward and Mary never did tie the knot.

To be angry is to revenge the faults of others upon ourselves.

Alexander Pope

When a man is wrong and won't admit it, he always gets angry.

Lord Haliburton

Man is a reaosnable animal who always loses his temper when he is called upon to act in accordance with the dictates of reason.

Oscar Wilde

Answer: West Virginia.

Notable Births

1614	Nicholas Rowe	1917	Lena Horne
1917	Buddy Rich	1918	Susan Hayward

Notable Events

1858 Joseph Heco became first Japanese to take American citizenship
1859 Blondin crossed Niagara Falls on a tightrope
1899 C.M. Murphy became first 60-mph bicyclist
1900 Fire at Hoboken, New Jersey docks took 326 lives
1903 Mining disaster at Hanna, Wyoming, killed 169 people
1963 Paul VI became pope

Who was that man who took over a failing business and turned it into the third-largest drug company in the country? And why didn't he want his picture taken? And what makes him so special?

Philip Musica was born in Italy in 1877, and came to America with his family when he was six. His father first had a barber shop on Manhattan's Lower East Side, and later was involved in importing food from Italy. Young Philip joined his father in this enterprise after leaving school at the age of sixteen. The business grew and prospered greatly, and for good reason: Someone was bribing customs officials to mark down the weights of the Musica's imports and Musica and Son were able to beat the prices of their competition easily. The authorities finally found out, Philip took the blame, and spent six months in the Tombs.

On his release, Philip got his family involved in the hair trade. The "Gibson Girl look" was the nation's latest craze, and it required substantially more hair than most women had. Knowing the importing business, and a quick buck when he saw one, Philip sent several family members to buy hair in Italy and set up a wholesale company in New York. Demand was so great that human hair went for as much as forty times its price in Italy. Musica built one success on another, and soon managed to enlist substantial banking money into his enterprise. Now in comfortable circumstances, he moved the family to a big home in Bay Ridge, adjacent to Brooklyn's most fashionable district. He lived a sophisticated life, enjoying fine restaurants and the opera.

But the success of the company was superficial. After Musica had parlayed a shipment of hair worth almost $350,000 as collateral for a $25,000 advance on a loan, one suspicious bank employee did some investigation and found that the bills of lading had been doctored. The six-figure shipment of hair turned out to be worth about $250, and no one was home at the Musica house. It was later discovered that Musica had duped twenty-two banks out of nearly two million dollars.

Musica and his family were apprehended in New Orleans, on the gangplank of a ship bound for Honduras. He was tried and convicted, but was not sent to prison this time. Apparently, some sort of arrangement was made, and he was paroled after three years to become William Johnson, a "special investigator" (actually, a stool pigeon) for the deputy attorney general of New York. This didn't last long, however. Musica had a talent for conning confessions from innocent people.

In the early 1920s, he was in business with an ex-convict named Brandino. It was really more of a service than a business: Musica and his partner followed hearses to gravesites, observed the festivities, and then stole the flowers for resale to local florists.

In 1923, encouraged by a man who had made a small fortune in hair tonic, Musica rented a small building in Mount Vernon, New York, and began to make toilet water, cosmetics, and "drugs." By this time he'd also done several things to conceal his past. He'd changed his haircut, grown a mustache, affected glasses, and changed from a flamboyant dresser to a very conservative one. He'd changed his name as well. Now he was his former landlord, Frank Donald Coster. He incorporated his operation as Girard and Company, and brought in three of his brothers to help run the business. They, too, assumed aliases. Except for the new name, it appeared that Philip Musica was going straight.

The little business did fairly well. Coster cleared $25,000 for his own salary in its second year. But there was more money than that to be realized from the operation, as Coster well knew.

Alcohol is an essential ingredient in toiletries manufacture. Alcohol was also an essential element in Prohibition. Girard and Company used most of the 5,250 gallons of alcohol alloted to them weekly for legitimate manufacturing purposes. Only a little leaked to bootleggers. Bootleggers paid more than legitimate customers, but because of Federal monitoring it was difficult to "lose" too much to them unless one had control of shipment records at both ends of a transaction. Aware of this, Coster set up the W. W. Smith company as a dummy distributor. It would decoy Federal agents away from Girard and Company's operations as well as provide it with a much greater volume of alcohol. Still, he'd have to make it look very "clean."

Coster quickly put his enterprise into legitimate order and had Price-Waterhouse audit his books. They were perfect. With a perfect audit and a successful business, it was easy to get an expansion loan for Girard, and with these two things accomplished, he went to the government and got a whopping increase in his alcohol allotment. A consequence of this new allotment was a lucrative little partnership with underworld lord, Dutch Schultz. Subsequently, Coster paid off his loan in six months instead of a year, and parlayed this quick repayment into a loan for $1.5 million to buy the ailing McKesson and Robbins drug company. Naturally, a *giant* pharmaceutical firm needed a *lot* of alcohol, and this was forthcoming. The deal, combined with good management of the company's legitimate undertakings, made F. Donald Coster president of the third largest drug firm in the country within two years.

The crash of '29 hit the company hard, but only for a time; medicine and alcohol being pretty much necessities in America, the Depression only temporarily cooled the business climate. Times were soon good enough for Coster to be able to buy a 134-foot yacht large enough for a twenty-man crew.

F. Donald Coster was, to say the least, hesitant about photographers. He made a point of it. Although he wasn't reclusive, he was careful about where he went, and whom he saw — and he certainly didn't want his picture taken.

Word of this apparently harmless idiosyncrasy got around, and finally a newsman bribed one of Coster's servants to get a shot of the mystery man. Some time later, the photo appeared in the financial pages of the *New York Times*. Coster was furious, but there was nothing he could do except hope for the best.

The best was not forthcoming. Soon enough, Brandino, the used-funeral flower magnate, sent Coster a letter. A little while later, he was on Coster's doorstep, demanding $10,000 hush money. He got it. Then Brandino got drunk and told some other ex-cons, old "friends" of Coster, about his new identity and the ready extortion money. Coster was besieged by blackmailers who "knew him when."

Coster's own finances began to run low because of this, and he tried to foist a phony wholesale "crude-drug" deal on the Board of Directors of McKesson and Robbins. What looked like a profitable subsidiary company was actually a ficticious name set up to pour M. and R. money into Coster's bottomless pocket. In time, events caught up with Coster. The managers couldn't help but be suspicious, and they found, after investigation, that their drug warehouse was, in fact, a vacant lot in Montreal. Coster's three brothers were arrested; then, as two Federal agents were walking to the door of Coster's Fairfield, Connecticut home, they heard a shot. Rushing into the house, they found Coster in his bathroom, a bullet through his head.

So, what is so special about him? Out of over 250,000 listings in eighty years, Philip Musica, aka William Johnson, aka Frank Donald Coster, is the only absolute imposter ever to get into the pages of *Who's Who in America*.

June 30

The tallest couple ever to be wed were married in 1871. At the time of the wedding, the Nova-Scotian Anna Swan stood seven feet, five-and-a-half inches tall. Her husband Martin Bates, a former Confederate Army Captain, was three inches shorter. Both were members of P.T. Barnum's collection of remarkable people, but their marriage was not simply a Barnum publicity campaign. They married for love, and wanted a family. They did have two children, who at birth weighed a total of forty-two pounds. Unhappily, both babies died on the same day they were born.

One of the quirks of Frederick William the First, who ruled Prussia from 1713 to 1740, was his fondness for giants. His devotion to them was so great, in fact, that he created a small army of men — some 2,400 soldiers — all of them six feet, six inches tall, or taller. Any Prussian man of extraordinary height was destined for the army, whether he wished to join or not, for Frederick's army recruiters sometimes went to extremes to ensure that they got their man. On one occasion, a body-hunter found a carpenter who stood about six foot seven. A few discrete queries convinced the recruiter that the man would not go willingly into the service, and so he commissioned the fellow to build a six foot, nine inch coffin, supposedly for a deceased friend of the recruiter. When the box was completed the soldier insisted it wasn't long enough. The carpenter insisted it was and furthermore, he himself would prove it. "I'm six foot seven;" he said, "and I can get into it easily." He climbed in, whereupon the recruiter slammed the lid on him and shipped the coffin to Frederick at Potsdam. Unfortunately, the carpenter smothered to death en route.

Another time Frederick paid $6,000 to the kidnappers who presented him with James Kirkland, six feet, eleven inches tall, an Irish giant they had taken a thousand miles through Europe to Prussia.

Another animal trial (see March 22): Barely sixty years ago, a horse was executed in Russia. The animal, Krepysh by name, wasn't brought to court for civil or criminal crimes, but rather for political ones. It seems he was the favorite steed of Czar Nicholas, and 1919 was a very bad year for Romanoffs generally. Krepysh was charged with being the holder of the Czar's Cup, with having won over $200,000 of the "people's money," and other crimes of guilt by association. Convicted of high treason, he was shot by a firing squad.

Perhaps the greatest marksmanship record ever set was achieved by a man named Adolph Tupperwein in December 1906. About every five seconds, for eight hours a day, twelve days straight, Tupperwein shot at two-and-a-half-inch wooden cubes tossed into the air. Of the 50,000 blocks he shot at the first eight days of this strange marathon, he missed but 4; and of the 72,500 he beaded on over the entire duration, he missed a total of 9.

Poor Nancy Turtle! Her husband done her wrong! Just how wrong is seen in this advertisement she took out in a Connecticut newspaper. It dates to about the year 1800.

> $100 REWARD—For the apprehension of Lewis Turtle, a tall man, about 50 years, has considerable money and a high forehead, long face and lantern jawed man, a bad man, with a fist like a giant, and has often beat me, and I want him to end his days in the Penitentiary where be belongs, and he wears a grey coat, with a very large mouth, and one blue eye, and one blind blue eye, and a hideous looking man, and now living with the 7th woman, and me having one child to him, and he has gone off, and I want him brought slap up in the law, with blue pants. He ought to be arrested and has a $100 of my money, and a bald headed rascal, full of flattery and receipt, and she is a bad woman, and her little girl calls him "papa" and is called Eliza Jane Tillis, and a boy blind of one eye, and he is not a man who has got any too much sense, nor her. And he stole $100 from me, and some of my gold and silver, and ought to be caught and I will never live with him again, no never, he is a disgrace. And I would like to have him caught up and compelled to maintain me and his child, as I am his lawful wedded wife, and have the certificate of marriage in my possession.
>
> NANCY TURTLE

Hawaii produces 80 percent of this country's pineapples. Can you name the only other state that grows them commercially?

It's Florida.

Leo (The Lion)
July 24 through August 23

JULY

JULY 1

Question: Can you figure out this cryptogram?

Wood
John
Mass

Edward Jenner delivered the first smallpox innoculation on this date in 1796, but early innoculations didn't always work. Sometimes there was too much vaccine or an over-virulent strain of the vaccine was given, or the needle was not sterile — any number of factors existed that resulted in killing someone instead of protecting him, as this verse indicates;

His Body mouldering here must lie —
Behold the amazing alteration
Effected by Innoculation —
The means improved his Life to Save
Hurried him headlong to the grave.
Full in the Bloom of Youth he fell.

If you dream of artichokes, good fortune will come to you from an unexpected source; but if you dream of cauliflowers, friends will slight you or kick you when you're down.

The word "dunce" once meant an exceptionally gifted person. The term was taken from the name of Joannes Duns Scotus, the thirteenth-century scholar and professor of theology at Oxford. When a student had given a good account of himself, he was called a "duns," which gradually developed into "dunce." A hundred years later, however, during a movement of scholarly reform, theologians felt that those who steadfastly followed the orthodox methods of Duns Scotus were obstinate, stupid fellows, and the word "dunce" came to mean a dull, and intransigent individual.

That which seems the height of absurdity in one generation often becomes the height of wisdom in another.
Adlai Stevenson

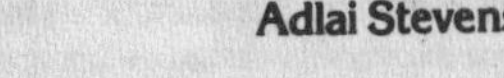

Notable Births

1646	Gottfried Leibniz	1925	Farley Granger
1804	George Sand	1931	Leslie Caron
1899	Charles Laughton	1941	Rod Gilbert
1902	William Wyler	1941	Twyla Tharp
1915	Jean Stafford	1942	Genevieve Bujold
1916	Olivia de Havilland	1942	Karen Black

Notable Events

1190	Richard the Lionheart started on Third Crusade
1796	Jenner delivered first smallpox vaccination
1845	D.L. Yulee of Florida became first Jewish senator
1847	First U.S. adhesive postage stamp issued
1859	First intercollegiate baseball game played, Amherst vs. Williams
1862	United States outlawed polygamy
1863	Battle of Gettysburg fought
1874	First kidnapping for ransom in United States; Germantown, Pennsylvania
1893	First wooden bicycle race track opened
1898	Charge up San Juan Hill led by Wood and Roosevelt

The practice of tarring and feathering is at least 800 years old. Here is part of a law directed at sailors, which was enacted in England during the reign of Richard the Lionheart, in about 1195:

> . . . if any man were taken with theft or pickery, and thereof convicted, he should have his head polled and hot pitch poured upon his pate, and upon that the feathers of some pillow or cushion shaken aloft, that he might thereby be known as a thief, and at the next arrival of the ships to any land be put forth of the company to seek his adventures without all hope of return unto his fellows.

King Kusinaba, a Hindu monarch, fathered 100 daughters, all of them hunchbacks.

Not all congressmen and senators go gallivanting off on "fact-finding" trips to the Bahamas at the expense of good government. Witness the Florida representative, Charles E. Bennett, who holds the record for the greatest number of roll-call votes made. Beginning in 1951, Bennett was present for 3,807 straight tallies. His record ended in 1974, when an unexpected motion for adjournment came up while he had stepped from the House floor for a few minutes.

A husband who had cremated four wives and kept their remains in separate urns eventually buried the ashes after the urns had upset and the contents had mixed together. The epitaph on their tombstone reads:

Stranger pause and shed a tear,
For Mary Jane lies buried here.
Mingled in a most surprising manner
With Susan, Marie, and portions of Hannah.

JULY 2

Notable Births

1877	Herman Hesse	1922	Dan Rowan
1885	Lotte Lehman	1925	Medgar Evers
1903	Olaf V of Norway	1925	Patrice Lumumba
1908	Thurgood Marshall	1937	Richard Petty

Notable Events

1778 Last pregnant woman hanged in Massachusetts; Bathsheba Spooner
1881 Garfield shot in Washington by Charles Guiteau
1900 First flight of a Zeppelin
1919 First-known airplane stowaway caught, East Fortune, Scotland
1937 Amelia Earhart last heard from
1954 Wartime rationing ended in Great Britain
1957 2,500 dead in Iranian earthquake
1961 Suicide of Ernest Hemingway

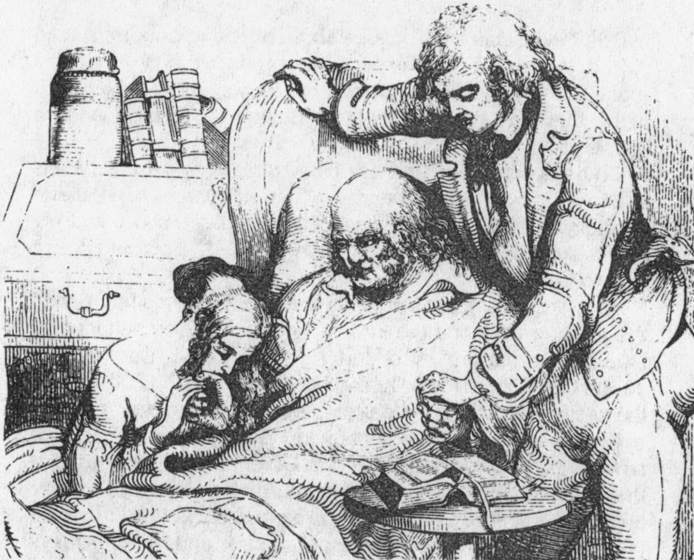

Here are some last words of famous people:

Sir Walter Raleigh exhorted his hesitant executioner thus: "Why dost thou not strike? Strike, man!"

Benjamin Franklin said to his daughter, who had suggested he change his position so he could breathe more easily: "A dying man can do nothing easily."

Fontanelle, the French writer, addressed friends at his bedside thus: "*Je ne souffre pas, mes amis, mais je sens une certaine difficulté d'être.*" ("I do not suffer, my friends, but I feel a certain difficulty of being.")

And John Adams said: "At least Thomas Jefferson still lives." But, unknown to Adams, Jefferson had died several hours before, with the last words: "I resign my soul to God, my daughter to my country." Both men died on July 4, 1826.

Henrik Ibsen was asked if he were feeling better: "On the contrary," he said. He expired immediately.

Socrates reminded a friend, before drinking the cup of poison: "Krito, we owe a cock to Aesculapius; discharge the debt and by no means forget it."

King William II asked his doctor: "Can this last long?"

General Sedgwick died at the Battle of Spotsylvania Courthouse with: "Come, come! They couldn't hit an elephant at this dis . . ."

The first requisite for immortality is death.

Stanislaw Lec

Questions: How can you divide nineteen apples equally among seven hungry boys?

Why does a watermelon have so much water in it?

Between 1889 and 1930 in the states that formed the Confederacy during the Civil War, there were a total of 2,882 lynchings, accounting for about 70 percent of the national total during those years. But don't get the impression that blacks were exclusively the victims of this heinous practice. Only 2,577 of those executed without trial were Negroes.

In contrast, there was not a single lynching, white or black, recorded during those years in the New England states.

Racism is the snobbery of the poor.

Raymond Aron

Sentence first, verdict afterwards!

Lewis Carroll

The following epitaph comes from a stone near Appomatox Courthouse, Virginia:

> Robert C. Wright was Born June 26th, 1772.
> Died July 2nd, 1815, by the bloodthrusty hand
> of John Sweeny, Sr., Who was massacre with the Nife,
> then a Loudon Gun discharge a ball pentrate the
> Heart that Give the immortal wound.

Time magazine reported in July 1943 that a marriage license had been taken out in Pryor, Montana, by Owen Smells and Mary Knows. The lady became Mary Knows Smells. The magazine also reported their divorce three years later.

Julius Caesar and Napoleon Bonaparte were both epileptics. Napoleon was also deathly afraid of cats.

A way to tell frogs and toads apart without a toadstool is to let them bite you. A toad will gum you; a frog has teeth. Be careful: Brazil's barking toad has a "gum" that can kill a horse.

Answers: Make them into applesauce.

Because it's planted in the spring.

JULY 3

Question: Within 10 years, when were the following invented?
military tank
telegraph
street car
steam boat

Notable Births

1738	John Singleton Copley	1906	George Sanders
1807	Otis Skinner	1909	Earl Butz
1878	George M. Cohan	1913	Dorothy Kilgallen
1883	Franz Kafka	1943	Geraldo Rivera

Notable Events

1608	Quebec founded by Champlain
1878	First flight of a modified dirigible
1893	First solo circumnavigation ended by J. Slocum; Fairhaven, Massachusetts
1898	Battle of Santiago Bay effectively ended Spanish-American War
1970	British jet crashed near Barcelona, killed 112 people
1976	Israeli commandos stage raid on Entebbe

Spain didn't have a chance in Teddy Roosevelt's "lovely little war" of 1898, but people on the home front didn't realize that until it was too late. In May, General Blanco cabled the Spanish government from Cuba that he had dispatched 827 men "to America" with the orders "to hold the country until reinforced."

Once the news reached Madrid, one newspaper felt obliged to enhance it a little. It reported that, "U.S. troops saw the Spanish gunboat and are now helplessly scattered from Boston to Chicago in Florida, where the Indians are killing them without resistance, for they had thrown away all their arms. Indeed, they are hopelessly entangled in the great swamps through which DeSoto pushed his way."

The first casualty when war comes is truth.

Hiram Johnson

On an inspection tour in 1915, a Lieutenant Cunningham of the British Royal Navy Service stopped alongside a dirigible and gave the fabric a plunk with his finger. According to a booklet put out by the Goodrich corporation, "an odd noise echoed off the taut fabric." Cunningham then imitated the sound: "Blimp!" Onlookers picked up the expression and the dirigible got its popular name.

This story can't really be taken as gospel, but it's as likely an origin for the word as any.

A New London, Connecticut, man named John Weeks died in 1798 at the age of 114. Eight years before, he'd married his tenth wife — she was sixteen — and he grew a new head of dark hair and cut several new teeth in the first year of their marriage. A few hours before he died, he ate three pounds of pork, three pounds of bread, and drank a pint of wine.

Don't ever, *ever* make a joke about hijacking or bombs at an airport, no matter how respectable you are, or how lightly you make the remark. Tilford Dudley did this on July 3, 1969, on a plane that was about to fly from Boston to Chicago, and he learned a hard lesson.

Dudley's convention in Boston had gone very well, and he was in a jovial mood. When the stewardess stopped by his seat and cordially inquired about his destination, Dudley, who later admitted he liked to tease pretty girls, jokingly asked, "How long does it take to Cuba?"

That was that. A few moments later the plane had returned to the loading area and the state police had Dudley handcuffed. Dudley was charged with disturbing the peace, and District Court Judge Guy Rizzoto found him guilty and fined him $200, despite the testimony of eleven passengers that the remark had not bothered them at all. In sentencing Dudley, Rizzoto cited the famous pronouncement of Judge Oliver Wendell Holmes, that the Constitutional guarantee of freedom of speech does not give anyone the license to cry "Fire!" in a crowded theater.

Dudley, a Harvard Law School graduate and the director of National Affairs for the United Church of Christ, appealed.

You hear about constitutional rights, free speech, and the free press. Everytime I hear these words I say to myself, "That man is a Red, that man is a Communist!" You never hear a real American talk like that.

Frank Hague

What do I care about the law? Ain't I got the power?

Cornelius Vanderbilt

Rodin's statue *The Thinker* is actually the sculptor's representation of the poet Dante.

Other senses do not improve after the sense of sight is lost. The brain simply learns to rely more on the other sense information it receives, and to interpret it more clearly.

Answer: 1914, 1835, 1836, 1783.

JULY 4

Question: Can you name the 5 most common American surnames?

Notable Births

1804	Nathaniel Hawthorne	1902	Meyer Lansky
1807	Giuseppe Garibaldi	1905	Lionel Trilling
1826	Stephen Foster	1911	Mitch Miller
1872	Calvin Coolidge	1918	Abigail Van Buren
1883	Rube Goldberg	1918	Ann Landers
1885	Louis B. Mayer	1924	Eva Marie Saint
1900	Louis Armstrong	1927	Neil Simon

Notable Events

1054	Chinese astronomers first noticed explosion of star that became Crab Nebula
1636	Roger Williams founded Providence, Rhode Island
1863	Vicksburg surrendered to Grant
1866	Fire destroyed large part of Portland, Maine
1883	First Wild West Show presented, North Platte, Nebraska
1884	First American bullfight held, Dodge City, Kansas
1955	First King Cobra snakes born in captivity, New York City

The Washington Monument took thirty-seven years to construct. The cornerstone was laid on July 4, 1848, but work was stopped in 1856 when the money privately subscribed for the obelisk was depleted and Congress refused to appropriate more. At that time the monument stood only 150 feet tall. Its completion was finally voted by Congress in 1877, twenty-one years later, and it was dedicated in 1885 on Washington's birthday.

It cost $1.3 million to build, and stands 555 feet, 5⅛ inches tall. There are 898 steps leading to the observation windows, 500 feet up the monument. It is sinking into the ground at the rate of .47 feet per century.

If you don't like the West Coast, go East, young man!

The California Supreme Court recently upheld Disneyland's ouster of two men who were dancing together at the park's "Date Night." It held that regulations that specified only male/female couples protected the rights of other dancers in a reasonable fashion.

But in Rhode Island in 1980, a young gay man's right to bring his boyfriend to the senior prom was upheld by a federal court. That court ruled that the young man had a right under the First Amendment to make such a "statement" and it must be guaranteed, even though the school feared that the incident might provoke violence from his heterosexual classmates.

In Chester, England, there is this epitaph on a potter's grave:

> Beneath this stone lies Catherine Gray,
> Changed to a lifeless lump of clay:
> By earth and clay she got her pelf,
> And now she's turned to earth herself.
> Ye weeping friends, let me advise,
> Abate your tears and dry your eyes;
> For what avails a flood of tears?
> Who knows but in a course of years,
> In some tall pitcher or brown pan,
> She in her shop may be again.

Answer: Smith, Johnson, Williams, Brown, Jones.

The New England Yankee has a reputation for thrift and for taking things literally. These two characteristics were certainly to be found in Calvin Coolidge, who was born in Vermont and served as governor of Massachusetts before becoming president in 1923. A visitor to the White House once asked if he might have one of the president's cigars, so he could present it to a friend who collected the cigar bands of famous people. Silent Cal immediately replied, "Certainly." He reached into his cigar box, took one out, stripped the band from it, and handed the band to his guest.

He [Coolidge] looks as if he'd been weaned on a pickle.

Alice Roosevelt Longworth

A liberal politician calls it share-the-wealth; a conservative calls it soak-the-rich.

Laurence J. Peter

In 1927, the legislature of South Dakota changed the name of Sheep Mountain to Mount Coolidge, in appreciation for the "high distinction" given their state by the president's vacationing there that summer. In Coolidge's home state of Vermont a similar resolution had been introduced earlier into the legislature there, but the fact that all the peaks in Vermont already had names baffled that august body's Yankee ingenuity.

The vision of a cat is about six times as acute as a human's.

JULY 5

Question: What herb cures all ills?

In 1844, the British painter Haydon was newly out of a debtors' prison. He put on a show of his work at Egyptian Hall in Piccadilly, to raise some money as quickly as possible. Although he had always made a profit by showing his work there before, this time it actually cost him money to even put on the exhibition. The reason for this was that Tom Thumb, P.T. Barnum's famous midget, was on exhibition around the corner from the gallery. Haydon indignantly wrote: "Tom Thumb had 12,000 people last week, B.R. Haydon 135½ (the half a little girl) . . . Exquisite taste of the British people!"

What garlic is to salad, insanity is to art.

Homer St. Gaudens

When you're down and out, something always turns up — and it's usually the noses of your friends.

Orson Welles

The first Macy's Parade didn't take place in New York City, and it didn't take place on Thanksgiving. Before Rowland Macy moved to New York, his dry goods store in Haverhill, Massachusetts, was struggling to stay alive. Hoping to attract new customers to his business, Macy planned a Fourth of July celebration in 1857. This was to include a small band and an address delivered by one of the area's leading citizens.

The band marched to Macy's store without incident, but the guest speaker never showed up, and Macy had to give the speech himself. He got out of it by reciting "George Washington, Solder and Statesman," a eulogy he'd once had to memorize in school.

The affair obviously didn't do much for Macy's. The next year the Macy family moved to New York, where the business and the parades fared much, much better.

When the French Academy was preparing its first dictionary, it defined "crab" as, "A small red fish which walks backwards." This definition was sent with a number of others to the naturalist Cuvier for his approval. The scientist wrote back, "Your definition, gentlemen, would be perfect, only for three exceptions. The crab is not a fish, it is not red and it does not walk backwards."

Fortunately, assassination of French language not a serious crime.

Charlie Chan

Notable Births

1709	Etienne de Silhouette	1889	Jean Cocteau
1801	David Farragut	1902	Henry Cabot Lodge
1810	P.T. Barnum	1909	Andrei Gromyko
1853	Cecil Rhodes	1948	Julie Nixon

Notable Events

1575	Jesuits landed in China
1770	Russians defeated Turks at Tchesme
1916	First transcontinental motorcycle trip by a woman began, New York City
1918	Czar and family executed at Ekaterinburg
1959	Ghana began boycott of all South African goods
1970	DC-8 crashed near Toronto, 108 dead
1978	Leslie Van Houton, Manson family member, lost appeal

In 1957, Colonal Stig E.C. Wennerstrom was awarded the Legion of Merit by the United States government in recognition of his services with the American military while he was on leave from the Norwegian armed forces. In July 1963, the colonel announced he was a Communist spy.

Some day the American people are going to erect a monument to [Senator Joe McCarthy's] memory.

Eddie Rickenbacker

The Council of Constance put the pope on trial in 1414 for crimes including piracy, rape, incest, murder, and sodomy. Other so-called scandalous charges were suppressed. The proceedings were attended by more than 700 prostitutes.

Of all sexual aberrations, chastity is the strangest.

Anatole France

Here is an epitaph from a Hartford, Connecticut cemetery:

Here lies two babies, so dead as nits;
De Lord he kilt dem mit his ague fits.
When dey was too good to live mit me,
He took dem up to live mit He,
So he did.

Answer: Thyme.

JULY 6

Notable Births

1886	Beatrix Potter	1927	Janet Leigh
1915	Laverne Andrews	1932	Della Reese
1925	Merv Griffin	1946	Sylvester Stallone

Notable Events

1415 John Huss burned at stake at Constance
1535 Execution of Thomas More
1808 Pope Pius VII taken prisoner by French after excommunicating Napoleon
1843 Fremont expedition to Pike's Peak began
1854 Republican party founded, Ripon, Wisconsin
1898 United States annexed Hawaii
1944 Fire in Hartford, Connecticut, circus tent killed 168 people
1964 Nyasaland became 37th independent African nation

Question: What's the state shown here?

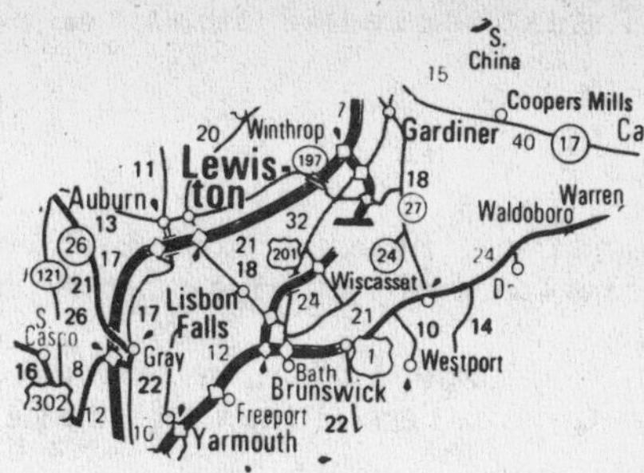

If it hadn't been for his headstrong wife and the felony she committed, John Charles Fremont's expedition to the West (begun on this date in 1843) might never have gotten underway.

Fremont was a young army lieutenant and a surveyor when he met fifteen-year-old Jessie Benton, the daughter of Senator Thomas Hart Benton. Jessie and John were immediately attracted to one another, but Senator Benton most definitely didn't approve of Fremont as a son-in-law. He used his influence to have the War Department transfer Fremont as far away from civilization as possible. In those days (some unkind people would say in these days as well) that meant Des Moines. Fremont performed so well in Des Moines that he was assigned to command a major expedition charged with mapping the passes through the Rocky Mountains to help determine the best overland route to California, which was then Mexican territory. He was ordered to Washington for instructions, and while he was there he and Jessie were secretly married.

When he left for Saint Louis to get the trek underway, Jessie went with him. It was a good thing that she did. While Fremont and his men were away for a week on a shakedown expedition, a message arrived ordering him back to Washington to explain his purchases of "unauthorized equipment" unconnected with the assignment. Jessie intercepted it and, believing her father had something to do with this unexpected turn of events, destroyed it. This was, of course, a felony. In its place she sent word to her husband to: "Proceed at once; ask no questions." Fremont did so, not suspecting the circumstances of her message. Everything went extremely well on the expedition, and he was welcomed home the next year as a hero.

Two years later, the twenty-two-year-old unconvicted felon Jessie Benton Fremont was the wife of the governor of California.

We should often be ashamed of our very best actions, if the world only saw the motives which caused them.

La Rochefoucauld

Sir Thomas More, the author of *Utopia*, was executed on this date in 1535. Among his last words, as he approached the scaffold, were; "Give me a hand going up; I shall fend for myself coming down."

Answer: Maine.

JULY 7

Question: Which came first, the chicken or the egg? Why? (There's a logical answer to this age-old question.)

This letter appeared in *Newsweek* on July 7, 1957.

You Americans wonder why you are so unpopular. Let me tell you:

You have no house burned to ashes, no window broken and no one had to dig out his beloved from what had once been his home.

Also, you continue the tradition of Prussian militarism. You make military considerations overrule everything else. Your unpopularity is not the consequence of bad behavior, but your utter lack of respect for other nations with another history and experience.

(signed)
West Germany

We'll blast them back into the Stone Age.
William Westmoreland

Thank heaven for the military-industrial complex.
Barry Goldwater

In July 1950, the *Postal Record*, the official publication of the National Association of Letter Carriers, noted that the fastest time in which the Pony Express had been able to deliver the mail between Saint Joseph and Kansas City, Missouri, was nine hours. It went on to note that the modern, streamlined post office was able to move the mail between the two cities in only two or three days.

Now, that's progress!

Did you know the Bible records seven cases of suicide?

Answer: The egg. Reptiles laid eggs for millions of years before chickens were even invented.

Notable Births

1860	Gustav Mahler	1907	Robert Heinlein
1884	Leon Feuchtwanger	1911	Gian Carlo Menotti
1899	George Cukor	1917	Lawrence O'Brien
1901	Vittorio De Sica	1922	Pierre Cardin
1906	Satchel Paige	1940	Ringo Starr

Notable Events

1842	Total eclipse of the sun in Europe
1863	First U.S. wartime conscription took effect
1917	Emma Goldman sentenced to 2 years for interfering with army registration
1930	Arthur Conan Doyle died, promising to return from spirit world
1941	United States occupied Iceland bases
1946	Mother Cabrini canonized
1960	Belgium sent troops into Congo
1960	Eisenhower banned Cuban sugar imports
1973	77 people died as floods swept two buses into river, Alway, India

On this date in 1863, the first conscription law in the history of the United States went into effect, so it may be appropriate to let a noted man of letters speak on the topic of war:

O Lord our Father, our young patriots, idols of our hearts, go forth in battle — be thou near them! With them — in spirit — we also go forth from the sweet peace of our beloved firesides to smite the foe. O Lord, Our God, help us tear their soldiers to bloody shreds with our shells; help us to cover their smiling fields with the pale forms of their patriot dead; help us to drown the thunder of their guns with the shrieks of their wounded, writhing in pain; help us lay waste their humble homes with a hurricane of fire; help us to wring the hearts of their unoffending widows with unavailing grief; help us to turn them out roofless with their little children to wander unfriended the wastes of the desolated land in rags and hunger and thirst..

Mark Twain

The Marine Corps . . . have a propaganda machine that is almost equal to Stalin's.
Harry S Truman

JULY 8

Notable Births

1838	Ferdinand Zeppelin	1913	Walter Kerr
1839	John D. Rockefeller	1914	Billy Eckstine
1907	George Romney	1917	Faye Emerson
1908	Nelson Rockefeller	1935	Steve Lawrence

Notable Events

1835 Liberty Bell cracked tolling death of Justice Marshall
1867 Customs treaty signed between north and south Germanies
1871 Prussia began *Kulturkampf* against Catholic Church
1911 First transcontinental horseback trip (solo) completed by a woman
1961 Portuguese ship *Save* wrecked off Mozambique, 243 died
1972 Russian wheat deal announced

Tasmanian natives have only three numbers — one, two, and many.

In July 1955, John McElroy, 35 years old, was arrested in Miami for appearing naked, in public. He explained to authorities that he'd disrobed because he felt the prison uniform he had been wearing was too conspicuous.

I wasn't really naked. I simply didn't have any clothes on.
Josephine Baker

Questions: If you see a counterfeit $20 bill on the street, why must you pick it up?

Why is a penny like a rooster on the fence?

In 1909, *Wide World* magazine estimated John D. Rockefeller's wealth at one billion dollars. The magazine also estimated that, if he worked forty hours a week, and counted out five dollars a second, it would take Rockefeller twenty-six years and six months to count all his fortune. *Wide World* calculated that one billion silver dollars would stretch 248 miles, and if a train were to carry the ore from which the dollars were manufactured, it would be fourteen miles long. If plain matches were used instead to represent the billion dollars, they would fit in twelve full freight cars.

I never hated a man enough to give him his diamonds back.
Zsa Zsa Gabor

In 1927, John D. Rockefeller, Sr., was stopped by an Officer Sproul in Matawan, New Jersey. The policeman requested the use of his chauffered car to overtake someone speeding a short distance up the road. He himself would ride on the running-board. Mr. Rockefeller agreed, with command: "Phillips! Drive on!" and a few minutes later the miscreant had been apprehended. Officer Sproul thanked Rockefeller for his kind assistance but JDR said "on the contrary," and handed the cop five shiny new dimes.

Generous people are rarely mentally ill people.
Karl Menninger

Money will buy a pretty good dog but it won't buy the wag of his tail.
Josh Billings

The Rockefellers have never been known to give a dime that they didn't get ten dollars back for.
Huey Long

Pancho Villa, despite his reputation as a bandit and outlaw, was one of the five largest grain producers in Mexico.

In July, 1956, a car belonging to Harry Owens of Chicago was stopped by police. The lawmen found in it a .44 revolver, 100 bullets, eleven daggers, three switchblades, lock-picking tools, a lock-puller, and a tear-gas gun. When he was asked for an explanation, Mr. Owens said "My hobby is shooting. I throw daggers and knives to amuse myself. I studied locksmithing, and I like to watch people cry."

All work and no play makes Jack a dull boy — and Jill a wealthy widow.
Evan Esar

Answers: Because you could be arrested for passing it.
Its head is on one side, tail on the other.

JULY 9

Question: There are said to be seven presidents born in log cabins or the equivalent. Can you name them?

The phrase "Kilroy was here" and the accompanying logo  spread throughout the world during World War II, courtesy of the United States Navy. It appeared on navy ships in the most amazing places.

For a while its origins remained a great mystery, and then all sorts of would-be authors began to claim it as theirs. It wasn't until the early fifties that the puzzle was solved.

James J. Kilroy was an inspector at the shipyard of the Bethlehem Steel Company in Quincy, Massachusetts, during the war, and his work required him to shimmy into all kinds of places on ships to check for proper workmanship. Once or twice his boss insisted that Kilroy reinspect certain hard-to-reach areas, believing that Kilroy had simply marked them inspected to avoid the arduous, dirty task a real on-site check would have required. After that, Kilroy began to chalk his signature wherever he'd been so he could challenge the foreman the next time he ordered a reinspection. When the ships went to war and sailors discovered Kilroy's peculiar little cartoon, like all good naval personnel they promulgated it throughout the world.

⚜

J.J. Greenough patented the first sewing machine in 1842. By 1855 there were 70 different machines and by 1867 the number had escalated to 843. In the next thirty-three years, six thousand various patents for sewing machines were granted.

Notable Births

1764	Ann Radcliffe	1878	H.V. Kaltenborn
1777	Arthur Henry Hallam	1887	Samuel Eliot Morison
1819	Elias Howe	1916	Edward Heath
1856	Nichola Tesla	1947	O.J. Simpson

Notable Events

1609	Royal Charter of Rudolf II allowed freedom of conscience in Bohemia
1755	French defeated English at Fort Duquesne
1847	New Hampshire enacted first 10-hour labor law
1872	Donut cutter patented by J.F. Blondel, Thomaston, Maine
1877	Riots in Pittsburgh left 100 dead
1961	Whittaker Chambers died
1966	Klansmen sentenced to 10 years in case of Schwerner, Chaney, and Goodman
1967	Typhoon Billie left 346 dead in Japan

About the year 1780 in Dublin, Ireland, a theater manager named Daly made a wager that within one day he could introduce a new word into the language. Throughout the city, that night, he chalked the letters "QUIZ" on every available space. The next morning the Irish awoke to find a "puzzling" new word all over their town, and for weeks wondered what it meant. By the time the nature of its origin was revealed, English had a new word, and Daly had his bet.

Answer: Lincoln, Jefferson, Jackson, Fillmore, Buchanan, Garfield, Arthur (supposedly, according to some accounts).

JULY 10

Notable Births

1509	John Calvin	1920	David Brinkley
1834	James McNeill Whistler	1923	Jean Kerr
1867	Finley Peter Dunne	1943	Arthur Ashe
1871	Marcel Proust	1945	Virginia Wade
1915	Saul Bellow	1947	Arlo Guthrie

Notable Events

1212	London fire claimed 3,000 lives
1835	Abolitionist riots in New York City
1877	Cork life preserver patented
1913	Russia declared war on Bulgaria
1923	All non-Fascist parties in Italy ordered dissolved
1943	Allies invaded Sicily
1946	United States announced price rise of 10 percent in two weeks
1962	Telstar launched

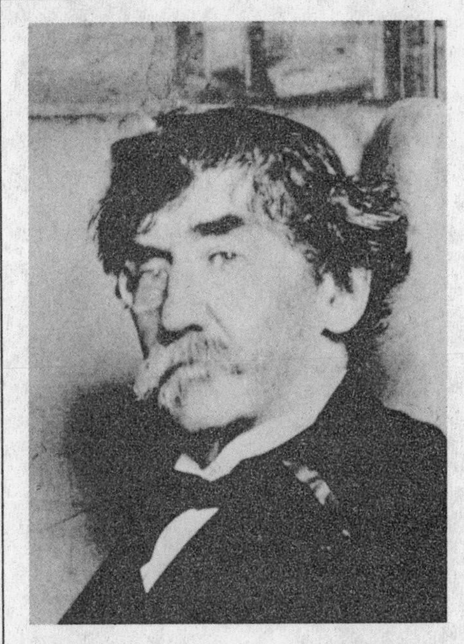

The artist Whistler had a poodle to which he was extremely attached. One day it became evident that the dog had an infected mouth, and Whistler had the gall to summon Sir Morell Mackenzie, England's foremost throat specialist. When he arrived at Whistler's and found the poodle was his patient, Mackenzie was not pleased; but he said nothing, treated the animal, and collected his fee.

The next day, Whistler received a note from Mackenzie asking him to come to his office as soon as possible. Thinking it concerned his dog, Whistler went immediately.

When he arrived, Mackenzie said in a somber tone, "How do you do, Mr. Whistler? I wanted to talk to you about having my front door painted."

People will forgive anything but beauty and talent. So I am doubly unpardonable.

James McNeill Whistler

Question: Why is a cold like a great humiliation?

At a July 10, 1976, Klonvokation near Georgetown, Illinois, KKK members held a cross-burning — or tried to. The meeting got underway an hour late, and when it came time to set up the cross, they found it was too heavy for them to be able to move it to the site. Klan members spent three hours chopping it down to a reasonable size, and then discovered they couldn't get it to ignite.

The first and great commandment is, Don't let them scare you.

Elmer Davis

⚜

The Salem, Massachusetts, Witch Trials of 1692 were initiated by the overactive imaginations of a nine-year-old-girl named Ann Putnam and her friends, and the subsequent executions were carried out because of the ignorance and hysteria of the townspeople. None of the victims had ever acted in any suspicious way, and were accused only because several of the little girls dared not face up to being punished for a childish game.

It all began when a West Indian woman name Tituba, working as a domestic in the Putnam house, started to entertain the children with stories of the voodoo and witchcraft of her native island. These tales fired the girls' sense of the dramatic and they began to playact as if they were indeed possessed. When their elders became angry at their behavior, they accused various townspeople of having bewitched them, as if Tituba's stories were possible, rather than face punishment. The little girls' indictments, the zealous and misguided writings of the theologian Cotton Mather, and the opinions of the local doctor, Griggs, who attributed any unknown disorder to possession by the devil, led to the trials of more than thirty people for sorcery. Ironically, those few individuals who admitted in court that they practiced the black arts were allowed to live. It was only those who maintained they were not witches who were sentenced to die.

Twenty-one of the accused were eventually found guilty. Twenty were sentenced to the gallows, but one was to meet a different fate. Bridget Bishop, the owner of two taverns and a debatable reputation, was the first to die, hanged on July 10, 1692. Nine days later, Rebecca Nurse, an elderly woman of a pious and spotless reputation, and four other women accused by the little girls suffered the same fate. Soon after, a man named Giles Corey was pressed to death under planks and stones. On August 19, the Reverend George Burroughs was hanged with five others. Burroughs's conviction was based on his ability to hold a musket straight out at arm's length on the strength of his index finger inserted in the barrel. The magistrates were sure the feat could not be done without witchcraft. Even though Burroughs recited the Lord's Prayer faultlessly just before the noose was placed around his neck, something deemed impossible for anyone in league with the devil, he was summarily hanged. It was not until eight more people had met their deaths that the hysteria began to die.

Shortly before her own death in 1706, Ann Putnam admitted her guilt in the situation, as several of her friends did later.

Incidentally, the trials themselves did not take place in Salem; they took place in Danvers. Until 1752, Salem wasn't even a town by itself — it was a village within the town of Danvers. Although Gallows Hill is located in what is now Salem, no one is quite sure which of two hills it is.

An honest God is the noblest work of man.

Robert G. Ingersoll

Answer: It brings the proudest man to his — sneeze.

JULY 11

Questions: When is a man in love like a tailor?

Why is the music of an organ grinder always considered classical?

Notable Births

1754	Thomas Bowdler	1920	Yul Brynner
1767	John Quincy Adams	1931	Tab Hunter
1899	E.B. White	1953	Leon Spinks

Notable Events

1804 Burr killed Hamilton in Hoboken duel
1861 Londoners voted to reject a free library
1937 Hitler guaranteed Austrian borders
1960 Tshombe proclaimed independence of Katanga Province
1973 Boeing 707 crashed near Paris, 122 killed
1974 Typhoon Gilda left 106 dead in Japan and Korea

Before Aaron Burr met Alexander Hamilton in their famous duel, he had to fight one of his own relatives for the privilege. Samuel Broadhurst, related to Burr by marriage, heard of the challenge, which came about because Hamilton refused to apologize for a remark Burr considered libelous, and went to Burr to try to negotiate an honorable settlement. He himself was challenged by Burr, and in the duel that followed (with swords), Burr drew blood first and so was declared the victor.

Unhappily, the Burr-Hamilton contest was fought with pistols. Hamilton's supporters insisted that he shot in the air, while those favoring Burr said Hamilton was aiming directly at the challenger when Burr's shot hit him and spun him around, causing Hamilton's ball to fire harmlessly. Burr's weapon was a twelve-inch flintlock, and Hamilton had a gun with equivalent firing power. The distance was ten paces, which caused one commentator to report that the duel was fought at "point blank range with miniature cannon."

Ironically, in 1797, when Hamilton and Burr were on better terms, Hamilton once challenged James Monroe over some minute slight, and Burr had intervened to make peace between them.

Man is a reasoning rather than a reasonable animal.
Alexander Hamilton

This is an epitaph from a tombstone near San Diego, in California:

> This yere is sakrid to the memory of William Henry Skaraken, who caim to his deth by bein shot by Colt's revolver—one of the old kind, bras mountid and of sutch is the kingdom of heavin.

On this date in 1745, the Battle of Fontenoy (in Belgium) was fought. Fifty thousand English, Dutch, and German troops lined up before seventy thousand Frenchmen, and the English commander, Lord Charles Hay, moved to the front. Very politely, he removed his hat and bowed to the French commander, offering him the courtesy of the first volley. With similar courtesy, the French general declined.

The allied troops then fired, and 810 Frenchmen fell dead.

Answers: When he is pressing his suit.

Because it is a production by Handle (*sic*).

Notable Births

100 B.C.	Julius Caesar	1904	Pablo Neruda
1730	Josiah Wedgwood	1908	Milton Berle
1817	Henry David Thoreau	1917	Andrew Wyeth
1854	George Eastman	1918	Jesse Owens
1895	George Eastman	1922	Mark Hatfield
1895	Kirsten Flagstad	1934	Van Cliburn
1895	Oscar Hammerstein II	1949	Lasse Viren
1895	R. Buckminster Fuller		

Notable Events

1543	Henry VIII married Catherine Parr
1822	General Hull invaded Canada
1862	Congressional Medal of Honor authorized
1934	Belgium prohibited uniformed political parties
1938	Hughes set round-the-world speed record, 3 days, 19 hours, 14 minutes
1961	South Korean dam burst, killed 250 people
1967	Race riots began in Newark, New Jersey

It is almost a certainty that Julius Caesar was *not* born by Caesarian section. For one thing, until about the year 1500 A.D., Caesarian deliveries were not made until the mother was dead. After 1500, they were occasionally performed on living women, but until the nineteenth century very few mothers survived the operation; and we know that Caesar's mother lived on many years after his birth.

The story of Cleopatra dissolving a pearl in her wine as a tribute to Mark Antony is also the fabrication of some ancient historian. Those who have had the wherewithal to try this have found it takes several days for a pearl to disintegrate even in the strongest vinegar, and it never really fully dissolves — the non-mineral components of the pearl remain as a residue. In ordinary wine, a pearl will remain a pearl for an indefinitely long time. Cleopatra may have dropped a pearl into her cup and swallowed it with the wine, thus fulfilling her pledge to drinking a fortune's worth of wine in toasting Antony in one evening; but she didn't dissolve it.

Question: Can you name the three states that were named after presidents of the United States?

History is an account, mostly false, of events, mostly unimportant, which are brought about by rulers, mostly knaves, and soldiers, mostly fools.

Ambrose Bierce

R. Buckminster Fuller is best known as the inventor of the geodesic dome and as the author of *Operating Manual for Spaceship Earth*, but he is the creator of hundreds of other inventions as well. Sadly, some of this inventions are so good, so sensible, and so inexpensive compared to their commercial counterparts that you'll never have a chance to see them.

The best example of a Fuller superinvention is the automobile he designed. Working with a team of skilled engineers in Connecticut during the early years of the Depression, Bucky built a streamlined three-wheeled car that could carry eleven adults, park in a smaller space than a contemporary Ford sedan, and turn in its own length. He called it the Dymaxion Car. Its front-wheel drive, shatterproof glass, air-conditioning, and above-spring suspension were all innovations, as was the use of aluminum for the body and aircraft steel for the frame. Because of the rear-mounted engine, there was also no drive shaft hump, so the entire floor space of the car was usable. Because of its streamlined appearance (it looked like a baby whale, more or less) and light-weight qualities, it could achieve the same performance with a ninety-horsepower engine that a 1933 conventional auto could with 300 horsepower. A later modification consisted of arranging three small (10-15 hp) engines in a series, which enabled the Dymaxion Car, loaded with ten passengers, to cruise at sixty to seventy miles per hour while getting forty to fifty miles per gallon.

This wonderful machine was to be displayed at the New York Auto Show of 1934, but its invitation was withdrawn without explanation at the last minute. At least one writer's guess is that the cancellation was caused by pressure from the Chrysler Corporation. Chrysler had paid dearly for a prime location to introduce its new "Air Flow" car — an automobile that would have appeared a very poor second beside Fuller's Dymaxion.

Had it gone into mass production, the Dymaxion could have been built for about the same money as a midsized Ford or GM product, but it was the wrong time for the right car. In the middle of the Depression, America's large automakers clearly could not afford to retool to make a superior auto, only to see it become dinosaur in an economic ice age. And it certainly didn't make much sense for manufacturers to build a product that would last four times as long as their present ones for the same profit — that would have been economic suicide. The Depression market and money supply also prevented other entrepreneurs from capitalizing on such a venture successfully, and so the idea of the Dymaxion Car (three were made, and one may still survive) died away as the country went to war. Had it gone into production, drivers over the past four decades could have saved billions of dollars every year on gas, and the United States would not be facing an energy crisis of the same magnitude today.

So much for a better idea from Fuller.

Answer: No. The only one is Washington.

JULY 13

Questions: What was the name of the astronaut who took the first American space walk?

Which astronaut stayed in the space capsule when man first set foot on the moon?

In the twelfth century, the Roman Catholic Church disapproved of men wearing their hair long, and announced that henceforth men would be excommunicated if they were alive, and refused the prayers of the church when they died, if they chose to do so. Louis VII of France (1137-80) heeded this advice, and it cost him dearly, at least on this earth. His queen, Eleanor of Aquitane, didn't like her husband's hair short, and insisted he grow it long again. He refused, one thing led to another, and they were divorced. She took her dowry with her, which included the provinces of Guienne and Poitou, and she later married Henry, Duke of Normandy, who eventually became King Henry II of England.

Oh, yes — the English and the French did go to war, for several decades in all.

And so, over the simple fact of the length of his hair, Louis caused a good portion of France to become officially English.

The wife of King Richard the Lionheart never set foot in England.

Answers: Edward White.
Michael Collins.

Notable Births

1816	Gustav Freytag	1913	Dave Garroway
1859	Sidney Webb	1954	David Thompson

Notable Events

1174 William the Lion captured by Henry II
1793 Marat stabbed in his bath by Charlotte Corday
1863 1,300 people killed in New York draft riots
1865 Edward Whymper became first man to conquer Matterhorn
1929 First Esperanto movie shown, New York City
1949 Pope excommunicated all Communists
1978 Lee Iococca quit Ford

In July 1940, Estelle Vandemark of Rochester, New York, was granted an annulment of her marriage, on the grounds that her husband chewed razor blades, ate glass, and sewed buttons to his flesh. She said these things made her "nervous."

Next to the wound, what women make best is the bandage.
Barbey D'Aurevilly

Marriage is the only adventure open to the cowardly.
Voltaire

When Los Angeles police told Harry Hetzler his car had been stolen, he insisted that that was impossible. The car was just outside, he said, and his dog was in it. If anyone had tried to steal it, the dog would have barked, which certainly would have awakened his ranch hand, Carl Thomas, and he'd have stopped the thief.

No, the police countered. The car was in Yuma, Arizona, the dog hadn't so much as growled, and Thomas had been arrested on one count of grand theft (stealing an auto).

I never trust a man unless I've got his pecker in my pocket.
Lyndon Johnson

Elmira Johnson and Vera Slotkin, of Braintree, Massachusetts, were two sisters who'd moved in together after their husbands died, hoping to make ends meet together until they, too, passed on. But despite owning their home and sharing expenses and Social Security payments, their Golden Years were tough ones, and they had to be continually vigilant about money.

One morning as they were walking to the corner market, Elmira spotted something shiny in the street.

"Look, Vera! A quarter!" she said.

Vera spotted it too, and quickly hobbled into the street to pick it up, whereupon she was immediately run over by a beer delivery truck.

Elmira just laughed and laughed, because she knew it was only a nickel.

For every credibility gap there is a gullibility fill.
Richard Clopton

Life is what happens to us while we are making other plans.
Thomas La Mance

JULY 14

Notable Births

1602	Cardinal Mazarin	1911	Terry-Thomas
1860	Owen Wister	1913	Jerry Ford
1880	Donald Meek	1918	Ingmar Bergman
1903	Irving Stone	1923	James Purdy
1904	Isaac Bashevis Singer	1932	Roosevelt Grier

Notable Events

1789 Bastille stormed
1853 Crystal Palace opened, New York City
1911 First airplane landed on White House lawn
1933 Nazis suppressed all other political parties
1958 Arab nationalists overthrew Iraqi government, Faisal II slain
1960 Fire in Guatemalan mental hospital took 225 lives
1965 Mme. Vaucher became first woman to climb Matterhorn
1966 Richard Speck killed 8 student nurses in Chicago apartment

Questions: Why is a nurse in a mental institution like the newest movie starlet?

What's the favorite subject for an artist to draw?

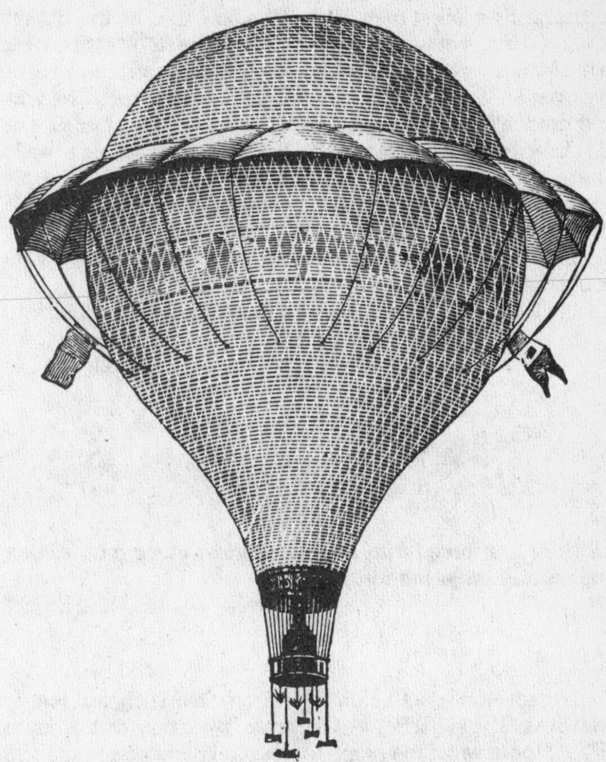

On this date in 1808, the first balloon duel in history took place, over the Tuilleries in Paris. A Monsieur de Grandpre sent his first ball through his opponent's balloon, and Monsieur Le Pique and his second plunged into the gardens below.

For forty years, the record for one-handed chin-ups stood at twelve, set by an Englishman named Cutler in 1878. One day in 1918, a circus performer named Leitzel came into Hermann's Gym in Philadelphia for a workout. Talk got around to the Cutler records, and Leitzel announced it could be broken. What was more, Leitzel, for a wager, would do it. The gym's population took one look at the diminutive thirty-six-year-old athlete (ninety-five pounds and four feet, nine inches tall), and the money flew. Leitzel then strode to the bar and did an incredible twenty-seven one-handed chins, and then for good measure added nineteen with the left hand.

Lillian Leitzel walked out of the gym a much wealthier woman than when she went in.

A woman, if she has the misfortune of knowing anything, should conceal it as well as she can.

Jane Austen

Man yet to be born who can tell what woman will do or will not do.

Charlie Chan

If you're a very senior citizen, and you think that things have become more and more crazy over the last century — you're right, up to a point. In 1880 there were just under 32,000 patients in state mental asylums. By 1910 that figure had risen to 159,096; and by 1930 to about 265,000. Happily, though the population has increased greatly since then, today there are fewer than 200,000 state mental patients in the country — although no figures are available for the private sector, of course, and a lot of folks who should be aren't, because their government jobs pay too much.

Anyone who goes to a psychiatrist ought to have his head examined.

Samuel Goldwyn

America is the only nation in history which miraculously has gone directly from barbarism to degeneration without the usual interval of civilization.

George Clemenceau

Answers: Because every one is crazy about her.
His salary.

JULY 15

Questions: What dance do bakers tend to like?

Why is a collection of convicts like a deck of cards?

The world's tallest man, Robert Wadlow, died on this date in 1940 at the age of twenty-two. At his death he stood either 8 feet 10 1/10 inches or 8 feet 10 3/10 inches, depending on the source of information, and weighed 491 pounds. Since puberty, Wadlow had gradually lost any sensation in his extremeties. Because of his size and morphology, he also came to need braces to walk. These two factors combined to cause his death. One of his braces fell out of fit, and his shin was rubbed raw to the muscle and bone without him feeling it. By the time the wound was discovered, it had become so badly infected that Wadlow's life could not be saved.

Here is the way Wadlow grew through one decade of his life:

Age	*Height*	*Weight*
12	6 feet 5 inches	210
13	7 feet 1 3/4 inches	255
16	7 feet 10 inches	400
22	8 feet 10 1/10 inches	491

All men are forced into two categories; those with eleven fingers and those without.

Ned Rorem

Clement Moore, author of "A Visit from Saint Nicholas" (better known as "The Night Before Christmas"), was born on this day in 1779. Moore wrote the poem for his family and never expected or tried to get it published. When it did appear in print, he refused for twenty-two years to have his name attached to it, and he never made a penny from it.

Kangaroos can travel at forty miles an hour, but they cannot walk.

Notable Births

1607	Rembrandt van Rijn	1889	Marjorie Rambeau
1779	Clement Moore	1919	Iris Murdoch
1796	Thomas Bulfinch	1946	Linda Ronstadt

Notable Events

1099	Jerusalem taken on First Crusade, population massacred
1895	Bulgarian premier Stambulov assassinated
1904	First U.S. Buddhist temple established, Los Angeles
1922	First duck-billed platypus in America exhibited, New York City
1933	First solo round-the-world flight begun, Wiley Post
1940	Robert Wadlow, world's tallest man, died
1965	Mariner IV sent close-up photographs of Mars

Here is the epitaph of Solomon Towslee, Jr., of Pownal, Vermont:

Who was killed in Pownal
Vt. July 15, 1846, while
repairing to Grind a sithe
on a stone attach'd to the
Gearing in the Woollen
Factory. he was entangled.
hes death was sudden and awful.

From *The Lady's Magazine and Musical Repository*, 1801:

Here lieth, aged three months the body of Richard Acanthus a young person of unblemished character. He was taken in his callow infancy from the wing of a tender parent by the rough and pitiless hand of a two legged animal without feathers.

Though born with the most aspiring disposition and unbending love of freedom he was closely confined in a grated prison and scarcely permitted to view those fields of which he had an undoubted charter.

Deeply sensible of this infringement of his natural rights he was often heard to petition for redress in the most plaintive notes of harmonious sorrow. At length his imprisoned soul burst the prison which his body could not and left a lifeless heap of beauteous feathers.

If suffering innocence can hope for retribution, deny not to the gentle shade of this unfortunate captive the humble though uncertain hope of animating some happier form; or trying his new fledged pinions in some happy elysium, beyond the reach of

Man

the tyrant of this lower world.

As I am sure you have guessed, that was about a bird.

Answers: A-bun-dance.

Because there's a knave in every suit.

Notable Births

1783	Joshua Reynolds	1907	Barbara Stanwyck
1821	Mary Baker Eddy	1911	Ginger Rogers
1872	Roald Amundsen	1912	Sonny Tufts
1880	Kathleen Norris	1942	Margaret Court

Notable Events

1662 Royal Society founded, London
1765 Grenville succeeded by Rockingham as British prime minister
1790 Washington selected to be U.S. capital
1935 First parking meter installed, Oklahoma City
1939 Fritz Kuhn, head of U.S. Nazi party, arrested for drunk and disorderly conduct
1945 First A-bomb tested, Alamogordo, New Mexico
1973 Butterfield revealed existence of White House tapes

Question: About how long do the following animals live?
Beaver
Guinea pig
Hippopotamus
Kangaroo

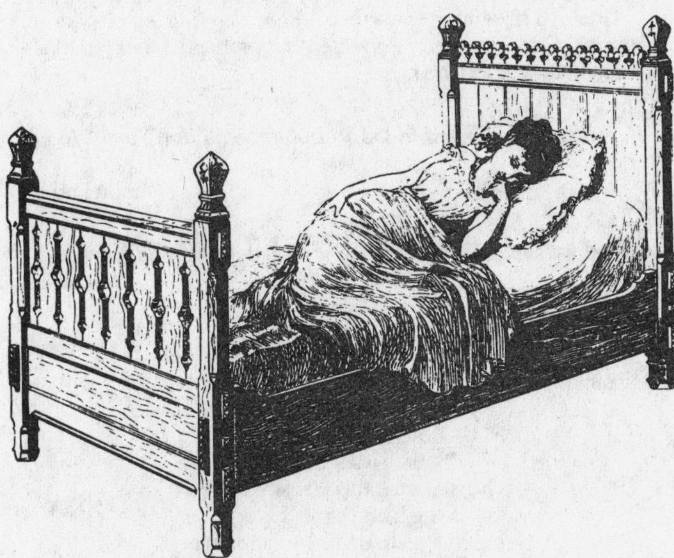

Mollie Fancher was known as the Brooklyn Enigma, and for very good reason. In 1876, when she was eighteen, a series of accidents left her blind, mute, almost totally paralyzed, and bedridden for life. For many years her legs were twisted under her and her right arm was locked up behind her head. Normally it would be a pathetic situation for a young girl to be faced with for the rest of her life, but Mollie Fancher was not a normal young girl. She was able to crochet and do embroidery by feeling behind her head for her needle work, but these were the least of her achievements. Somehow, although blind, she could "see" an object if it were placed on her forehead or at the top of her skull. She could also name colors by touch and could read a letter that was still in its envelope if someone would but hold it up to her head. She could also identify people she had never met before, who were only acquaintances of her other friends. On one occasion when Judge Abram Daily visited her (he was also her biographer), she wrote down on her slate that he had entertained a tall, thin man with a dark complexion, on the previous evening. She was correct. The judge was astonished, for there was no way that Molly could have been aware of it. He asked her how she'd known this, and she replied that in her own way, she had been there. A few days later, Judge Daily came in with two men and asked Mollie, "Do you know either of the gentlemen with me?" She told him she did not know the man on the left, but the man on the right was the person he'd had over to dinner several nights earlier. Mollie was right, again.

On another occasion, Louis Sherk instructed an assistant to hang a picture in the front room of Mollie's house, a room Mollie had not been in for many years. She had not been told he was coming, and as usual was upstairs in bed when he arrived. When the man deliberately chose a bad place for the painting he heard a voice say, "No, not there, you fool! On the opposite wall — the light is better."

Mollie could also find lost or hidden items for people, and could precisely describe changes in Brooklyn that occurred long after she'd lost her sight and become bedridden. According to all accounts of her abilities, she must have had extraordinary psychic abilities, and was certainly gifted with the power of astral projection.

Some things have to be believed to be seen.
Ralph Hodgson

A nose that can see is worth two that sniff.
Eugene Ionesco

The model for the Indian Head penny, designed by sculptor James Barton Longacre, wasn't an Indian at all. It was his ten-year-old daughter Sarah.

She was so ugly she'd make a train take a dirt road.
Tom Rush

Answer: Five, four, twenty-five, and seven years respectively.

JULY 17

Question: What do the following people have in common?
Arnold Palmer
Nellie Bly
Wiley Post
Howard Hughes

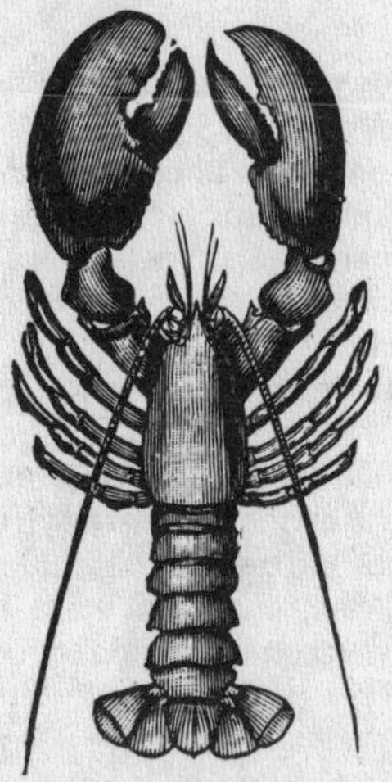

There's a well-known "Bert & I" story in which the two Maine lobstermen pull up a "sea monster" in the form of a skindiver who had been poaching lobster. Bert suggests they turn the creature over to a museum, but his companion, impressed by the number of lobsters he has in his sack, and aware they were undoubtedly poached from their traps, says "no way." Instead, he tells Bert, they should weight him down with rocks, tie a line and a buoy to him, and "set 'im agin."

In July 1958, a man named George Vasquez was surfishing from a beach near Hyannis, Massachusetts, and actually did hook a skindiver and reel him ashore. The diver stood 5 feet, 10 inches, well above the legal limit.

Another fishy story occurred that same month and year in Crestline, California. Frank Indovina had run out of worms before he'd caught a thing, had switched to processed American cheese, and again had come up empty-hooked. Disgusted, he wadded up some supermarket trading stamps and speared them on the hook. By the time he'd quit for the day, he'd landed seven bass, two bluegill, and a trout.

If that weren't enough, in July 1958, the city of Dallas, Texas, paid $43.25 in medical bills for the treatment of a job-related injury suffered by one of its employees. Garbageman C.E. Haddock stepped on the fin of a dead catfish, puncturing his foot. Medical attention had been provided by Doctor D. C. Gill.

The famous phrase from Lincoln's Gettysburg Address, "Government of the people, for the people, and by the people," hardly originated with the president. A man named Thomas Cooper had used the phrase "of the people and for the people" in 1795, and Chief Justice Marshall echoed it in a speech of his own some years later. In 1830, in a letter to Senator Robert Hayne of South Carolina, Daniel Webster spoke of a government "made for, by, and answerable to" the people. In a book of speeches published in Boston in 1850, a man named Theodore Parker used substantially the same phrase as Lincoln did thirteen years later — and Lincoln owned a copy of Parker's book.

Answer: They all made celebrated round-the-world trips.

Notable Births

1763	John Jacob Astor	1912	Art Linkletter
1810	Martin Tupper	1917	Phyllis Diller
1863	David Lloyd George	1917	Lou Boudreau
1891	Haile Selassie	1935	Diahann Carroll
1900	James Cagney	1941	Daryle Lamonica

Notable Events

1890	Cecil Rhodes elected governor of Cape Colony
1936	Spanish Civil War began
1938	Wrong Way Corrigan set off from New York to California, ended up in Ireland
1944	Port Chicago, California, explosion, 322 dead
1954	Brooklyn Dodgers became a majority black team
1975	U.S. Apollo, Soviet Soyuz space link-up

Until 1878, eunuchs were in great demand as singers in Vatican City. That year, Pope Leo XIII prohibited their employment in the Papal Choir.

If you're not allowed to laugh in heaven, I don't want to go there.

Martin Luther

Religion is excellent stuff for keeping common people quiet.

Napoleon

Epitaph from North Andover, Massachusetts.

Erected in Memory of
Mr James Bridges
Who departed this life July 17 1747
in the 51st year of his age
Being melted to death by extreem heat.

Nero didn't fiddle while Rome burned — the violin only goes back to the fifteenth century. Besides, the historian Tacitus tells us that Nero was at his villa fifty miles from Rome during the conflagration. Nero did, however, blame the Christians for setting the fire.

Anna Hopewell, Enosburg, *Vermont*

Here lies the body of our Anna
Done to death by a banana
It wasn't the fruit that laid her low
But the skin of the thing that made her go.

JULY 18

Notable Births

1747	John Paul Jones	1911	Hume Cronyn
1811	William M. Thackeray	1913	Red Skelton
1906	Clifford Odets	1921	John Glenn
1906	S.I. Hayakawa	1933	Yevgeny Yevtushenko

Notable Events

64	Rome began to burn; fire lasted 8 days, Nero blamed Christians
1203	Constantinople taken in Fourth Crusade
1870	Doctrine of papal infallibility promulgated
1918	Joyce "Trees" Kilmer killed in action, France
1947	Thor Heyerdahl reached Marquesas in *Kon-Tiki*
1955	First commercial use of atomically generated power, Schenectady, New York
1969	Kennedy drove off bridge at Chappaquidick

Roughly 800 years ago, the merchants of Venice bought about half the Roman Empire for half a million dollars (in Venetian currency of course). On the Fourth Crusade, the Christians of Western Europe needed transportation and provisioning for their attack on the Holy Land. The problem was that they had no money. Venetian businessmen managed to strike a deal with the leaders of the crusade, promising to supply their needs if the Christians would first capture the town of Zara, in Dalmatia, for Venice. The Crusaders agreed, and did so — so expeditiously, in fact, that the Doge of Venice volunteered to support their much greater efforts against the Turks in Constantinople. The Christians were successful in taking the city on July 18, 1203, and as repayment on the loan, Venice eventually got about half of what was left of the Roman Empire at that time.

Question: Can you figure out this cryptogram?

hiBve

"Get" is a versatile word. In the following passage the verb "to get" is used twenty-eight times in various forms, all correctly:

> I got on horseback within ten minutes after I got your letter. When I got to Canterbury, I got a chaise for town; but I got wet through before I got to Canterbury, and I have got such a cold as I shall not be able to get rid of it in a hurry. I got to the Treasury about noon, but first of all I got shaved and dressed. I soon got into the secret of getting a memorial before the Board, but I could not get an answer then; however, I got intelligence from the messenger that I should, most likely, get one the next morning. As soon as I got back to my inn, I got my supper and got to bed. When I got up in the morning, I got my breakfast, and then got myself dressed that I might get out in time to get an answer to my memorial. As soon as I got it, I got into the chaise, and got to Canterbury by three, and about tea-time I got home. I have got nothing for you.

Take that, S.I. Hayakawa!

A big elm tree will produce about six million leaves in a season.

Answer: A big bee in a little hive.

JULY 19

Questions: Why don't jokes last as long as church bells?

If you split your sides laughing, what should you do?

Notable Births

1814	Samuel Colt	1917	William Scranton
1834	Edgar Degas	1922	George McGovern
1860	Lizzie Borden	1923	Patricia Medina
1883	Benito Mussolini	1942	Vicki Carr
1898	Herbert Marcuse	1946	Ilie Nastase

Notable Events

1812	United States declared war on England
1848	First Women's Rights Convention held in United States, Seneca Falls, New York
1848	Bloomers introduced in Seneca Falls
1870	France declared war on Prussia
1885	President Cleveland ordered cattlemen to vacate Indian lands
1956	United States withdrew offer of help to Egypt for Aswan Dam
1964	Wallace withdrew from presidential race

In many parts of rural Europe, it is still the large, "peasant-looking" woman that is deemed the sexiest, and is much preferred to the gaunt version of femininity we have in fashion magazines. In Nigeria, too, they like their woman a tad on the substantial side. Members of the Efik tribe actually wait hand and foot on an engaged girl for up to two years to ensure that she doesn't exert herself and to see that she gets *plenty* to eat. She is secluded in a hut, practically immobilized, and stuffed with fatty foods for all that time.

And on her wedding day, symbolic of her ordeal and as an augury of good luck, she wears a chicken around her neck.

If you're watching a western or a cop show on the tube and there's a gunfight, count to see how many shots one of the combatants fires before reloading or surrendering because he's out of ammunition. If the number is six, the scriptwriter has fallen prey to a common mistake. Any lawman or outlaw who wasn't a damn fool would never load up all the chambers of a six shooter. To do that would mean that sooner or later he'd shoot himself in the leg. A real professional would always load up so that a handgun's hammer rested on an empty chamber.

Facts do not cease to exist because they are ignored.

Aldous Huxley

Mrs. Caroline Squires of Cincinnati filed for a divorce from her husband in 1949 on grounds of desertion. She testified he'd stepped out "for a beer" on the Fourth of July, 1917, and had never come back.

July 19, 4236 B.C. may be the earliest definitely recordable date of historical significance. On that date over 6,200 years ago, the first 365-day calendar was introduced at Heliapolis, Egypt. It began with the heliacal rising of the star Sirius, which, at that location, was on the nineteenth of July.

We Americans are the best informed people on earth as to the events of the last twenty-four hours; we are not the best informed as to the events of the last sixty centuries.

Will and Ariel Durant

The gecko lizard has no bone, and very little brain, between its ears. When it is held up to the light, it appears as if it has a skylight in its head.

Answers: Because after they've been toll-d a few times they're worn out.

Run until you get a stitch in them.

Notable Births

1304	Francesco Petrarch	1934	Sally Ann Howes
1919	Sir Edmund Hillary	1938	Diana Rigg
1921	Elliot Richardson	1938	Natalie Wood
1924	Thomas Berger	1940	Tony Oliva

Notable Events

1801 Largest cheese in the world to date pressed in Cheshire, Massachusetts, as gift for Jefferson
1871 British Columbia joined Canada
1876 First intercollegiate track meet, Saratoga, New York
1880 Cleopatra's Needle arrived in New York
1944 Attempted assassination of Hitler
1951 Jordan's King Abdullah assassinated
1969 Apollo 11 landed on the Moon
1976 Viking I landed on Mars

The term "lynching" derives from a Virginian named Charles Lynch, who meted out semi-legal justice during the disruptive years of the American Revolution when the country's legal system was often in limbo. Although Lynch never sentenced a man to death, his name somehow came to be associated with that form of extra-legal justice.

Interestingly, 300 years before Charles Lynch, there was an Irishman named James Fitz-Steven Lynch, mayor of Galway, who in 1493 sentenced his own son to death for murder. Afraid that the boy's friends would rescue him from jail, he had the young man brought to his own home straight from the court and hanged him from a tree in front of the house.

Perfect courage means doing unwitnessed what we would be capable of with the world looking on.

La Rochefoucauld

Frank Defatta, an Italian immigrant living in Talulah, Alabama, was not a popular man in his neighborhood. It seems he would not keep his goats at home. This used to bother Dr. J. F. Hodges, who lived nearby. The Defatta goats found the Hodges residence a particularly attractive place to spend their time. They continually fouled the doctor's porch and doorstep, and even began to eat the house. Defatta was warned several times by Hodges and the local authorities that this kind of irresponsibility could not be tolerated. Defatta ignored these warnings. On July 19, 1899, Dr. Hodges could stand it no longer, and he shot and killed one of the goats. On July 20, 1899, Defatta and four of his friends shot and killed Dr. Hodges over the incident.

The Italians were arrested and jailed, but popular opinion overcame the power of the Louisiana authorities to protect them (three of the accused were suspected of being involved in another murder several weeks before), and they were pulled from their cells and lynched.

On the surface, this seems to be a tragic, but relatively insignificant incident, since lynching was a fairly common practice in that part of the country at the time — except that Italy came within a hair's breadth of declaring war on the United States because of it.

The Italians — you can't find one who is honest.

Richard Nixon

Answers: They quack up.

A shoe.

Questions: Why don't ducks fly upside down?

What has a tongue yet cannot speak?

For an inhabitant of a space colony on the moon, there would be no such thing as a romantic earth-rise. Because the moon rotates on its axis in the same period that it revolves around the earth, it always keeps the same face towards our planet. It doesn't have the kind of quick rotation the earth does, which provides us with the illusion that the sun and the moon both rise. The earth would appear as a new earth, crescent earth, or full earth at various times, and only from the lighted face, never from the dark side of the moon (which never faces the earth). Astronauts who report on the beauty of an earth-rise from a lunar orbit actually mean the way in which the earth seems to climb in the sky as their space capsules come from behind the moon and our planet reappears in their line of sight.

Oysters only eat when the moon shines.

JULY 21

Questions: What is it one always wants and forgets about when it comes?

What's black and white and red all over?

Think what you will about radical conservationists, but evidence abounds that man must carefully weigh his every act regarding the treatment of his environment. The smallest change can have unforeseen circumstances of the gravest import.

Take the case of Laysan Island. This tiny islet of the Leewards, the chain of atolls that extends northwest from Hawaii and includes Midway Island, was until the middle of the nineteenth century a bird rookery. Then it became economically feasible to harvest the rich deposits of guano there and transport them all the way to fertilizer-starved Europe. But, by 1909, the deposits were exhuasted, and all the people who had been working them left the island. Laysan was sanctuary once again, this time an official one.

But someone left behind a single pair of rabbits when he left.

To Adam and Eve Rabbit it was a lush Eden, and their progeny multiplied and flourished, subdued the land, and had dominion over all the birds, until there were too many rabbits and too little food. They died by the scores of thousands. When trustees of the sanctuary visited Laysan in 1923 they discovered that, except for four trees, it was completely devoid of vegetation. Every plant, every shrub, every blade of grass had disappeared, and the skeletons of sea birds and rabbits were piled high over the footpaths. The visitors killed the few surviving rabbits, and in a decade the island had once again become a tropical atoll and a haven for birds.

If all these nature kooks had their way, America would still be a wilderness from coast to coast. Thank God there are at least a few businessmen who care about the Gross National Product.

Harley G. Waller

Notable Births

1863	C. Aubrey Smith	1899	Hart Crane
1885	Frances Parkinson Keyes	1911	Marshall McLuhan
1899	Ernest Hemingway	1933	John Gardner

Notable Events

1773 Pope Clement dissolved the Jesuits
1861 First Battle of Bull Run
1918 First shots of World War I landed in United States, Meeting House Pond, Massachusetts
1944 United States forces landed on Guam
1961 Space flight of Gus Grissom
1978 White House staff marijuana inquiries began after resignation of Dr. Peter Bourne

This passage is taken from the *People's Advocate*, a progressive magazine of the late nineteenth century:

When Babylon went down, two percent of her population owned all of her wealth. The people were starved to death.

When Persia went down, one percent of her population owned all the land.

When Rome went down, 1,800 men owned all the whole world.

There are about forty million people in England and Wales, and 100,000 men own all the land in the United Kingdom.

For the past twenty years the United States has rapidly followed in the steps of those old nations. Here are the figures: In 1850, capitalists owned thirty-seven and one-half percent of the nation's wealth. In 1870 they owned sixty-three percent. In 1880, about 30,000 owned three-fifths of the entire wealth.

In America today, about fifteen percent of the population owns eighty percent of the wealth, and, through stock control and board representation, a few thousand men have practically absolute power over America's economy.

I see in the near future a crisis that unnerves me, and causes me to tremble for the very safety of my country. As a result of the war, corporations have been enthroned, and an era of corruption in high places will follow, and the money power of the country will endeavor to prolong its reign by working upon the prejudices of the people until wealth is aggregated in a few hands, and the republic is destroyed. I feel, at this point, more anxiety for the safety of my country than ever before, even in the midst of war.

Abraham Lincoln

The wrecks of the past were America's warnings.

George Bancroft

A government that robs Peter to pay Paul can always depend on the support of Paul.

George Bernard Shaw

Put God to work for you and maximize your potential in our divinely ordered capitalist system.

Norman Vincent Peale

Answers: Sleep.
A blushing zebra.

Notable Births

1822	Gregor Mendel	1898	Alexander Calder
1849	Emma Lazarus	1898	Stephen Vincent Benét
1882	Edward Hopper	1923	Robert Dole
1890	Rose Kennedy	1932	Oscar de la Renta

Notable Events

1795 Peace made between France and Spain
1933 Wiley Post completed first solo air circumnavigation, 7 days, 18 hours, 45 minutes
1934 John Dillinger killed by FBI agents, Chicago
1950 Leopold III of Belgium returned from exile
1961 Zinjanthropus age estimated to be 1,750,000 years
1964 GM announced 6-month profit of 1.138 billion
1970 Himalayan flood killed 500
1977 Gang of Four expelled from Communist party, Teng replaced in China

Question: What's the state shown here?

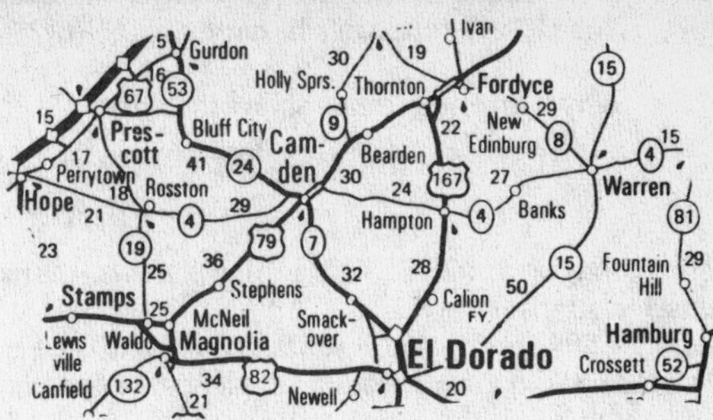

July 22, 1376, was the date that the Pied Piper led the plague of rats away from Hamlin, Germany. When the city government refused to pay him as they had contracted to do, he whistled away all the town's children.

In July 1812, the British frigate *Swallow* was engaged with a French ship off Majorca. On board the *Swallow* were a sailor named Phelan, his wife, and their three-week-old son, Tommy. In the course of the action, many of the English were badly wounded, and Mrs. Phelan attended to them as best she could. Then her own husband was seriously hurt, and she rushed to his side. As they embraced, Mrs. Phelan's head was preemptorily removed by a cannonball. The shock of seeing his wife decapitated in his arms killed Phelan as well. The now orphaned Tommy would also have perished after the battle for want of milk, but fortunately there was a Maltese goat on board the frigate, and Tommy and the goat learned to get along just fine, thank you.

Parents can never do too much for their children to repay them for the injustice of having brought them into the world.

Elizabeth Cady Stanton

In July 1854, the *Baltimore Sun* reported that "Major William Keller died at Cumberland, Maryland, on the 22nd instant. His death, it is said, was hastened by a wound received in the war of 1812."

Billy and Jane were parked in Lovers' Lane one dark and moonless night. Suddenly, Billy said, "Why Jane, it's so dark I can't even see my hand in front of my face!"

Jane just laughed and laughed.

Why? (answer later)

"Preposterous" is a curious word. Its roots in Latin mean "before and after," and, in fact, the word is put together to describe the folly of placing something first that ought to be last.

Answer to puzzle: Jane knew Billy's hand was nowhere near his face.

Answer: Arkansas.

JULY 23

Questions: A nickel and a dime were crossing a high bridge. The nickel jumped off; the dime didn't. Why?

Why is an empty purse always the same?

The sun comes up at 4:28 EST today. How long was the night, from sunset to sunrise?

Eight hours, fifty-six minutes. If you take Standard Time clock time of sunrise and double it, you get the length of the night in hours and minutes.

On July 24, 1837, over Greenwich, England, Robert Cocking was involved in the first fatal parachute jump in history. He was testing a new parachute design.

It performed poorly.

Notable Births

1874	Sunny Jim Fitzsimmons	1912	Michael Wilding
1888	Gluyas Williams	1924	Gloria DeHaven
1888	Raymond Chandler	1928	Hubert Selby, Jr.
1894	Arthur Treacher	1936	Don Drysdale

Notable Events

1784	Erzeroum earthquake killed 5,000 people
1959	Nixon left for Russia on "Kitchen Debate" trip
1964	Bone, Algeria, munitions explosion killed 100
1967	Detroit race riots began
1973	Nixon claimed executive privilege in matter of tapes
1978	White Rhodesian leaders' scheme to put arms money in Swiss banks revealed

Answers: It had more cents than the nickel.

Because there's never any change in it.

JULY 24

Notable Births

1783	Simon Bolivar	1895	Robert Graves
1802	Alexander Dumas (père)	1898	Amelia Earhart
1864	Frank Wedekind	1920	Bella Abzug
1878	Lord Dunsany	1936	Ruth Buzzi

Notable Events

1704 British took Gibraltar from Spain
1785 League of German Princes formed
1847 Mormons reached Great Salt Lake
1851 British window tax abolished in effort to encourage homes with windows
1865 Agassiz expedition left Rio for Upper Amazon
1865 Tennessee readmitted to Union
1924 Scopes found guilty in Monkey Trial
1929 Kellogg-Briand Treaty effective
1934 First ptarmigan hatched in captivity, Cornell University
1937 5 of 9 Scottsboro defendents freed
1941 United States imposed trade restrictions against Japan
1956 Floods claimed 300 lives in Iran
1974 Supreme Court ordered Nixon to release 64 tapes

"Ape-Grape"

The Apes, from whom we are descended,
Hang ape-x down from trees suspended,
And since we find them in the trees,
We term them arbor-ig-i-nes.
This quite explains the monkey shines
Cut up by those who pluck from vines
The Grape, and then subject it juices
To Bacchanalian abuses.

Robert Williams Wood

Dionysius, the Tyrant of Heraclea (yes — *that* Dionysius!) had needles put in his chairs to keep him from falling back, if he fell asleep. He was so fat he would have suffocated in that position.

Answer: Show Me State, Granite State, Buckeye State, Volunteer State.

Question: What are the nicknames of the following states?
Missouri
New Hampshire
Ohio
Tennessee

The number 142,857 is a real oddball. If you multiply it by the numbers 1 through 6 you get the same digits in the same order, though in different positions: 142,857, 285,714, 428,571, 571, 428, 714,285, and 857,142. When multiplied by 7 the product is 999,999, and by 8 it's 1,142,856, 1 less than a 1,000,000 more than the number you started with.

Anyone who thinks there's safety in numbers hasn't looked at the stock market pages.

Irene Peter

On July 24, 1485, King Richard III of England had postriders placed on the highways of Britain, with the instruction that his official messages be carried at no less than seven miles in an hour in summer, and five in winter. With this action he initiated the first regular postal service in Europe, although hundreds of years earlier the Chinese had a postal system more efficient than anything the Western world had until the seventeenth century.

Among the cargoes the *Nantucket Enquirer* listed as having arrived in that island's harbor in the summer of 1824 was this rather odd one: "American sloop *Henry* from Falmouth; passengers, four ladies, three musicians, one lion, one lama [llama] one Shetland pony, a monkey, a baboon, and two lawyers."

The following is an inscription on a tombstone at Saint Andrews church in Plymouth, England:

Here lies the body of James Vernon, Esq.,
the only *surviving* son of Admiral Vernon:
died July 23rd, 1753.

And here is one from Saint Edmund's Bury:

Here lies Joan Kitchen,
who, when her glass was spent,
Kicked up her heels and away she went.

The invention of shatterproof glass was an accident, caused by a laboratory assistant's negligence. In 1904, a French scientist named Bendictus knocked an unstoppered bottle from a shelf and onto the floor. To his amazement, although the glass was shattered, the bottle remained intact. Bendictus discovered the bottle had once contained a solution that had evaporated and left a celluloid film on the inside of the glass. This had acted rather like a frame of glue and prevented the glass from breaking into hundreds of shards. The concept behind safety and shatterproof glass was discovered.

If at first you don't succeed, you're running about average.

H.L. Mencken

JULY 25

Questions: What's a Solar in Ecuador?

What's a Stone in England?

What's a Stoop in Holland?

The island of Puerto Rico was originally called San Juan. Its capital city, San Juan, was originally called Puerto Rico.

Some Seventeenth-Century English Nostrums:

To overcome cowardice, wear a pin taken from the shroud of a corpse.

To ensure pregnancy, tie a bell to the woman's girdle and ring it three times before making love.

To get rid of warts, tie the same number of peas in a rag as you have warts, and throw the bundle on the turnpike. When a passerby picks up the rag, he will receive your warts and yours will disappear.

To cure a toothache, solicit alms in the name of Saint Lawrence.

There is one thing stronger than all the armies in the world, and that is an idea whose time has come.

Victor Hugo

A man from Liverpool, England, named Eddie McAlea ws arrested in early 1980 and charged with the attempted robbery of a jewelry store. McAlea had entered the store brandishing a gun and had ordered the owner to fork over some rings and other loot. The properietor would have none of it, however — not when he saw that McAlea's gun still had the cork plug stuck in its barrel.

Answers: .43 acres, 14 pounds, 1.32 gallons of beer.

Notable Births

1844	Thomas Eakins	1883	Alison Skipworth
1848	A. J. Balfour	1894	Walter Brennan
1870	Maxfield Parrish	1924	Frank Church

Notable Events

1261	Constantinople taken by Greeks
1840	American officers exploring Fiji massacred
1932	Poland and Russia signed non-aggression pact
1934	Dollfuss, the Austrian chancellor, assassinated by Nazis
1948	Bread rationing ended in England
1952	Puerto Rico became a commonwealth
1957	Japanese floods kill 513 people
1972	Eagleton admitted electro-shock treatments

"Biscuit" is a word developed from Latin and French, and has a nautical origin. When European seafarers began to take long voyages, they needed a bread which would not go stale or putrify. Biscuit—*bis*, "twice" in Latin, and cuit, "cooked" in French—was the answer. For extended voyages the biscuits might be cooked as many as four times.

One of the major criticisms of capital punishment over the years has been that at heart it is more revenge for, rather than a deterrent to, crime, especially in the way it is usually administered. The authorities have seldom allowed a criminal to take his own life, and there are numerous instances in which a would-be suicide was "rescued" from death and revived so he could face a state-administered execution.

Convicted murderer Johnny Reo, on Death Row at Sing Sing, vowed he'd never let them kill him. He simply wasn't going to give them the satisfaction. Because his suicide threat seemed genuine, special guards were assigned to him to ensure he had no opportunity to deprive the law of its proper revenge.

But Reo was just a little smarter than his keepers. About two months before the execution was scheduled, he covertly began to eat things he shouldn't. Within a few days, his stomach started to hurt, but he kept it up. Soon the pain became unbearable even for tough little Johnny Reo, and he was taken to the hospital. He wouldn't cooperate with the doctors, but an X-ray gave them a pretty good idea of what he'd been up to. They operated on his stomach and took out six large screws, a handful of gravel, and a total of twenty-five feet of bedsprings, broken off in tiny pieces.

They sewed him up, and he was executed on schedule.

In the 1977 occasion of the annual Norfolk, England, fishing derby, a smelt weighing one-sixteenth of an ounce took the trophy for largest fish. The shame of it is that this smelt was not the only fish caught. It beat out 107 others!

When police in Simcoe, Ontario, arrested Anthony Spellag as a vagrant, they found on his person four flashlights, four screwdrivers, three wrenches, two extension cords, a tube of sealing compound, a steel measuring tape, a windshield wiper, a gearshift knob, a rear-view mirror, ten pounds of sugar, a bag of candy, a skirt, a bra, and a pair of women's gloves.

You were expecting a partridge in a pear tree, too?

Notable Births

1796	George Catlin	1897	Paul Gallico
1796	Jean Corot	1906	Gracie Allen
1856	George Bernard Shaw	1922	Jason Robards, Jr.
1875	Carl Jung	1923	Hoyt Wilhelm
1885	Andre Maurois	1928	Stanley Kubrick
1892	Pearl S. Buck	1944	Mick Jagger
1894	Aldous Huxley	1954	Vitas Gerulaitis

Notable Events

1757	French defeated English at Hastenbeck
1788	New York ratified Constitution
1805	Earthquake in Italy claimed 20,000 lives
1939	United States abrogated Japanese trade treaty
1952	King Farouk of Egypt forced to abdicate
1958	Last debutantes presented at British court

Question: Why is a defeated team like some wool?

The First Crusade was partly inspired by a monk of Amiens, in northern France, called Peter the Hermit. Late in the eleventh century, pilgrimages were incredibly popular in Christendom, and thousands of people flocked every year to one holy place or another. Peter the Hermit took the grandest pilgrimage of all, to Jerusalem. While he was there, he was appalled by the Moslems' treatment of the Christians, and he promptly had a vision from God in which Jesus Christ told him that he had been chosen to lead an army to liberate the Holy Land from Islam.

On his return to Europe, Peter met with Pope Urban II, who supported the idea, and also received the endorsement of the Greek patriarch, Simeon. Raising an army proved to be relatively easy for Peter since contemporaries described him as: "Enthusiastic, chivalrous, bigoted . . . not far removed from insanity." He rode barefoot through Europe on the back of a mule, and was received everywhere as a living saint. Tens of thousands of people determined to join the holy army.

In March 1095, word of impending trouble from the Turks hastened the force's timetable considerably, and shortly after Peter set out at the head of one hundred thousand ill-prepared soldiers, the advance group. Most of the men were rustics, many didn't know where Jerusalem was (or had no appreciation of the distance), and few brought money or provisions. They were assured that God would provide and that they could beg alms as they traveled, although there was no way an army of one hundred thousand men could live off the sparsely populated, poverty-striken medieval countryside. A second group of soldiers was headed by Walter the Penniless.

Neither man was an administrative or military genius. By the time their armies got through western Europe their reputations had long since preceded them, and they had to fight large-scale wars with Hungarian and Bulgarian Christians to earn the right to pass through those countries. Populations fled *en masse* as the Crusaders approached, taking their provisions and livestock with them, and scorching the earth behind them. When Peter reached Constantinople he had lost seventy thousand men, and Walter arrived with but three thousand of his original force of twenty-five thousand. The Emperor Alexis graciously hurried them on their way across the Bosporus. He thought they were rabble and wanted nothing to do with them *or* their mission.

By this time, Peter had probably become genuinely insane, and although nominally he still gave the orders, no one listened to him any more. What was left of the armies split up along national lines, though all remained intent on saving Jerusalem. A fellow named Renaud took the Italians and the Germans to Nicea, where they were destroyed by the Turks. Hearing of that loss, the larger army regrouped and started to Nicea to avenge the defeat. Then *they* were destroyed by the Turks.

Fortunately (for the Europeans) the main army raised by the Western aristocracy then arrived. They were better equipped, provisioned, and disciplined, and things began to turn around. Peter joined his forces to theirs and they paid him lip service, but tactically he was out of the picture. He twice tried to run away, but each time was captured and brought back. (He was after all, though crazy, the inspiration for the whole movement.) The Crusaders took Nicea in 1097, and Jerusalem two years later.

It has been estimated that this crusade cost three hundred thousand lives, and achieved results that might have been produced by one day's worth of diplomacy.

The First Crusade . . . set off on its two-thousand-mile jaunt by massacring Jews, and plundering and slaughtering all the way from the Rhine to the Jordan. "In the Temple of Solomon," wrote the ecstatic cleric Raimundus de Agiles, "one rode in blood up to the knees and even to the horses' bridles, by the just and marvelous Judgment of God!"

Herbert J. Muller

Answer: Because it is worsted.

JULY 27

Question: What can you take with you wherever you go?

Notable Births

1824	Alexander Dumas (fils)	1906	Leo Durocher
1870	Hilaire Belloc	1916	Keenan Wynn
1872	Paul Laurence Dunbar	1948	Peggy Fleming

Notable Events

1866	First messages exchanged over Atlantic cable
1884	Divorce legalized in France
1894	Japan and Korea declared war against China
1915	Revolution began in Haiti
1915	Direct wireless communication between United States and Japan established
1933	Death penalty for kidnapping established in Kansas City
1953	Korean armistice signed
1978	United Nations approved Namibian War settlement plan

There's a reason why all British lawyers practice in black robes, and it's not tradition. When Queen Mary died, her husband King William III directed all court functionaries to don black mourning garb in her memory. That was in 1694, and the order has never been rescinded.

The oldest business sign ever found was unearthed from the ruins of Memphis, Egypt, and dates to before 500 B.C. It belonged to a man whom we would now call an oneirologist, and reads: "I Rhino of Crete Interpret Dreams by God's Command."

"An apple a day . . ." is good, cheap advice. Equally good, but not nearly as cheap, is the counsel found in a book entitled *The Onliest and Deepest Secrets of the Medical Arts*. This curious book was written by a famous Dutch physician of the eighteenth century named Boerhave. It achieved much notoriety during Boerhave's lifetime because of his excellent reputation, and because he had expressly instructed that the book was to remain sealed until after his death. Then it was sold when his estate went up for auction, and the highest bidder would know the "onliest" secrets.

The doctor died in 1738, and the volume brought a high bid of about $10,000. The seal of the 100-page text was then broken. The first ninety-nine pages were blank. On the final page Boerhave had penned: "Keep your head cool, your feet warm, and you'll make the best doctor a poor man."

A French Government study released in the late 1930s revealed that of all the major crimes committed in the whole country between 1900 and 1930, fully 75 percent of them had been perpetrated by people who had been born in or had at one time lived in the southern port city of Marseilles.

You can get much farther with a kind word and a gun than you can get with a kind word alone.

Al Capone

Answer: Your name.

Notable Births

1844	Gerard Manley Hopkins	1929	Jacqueline Kennedy
1892	Joe E. Brown	1937	Peter Duchin
1898	Charles Mayo	1943	Mike Bloomfield
1901	Rudy Vallee	1943	Bill Bradley
1909	Malcolm Lowry	1948	Sally Struthers
1927	John Ashbery	1949	Vida Blue

Notable Events

1742 Peace of Berlin betwaen Austria and Prussia declared
1750 Johann Sebastian Bach died
1794 Robespierre and 70 followers executed
1821 Peru declared independence from Spain
1915 Marines landed in Haiti to quell revolution
1932 MacArthur drove Bonus Army from Washington
1948 Army bomber flew into Empire State Building
1948 Explosion at Farben Works, Germany, killed 184 people
1961 Picasso and Miro paintings stolen in Pittsburgh
1976 Chinese earthquake killed 655,235 people

Question: Within ten years, when were the following invented?
aerosol spray
breech loading rifle
diesel engine
pendulum clock

One of the members of the Roman Triumverate, Livinius Crassus (114-53 B.C.), was a pretty crass fellow. He set up a fire-fighting department of 500 men under this direction. When a blaze broke out, the fire brigades and Crassus would rush to it, just as one would expect. But when they reaced the scene, Crassus would offer to buy the burning property from its owner for a ridiculously cheap sum. If the man refused to sell, Crassus and his men went home. Otherwise, Crassus took title, and later sold the property at its real market value. In this way he amassed a fortune that would be worth over four billion dollars in today's money.

France acquired its Equatorial and West African colonies in a way that makes Peter Minuit's Manhattan coup pale by comparison. All it took was thirteen men and a small bribe.

In 1890, a young lieutenant colonel named Charles-Parfait Monteil began a journey of exploration and acquisition in Africa. He had only a dozen men with him. They traveled with very little baggage, but the French government had had the foresight to outfit them with about $16,000 in gold. "Get as much land as you can for it," Monteil was instructed. In twenty-seven months, this group trekked over 5,000 miles through some of the worst jungle the Dark Continent had to offer. By the time they emerged in 1893, they were broke, but in return for the money they'd given up they had picked up title deeds from two-dozen ranking chiefs in the region. For less than a half a cent a square mile, and without the loss of a single French life, France acquired territory fourteen times larger than itself.

The nerve!

A Michigan judge was recently removed from office by that state's judicial tenure board for his conduct on the bench, which it found to be "flagrantly dishonest." He then failed to win reelection after his ouster. Charles Probert, now a despondent man, subsequently tried to commit suicide. He succeeded only in blowing out his eyeball. Subsequently, he sued for $50,000 and $200 a week for life, claiming the injury was job related and that he should be eligible for Workman's Compensation.

The starling has been in the Western Hemisphere for less than a century, and the arrival of the first birds can be traced to the day they were set free.

A fellow named Ernest Scheifflin was responsible. It was his decision that a pleasant, *cultural* thing to do would be to introduce to America all of the birds mentioned in Shakespeare's plays. This he did. Most of his immigrants did fairly well here, gradually assimilated, and kept out of trouble.

Not so the starlings. They have done so well at the expense of other feathered creatures and man that their roosts have grown so unruly in some parts of the country that the United States Army has had to be called in to keep them under control.

Scheifflin began the whole thing when he released eighty starlings in New York City's Central Park in 1890.

Solely to make it more palatable, a Frenchman named Ferdinand Flocon set that nation's entire civil law code — over 2,200 articles containing over one hundred thousand words — into a poem, perfect in rhythm and meter. After this death in 1866, his widow was offered an annual pension of over six thousand francs by a grateful Napoleon III. She refused it though, saying her husband had bever been a supporter of the emperor's policies.

We've mentioned elsewhere that the natives of Tasmania have an unusual counting system, consisting of the numbers one, two, and many. Not to be outdone, the Yuki Indians, a California tribe, used to be embarrassed because they sometimes had to count on their fingers. They solved this silly phobia by counting on the spaces *between* their fingers.

An old custom of the natives of Siberia translates roughly into the equivalent of the debutante ball. Until a century or so ago, it was the custom for a young girl to appear before a man she fancied and throw dead lice at him. This action indicated to all concerned that she was available for marriage.

Answer: 1941, 1810, 1892, 1656.

JULY 29

Question: Why is a young woman like an umbrella?

On July 29, 1667, according to the diaries of Samuel Pepys, a naked Quaker marched through Westminster Hall with a chafing dish full of fire balanced on his head, crying, "Repent! Repent!"

In July 1956, Luigi Capuano of Turin, Italy, was freed after spending four months in jail. When he reached his home, he discovered his wife was not there. He later discovered her in a nearby hotel with another man. Mad as hell, Capuano beat up his wife's lover and threw him into the street. Capuano was promptly arrested, and later got eighty-two days in jail for the "immoral act" of forcing a naked man to appear in a public place.

A man does not look behind the door unless he has stood there himself.

Henri DuBois

I have always believed that to have true justice we must have equal harassment under the law.

Paul Krassner

It's only coincidence, but the word *nasa* in Hebrew means "to go up."

An Old English Epitaph

Here lies John Plumpudding of the Grange,
Who hanged himself one morning for a change.

In 1973, a gentleman from Eastport, England, grew a whopping 4½-pound tomato. He attributed his unique success to his idea of playing music to the tomato through the stereo headphones placed on it.

Notable Births

1805	Alexis de Tocqueville	1905	Stanley Kunitz
1869	Booth Tarkington	1905	Dag Hammarskjold
1878	Don Marquis	1905	Clara Bow
1887	Sigmund Romberg	1907	Melvin Belli
1892	William Powell	1918	Edwin O'Connor
1905	Thelma Todd	1942	Stephanie Powers

Notable Events

1617	Treaty of Succession between Austrian and Spanish Hapsburgs
1794	Bethel African Methodist Episcopal Church founded, Philadelphia
1890	Suicide of Vincent Van Gogh
1900	King Humbert I of Italy assassinated
1914	Cape Cod Canal opened
1937	King Farouk enthroned in Egypt
1958	NASA authorized
1973	Bertha Bratton became first woman to win Illinois state fiddlers' contest

Here's a neat rainy day project for your next rainy day — making a show bottle of six different-colored liquids, which won't mix together *if the bottle's kept upright.*

Take a tall bottle or jar. Put in it, in equal or unequal parts to your fancy, the following (in this order): sulfuric acid tinted with indigo dye; chloroform; glycerine tinted with caramel; castor oil colored with alkanet root; 40 percent alcohol tinted with aniline green; and cod liver oil with 1 percent of oil of turpentine.

Of course it helps if you live in a pharmacy, and/or don't mind having such things as sulfuric acid and chloroform sitting around on your windowsill where the cat could knock it — oh, well!

Experience is the one thing you have plenty of when you're too old to get a job.

Laurence J. Peter

Henry Harris Jr.
Winsport, PA

Born June 27, 1821, of Henry Harris
and Jane his Wife
died on the 4th of May, 1837
by the kick of a colt in his bowels

It cost about seventy-five cents in Julius Caesar's time for one soldier to kill another in a war. In the American Civil War the price had gone up to about $5,000, and by World War I to $25,000. The price tag in World War II climbed to $50,000. By 1966 it was costing Americans in Vietnam over $100,000 to dispatch an enemy soldier, and by the time our active involvement in that war ended, the cost was something close to $400,000.

It was often suggested the the United States could buy off a Viet Cong for far less money than it took to kill one, but neither Johnson nor Nixon seriously considered this alternative.

Answer: She's made out of ribs, must be dressed in silk to look her best, goes up in the air at the least hint of a storm, is accustomed to reign, and is usually taken away from you by your best friend.

Notable Births

1818	Emily Brontë	1890	Casey Stengel
1822	Oliver Optic	1898	Henry Moore
1857	Thorstein Veblen	1939	Peter Bogdanovich
1863	Henry Ford	1941	Paul Anka

Notable Events

1626 Italian earthquake left 17,000 dead
1899 Peace conference at The Hague ended
1916 Explosion at Jersey City munitions dock caused $40 million damage
1945 Churchill refused knighthood
1961 U.S. Public Health Service ordered syphilis study
1971 Boeing 727 and Japanese jet collided, 162 dead
1975 Jimmy Hoffa disappeared

Question: Who were their vice-presidents?
Harry Truman
Herbert Hoover
Calvin Coolidge
Woodrow Wilson

At about the turn of the century, 20 percent of the men of the British Army were treated for syphilis *yearly*.

Despite his reputation as a tyrant, Henry VIII of England ruled well during the early years of his reign. In fact, if it had not been for the syphilis that finally drove him almost insane during his later years, he might very well have gone down in history as England's greatest king.

His early state papers reveal a wise, compassionate, and fair man — a true ruler of the Renaissance. In his correspondence with his court and state officials he was direct, yet simple and warm; and in their letters, his civil servants showed that Henry was no huge, egotistical demigod who insisted on fawning praise and instant compliance. There is a decided tone of respect and consideration on both sides, which indicates that Henry was much more a leader than a ruler, good-natured and good-humored in private as well as in public.

He was also among the best-educated men in the England in his day. He was musical, spoke and wrote four languages, and was as expert in many things as some specialists are in one. Henry ranked with the best contemporary minds in medicine and theology (he read religious books incessantly and attended mass three times a day before the schism with the Roman Catholic Church over Anne Boleyn). He was also a superb engineer, and made a significant number of improvements in his army's artillery, as well as inventing several new shipbuilding techniques and procedures. And at tournaments, until he grew too fat, no one was his equal.

For the first half of his reign, he was an eminently popular king, successful in war and peace, and ever watchful of the welfare of his people. Extraordinarily handsome and as athletic a man as there was in England, he had the ability and the inclination to be among the stellar monarchs of history, but, as the Down East sage Bert says, "The dirt just drug him down."

Actions of the last age are like almanacs of the last year.
Thomas Denham

He learned the arts of riding, fencing, gunnery,
And how to scale a fortress — or a nunnery.
Lord Byron

Answer: Alben Barkley, Charles Curtis, Charles Dawes, Thomas Marshall.

There is a kind of parrot native to New Zealand called the kea, or mountain nestor, which formerly lived almost solely on insects. However, in just the past century, the kea has adapted to changes in its environment and has learned to kill ranch sheep with its sharply hooked beak. Hunting parties of these parrots dig at the sheep's back until they are able to pull out the intestines, thus killing it.

In a town in Connecticut a man died who had a large growth on his head. On his tombstone are this illustration and these lines:

Our father lies beneath the sod,
His spirit's gone unto his God;
We never more shall hear his tread
Nor see the wen upon his head.

JULY 31

Questions: What's a Sun in Japan?

What's a Yen in Japan?

What's a Yen in Vietnam?

The Marquis de Lafayette was made a major general in George Washington's Continental Army at the age of nineteen. His real name, in full, was Marie Jean Paul Yves Roche Gilbert du Motier.

On the last day of July 1664, the Dutch swapped their New Netherlands colony for Britain's South American colony in Surinam. You hear a lot more about New York City these days, but the Dutch got fifty thousand times as much land as the English did in the transaction.

Perhaps the greatest nine-day wonder in the toy business was the Hula Hoop. They're still around, but the big year was back in 1958, when forty-five-million-dollars worth of them were sold in the United States alone.

The Hula Hoop phenomenon covered the globe, with varying effects. In the Netherlands, building construction stagnated for want of the plastics used in plumbing fixtures, plastics which had been diverted to hoop manufacture. In South Africa, Hula Hoops were given away to black children by charitable organizations because only white kids could afford the price tag (equivalent to 65 cents). In Japan, even though Prime Minister Kishi got one for his sixty-second birthday, the government banned their use in certain areas because it felt they were too dangerous. Indonesia banned them outright, because that country's conservative government was afraid they "might stimulate passion." The Russian press announced that they reflected "the emptiness of American culture," while Poland, East Germany, and Yugoslavia welcomed the hoop into their countries.

Quite a set of accomplishments for a toy that started out as a humble three-foot-diameter bamboo ring used in Australian gym classes!

No one ever went broke underestimating the taste of the American public.

H.L. Mencken

Although the romantic notion of a typical suicide pictures a gaunt young poet starving and freezing to death in a winter garret, heart broken by unrequited love, studies have shown that a "typical" suicide is more likely to be a fat old man from San Diego who kills himself in May.

Back in 1654, Archbishop James Ussher proved to his own and the Church of England's satisfaction that Adam was placed on the earth at nine in the morning on October 26, 4004 B.C. That means the seximillennial anniversary of Creation is coming up in less than twenty years.

See you there!

Answers: 1.19303 inches; a unit of money measurement; 13.33 pounds.

Notable Births

1831	Madame Blavatsky	1929	Don Murray
1912	Milton Friedman	1951	Evonne Goolagong

Notable Events

1777 Lafayette landed in America
1789 Turks defeated by Russians and Austrians at Focshain
1932 War began between Bolivia and Paraguay
1959 Nehru dismissed his cabinet
1960 Typhoon Shirley killed 104 on Taiwan
1964 Ranger 7 landed (crashing) on moon
1976 Big Thompson Canyon, Colorado, flood killed 130 people

Some varieties of this animal have no legs, some have only tiny hind legs, some have weak legs both fore and aft, and some have exceptionally strong legs. Do you know what it is? (No, this is not a riddle; this is a real family of lizards.) (the skink)

James Stewart, twenty-two, of Brighton, Massachusetts, was arrested in 1951 and charged with possession of a stolen calf. Stewart explained to police that he was only borrowing the animal for a while. His son had never seen a cow before, and he was almost three years old.

The name "derrick" for a type of crane may have its origin in an unusual circumstance of war. During England's conflict with Spain at the end of the sixteenth century, two-dozen English sailors were captured during a raid on the port of Cadiz. They were sentenced to death, but no Spaniard could be found willing to execute so many men. The authorities made a deal with one of the prisoners, Derrick by name, promising to pardon him if he would agree to execute his twenty-three countrymen. He apparently accepted the offer, and later went on to become the executioner at Tyburn in London. His name and notoriety were eventually applied to the Tyburn gallows, which resembled a modern crane.

Virgo (The Virgin)
August 24 through
September 23
AUGUST

AUGUST 1

Questions: How can you make a fire with three sticks?

What do kangaroos have that no other animal has?

Notable Births

1769	Napoleon Bonaparte	1819	Herman Melville
1770	William Clark	1899	William Steinberg
1779	Francis Scott Key	1921	Jack Kramer
1815	Richard Henry Dana	1936	Yves Saint-Laurent

Notable Events

1291 Swiss defensive league formed against House of Hapsburg
1493 Columbus discovered South American continent
1790 First U.S. census began
1834 Effective date of abolition of slavery in British Empire
1854 Yellow fever epidemic began in New Orleans
1893 Shredded wheat patented
1914 France mobilized, Italy declared neutrality
1931 Lady Astor declared Russia best country in world
1957 First solar-heated commercial building completed, Albuquerque, New Mexico
1971 Typhoon Rose killed 130 in Hong Kong

Syphilis was not imported into the Old World by Columbus and the other early explorers. It had been a part of European culture for centuries. Its prevalence throughout Europe at the time of the explorations gave rise to the impression that the native Americans were responsible, but that is not the case. It is probable, however, that the explorers did introduce a particularly virulent strain of the disease that was previously unknown to Europeans.

On a sunny summer day, the heat of the sun on one acre of pond can equal the energy of 4,500 horsepower.

The moon actually does impart some heat to the earth. Over a century ago, the Italian scientist Mellini took a three-foot-diameter lens and focused moonlight on a thermometer. The mercury rose from .6 degrees to 4.8 degrees Fahrenheit, according to the phase of the moon and the atmospheric conditions.

Mrs. Carrie M. Crandall of Westerly, Rhode Island, wrote a letter to the city clerk of Worcester, Massachusetts, in August 1949, in which she said: "I fell into an open coal chute in front of the Hotel Pleasant . . . and I think the city should pay me something for my injuries." She went on to say that she thought this "occurred in 1889 or 1890."

Crocodiles and alligators are surprisingly fast on land — not that one could catch a Bob Hayes, but certainly a portly matron might easily become dinner — if they could find one. Although they are rapid, they are not agile; so if you ever find yourself chased by one, run in a zig-zag line. You'll lose him or her every time.

On the other hand, the average hippopotamus is faster than a world-class human sprinter.

Answers: Be sure one's a match.
Baby kangaroos.

AUGUST 2

Notable Births

1754	Pierre L'Enfant	1924	James Baldwin
1871	John Sloan	1924	Carroll O'Connor
1905	Myrna Loy	1933	Peter O'Toole
1914	Gary Merrill	1946	Bob Beamon

Notable Events

1819 First parachute jump from a balloon made, Charles Guille, New York City
1830 Charles X of France abdicated
1858 First street mailboxes introduced, Boston
1858 British Columbia organized as a colony
1876 Wild Bill Hickok shot in back by Jack McCall
1914 Germany occupied Luxembourg
1934 Von Hindenburg died, Hitler took over as chancellor
1943 Patton slapped and kicked Private C.H. Kuhl
1943 *PT-109* rammed and sunk by destroyer *Amigiri*
1944 Turkey broke relations with Germany
1964 Gulf of Tonkin incident

Questions: What's the surest way to double your money at a race track?

When does an Englishman double his money?

On August 1, 1876, from the doorway of Carl Mann's saloon in Deadwood, Dakota Territory, Wild Bill Hickok stood gazing out into the street. Talking with his friend Tom Dosier, he said he felt he would soon be killed. Dosier told Bill to "knock it off," but Hickok wrote to his wife that night:

Agnes Darling:
If such should be we never meet again, while firing my last shot, I will gently breathe the name of my wife — Agnes — and with wishes even for my enemies I will make the plunge and try to swim to the other shore.

J.B. Hickok

The next afternoon, a little after four, Carl Mann, Charlie Rich, and a man named Captain Massey were having an amiable game of poker with Wild Bill when Jack McCall sauntered in through the open rear door of the saloon. McCall walked towards the bar, then casually moved towards the table where the game was in progress. He took a quick look at Bill's hand — aces and eights — then drew his Colt .45 and shot him in the back of the head. Wild Bill slid from his stool to the floor, his hand still crimped from holding his cards.

Some interesting details should be noted here:

It was the first time anyone had ever seen Hickok sit with his back to a door. From his seat, Wild Bill faced the front door, but McCall entered from the rear. Bill had asked Charlie a couple of times to change places with him so he could more easily keep an eye on both entrances, but Charlie, kiddingly, had refused. Rich later blamed himself for Hickok's murder.

A man named Doc Peirce was the only one in the area with any medical training, and so the chore of preparing Bill's body for burial fell to him. Of this experience he once said, "I have seen many dead men on the field of battle and in civil life, but Wild Bill was the prettiest corpse I have ever seen." It was Peirce who closed the bullet's exit wound in Hickok's cheek so it was "barely noticeable."

All six chambers in the murderer's gun were loaded, but later tests showed that none of the other cartridges were capable of firing. McCall, unknowingly, beat a five-to-one chance of becoming Wild Bill's thirty-seventh victim. (It must be said in Hickok's defense that trouble usually went looking for him, not vice versa.)

Wild Bill was buried the next day at a scenic spot nearby called Ingleside. A wooden plank had been roughly inscribed overnight to stand at the head of his grave:

> A brave man, victim of an assassin,
> J.B. Hickok (Wild Bill) age 39 years;
> murdered by Jack McCall, Aug. 2, 1876

Three years later, Deadwood had grown so much because of a gold strike that the town threatened the ground where Wild Bill was buried. On the anniversary of his interment his remains were removed by his friends to the Mount Moriah Cemetery, and a marble tombstone was erected. It gave much the same information as the earlier plank had, and added this epitaph:

> Pard, we will meet again in the happy
> hunting grounds to part no more.

Within a decade this stone was gone, victim to pilgrims and souvenir hunters who'd chipped away pieces of it as relics. A third marker was eventually enclosed by an iron fence.

Lastly, the co-owner of the saloon in which Wild Bill Hickok was murdered was named Jerry Lewis.

How much do you think I'll get for my autobiography?

Arthur Bremer

The Romans were avid gamblers. Both Caligula and Augustus were addicted to craps, and Augustus loved to win big so much that he'd often bankroll his friends and opponents just to increase the size of the pot. Nero was a domino freak, and Claudius carried a collection of gaming tables wherever he went. The Emperor Commodus had a whole casino built in his palace.

Eventually, things got out of hand in Rome, and laws had to be passed prohibiting people from gaming in taverns. Too many people were getting killed.

In Pueblo, Colorado, in August 1950, as rookie policeman James Scanlon was explaining how a fellow rookie had accidentally shot himself in the leg, he accidentally shot himself in the leg.

Answers: Fold it in your pocket.

When he makes one pound, two every day.

AUGUST 3

Question: Can you name the world's five busiest airports, in terms of passengers per year?

Notable Births

1887	Rupert Brooke	1921	Marilyn Maxwell
1900	Ernie Pyle	1921	Hayden Carruth
1901	John Stennis	1924	Leon Uris
1905	Walter Van Tilburg Clark	1926	Tony Bennett
1905	Dolores Del Rio	1940	Lance Alworth

Notable Events

1907	Kaiser Wilhelm and Czar Nicholas met to discuss Baghdad railroad
1914	Germany declared war on France, invaded Belgium
1940	Suicide of Willard Hershberger
1961	Three Philadelphia city officials indicted on 136 counts of bribery and conspiracy
1975	Boeing 707 hit Moroccan mountain, 188 people killed

As we've mentioned in connection with the siege of the Alamo, Davy Crockett has had what is known as a good press. His terms in Congress as a representative from Tennessee were characterized by a lot of sleeping and quiet snoring, although it must be said that when there was a issue he felt strongly about, he waxed truly eloquent.

Perhaps the most memorable speech he made as a legislator occurred in the midst of the debate on whether or not the sale of whiskey should be legalized within the confines of the Capitol Building. Crockett had a better idea. He declared, "Congress allows lemonade to members and it is charged under the head of stationery. I move that whiskey be allowed under the item of fuel."

For 200 years, residents of the town of Dubalhati in India had to pay a tax of twenty-thousand fish to the Indian emperor every year. It started in the sixteenth century when the Emperor Akbar was informed that the district was so poor no taxes could be taken from it. Akbar felt sure there was something he could collect from the destitute villagers, and set out to investigate the place. There he discovered that a river was the home to thousands of walking perch. These fish were about six inches long, inedible and useless, but they did possess the curious ability to "walk" on dry land, and even to climb trees after a fashion, much like our own more familiar lungfish. Akbar ordered a yearly tribute of twenty-thousand fish from the town. For two centuries at tax time the people of Dubalhati harvested the odd little fish and sent them under escort (they represented revenue, after all) to the imperial treasury. The tax was finally rescinded in the late seventeenth century.

The word "arctic" comes from the Greek *arktos* — a bear — but not a polar bear, as you might think. It derives its meaning from the constellation of the Big Dipper, *Ursa Major* in Latin, the "Great Bear."

A Belgian coal miner, Celestian Jadot, had his pension cut unexpectedly in 1948, so he went to Brussels to find out why. He was told he had not worked in Belgium as long as he'd said he had, or as long as the pension bureau had originally thought. It happened that a coal shaft in which he'd worked for a decade extended beneath French territory, so they had cut his benefits accordingly.

Answer: O'Hare (Chicago), Atlanta, Los Angeles, Heathrow (London), Tokyo.

In fourteen years, between 1856 and 1870, the ruling Gaikwar of Baroda, India, spent over two million dollars on state weddings for his pets. With all the pomp and ceremony due members of the royal household, the Gaikwar presided at the nuptials of fourty-two pairs of his favorite pigeons. Each wedding cost the equivalent of $50,000.

Notable Births

1792	Percy Bysshe Shelley	1910	William Schuman
1859	Knut Hamsun	1956	Joni Huntley

Notable Events

1730 Frederick, Crown Prince of Prussia, imprisoned by father
1734 John Peter Zenger acquitted in famous newspaper case
1789 Feudalism abolished in France
1889 Special Delivery initiated
1914 Britain declared war on Germany
1964 Bodies of Schwerner, Chaney, and Goodman identified

Question: Within ten years, when were the following invented?
electron microscope
life preserver
machine gun
long-playing record

In August 1622, a small band of Puritans began a settlement at what is now the Wollaston section of Quincy, Massachusetts about ten miles south of Boston. The colony at the time was known by its Indian name, Wassaguscus. By the end of the first winter, the settlers were in perilous circumstances. They were nearly out of food, and the Indians, whom they had treated very badly, were becoming decidedly unfriendly. John Saunders, the leader of the band, decided he'd have to sail for the tiny villages up the coast in the hope of finding one with surplus food. Before he left, he cautioned his people not to trespass against the Indians in any way, and instructed Edward Johnson, his second-in-command, to deliver any troublemaker to the natives themselves for punishment.

While Saunders was gone, the settlement's cobbler found the Indians' corn cache. Unmindful of Saunders's admonition, he "liberated" most of it for his fellow Christians. When the Indians discovered their food had been stolen, they went to the English and demanded that the guilty party be turned over to them.

Johnson, rather than risk the lives of all the colony members by refusing or fighting, said he would hand over the man within the hour. A huge debate then ensued within the stockade as to who that man should be. The cobbler admitted he had stolen the corn, and was willing to turn himself over to face the consequences. But other settlers insisted he had saved their lives by the theft, and moreover, as the only bootmaker and leather-worker among them, he was far too valuable to be sacrificed. Other innocent individuals were passed over because of their skills, or their family needs, or for other reasons.

But the colony's wool-sorter insisted on justice. He insisted adamantly that the guilty party should be the one punished, regardless of the circumstances, and he recalled Saunders's instructions. He said he could not believe that his fellows were willing to sacrifice an entirely innocent individual simply because the guilty party happened to have a certain skill.

Then one of the other men pointed out that this very wool-sorter had no kin in the colony; indeed, there was not even any wool for him to sort. By acclamation, this young man who had spoken out for justice was chosen as the scapegoat of injustice.

Edward Johnson turned his back as the men of the little village carried the wool-sorter out of the fort to be delivered to the Indians.

Common sense in an uncommon degree is what the world calls wisdom.

Samuel Coleridge

Since 1975, people found guilty of bathing nude in the Corsican town of Oliastro have been punished by being painted blue.

Answer: 1939, 1805, 1862, 1948.

AUGUST 5

Questions: A woman works in a candy store. Her measurements are 40-28-38, she's 5 feet, 4 inches tall, and wears a size eight shoe. Guess what she weighs.

Why is ardent love like a three-ring circus?

Notable Births

1850	Guy de Maupassant	1911	Robert Taylor
1889	Conrad Aiken	1930	Neil Armstrong
1906	John Huston	1940	Roman Gabriel

Notable Events

1772	Poland partitioned among Prussia, Russia, and Austria
1864	Farragut took Mobile, Alabama
1884	Cornerstone of Statue of Liberty placed
1911	First intercity air race held, New York to Philadelphia
1914	First electric traffic lights installed, Cleveland
1914	Austria-Hungary declared war on Russia
1926	First talking movie shown, New York City
1936	General Metaxas declared Greece a dictatorship
1940	Estonia and Latvia incorporated into USSR

Shortly after the first use of the electric chair in America on this date in 1890, the Abyssinian emperor, Menelik II, ordered three chairs for his country. When they arrived, he discovered there was a problem — Abyssinia had no electricity.

Menelik made the best of a bad situation and had one of the chairs converted into his throne.

Never invest your money in anything that eats or needs repairing.

Billy Rose

On August 5, 1858, the laying of the Atlantic Ocean telegraph cable was completed, and the American financier, Cyrus Field, is generally recognized as the driving force behind the project. Actually, Field was one of three men who signed an agreement in 1856 declaring their goals and their equal partnership in the venture. The next year, their Atlantic Telegraph Company undertook the challenge, with the Englishman Sir Charles Bright as engineer-in-chief, and Field as general manager. Throughout the endeavor, Bright was a more important factor than Field. If any one man deserves the credit for this great engineering success, it is Charles Bright, but you won't find his name in most American history books.

We all have strength enough to endure the misfortunes of others.

La Rochefoucauld

Ralph R. Upton was a Seattle high school teacher who created the phrase "Stop, look, and listen," the dictum for automobiles in the days before traffic lights.

He was killed on this day in 1935 — the twenty-fourth anniversary of the first electric traffic light's installation — in a car accident.

A pessimist is a man who looks both ways before crossing a one-way street.

Laurence J. Peter

Answers: Candy.
It's always intense.

Notable Births

1651	François Fenelon	1893	Louella Parsons
1809	Alfred Lord Tennyson	1910	Lucille Ball
1881	Alexander Fleming	1916	Richard Hofstadter
1883	Scott Nearing	1917	Robert Mitchum

Notable Events

1762	Traditional date of invention of sandwich
1774	Shakers arrived in New York City
1832	J.G. Spurzheim, first phrenologist in America, landed at New York City
1857	First Atlantic cable laid out
1872	Connecticut passed opium laws
1890	First electrocution execution
1914	Serbia and Montenegro declared war on Germany
1926	Gertrude Ederle became first woman to swim English Channel
1929	Judge Crater vanished
1945	A-bomb dropped on Hiroshima
1948	Teenager Bob Mathias won Olympic decathlon
1964	Sam Sheppard released from prison

In the fifteenth century, on the Isle of Sheppy, England, Sir Robert de Shurland was in love with a girl who subsequently died. This love story went on to have a bizarre conlusion.

The local priest refused to bury the girl with the rites of the church because she had neither been baptized nor confirmed. This enraged the grief-stricken lord, and he ordered his servants to bury the priest alive. He later said he didn't really mean it, but his men had taken him at his word and thrown the priest (who was very much alive) into an untimely grave. Once he realized his crime, de Shurland decided the king might be merciful if he went and confessed the murder immediately. He leapt on his steed, crossed the strait, and headed for London. There he explained, apologized, and gave a handsome donation to the church as a token of repentance. The King pardoned him.

When he returned to Sheppy, an old woman who had reputation for being a witch warned him that the horse that had so gallantly carried him on his journey would some day cause his death. Taking no chances, he had the horse killed, and then thrown into the ocean with a stone around his neck. "Prudence is superior to fate," he told himself.

Twenty years later, he came upon a skeleton on the beach. He noticed a stone among the bones and so recognized the remains of his old horse. "So the old hag thought you'd kill me, did she? Ha!", he said, and gave the skeleton a good hard kick.

One of the sharp vertabrae cut his toe. The wound became infected and de Shurland developed gangrene. The rot spread throughout his body and he was dead in a few weeks.

He that is born to be hanged shall never be drowned.

Thomas Fuller

The clemency of princes is often a mere tactic for gaining their subjects' affections.

La Rouchefoucauld

There are over 3,500 species of cockroaches in the world.

Question: What are the nicknames of the following states?

Colorado
Maryland
Minnesota
Nevada

Telling fortunes with coffee grounds is called hyromancy; communicating with the dead is necromancy; and foretelling the future by dreams, oneiromancy. There are dozens of other ways to divine the future — here is a list of just some of them:

aeromancy	**divining by**	air
pyromancy		fire
hydromancy		water
geomancy		earth
theomancy		spirits
demonomancy		devils
idolomancy		idols, images
psychomancy		men's souls and affections
antinopomancy		entrails
theriomancy		beasts
ornithomancy		birds
ichthyomancy		fish
botanomancy		herbs
lithomancy		stones
cleromancy		lottery
onomatomancy		names
arithmancy		numbers
logarithmancy		logarithms
sternomancy		the body, breast to stomach
gastromancy		sounds of the stomach
omphelomancy		navel
chiromancy		hands
pedomancy		feet
onychomancy		fingernails
cephaleonomancy		a donkey's braying
tuphramancy		ashes
capnomancy		smoke
livanomancy		burning frankincense
carromancy		melting wax
lecanomancy		a basin of water
catoxtromancy		looking glasses
chartomancy		maps
macharomancy		knives or swords
chrystallomancy		glasses
dactylomancy		rings
coseinomancy		sieves
axinomancy		saws
cattabomancy		vessels of brass
roadomancy		the stars
spatalamancy		skin, bones
sciomancy		shadows
astragalomancy		dice
oinomancy		wine
sycomancy		figs
typomancy		coagulation of cheese
alphitomancy		rye meal or bread
crithomancy		grain or corn
alectromancy		roosters and hens
gyromancy		circles
lampadomancy		candles and lamps
clidomancy		keys

No matter how thin you slice it, it's still baloney.

Al Smith

Answer: Centennial State; Old Line State; North Star, or Gopher State; Sagebrush State.

AUGUST 7

Questions: Why is a lucky gambler like a popular man?

What is the most useful bet ever made?

Notable Births

1852	Doctor Watson	1904	Ralph Bunche
1884	Billie Burke	1929	Don Larsen
1903	Louis Leakey	1950	Dave Wottle

Notable Events

1789	War department created
1844	Twelve crushed to death in crowd at hanging in Nottingham, England
1888	Revolving door patented
1888	Mary Anne Nicholls became Jack the Ripper's first victim
1941	Death of Rabindranath Tagore
1942	India Congress Party outlawed, Gandhi jailed
1968	Storms in India killed 1,000 people
1972	Floods in Philippines took 454 lives

In the village of Bijori in India's Central Provinces, it rains beads of various colors, already bored for stringing. As of 1963, "Ripley's Believe It or Not" had no idea why or how.

A man named James Morton was hauled into court in Berkeley, California, a while ago because he hadn't paid a traffic fine. He explained to the judge he'd long before given his wife the money to pay the fine, but she had used it instead to hire a lawyer to initiate divorce proceedings.

The following comes from England and dates from about 1500. It is presented without editorial comment:

A pretty petty parly about a Fart

Why what's a fart? wind, or aire, or sound, or so,
But presently his back-parts they cry no.
By me fay, saies one, for all your winking,
The answers good, were it not for stinking.
Nay quoth another, in it's no evill,
But that to mee it seeme's so uncivill.
Yet sayes the sagest, young men are too bold,
The priviledge belongs to us that'r old.
Nay quoth an heire this may well be done,
Farts be entaild from the father to the son.
Why sayes another, upon my conscience
It may be reform'd by some frankinsence.
Quoth an astronomer, if you'll not laffe,
I'le measure this fart with my Jacob's staffe.
Fie, sayes Sir John, I like not this passage,
Farts interpos'd in midst of a message;
Yet gentlemen, this before our departing,
In rhetoricke is no figure of farting.
Nay more than all this, sayes little Jack Straw,
A fart's not in compasse of th' civill law,
'Tis true sayes Sir John, I dare assure'm,
'Tis *contra modestiam*, not *contra naturam*,
Your words sayes another are all but wind,
For I do not like those motions behind:
I'le lay my cap, quoth Will with the red hose,
That the *major* part will goe with the nose.
Well sayes th'other, I'me asham'd to tell it,
For all that are here, may easily smell it;
Then I that stood by said, surely this fart,
Is voyce of the belly and not of the heart.
In compasse of ten mile about,
(Saies one) such a fart there never came out.
A pursevant then humbly on his knees
Would faine have the fart, but it payes not fees:
But sayes the delinquent, pray let mee speake,
Now I assure thee, my shoes did but creake.
O strange quoth one, 'tis most wondrously,
The gentleman speaketh as well as I.
So (gentle reader) our dispute did bend,
To one onely center; and there's an end.

If I break wind in Wittenberg they smell it in Rome.
Martin Luther

Answers: Both have winning ways.

The alphabet.

AUGUST 8

Notable Births

1763	Charles Bulfinch	1910	Sylvia Sidney
1819	Charles A. Dana	1919	Dino De Laurentiis
1882	Leopold Stokowski	1923	Esther Williams
1884	Sara Teasdale	1936	Frank Howard
1896	Marjorie Kinnan Rawlings	1937	Dustin Hoffman
1908	Arthur Goldberg	1938	Connie Stevens

Notable Events

1540	Henry VIII married Lady Catherine Howard
1866	Queen Emma of Hawaii visited United States
1914	Britain and France occupied Togoland
1942	Marines landed in Solomon Islands
1945	Russia declared war on Japan
1963	British mail train robbed, $7 million taken
1974	Nixon announced resignation

On August 8, 1492, Ferdinand V of Aragon and Isabella of Castile and Lyon ordered the two hundred thousand Spanish Jews they ruled to leave the country. The next day, Columbus (who probably had some Jewish blood) set sail on his voyage of discovery. Among his crew were at least three Jewish sailors, and the major portion of his voyage was funded by Jews who refused to charge interest on the loans they made to the captain.

Laws and institutions must go hand in hand with the progress of the human mind.

Thomas Jefferson

Question: What part of a brand new clock has always been used before?

The first book banned in modern Boston was a crusade against prostitution entitled *The Woman Who Did*, which was published in 1894. The censors found fault with the way author Grant Allen handled his material, not the book's motivation.

Among the other works Boston has banned for one reason or another are *A Farewell to Arms*, *An American Tragedy*, *Candide*, and the film *Gone With the Wind*. Even Walt Disney's *Snow White and the Seven Dwarfs* was censored.

A censor is a man who knows more than he thinks you ought to.

Laurence J. Peter

A sodomite got very excited looking at a zoology text. Does this make it pornography?

Stanislaw Lec

⚜

Queen Salote of Tonga stood six foot, three inches tall and weighed 280 pounds.

⚜

Originally, the children's story "Little Red Riding Hood" was veiled criticism of the way Henry VIII (the Wolf) was gobbling up the property of the English monks (Little Red Riding Hood). One had to be careful with Henry — criticism of His Royal Personage was considered treason, and you know what that meant.

Answer: The second hand.

AUGUST 9

Question: If it is noon in Chicago, what time is it in:
Denver
Nashville
Indianapolis
San Francisco?

On August 9, 1796, a two-day cricket match began between two teams of Greenwich Hospital war pensioners. The first consisted of men with only one arm; the second of men with only one leg. Surprisingly, the one-legged team won by 103 runs, and split a bet of one thousand pounds among them.

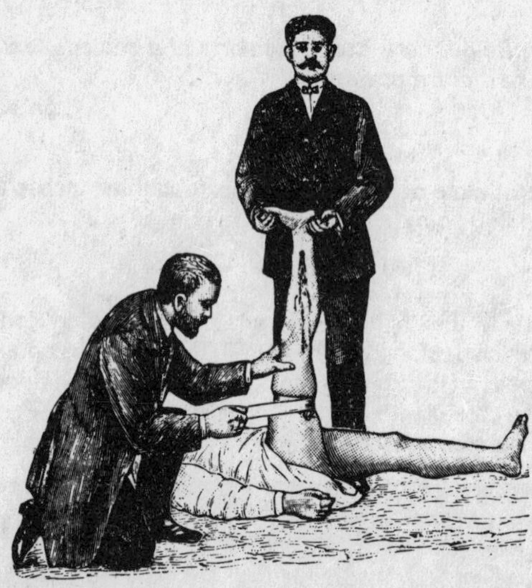

Whenever John Dryden was about to embark on a period of creative endeavor, he always took an enema and had himself bled to freshen his mind.

President Grover Cleveland was an inveterate fisherman and, like most of them, some of the fish he caught grew with the telling. When his second child was born, the attending physician asked Cleveland if he happened to have a scale so he could weigh the baby. Cleveland replied that yes, he had the one he weighed his prize fish on, and he brought it for the doctor.

The child weighed in at twenty-six pounds, four ounces.

Practical politics consists in ignoring facts.

Henry Adams

Epitaph from a cemetery in Bayfield, Wisconsin:

BASIL, child of Jos. Davis,
& Fleuvis Davis. Died
On August, 1864, aged 4 years & 4 mths & 18 days.
Struck
by
Thunder.

Answer: 11:00 a.m.; noon; 1:00 p.m.; 10:00 a.m.

Notable Births

1593	Izaak Walton	1913	Herman Talmadge
1631	John Dryden	1922	Philip Larken
1653	John Oldham	1928	Bob Cousy
1896	Jean Piaget	1938	Rod Laver

Notable Events

1615	Second civil war began in France
1893	First bowling magazine published
1898	Spain formally accepted U.S. peace terms
1931	Revolution failed in Cuba
1934	United States nationalized silver
1940	FDR called chances of U.S. Army fighting overseas 100-1
1954	Turkey, Greece, and Yugoslavia formed alliance
1970	Plane crash in Peru killed 101 people
1974	Ford sworn as president

Some kinds of eels have a particularly difficult time propagating their species. Spawned in the sea, they migrate to fresh water as one-inch elvers, sometimes reaching rivers and ponds as high as eight thousand feet in elevation. Once there, they grow for eight or nine years (to lengths as long as five feet) and mature sexually, but remain "celibate." When it comes time to spawn, they turn from blackish to silver in color, and then race to the sea. Their drive to reach the ocean often leads the eels to take shortcuts, and they have been known to travel over a mile through dewy meadows.

AUGUST 10

Notable Births

1874	Herbert Hoover	1924	Martha Hyer
1900	Norma Shearer	1928	Jimmy Dean
1911	Jane Wyatt	1928	Eddie Fisher
1923	Rhonda Fleming	1933	Rocky Colavito

Notable Events

1627	Richelieu began siege of La Rochelle
1787	Turkey declared war on Russia
1792	Mob stormed Tuilleries; Swiss Guard massacred
1914	France declared war on Austria-Hungary
1945	Japan offered to surrender
1964	Pope Paul VI issued *Ecclesiam Suam*, offered to intervene for peace in Vietnam
1977	United States and Panama agreed to Panamanian control of canal

Question: Can you name the sixth through the tenth most common American surnames?

Three years into the Great Depression, President Hoover ventured out of the Rose Garden and went to Charlestown, West Virginia, to dedicate a new public building. West Virginia's economy, heavily based on coal, had been especially hard hit by the worldwide stagnation, and Hoover and his policies were not great favorites in the region. Still, protocol required that the president receive a twenty-one-gun salute, and in this instance the guns were cannon stationed near the presidential platform. They were fired with a tremendous roar and great billows of smoke. When the air cleared, a loud voice near the front of the crowd bellowed out, "By God! They missed him!"

We're all on the same side — we're out to get me.

Bob Schneider

Once upon a time my political opponents honored me as possessing the fabulous intellectual and economic power by which I created a world-wide depression all by myself.

Herbert Hoover

Louis XIV of France really was as unpleasant a fellow as he's been depicted. In 1674, when he was visiting a school at Clermont, he heard from the school's authorities that one of the children, a nine-year-old Irish lad named Francis Seldon, had made a pun about the king's bald pate.

Louis was furious. He had a secret warrant drawn up for the child's arrest, and young Seldon was thrown into solitary confinement in the Bastille. His parents, members of one of Europe's richest merchant families, were told simply that the child had disappeared.

Days turned to months, months to years, and Louis himself passed on. But Francis spent sixty-nine years "in the hole" for making fun of the king's baldness.

The warship *Vasa* was to be the pride of the Swedish Navy. Forty acres of prime timber had gone to supply the wood for the huge (for its time) 180-foot square rigger, and hundreds of shipwrights had labored on her for years.The ship boasted 300 soldiers, a crew of 133 men and, sixty-four guns. On August 10, 1628, it seemed that half of Sweden had turned out for her launching. Speeches were made, proclamations read, everyone congratulated everyone else. The *Vasa* was christened and slid proudly into the water.

Within an hour she had sunk — less than a mile from shore, — in a small but nasty squall, and taking all but a handful of her sailors to the bottom. She had never even raised her full complement of sails.

In August 1949, the Interstate Commerce Commission recommended that one of the ways the ferry operating between Weehauken, New Jersey, and Manhattan could help meet higher overhead costs would be to raise its tariff for carrying uncrated elephants between the two ports from $1.40 to $2.80.

There's always an easy solution to every human problem — neat, plausible, and wrong.

H.L. Mencken

Answer: Miller, Davis, Martin, Anderson, Wilson.

AUGUST 11

Question: Which weighs more, a pound of feathers or a pound of gold?

The words "monastery" and "convent" are opposites, despite the fact that both are names for religious houses. "Monastery" comes from the Greek root *monos*, and means "a place to be alone." "Convent" comes from the Latin *conventum*, and means "to come together."

You know how they say that the best place to hide something is right under a person's nose? It didn't work for Arlene Gibson. In 1948 she wore her stolen jewelry to the policeman's ball and ended up in jail.

If you like figures, you'll love the number nine. Multiply nine by any other number, and the sum of the digits in the product will always total nine. For example, $9 \times 7 = 72; 7 + 2 = 9; 9 \times 339 = 3{,}051; 3 + 5 + 1 = 9$; and so forth. (This has to be modified sometimes—$9 \times 5{,}071 = 45{,}639; 4 + 5 + 6 + 3 + 9 = 27; 2 + 7 = 9$—but it always works one way or the other.) If you take any row of figures and reverse them, then subtract the reversed number from the first, the digits in your answer will add up to nine in the same way. This also works when any number you select is raised to its square or cube. Also, if you write down any number at all, total the sum of its digits, then subtract this figure from the original number, the digits of the product will always total nine.

Answer: It's debatable. A pound of feathers is sixteen ounces avoirdupois, a pound of gold is twelve ounces troy.

Notable Births

1865	Gifford Pinchot	1911	Angus Wilson
1897	Louise Bogan	1912	Jean Parker
1902	Lloyd Nolan	1921	Alex Haley
1907	Bobo Newsom	1925	Mike Douglas
1908	I.W. Abel	1928	Arlene Dahl

Notable Events

843	Treaty of Verdun separated France and Germany
1807	First voyage of Fulton's steamboat
1834	Protestant mob stormed Ursuline Convent, Charlestown, Massachusetts
1853	200 people died in New York City from heat stroke
1934	Beebe descended ½ mile in bathysphere
1949	U.S. Department of Defense established
1961	Warren Spahn won 300th game
1965	Race riots began in Watts
1969	Nixon proposed $4 billion welfare program

Here is an epitaph from Iver, Bucks, England:

Near this place lieth the body of Mrs. Elizabeth Farrington, late wife of Mr. Richard Farrington, Citizen and Distiller of London, and daughter of Joseph How, late of this Parish, Gent, who departed this life on the 11th of Aug. 1724, aged 40 years. Also twelve sons and daughters of the above said Richard and Elizabeth Farrington:

					Y	M	D
Elizabeth	died	7 Sept.	1706	aged	0	0	7
Hester		9 Dec.	1711		2	3	10
Sarah		22 Sept.	1714		0	1	19
Anne		15 Nov.	1716		1	1	27
Margaret		30 May	1717		4	0	22
Sarah		1 Sept.	1717		0	11	10
Robert		14 Dec.	1721		0	7	21
Joseph		16 Dec.	1721		0	7	23
Martha		20 Sept.	1722		0	5	2
Thomas		24 Aug.	1723		0	1	25
Anna Christina		10 Mar.	1725		0	7	9
Mary		24 June	1725		7	2	8

R^{d}. F. the father of the above children, died April 24, 1750, in the 74th year of his age. Two other children, Anna Maria died on the 20th Nov. 1731, in the sixth year of her age, and Elizabeth, June 25th, 1741, aged 34 years.

On this date in 1746, the British Parliament passed a law which forbade the Scots to wear their kilts. It was nothing to do with the kilt being "effeminate" but was an attempt to quell the spirit of Scottish nationalism to which the traditonal kilt most decidedly contributed, in the opinion of the British government.

The term "knuckle under" commonly means to submit, and it originated in a time when knuckle meant more than just the joints of one's hands. "Knuckle" then referred to any joint, usually the knee. Thus, to knuckle under was to kneel, the posture of submission.

AUGUST 12

Notable Births

1774 Robert Southey
1818 Lucy Stone
1876 Mary Roberts Rinehart
1880 Christy Mathewson
1881 Cecil B. DeMille
1911 Cantinflas
1921 Marjorie Reynolds
1931 William Goldman
1939 George Hamilton

Notable Events

1585 First letter written in English sent from America
1816 Lord Amherst refused to kowtow to Chinese emperor, scandal ensued
1914 Britain declared war on Austria-Hungary
1935 "L'il Abner" comic strip began
1936 Hitler promised not to interfere in Spain
1941 Petain called on French to support Hitler
1953 Russia tested first H-bomb
1961 Berlin Wall erected
1970 U.S. Post Office became Postal Service
1972 Floods in Bangladesh killed 2,500

Questions: Why will the condition of a sick man improve if he makes a nickel wager with someone?

Why is a man who doesn't gamble just as bad as one who does?

According to the investigation conducted after the Tacoma suspension bridge swung itself into oblivion on this date in 1937 (you've probably seen the film account of the celebrated incident), the span toppled because poor engineering put together a fatal combination of bridge length and the physical laws of wave lengths and frequencies. Another plausible explanation can be seen from the "translation" of engineering jargon listed here:

Engineers' Dictionary

Major technological breakthrough: Back to the drawing board.
Developed after years of intensive research: It was discovered by accident.
Project slightly behind original schedule due to unforeseen difficulties: We are working on something else.
The designs are well within allowable limits: We just made it, stretching a point or two.
Close project coordination: 1. We should have asked someone else, 2. Let's spread the responsibility for this screw-up.
Customer satisfaction is believed assured: We were so far behind schedule we think the customer is happy to get it at all.
The design will be finalized in the next reporting period: We haven't started yet.
A number of different approaches are being tried: We don't know where we're going, but we're on our way.
Preliminary operational tests were inconclusive: It blew up when turned on the switch.
Extensive effort is being applied on a fresh approach to the problem: We just hired three new guys; maybe they can figure it out.
Test results were extremely gratifying: It worked, and are we surprised!
The entire concept will have to be abandoned: The only guy who understood it quit.
Modifications are underway to correct certain minor difficulties: We threw the whole thing out and are starting from scratch.

All five games of the 1905 World Series between the New York Giants and the Philadelphia Athletics were shut-out affairs. Christy Mathewson pitched three of them for the Giants, but had his name misspelled in his team's home-town program.

Answers: It makes him a little better.
Because he is no better.

AUGUST 13

Question: What are the six deepest seas or oceans, in order?

Merriwether Lewis, born on this date in 1774, was only twenty-nine when he commanded the famous Lewis and Clark expedition. He was only thirty-five when he committed suicide.

The French writer Montaigne related this story of the first group of American Indians to visit France in the sixteenth century.

While they were in Rouen with the French king, Charles IX, the Indians were asked what, out of all they had seen had most affected them. They remarked that they were most struck by the docility of the French poor. They could not understand why so many people who were starving and suffering amid such luxury "did not take the others by their throats, or set fire to the houses."

I would rather have my ignorance than another man's knowledge, because I have so much more of it.

Mark Twain

The most dangerous thing in the world is to leap a chasm in two jumps.

David Lloyd George

Handicapping had its origins in a bartering system used in England five centuries ago, known as "hand in cap." When two men wanted to trade services or goods, but could not agree on the value or amount, a third man was asked into the transaction as an umpire. All three then put a token amount of money into a cap, and the third man was asked to suggest a fair exchange price for the commodities in question. If the figure was acceptable to one trader, but not the other, there was no deal, but the man willing to make the deal was allowed to put his hand into the cap and take the money. If the exchange was acceptable to both or neither man, the umpire claimed the spoils. By the seventeenth century, a similar system had been developed to determine appropriate weight "handicaps" for horse races.

Weep, Stranger, for a father spill'd,
From a stage-coach and thereby killed;
His name was John Sykes, a maker of sassengers,
Slain with three other outside passengers.

Probably the world's record for eating spinach belongs to a Tokyo doctor named Kakuji Yoshida. In six years he ate over 8,200 pounds of the leafy children's favorite, better than three pounds a day.

Herbert E. Rasmussen of Chicago was arrested for arson in January 1948. The fire had resulted in $125,000 damage. He admitted to police he was trying to destroy the evidence of a $16 burglary.

Notable Births

1422	William Caxton	1899	Alfred Hitchcock
1743	Antoine Lavoisier	1902	Regis Toomey
1842	Albert Sorel	1913	Archbishop Makarios
1860	Annie Oakley	1920	George Shearing
1895	Bert Lahr	1927	Fidel Castro

Notable Events

1521	Cortez completed conquest of Mexico
1587	Manteo became first Indian convert to Protestantism
1792	French royal family imprisoned
1868	Earthquake claimed 25,000 lives in Peru and Equador
1873	Franz Josef Land discovered
1896	Nansen reached 86 degrees latitude
1919	Man o' War lost his only race, to Upset, at Saratoga
1935	First roller derby held, Chicago
1940	United States recalled consuls from Latvia, Lithuania, Estonia
1961	2-million-dollar Cezanne stolen from Aix-en-Provence
1964	Lester Maddox closed restaurant rather than admit blacks
1964	Death of Ian Fleming

Captain S.L. Hinde of England had some curious things to report about the art of cannibalism in the Congo in 1895. He said that in many places in the Congo people were used as food, pure and simple, without the religious or military justifications present in other cannibalistic societies. The members of the Bengala tribe, he noted, were decided gourmets. They would break the arms and legs of their dinner a few days before he or she was to be consumed, and leave the live victim balled up in a filled cookpot for several days while the flesh was softened by the water. In Baletela country, Hinde said he'd seen no old, grey, or lame people in any of the tribes, and surmised that the reason was the cannibalism of the infirm.

A converted cannibal is one who, on Friday, eats only fishermen.

Emily Lotney

Answer: Pacific, Indian, Atlantic, Caribbean, Japan, Mediterranean.

AUGUST 14

Notable Births

1863	Ernest Thayer	1925	Russell Baker
1867	John Galsworthy	1926	Buddy Greco
1924	Maurice Richard	1930	Earl Weaver

Notable Events

1040 Duncan slain by Macbeth
1848 Sale of beer during church hours prohibited in Britain
1851 Earthquake in Italy left 1,000 dead
1901 First airplane flight made by Gustave Whitehead, Bridgeport, Connecticut
1940 Atlantic Charter formulated
1945 United States accepted unconditional surrender from Japan
1962 U.S. mail truck robbery netted $1.5 million, Plymouth, Massachusetts
1972 East German airliner crashed in East Berlin, 156 killed

Question: Can you match the monetary unit with its country?

a) Tugrik	1. Morocco
b) Dirham	2. Malaysia
c) Ringgit	3. Mongolia
d) Kip	4. Laos

Although the stereotypical Englishman is sober and stuffy, historically the English have had a real problem with alcohol. Drunkenness was so bad among the Britons that the Emperor Diocletian had to order the destruction of half the country's vineyards 1,900 years ago. People's fondness for drink continued, however, and during the Dark Ages the English came to have an international reputation. It is recorded that in the year 1000, Kink Sweyne of Denmark heard that Britain's King Ethelred was a "driveller . . . wholly given up to wine." The sober Dane immediately decided to invade the kingdom of the soused monarch. He didn't succeed against the English, but a Norman a few years later did, and his victory was probably owed in part to spiritous factors. The armies of William the Conqueror spent the night before the Battle of Hastings in fasting and prayer, while Harold's men feasted and drank. The Norman forces had a surprisingly easy time the next day battling hung-over Englishmen.

But the conquered English managed to pass on their traditional fondness for liquor to their conquerors. One chronicler on crusade a few hundred years later wrote, "The merchants of the country . . . could hardly credit what they saw was true, that a single people . . . small in number, should consume three times as much bread, and one hundred times as much wine, as that on which many nations of the heathen . . . lived." Centuries later, during the reign of Queen Elizabeth, alcohol had apparently developed outstanding medical qualities. One advertisement for a patent remedy of the era claimed:

> It sloweth age; it strengthens the youth; it helpeth digestion; . . . it abandoneth melancholie; it relisheth the heart; it lighteneth the mind; it quickeneth the spirits; . . . it keeps the hands from shivvering; the sinews from shrinking, the veins from crumbling; the bones from aching.

The sensible, health-conscious Englishman could hardly be expected to resist this. Nor was a prescription needed. A Frenchman describing contemporary England said simply, "As for taverns, London is composed of them."

Temperance measures and movements finally got underway in the 1830s. The consumption of hard liquor had grown enormously in the past few decades, and many Englishmen, although capable of handling vast amounts of ale and beer, were as immoderate with whiskey and rum as the American Indian— with the same disastrous results. Parliament tried to encourage beer drinking instead, and the Beer Act of 1830 was passed. Under this law any householder was permitted to brew and sell malt liquors. It was hoped that this act would aid British agriculture by creating a greater demand for hops and barley for brewing, and that the behavior and economy of the British workingman would be improved by drawing him away from more potent and expensive spirits.

The plan backfired. In 1831, 24,000 new pubs were opened in England, and the number continued to grow to such an extent that, later in the century, there were three pubs for every 100 adult men in the country. Legislator Sidney Smith, who formerly had supported the bill, wrote, "The new Beer Bill has begun its operations. Everybody is drunk. Those who are not singing are sprawling. The sovereign people are in a beastly state."

Private and church temperance societies also fared poorly during the first few years of the movement's existence. When a temperance group in Bradford disbanded, a ranking member explained, "Here there was no want of zeal, talent, or piety . . . and yet in nearly five years, we did not succeed in reforming a single drunkard."

A number of the societies survived, though, and the rolls of people pledged to temperance grew. Joseph Livesley, a cheese merchant, founded the British Teetotal Temperance Society in 1832, and by 1837 it claimed 110,000 members.

One champion of the cause chose to demonstrate the virtues of temperance by personal example. He was E. P. Weston, the Temperance Walker. He toured the world performing amazing feats of endurance, which he insisted he would be incapable of were he a drinker. In an 1875 exhibition at Nottingham, he walked fifty-five miles in twelve hours around a cricket pitch, and then played a half hour's worth of trumpet solos with a local temperance band. Seven years later, Weston walked a world-record five thousand miles in 100 days, forever detailing the benefits of abstinence to anyone who would listen.

During the last twenty years of the century, temperance also became associated with the British suffragette movement. In 1898, the classic *Intemperance and Tight Lacing* appeared. This didactic work warned of the synergistic consequences of mixing corsets and cocktails, and showed how liquor stimulated amorousness, licentiousness, and obscenity. It also explained how tight girdles interfered with the proper circulation of blood below the abdomen, inflaming certain areas of the lower part of the body. This tract concluded by asking its reader, "Do you think our Saviour thinks any more of you for being corseted?"

A woman drove me to drink and I never even had the courtesy to thank her.

W.C. Fields

An Epitaph from Oxfordshire, England

Here lies the body of John Eldred,
At least he will be here when he is dead:
but now at this time he is alive,
The 14th of August sixty five.

Answer: Tugrik - Mongolia; Dirham - Morocco; Ringgit - Malaysia; Kip - Laos.

AUGUST 15

Questions: What part of the refrigerator should you never take in vain?

How long will an eight-day clock go without winding?

There's no evidence that Sir Walter Raleigh ever laid his cloak across a mud puddle for Queen Elizabeth. The incident appears in Walter Scott's novel *Kenilworth*, which is probably its source. Scott was imaginative writer, and given to considerable embellishment of historical fact.

In August 1848, Ford Sanders of Topeka, Kansas, had to be treated at the hospital for injuries inflicted on him by his thirteen-year-old son. He professed he had no idea why the boy all of a sudden attacked him: "I was just going to whip the wife a little when he hit me on the head with a brick."

Why should the Devil have all the good times?

Anonymous

Gross ignorance — 144 times worse than ordinary ignorance.

Bennett Cerf

After Queen Victoria's husband, Prince Albert, died in 1861, she had her servants lay out a fresh suit of his clothes and fill his wash basin with warm water every evening until her own death, nearly forty years later.

Answers: The maker's name.

It won't go at all without winding.

Notable Births

1771	Sir Walter Scott	1898	Lillian Carter
1785	Thomas De Quincy	1904	Bil Baird
1859	Charles Comiskey	1912	Julia Child
1860	Mrs. Warren Harding	1912	Wendy Hiller
1879	Ethel Barrymore	1925	Mike Connors
1887	Edna Ferber	1925	Oscar Peterson
1888	T.E. Lawrence	1931	Janice Rule

Notable Events

309 B.C.	Eclipse recorded in Greece
1057	Macbeth slain by Malcolm
1635	First American hurricane recorded, Plymouth, Massachusetts
1840	Monument to Sir Walter Scott unveiled, Edinburgh
1848	Dental chair patented
1914	First ship passed through Panama Canal
1925	Norway annexed Spitsbergen
1935	Will Rogers and Wiley Post killed in plane crash, Alaska
1940	150 German planes shot down over Britain
1950	Earthquake in Assam, India, 1,500 perished
1971	Nixon established 90-day wage and price controls

A young man who was just getting his business started was being given some advice by an old friend of the family, himself a successful and wealthy businessman. "And remember," the gentleman told him, "that honesty is always the best policy."

The new merchant said he'd remember that, and practice it faithfully.

As they shook hands on leaving, the older man added, "And you might want read up on business law. You'd be surprised what can be done in a businesslike way and still be honest."

Ethics stays in the prefaces of the average business science book.

Peter Drucker

It's queer the way the likes of me do be telling the truth, and the wise are lying all the times.

J.M. Synge

Tharnmidsbe L. Praghustspondgifeem (né Edward L. Hayes) petitioned the courts in San Francisco in the summer of 1944 to change his name once again, because he'd come up with a new set of syllables that he considered were "good omen" sounds, more propitious than the ones in his present name. He wanted the new legal name "Miswaldpornghuestficset Balstemdrignshofwintplausjof Wrandvaistplondqeskycrufemgeish." Three years later, perhaps inspired by M.B.W. (I wouldn't put you through that again), a fellow named Miswald Cends Wrandvakist said his name was *un*lucky, despite its similarity to M.B.W.'s, and wanted to change it to Linkols Dislgrowels Wrandvausgilmokets.

Take heart! Did you know there are something like six hundred thousand John Smiths in this country.?

The force exerted on a flea's body when it leaps is about 150 Gs, and it goes from 0 to 100 cm per second in less than .002 seconds. That's about the same G-force a human would receive from crashing directly into a brick wall at 200 mph.

Notable Births

1861	Edith Roosevelt	1928	Ann Blyth
1862	Amos Alonzo Stagg	1930	Frank Gifford
1868	Bernarr Macfadden	1931	Eydie Gorme

Notable Events

1780	American force defeated at Camden
1812	British captured Detroit
1829	Cheng and Eng arrived in Boston
1945	Marshall Petain found guilty of treason
1955	Fiat Motors ordered first private atomic reactor
1978	Xerox fined $25.6 million for excluding SCM from copier market

Question: What's the Canadian Province shown here?

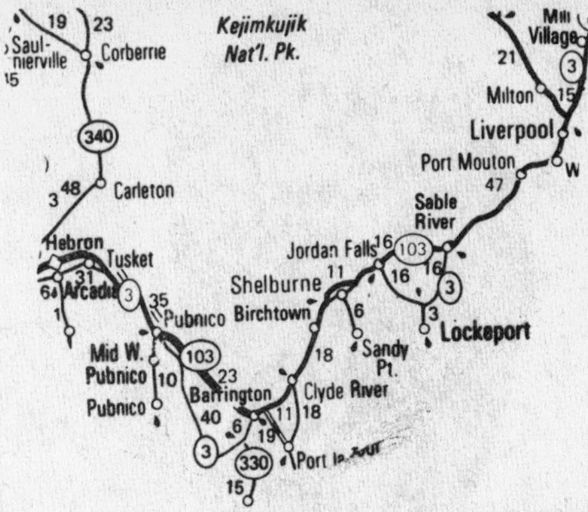

The jig was up for New York lawyer Joseph Feldman when firemen made a routine inspection of his apartment after a blaze in a downstairs business several years ago. The men in red found Feldman's lodgings packed to the brim with some fifteen thousand books, most of which were the property of the New York Public Library.

When authorities questioned him, Feldman explained that he liked to read. It turned out he didn't even have a library card.

On August 16, 1965, at a small social service organization summer camp (which shall remain nameless) the scheduled evening activity was a snipe hunt. For those unfamiliar with this traditional camp diversion, youngsters are given a paper or burlap bag and sent out into the woods with a variety of ludicrous instructions for catching snipe; which, though they are real birds, are either not native to the area, or are certainly not capturable by children. The hunt is usually conducted late in the camping season and serves to make complete fools of the kids, which in turn affords their counselors an ego boost sufficient to get them through the last few weeks of summer.

On this particular safari, eighty-five campers entered the woods at seven in the evening, but only seventy-eight returned to camp when the bugler blazed the "call to quarters." The missing seven were discovered the next day, pecked to death by irate snipe!

A lot of parents pack up their troubles and send them to summer camp.

Raymond Duncan

The Colorado Supreme Court recently ordered a man to pay a (former) friend $24,600 because he lost to him at golf. Apparently, it started out as a friendly but rather heavy wager, and Lloyd Hammer must have had a really bad day on the links. By the time the round was over, he owed the $24,600 to his opponent, Federick Berckfeldt. Hammer refused to pay, so the other man sued. The state's highest court ruled that, even though gambling is illegal in Colorado, the match came under the term "bona fide social relationship," and thus was out of the purview of the law.

It's not dramatic enough for the plot of *The China Syndrome — Part II*, but it's true: the cooling system of a nuclear reactor at the University of Florida used to malfunction whenever a toilet was flushed in the building. There was a sign that asked people not to flush the john when the reactor was running, but between 1975 and 1977 the reactor had to be shut down five times when someone pulled the chain at the wrong time.

The Atomic Age is here to stay — but are we?

Bennett Cerf

In August 1940, forty-five dozen socks which had been stolen from a salesman's car were found scattered over several acres of fields in New York State. The thief who dumped them there discovered too late that no two of the 540 socks formed a pair.

America is the country where you buy a lifetime supply of aspirin for one dollar, and use it up in two weeks.

John Barrymore

In 1497, a giant pike was caught in Mannheim, Germany, which had been tagged with a metal plate bearing this inscription (in Greek): "I am the first fish that was put in this pond by the hands of Frederick the Second, on the third day of October, 1262." In 235 years, the fish had grown from a fingerling to a mature fish weighing 350 pounds and stretching nineteen feet from head to tail. This was the first successful fish-tagging in history.

Answer: Nova Scotia.

AUGUST 17

Question: What are the five largest islands in the world?

Have you ever wondered why the cuffs of men's coats have buttons on them? Centuries ago, it was a custom among the troops of the British armed forces to use their sleeves as napkins and handkerchiefs. This sometimes made for a less than natty appearance at parade time. Some martinet had the brilliant idea of sewing metal buttons on the cuffs to discourage these practices, and the buttons have been there ever since.

Answer: Greenland, New Guinea, Borneo, Madagascar, Baffin.

Notable Births

1786	Davy Crockett	1893	Mae West
1888	Monty Woolly	1921	Maureen O'Hara

Notable Events

1786	Death of Frederick the Great of Prussia
1807	Fulton completed first steamboat run, New York City to Albany
1815	Napoleon arrived at Saint Helena for beginning of exile
1835	Gold discovered in Klondike
1930	Air endurance record of 647 hours set over Saint Louis
1969	Hurricane Camille killed 258 in Mississippi and Alabama
1976	Philippines earthquake took 8,000 lives

Some prospectors did get rich — very rich — out of the Klondike gold rush, but proportionately far more enterpreneurs made far more than the miners. Jack London sometimes made over a thousand dollars a day ferrying would-be tycoons up a set of rapids in the Yukon River — the gold fever was so hectic that many paid him exhorbitant sums just to save the few hours extra the normal portage route would have taken. In the first winter of the big rush in Whitehorse, the grocer set the pace: food was so scarce that a single chicken egg went for as much as five dollars — no checks, sir; gold if you please.

One of the greatest opportunists in the stampede for gold was the telegraph operator in Skagway, the jumping-off point for the White Pass Trail into the Klondike gold fields. His name was Soapy Smith. For five dollars, Soapy would send out a wire to anywhere in the United States or Canada, and he'd usually have an answer back in a few hours, for five dollars, collect. This meant a lot to men who might not have seen their families for several months as they traveled to the Yukon.

Smith was brilliant. At the time, Skagway had no telegraph connections to anywhere.

In his private heart no man much respects himself.

Mark Twain

Ancient peoples looking for gold used to toss loosened earth in the air and let the wind blow away the worthless soil, while the heavier gold flakes and dust remaining behind, much in the way that grain is winnowed. Ground was also loosened and sifted in a similar manner when they looked for precious stones. Our word "analyze", comes from this process. The Greek words *ana*, "up" and *lyo*, "to loosen", make up the word.

In the summer of 1972, it was discovered that all the seventy-two panes of one-way glass in the bathroom windows of a Greenfield, Massachusetts, housing project had been installed backward.

A doctor can bury his mistakes, but an architect can only advise his client to plant vines.

Frank Lloyd Wright

My mistake was buying stock in the company. Now I worry about the lousy work I'm turning out.

Marvin Townsend

Notable Births

1587	Virginia Dare	1927	Rosalynn Carter
1834	Marshall Field	1933	Roman Polanski
1893	Burleigh Grimes	1934	Roberto Clemente
1922	Alain Robbe-Grillet	1935	Rafer Johnson
1922	Shelley Winters	1937	Robert Redford

Notable Events

1777	Battle of Bennington
1834	Mount Vesuvius erupted
1892	Gladstone began fourth ministry
1944	Dunbarton Oaks Conference opened, led to formation of United Nations
1947	Cadiz, Spain, munitions explosion killed 400
1951	Hurricane in Caribbean left 260 dead
1953	Mossedegh overthrown in Iran by Shah and CIA
1955	Hurrican Diane hit East Coast, left 400 dead
1976	Two U.S. officers killed by ax-wielding North Koreans in Border incident

Questions: What's the easiest thing for a miser to part with?

Why is a greedy man like a fellow with a short memory?

Remember Virginia Dare, the first English child born in North America? She was born on this day in 1587, at the Roanoke colony founded that year under Sir Walter Raleigh's charter by John White and a hundred or so settlers. You may associate the mysterious word "Croatoan" with this colonization attempt, too.

White soon found that it was necessary for him to return to England to procure tools and equipment the colonists needed to survive, and in 1588 he took a skeleton crew of fifteen sailors and headed back across the sea. He left instructions for the settlers to leave their destination in a conspicuous place if they had to move, or if they were taken away by hostile Indians or other European explorers.

When White returned from England in 1590, he found the colony deserted and the fort ransacked. The only clue was the word "Croatoan" carved into a post of the fort. He guessed that the colonists had moved voluntarily, despite the condition of the fortress, since Croatoan was the name of an island to the south inhabited by friendly Hatteras Indians. Other hostile natives had probably destroyed the fort after the colonists had left, as there were no signs of carnage. But for some reason, White was unable to search for them at the time, and for 20 years the whereabouts of the settlers remained a mystery.

Then, late in the eighteenth century, settlers on the Lumber River in North Carolina came upon a tribe of light-skinned, grey-eyed Indians whose language was a strange kind of English, and who said their ancestors could "talk in a book." It was even surprising that some of these Lumber Indians had blue eyes and blondish hair — and among their surnames were forty-one of the ninety-five names of the Roanoke colonists.

Many historians today believe that the colonists were either taken by the Hatteras to Croatoan or went to them for help. There, isolated from the later white explorers and settlers, they intermarried with the Hatteras and migrated to the mainland in about 1650.

Two pithy epitaphs from unknown places:

He lived and died a true christian,
He loved his friends and hated his enemies.

The manner of her death was thus:
She was druv over by a bus.

Caesar salad has nothing to do with any of the Caesars. It was first concocted in a bar in Tiajuana, Mexico, in the 1920s.

Answers: His comb.

Both are always for-geting.

AUGUST 19

Question: Can you match the traditional gift with wedding anniversary?

a Bronze — *1* 13th
b Lace — *2* 15th
c Leather — *3* 8th
d Crystal — *4* 3rd

Planned obsolescence isn't just the recent invention of automobile and appliance manufacturers. It's been around for a long time. Manufacturers for thousands of years have known that they can't afford to make something so well that it won't wear out or break eventually. It's bad business. Those who don't appreciate this have often found out soon enough, and sometimes the hard way. Take this example from the reign of Tiberius:

The time is about 34 A.D. The Roman Empire and its citizens are enjoying prosperity, growth, and influence greater than any that has been known in the world up to this time. Manufacturers and merchants become wealthy men. Trade flourishes — the king of distant Ceylon boasts that he has a complete collection of Roman coins. The last thing Rome needs is for a wrench (not yet invented) to be thrown into this well-oiled mercantile machinery.

A common artisan, a glassblower, seeks an audience with Tiberius. Normally the emperor is too busy and important a man to bother with a mere tradesman, but this fellow intrigues him. He says he has found a way to blow unbreakable glass, and Tiberius has heard from reliable source that this is indeed so. The emperor must see this wonderful thing for himself, and an appointment is made.

The artisan brings the emperor a sample of his wares, which Tiberius duly examines. The goblets and cups are indeed glass, thin-walled, and well made. After this inspection, the glassblower takes a few of the pieces and smashes them into the tile floor and stone walls of the chamber. None of them shatter. He invites Tiberius to do the same, so he won't be suspected of tricking him. Tiberius hurls glasses, goblets, and flasks everywhere, and some dent, but not one cracks or breaks. The glassblower then retrieves them and hammers out the dents with a mallet, as if they had been made of tin or bronze. Tiberius is astonished, and the inventor muses silently on his rich and leisurely future.

Tiberius asks the craftsman if any other people know how to make glass like this. No, he replies, he is the only one. The emperor calls in his guards and orders the man beheaded immediately.

The process has never been duplicated.

Planned obsolescence is another word for progress.
James Jeffrey Roche

A young Rhode Islander named Martin Dalton was convicted of murder in 1898 and sentenced to life imprisonment. When he was offered a pardon in 1930 he refused it, explaining that he no longer had a family, nothing to do, and nowhere to go. He remained in prison until his death in 1960. During the last sixty-one years of his confinement he didn't have a single visitor, and the last letter he received came to him in 1939.

When I see the* Ten Most Wanted Lists . . . *I always have this thought: If we'd made them feel wanted earlier, they wouldn't be wanted now.
Eddie Cantor

Notable Births

1785	Seth Thomas	1903	James Gould Cozzens
1870	Bernard Baruch	1915	Ring Lardner, Jr.
1871	Orville Wright	1919	Malcolm Forbes
1892	Alfred Lunt	1931	Willie Shoemaker
1902	Ogden Nash	1940	Jill Saint John

Notable Events

14	Accession of Tiberius
1601	Michail of Wallachia murdered by Hungarians
1604	Peace concluded between England and Spain
1772	Revolution in Sweden backed by France
1948	Alger Hiss refused to take lie detector test
1960	USSR orbited two dogs
1961	Francis Gary Powers sentenced to ten years in U-2 incident
1966	Earthquake in Turkey left 2,520 dead

An Epitaph from Maine

Sacred to the memory of James H. R   m, who died Aug. the 6th, 1800. His widow who mourns as one who can be comforted, aged 24, and possessing every qualification for a good wife, lives at   street, in this village.

The mantelpiece above a fireplace got its name because it was originally just a board with pegs on it from which wet mantles or other clothing would be hung to dry.

Answer: a-3, b-1, c-4, d-2.

AUGUST 20

Question: What are the five highest peaks in the United States?

Notable Births

1591	Robert Herrick	1886	Paul Tillich
1625	Thomas Corneille	1890	H.P. Lovecraft
1785	Oliver Hazard Perry	1916	Van Johnson
1833	Benjamin Harrison	1921	Jacqueline Susann
1881	Edgar Guest	1942	Isaac Hayes

Notable Events

1910 J.E. Fickel fired first gun from airplane, over Long Island
1915 Italy declared war on Turkey
1939 Johnny Weissmuller married Beryl Scott
1940 Trotsky assassinated in Mexico
1964 Queen Hope (Cook) of Sikkim arrived in New York to visit World's Fair
1968 Warsaw Pact nations invaded Czechoslovakia

A little after the Civil War, up in the Walla Walla Valley of Washington, a gentleman called "Doc" Baker figured that what was needed to make the area a growing concern was a railroad. He talked to some of his friends about the idea and they decided it was feasible except for one thing: money. It wasn't *simply* money, really, it was a combination of problems that only an ample money supply would cure. Here's more or less what happened.

Baker and his associates carefully figured out their needs and assets, and discovered that they could afford two locomotives, but very little else: no iron rails, no real railroad cars, no tribute. The tribute was needed for the Chinook Indians. In order to get the locomotives to Walla Walla, they would have to go through Chinook Territory, and the Chinooks had a thriving little mafia going at Wishram Rapids, on the Columbia River. There, goods had to be portaged to a barge upstream, and, in addition to collecting a passage toll, the Indians were the only available labor, so they charged what the market would bear. Baker knew that the Indians would want an exhorbitant amount of money to move two locomotives, more than he and his partners could afford to pay.

But he had a plan. Along with the locomotives and 100 pair of train wheels, Baker ordered one thousand silk hats. It seemed a Chinook named Seekolicks had befriended him at one time, and Baker had made him the gift of a fancy set of clothes and a fine top hat. The other young men of the tribe were intensely jealous of the effect this had had on the young women. Once the barge reached Wishram, Baker promised each man who helped him a fine top hat. He was deluged with applicants, and had the engines and the other material up river in short order.

In due course, the barges reached the Walla Walla Valley, where Baker had taken care of the dual problem of no cars and no rails with a single solution: wood. Timber was plentiful in the region, and the railroad men had taken the money which would have purchased "very little else" and used it to build wooden rails and a whole fleet of wooden rail cars. An ox team pulled the locomotives to the terminus (supervised by an engineer on a donkey), the cars were mounted on the wheels, and the railroad was born. It was an immediate success, and the area's economy boomed.

Still, there were some other problems. The economic lifeblood of the valley was cattle, and a railroad that killed too many cattle on its tracks wouldn't last long. The train dispatcher at Wallula provided a brilliant solution. He told the owners of the railroad to take the cowcatchers off, since they served to protect the locomotives from the cows rather than vice versa, and to put platforms in their place. Two dogs, Ponto and Thor by name, were taught to ride the platforms and to jump off and chase away any cows they spotted near the tracks. These dogs performed their work so admirably that the Walla Walla Railroad paid fewer claims for killed livestock than any other railroad of its size in the world, despite the fact that it ran almost entirely through unfenced range land.

The other problem was that the locomotives' treads and flanges chewed up the wooden rails rapidly, and they had to be continually replaced. Fortunately, Doc Baker was aware of the marvelous qualities of good old rawhide. Called the "Cowboy's Metal," it was so durable that Baker ordered the rails covered with it. After a few rains and the baking of the summer sun, it became as sturdy as steel and served the road well for many years. Later on, Baker's use of rawhide would have amazing consequences, though at the time he had no inkling of its great future.

Sometime in the 1880s the Pacific Northwest was hit by the most severe winter in memory. The railroad had to cease normal operations early and the last shipments of feed for the animals could not be transported. The severe weather continued, and the cattlemen soon used up all their fodder. There was nothing left for them to do but turn their herds out to forage as best they could on the grasses beneath the snow. Things got so bad that even the wolves in the mountains began to hunt in packs, an extremely unusual thing. Once they'd wiped out the deer population they moved to the valleys and began to devour the carcasses of beef littering the flatlands. Still the weather raged, and the wolves moved ever closer to the settlements.

The population of Walla Walla and the other little towns grew increasingly alarmed. Evacuation was impossible, so they hoarded their stores, boarded their windows, and readied their weapons.

Suddenly one night, in the middle of yet another vicious storm, Seekolicks and a companion appeared at Doc Baker's door. He let them in, and immediately the half-frozen Indians threw themselves before the fire. Excitedly, in a mixture of Chinook and English, they tried to tell him something crucially important. All Baker could understand was the single word "Wolves!" He was terrified.

Then Seekolicks explained further: "Railroad — him gonum hell. Damn wolves digum out — eatum all up — Wallula to Walla Walla!"

Over the next week there was a remarkable thaw, and the wolves returned to the hills. The communities of central Washington recovered. This time they put iron strips atop the wooden rails, which lasted until another railroad bought up the WWRR and incorporated it into their line, replacing its unique rails with their own more conventional ones.

Answer: Mount McKinley, Mount Saint Elias, Mount Foraker, Mount Bona, Mount Blackburn.

AUGUST 21

Questions: Why is a marine painter like a ship?

Why do architects make good actors?

Notable Births

1561	James (The Admirable) Crichton	1906	Count Basie
1872	Aubrey Beardsley	1936	Wilt Chamberlain
		1946	Patty McCormack

Notable Events

1492	Columbus set sail on first New World voyage
1841	Venetian blinds patented
1857	Charter Oak blown down in Hartford storm
1858	First Lincoln-Douglas debate
1897	"Yes, Virginia, There Is a Santa Claus" published
1908	Prussian universities agreed to admit women
1912	A.R. Eldred became first Eagle Scout
1935	Senate voted neutrality on Ethiopian situation
1941	Siege of Leningrad began
1961	Goya's *Duke of Wellington* stolen from National Gallery
1963	Martial law declared in Vietnam
1964	Bolivia broke diplomatic relations with Cuba

The term "gigolo" comes from Venice. At the end of the seventeenth century, styles called for increasingly higher heels for women. The situation became so extreme that women's shoes were more stilts than footwear, and walking, even standing, was nearly impossible without assistance. Fashionable ladies were forced to hire lackeys to accompany them wherever they went. These escorts were called *cicisbeos*, Italian for cavalier servants. In time, *cicisbeo* became "gigolo" in English, and came to mean the professed gallant of a married woman.

High heels were invented by a woman who had been kissed on the forehead.

Christopher Morley

Some Iraqi peasants make their rather drab farms a little more colorful by painting their animals. They do this according to a strict color code designed to insure that an animal is safe from evil spirits and pleasing to the good ones. Chickens are tinted green, calves' faces are done in royal purple, and the top part of the cows' udders are bright red. Beef cattle are the most precious of all animals and have their genital areas painted a striking blue.

Members of the Indian tribe known as the Saival are forbidden to marry anyone who cannot prove his or her ancestors have been vegetarians for over four thousand years.

Answers: Because he draws so much water.

They're good at drawing large houses.

King Richard II of England had a law passed requiring all the women in his country to ride horses sidesaddle, because his first wife, Anna of Bohemia, had a deformity that prevented her riding astride.

Among the many other interesting things that Richard did during his reign was to marry his second wife, Princess Isabella of France, when she was seven.

AUGUST 22

Notable Births

1862	Claude Debussy	1929	Honor Blackman
1891	Jacques Lipchitz	1939	Carl Yastremzski
1893	Dorothy Parker	1940	Valerie Harper

Notable Events

1654 First Jew arrived in America, Jacob Barsimson
1771 First Dwarf exhibited in America, Boston
1851 First America's Cun race held, *America* defeated *Aurora*
1865 Liquid soap patented
1910 Japan annexed Korea
1911 Mona Lisa stolen from the Louvre
1927 Sacco and Vanzetti executed
1964 CIA official announced victory in Vietnam "doubtful"

Question: Within ten years, when were the following invented?
iron plow
sewing machine (early)
rifle
refrigerator

On this date in 1911, the Mona Lisa was stolen from the Louvre in Paris. It was recovered in Florence two years later, and returned to the French museum. In 1935, five different Americans were convinced that the recovered painting was a forgery, and each paid an average of $300,000 for the "original" work of art — but only the canvas in the Louvre has da Vinci's fingerprints.

Speaking of art forgeries, Dr. George de Cornell, former director of the Fine Arts Guild of America, once pointed out that "of three thousand Corots, eight thousand are in the United States and England — only Corot never painted three thousand pictures."

This is either a forgery or a damn clever original!
Frank Sullivan

United States Marines, take note: There's such a thing as a sergeant fish. It's called that because it's big, hungry, nasty, has stripes down its side, and a big mouth.

There's enough fat for seven bars of soap, enough lime to whitewash a small shed, enough phosphorous for 2,200 matches, and enough iron to make a nail — all in the human body.

Be you a fan of Rod McKuen or a detractor, the fact remains: That poet's syrupy verse has earned him more than the poets Yeats, Eliot, and Frost made together during their lifetimes.

Answer: 1784, 1790, 1520, 1858.

AUGUST 23

Question: Within ten years, when were the following invented?

steam engine
slide rule
circular saw
revolver

Notable Births

1754	Louis XVI	1868	Edgar Lee Masters
1769	George Cuvier	1912	Gene Kelly

Notable Events

1839	Hong Kong taken by British
1904	Automobile tire chain patented
1930	Bodies of 1896 North Pole balloonists found
1958	China began bombardment of Quemoy
1966	Red Guard movement initiated in China
1975	Pathet Lao completed takeover in Laos

In 1952, New York State had 13,000 miles of paved roads. If all the cars and trucks registered in the state that year had been taken from their driveways and placed on the roads bumper to bumper, they would have stretched 14,000 miles.

The so-called Opium War of 1838-42 between Britain and China was just that: a war over opium. Don't get the idea that the conflict resulted from the British trying to curb drug use by the Chinese — the British were the pushers.

The idea of marketing opium in China belonged to the noble British East India Company. Until about 1794 it was a half-hearted and half-successful effort, but then things started to boom. Opium volume continued to grow during the next few decades, and in 1821 the British appropriated Lintin Island at the mouth of the Canton River for use as a smuggling headquarters. At this time, traders were sending out about seven thousand chests annually, for the equivalent of a few hundred dollars a chest.

The Chinese government became frantic. It pleaded with British representatives to stem the tide of the trade in the illegal drug, but there was too much money in it for the British. In 1834, the Chinese emperor called for the public execution of traffickers and users. Even that didn't help the situation. Finally, in 1838, the Chinese government seized about a half year's import of opium — some twenty thousand chests with a "street" value of over twelve million dollars.

That pushed the pushers too far. It wasn't much of a war by contemporary British standards, and they eventually settled with the emperor for the district of Canton, which includes the port of Hong Kong. Once there, the first significant act of government was to legalize the opium trade. In the first year they made the equivalent of thirty-two million pounds. Between the early decades and the middle of the nineteenth century, the British did millions and millions of pounds of drug deals in China, and the money was worth a lot more then than it is now.

Beauty of poppy conceals sting of death.

Charlie Chan

First war profiteer like early bird — look for big fat worm.

Charlie Chan

We are the first race in the world, and the more of the world we inherit the better it is for the human race.

Cecil Rhodes

A widow in Portsmouth, England, caused the following lines to be placed on the tombstone of her husband:

Here lies Jemmy Little, a carpenter, industrious,
A very good natured man but somewhat blusterous.
When that his little wife his authority withstood,
He took a little stick and bang'd her as he would.
His wife now left alone, her loss does so deplore,
She wishes Jemmy back to bang her a little more;
For now he's dead and gone this fault appears so small,
A little thing would make her think it was not fault at all.

Answer: 1628, 1620, 1777, 1835.

Notable Births

1759	William Wilberforce	1889	Jorge Luis Borges
1872	Max Beerbohm	1898	Malcolm Cowley

Notable Events

79	Mount Vesuvius erupted, buried Pompeii
410	Alaric sacked Rome
1572	Saint Bartholomew's Day Massacre in Paris
1869	Waffle iron patented
1891	Edison applied for motion-picture camera patent, granted 1897
1939	Hitler and Stalin agreed to 10-year nonaggression pact
1944	Allies liberated Paris
1954	Communist party outlawed in United States
1960	Bus plunged into river, Turvo, Brazil, 60 dead
1964	American Nazis demonstrated in Atlantic City, New Jersey

Questions: Why is it allowed to pick the pocket of someone who owns an art gallery?

Is there something some men with a camera will never take?

As the Roman governor of Sicily, Caius Verrus was responsible for maintaining a strong navy to protect merchant vessels and coastal villages against Mediterranean pirates. But Caius had a taste for wine and women, and was also as corrupt as any other politician. It is not surprising, then, that the Sicilian naval force was so ineffectual. Word eventually reached Rome of the condition of the Sicilian navy, and Caius was instructed to get his act together. Piqued, he proceeded to order an attack against a pirate enclave, which, to no one's surprise, failed miserably.

But Caius was not one to pass over *any* opportunity. Because they lost the skirmish, he ordered all the captains to be executed. To make a little money on the side, he charged the families admission before allowing them to see the condemned men. He also extracted huge bribes from the grieving families by promising to have their sons, husbands, and fathers killed mercifully—for certain monetary considerations of course.

Caius was finally brought to trial, and the famous Cicero was the prosecuting attorney. When Caius saw how things were going in court, he tucked a bundle of booty under his arm and skipped town. He was never formally brought to justice.

Be yourself *is the worst advice you can give to some people.*
Tom Masson

On August 23, 1572, King Charles IX of France was incredibly angry. His sister had married a Protestant, of all things. His mother, Catherine de Medici was incensed, too. The assassination of a leading Protestant, Admiral Coligny, which she had personally arranged, had failed the day before.

Their joint anger and frustration came together the next day (August 24) in the form of the Saint Bartholomew's Massacre. Over ten thousand Protestants were dispatched overnight, and Charles bragged in his report to the pope that he had personally killed many of them.

The pope was overjoyed. He ordered a *Te Deum* to be sung in honor of the event, and later issued a bull calling for the entire Catholic population of France to celebrate itself and its good works the following December.

It is the test of a good religion if you can joke about it.
G.K. Chesterton

In the funeral industry, retail markups on caskets often range from 400 to 900 percent (substantially more than on vacuum cleaners sold door to door). The highest markups are generally on the cheapest, worst-looking coffins. This tends to make the customer purchase a more expensive casket, on which the gross profit for the funeral director is much higher.

Funeral pomp is less concerned with the honor due the dead than with the vanity of the living.
La Rochefoucauld

Piston-cylinder hand pumper fire engines aren't that recent an invention. They date back to at least the second century A.D. Early ones had hoses made of oxen intestines.

When Malcolm Cowley, the poet and critic, was first asked to give information about himself for *Who's Who*, he felt embarrassed because he wasn't a member of any prestigious organization, so he made himself a member of the Bibliophage's Club. Twenty years later, after his membership in that fictitious fraternity had been listed in every edition of *Who's Who* since 1932, he told the editors about his small deception. The amused publishers have allowed the listing of the nonexistent organization to remain in every subsequent volume, and it is perhaps the only canard (except for that of F. Donald Coster) to have escaped their watchful eyes in over eighty years.

Answers: Because he had pict-ures.
Yes — a hint.

AUGUST 25

Question: What are the nicknames of the following states?
California
Hawaii
Iowa
Maine

Notable Births

1836	Bret Harte	1917	Don DeFore
1850	Bill Nye	1918	Leonard Bernstein
1884	Will Cuppy	1919	George Wallace
1909	Ruby Keeler	1921	Brian Moore
1909	Michael Rennie	1927	Althea Gibson
1913	Walt Kelly	1930	Sean Connery

Notable Events

1770 Suicide of Thomas Chatterton
1814 British invaded Washington and burned Capitol
1830 Tom Thumb railroad lost race to horse-drawn vehicle
1930 Pilsudski ministry formed in Poland
1939 Britain voted war powers to Parliament
1940 First parachute wedding performed, New York City
1966 George Lincoln Rockwell assassinated, Arlington, Virginia
1969 Floods in western Virginia took 189 lives

Yes, Virginia, there was a John Henry, and yes, he was a steel-driving man. He worked for the Chesapeake and Ohio Railroad, pounding steel drills to make holes for explosives in the laying out of new roadbeds.

His hammer was mounted at the end of a unique handle made of a special wood, which was only half-an-inch thick. Greased with tallow to make it even more flexible, it was so limber that when Henry held it out straight, the heavy end of the sledge dipped at a forty-degree angle, and he used it like a whip when he pounded. Standing nearly six feet behind the drill, he'd start his stroke behind him with the hammer head down below his knees, then in a lightning-quick stroke, bring it over his head and onto the tap. When he felt like it (usually for an audience, and he'd often draw hundreds of spectators), he could swing two hammers, one with each arm, all the ten-hour-workday long, and hardly break a sweat.

The rest of his story is a little less clear, but it is documented well enough for us to know he did indeed face off against a steam engine, and that he won the contest. It took place in about 1870, either in or near the Big Bend Tunnel on the C & O road. The Big Bend was the longest tunnel excavation ever attempted up to that date, a mile and a quarter through a West Virginia mountain, and the C & O had bought a new steam driver for the project. When it arrived, a match between it and the thirty-four-year-old John Henry was a natural. Henry was to get $100 if he won; if not, it was expected that he would permanently withdraw his boast that he could outwork any machine.

The battle lasted thirty-five minutes, and when it was over, John Henry, swinging two *twenty* pound hammers for the occasion, had drilled two holes seven feet deep. The engine had driven only one, nine feet deep.

Accounts of what happened next differ. One says that he went home to his wife complaining of a headache, ate sparingly at dinner, went to bed, and died in his sleep of a brain hemorrhage. The other story reports that he showed no ill effects from the ordeal, but was killed in a cave-in a short time later.

In an economy drive during the 1930s, forty people with adding machines were replaced in the Polish Treasury department by a prodigious mathematician and memorizer, Dr. Salo Finkelstein, of Warsaw. He worked for the treasury for five years, and not a single mistake has ever been found in the figures he produced, though he did all the calculations in his head.

When we got into office, the thing that surprised me most was to find that things were just as bad as we'd been saying they were.

John F. Kennedy

If you believe that the saying, "Still water runs deep," holds true, you're absolutely wrong. When was the last time you saw still water run, deep or shallow?

George Lumley, aged 104, married Mary Dunning, aged 10, in Nortallerton, England on August 25, 1783. She was the great-great-granddaughter of the woman who'd broken her engagement to Lumley, eighty years before.

Patience — a minor form of despair disguised as a virtue.

Ambrose Bierce

A man is only as old as the woman he feels.

Groucho Marx

Answer: Golden State, Aloha State, Hawkeye State, Pine Tree State.

AUGUST 26

Notable Births

1819	Prince Albert	1901	Maxwell Taylor
1838	John Wilkes Booth	1904	Christopher Isherwood
1880	Guillaume Apollinaire	1921	Benjamin Bradlee

Notable Events

1619	Ferdinand of Bohemia deposed
1847	Liberian independence
1873	First U.S. kindergarten established
1883	Krakatoa exploded, 36,000 dead
1893	British East Africa Equatorial Railroad established
1920	Women's suffrage amendment effective
1933	Rioting in Havana left 26 dead
1961	Buddhism made state religion in Burma
1978	CAB allowed 50-70 percent reductions in airline fares

Questions: What's black and white and red?

Why did the man take hay to bed?

Falcon Island, an atoll situated some two thousand miles east of Australia, has had a volatile career as islands go. It wasn't discovered until 1865, probably because it wasn't there. The island is at the mercy of the "Ring of Fire," the Pacific's earthquake and volcanic activity, and it comes and goes according to whatever geological forces are currently working on it.

It was reported to have disappeared in 1877, then reappeared in 1884, sank on April 14,1894, reappeared later that year, and sank again the following year. Up in 1900, down in 1913, and up again in 1926. Where it's situated today is anybody's guess. So far, its maximum dimensions have been a square mile in area and 530 feet in elevation.

Hey! Buddy! Wanna buy some real estate, cheap?

There is a water plant native to British Guinea called *Victoria regia.* It resembles a huge lily pad, grows as large as four feet in diameter, and is so sturdy that a six-year-old child can sit on it without sinking.

To prove his point that the electoral process was not foolproof, and the voters were careless, the Democratic mayor of Milton, Washington, managed to get a mule named Boston Curtis on the town's election ballot in 1938. The mule was elected as a Republican committeeman by fifty-one votes.

Here is random selection of some advertisements from English newspapers of 1664-1690:

Whereas John Pippin, whose grandfather, father, and himself have been for above 190 years past famous throughout all England for curing the rupture, making the most easie trusses of all sorts, both for men, women, and children, being lately deceased; This is to certifie to all persons that Eleanor Pippin, the widow, who in his lifetime made all the trusses that he sold, lives still at "The Three Naked Boys," near the Strand Bridge, where she makes all manner of trusses. She also hath a gentleman to assist her the fitting of them upon men, he being intrusted by the said John Pippin in his lifetime.

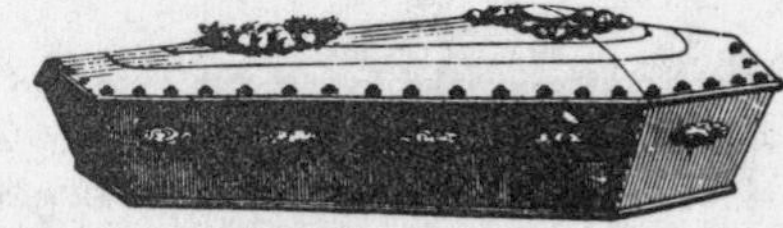

At the sign of "The Golden Pall and Coffin", a coffinmakers shop, at the upper end of the Old Change, near Cheapside, there are ready made to be sold, very fashionable laced and plain dressings for the dead of all sizes, with very fashionable coffins, that will secure any corps above ground without any ill scent or other annoyance as long as shall be required.

One Robert Taylor, a dancing-master, being in company of several neighbours in Covent Garden on Monday night last, about 10 of the clock, upon the occasion of some three words, killed one Mr. Price, of the same place, at the "Three Tuns" Tavern, in Shandois Street. The said R. Taylor is a person of middle stature, hath a cut across his chin, a scar in his left cheek, having two fingers and a thumb of one hand burnt at the ends shorter than the other, round visaged, thick lipt, his own hair being of a light brown under a periwig; he lived in James Street, in Covent Garden. Whoever apprehends him, and gives notice thereof to Mr. Reynolds, bookseller, in Henrietta Street, Covent Garden, shall have 10 pounds reward. And whereas it was printed in last week's *Intelligence* that he was taken, you are to notice that it is most notoriously false.

At Tobias' Coffee-house, in Pye Corner, is sold the right drink, called Dr. Butler's Ale, it being the same that was sold by Mr. Lansdale in Newgate Market. It is an excellent stomack drink, it helps digestion, expels wind, and disolves congealed phlegm upon the lungs, and is therefore good against colds, coughs, ptisical and consumptive distempers; and being drunk in the evening, it moderately fortifies nature, causeth good rest, and hugely corroborates the brain and memory.

At the "Miter," near the west end of St. Pauls, is to be seen a rare collection of curiosityes, much resorted to, and admired by persons of great learning and quality; amongst which a choyce *Egyptian Mummy,* with hieroglyphics; the *Ant-Beare* of Brazil; a *Remora*; a *Torpedo*; the huge *Thigh-bone of a Gyant*; a *Moon Fish;* a *Tropick-bird,* &c.

Answers: A skunk with a heat rash.

To feed his nightmares.

AUGUST 27

Questions: In what room of a house is a burglar most likely to be interested?

When is a man in jail most like a boat?

Notable Births

551 B.C.	Confucius	1899	C.S. Forester
1770	George Hegel	1908	Lyndon Johnson
1871	Theodore Dreiser	1916	Martha Raye
1882	Samuel Goldwyn	1929	Ira Levin
1890	Man Ray	1943	Tuesday Weld

Notable Events

1618	Five Articles of Perth created
1783	First hydrogen balloon flight, Paris
1788	Recall of Necker to office in France
1791	Austria and Prussia mobilized to attack France
1859	Edwin Drake drilled first oil well, Titusville, Pennsylvania
1932	First public loop-the-loop in an autogyro performed
1964	Gracie Allen died
1966	Francis Chichester began solo circumnavigation in *Gypsy Moth IV*

Samuel Goldwyn's genius did not always extend itself to other fields besides the movies, and there are hordes of stories about him still circulating in Hollywood. When Radclyffe Hall's sensational (at the time) novel, *The Well of Loneliness*, was published in 1928, Goldwyn took note of its enormous sales and expressed an interest in the movie rights. "You can't film that," he was told by his advisors, "it's about lesbians."

"So, all right," Goldwyn said. "Where they got lesbians, we'll use Austrians."

There is a correlation between the creative and the screwball. So we must suffer the screwball gladly.

Kingman Brewster

One of the many sensational things that Lyndon Johnson did as president was the exhibition of his gall bladder scar to the media in 1964. Many people in the country thought this was entirely unnecessary — if not just plain disgusting — but Johnson, a consummate politician who was aware of the most trivial aspects of public office, had good reason for doing it. There had been persistent rumors that his operation had, in fact, removed a cancerous tumor. He asked his physicians if somebody knowledgeable seeing the scar, would think it was for anything other than a gall bladder job. He was assured that the scar indicated a classic GB operation, and could not be confused with another procedure.

So he hiked up his shirt and showed the stitches to the nation, and any rumors that he had cancer were immediately quashed.

It is the President's decision to choose how to impart information to the people.

John Ehrlichman

I sleep each night a little better, a little more confidently, because Lyndon Johnson is my President.

Jack Valenti

On the morning of August 27, 1891, at 924 Washington Street, Buffalo, New York, Mrs. Magdalene Mochel awoke to find her mother, Mrs. Barbara Luker, dead on the bedroom floor. Mrs. Mochel, an elderly woman herself, did what little she could. She covered her mother up where she lay, and waited for the police.

When the police arrived, it was the sixth of November.

In August 1948, Vernon Dobson of Detroit bought a car with a rubber check. Then he got worried about what might happen to him when the check bounced, so he sold it to another man to get enough money to cover the amount of the bad check. Poor Vernon — the fellow who bought it gave *him* a rubber check, and Vernon ended up getting arrested.

The two most beautiful words in the English language are: "Check enclosed."

Dorothy Parker

In 1969, little Audrey Sharples, aged ten, of Swarthmore, Pennsylvania, invited her aged and blind grandfather to go swimming with her in Crum Creek, a rather dubious body of water that flows through the campus of Swarthmore College. The old man was reluctant at first, but Audrey told him he shouldn't be afraid of having a good time, and he finally assented. In fact, as they were walking through the meadow towards the river, his childhood memories came back to him and he became excited about the idea of once again frolicking in the crystal clear Crum. He asked his granddaughter if the big tree with the overhanging branch was still there, the one he used to dive off when he was little. She assured him that it was, and he announced that, by golly, the first thing he'd do was dive in head first from it!

She brought him up to it, and he carefully picked his way along the thick, horizontal branch. "O.K. now, Audrey?" he asked.

"O.K. Gramps!"

The courageous elder stood, stretched, and executed a perfect swan dive.

But little Audrey just laughed and laughed, because she knew it was August and the creek had dried up.

Smart is when you believe only half of what you hear. Brilliant is when you know which half.

Robert Orben

In the country of the blind the one-eyed king can still goof up.

Laurence J. Peter

It's a good thing that beauty is only skin deep, or I'd be rotten to the core.

Phyllis Diller

Answers: In the haul.
When he requires bailing out.

AUGUST 28

Notable Births

1749	Goethe	1908	Roger Tory Peterson
1828	Leo Tolstoy	1916	C. Wright Mills
1899	Charles Boyer	1930	Ben Gazzara

Notable Events

1619 Deposed Ferdinand of Bohemia made Holy Roman Emperor
1798 First successful U.S. vineyard begun, Lexington, Kentucky
1833 Britain voted to outlaw slavery in Commonwealth
1893 Hurricane in southeastern United States killed 1,000 people
1956 Floods in Turkey claimed 138 lives
1957 Strom Thurmond set filibuster record of 24 hours, 18 minutes
1963 Martin Luther King delivered "I have a dream" speech

And now an anti-Lincoln epitaph from Stanstead, Quebec:

Eleazer Albee
Born in Rockingham, Vt.
Died in Stanstead Aug. 28, 1864
He went into Voluntary Banishment from his
Beloved Native Country, during the Reigning
Terror in the Third Year of the
Misrule of Abraham the First.

In New Amsterdam (now New York City) there were 700 people, 150 houses, and forty taverns in 1647.

Question: What do the following have in common?
Rhodesian Ridgebacks
Akitas
Vizkas
Briards
Papillons

One day in 1842, Madame Regnier, the wife of the attorney to the French royal family, was prattling on about nothing in particular at their home in Versailles. Her husband was annoyed by her chatter, and told her, "Be silent, woman, you talk nonsense!"

Madame Regnier shut her mouth, and said not another word for the remaining thirty years of her life.

The trouble with her is that she lacks the power of conversation, but not the power of speech.

George Bernard Shaw

If a man hears much that a woman says, she is not beautiful.

Haskins

Try praising your wife, even if it does frighten her at first.

Billy Sunday

The only question left to be settled now is, are women persons?

Susan B. Anthony

They're not all crooks, folks! In 1975, William Natcher, a Democrat congressman from Kentucky, was allowed $238,584 for office expenses. He returned the unused portion of $166,000 to the taxpayers the following year.

Answer: They are all dog breeds.

AUGUST 29

Question: If people lived forever, which of these folks would be the oldest? The youngest?

Ben Franklin
Marquis de Sade
Giovanni Casanova

Notable Births

1632	John Locke	1916	Ingrid Bergman
1780	Jean Auguste Ingres	1916	George Montgomery
1809	Oliver Wendell Holmes	1929	Thom Gunn
1862	Maurice Maeterlinck	1938	Elliott Gould
1912	Barry Sullivan	1947	Bob Lutz

Notable Events

1664	British annexed New York
1758	First state Indian reservation established, New Jersey
1779	John Paul Jones said, "I have not yet begun to fight!"
1833	Factory act limited child labor to 9 hours daily
1862	Second Battle of Bull Run began
1866	Mount Washington Cog Railway demonstrated
1885	Rock Spring, Wyoming, massacre of Chinese by white miners
1892	Billy Schreiber became first to catch baseball dropped from Washington Monument
1896	Chop Suey first made, New York City
1934	Queen Astrid of Belgium killed in car accident in Alps
1960	Premier Hazza el-Majali of Jordan assassinated

So you think there are a lot of nuts out on the road, huh? Well, out of 10,000 problem drivers referred to a special Detroit traffic clinic in the early fifties, 1,000 were found to be former inmates of mental institutions, 850 were feeble-minded, and 100 were commitably insane when they reached the clinic.

Statistics are like a bikini. What they reveal is suggestive, but what they conceal is vital.

Aaron Levenstein

Hops will comb a pole from left to right, but pole beans climb from right to left.

As late as the Reformation, Catholic priests in England were of the opinion that Hebrew was a new, not an ancient, language, and that anyone who learned it would be mystically transformed into a Jew.

The Jew is like anyone else, only more so.

Arnold Forster

In 1620, on the property of Richard de Clare, Earl of Gloucester, a Jew from Tewkesbury fell into a hole one Saturday morning. Out of reverence for his sabbath, the Jew would not allow himself to be rescued that day. Gloucester, feeling rebuked by an infidel, but supposedly out of respect for *his* sabbath, refused to rescue him on Sunday. They finally pulled him out on Monday, dead.

I never knew any man in my life who could not bear another's misfortunes perfectly like a Christian.

Alexander Pope

The Jews and the Arabs should settle their dispute in the true spirit of Christian charity.

Sir Alexander Wiley

There is a famous book of records on the market (we won't mention any names) which states that the Washington Monument is sinking at the rate of six inches a year. At that rate, the 555-foot, 5-inch-tall obelisk will disappear into the earth around the year 3000.

Not to worry! In 1973, the National Geodetic Survey studied the problem and reported the memorial is only sinking at the rate of .47 feet (5.64 inches) per *century*, and will be with us until the year 113,073.

You can observe a lot just by watching.

Yogi Berra

The words "scruple" and "scrupulous" come from the days of the ancient Roman merchants and traders. Before scales were made of metal, a sharp stone was used as the fulcrum for the wooden balances, and a much smaller stone, the scrupulus, was used as a counterweight during transactions. In weighing small quantities, both the seller and the buyer had to watch the beam with scrupulous attention to avoid either selling too much or receiving too little; so you can see how our word was derived. Similarly, to have a scruple left is still to have some anxiety about the propriety of an arrangement even after looking at it carefully.

In February 1955, for "reasons of economy and efficiency," the Indiana State Senate voted to abolish its Committee on Efficiency and Economy.

The formula for cold cream has changed hardly at all in the 1,700 years since it was originally made by the Roman physician Galen.

Answer: Ben Franklin, Giovanni Casanova.

AUGUST 30

Notable Births

1797	Mary Shelley	1908	Fred MacMurray
1870	Maria Montessori	1909	Shirley Booth
1893	Huey Long	1912	Joan Blondell
1896	Raymond Massey	1918	Ted Williams
1901	John Gunther	1943	Jean-Claude Killy
1901	Roy Wilkins	1943	R. Crumb

Notable Events

30 B.C. Suicide of Cleopatra
1637 Anne Hutchinson banished from Plymouth Colony
1791 Peace of Sistova between Austria and Turkey
1874 Factory Act in Britain limited work week to 56½ hours
1932 Goering elected Reichstag president
1935 Selassie gave United States and Britain oil rights in Ethiopia in attempt to stop Italy
1945 MacArthur landed in Japan

Cleopatra was not an Egyptian. She was a Greek.

There was once a king of Egypt named Pheron, who, it was said, went blind because he dared to throw a dart in the Nile. His affliction had lasted for a decade when an oracle told him his blindness would cease if he washed his eyes with the urine of a woman who had never lain with anyone except her husband. He tried his own wife's but it didn't work. He tried another woman's — and another — and another — but to no avail. Finally he found a woman whose water did the trick, and his sight was restored. Pheron ordered the two thousand or so women whose marital fidelity had proved questionable, (including his own wife) to be imprisoned in a nearby town, and then incinerated the town. Pheron proceeded to marry the woman who had cured him and who, history tells us, proved to be less than chaste afterwards. When the Pheron wanted to know why she'd been loyal earlier, but was no longer, she replied that no one had ever asked her before.

Nine-tenths of the people were created so you would want to be with the other tenth.

Horace Walpole

On August 30, 1146, a conference of European leaders outlawed the crossbow, the era's most effective weapon. In banning the machinery, they believed they had ended wars for all time.

You can't say that civilization don't advance, for in every war they kill you in a new way.

Will Rogers

The word "blackguard" did not originally have its present connotation. A blackguard was a servant who took care of the pots and pans when a lord's household moved, or a royal tour of the countryside was undertaken.

Answer: 1899, 1608, 1783, 1858.

Question: Within ten years, when were the following invented?

tape recorder (first one)
telescope
parachute
washing machine

Because of fertility drugs, multiple births are becoming far more common. Several years ago, there was even an instance of nonuplets (nine) in Mexico City, but this doesn't begin to approach the legendary records for babies born at the same time.

Anne Hutchinson, who was banished from several Puritan colonies in Massachusetts and Connecticut for her religious opinions, was once accused by the Reverend Samuel Clarke of having given birth to thirty children at once, one for each of her well-known heresies, and each one a devilish monster. Many people believed the accusation. And on January 20, 1269, it was duly recorded that the Countess of Cracow, Poland, delivered thirty-six babies.

But all-time champion of multiple births has to be the Dutch countess, Margaret of Henneberg. Because she had refused to give alms to a poor woman with two children while she herself was pregnant, she was said to be the victim of a terrible curse. On the Friday before Palm Sunday, 1276, she delivered 365 children, all the size of mice. There were, according to reports, 182 boys, 182 girls, and one child of indeterminate sex. It was clear that these children would not live long, and so the Bishop of Utrecht was sent for to baptize them immediately. All the boys were named John, and all the girls were christened Elizabeth. It is not known what name was given to the odd baby.

Moments after the baptism, the countess and all her children died.

We all worry about the population explosion, but we don't worry about it at the right time.

Arthur Hoppe

AUGUST 31

Questions: What kind of grain is usually sown at night?

How can you make fifteen bushels of corn from just one?

When Edward I of England was on what he thought was his deathbed, he swore to God that he would go on a crusade to free the Holy Land from the Moslem infidels if the Lord saw fit to let him live. Edward recovered, but the prospect of another long, expensive crusade did not appeal to him once he regained his health. He decided God would be quite happy if he banished the Jews from England instead.

The king hoped to achieve several things by this action. First of all, he would secure a place in Heaven for his Christian piety. Second, and perhaps more importantly, he wanted to restore England's economy. Crusades and wars had left the country impoverished and heavily in debt to Jewish merchants. If they were banished, the Jews would be forced to cancel all the debts owed them, and under the laws of the time their property would be forfeited to the king. This would, of course, make Edward a *very* rich man. To assuage the jealousy the church and nobility were bound to feel over this unexpected royal wealth, he promised a tenth of the confiscated property to the church and a fifteenth to the nobility. That made his pogrom unanimously popular.

On August 31, 1290, he issued the expulsion order, which declared that all Jews must leave England by the first of November or suffer death. They were also advised of the availability of safe-conduct passes issued by the king — for his usual fee. Many Jews bought them, but they were heeded by few Englishmen. As they fled to the seaports, thousands of Jews were robbed and beaten, and hundreds slain. Once on board, many of them were no safer. One captain purposely grounded his ship on a shallow bar and then invited the Jews on board to walk out with him on the exposed shoal during low tide. Everyone debarked. When the tide started to come in, the captain raced back to the ship had himself hauled aboard, and ordered the ladders to be pulled up before any of the Jews could reach them. At high tide he freed the boat and sailed away, leaving the Jews to drown. His story was told to King Edward, who congratulated the man for his quick wit, and rewarded him with a portion of the cargo.

Altogether, some fifteen thousand people were deported, and Jews were not officially allowed to be on English soil again until 1656.

I think Hitler was too moderate.

J.B. Stoner

In the late summer of 1978, several University of Iowa football players reported for practice with shaved heads. The State Barbers' Examining Board immediately brought suit against them for practicing "cosmetology and/or barbering without license."

Justice is incidental to law and order.

J. Edgar Hoover

Properly speaking, a two-storey house must have three floors. The word "storey" is derived from French and Latin words meaning "built up," and the first storey cannot be on the ground.

Notable Births

12	Caligula	1919	Richard Basehart
1875	Eddie Plank	1922	Barbara Bel Geddes
1897	Fredric March	1928	James Coburn
1903	Arthur Godfrey	1934	Buddy Hackett
1908	William Saroyan	1935	Eldridge Cleaver
1908	Alan Jay Lerner	1935	Frank Robinson

Notable Events

1030	Eclipse occurred during Battle of Stiklastad
1535	Pope Paul III deposed and excommunicated Henry VIII
1932	Germany demanded arms parity
1934	Huey Long entered New Orleans with troops
1935	First national skeet-shooting tournament held, Indianapolis
1964	Census Bureau declared California most populous state
1969	Rocky Marciano killed in plane crash

On June 12, 1883, the U.S.S. *Lancaster* was in the port of Kronstadt, Russia, in honor of the coronation of Czar Alexander II. As navy personnel have traditionally done, the officers and men of the *Lancaster* feted their Russian counterparts grandly. The ranking officer of the Russian delegation, the general commanding the forts of Saint Peter and Saint Paul, carried on in the best of that tradition as well, and proceeded to imbibe a significant portion of the wine in the mess.

When he departed, at *least* three sheets to the wind, the *Lancaster* gave him the customary fifteen-gun salute. The general, his recall of protocol dimmed by the alcohol, thought the Americans were firing on Kronstadt, and he immediately ordered the forts to return the fire.

By the time he realized what he'd done and rescinded the order, the Russian cannons had fired sixty-five rounds at the *Lancaster* — all misses.

Do you know what you can do with this design?

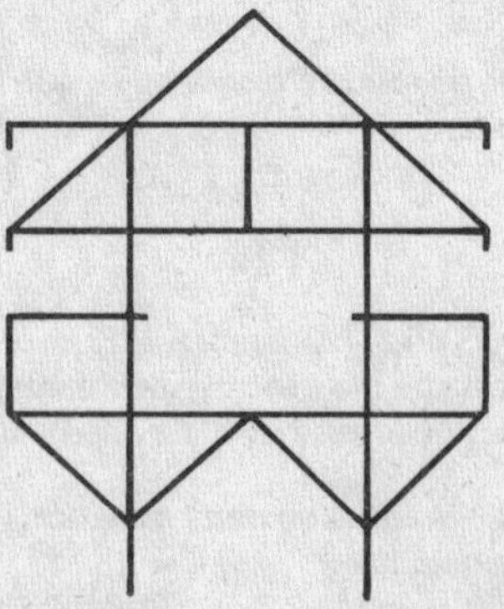

All the letters of the alphabet can be traced in it.

In his lifetime, Charles Wesley, whose brother John founded the Methodist Church, wrote over 6,500 hymns.

Answers: Wild oats.
Pop it.

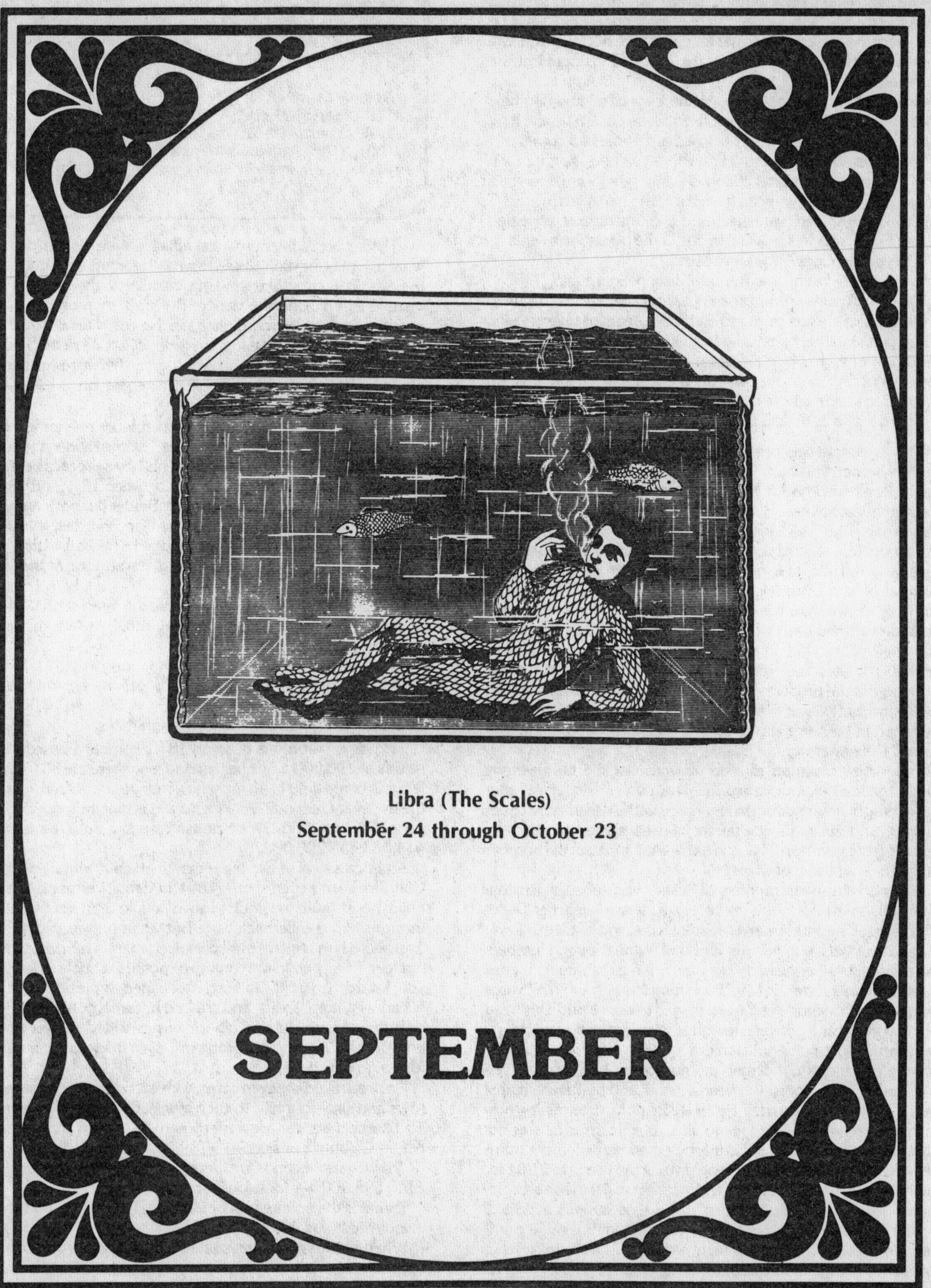

Libra (The Scales)
September 24 through October 23

SEPTEMBER

SEPTEMBER 1

The story is told of a Southern lawyer who had a slave named Sam. Sam's memory was a source of local pride. For a while he even became the court reporter for the district, because he could hear a case and at any time in the proceedings could give a complete oral transcription of testimony up to that point.

One day, the Devil appeared to the lawyer and told him he'd come for Sam. The lawyer protested that he couldn't spare him, but the Devil said he couldn't help it, Sam's time had come.

"Look," said the lawyer, "I know that you're a sporting man who'll strike a fair bargain. If Sam's memory is failing, then he's no good to me, and you can have him. Give him a test."

The Devil agreed, vanished, and a moment later appeared before Sam, who was plowing in one of the plantation's fields.

"Do you like eggs?" the Devil asked.

"Yes," replied Sam, and the Devil disappeared again.

The Revolutionary War broke out soon after and Sam served in the conflict. He was captured and imprisoned for several years. When peace came, he returned to his former owner. The lawyer freed him and gave him a small piece of ground to work. A few years went by, then one day the Devil appeared once again before Sam and, without introduction, asked simply, "How?"

"Fried," said Sam, and the Devil left for good.

This anecdote was probably originally told in the eighteenth century about Thomas Fuller, a slave known as the "Virginia Calculator," who had a great reputation for his memory and mathematical abilities. His peculiar talents came to be known to his owner, who used him for bookkeeping purposes on the plantation, but who did not exhibit him formally. When Fuller was seventy years old, two gentlemen asked him to calculate the number of seconds in eighteen months, which Fuller answered correctly in two minutes. Then they asked him how many seconds a man had lived who was seventy years, seventeen days, and twelve hours old. In one minute he gave them the answer. Several minutes later, one of the gentlemen who had been working out the problem on paper came up with an answer and told Tom that he was wrong. Tom took a look at the figure the man had in his hand and said, "No, massa. You forgot the leap years." Fuller was right.

Fuller never learned to read or write, nor did he have any mathematical training. He explained he'd developed his skill after being taught how to count to ten. After that, he'd learned to count to 100, and subsequently taught himself higher numbers by counting the number of hairs in a cow's tail and then the number of grains in a bushel of wheat.

A remarkable contemporary of Fuller's was Jedediah Buxton, an Englishman. Although his father was a schoolteacher, Jedediah himself never learned to read or write, and made his living throughout his life in various forms of manual labor. Numbers were his gift. When asked how many one-eighth cubic inches there were in a form 23,145,789 yards wide by 5,642,732 yards long by 54,965 yards deep, he managed to work it out in his head while working and conversing with a huge group of men. He got the twenty-eight-place solution exactly right. One major calculation he undertook concerned the number of barley corns, vetches, peas, wheat, oats, rye, beans, lentils, and human hairs that would fit in 360 cubic miles. He had to begin by determining how many of each element it took to fill a cubic inch, as he was not given this information. He did this by experimentation: the numbers he found ranged from twenty-five for the beans to 2,304 for the hairs, and he said that it took him longer to get the one-cubic-inch figures that it did the final sums. One curious aspect of Buxton's figuring was his original terminology for huge numbers. He devised his own system, working up from millions of millions. First he had thousands of millions of millions; then he used tribes, and thousands of tribes, etc., up to thousands of millions of millions of tribes; and the next unit up he called cramps; so there were thousands of cramps, etc., through tribes of tribes of cramps.

Notable Births

1875	Edgar Rice Burroughs	1920	Liz Carpenter
1898	Jimmy Hatlo	1922	Vittorio Gassman
1907	Walter Reuther	1922	Melvin Laird

Notable Events

1726	Earthquake in Italy took 4,500 lives
1878	Emma Nutt became nation's first telepone operator
1891	DAR chartered as national organization
1910	First transcontinental trip on horseback by woman ended

In other areas his numerical abilities were also evident. If he went to a play, he didn't listen to what the actors said, but counted the words they spoke; and he calculated the dancers' steps instead of enjoying the dance. Buxton's memory for ordinary events was quite extraordinary, too. He could recall what he had done and what he had eaten every day of his life since childhood, and once listed all the people who'd given him a free glass of beer since he was twelve — fifty-seven people on 2,130 different occasions.

Another Englishman displayed even more phenomenal powers in the nineteenth century. He was George Bidder, the son of a stonemason. His father recognized his boy's precocity early, and exhibited him throughout England between 1812 and 1820. As a consequence of his travels, young Bidder did not learn to read or write before he was ten. Unlike similar prodigies, whose powers often decline or disappear altogether as they grow older, Bidder's improved. The following gives an idea of the youngster's progress:

At age ten he was asked: "What is the interest of £4,444 for 4,444 days at 4½ percent per annum?" In two minutes he replied: "£2,434, 16s, 5½p."

At age eleven the question was: "How long would it take to fill a cubic mile cistern at a rate of 120 gallons per minute?" He calculated almost immediately that it would take 14,300 years, 285 days, twelve hours, and forty-six minutes.

Two days before his death in 1878, someone asked, "If light travels at 190,000 miles per second, and there are 36,918 wavelengths of red light to an inch, how many waves of red light strike the eye every second?" As a friend was instinctively reaching for a pencil, Bidder said, "Your needn't work it out. The answer is 444,443,651,200,000."

America's rival to Bidder in the nineteenth century was Zerah Colburn, born September 1, 1804, in Cabot, Vermont. As a small child he showed no indication of genius; in fact, most folks thought him a trifle backward. But when he was six, his father overheard him reciting multiplication tables to himself, a surprising feat for any child with only two months schooling, let alone a "backward" one. Mr. Colburn proceeded to probe the depth of his son's natural ability, and realized he had a gold mine. For the next three years, Zerah Colburn was exhibited all over America and Europe. Among the problems given the youngster were the following questions:

"In a cornfield of seven acres, with each acre having seventeen rows and sixty-four hills to each row, each hill has eight ears with 150 kernels per ear. How many kernels of corn are there in the field?" Colburn's answer — 9,139,200 — took twelve seconds.

"How many seconds are there in eleven years?" The answer — "346,896,000" — took four seconds.

"What is the square root of 998,001?" In four seconds he had calculated it was 999.

When he was asked the square and cube roots of numbers to nine places, Colburn commonly produced the right answers before the numbers could even be written on a blackboard.

Ironically, when he toured in England, the British press often reported that he was Russian; the public obviously felt that an American could not possibly be that clever.

SEPTEMBER 2

Notable Births

1852	Paul Bourget	1918	Martha Mitchell
1839	Henry George	1923	Marge Champion
1850	Eugene Field	1933	Marv Throneberry
1917	Cleveland Amory	1948	Terry Bradshaw
1918	Allen Drury	1952	Jimmy Connors

Notable Events

962	Otho III crowned emperor of Germany
1666	Great Fire of London devastated city
1752	England and colonies adopted Gregorian calendar
1792	Massacres began throughout French prisons
1864	Sherman took Atlanta on "March to Sea"
1865	Second Maori War ended
1894	Fire in Hinckley, Minnosota, mine killed 500 men
1945	War with Japan ended, truce signed
1964	Sergeant York died

Question: What's the special name for a group of these animals?

ducks
ants
hawks
badgers

Back in Shakespearean England, every grouping of animals had a specific name, and woe be unto him who classified all gatherings of feathered or furry creatures as flocks or herds. Books describing animals were called "bestiaries," and the name has come to mean any collection of words for animal groups. Here's a bit of bestiary; the animals themselves and their collective names.

lions	pride
leopards	leap
deer	herd
roes	bevy
bears	sloth
boars	singular
wild swine	sounder
tame swine	doyft
wolves	rout
horses	harras
colts	rag
mares	stud
asses	pace
mules	barren
oxen	team
kine	drove
sheep	flock
goats	tribe
foxes	skulk
badgers	cete
martins	richness
ferrets	fesynes
hares	huske, *or* down
rabbits	nest
cats	clowder
young cats	kindle
apes	shrewdness
moles	labour

When an animal is resting, it was said to be:

hart	harbored
buck	lodged
roebuck	bedded
hare	formed
rabbit	set

Additionally, two greyhounds were called a brace, while three were a leash; however, two spaniels were a couple. A number of hounds was a mute, a number of raches, a kennel, several whelps, a litter, and a group of curs was a cowardice.

The practice of naming groups was eventually expanded to include collections of people and their professions as well, usually with a certain tinge of sarcasm. Here's a bit of that kind of a "humanitary":

princes	state
friars	skulk
thieves	skulk
hermits	observance
sergeants	subtiltie
porters	safeguard
foresters	stalk
hunters	blast
butlers	draught
cooks	intemperance
harpers	melody
pipers	poverty
cobblers	drunkenship
tailors	disguising
tinkers	wandering
beggars	fighting
knaves	ragful *or* netful
boys	blush
ladies	bevy
women	gaggles
wives	non-patience

It is a very sad thing that nowadays there is so little useless information.

Bertrand Russell

Answer: Brace; colony; cast; cete.

SEPTEMBER 3

Questions: Why are newly planted seeds like gateposts?

If I saw you riding on a jackass, what fruit might I be reminded of?

Notable Births

1849	Sarah Orne Jewett	1926	Anne Jackson
1873	Emily Post	1926	Alison Lurie
1913	Alan Ladd	1943	Valerie Perrine

Notable Events

1189	Jews massacred at coronation of Richard the Lionheart
1639	First lawyer disbarred in America, Thomas Lechford, Massachusetts
1783	Peace of Versailles ended Revolutionary War
1895	First pro football game played, Latrobe, Pennsylvania
1930	Hurricane killed 2,000 people in Santo Domingo
1935	State Department forced oil companies to give up Ethiopian oil rights
1939	Britain declared war on Germany
1958	First American casualty at Quemoy-Matsu
1964	Luci Johnson danced the frug with Killer Joe Piro
1964	Bobby Kennedy resigned as attorney general
1976	*Viking II* landed on Mars

The word "etiquette" has as its source the French word for a ticket or a little card. On ceremonial occasions in Europe, it would be customary to hand out notes to the guests with instructions for their behavior during each part of the proceedings — when to rise, sit, etc. The association of this note with proper decorum derived from this practice.

Before the days of glass, windows in a house were for ventilation rather than light. The word itself reflects this — it comes from the Icelandic *vindauga*, which literally means "wind-eye."

A fiasco isn't a debacle, it's just a glass bottle — at least in Italian. Venetian glassblowers used to turn what started off as a delicate piece of work into a common flask (*fiasco* in Italian) if there were mistakes made in its production. So fiasco, properly speaking, is a fault that makes something beautiful into something ordinary, although most people associate it with a complete failure.

There's a certain amount of decided snobbishness that seems to be a natural part of the "established" families of America. In Massachusetts they say, "The Lodges speak only to the Cabots, and the Cabots speak only to God." (This was before the advent of the parvenu Kennedys, of course.) On the Main Line of Philadelphia, the quickest definition of the hierarchy is that *the* families are the Ingersolls and the Biddles, the subtle difference between them being that, "When a Biddle gets drunk, he *thinks* he's an Ingersoll."

All of which is fine if you're into that sort of thing, or until you start looking stupid.

At one society function some time ago, a reigning lady of the Boston set was introduced to a gentleman. They exchanged greetings, and she asked, "And where are you from?"

"Idaho," was the reply.

"Oh, I hope you don't mind my saying this, dear," she replied, "but it's pronounced 'Ohio.'"

On another occasion, one of the Mrs. Cabots of Boston was seated next to a Chicago matron at a tea party. The Chicago woman was not quite up to Mrs. Cabot's standards, and throughout their conversation the Boston woman had been decidedly cool. In discussing the respective cities' "400s," Mrs. Cabot said, with a tinge of haughtiness in her voice, "In Boston, we place all our emphasis on *breeding*."

The other woman smiled slyly and rejoined, "In Chicago, we think it's a lot of fun, but we *do* manage to foster a great many outside interests."

There are bad manners everywhere, but an aristocracy is bad manners organized.

Henry James

She balanced her dignity on the tip of her nose.

Heywood Broun

When I sell liquor, it's called bootlegging; when my patrons serve it on silver trays on Lake Shore Drive, it's called hospitality.

Al Capone

Answers: Because they prop-a-gate.
A pair.

SEPTEMBER 4

Notable Births

518 B.C.	Pindar	1908	Richard Wright
1768	Chateaubriand	1917	Henry Ford II
1818	Richard Congreve	1929	Thomas Eagleton
1848	R.R. Bowker	1930	Mitzi Gaynor

Notable Events

1790 Necker resigned in France
1833 Barney Flaherty became America's first newsboy, New York City
1882 First electric power station on line, New York City
1887 Fire in Exeter Theater, England, took 200 lives
1939 Field Marshall Smuts became South African premier
1939 France declared war on Germany
1939 Liner *Athenia* blown up off Scottish coast, 1,400 killed
1941 Shoot-on-sight order given to Coast Guard boats
1949 Longest pro tennis game played, Pancho Gonzalez and Ted Schroeder, 67 games in 5 sets
1970 Hurricane Diane claimed 148 lives in Caribbean and United States

It may surprise you, but the Frisbee has been around for twenty-five years. In fact, it was so popular in some sections of the country that it merited *Newsweek's* attentions in 1957. The article said it was "a great game for ersatz athletes, for it requires neither intelligence, timing, endurance, stamina, nor wind." Within two months that spring, the stupid, inept, weak collegiates of Princeton University bought 5,300 of the discs from a store adjacent to the campus. *Newsweek* also said the Frisbee could cut a figure eight, which it can't, and that it was a passing fad, which it certainly has not proved to be.

Answer: 1882; 1709; 1870; 1916.

Question: Within ten years, when were the following invented?
electric fan
piano
stock ticker
stainless steel

Good neighbor, Ben!

Californian Anna Steinach hired her neighbor Ben Werner to look after her farm while she was in the hospital in the autumn of 1940. When she was released from the hospital, she practically had to look *for* her farm. Werner had sold all her poultry, and as many of her goats as he could catch. He himself ate all the rabbits she'd been raising. He killed her dog (he claimed it ate too much), and for ten dollars sold Pete, her horse, to a dog-food manufacturer. Having wiped out the animal population on the Steinach spread, Werner then tore down her barn (nothing left to keep in it anyway) and sold the lumber. After he discovered a strongbox containing $630 in the cellar of the house, he proceeded to chew up her cellar floor, tear into the house's walls, and dig holes all over the property looking for more treasure.

Surprisingly, there's no evidence that Mrs. Steinach suffered a relapse when she discovered her neighbor's destruction of her property.

It is easier to love humanity as a whole than to love one's neighbor.

Eric Hoffer

He is a fine friend. He stabs you in the front.

Leonard Lewis Levinson

It has been recorded that, in ancient Rome, the typical "girl and pony" show included bulls, giraffes, leopards, cheetahs, boars, asses, dogs, and apes, as well as stallions. Many of these animals were specially trained, and often became rapists if denied the "pleasures" they had become accustomed to.

The so-called new morality is too often the old immorality condoned.

Lord Shawcross

Among the porcupines, rape is unknown.

Gregory Clark

SEPTEMBER 5

Question: What are the nicknames of the following states?
Vermont
Oklahoma
South Carolina
Utah

Notable Births

1585	Cardinal Richelieu	1912	John Cage
1638	Louis XIV	1918	Frank Yerby
1847	Jesse James	1929	Bob Newhart
1902	Darryl F. Zanuck	1932	Carol Lawrence
1905	Arthur Koestler	1942	Raquel Welch

Notable Events

1774	First Continental Congress opened, Philadelphia
1813	Denmark declared war on Sweden
1822	Earthquake in Syria killed 22,000 people
1836	Sam Houston elected president of Republic of Texas
1933	Batista seized control in Cuba
1939	United States declared neutrality in European conflict
1958	First color videotape recording made
1964	Typhoon Ruby claimed 735 lives in China and Hong Kong
1972	Israeli Olympic team members taken hostage by Black September guerrillas
1975	Attempted assassination of Ford by Squeaky Fromme

By blood and/or marriage, Franklin Roosevelt was related to eleven former presidents: Washington, John Adams, John Quincy Adams, Madison, Van Buren, William Harrison, Taylor, Grant, Benjamin Harrison, Teddy Roosevelt, and Taft. Madison and Taylor were themselves second cousins.

James Monroe's wife was only seventeen when they were married. He was twenty-seven. The future president who married the youngest girl was Andrew Johnson. He was all of eighteen when he married his sixteen-year-old wife.

The greatest age difference between a president and his wife was that of the John Tylers. He married his second wife when she was twenty-four and he was fifty-four. Tyler also fathered the greatest number of children, fifteen in all.

Only five presidents have married women older than themselves. They are Washington, Fillmore, (his first wife), Benjamin Harrison (again, his first wife), Harding, and Nixon.

The first wife of William Henry Harrison, Anna Symmes, was the sister of John Cleves Symmes, the fellow who proposed the Hollow Earth theory (September). Harrison's grandson, President Benjamin Harrison, had a daughter who was younger than four of his grandchildren.

The following letter was written as a recommendation for a young man by Cardinal Richelieu to the French ambassador in Italy. Read across the page, it is a glowing testimony to the man's qualities, but what the cardinal really had to say about M. Compigne is all contained in the left-hand column. This form of literary trick is called an Equivoque.

Sir:

M. Compigne, a Savoyard by birth,   a Friar of the Order of St. Benedict,
is the man who will present to you   as his passport to your protection,
this letter. He is one of the most   discrete, the wisest and the least
meddling persons that I have known   or have had the pleasure to converse with.
He has long earnestly solicited me   to write you in his favor, and
to give him a suitable character,   together with a letter of credence;
which I have accordingly granted to   his real merit; rather I must say, than to
his importunity; for, believe me, Sir,   his modesty is only exceeded by his worth.
I should be sorry that you should be   wanting in serving him on account of being
misinformed of his real character;   I should be afflicted if you were
as some other gentlemen have been,   misled on that score, who now esteem him
and those among the best of my friends;   wherefore, and from no other motive
I think it my duty to advise you   that you are most particularly desired
to have especial attention to all he does,   to show him all the respect imaginable
nor venture to say anything before him,   that may offend or displease him
in any sort; for I may truly say there is   no man I love so much as M. Compigne
none whom I should more regret to see   neglected, as no one can be more worthy to be
received and trusted in decent society.   Base, therefore, it would be to injure him.
And I well know, that as soon as you   are made sensible of his virtures,and
shall become acquainted with him   you will love him as I do; and then
you will thank me for this my advice.   The assurance I entertain of your
Courtesy obliges me to desist from   urging this matter to you further, or
saying anything more on this subject.   Believe me sir, etc.   *Richelieu*

Answer: Green Mountain State; Sooner State; Palmetto State; Beehive State.

SEPTEMBER 6

Notable Births

1757	Marquis de Lafayette	1878	Henry Canby
1782	Mrs. Thomas Jefferson	1899	Billy Rose
1860	Jane Addams	1937	Jo Anne Worley

Notable Events

1713 Jacobites rebelled in Scotland
1781 Benedict Arnold burned New London
1810 First Pacific-coast colonists left New York City
1869 Mine collapse in Plymouth, Pennsylvania left 110 dead
1901 McKinley shot at Buffalo by Leon Czolgosz
1975 Earthquake in Turkey killed over 2,300 people

Questions: Why is a man committing murder like a chicken crossing the street?

Why is a window in a prison like a nutmeg?

The little ridges on American coins from the dime on up weren't put there just for decoration. In the nineteenth century, when coins contained about their real value in gold or silver, many people made themselves a "little extra money" by filing off the edges of the coins. The milling of coins was instituted to make it easier to determine if a coin had been tampered with in this fashion.

Of course, nowadays, unless your thing is tin or aluminum . . .

The Equivoque letter form was also used by women imprisoned by marriages they disliked to convey their real feelings to their friends without their husbands' knowledge. Unless a man was privy to the trick, he would be wildly flattered by his wife's adulation if he happened to see (or intercept) the letter, and the woman would remain safe from his revenge. Here's a good example of an Equivoque from Victorian England. Read the first and then every other line to gather the woman's real feelings.

To Miss M---.

— I cannot be satisfied, my dearest friend!
blessed as I am in the matrimonial state,
— unless I pour into your friendly bosom,
which has ever been in unison with mine,
— the various sensations which swell
with the liveliest emotion of pleasure,
— my almost bursting heart. I tell you my dear
husband is the most amiable of men.
— I have now been married seven weeks, and
never have found the least reason to
— repent the day that joined us. My husband is
both in person and manners far from resembling
— ugly, cross, old, disagreeable, and jealous
monsters, who think by confining to secure
— a wife, it is his maxim to treat as a
bosom friend and confidant, and not as a
— plaything, or menial slave, the woman
chosen to be his companion. Neither party
— he says, should always obey implicitly;
but each yield to the other by turns.
— An ancient maiden aunt, near seventy,
a cheerful, venerable, and pleasant old lady,
— lives in the house with us; she is the delight of both young and old; she is ci-
— vil to all the neighborhood round,
generous and charitable to the poor.
— I am convinced my husband loves nothing more
than he does me; he flatters me more
— than a glass; and his intoxication
(for so I must call the excesses of his love)
— often makes me blush for the unworthiness
of its object, and I wish I could be more deserving
— of the man whose name I bear. To
say all in one word, my dear, and to
— crown the whole——my former gallant lover
is now my indulgent husband; my husband

— is returned, and I might have had
a prince without the felicity I find in
— him. Adieu! may you be blessed as I am unable to wish that I could be more
— happy.

Answers: Because it's a fowl proceeding.
It has to be grated to be useful.

SEPTEMBER 7

Question: Give me your huddled masses . . .

Can you name the five countries that sent the most immigrants to the United States in the decade 1961-70?

Notable Births

1533	Queen Elizabeth I	1900	Taylor Caldwell
1860	Grandma Moses	1909	Elia Kazan
1867	J. Pierpont Morgan	1913	Anthony Quayle
1885	Elinor Wylie	1924	Daniel Inouye

Notable Events

1565	Saint Augustine, Florida, founded by Melendez
1736	Porteous Riots in Edinburgh
1776	American *Turtle* battled British *Eagle*
1797	United States frigate *Constitution* launched
1858	Eclipse in South America
1880	Clay pigeon patented
1901	Peace of Peking ended Boxer Rebellion
1908	Nation's first Esperanto club organized, Chautauqua, New York
1940	London *Blitzkrieg* began

Some interesting laws were passed during Queen Elizabeth I's reign. Staying with a gypsy band for more than a month was made a felony, punishable by death. All persons over the age of seven had to wear a woolen cap, of English wool and manufacture, on all Sundays and holidays. The fine for noncompliance was three shillings, four pence. Any person slandering the queen was to have his ears cut off. If he put it in writing, it became libel, and the penalty was death.

The following commentary on the vagrancy laws of Queen Elizabeth's time is taken from a history written some fifty years after her death in 1603, and dates from the period of the Commonwealth when Cromwell ruled instead of the king.

> Queen Elizabeth, in the fourteenth and eighteenth years of her glorious reign, two acts were made for idle vagrant and masterless persons, that used to loiter, and would not work, should for the first offense have a hole burned through the gristle of one of his ears of an inch compass. And for the second offense commited therein, to be hanged. If these and such like laws were executed justly, truly, and severely, (as they ought to be,) without any respect of persons, favor, or friendship, this dung and filth of idleness would easily be rejected and cast out of this Commonwealth, there would not be so many loitering idle persons, so many Ruffians, Blasphemers, Swing-Bucklers, so many Drunkards, Tosspots, Dancers, Fiddlers, and Minstrels, Dice-players, and Maskers, Fencers, Thieves, Interlude-players, Cut-purses, Cousiners, Masterless Servants, Jugglers, Rogues, sturdy Beggars, counterfeit Egyptians, &c., as there are, nor yet so many plagues to be amongst us as there are, if these Dunghills and filth in Commonweals were removed, looked into, and clean cast out, by the industry, pain, and travail of those that are set in authority, and have government.

The law, in its majestic equality, forbids the rich as well as the poor, to sleep under bridges, to be in the streets, and to steal bread.

Anatole France

The New York Giants baseball team, now in San Francisco, originally got their club's name in about 1889, when many of the players were over 6½ feet, and most of them weighed over 200 pounds.

Answer: Mexico, Canada, Italy, Great Britain, Cuba.

POLO GROUNDS, 1889.

SEPTEMBER 8

Notable Births

1157	Richard the Lionheart	1922	Sid Caesar
1837	Joaquin Miller	1924	Grace Metalious
1841	Antonin Dvorak	1925	Peter Sellers
1911	Euell Gibbons	1930	Nguyen Cao Ky

Notable Events

1636 Harvard College established
1664 New Amsterdam renamed New York
1900 Galveston hurricane and floods killed 7,000 people
1923 7 navy destroyers ran aground, Santa Barbara, California
1934 *Morro Castle* burned off Asbury Park, New Jersey killed 130 people
1943 Italy surrendered to Allies
1946 King Simeon II of Bulgaria deposed as nation abolished monarchy
1964 Uruguay broke diplomatic relations with Cuba
1974 Ford granted Nixon unconditional pardon

Thomas Paine, whose writings had a tremendous influence on the course of the American Revolution, was not an altogether admirable character. Among his are noticeable faults was his lack of personal hygiene. An American named Watson who traveled with him for a time in France recounted:

> I often officiated as his interpreter, although humbled and mortified by his filthy appearance, and awkward and unseemly dress . . . at L'Orient he was absolutely offensive and perfumed the whole apartment. He was soon rid of his respectable visitors, who left the room with marks of astonishment and disgust.

Birds do not sleep in their nests. They may occasionally nap in them, but they actually sleep in other places.

Question: Can you figure out this cryptogram?

B
faults husband quarrels wife faults

Richard the Lionheart has to be considered one of England's worst kings, despite his exalted reputation. He was in the country for less than a year of his decade-long reign, and he didn't even speak the language. He ruined the country economically to finance his part in the crusades, which he undertook not out of any real desire to free the Holy Land, but to further his own vainglory.

Upon returning from the crusades, Richard so offended Leopold of Austria and Henry VI of France that they captured him and held him for ransom, and this forced payment for all practical purposes bankrupted England. It was many, many years before the country recovered from his excesses.

The louder he talked of his honor, the faster we counted the spoons.

Ralph Waldo Emerson

In the time of Richard the Lionheart and the Third Crusade, the following law was in effect for those traveling to the Holy Land:

> He who kills a man on shipboard, shall be bound to the dead body and thrown into the sea; if a man is killed on shore, the slayer shall be bound to the dead body and buried with it. He who shall draw his knife to strike another, or who shall have drawn blood from him, to lose his hand; if he should only have struck him with the palm of his hand without drawing blood, he shall be thrice ducked in the sea.

The first president of Harvard College was a good Puritan named Nathaniel Eaton. He built a six-foot fence around the institution to keep his nine students from escaping, and often beat them black and blue when they failed to learn their lessons properly. In 1638 (the college was founded on this day in 1636), he was charged with embezzling the funds of John Harvard's endowment and fled to England, where he died several years later, a pauper in a debtor's prison.

To err is human, but when the eraser wears out ahead of the pencil, you're overdoing it.

J. Jenkins

The word "zest" is derived through the French from the Latin *schistus*, which means "divided," and is used specifically in referring to a lemon peel. Hence "zest" denotes an element that gives a pleasant, tangy taste to something.

Answer: Be above quarrels between husband and wife, there are faults on both sides.

SEPTEMBER 9

Questions: What is the worst kind of assassin?

What relation is a door mat to a door step?

When Leo Tolstoy and his brother were children, they created a club with a peculiar, almost impossible initiation ceremony. In order to become a member, one had to stand in a corner for a half an hour and *not* think of a white bear.

Nothing fixes a thought so in the memory as the wish to forget it.

Michel de Montaigne

Benjamin Franklin was the first postmaster general of the United States, appointed to that office shortly after the colonies declared their independence. Ironically, some years later, another postmaster general banned two of Franklin's own books from the mails because he judged them to be obscene. Thomas Jefferson had once called one of the banned books his favorite work.

I am going to introduce a resolution to have the Postmaster General stop reading dirty books and deliver the mail.

Gale McGee

Originally the canary bird was literally the "dog-bird," but this had nothing to do with any resemblance to a canine on the bird's part. When Augustus Caesar first heard accounts of some islands off the coast of Morocco, he was impressed by the description of the huge dogs found on them. The group of islands therefore named Canaria, or Dogland, from the Latin *canis*, for dog. The first caged songbirds came from "Dogland," and were simply called canaries.

The population of Chicago increased from 350 inhabitants in 1830 to 112,000 in 1860, and 1,099,000 in 1890.

Notable Births

1828	Leo Tolstoy	1911	Paul Goodman
1887	Alf Landon	1925	Cliff Robertson
1899	Waite Hoyt	1927	Robert Shaw
1900	James Hilton	1932	Sylvia Miles

Notable Events

1830	First balloon flight by a native-born American, C. F. Durant
1898	First national log-rolling championships held, Chicago
1954	Earthquake in northern Africa killed 1,657 people
1976	Death of Mao Tse-tung
1978	Illinois legalized use of pot for cancer and glaucoma treatment

In September 1947, an already injured Indianapolis resident named Russell Mitchell had one of his crutches break under him. He stumbled, fell down a flight of stairs, and bashed his head against a wall.

He was quickly arrested for using profane language.

I see no wisdom in saving up indignation for a rainy day.

Heywood Broun

The* shlemiehl *lands on his back and bruises his nose.

Yiddish Proverb

A Chicago teenager, Barbara Avery, was invited to a birthday party in her honor a couple of years ago, and immediately got on the phone to line up a babysitter for her child. She called everyone she knew, but no one was available. Unwilling to miss the festivities, she dumped the baby down her building's incinerator/compactor, turned the machine on, and drove to the party.

The best substitute for experience is being 16.

Raymond Duncan

Like its politicians and its wars, society has the teenagers it deserves.

J.B. Priestley

Chicago has a strange metaphysical elegance of death about it.

Carl Sandburg

What Paul Bunyan was to the logger, and Pecos Bill was to the cowboy, Joe Magarac was to the immigrants from central and eastern Europe who slaved in the steel mills of Pennsylvania and Ohio. Interestingly enough, "Joe Magarac" can be literally translated from the Hungarian and Slovakian languages to mean: "One who works and eats like a jackass."

Answers: One who takes life cheerfully.

A stepfa'ther.

SEPTEMBER 10

Notable Births

1886	Hilda Doolittle	1929	Arnold Palmer
1910	Fay Wray	1945	José Feliciano
1915	Edmund O'Brien	1946	Jim Hines

Notable Events

1775 American forces invaded Canada
1813 Battle of Lake Erie
1913 First coast-to-coast paved highway opened
1933 German Jews began antiboycott boycott
1943 Nazis took Rome
1952 West Germany agreed to pay Israel $822 million in reparations
1964 Xavier Cugat announced engagement to Charo
1964 Senate voted to reopen Bobby Baker investigation

William the Conqueror of England had an interesting courtship — and death. As the story goes, he saw his future wife, Mary, in the street. He made advances to her, but she refused his attentions. The next time he saw her, she rebuffed him again, so he broke her arm, knocked her unconscious, and dragged her to the chapel.

His death was occasioned by his going to war with Philip I of France in 1087. The French king had made a witty remark about William's corpulence (something to the effect that he hoped his child was due soon — William weighed over 300 pounds). The Norman took affront, and vowed Philip's kingdom would be his.

Question: All the women in a new company are economists; one third of the economists in the company are women. There are twelve new employees and nine women. A third of the new employees are economists. None of the women are new employees. How many economists are male and are *not* new employees?

While his army was advancing in France, William's horse stumbled under his weight and he was thrown to the ground. His wounds became infected and caused his death on September 10, 1087, at the age of sixty-one.

William was decidedly unpopular with his army, and they abandoned his corpse to rot. It was finally taken away by the monks of a local monastery. By this time the body had begun to swell and putrify, and there was no coffin available that would encompass the royal form. When the monks tried to force it into a masonry crypt, it burst, sending a stench throughout the church, which was relieved only after weeks of airing, incensing, and perfuming.

The body of a dead enemy always smells sweet.

Guy de Maupassant

There is nothing more natural, or more mistaken, than to suppose that we are loved.

La Rochefoucauld

Imprisoned in every fat man, a thin one is wildly signalling to get out.

Cyril Connolly

Brandeis University, in Waltham, Massachusetts, selected Antonio Magliocci as its "Man of the Year" for 1977. In 1964 and 1970, Magliocci appeared on the lists of suspected organized crime figures put out by the United States Department of Justice, and New York police department files have linked him closely with the Columbo family.

A preacher in a small New England town announced to his congregation that the subject of the next Sunday's sermon would be "Lying."

"In preparation for what I am going to say, I'd like you all to read the nineteenth chapter of Mark, which is appropriate to it."

When he began his sermon the next week, the minister first called on the congregation. All those who had read the recommended chapter were asked to raise their hands. Nearly everyone's hand went up.

"Good!" he exclaimed. "You are exactly the people I want to address. There is *no* nineteenth chapter of Mark."

Nothing is more unpleasant than a virtuous person with a mean mind.

Walter Bagehot

Answer: Six

SEPTEMBER 11

Question: About how long do these animals live?
grizzly bear
cow
giraffe
lion

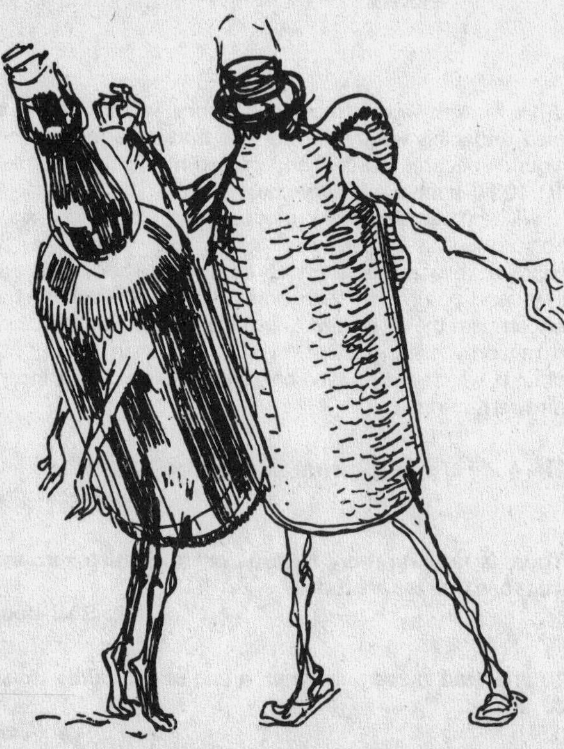

In 1612, a petition was signed by nineteen residents of Bayton, England, and sent to Parliament, requesting that that august body do something about two taverners in their town who sold ale that was too strong. Below are a few of their manifold reasons for asking for greater regulation of the generous barkeepers:

. . . that John Kempster and John Byrd do not sell their ale according to the law, but do sell a pint for a penny, and do make it so extraordinary strong that it draws diverse idle persons into the said alehouses, by reason whereof sundry, assaults, affrays, bloodsheds, and other misdemeanors, are there committed by idle and drunken company which do thither resort and there continue their drunkenness three days and three nights together, and also diverse men's sons and servants do often resort and continue drinking in the said houses day and night, whereupon diverse disorders and abuses are offered to the inhabitants of Bayton aforesaid, as in pulling down styles, in carrying away of yerts, in throwing men's waynes, plows, and such like things, into pools, wells, and other byplaces, and putting their yokes for oxen into lakes and miry place, &c.

We lived for days on nothing but food and water.

W.C. Fields

The chestnut tree gives a chestnut, the pine tree a pine cone, the blueberry bush blueberries — so why does an oak yield an acorn? Actually, hundreds of years ago, oak was spelled without an *o*, as were other words like "oath," "oar," and "oats." The nut it produced was called a kern, which meant a seed (today's kernel): So the acorn was originally an akkern, or oak seed. Not so very different from a chestnut after all.

Notable Births

1524	Pierre de Ronsard	1909	Anne Seymour
1862	O. Henry	1917	Jessica Mitford
1885	D.H. Lawrence	1949	Marty Liquori

Notable Events

1850 American debut of Jenny Lind
1857 Lee's Mormons massacred 120 people in wagon train attack
1911 Attempt to repeal Prohibition in Maine defeated
1947 Australia received first export of radioactive isotopes
1952 First implantation of artificial aortic heart valve
1967 New York teachers out on strike, one million kids out of school
1973 Allende overthrown in Chile by military junta

In the fall of 1940, the Alcoholic Beverage Control Board of Washington, D.C., suspended a club's license because the owners had served liquor to a minor and had allowed foul language to be used on the premises. By the time the order was handed down, the club had gone out of business, and the former owners notified the ABCB of this. The board responded by ordering them to reopen the club so that it could then remain closed for the first seven days of the reopening to fulfill the suspension, after which time it could then go out of business.

If you can't convince them, confuse them.

Harry S Truman

One-seventh of the human brain and spinal column is pure cholesterol. Think about that the next time you sit down to a nice plate of polyunsaturates.

Sheep in Australia outnumber people by thirteen to one.

After Albert Einstein had been at Princeton for some months, local newshounds discovered that a twelve-year-old girl happened to stop by the Einstein home almost every afternoon. The girl's mother hadn't thought to ask Einstein about the situation until the newspapers reported it, but when she got the opportunity after that she did so. What could her daughter and Einstein have in common that they spent so much time together? Einstein replied simply, "She brings me cookies and I do her arithmetic homework."

What are our schools for if not indoctrination against Communism?

Richard Nixon

Answer: 25, 15, 10, 15 years respectively.

Notable Births

1829 Charles Dudley Warner
1880 H.L. Mencken
1891 Arthur Sulzberger
1892 Alfred Knopf
1898 Maurice Chevalier
1907 Louis MacNeice
1918 Jesse Owens
1940 Mickey Lolich

Notable Events

1722 Russia took Baku and Derbent from Persia
1869 National Prohibition party founded in Chicago
1916 First transcontinental motorcycle trip by a woman completed
1928 Hurricane in the West Indies killed over 4,000 people
1940 Italy invaded Egypt
1942 Nazis stopped Russians at Stalingrad
1944 United States forces entered Germany
1949 Heuss elected president of West Germany
1974 Haile Selassie deposed in Ethiopia

Question: What's the state shown here?

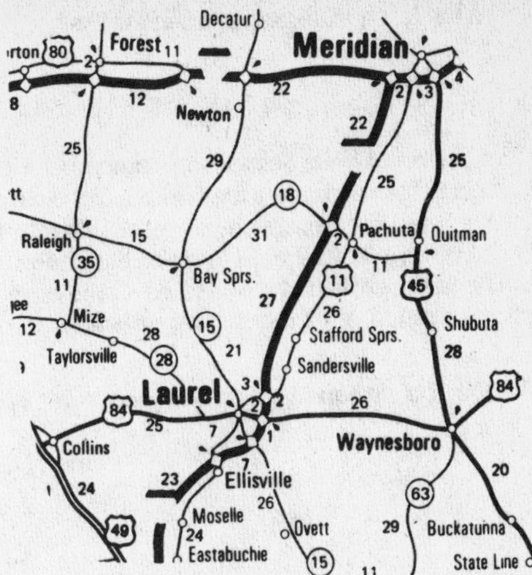

The amazing Mike Fink, Davy Crockett's riverboat pal in many of the books and movies that have been made about Crockett's life, was a real person, albeit a little older than he's usually portrayed. He was a superlative frontier scout and hell raiser, whose practical jokes often bordered on felony. After a series of spectacular escapades on the Mississippi had made the local authorities a bit more concerned about him than Mike Fink would have liked, he headed up the Missouri River as the leader of a trapping expedition for the Mountain Fur Company.

Near the mouth of the Yellowstone River, he and the fifty or sixty other men in the expedition built a stockade they named Fort Henry, which they used that summer as a base of operations. As winter approached, they dug a more serviceable cave in bluff somewhat further down the Missouri for their winter quarters.

Apparently, some time during the winter of 1821-2, Fink and his best friend, a man named Carpenter, had a vicious argument over an Indian woman, and it was only the intervention of the other leaders that kept them from killing each other. They managed to make an uneasy truce for the remainder of the season.

The next spring, back at Fort Henry, the rivalry was revived over some whiskey. Again, friends broke it up, and ostensibly Fink and Carpenter patched up their differences. But then Fink said he wanted to formalize the treaty in the traditional way he and Carpenter demonstrated their mutual respect and trust.

The tradition called for both of them to shoot a tin cup of whiskey off the other man's head at a distance of sixty or seventy yards. Both men agreed that this seemed fine. Fink was a man of honor, in his own way, and the two were considered to be about the best shots in the country. Neither man had trimmed so much as a hair on the other's head in the dozens of times they'd done this feat in shooting exhibitions, so it seemed a good way to make things right once and for all between the two of them.

Carpenter was not as trusting of Fink as he once had been, however. Fink had been drinking heavily, as usual — he could put away a gallon of hard liquor a day and, outside of his temper, it had no noticeable effect on him — and he believed somehow that Fink's rage over the squaw situation went deeper than the others realized. Yet he could not very well refuse the conditions of the truce without showing Fink he distrusted him. After a coin toss, which Mike won, Carpenter told a mutual friend of theirs named Talbot that it anything went wrong he wanted him to have his gun and other equipment. He then filled a cup to the brim with whiskey and marched off. Sixty yards away he stopped, turned around, and placed the cup on his head.

Fink took a bead on the cup, then lowered his rifle and said, "Hold your noodle steady, Carpenter! Don't spill the whiskey! I shall want some presently."

Again he aimed, and this time he fired. Carpenter fell dead without a sound. The ball had struck him square in the middle of his forehead.

Fink calmly set his rifle down and blew the smoke out through the touch-hole, never taking he eyes off Carpenter. Finally he said, "Carpenter! Have you spilt the whiskey?" The man over Carpenter's body shouted back that he was dead.

"It's all an accident," Fink hollered. "I took as fair a bead on the black spot on the cup as ever I took on a squirrel's eye." He then proceeded to curse the gun, the bullet, the powder, and himself. None of the other men bought his sincerity, but under the circumstances there wasn't much in a legal way that could be done.

However, Talbot resolved to avenge the death. It was several months before an opportunity presented itself, but finally, after a big bout of drinking, Fink bragged that he'd killed Carpenter in cold blood, and that he had no regrets about having done so.

Talbot pulled out the dead man's gun and shot Fink through the heart. Mike Fink died instantly, and no one ever bothered to make Talbot answer legally for the crime.

It's far easier to forgive an enemy after you've got even with him.

Olin Miller

Like challenging a school of piranhas to a game of water polo.

Thomas Middleton

More adults than children were reported lost at Japan's Expo '70 world's fair.

Answer: Mississippi.

SEPTEMBER 13

Questions: Why is a barn so noisy?

What has a trunk and a tail and walks?

After the deposition of Haile Selassie on September 12, 1974, the ruling junta in Ethiopia charged the families of the old regime leaders they executed the equivalent of seventy-five American dollars. Only then were they allowed to claim the bodies of their loved ones. The junta explained it was to cover the costs of the bullets, the firing squads, and other similar expenses.

Do not take life too seriously. You will never get out of it alive.

Elbert Hubbard

Two Epitaphs

The following lines are over the remains of Robert Trollop, architect of the Exchange and Town Hall at New Castle, England:

Here lies Robert Trollop,
Who made yon stones roll up.
When death took his soul up,
His body filled this hole up.

To the memory of Ric Richards who by a gangrene
first lost a toe, then a leg and lastly his life.
Ah cruel Death to make three meals of one,
To taste and eat, and eat till all was gone.
But know thou tyrant when the trump shall call,
He'll find his feet, and stand where thou shalt fall.

The word "fee" comes from the Anglo-Saxon word for cattle, *feoh*. Livestock was a principal form of exchange throughout early Europe, and *feoh* was often collected as a payment for services rendered.

The ancient Greeks had a fairly civilized way of dealing with individuals who proved to be more trouble than they were worth: banishment. From time to time, a voting day would be announced, and citizens would gather at a certain place to make nominations and cast their ballots. If a man felt someone should be ostracized for some misdeed or another, he simply nominated him a candidate for banishment. Once the nominations were in, each citizen used an oyster shell or a pottery shard to scratch the name of any one on the list he felt should be compelled to leave Greece. If the number of votes for one individual reached six thousand he would be expelled from the country, without any recourse to trial or appeal. The exiled man was given ten days in which to set his domestic and business affairs in order, and then he had to leave, usually for a period of ten years. There were no other punishments involved, however; no property was confiscated, no fines imposed, and no one imprisoned. At the the end of the decade, the man was allowed to return and resume his business as if nothing had happened.

Notable Births

1818	Richard Gatling	1894	J.B. Priestley
1851	Walter Reed	1905	Claudette Colbert
1860	John J. Pershing	1916	Roald Dahl
1874	Arnold Schoenberg	1925	Mel Torme
1876	Sherwood Anderson	1944	Jacqueline Bisset

Notable Events

1759	Battle of Quebec
1788	New York City named capital of United States
1788	First U.S. Federal election held
1814	"Star Spangled Banner" written
1826	First rhinoceros in United States exhibited, New York City
1899	H.H. Bliss of New York City became nation's first auto fatality
1970	Attica prison stormed by 1,000 N.Y. State Troopers

The stomach of a hippopotamus can hold about 400 pounds.

During the fall of 1944, a detachment of United States Marines was temporarily headquartered in the Russell Islands while it awaited the go-ahead for the invasion of Okinawa. There, the Marines had the opportunity to mingle with the native population, and many of the Leathernecks were fascinated by the witchcraft the islanders employed. One old chief appeared to have quite uncanny powers, a suspicion that was confirmed when he prophesied the beginning of the rainy season to the very day.

A marine officer finally cornered the old man and asked him how he did it. The chief told him in his best pidgin English:

"Blackfella looksee coconut tree, looksee bird, looksee topside, alleesame savvy by n' by come rain. Blackfella alleesame savvy pretty damn sure come rain quick when he looksee Marinefellas, sailorfellas draw plenty raincoats from small stores."

Answers: All the cows have horns.

A mouse going on vacation.

SEPTEMBER 14

Notable Births

1769	Alexander von Humboldt	1923	Charles Evers
1860	Hamlin Garland	1934	Kate Millett
1886	Jan Maseryk	1944	Joey Heatherton

Notable Events

1509 Earthquake claimed 3,000 victims in Constantinople
1807 Fulton's steamboat tested on Hudson River
1812 Russians destroyed Moscow on approach of Napoleon
1847 U.S. Army entered Mexico City
1886 Typewriter ribbon patented
1911 Peter Stolypin, Russian premier, assassinated
1940 First peacetime conscription bill enacted in United States
1951 Red Chinese invaded Lhasa
1964 Floods in South Korea killed 563 people

Questions: How's your movie memory? In what years were these films Academy Award winners?
Annie Hall
My Fair Lady
From Here to Eternity
Marty

Cortez Peters of Washington, D.C., wearing mittens in zero-degree cold, once typed 184 words per minute.

Several years ago, as part of some research it was doing on America's love affair with the boob-tube (an increasingly accurate term, I might add), the *Detroit Free Press* offered 120 families $500 if they would go without television for one month. Only 27 of them accepted the offer.

Getting an award from TV is like kissing someone with bad breath.

Mason Williams

Not too long ago, better than one out of every six members of the United States Communist party was an FBI agent, and the bureau, through the dues paid by their spies, was the biggest financial supporter of communism in the United States.

I don't know much about Americanism, but it's a damned good word with which to carry an election.

Warren G. Harding

The Emperor Diocletion once "hired" 40,000 Christians to build his baths. They labored seven years, and 27,800 of them died during that time. When the buildings were completed, Diocletian rewarded the survivors' efforts by executing all of them. Their leader, Zeno, later became a saint.

Hitler had the best answers to everything.

Charles Manson

It wasn't the severe Russian winter that kept Napoleon from taking Moscow in 1812. The early part of that winter, the period when Napoleon retreated, was unusually mild. The French withdrew from Moscow on October 19, and it wasn't until October 27 that the first overnight frost occurred in the region. By November 8, temperatures were generally colder, but not severely so. In fact, Napoleon's advance to the rear was hampered because the Beresina River, often frozen by the end of November, was still open water on November 26. When Napoleon left his army at Smorgani on December 5, temperatures still hadn't dropped below the twenties.

The event that had taken the greatest toll of the French Army was a long history of illness, which began with sunstroke in the summer and progressed to dysentery, diphtheria, and typhus in the months that followed. Poor medical care and inadequate supplies compounded the army's ill-fortune. Even though it was a mild early winter, it was enough to kill thousands of Napoleon's troops who were already ill or wounded.

History is mostly guessing. The rest is prejudice.

Will and Ariel Durant

Answer: 1977, 1964, 1953, 1955.

SEPTEMBER 15

Questions: Why is a butler like a mountain?

Which will burn longer, a thin wax candle or a fat tallow one?

Notable Births

1789	James Fenimore Cooper	1903	Roy Acuff
1857	William Howard Taft	1913	John Mitchell
1889	Robert Benchley	1915	Robert McCloskey
1890	Agatha Christie	1922	Jackie Cooper
1894	Jean Renoir	1924	Bobby Short
1899	Milton Eisenhower	1938	Gaylord Perry

Notable Events

1776	Washington abandoned New York City
1853	First woman ordained minister in United States, A.B. Blackwell
1863	Lincoln suspended Habeas Corpus for remainder of war
1904	Wilbur Wright made first turn in airplane
1913	Important goat show opened in Rochester, New York
1915	Germans in New Guinea surrendered
1935	Nuremburg Laws made Jews outlaws and swastika state flag
1950	MacArthur took offensive at Inchon
1959	Khrushchev began U.S. tour
1969	South Korean floods killed 250 people

Most everyone knows that Daniel DeFoe's novel *Robinson Crusoe* was based on the experiences of a real seaman named Alexander Selkirk, who was marooned on Juan Fernandez Island, off the coast of Chile, for nearly 4½ years.

Selkirk was born Alexander Sel*craig* in Largo, Scotland, in 1676. His father was a sober shoemaker, but the boy was rebellious and undisciplined. In 1703, he saw handbills advertising berths for able sailors in Captain William Dampier's mission to plunder French and Spanish ships (these countries were at war again, as usual, with England), and he journeyed to London to sign on. He went aboard the second ship in Dampier's expedition, the *Cinque Ports*, which was commanded by William Pickering. Holding the rank of sailing master, Selkirk was third or fourth in the chain of command. Although he thought Pickering an excellent seaman and a good officer, he came to detest his immediate superior, a Lieutenant Stradling. As luck would have it, Pickering died early on in the voyage, and Stradling was elevated to the command of the ship.

He must have been a miserable man to sail under, for when the two vessels put into Juan Fernandez for provisions and water, Selkirk and forty-two other men vowed to remain on the island. Dampier finally had to bribe them all to return to Stradling's ship. Then, in March and April 1704, Dampier collected five prizes, but they did not carry especially valuable cargoes. This led to a rift between the greedy Stradling and Dampier, and they agreed to split up for a time. Members of both crews were then given the opportunity to change captains, but only five did. Selkirk himself stayed with Stradling, believing Dampier to be one of the least seaworthy skippers sailing. The *Cinque Ports* journeyed forth to Central America while Dampier's ship, the *Saint George*, remained off the South American coast.

Plunder was thin for the *Cinque Ports*, and she was badly damaged in a storm that summer. By September, she had returned to Juan Fernandez. During those months the relationship between Stradling and Selkirk had further deteriorated. In October, when Stradling gave the order to sail in what Selkirk considered to be a half-repaired boat, Selkirk insisted he be put ashore. He expected that other sailors would also refuse to sail, but he was wrong. The captain took him at his word and dispatched him in the long boat. After the boat had left him on the island, Selkirk changed his mind and called after it to return, but his entreaties fell dead in the water. Robinson Crusoe had landed.

According to Selkirk's own account of his marooning, he spent his first eight months in a cave, sometimes bored, sometimes fearful, often brooding, occasionally suicidal. Then the words of his Bible finally reached him, and he set about making as decent a life for himself as was possible under the circumstances. He moved from the cave and built a hut. He journeyed inland, where he found, in addition to many wild fruits and vegetables, acres of such things as radishes, turnips, and plum trees, which had been sown by early sailors and castaways. Wild goats abounded on the island, and after the one pound of powder he had brought for his musket ran out, he learned to catch them alive. He domesticated some of the animals, and lamed others as a precaution. He also trapped and tamed the descendents of the ships' cats, which had escaped onto the island. He said that by the time of his rescue, hundreds of cats slept next to his bed. Several times enemy ships visited the island and Selkirk had to go into hiding. The closest he ever came to being captured was when a Spanish sailor urinated on the trunk of the tree he was hiding in.

On February 1, 1709, Selkirk spotted the English vessel, the *Duke and Duchess*, several miles offshore, and set bonfires to attract the crew's attention. That almost proved a mistake, because the master, a Captain Rogers, feared the fires came from a Spanish garrison, and so he almost didn't put ashore.

Selkirk was eventually made sailing master of a ship the Rogers's expedition captured (its purpose was the same as Dampier's) and earned £800 as his share of the booty during the 2½ years he sailed with Rogers. When they returned to London in October 1711, Alexander Selkirk had been gone over eight years, and had spent more than half of that time in total isolation.

He spent the next thirty months in London, alternately debauched and depressed. When his money ran out he returned home, where it was said he spent much of his time alone, gazing out over the ocean. In 1716, he left for London with a girl named Sophia Bruce, whom he had met during one of his protracted soliloquies. They lived together there for a year or two, until he took a commission as a lieutenant in the Royal Navy. He returned to her after one voyage, but soon left her again, this time for a woman named Frances Cavendish, whom he'd met once while he was waiting for his ship to get underway. They married shortly before his death (occasioned either by malaria or yellow fever), which occurred off the east coast of Africa in December 1720.

A footnote: Shortly after Stradling stranded Selkirk, the *Cinque Ports* herself was stranded off Columbia, and her crew was captured by Spaniards and thrown into prison. Most of them were dead by the time Selkirk had been marooned for a year.

The hot-headedness of youth causes no more damage than the apathy of old age.

La Rochefoucauld

Answers: Because he looks down on the valet.

Both burn shorter.

Notable Births

1823	Francis Parkman	1925	B.B. King
1880	Alfred Noyes	1926	John Knowles
1914	Allen Funt	1927	Peter Falk
1922	Janis Paige	1930	Anne Francis
1924	Lauren Bacall	1934	Elgin Baylor
1925	Charlie Byrd	1948	Rosie Casals

Notable Events

1620	Puritans left Plymouth, England, for America
1862	Battle of Antietam began
1891	H.M. Converse became first white woman to become Indian chief, Six Nations Tribe
1938	Britain and France urged the Czechs to give up Sudetenland
1941	Shah of Iran abdicated
1974	FBI found guilty of perjury and suborning perjury in Wounded Knee trials
1978	Earthquake in Iran killed several thousand people

Question: How's your movie memory? In what years were these films Academy Award winners?

The Godfather
Ben-Hur
On the Waterfront
A Man for All Seasons

In 1795, a sea captain named Jacob Crowninshield had his vessel, the *America*, docked in Bengal, India, when it occurred to him that there weren't any elephants back home. A shrewd Yankee, he reasoned that an elephant would fetch a good price from some entrepreneur who wanted to display this beast, then considered the ultimate attraction of the time. He proceeded to purchase a two-year-old female for the princely sum of $450.

The *America* docked in Manhattan on April 11, 1796, and within a week Crowninshield's hunch was confirmed: in a few days he'd sold the elephant for $10,000. The new owner did make a fortune from her, and Crowninshield ended up in Congress.

Perhaps he had heard the story, or seen the elephant in his youth, for a Mr. Albert Richardson tried to cash in thirty-eight years later in the same way. Richardson was a ship owner in Boston in 1834, and he was not considered to be an easy man to deal with, especially in business matters. When Captain Brown of the *Sachem* returned from Bangkok, and mentioned that Captain Elias Davison had been loading an elephant on board another of Richardson's ships when he departed from Thailand, Richardson's greed became overriding. He *would* have the elephant, and at his price.

Captain Davison reached Boston a fortnight later and went immediately to Richardson. He reported that all his accounts were in order, and he had drawn about $300 against his pay on the voyage.

"What about the elephant?" asked the owner.

Davison admitted he had an elephant on board, but he didn't understand what that had to do with anything.

"Freight, man, freight!" said Richardson.

The captain explained that, since he had ample room under the hatch and no cargo had been passed over for the elephant's sake, he hadn't thought that Richardson would charge him for freight.

Well, the miser said, the vessel and all the space in it were his and he was entitled to a freight charge. He named an exhorbitant figure.

"Then I wish, sir, that I had been carrying the elephant on your account instead of on my own."

"Yes," agreed Richardson, "and then I instead of you could have sold the beast to a menagerie." The shrewd businessman paused for a moment and then continued, "I tell you what I'll do. I'll write off the $300 you owe me and the freight charges, and I'll take the elephant!"

Davison looked crestfallen. "Couldn't you do a little better than that, sir?"

"Not a penny more." (He knew he had the captain under his thumb.) "Take it or leave it."

Davison took it; he had no other choice. A contract for the transaction was quickly drafted and signed, and Richardson then hurried down to the wharf to see his new possession. He got there just as the deckhands were preparing a block and tackle to haul the beast out.

"Be careful!" he called to the mate. "That's my elephant now. Don't hurt him!"

"Take a might of pounding to hurt this elephant," the mate hollered back. "He died last night off Cape Cod."

Answer: 1972, 1959, 1954, 1966.

SEPTEMBER 17

Question: What are the average elevations of these states?
Maine
Louisiana
Minnesota
Illinois

Notable Births

1730	Friedrich von Steuben	1916	Mary Stewart
1883	William Carlos Williams	1928	Roddy McDowell
1898	Frank Frisch	1929	Sterling Moss
1907	Warren Burger	1931	Anne Bancroft
1915	Arthur Miller	1935	Ken Kesey

Notable Events

1787	U.S. Constitution adopted at Philadelphia
1908	First airplane fatality; Orville Wright injured
1953	First successful separation of Siamese twins
1959	Typhoon Sarah killed 2,000 people in Asia
1961	Typhoon Nancy left 137,000 homeless in Japan

Though, of course, no European a few centuries ago would ever admit to having attended one, most people knew exactly what went on at a witches' Sabbath. Witches' Sabbaths were usually held at the intersection of four corners or near a lake, and one could tell where a coven had held a meeting because the demons' footprints scorched the earth so severely that nothing would ever grow in those places again. When a witch was going to or coming from a Sabbath it was impossible for him or her to go through a door or a window. That problem was solved by leaving through the chimney and returning through the keyhole. In order to conceal an absence from home, his or her form was taken by one of the animal familiars (often cats) the witch kept, which would feign illness until the master returned.

At the site of the ceremonies, newcomers were stopped and checked for the Devil's mark, then made to renounce their salvation, spit on the Bible, and swear allegiance to, and kiss the Devil. Then the singing and dancing began. One popular dance involved the witch stripping naked and dancing with two cats, one tied around the neck, the other to the belt. After an exhausting period of dancing, the witches would then sit in a circle and brag about the evil they had done recently. Those whose conduct was judged to be insufficiently bad would be flogged. Later, the witches would feast on blood and flesh and were entertained by thousands of terpsichorean toads, which generated spontaneously from the ground.

Then they'd all go home, get some sleep, and go to their government jobs in the morning.

People only think a thing's worth believing in if it's hard to believe.
Armiger Barclay

From the time of James I (1603-25) to the middle of the eighteenth century, about four thousand people were burned or hanged as witches in England. During the height of the witch mania in Germany, there were dozens of executions daily for many years.

Answer: 600', 100', 1,200', 600'

SEPTEMBER 18

Notable Births

1709	Samuel Johnson	1905	Eddie Anderson
1787	William Collins	1909	Kwame Nkrumah
1895	John Diefenbaker	1933	Jimmy Rodgers
1905	Greta Garbo	1940	Frankie Avalon

Notable Events

1634 Anne Hutchinson arrived in Boston
1792 6 of 10 *Bounty* mutineers found guilty, later hanged
1793 Cornerstone of Capitol Building laid
1813 Michael McIlvena hanged for illegally performing marriage ceremony
1873 Panic of 1873 began
1926 Gulf Coast hurricane killed 372, left 40,000 homeless
1937 First night skywriting accomplished, Andy Stinnis, New York City
1959 Floods in Surat, India, left 500 dead
1961 Dag Hammerskjold killed in Congo plane crash
1975 Patty Hearst captured

Questions: Grammatically, should you say "nine and five *is* thirteen," or "nine and five *are* thirteen"?

How do we know that *Uncle Tom's Cabin* was not written by a female hand?

More last words of famous people:

Quick, Puss, chloroform — ether — or I am a dead man!
Sir Richard Burton, to his wife

Come on, boys, come on!
Major Henry Camp, at the Battle of Richmond

Moose . . . Indian . . .
Henry David Thoreau

Stop! Turn home! I'm bored! I'm bored!
D'Annunzio, to his chauffeur

I am mortally wounded, I think.
Stephen Decatur

Put your hands on my shoulders and don't struggle.
W.S. Gilbert, rescuing a drowning woman

I wonder why he shot me?
Huey Long

Mozart!
Gustav Mahler

I have a terrific headache.
Franklin D. Roosevelt

But . . . but . . . Mr. Colonel . . .
Benito Mussolini

Mussolini must not die!
Petracci, Mussolini's mistress

"Texas . . . Texas . . . Margaret . . ."
Sam Houston

"Let me die in my old uniform. God forgive me for ever putting on another."
Benedict Arnold, asking for his uniform as a major general in the Continental Army

"So little done. So much to do."
Alexander Graham Bell

"Smite my womb."
Agrippina, to the assassins her son Nero had sent to kill her

"Waiting are they? Waiting are they? Well, goddam' em, let 'em wait!"
Ethan Allen, when told by a parson that the angels were waiting for him

"José! Bring the luggage. They do not want us here."
Simon Bolivar

"I thought I did for the best . . . Useless! Useless!"
John Wilkes Booth

"Follow the path for another fifty yards. I am going back to the foot of the rocks to make another climb. If I feel in good form I shall take the difficult way up; if I do not I shall take the easy one. I shall join you in an hour."
King Albert of Belgium

"I am about the extent of a tenth of a gnat's eyebrow better."
Joel Chandler Harris

"I am better now."
D.H. Lawrence

"I've never felt better."
Douglas Fairbanks

And one last word to rival that last syllable of General Sedgwick. It was uttered by freedom fighter, Robert Emmett, when the hangman asked him if he were ready:

"Not—"

You know what I think about violence. For me it is profoundly moral, more moral than compromises and transactions.
Mussolini

Because it was written by Harriet Beecher S towe.

Answers: Nine plus five equals *fourteen*.

SEPTEMBER 19

Question: What's a Fen in the People's Republic of China?

What's a Fun in Hong Kong?

Epitaph from New Ipswich, New Hampshire:

Mr Gilman Spaulding
Was kil'd with an axe
By an insane Brother
Sept. 19,1842
Aet. 38

The following is an accurate sketch of a tombstone in East Haven, Connecticut. Mrs. Bradley had nine other children:

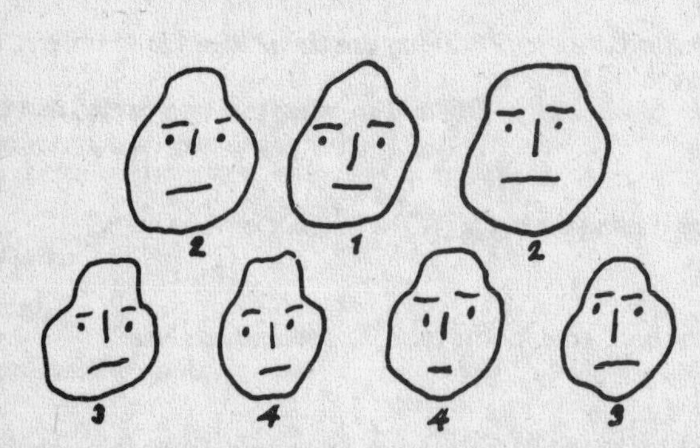

In memory of Urial, first son of Mr. Edmun & Mrs. Lydia Bradley, who died Sept. 29th, A.D. 1788. Also of three pair of twins, who died A.D. 1788/89, & 1793/4.

See death remove the eldest son,
Just as the family begin;
And three pair of twins in a short space
To quicken us in the Christian race.

The word "ye, often found in old books and on monuments and tombstones, is not pronounced "ye." It's pronounced "the" — in fact, it *is* "the." In the early days of bookmaking, when their art and equipment were rather primitive, printers had problems spacing out a line of type to give an even margin. When they had to, they would use a *Y* as a corruption of the Old English thorn letter þ, which came from the Latin alphabet and was used in the Celtic and Old English languages. Its sound was *"th."* Similar spacing considerations (and sometimes just poor planning) led to its use by stonecutters on memorial stones, plaques, and statue legends. After a time, the origins of "ye" were forgotten and it was used by convention, even when there was no need to do so.

Answer: .1312 inches; .14625 inches.

Notable Births

1890	Ernest Truex	1926	Duke Snider
1901	Joseph Pasternak	1926	Lurleen Wallace
1910	Margaret Lindsay	1933	David McCallum
1910	Frances Farmer	1936	Al Oerter
1911	William Golding	1943	Joe Morgan
1914	Rogers Morton	1949	Twiggy

Notable Events

1796	Washington delivered farewell address
1863	Battle of Chicamauga began
1870	Seige of Paris by Prussian forces began
1876	Carpet sweeper patented, M.R. Bissell
1928	First animated sound cartoon shown, *Steamboat Willie*
1955	Peron deposed in Argentina
1955	Hurricane Hilda left 200 people dead in Mexico
1976	Turkish 727 struck mountain in Turkey, 155 people dead

It sounds incredible, but there were vacuum cleaner salesmen in ancient Rome. There *must* have been! Witness this passage from Ovid:

A lewd dealer will come to your mistress in a buying mood, and will spread his wares before her, while you sit in misery. And she . . . will ask to inspect them. Then she will kiss you. Then she will ask you to buy. She will swear that this will satisfy her for many a long year, that she needs it now, that now is a good time to buy it. If you make the excuse that you have not the cash at home, she will ask you for a check — lest you ever be glad you learned to write.

The most essential gift . . . is a built-in shock-proof shit detector.

Ernest Hemingway

The tennis term "love" comes from the French *l'oeuf*, which means "egg."

Following a number of committee reports and extensive meetings of program executives, stars, sponsors, and members of the advertising industry, The National Broadcasting System decided in December 1947, that it was permissible to use the word "diaper" on the air.

Bananas are grown with great commercial success north of Seattle, Washington. Locally, they call the region the "Banana Belt."

Have you ever wondered how much food a squirrel stores away for winter? Professional squirrel watchers have estimated that a single squirrel can secrete as much as twenty bushels of food in dozens of locations; however, unlike (or like, if you wish) the elephant, the squirrel forgets. It seldom remembers where it hid even a tenth of its stockpile.

Question: What are the largest continents, in order?

Notable Births

356 B.C.	Alexander the Great	1905	Ellery Queen
1878	Upton Sinclair	1934	Sophia Loren

Notable Events

1860 Prince of Wales arrived at Detroit
1902 115 people perished in Birmingham, Alabama, church fire
1934 Hauptmann arrested in Lindbergh baby kidnapping
1973 Riggs-King tennis match, King won 6-4, 6-3, 6-3

Dwight D. Eisenhower wore three coats of clear nail polish.

Up until at least 1938, and probably for some years thereafter, hydraulic brake fluid was basically an equal mixture of castor oil and denatured alcohol.

Some people would argue that, "Cats are cats, and more trouble than they're worth," but not one particular New York man. This gentleman's family kept ten cats, and with that many felines, there was generally some sort of trouble. Their antics continually pushed the man toward the breaking point, and finally, after one incorrigible cat defecated for the umpteeth time on the rug, the fellow broke. He lit out after it with a sixteen-gauge shotgun, and cornered it beneath a chair. To get a clear shot, the man tried to prod the transgressor out, using the butt of the gun. The weapon went off and blew the fellow's brains all over the room.

The cat escaped without a scratch.

In classical times, the color and quality of a person's hair was felt to be an indicator of his personality. Straight hair was associated with cowardice, while frizzy hair was associated with clumsiness and coarseness. Curly hair that ended in ringlets was the most esteemed. Reportedly, Achilles and Ajax had this kind of hair and the curls of Augustus Caesar were said to be unsurpassed in Rome. Auburn or light brown hair supposedly indicated intelligence, industry, a good disposition, and sexual prowess. Black was a neutral color, but red hair was an object of aversion, and was thought to be a mark of reprobation. Even red animals were viewed with scorn, and it was the habit of the Copts in Egypt to hurl a red donkey annually from a high wall as a sacrifice.

In September 1954, the K-9 Corps of Phenix City, Alabama, really showed its stuff. Purportedly on the track of an escaped convict, the three bloodhounds steadfastly refused to enter a thick woods until a path had been cleared for them by a reporter. Once in the woods and on the criminal's scent, one dog got lost, and a second followed the track of a policeman all day. Later on, the third dog got carsick. All three of the bloodhounds later developed hay fever from the ordeal.

Did you know that Dwight Eisenhower played fourteen games as a minor league outfielder for the Junction City, Kansas, team back when he was a teenager? Under an assumed name, too. It was reported that this "Wilson" was so good that he attracted the attention of several major league scouts in that short time.

Here is a famous English epitaph:

Here lies John Bun
Who was killed by a gun;
His name wasn't bun, his real name was Wood,
But Wood wouldn't rhyme with gun,
so I thought Bun should.

Answer: Asia, Africa, North America, South America, Antarctica, Europe, Australia.

SEPTEMBER 21

Questions: Why is a baseball game like an angel cake?

Why is a baseball game like yesterday?

Notable Births

1452	Girolamo Savanarola	1849	Edmund Gosse
1756	John McAdam	1932	Melvin Van Peebles
1866	H.G. Wells	1944	Hamilton Jordan
1874	Gustav Holst	1949	Artis Gilmore

Notable Events

1774	First Colonial Congress met, Philadelphia
1792	French Republican Convention opened
1934	4,000 people died in Japanese typhoon
1938	Hurricane of 1938 left 600 dead in New England and tremendous damage
1945	Henry Ford retired as head of Ford Motors
1953	North Korean pilot landed MIG at U.S. base, collected $100,000 reward
1957	Death of Haakon VII of Norway

One of the greatest hoaxes of all time, ranking right up there with the London lion washing, was the Marie Antoinette necklace case. In 1772, Louis XV's mistress, Madame Du Barry, insisted that he have the most expensive necklace in the world made especially for her. The court jeweler, a man named Boehmer, was commissioned to fashion it. He collected 600 stones, worth about $7,000,000, and over many months made a stunning piece of jewelry. He was waiting to be called to Versailles to present it when Louis died. For some reason, neither Louis XVI nor Marie Antoinette wanted it and it remained with Boehmer.

Several years passed before the two principals in the case arrived on the scene. One was a woman associated with the court named Jeanne de la Motte. She had some royal blood in her, and a lot of ambition. The other individual was the Cardinal de Rohan, a man whom Marie Antoinette hated, but who desperately wanted to be in her good graces. He was compulsive, unimaginative, and immoral — in short, a good man to try to bribe.

Jeanne managed to convince de Rohan that she could help him win favor with the queen. Then, working with a forger, she produced letters that indicated a willingness on the part of the queen to reconcile their differences. Some time later, after more of this kind of intrigue, Jeanne arranged a short, nighttime meeting between de Rohan and an imposter pretending to be the queen, possibly Jeanne's sister. The imposter gave de Rohan a rose as a token of the queen's love for him, though not a word was spoken betwen them. Finally, the cardinal received a letter authorizing him to get the necklace for her, using Jeanne as the intermediary. It also urged him, and whomever he dealt with, not to breathe a word about it to anyone, as she wanted surprise her husband.

Jeanne got the necklace, and her husband immediately smuggled it to England. There he sold the stones, and sent most of the money back to Jeanne who was still in Paris. She lived extremely well on it for a time.

Then, about six months after the theft, Cardinal de Rohan, puzzled by the real queen's continued coolness toward him, finally asked her about the necklace. She was shocked and outraged. "Necklace? *What* necklace?"

Jeanne de la Motte was arrested, tried, and thrown into prison. What monies she had left were confiscated. By this time the French Revolution was brewing, however, and with the help of some rebels, whose cause she supported, she escaped and joined her husband in England. There she worked incessantly against the French monarchy.

Her life ended in 1791 when she jumped out of a window to avoid her creditors.

What female heart can gold despise?
What cat's averse to fish?

Thomas Gray

Woman's virtue is man's greatest invention.

Cornelia Otis Skinner

Behind every great man is a woman with nothing to wear.

L. Grant Glickman

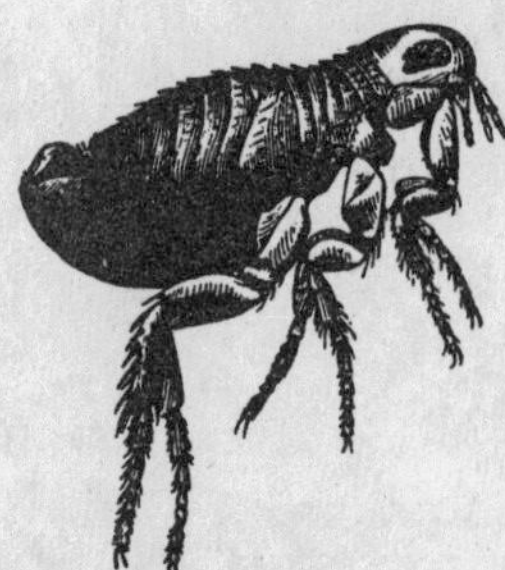

The Icelandic word for flea is *flo*, the German is *floh*, and the Dutch is *vloo*. All have the root word *plu* in common, which means "to fly or jump" in both the seminal Germanic and Sanskrit languages. A flea can jump over thirty times its own height, and pull eighty times its own weight.

Answer: It depends on the batter.
Because it's a pastime.

SEPTEMBER 22

Notable Births

1694	Lord Chesterfield	1895	Paul Muni
1796	Michael Faraday	1902	John Houseman
1885	Erich von Stroheim	1914	Martha Scott
1895	Babette Deutsch	1920	Bob Lemon

Notable Events

1241 Death of Snorri Sturlason, Icelandic poet
1609 Moors expelled from Spain
1656 First female jury in American sat, Patuxent, Maryland
1734 George Boehnisch, first Moravian in American, arrived, New York City
1776 Nathan Hale hanged
1862 Emancipation Proclamation issued
1927 Dempsey-Tunney "Long Count" issued
1955 Hurricane Janet left 500 dead in Caribbean
1958 Sherman Adams resigned as Ike's assistant
1975 Attempted assassination of President Ford by Sara Jane Moore

It was a common belief among the Irish that rats could be rhymed to death. Many believed that rats were so strongly cannibalistic (they are) that they would literally eat each other inside out (they don't).

Before he became president, Dwight D. Eisenhower was president of Columbia University; however, that resulted from a misunderstanding. The trustees of the university had selected Dwight's brother Milton, a noted educator, for the position. Their messenger to Milton misinterpreted his mission and contacted Ike instead, who immediately accepted.

Saint Francis of Assisi must have been a remarkable man. He was supposedly able to levitate in his cell, even though he weighed over 300 pounds.

Snoring is grounds for divorce in sixteen states.

Question: What are the young of these animals called?

hare
turkey
pigeon
tiger

In the Mexican town of Coacalco several years ago, police killed a man who, in the opinion of the four thousand townspeople, did not deserve it. These enraged citizens stormed the mayor in his office, forced him to eat twelve pounds of bananas and then resign.

Despite the fact that they all spoke English in the Buster Crabbe TV series, in 1937, 90 percent of the men of the French Foreign Legion were German.

The invention of the sandwich is often attributed to the fourth Earl of Sandwich. Supposedly, he had been gambling without sleep or food for twenty-four hours straight when he suddenly felt an urge to eat. He called for something to be brought immediately. The only victuals handy were a slice of meat and two pieces of bread. The earl purportedly slapped the meat between the bread, and the sandwich was born.

Sandwich might have rediscovered the form, but he did not invent it. In his *Life of Tiberius Claudius Caesar*, Suetonius mentioned the sandwich nearly two-thousand years ago.

It was the practice of the ancient Egyptians to conduct trials in dark chambers so that the judge could not see the plaintiff, the defendent, or any of the lawyers. It was felt that cases could thereby be decided on their merits, and without the interference of any visual prejudice.

In most law courts a man is considered guilty until he is proven influential.

Laurence J. Peter

Answer: Leveret; poult; squab; whelp.

SEPTEMBER 23

Question: Do you know the common denominator of the following terms?

Harrier
Malinois
Clumber
Kuvaszok
Pulik

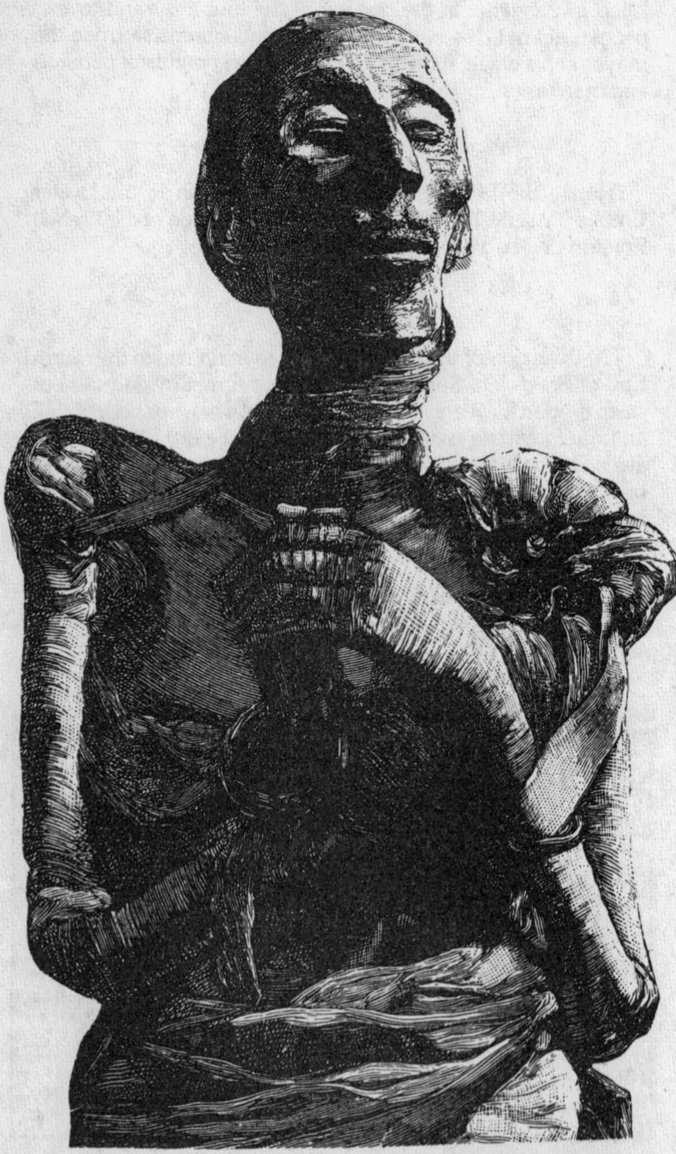

Natives of the province Imerina in the Malagasy Republic dig up the bodies of their dead each September and give them a fresh change of clothing. If the family of the deceased has had a good year financially, the corpse will also get a better grave. This goes on until the bereaved themselves die or the bodies wear out.

In Liechtenstein, an obituary is printed in the principality's newspaper whenever a cow dies.

Answer: They are all breeds of dogs.

Notable Births

480 B.C.	Euripides	1920	Mickey Rooney
63 B.C.	Augustus Caesar	1932	Ray Charles
1800	William McGuffey	1938	Romy Schneider
1889	Walter Lippman	1942	Woody Woodward
1898	Walter Pidgeon	1949	Bruce Springsteen

Notable Events

1719	Liechtenstein became first independent principality in Europe
1745	First native-born American knighted, William Pepperell
1780	Major Andre arrested; Arnold's treason exposed
1806	Lewis and Clark returned to Saint Louis
1845	Knickerbocker baseball club organized
1930	Mellon bought $800,000 worth of old masters
1952	Nixon delivered "Checkers" speech

Inflation hit the Roman Empire with a vengeance between 280 and 300 A.D. Using our own currency to illustrate the appalling situation there, a home that sold for a thousand dollars in 280 A.D. would have been worth two million by the year 300 — that is, if you could get a mortgage.

A study of economics usually reveals that the best time to buy anything is last year.

Marty Allen

Frank Speck of Philadelphia had a vasectomy in 1974. Some time afterward, his wife became pregnant. They decided that she would have an abortion, which was in due course performed. A few months later Mrs. Speck gave birth to a baby girl.

The Specks sued both their physicians.

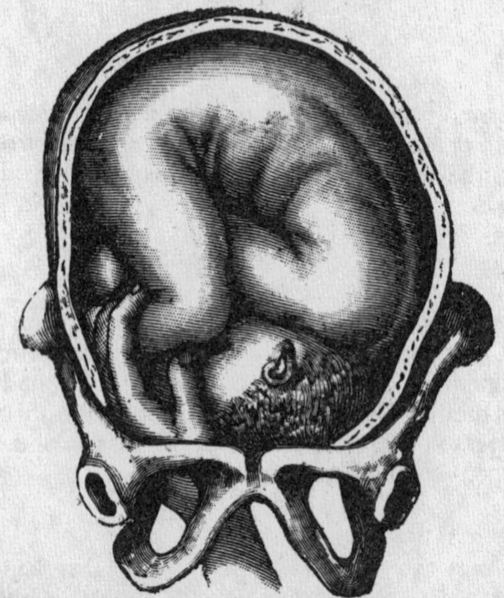

A vasectomy is never having to say you're sorry.

Rubin Carson

It is now quite lawful for a Catholic woman to avoid pregnancy by a resort to mathematics, though she is still forbidden to resort to physics and chemistry.

H.L. Mencken

Notable Births

1717	Horace Walpole	1896	F.Scott Fitzgerald
1755	John Marshall	1903	George Raft
1837	Mark Hanna	1924	Sheila MacRae
1890	A.P. Herbert	1941	John Mackey

Notable Events

787	Council of Nicea met to regulate image worship
1657	First autopsy and verdict of coroner's jury recorded in America, Maryland
1852	First flight of a dirigible, by Henri Giffard
1869	Black Friday on Stock Market
1906	Devil's Tower, Wyoming, made first national monument
1955	Eisenhower suffered heart attack
1966	Hurricane Inez left 293 dead in Caribbean

The modern meaning of the word "clue" comes from medieval England. When the story of Theseus was told in England, (he slew the Minotaur and found his way back out of the Labyrinth by following a string), the English associated their word for a ball of thread, a "clew," with the solution to Theseus' problem. This was the origin of its present definition.

Before the European explorations, bedbugs were unknown in the Western Hemisphere.

Up in Alaganik, Alaska, in late 1947, one Jimmy La Gasa decided to see what would happen if he fired a shot at a powder magazine.

If the leg the search party found could only talk . . .

In nature there are neither rewards nor punishments — there are only consequences.

Robert B. Ingersoll

Man who flirt with dynamite sometime fly with angels.

Charlie Chan

Giuseppe Cavallo was arrested in Sicily in September 1956, for attempting to commit suicide without a firearms permit for the gun he used.

The word "anathema" did not originally mean a curse. It came from the pagan Greek and Roman practice, still carried on in some form by the Catholic Church, of bringing a votive offering to be set up in a temple. A sailor who had returned safely from a voyage might have brought a model of his ship — *anathema*, from the Greek *ana*, "up" and *tithēmi*, "to set." An offering refused by the priest was *an-anathema* — not set up — which was gradually shortened to just *anathema*, while retaining its negative meaning.

Questions: How can the final score of a ballgame be four to two if not a man on either team reaches base?

Why is tennis so noisy?

School's been open for a couple of weeks now, and the weather is getting chilly enough to take its toll on attendance. Below are a number of excerpts from parents' notes to a high school nurse explaining why their children missed school:

"Dear school: Pleas exkuse John for being absent on January 28, 29, 30, 31, 32, and 33."

"Chris have an acre in his side."

"Mary could not come to school because she was bother by very close veins."

"John has been absent because he had two teeth taken out of his face."

"I kape Billie home because she had to Christmas shopping because I didn't no what size she wear."

"John was absent yesterday because he had a stomach."

"Please excue Gloria, She been sick and under the doctor."

"My son is under the doctor's care and could not take P.E. Please execute him."

"Lillie was absent from school yesterday as she had a gang over."

"Please excuse Blanch from P.E. for a few days. Yesterday she fell out of a tree and misplaced her hip."

"Please excuse Joyce from jim today. She is administrating."

"Please excuse Joey Friday, he had loose vowels."

"Carlos was absent yesterday because he was playing football, he was hurt in the growing part."

"My daughter wouldn't come to school Monday because she was tired. She spent the weekend with some Marines."

"Please excuse Sandra from being absent yesterday. She was in bed with gramps."

"Ralph was absent yesterday because of a sour trout."

"Please excuse Wayne for being out yesterday because he had the fuel."

from *Urban Folklore from the Paperwork Empire*

There is no substitute for education, unless it is the American school system.

Laurence J. Peter

Nine times out of ten the man who listens to reason is thinking of some way to refute it.

Laurence J. Peter

Answers: The players are all women.
Each player raises a racket.

SEPTEMBER 25

Question: Can you rank these countries according to the number of newspapers bought per person (from the greatest to the least)?

A. Iceland
B. Sweden
C. USSR
D. United States

Notable Births

1613	Claude Perrault	1918	Phil Rizzuto
1897	William Faulkner	1931	Barbara Walters
1905	Red Smith	1936	Juliet Prowse
1906	Dimitri Shostakovich	1951	Bob McAdoo

Notable Events

1513	Balboa discovered the Pacific
1789	Congress passed the Bill of Rights
1933	First state poorhouse opened, Smyrna, Delaware
1942	Wendell Willkie visited Moscow battlefront
1951	Battle of MIG Alley
1953	Typhoon in China Sea claimed 1,300 lives
1956	Transatlantic telephone system began operation
1959	Attempted assassination of S. Bandaranaiki, Ceylon
1964	UAW out on strike against GM

When Lawrence Nelson was buried in Lenoir, North Carolina, his widow ordered the inscription on his tombstone to read: "Robbed and murdered by Harry Kendall and John Vickers, September 25, 1906." In part because of circumstantial evidence, and in part because of the publicity the curious epitaph received, Kendall and Vickers were convicted and were given life sentences. Their appeals for a new trial were denied, and each served eleven years before a man was arrested who confessed to Nelson's murder, more than a decade before.

The two were immediately freed, but Vickers died soon thereafter. Kendall spent the next thirty years of his life trying to get the monument destroyed, or at least to have the statement of his guilt erased from it, but to no avail. Entreaties to the murdered man's family and to the state legislature fell on deaf ears. Kendall finally took the state to court in the late forties. In 1949, the legislature voted to give Kendall $5,000 in damages in an out-of-court settlement (much less than his own accumulated court costs, and certainly very little compensation for eleven years of wrongful imprisonment). The legislators also passed a law prohibiting monuments charging people with crimes, but it left the question of the offending tombstone unresolved.

The tombstone is about the only thing that can stand upright and lie on its face at the same time.

Mary Wilson Little

The Indian Ocean boasts a very special crustacean. This arthropod is to crabs what Yogi is to bears — smarter than average. To defend itself, the shore crab always carries a pair of sea anemones along with it, one held in each of its claws. When an enemy approaches, the crab lunges towards it, pincers held high. One taste of the stinging tentacles of the anemone is usually enough for any predator.

Balboa, who is given credit for being the first European to see the Pacific from its eastern shore, got to the New World as a common seaman, not as an expedition leader, as many would assume. Although he was a deckhand, he so impressed those in charge of the voyage that he was placed in command of the settlement they established at Panama. It was on a reconnoitering mission several months after he reached the isthmus that he climbed that peak in Darien (on this day in 1513) and insured his place in history.

Tides in the Mediterranean Sea are very slight, ranging from nine inches at Zante to about three feet in Venice.

An empty gallon can will hold one gallon of ammonia gas. A gallon can filled with water will hold 600 gallons of ammonia gas.

The lavender plant got its name from the manner in which it was used in the Middle Ages. The word "lavender" comes from the Latin root *lavāre*, to wash. Small brooms made of sweet lavender were used for cleaning delicate fabrics. This was instead of subjecting them to the usual method of beating materials on a stone in the river. The garment would be washed with soap and water, gently brushed with a lavender broom, and then rinsed.

The real name of Daniel DeFoe, author of *Robinson Crusoe* and *Moll Flanders*, was simply Foe. Both he and his identically named father were active dissenters who wrote a large number of political and religious tracts. To distinguish their authorship, Foe the younger began to sign his works D. Foe. This appellation caught on with the public, and by 1705 he had adopted Defoe as his signature.

Answer: (based on 1975 data) a, b, c, d.

SEPTEMBER 26

Notable Births

1875	Edmund Gwenn	1897	Pope Paul VI
1888	T.S. Eliot	1898	George Gershwin
1889	Martin Heidegger	1926	Julie London
1891	Charles Munch	1947	Lynn Anderson

Notable Events

1777 Philadelphia taken by British
1831 Anti-Masonic party convention opened
1898 Supposed remains of Columbus unearthed in Cuba
1934 *Queen Mary* launched
1959 Typhoon Vera killed 4,500 in Japan
1960 First Nixon - Kennedy debate
1946 Russians denounced Sherlock Holmes on grounds he protected private property

Question: In terms of numbers of ships registered, what are the four greatest maritime nations?

The name of the ocean liner *Queen Mary* was supposed to be *Queen Victoria.* When the president of the Cunard Line went to tell George V of his company's plans for the ship, he said simply that they were going to name her after one of England's most noble queens, meaning Victoria. The king immediately thought the man meant his own wife, and exclaimed, "Oh, Her Majesty will be so pleased!" And that was that.

How come nobody wants to argue with me? Is it because I'm always right?

Jim Bouton

Between 1870 and 1880, according to the United States Census, the total wealth of Americans rose by some 80 percent, from about twenty-four billion to over forty-four billion dollars. During that same time, the average workingman's wages fell from over $400 to about $300 a year.

Civilization and profits go hand in hand.

Calvin Coolidge

What has destroyed every previous civilization has been the tendency to the unequal distribution of wealth and power.

Henry George

The people came to realize that wealth is not the fruit of labor but the result of organized protected robbery.

Frantz Fanon

The word "sardonic," denoting a humorous mood in which there lurks some evil, comes from a legend of the Italian island of Sardinia. An herb that could cause the death of a person through unsuppressible laughter supposedly grew there, and many peasant stories were told about it.

Nobody ever died of laughter.

Max Beerbohm

Shortly after President Nixon left office, a Parisian company marketed cassette tapes of his resignation speech, complete with transcripts in both English and French. Unfortunately, Nixon's speech was too short to fill the tapes completely, so the company tacked on readings of several of the poems of John Keats.

When Hitler committed suicide shortly before Germany's surrender in World War II, he was a rich man. Not so much because of his salary — that was substantial, but not lavish — but because of a brilliant idea of Martin Bormann's. The Fuhrer's portrait appeared on almost all German stamps between 1933 and 1945, and Bormann reasoned that it was only fair for Hitler to receive a royalty for it. Although the royalty was only a small fraction of a pfennig, it made Hitler millions of marks.

That poisonous snake, the viper, has a harmless origin as far as its name is concerned. In Latin, *vivapara* means only "she who produces live young."

One year after the end of World War II there was a severe meat shortage in America. Several incidents were recorded of people jokingly ordering a steak at a restaurant, getting it, and dropping dead of heart failure. In September 1946, Marlin Perkins, later the host of the television program "Wild Kingdom," but then the director of the Lincoln Park Zoo in Chicago, noted that his diet hadn't been much affected by the dearth of beef. He went on to say that Americans should try alternative kinds of flesh, and recommended his favorite: fried rattlesnake meat.

America is an enormous frosted cupcake in the middle of millions of starving people.

Gloria Steinem

Answer: Liberia, Russia, Greece, Panama.

SEPTEMBER 27

Questions: Why is a former boxer like a beehive?

What kind of paper makes the best kite?

Notable Births

1722	Samuel Adams	1920	William Conrad
1792	George Cruikshank	1922	Arthur Penn
1840	Thomas Nast	1926	Jayne Meadows
1917	Louis Auchincloss	1929	Sada Thompson
1919	Charles Percy	1939	Kathy Whitworth

Notable Events

1290	Earthquake in China claimed 100,000 lives
1741	George II secured Hanoverian neutrality
1760	Secret treaty by East India Company made Mir Kasim Nawab of Bengal
1892	Book matches patented
1919	Democratic National Committee voted to admit women
1922	King Constantine of Greece abdicated
1937	First Santa Claus school opened, Albion, New York
1964	Warren Commission report issued

> Fake, small-appearing feet, which French heeled shoes and pinched toes develop, have a great power to make a man look down, which means to get down to sex. Small-footed women have a fascination over man to escape the delay in progression which big feet indicate. Man was created in a woman's brain, and since he is under the Divine Law to move forward he must move his interest from a woman's feet and get past them — complete his cycle — where he can feast on her through her head and brain which is typical of returning to the Garden of Eden, the holy place waiting for him.

> It is absolutely true, that only our Great Creative Gentile White race of people have an absolute monopoly on Christianity, yet all others are allowed to receive blessings from us Christians and in the near future, it will be publically announced, that negroes and orientals will be given a new religion, because their present original belief is worthless, the same as nothing, because it does nothing for them. As everyone knows, they have to cater to us White race people for intellectual help . . . The Christian White man means as much to negroes and orientals as does Christ mean to the Intelligent White Man. Therefore, "WHITEMANISM" is the only true religion for them.

One of the great things about America is that you can say and do whatever foolishness you feel like so long as you've got a religion to excuse it. One fellow who really took advantage of this freedom, and built himself an empire, was William Edwin Riker, the Promised Comforter and founder of Holy City, California, and the Perfect Christian Divine Way.

Until he was 36 years old, Riker was just another religious fanatic and self-proclaimed healer, without much to distinguish him from hundreds of others. Then in 1909, his wife, who had just given birth, discovered that he was keeping another "wife." Riker compounded the problem by threatening to kidnap the baby. The newspapers picked up the story and had a field day with it. Riker ended up fleeing Oakland in a "heavy, false beard", and took refuge in British Columbia. Neither woman pressed bigamy charges, however, and the furor subsided.

From various bases in the next ten years, Riker continued to proselytize his peculiar faith. He won a few dozen converts, and another wife, Lucille. In 1918 the group moved the Perfect Christian Divine Way to a couple of acres on the highway between Santa Cruz and San Jose. Here they began to erect Holy City, Riker's planned Utopia. From this location, Riker spread his strange gospel for over forty years.

> Any person who dares accuse me of racial prejudice . . . I will have to accuse him of being an educated fool with a ruptured brain or he may have an infantile or paralitic brain and is 100% stupid, non-progressive, nonintelligent, anti-Christ, and besides all this he is blind as a bat and in my opinion, he was mentally born upside-down. . . . Here is what I claim to be, a 100% Spirit of California, God's country intelligent citizen.

Somehow, this kind of message began to draw converts to Riker's scheme, and Holy City began to grow. Believers signed over all their worldly goods to Riker in return for the privilege of living and working at the Headquarters of the World's Perfect Government.

Holy City grew and flourished. It came to include cabins, a gas station, a grocery store, a restaurant and bakery, a zoo, an observatory, and shops for a printer, a barber, and a cobbler. It also boasted its own radio station for a time, until the FCC shut it down for "not operating in the public interest" and other "gross violations." The grocery sold Holy City-brewed ginger ale and Golden Glow beer. Another building had peep show machines disguised as small churches. For a penny the curious could watch pretty girls *religiously* cavorting.

Flushed by his successes with Holy City, Riker in 1937 announced his candidacy for governor of California. A typical campaign flier read: "CALIFORNIA IS A WHITE MAN'S HOME and WILLIAM E. RIKER Your Next Governor Says: 'Orientals prepare to accept a job and get out of our white race man's business, as we don't need your help in any way . . . Our new Government will see that you get a job. Their polluting, undermining system of business must eternally stop in Our White Man's Home and besides this, they must keep their polluting hands off our White Race Women." He also advocated the deportation of full-blooded blacks to Africa, where he felt they would return to their "head-hunting, low-grade human rhinoceros eating tactics." Mulattoes could stay, he said, "to do the work." Needless to say, Riker wasn't a factor in any of the elections he entered.

By 1942 the golden age of Holy City had passed. The State of California had purposely rerouted the major highway away from Riker's empire a few years before and as business dwindled, so did the population. By 1948, only 20 of the former 200 converts lived there, and the town was rapidly falling into disrepair. In 1966, at the age of ninety-four, Riker was taken from his beloved Holy City and placed in a succession of mental hospitals. It was in one of these that he died in 1969. Today, the only resident of the community is an anonymous figure known locally as Crazy Harry, who spends most of his time guarding the battered and peeling Holy City signs, which are stacked in a garage where Riker's Cadillacs once were.

Answers: An ex-boxer is an ex-pounder, and an expounder is a commentator, a common 'tater is an Irish 'tater, an Irish 'tater is a specked 'tater, a spectator is a beholder, and a bee holder is a hive.

Flypaper.

SEPTEMBER 28

Notable Births

1839	Frances Willard	1901	William Paley
1841	Georges Clemenceau	1902	Ed Sullivan
1856	Kate Douglas Wiggin	1909	Al Capp
1892	Elmer Rice	1916	Peter Finch

Notable Events

929 Wenceslaus of Bohemia murdered by his brother
1213 Queen Gertrude of Hungary murdered by Magyars
1396 Turks massacred 10,000 Christians after Battle of Nicopolis
1795 Triple Alliance formed
1939 Poland surrendered to Nazis and Russians
1945 First American black sang major role in opera
1964 Nixon accepted honorary chairmanship of Youth for Goldwater
1971 Allende nationalized Kennecott and Anaconda Copper in Chile

The number of possible combinations of cards if four thirteen-card hands are dealt is 16,250,563,659,176,029,962,568,164,794,000,749,006,367,006,400.

A Ms. Gertrude Dorman was found guilty of smoking in bed in a Memphis hotel back in 1955, and fined $51. It seems the mattress had caught fire, and very nearly burned the place down. Ms. Dorman had pleaded "not guilty," insisting, "It was on fire when I got in bed."

Answer: a-3; b-4; c-1; d-2.

Question: Can you match the month with its traditional birthstone(s)?

a January	*1* Opal or tourmaline
b April	*2* Turquoise or zircon
c October	*3* Garnet
d December	*4* Diamond

On September 28, 1947, Morton Krouse put a penny in a vending machine in a New York subway station to get some peanuts. No peanuts came. Undaunted, he kept trying regularly for several months, but without ever getting a peanut from the machine. The next spring Krouse brought suit against the city for forty-six cents, which he said he'd deposited in the previous months without ever getting a peanut.

Maybe this world is just another planet's Hell.

Aldous Huxley

Voltaire relates that the German emperor, Wenceslaus, once roasted one of his cooks alive because he didn't like the way his meal had been prepared. He also tells us that Wenceslaus's closest friend in Czechoslovakia was the executioner of Prague, but he had this man put to death as well. It seems that Wenceslaus had ordered the executioner to kill him, and had knelt for the blow. The man refused, but orders were orders, and Wenceslaus had the executioner killed for disobeying him.

What is great in man is that he is a bridge and not a goal.

Friedrich Nietzsche

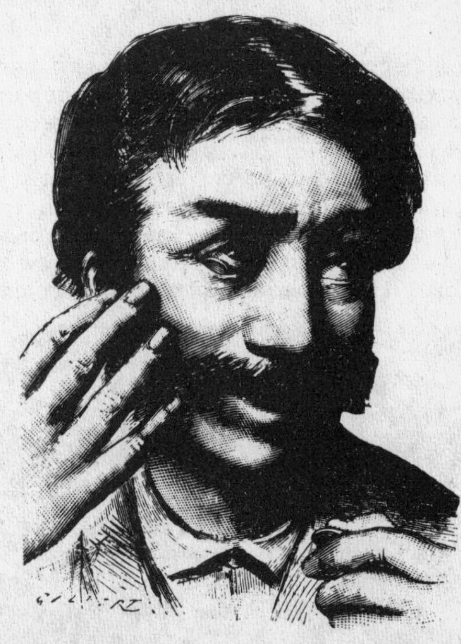

One of the more interesting pieces of medical trivia is that the group of people who suffer the fewest headaches are mental patients.

There's no word for the affliction in Albania, so perhaps the Albanians don't get them, either.

SEPTEMBER 29

Question: What is the state shown here?

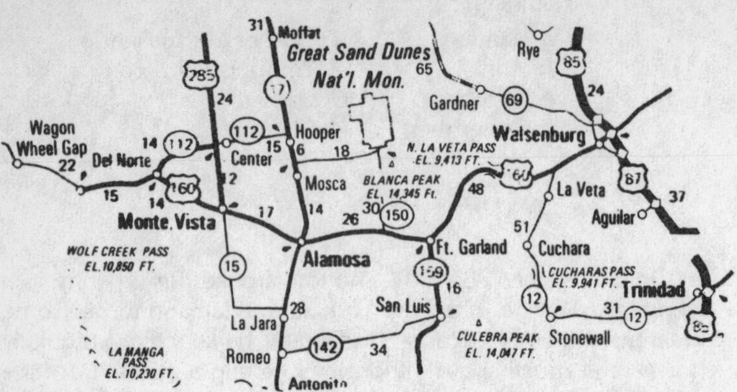

Notable Births

1547	Miguel de Cervantes	1912	Michaelangelo Antonioni
1758	Horatio Nelson	1913	Stanley Kramer
1810	Elizabeth Gaskell	1916	Trevor Howard
1901	Enrico Fermi	1925	John Tower
1907	Gene Autry	1927	Pete McCloskey
1908	Greer Garson	1931	Anita Ekberg

Notable Events

1784	First warrant for a black Masonic lodge issued
1853	Immigrant ship *Annie Jane* sunk off Scotland with 348 aboard
1892	First night football game played, Mansfield, Pennsylvania
1915	Transcontinental radio-telephone demonstrated
1918	Hindenberg demanded immediate peace from Allies
1961	Syria quit United Arab Republic
1964	Vatican allowed mature married men to become deacons

Rosemary McCarthy, twenty-seven years old and no doubt a comely miss, had to ask the Los Angeles police to protect her from a guy named John Hall in 1949. She complained that he followed her to work, tried to take her home, chased her and whistled at her all the time, and scared her "witless" by jumping out at her from doorways and behind trees.

Protested Hall in his own defense: "This is proper conduct for a man wooing a woman."

Perhaps in his day, but not in 1949. Hall was seventy-four years old at the time.

Some folks have all the luck.

One winter's day in 1949, Ellis Stackfleth of Manhattan, Kansas, was called on by an insurance salesman. Busy at the time, Stackfleth told the man he'd be happy to speak with him later, escorted him to the door, slipped on a patch of ice on the stoop, and broke his leg.

Out of all the countries whose sons and daughters immigrated to America, Ireland and Norway lost the highest proportion of their populations. Ireland lost a quarter of her people; Norway slightly less.

Although the living conditions and death rates for blacks traveling in the holds of seventeenth and eighteenth century slave traders are notorious, the situation was nearly as bad for some European immigrants up to fifty years after the slave trade ended. The following examples are representative of dozens of cases in which these ships lost a quarter or more of their populations to starvation and disease en route to the New World.

In 1710, after the War of the Spanish Succession, England granted some lands in America for the settlement of Palatine Germans. Because of the horrible conditions on board, nearly one thousand of the three thousand Germans who began the journey did not complete it, and many succumbed to disease soon after they arrived. Several years later, a ship sailing from Rotterdam to Philadelphia was delayed for six weeks waiting for its cargo and a change in adverse winds. During this time, the passengers lived on board and had to eat the provisions intended for the voyage. Although the vessel was originally supplied for a crossing of no more than twelve weeks duration, its owners refused to resupply it before it set sail, and it got underway with only six weeks' supplies. For the first eight weeks at sea, the passengers were on short rations; for the next twelve, all they had was bread and biscuits. During the final month they subsisted on what they could catch. Mice and rats were commodities worth more than gold. By the time the ship docked in Rhode Island, after a twenty-five-week passage, 108 of the 156 passengers on the manifest had died.

In some cases, the situation had not improved much by well into the nineteeth century. When the *Virginus* arrived in Canada, 344 of her 496 passengers were dead or near death; and the *Larch*, a ship sailing from Ireland in 1847, lost a quarter of her passengers and arrived with half her survivors gravely ill.

It is so stupid of modern civilization to have given up believing in the devil when he is the only explanation of it.

Ronald Knox

Answer: Colorado.

SEPTEMBER 30

Notable Births

1915	Lester Maddox	1927	W.S. Merwin
1917	Park Chung Hee	1928	Elie Wiesel
1921	Deborah Kerr	1931	Angie Dickinson
1924	Truman Capote	1935	Johnny Mathis
1926	Robin Roberts	1943	Jody Powell

Notable Events

1630 First execution in colonial America; John Billington hanged
1791 French National Assembly dissolved
1830 France recognized independence of all South American republics
1846 William Morris first used ether for a tooth extraction
1902 Rayon patented
1938 Neville Chamberlain announced, "Peace in our time."
1953 Ike announced appointment of Justice Warren to Supreme Court
1955 James Dean killed in car accident

Question: Can you match the unit of money with its country?

A. Bangladesh — 1. Cruzeiro
B. Brazil — 2. Peso
C. Chile — 3. Krone
D. Denmark — 4. Taka

Undoubtedly the greatest imposter in American history, and quite possibly of all time, is a man named Ferdinand (Fred) Waldo Demara, Jr. It would take a whole book to give even the briefest history of Demara's exploits (it did, in fact: see *The Great Imposter* by Robert Crichton, published by Random House in 1959), so these few words cannot possibly do his story justice — but the temptation is irresistible.

Fred Demara was born on December 12, 1921, in Lawrence, Massachusetts, son of a self-made man who lost everything in the Depression. In school, Fred was extremely bright but preoccupied with other things beside his books and he had a tendency to get into minor trouble (pulling a loaded gun on a classmate at recess, for example). From the time he was ten or so, the idea of a life in the service of the Catholic Church fascinated him, and when he was sixteen he dropped out of school to join a Trappist monastery in Valley Falls, Rhode Island. From that point on, to simplify a complicated but short career, Fred Demara proceeded to adopt at least three aliases, steal two cars, join the army and navy and become a deserter from both of them, successfully pass a graduate level course of study in theology, pose as two different people with Ph.D.s, teach at one college and become dean of the school of philosophy at another, fake a suicide, and be in and out of eleven different Catholic religious orders — all before he was twenty-five!

By that time he was associated with the Brothers of Saint John of God, and was working in a geriatric hospital in Los Angeles. But, as usual, Demara found this wasn't his vocation, and he moved on to a Benedictine house, Saint Martin's Abbey in Olympia, Washington. As usual, he swept through the small college the monks ran there like a beneficent tornado, becoming Mr. Everything to almost everyone. He also began to hobnob with the local elite, and was made an honorary sheriff, an honorary fire department official, and a notary public. It was just after he'd placed an application to become a justice of the peace that Demara's luck ran out. The abbot of Saint Martin's, Father Heider, had gotten wind of a possible scandal in Demara's past, and had investigated his background. One day, the FBI appeared and took the young brother into custody for desertion from the navy.

Although desertion in time of war could legally warrant the death penalty, Demara became a lawyer and pleaded his own case. He was sentenced to six years in a naval prison. While he was incarcerated, the army also found him, but charges against him for the other desertion were dropped. He was eventually released after only eighteen months —a rehabilitated model prisoner.

Demara then went to Boston and worked in several different hospitals for a time, before becoming C.B. Hamann, a zoologist with a Ph.D. (his third) from Purdue University. Having enjoyed his three previous abbreviated associations with small colleges, Demara followed up on a lead he picked up and approached LeMennais College, in Alfred, Maine. This institution, run by the Brothers of Christian Instruction, was at the time the smallest (twenty-five students) accredited four-year college in the country. He managed to talk the Order into a scheme of his to charter a school, the Institute Notre Dame, over which he expected to preside. But when the charter was granted and the school's catalog printed, instead of being named its president, Demara appeared only as an instructor in Biology. Furious, he packed, bought some wine, stole a car, and headed once again for Boston.

His time spent at LaMennais was by no means wasted, however, for it was there that he met a Canadian doctor named Joseph Cyr. This was the beginning of Demara's most fantastic imposture, which also made him famous the world over. A decade of aliases had taught Fred that it never hurt to have another identity up your sleeve, so when Cyr happened to mention that he's like to get accreditation to practice in the United States, Demara (as C.B. Hamann) offered to help. He advised Cyr to send for his professional credentials and personal identification materials and give them to him, promising to expedite the lengthy certification process through his contacts. Naturally, he made a set for himself.

When Fred Demara reached Boston that day in 1951, there were suddenly two doctor Cyrs in New England. That March he wrote to the Canadian Navy about the possibility of a commission as a doctor. Less than two weeks later he was mustered into the Canadian service. Demara had planned, or at least hoped, for a cushy job on a nice mainland naval base where "if penicillin didn't cure it, [he could] send it to another doctor." No such luck. Within a few months he was bobbing on the Pacific, headed for the waters off Korea. In addition, the first day he was on board, the vessel's skipper, Captain James Plomer, had several infected teeth that were causing him severe pain. He insisted that "Dr. Cyr" remove them immediately. Fred Demara in his life had never touched a tooth, but after hurriedly consulting the textbooks in the ship's sick bay, he did yeoman-like work. The Captain told him later it was the nicest job of extraction he'd ever experienced.

For the first few weeks, there was little for Fred to do medically. He dispensed penicillin when it was appropriate, and voraciously studied medical texts. The honeymoon ended one afternoon when a boat carrying nineteen wounded Koreans pulled alongside. Sixteen of the cases were relatively routine, but there were three people who were critically hurt. Altogether, he worked on them for over twenty-four hours straight, and on two of them he was forced to cut to the surface of their hearts. They all lived, and recovered nicely. Later he went to their village of Chinnampo to

Answer: a-4, b-1, c-2, d-3.

follow up on their progress, and was appalled at what he found there. He proceeded to make it his personal crusade to clean up the filthy conditions and to give the people of the area "real" medical treatment for the first time. They flocked to him, and he even performed a complicated lung resection operation, relying solely on an account of the procedure he'd read in the medical journal *Lancet*.

It proved to be his undoing. A well-meaning Canadian Navy publicity story led to his discovery, and he was eventually discharged in "disgrace," the next-to-lowest discharge category.

Demara was a *cause célèbre* for some time, appearing in the pages of *Time* and *Newsweek*, and in a *Life* interview, but soon he was reduced to working in a state hospital for the insane in Massachusetts. This didn't last long, though, and after another extended period of rambling, Fred Demara created a new alias —B.W. Jones. By now he had the temerity to list the name Demara and someone he invented called Tommy Barefoot as references on job applications. His reasoning was, he later recounted, that he was convinced that no one would believe that a person who gave those names as references could possibly be lying.

B.W. Jones ended up as an employee of the Texas prison system, and his ambition and ability got him quickly promoted through the ranks. He was about to be given an important state-wide corrections job when someone put him together with the *Life* article. Once more he fled, this time to Key West, Florida, where he was arrested when he tried to cash a check. Although he faced a maximum of forty-seven years in prison in Texas for his escapades, the state refused even to attempt to extradite him to avoid the embarrassment he would have caused Texas.

After a short stint in a Florida jail for drunkenness, he returned home to Lawrence, and worked in several children's homes. Then he taught school for a time as Martin Godgart on North Haven Island in Penobscot Bay, Maine, but again his past caught up with him, and he was dismissed. He used Godgart's credentials one more time and landed a teaching job in Barrow, Alaska, of all places, but even at that lonely spot he was doomed to discovery. A trapper who "never forgot a face" had seen the, by now, years-old *Life* interview, and Demara was on the road again. This time he visited Cuba and Mexico before returning to Massachusetts as a language teacher in the town of Winchendon during the 1958-59 school year.

Since that time, Fred Demara has remained pretty much out of the public eye.

But how long did you say you've known your family doctor?

It is always the best policy to speak the truth, unless, of course, you are an exceptionally good liar.

Jerome K. Jerome

No one quite knows exactly why cats purr; however, speculation is that Brahma bulls purr when they're happy.

The puff adder (or hog-nosed snake) is a tough customer. When riled, it reacts by "spreading its neck, hissing, and striking viciously at its annoyer." Scary! Of course, if the annoyer is patient and unperturbed by these antics, it will proceed to have fake convulsions, and finally to droop its tongue from its mouth, roll over on its back, and play dead. If it is moved while playing dead, it will roll over on its back again, and again, and again.

The alligator snapping turtle can snap a broom handle between its jaws.

There is a type of sea (herring) gull, called Franklin's gull, which lives entirely away from large bodies of water. It feeds almost exclusively on grasshoppers.

In 1839, at the dawn of the reign of Queen Victoria, there were an estimated 1,800 whorehouses in London. That's roughly the equivalent to twenty brothels in a town of 12,000 people.

That ratio today would give New Orleans, rightly or wrongly associated with prostitution, about one thousand houses of some repute.

Scorpio (The Scorpion)
October 24 through
November 22
OCTOBER

OCTOBER 1

Question: Can you define these ancient words?
crug
ilimp
sparrowfart
maily

Notable Births

1760	William Beckford	1924	Jimmy Carter
1871	Cordell Hull	1924	William Rehnquist
1885	Louis Untermeyer	1928	Laurence Harvey
1904	Vladimir Horowitz	1933	Richard Harris
1911	Fletcher Knebel	1934	Julie Andrews
1920	Walter Matthau	1936	Stella Stevens
1921	James Whitmore	1939	George Archer

Notable Events

1768	British troops landed in Boston to enforce Stamp Act
1791	Legislative Assembly met in Paris
1861	American Balloon Corps organized
1914	Seagull monument unveiled, Salt Lake City
1932	Ruth's "called" home run, off Charlie Root
1937	First trailer church opened
1938	Nazis invaded Czechoslovakia
1940	Einstein became U.S. citizen
1949	Communist People's Republic of China proclaimed
1961	Maris hit 61st homer, off Tracy Stallard
1969	Tunisian floods killed 500 people

Robert Louis Stevenson's character, Dr. Jekyll, who becomes the treacherous Mr. Hyde by drinking a mysterious draught, was based on a real man, a carpenter and official of Edinburgh, Scotland, named William Brodie. For nearly two decades, Brodie was by day a successful, respected man, and by night a drunken, profligate gambler and thief.

Brodie was born on September 28, 1741, the eldest of the eleven children of Edinburgh's most prosperous cabinetmaker. As a young boy he was very well educated (music and literature were part of his studies, a rare thing at that time for a tradesman's son) and apparently he seemed kind, honest, and polite, and this earned him the respect of the townspeople, while he was very young. At the age of twenty-two he was elected a burgess, and later on, after his life of crime was well underway, he was chosen as one of the city councillors. Since he was a partner in his father's carpentry business, he was also a fairly well-to-do individual, known for his fashionable wardrobe and his liberal spending money.

But at some point in his young life, he acquired some very expensive habits: women, wine, cards, and cockfights. Although he never married, he kept two mistresses for thirteen years, giving both of them their living and lodging expenses as well as maintaining their five children. This alone was an expensive situation, but it became unbearable when it was compounded by his drunken gambling. By the time he was twenty-six, Brodie could no longer afford his lifestyle, but he refused to give it up.

His work and reputation gave him access to most of the city's banks and businesses, and Brodie soon mastered the skill of taking lock impressions. His first robbery came in 1768, when he stole £800 from the banking house of Johnson and Smith. This lasted him only a little while, however, and he was quickly looking around for more money. In the next eighteen years, working alone or with several trustworthy accomplices, Brodie perpetrated hundreds of small and medium-sized robberies to finance his double life. During those years, his position and reputation served him well. On several occasions, he was recognized by witnesses who could not believe it was Brodie they saw, and consequently made no accusations.

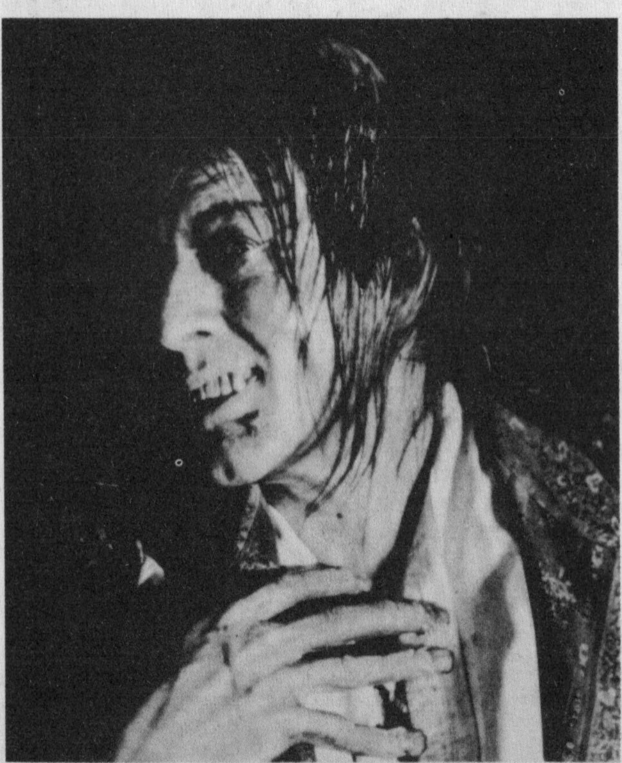

His life caught up with him in 1788 when he and his partners tried to rob their first major target, the Scottish General Excise Office. Although the theft was planned carefully, a watchman returned to the offices unexpectedly and one of Brodie's men missed the danger signal. Brodie himself got away without being seen, but one of the gang was caught, and told the whole story of Brodie's exploits. Advised of his imminent arrest, the carpenter fled just before the authorities reached his lodgings. He managed to evade capture in England for several months, but he was finally taken in Amsterdam the night before he was to sail to America. He was extradicted to Scotland, tried, convicted, and sentenced to be hanged.

On October 1, 1788, forty thousand Scots crowded the Edinburgh prison yard to witness his execution. The hanging was "successful," but it was discovered afterwards that Brodie had done everything possible in his attempt to beat the gallows. He had bribed a physician to insert a metal tube in his throat, and he had wired his suit to reduce the jerk of the rope as he dropped and the noose tightened around his neck. He'd also had his friends bribe the hangman to keep the rope short, again to lessen the force of the noose's jerk in the hope that it would not break his neck or crush the tube.

But he miscalculated. The drop did break his neck, barely, and it took him an especially long, miserable time to die.

Nearly seventy years later, Alice Cunningham, Stevenson's nanny, told him the story of Deacon Brodie, which her grandmother had told her; and the seed of Dr. Jekyll was planted. It sprang to life from Stevenson's hand one morning after he had had a strange dream in which he recalled most of the details of his nanny's story.

If England treats her criminals the way she has treated me, she doesn't deserve to have any.

Oscar Wilde

Answer: Edibles; to occur; the dawn; bespeckled.

OCTOBER 2

Notable Births

1720	Elizabeth Montagu	1890	Groucho Marx
1738	Chevalier d' Eon	1898	Bud Abbott
1847	Paul von Hindenburg	1904	Graham Greene
1851	Marshall Foch	1906	Willy Ley
1869	Mahatma Gandhi	1925	Clay Felker
1879	Wallace Stevens	1940	Rex Reed

Notable Events

1721 First camel imported and displayed in Boston
1866 Tin cans with key openers patented
1893 Tornadoes in Louisiana claimed 2,000 lives
1918 Lost Battalion was lost
1930 Haile Selassie crowned emperor
1939 U.S. government recognized Polish government-in-exile in France
1942 *Queen Mary* rammed British cruiser, 338 dead
1967 Thurgood Marshall became first black justice of the Supreme Court

Question: How's your movie memory? In what years were these films Academy Award Winners?

How Green Was My Valley
All About Eve
All the King's Men
Grand Hotel

Toward the close of the First World War, a German delegation went to the French leader Marshall Foch to discuss armistice terms. Foch picked up a piece of paper on his desk and read out a list of conditions. When he was through, the German leader was flabbergasted. "But those are terms which no civilized nation could impose on another!"

"Precisely," said Foch. "No, gentlemen, these are not our terms. They are the terms imposed on Lille by the German commander when that city surrendered."

I tremble for my country when I reflect that God is just.

Thomas Jefferson

In Galloway, Scotland, in 1785, a fellow named James Mossman was hanged for violating one of the laws of his time. His crime was that he was a resident of a neighboring district, found on the highway without good reason.

Theda Bara's movie contract with the Fox Studios back in the twenties stipulated that the actress:

could not marry for three years
must remain heavily veiled while in public
could not use public transportation
could not appear in the theater
could not attend a Turkish bath (this for a woman whose stage name was an anagram of Arab Death, yet!)
had to keep her limousine curtains closed at all times and could go out only at night.

In 1943 and 1944, William T. Fleming was arrested for impersonating an army captain. In 1945, he was arrested for pretending to be a second lieutenant. In October 1947, he was picked up in Detroit by FBI agents and charged with impersonating a first sergeant.

With his service record it's no wonder he'd been busted in rank.

For many years, the question asked outside of photographic circles was, "Is photography an art or simply a science or craft?" Photographers, of course, felt it was an art. One argument in their favor would seem to be this photo of a high jumper clearing the bar, which was taken by Roger Williams at a Rhode Island track meet in 1947. Printed correctly, it won second place in two major competitions in 1948 and 1950. The *Encyclopedia Brittanica* printed it, upside down, in a press booklet in 1950, and it looked good that way, too. Upside down it won The National Press Photographers first prize in 1951, and two other big competitions. With the negative reversed, it was also a prizewinner.

Well, sculpture is supposed to look good from any angle, and sculpture is art, right?

Each leg of a "daddy longlegs" spider contains about fifty joints.

Answer: 1941, 1950, 1949, 1932.

OCTOBER 3

Questions: Why is dancing like milk?

What is the best dance to end a musical comedy with?

Notable Births

1835	Charles C. Saint-Saens	1897	Louis Aragon
1873	Emily Post	1900	Thomas Wolfe
1880	Warner Oland	1925	Gore Vidal
1886	Alain Fournier	1936	Jim Perry

Notable Events

1777	Washington defeated at Germantown
1838	Opium War flared up with British sacking of junks in China
1959	First international cricket tournament held, Hoboken
1933	Dollfuss wounded in assassination attempt
1951	Bobby Thompson's homer lifted Giants over Dodgers
1952	First videotape recording made
1952	USSR expelled Ambassador George Kennan
1952	Britain tested its first A-bomb
1964	Malcolm X denounced racism
1964	57 people escaped East Berlin through tunnel

On October 3, 1947, in game four of the World Series between the Yankees and the Dodgers, Yankee pitcher Bill Bevens came within a strike of pitching the first no-hitter in series history.

There was one out in the bottom of the ninth in Ebbets Field that day, the bases were empty, and the Yankees were leading two to one. Bevens's wildness (eight walks up to that point) had cost him a run, but otherwise he had pitched superbly. Then Carl Furillo stepped up to the plate and Bevens walked him to tie the record of the most walks by a pitcher in a series game. Al Gionfriddo was sent in to run for Furillo, and promptly stole second. Third baseman Spider Jorgensen fouled out. Two down. Going with the LHB versus the RHP percentage, Dodger manager Burt Shotton sent in the left-handed batter, Pete Reiser to pinch-hit. Yankee mentor Bucky Harris countered by ordering Bevens to walk Reiser intentionally to set up the force play. Reiser went to first, and Eddie Miksus was sent in to run for him.

Then Shotton selected aging Cookie Lavagetto to bat for Eddie Stanky. Bevens got two strikes on Lavagetto, but the Cookie nailed the next pitch off the wall in right field. The ball bounded away from Tommy Henrich, and both Giofriddo and Miksus came around to score.

The Yankees and Bevens lost the one-hitter three to two, and instead of becoming a famous baseball name, Bill Bevens became an answer in trivia quiz. He pitched a good inning for the victorious Yankees in the seventh game, and certainly earned his World Series ring, but he never again pitched in the big leagues.

Two of the other players who figured prominently in the historic ninth inning fared no better. Lavagetto's hit was the last one of his baseball career, and speedy Gionfriddo, although only twenty-five years old at the the time, never played a major league game after the 1947 World Series.

On October 7, 1746, Mary Hamilton went on trial in London on a charge which might be called aggravated polygamy. Disguised as a man, she had married fourteen women over the period of several years.

Answers: Both strengthen the calves.
A reel.

OCTOBER 4

Questions: What's a Li in Red China?

What's a Li in South Korea?

Notable Births

1822	Rutherford B. Hayes	1896	Buster Keaton
1861	Frederick Remington	1914	Brendan Gill
1884	Damon Runyan	1924	Charlton Heston

Notable Events

1793 Christianity abolished in France
1878 First Chinese ambassador arrived in United States
1909 First dirigible balloon race held, Saint Louis
1932 First anti-vivisectionist play presented, Philadelphia
1940 Pope Pius XII called on women to reject immodest fashions
1957 Sputnik I launched
1963 Hurricane Flora left 6,000 people dead in Cuba and Haiti

Cleopatra's romantic achievements are well-known. In addition to her conquests of Caesar and Antony she numbered hundreds of other lovers, including several members of her own family. She even married two of her brothers, though their unions were purely for reasons of state.

But it was not only her charming personality that won the hearts of so many men. Cleopatra anticipated the modern woman by two thousand years in her use of cosmetics. Her brows were lengthened and darkened with antimony paste, and her cheeks were reddened with an iron oxide cream. The formulas she used were basically the same ones found in eyebrow pencils and rouge today. Her eyelids and lashes were stained blue to flatter her dark eyes, and her nails were died red with henna. Max Factor would have loved her.

But by the eighteenth century, this kind of thing had clearly gotten out of hand, in England at least. In 1770, the following bill was introduced in the British Parliament. It wasn't passed, but it does provide a good picture of the serious state of affairs that matters of the heart had reached, thanks to cosmetics:

> That all women, of whatever age, rank, degree, or profession, whether virgins, maids, or widows, who shall from and after such an act impose upon, seduce, or betray any of His Majesty's subjects, by scents, paints, cosmetic washes, artificial teeth, false hair, Spanish wool, iron stays, hoops, high heeled shoes, or bolstered hips, shall incur the penalty of the law in force for witchcraft and like misdemeanors, and that the marriage, upon conviction, shall stand null and void.

An absence, the decline of a dinner invitation, an unintentional coldness, can accomplish more than all the cosmetics and beautiful dresses in the world.

Marcel Proust

In the ninth inning of the first game of the 1923 World Series, Casey Stengel, playing for the Giants, hit an inside-the-park home run to beat the Yankees one to nothing. It was the first World Series game ever played at Yankee Stadium. Earlier in his career, Stengel had stolen second base while one of his teammates had been on it. It prompted one baseball commentator to call Stengel the greatest player the game had ever seen "from the neck down."

Answers: 546.8 yards, 2.44 miles.

OCTOBER 5

Question: What are the nicknames of the following states?
Virginia
Washington
West Virginia
Wisconsin

Notable Births

1703	Jonathan Edwards	1919	Donald Pleasance
1713	Denis Diderot	1923	Glynis Johns
1717	Horace Walpole	1923	Philip Berrigan
1829	Chester Alan Arthur	1933	Diane Cilento

Notable Events

1789	Women marched on Versailles to force Louis XVI to move to Paris
1854	First baby show in America staged, Springfield, Ohio
1864	Cyclone in Calcutta killed 70,000 people
1869	Water velocipede patented
1892	Dalton Gang nearly exterminated near Coffeyville, Kansas
1931	Herndon and Pangborn made first crossing of Pacific by airplane (non-stop)
1939	Latvia became Soviet satellite

Frederick Woods, a professor at MIT, once tracked down the descendents of the great colonial leader and churchman, Jonathan Edwards. In 1913 they included thirteen college presidents, sixty-five professors, 100 lawyers, thirty judges, sixty writers, three mayors, three governors, one vice-president of the United States, and a number of senators and congressman.

None of the desperadoes whose graves are marked in the Boot Hill Cemetary in Dodge City are actually buried there. Bodies that were once in the graveyard have been moved to a secret location to deter souvenir hunters. In any case, here are some of the interesting epitaphs to be found there:

Dead eye
Steve O'Hara
Killed 1875
—
Red-eye ruined
his dead-eye
and he was killed
in a fair fight.

Little
Joe Blackburn
Killed 1871

From where
he stood he
saw the moon
above the
caliboose
looking down
in brilliant
unconcern
as all hell
was breaking
loose.

Mule Skinner
Pete
—
He made the
mistake of not
keeping his eye
on the mule.

Toothless Nell
(Alice Chamber)

Killed 1876 in a
Dance Hall brawl
Her last words:
"Circumstances
led me to this end."

Tom
Henry
185?-1872

Shot by
the Sheriff
in a
Saloon fight.
He was just
a wild kid.

Jack
Wagner
killed
Ed Masterson
April 9, 1878
killed by
Bat Masterson
April 9, 1878

He argued with
the wrong man's
brother.

Shoot-Em-Up-Jake

Run for Sheriff 1872
Run from Sheriff 1876
Buried 1876

And a couple from Tombstone, Arizona:

Here
lies
Lester Moore

Four slugs
from a .44
No Les
No Moore

George Johnson

Hanged by mistake

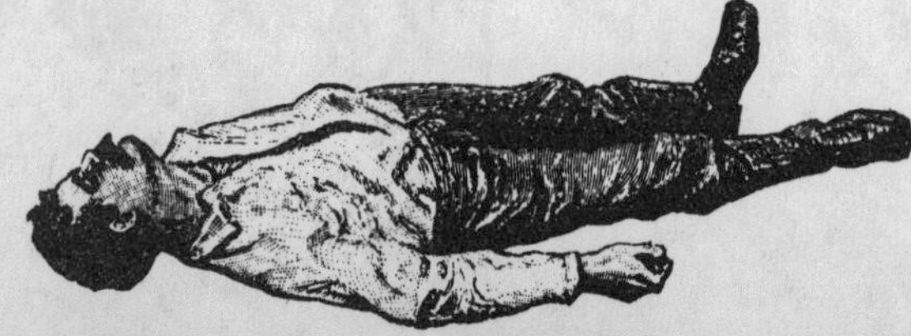

Justice can be brought to dead men.

Charlie Chan

Since we have to speak well of the dead, let's knock them while they're alive.

John Sloan

Answer: Old Dominion State, Evergreen State, Mountain State, Badger State.

OCTOBER 6

Notable Births

1820	Jenny Lind	1905	Helen Wills Moody
1846	George Westinghouse	1906	Janet Gaynor
1887	Le Corbusier	1908	Carole Lombard

Notable Events

1825 Patrick McGee, first giant exhibited in United States, arrived New York City
1859 John Brown seized Harper's Ferry Arsenal
1890 Mormons denounced polygamy
1927 *The Jazz Singer* first shown
1954 E.L.T. Lyon became U.S. Army's first male nurse
1956 House subcommittee convened to investigate rigged TV quiz shows
1973 Yom Kippur war began

For many years, an Englishwoman named Mrs. Hamilton was a great favorite with Czar Peter the Great of Russia. His mistress, in fact.

But hell hath no fury like a czar scorned. When he found out Mrs. Hamilton herself had been playing around, Peter ordered her beheaded, forthwith.

Yet he had fond memories, and may even, in fact, have regretted his order for her summary execution — for dozens of years from the incident to the time of his death, the Czar kept her head in a jar of formaldehyde next to the bed.

Although it is no longer so, attempted suicide in England was a capital crime, punishable by death. A Rochester, New York, policeman named McCoy found out recently that American law also has progressed in this area. McCoy shot a man who had been threatening to kill himself with a knife, and the police chief of the city had subsequently reassigned McCoy because of the incident. The officer appealed his transfer to a desk job, but the state Supreme Court ended up ruling that the chief's decision was proper. It added that shooting an individual was not an acceptable way to prevent the man from taking his own life.

Poor Cornelius Lehman! He ordered a tombstone from a monument maker in his home town of Goshen, Indiana, recently. When it was ready, he had it loaded into a trailer and started to transport it to the place where he wished to be buried, *eventually*, in Michigan. But shortly after he began the trek, the trailer came off its hitch and the gravestone was deposited in the street. Lehman, aged fifty-seven, tried mightily to move it, but to no avail. He finally decided that the best way to get it back into the trailer would be to use the front end loader which he had at home.

As he was driving the loader to the scene of the accident, Lehman suffered a fatal heart attack.

According to Robert Ripley's "Believe It or Not," the Saint Anne's River near Quebec City, Canada, cascades in seven waterfalls down a precipice three miles high. According to the *World Book Encyclopedia*, the highest point in Quebec is Jacques Cartier Peak, at 4,160 feet.

Questions: If a ton of coal costs $15, what will a cord a wood come to?

Bill Smith paid Forty eight dollars for his car, and then sold it for sixty dollars. What was his profit?

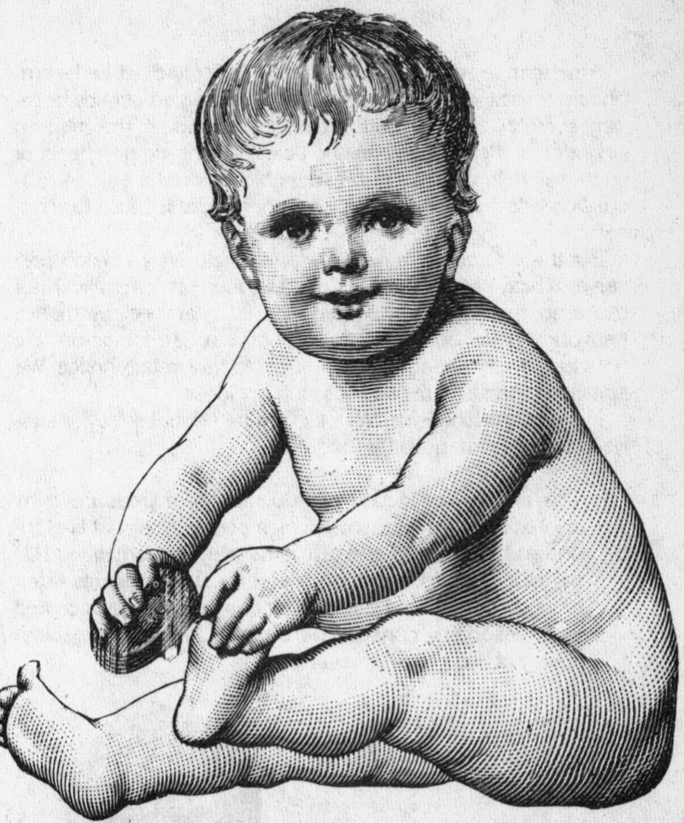

The first American baby show was held on this date in 1854 in Springfield, Ohio. It was at this pageant that one of the most famous remarks ever recorded about babies was uttered: "A baby is an alimentary canal with a loud noise at one end and no sense of responsibility at the other." It is supposed to have been said by one of the judges of the competition.

"Oz." is the abbreviation for ounces, and "viz." is the abbreviation for "namely" (from the Latin *videlicet*). Although neither word contains a *z* in its written form, both abbreviations do. This is because there used to be a punctuation mark that looked like a *z* with a tail which was used at the end of sentences. The *z* gradually intruded itself into these abbreviations from this punctuation mark.

Lopé de Vega, the famous Spanish writer whose works include *The Barber of Seville* and *Don Juan*, wrote an average of sixty plays a year during the last decade of his life.

Genius does what it must, talent does what it can.
Edward Bulwer-Lytton

Answers: Ashes.
$52 — the man's name was Forty.

OCTOBER 7

Question: Within ten years, when were the following invented?
friction match
nylon
metronome
parking meter

Notable Births

1849	James Whitcomb Riley	1913	Elizabeth Janeway
1885	Neils Bohr	1914	Sarah Churchill
1888	Henry Wallace	1916	Walt Rostow
1905	Andy Devine	1923	June Allyson
1907	Helen MacInnes	1934	LeRoi Jones

Notable Events

1765 First Colonial Congress held, New York City
1949 German Democratic Party established
1949 Tokyo Rose sentenced to 10 years for treason
1960 Second Nixon-Kennedy debate
1968 780 perished in floods in north-east India
1950 Chinese invaded Tibet

American television is almost universally criticized for its emphasis on sex and violence and for providing an already decadent society with even more decadent role models. The criticism is hotter and heavier when the possible long-range effects of such entertainment on impressionable children are under discussion. Most people would admit there's great cause for concern.

But there's another medium, almost exclusively a child's preserve, which should be scrutinized at least as carefully, if not more so than television. Often it is far more vicious than a network show, but because the grotesque goings-on are couched in rhyme, adults don't seem to take much notice. We speak, of course, of the famous Mother Goose.

In 1952, the Englishman writer Geoffrey Handley-Taylor analyzed the situation quite thoroughly:

> The average collection of 200 nursery rhymes contains approximately 100 rhymes which personify all that is glorious and ideal for the child. Unfortunately, the remaining 100 rhymes harbour unsavoury elements. The incidents listed below occur in the average collection and may be accepted as a reasonably conservative estimate based on a general survey of this type of literature.

8 allusions to murder (unclassified),
2 cases of choking to death,
1 case of death by devouring,
1 case of cutting a human being in half,
1 case of decapitation,
1 case of death by squeezing,
1 case of death by shrivelling,
1 case of death by starvation,
1 case of boiling to death,
1 case of death by hanging,
1 case of death by drowning,
4 cases of killing domestic animals,
1 case of body-snatching,
21 cases of death (unclassified),
7 cases relating to the severing of limbs,
1 case of the desire to have a limb severed,
2 cases of self-inflicted injury,
4 cases relating to the breaking of limbs,
1 allusion to a bleeding heart,
1 case of devouring human flesh,
5 threats of death,
1 case of kidnapping,
2 cases of torment and cruelty to human beings and animals,
8 cases of whipping and lashing,
3 allusions to blood,
4 cases of stealing and general dishonesty,
15 allusions to maimed human beings and animals,
1 allusion to undertakers,
2 allusions to graves,
23 cases of physical violence (unclassified),
1 case of lunacy,
16 allusions to misery and sorrow,
1 case of drunkenness,
4 cases of cursing,
1 allusion to marriage as a form of death,
1 case of scorning the blind,
1 case of scorning prayer,
9 cases of children being lost or abandoned,
2 cases of house burning,
9 allusions to poverty and want,
5 allusions to quarrelling,
2 cases of unlawful imprisonment,
2 cases of racial discrimination.

It is a far, far better thing to have a firm anchor in nonsense than to put out on the troubled seas of thought.
John Kenneth Galbraith

Answer: 1827, 1935, 1816, 1935.

OCTOBER 8

Question: How can you leave a room with two legs and come back with six?

Notable Births

1833	Edmund Stedman	1890	Eddie Rickenbacker
1838	John Hay	1895	Juan Peron
1872	John Cowper Powys	1941	Jesse Jackson

Notable Events

1871 Chicago Fire began; 250 died, 100,000 homeless, $200,000,000 damage
1895 Queen of Korea assassinated
1904 First offical auto race held, Hicksville, New York
1951 Egypt abrogated 1936 treaty with Britain
1956 Don Larsen pitched only perfect World Series game
1978 Senate extended ERA deadline to June 30, 1982

One of the greatest single-handed feats in military history was that of Sergeant Alvin York during World War I. You probably remember the name, and have some idea what he did; here then, are the details.

On October 8, 1918, a small American force found itself swallowed up behind an advancing German line in the Argonne Forest. The Americans had suffered many casualties, and there were enemy machine-gun nests all around them. The unit's sergeant was too badly injured to continue as its leader, so he passed on his command to a young man from Fentress County, Tennessee, Corporal A. York. Surrender seemed the only course of action, but before York could even think about it, a dozen Germans rushed down a hill towards his position. He jumped behind a tree and began firing. All twelve fell. Eight more charged, and they were shot down by York's machine gun. Thinking themselves to be greatly outnumbered, the Germans surrendered — all ninety-two of them.

York was on the spot. How was he going to get all these prisoners back to his own lines while he was still surrounded by Germans, and outnumbered ninety-two to one to boot? He did the only thing he could do, short of revealing the real situation. He ordered the Germans to march ahead of him and not look back. He then gathered the six men in his command who were walking wounded and set off. On the way, as new pockets of soldiers and machine guns were encountered, York ordered them to give themselves up. Seeing a hundred or so of their countrymen marching as prisoners convinced these front-line Germans they had no choice, and they all joined the captive band without resistance. By the time York reached the American forces, he had cleaned out thirty-five machine-gun positions and taken a total of 135 prisoners, nearly single-handed.

Some men have been thought brave because they have been afraid to run away. **Thomas Fuller**

⚜

Legend has it that the Chicago Fire was started when Mrs. O'Leary's cow knocked over a lantern in the barn and caught some straw on fire, but the most probable explanation is somewhat different. Apparently, two young women who had been partying nearby were sent to steal milk from the udders of the famous bovine. Once in the barn they were startled by footsteps outside, and in her surprise one of the girls dropped the lantern she'd been carrying. Strong winds and a lack of rainfall fed the fire, which raged for three days. Ironically, the cow survived, and Mrs. O'Leary's house was left undamaged.

Answer: Return with a chair.

OCTOBER 9

Questions: What should you do if you had a dime and a buggy top?

What's the difference in value between an old Buffalo nickel and a new Liberty quarter?

Notable Births
1940 John Lennon
1948 Jackson Browne

Notable Events
1617 Peace made between Spain and Savoy
1804 Founding of Hobart, Tasmania, Australia
1807 Prussian serfs emancipated
1871 Peshtigo, Wisconsin, fire killed 1,152 people
1888 Washington Monument opened to public
1946 First electric blanket manufactured
1963 Dam collapse at Verona, Italy; 1,800 victims

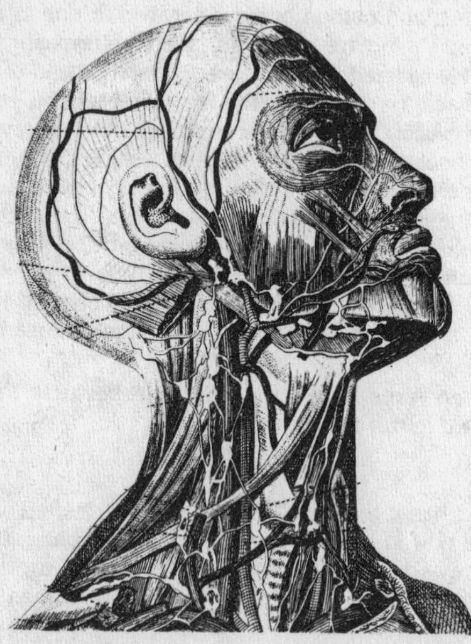

Because of a hereditary defect that affects the throat and vocal chords of their tribe, none of the 40,000 members of the Bolivian natives called the Quruñguas can speak a word.

Except for Russia, almost all railroads in the world have a standard distance of 4 feet 8½ inches between rails. Remarkably, the origin of the particular measure can be traced back over two thousand years.

When Caesar's armies invaded Great Britain in 55 B.C., many of the conquered Celts were put to work making chariots. The axle length on these chariots was a standard 4 feet 8½ inches. Because of the ruts these wheels created in the early roads of the island, it soon became foolish to attempt to build wagons or other conveyances with axles of any other lengths. The custom was perpetuated into the days of the railroads, and it was natural for the early railways to adopt that distance for their standard gauge, too.

One of the unforeseen problems in the building of the Grand Coolee Dam was the difficulty of pushing stiff cables through crooked, narrow, drainpipes over 500 feet long. It seems no one had anticipated it in the planning stage. The eventual solution proved quite simple. A string was tied to a cat's collar and the cat wisely was encouraged to head for the far end of the pipe by a large fan placed at the entrance to the twenty-four-inch-diameter pipe. The cat emerged, the string was used to pull a sturdy rope through the pipe, and the rope was used to pull the cables.

One of France's greatest modern scientific minds, Professor P.A.E. Lenard, who won the Nobel Prize for Physics in 1905, had an extraordinary phobia — he could not bear to hear Isaac Newton's name. Whenever he had to mention that great man in the course of a lecture, one of his students would write "Newton" on the blackboard, and then erase it so Lenard could go on. To see the name in print or hear it spoken plunged the Frenchman into horrible fits.

A lawyer from Washington, D.C., Charles S. Geier, filed suit in 1955 against the membership of an exclusive club in that city after he had been ousted from it. He sought damages of thousands of dollars because, his suit claimed, the club's action had harmed him "emotionally, physically, socially, financially, and professionally."

The club in question was an organization of Ping Pong players.

Ours is a world of nuclear giants and ethical infants.
General Omar Bradley

Answers: Buy a comb with the dime and comb the bugs out.
20 cents.

OCTOBER 10

Notable Births

1731	Henry Cavendish	1900	Helen Hayes
1738	Benjamin West	1914	Dorothy Lamour
1790	Reverend Toby Mathew	1918	Thelonius Monk
1813	Giuseppe Verdi	1930	Harold Pinter
1861	Fridtjof Nansen	1930	Adlai Stevenson III
1876	Rube Waddell	1946	Ben Vereen
1895	Lin Yu-tang	1956	Martina Navratilova

Notable Events

1886	First tuxedo introduced, Tuxedo Park, New York
1920	Bobby Wamsganss made first World Series unassisted triple play
1951	Mutual Security Act approved by Congress
1960	Tidal wave in Bangladesh claimed 6,000 lives
1961	Volcanic eruption on Tristan da Cunha forced evacuation
1973	Agnew resigned in wake of kickback scandal

The political corruption of Tammany Hall probably peaked in 1868 with the New York County Courthouse construction scandal. Although it was estimated to cost only $250,000, the final pricetag soared to over $13,000,000! Plastering alone came to $531,000, and that was before $1,294,000 in repairs were done to the original plastering prior to the building's opening. Brooms to keep it clean cost $41,000.

No one should expect the government to act in accordance with the moral code appropriate to the conduct of the individual.

Baruch Spinoza

Question: Can you define these ancient words?

boose
chinkers
hoodpick
kell

One of England's greatest opera singers — acknowledged to be the finest voice of her day — was a woman named Elizabeth Billington. Few singers have ever equalled her voice's quality, and none approached its strength. The power of her singing almost cost her her life, in fact.

When Madame Billington was in Naples in 1794, she sang the opera *Inez di Castro*, which had been specially written to show off her voice to its best advantage. The Italian audiences went wild; that is, until Mount Vesuvius erupted. The cataclysm was immediatly blamed on the singer; she was said to have upset the volcano's delicate geological balance, and a lynch mob gathered beneath her lodgings one night, intent on silencing the voice for good. She had to flee the country in disguise.

One of the criticisms often levelled at Congress is that some of the niggardly haggling that goes on there is the result of so many congressmen being lawyers. Cheer up, Bunkie, 'twas ever thus. Of the fifty-six signers of the Declaration of Independence (a fifty-seventh signature was added several years later) thirty-three were lawyers, thirteen were farmers, five were doctors, two were mechanics, one was a bricklayer, one a minister, and one a surveyor.

Answer: A place for a cow; metal money; a cheapskate; a woman's hat.

OCTOBER 11

Question: What's the special name for a group of these animals?

swans
chicks
larks
kittens

Notable Births

1658	H. Boulainvilliers	1910	Joseph Alsop
1884	Eleanor Roosevelt	1918	Jerome Robbins

Notable Events

1737	Earthquake in India killed 30,000 people
1899	Boer War began
1910	Roosevelt became first president to fly
1922	Exchange rate for German mark reached $1 for 2,000,000,000 marks
1938	Glass wool patented
1962	Vatican Council opened in Rome

Before German inflation rocketed into space in the early 1920s, Prince Frederick Leopold of Prussia borrowed eighteen million marks from the finance minister to pay off some debts. That figure represented about $330,000. When the loan fell due, (both principle and interest), it cost the prince the equivalent of $625 to wipe the debt clean.

A banker is a person who is willing to make a loan if you present sufficient evidence to show you don't need it.

Herbert V. Prochnow

When Teddy Roosevelt was police commissioner of New York City, it was announced that Ahlwardt, the anti-Semitic preacher from Germany, was coming to New York to make a speech advocating a crusade against the Jews. A number of Jewish leaders came to Roosevelt to ask that Ahlwardt not be allowed to speak, or at least that he be refused police protection. Although he was as aware of the possibilities of trouble as the Jews were, Roosevelt nevertheless insisted that the man could not be denied the American freedom of speech. He did, however, promise to do something to deflate Ahlwardt's diatribes.

The German did indeed give his speech, and Roosevelt appointed his security guard personally — forty policemen, all of them Jewish.

Nothing fortifies a friendship as a belief on the part of one friend that he is superior to the other.

Honoré de Balzac

In London in about 1903, two Irishmen came upon a beggar in a British soldier's uniform. The man was a pitiful sight. He'd lost an arm, a leg, and an eye in the recent Boer War. One of the Irishmen emptied his pockets into the cup of the poor devil, to the great astonishment of his companion. After they had passed out of the beggar's earshot, the amazed partner asked his friend, "What did you do that for? Did you not see he was a British soldier, and a foe to Ireland?"

The generous fellow said he did know that, certainly. "But he can have all I have," he said. "He's the only Englishman I've ever seen trimmed up enough to suit my taste!"

Traffic accidents kill between forty thousand and fifty thousand people in the United States every year. India loses far fewer citizens than this on her roads, but ten thousand people fall victim annually to the venom of the cobra.

Subtle has a range of meanings: fine, delicate, crafty, and acute. They all derive from the word's unique source. The Latin *subtela* means "under a [spider] web."

The origin of the word "syphilis" is probably the Greek *suphilos*, meaning "lover of pigs."

Roman socks had toes.

Answer: Bevy; clutch or brood; exaltation; kendle.

OCTOBER 12

Questions: Why is a woman like an angel?

What are the three acts of every woman's life?

Notable Births

1844	G.W. Cable	1903	Grayson Kirk
1855	Wilberforce Eames	1906	Joe Cronin
1872	Ralph Vaughn Williams	1922	Kim Hunter
1875	Aleister Crowley	1935	Luciano Pavarotti

Notable Events

1492 Rodrigo de Triana, on the *Pinta*, spotted land at 2 A.M.; America "discovered"
1773 First state hospital for the insane opened, Virginia
1892 First discovery of a comet from photographs
1918 Cloquet, Minnesota, forest fire took 400 lives
1921 League of Nations suggested partition of Upper Silesia
1928 First iron lung used, Boston
1940 Tom Mix died
1945 First Congressional Medal of Honor awarded to commissioned officer
1954 Hurricane Hazel hit Haiti and United States, 347 perished
1964 Russia launched first 3-man space capsule

Imagine a nice, middle-aged lady with a youngish "Mrs. Santa Claus" face, plump, cheery cheeks, and a sweet voice, and a nurse to boot. Don't you start thinking of hot, home-baked cookies and pies?

Please don't. This sweet woman was Miss Jane Toppan, a Lowell, Massachusetts, resident, and one of the foremost poisoners in history.

She ran a boarding/nursing home, and was much beloved by the citizens of the community for her compassionate and tireless care of her patients. She often succeeded in restoring to vitality people who looked as if they'd been bathing in the Styx. Of course, some folks did die there, but people die everywhere, don't they?

Jane's *modus operandi* was fairly simple. She'd take in a convalescent and administer the finest medical care for a time, until the patient was well enough not to need the regular attentions of a doctor. Then Jane would begin to administer her special poison, one that could not be detected in an autopsy unless a particular test was run. She was eventually convicted of thirty-one murders, but many families of other patients who may well have been her victims refused to allow the courts to exhume the remains for analysis. A better estimate of Jane's personal total would be around 100.

At her trial she calmly told an unbelieving court: "This is my ambition, to have killed more people — more helpless people, than any man or woman has ever killed."

Later, describing the murder of her stepsister, she tried to say exactly how she felt about it: "I can't quite describe the sensation. I wanted to laugh. I would kiss the patient, simply because I was happy. I remember kissing Edith. I remember Edith still thought I was trying to save her. If it hadn't been for her, I never would have been a nurse — and now I was paying her back . . . I don't know [why]. She had been very kind to me."

Jane Toppan died in the nut house.

When a patient is at death's door, it is the duty of the doctor to pull him through.

Laurence J. Peter

Never sleep with a woman whose troubles are worse than your own.

Nelson Algren

Several years ago, a National Airlines plane crashed and killed fifty-eight passengers. Because of the way the insurance arrangements were set up, the carrier received $1,500,000 more than the value of the plane; income to National that translated to a ticket price of over $25,000 for each of the people killed on the fatal flight.

It's easy to tell rabbits and hares apart as adults. Hares are larger, and have longer rear legs and ears. It's also simple to distinguish them as babies. Rabbits are born blind, hairless, and helpless, unlike hares. But as adolescents, hares and rabbits are almost identical.

Answers: Because she's usually up in the air, always harping on something, and never has anything to wear.

Attract, contract, and detract.

OCTOBER 13

Question: Why does a maid have more lives than a cat?

Notable Births

1754	Molly Pitcher	1919	Laraine Day
1890	Conrad Richter	1921	Yves Montand
1902	Luther Evans	1925	Margaret Thatcher
1909	Herblock	1931	Eddie Mathews

Notable Events

1781	Freedom of press granted in Austria
1792	Cornerstone of White House laid
1843	B'nai Brith founded
1930	107 Nazis took seats in Reichstag
1933	Construction of Alacatraz announced

The first of the great flagpole sitters was Saint Simeon Stylites, who lived during the early part of the fifth century. When he was about thirteen, he gave up his work as a shepherd and joined a Syrian monastery. This order was not disciplined enough for him, however, and he left it for the mountains forty miles east of Antioch to undertake a life of meditation. First he confined himself within a small circle of stones for several months, but this wasn't enough of a penance. He then found himself a nine-foot pillar, and proceeded to occupy progressively higher and narrower pillars of stone as time went on. He finally settled on one sixty feet high and three feet in diameter. Naturally enough, he secured a reputation as a holy man, and people flocked to see him. From his railed perch, resplendent in animal furs and an iron collar, he exhorted crowds twice daily to live the holy life. When he was not exhorting the faithful, he assumed devotional postures and did calisthenics. (It was reported he once touched his head to his feet 1,420 times in succession.) He died in 459, after thirty years atop his pillar.

Despite Saint Simeon's achievements, and although his successor Simeon the Younger was supposed to have spent sixty years on a stone pillar, the best known of all the perchers in history was Alvin "Shipwreck" Kelly.

Kelly, an orphan raised by the man responsible for his father's accidental death, made his living sitting atop flagpoles. Supposedly — although Kelly was notoriously inconsistent about this — he got his start in 1920, just before the Jack Dempsey-Georges Carpentier heavyweight title fight at Boyle's Thirty Acres in New Jersey. As Shipwreck told it, he'd been defending Dempsey before a group of that boxer's detractors, and they heaved him out of a third floor window. He grabbed a flagpole to break his fall, and a career was born. More probably, his vocation got underway in 1924 when, as a movie stuntman, someone bet him he couldn't spend ten hours on a flagpole. He spent thirteen hours, thirteen minutes up there, made some much-needed money, and had a lucky number for life.

The name "Shipwreck," according to his publicist, came from the fact that he'd survived thirty-two (occasionally the number was sixty-two) maritime disasters. A much more likely origin is that at various times he'd been a sailor. He also boxed for a living, but his pugilistic skills weren't of a high caliber, and his audiences used to groan, "The sailor's been shipwrecked again." when Kelly hit the canvas. Flagpole sitting was Shipwreck's forte.

In 1927, he set a record of seven days, thirteen hours, and thirteen minutes in Saint Louis. He broke that record shortly after at the Saint Francis Hotel in Newark, New Jersey, where he balanced on a fifty-four-foot pole for thirteen days as a publicity stunt for a coffee manufacturer. (He allegedly subsisted only on his sponsor's product the whole time, but this is doubtful.) He was paid $6,000 for these two weeks of perching.

Later that same year, he stood on an eight-inch platform in Madison Square Garden for 21 hours a day for 22 days while a dance marathon was being conducted beneath him. The next year, he was paid $29,000 for 145 days work on various platforms. In 1930, he spent 1177 hours (49 days) on a pillar in Atlantic City, smashing the record of a pretender who'd stayed up for 42 days. During his sojourn, Kelly endured a number of showers, three thunderstorms, and a hailstorm.

Kelly's last great stunt was performed on Friday, October 13, 1939, when he ate thirteen donuts while standing on his head on a pole stretched from the fifty-sixth floor of the Chanin Building in New York City. He was at least forty-seven, and probably fifty-four, years old at the time.

From this point on his life deteriorated rapidly. Over the course of his career, Kelly (who'd copyrighted his name and his act) managed to have seventeen imposters arrested in an attempt to maintain his preeminence. He did indeed remain first in his field, but his success could not go on forever. By 1942 he was painting, not perching on, flagpoles. As the forties wore on, even flagpole painting became a welcome occupation for the performer who was once so popular. At the time of his death — he was discovered lying between two cars in Manhattan in 1952, an apparent heart-attack victim — he was a forgotten man, living on a monthly city welfare check, his past glories forgotten.

Martyrdom is the only way a man can become famous without ability.

George Bernard Shaw

Answer: Because she comes to dust every day.

OCTOBER 14

Notable Births

1644	William Penn	1894	e.e. cummings
1882	Eamon de Valera	1896	Lillian Gish
1888	Katherine Mansfield	1906	Hannah Arendt
1890	Dwight Eisenhower	1950	Sheila Young

Notable Events

1066	Battle of Hastings; England taken by William of Normandy
1933	Germany quit League of Nations
1936	Belgium renounced alliance with France
1947	Sound barrier broken
1954	Chaplin donated Russian "peace prize" money to charity
1964	Martin Luther King awarded Nobel Peace Prize
1964	Khrushchev ousted
1970	Typhoon killed 583 people in Philippines

In late 1838, a stone was found at Grace Creek Mound, West Virginia, which was inscribed with curious markings. For years it puzzled the world's most noted archaeologists. Antiquarians studied the markings for seven decades, without ever reaching agreement as to what they said or meant, or even what language they were in. Fourteen believed the were Celtiberic, fourteen believed they were Old British; ten thought they were Phoenician; other authorities said they were Runic or Etruscan; and another cast his vote for Ancient Greek. In 1856, one learned man translated the stone thus: "The Chief of Emigration who reached these places has fixed these statutes forever." A later translation went, "The grave of one who was assassinated here. May God avenge him, strike his murderer, cutting off the hand of his existence." Another reader believed the inscription was Canaanite for, "What thou sayest, thou dost impose it, thou shinest in thy impetuous clan and rapid chamoid," whatever that means.

The whole debate got nowhere until one day in the early 1900s. Andrew Price, the president of the West Virginia Historical Society, happened to glance at the stone sideways. In a moment or two he'd figured the whole thing out. The inscription was carved in modern English and read: "Bill Stumps Stone / Oct. 14,1838."

The rock was not the key to a prehistoric exploration from Europe or the Mediterranean, it was simply the work of a prankster or more probably an idler who read books. Charles Dickens's *Pickwick Papers* had been published in 1837, and in one of Mr. Pickwick's first adventures he acquired, at great price, a mysterious, inscribed rock, which he believed to have enormous historical value. Later, he discovered that the inscription:

X

BILST
UM
PSHI
SM
ARK

really said only "X — Bil Stumps — His Mark." The author of the stone had no doubt read the book or heard the story, and one day, idly carved out the message that so baffled the "experts."

Answer: This can't be determined. *Velocity* is a measure of *straight* line speed only.

Question: A man on a winding road drove his car twenty mph for a mile, then thirty-four mph for 2.43 miles. What was his average velocity?

Originally, the word "farce" was a verb, meaning "to stuff or to pad." In the Middle Ages, when mystery plays based on biblical stories toured England for the religious edification of the illiterate population, the actors would often farce them; that is, add humorous asides and extra lines in order to keep the audience interested. By the end of the seventeenth century, this kind of jocular farcing had become so popular in the theater that plays were written as farces in their own right.

The tombstone erected by Dickens for his pet canary reads this way:

> This is the Grave of Dick, the Best of Birds. Born
> at Broadstairs, Mid's, 1851. Died at Gad's Hill Place,
> 14th October 1866.

An Epitaph from Colchester, Connecticut

Jonathan Kilborn
Died Oct. 14,1785 AEt. 79
He was a man of invention great
Above all that lived nigh
But he could not invent to live
When God called him to die

OCTOBER 15

Questions: For what two reasons is a paper dollar more valuable than a silver one?

Why is gooseberry jam like old money?

Notable Births

70 B.C.	Virgil	1900	Mervyn LeRoy
1830	Helen Hunt Jackson	1905	C.P. Snow
1844	Friedrich Nietzsche	1908	John Kenneth Galbraith
1854	Oscar Wilde	1917	Arthur Schlesinger, Jr.
1881	P.G. Wodehouse	1920	Mario Puzo
1884	Jane Darwell	1926	Jean Peters
1892	Ina Claire	1945	Jim Palmer

Notable Events

1783	DeRozier made first human ascent in captive balloon
1839	Victoria proposed to Albert; he accepted
1881	First American fishing magazine published
1894	Dreyfus arrested on charge of treason
1915	Britain declared war on Bulgaria
1917	McKinley Municipal Building dedicated, Niles, Ohio
1942	Hurricane in Bengal, India, left 40,000 dead
1961	Pakistani camel driver Bashir Ahmed began U.S. tour, at LBJ's request
1964	Harold Wilson elected prime minister of England

Perhaps America's most gruesome cannibal was a kindly old housepainter from New York City named Albert Fish. He killed and ate at least seventeen children before he was apprehended, usually preparing the meat in a stew with carrots and onions. Sentenced to death, he reportedly viewed his electrocution with delight, even helping the guards to adjust the shackles on the electric chair so they'd fit just right.

He was dispatched one winter morning in 1916.

They don't make them like they used to:

Isham Harris was governor of Tennessee when the Civil War broke out. He sided with the Confederacy, and was soon expelled from office by the Union Army. He signed on as a Confederate private and spent four years in the infantry. When the war was over, he lived for short periods in Mexico and England before finally returning to Tennessee in 1867. What makes Harris's biography most interesting is that for those six years, though he himself was often starving and in need for clothing and shoes, he carried $650,000 on his person. The money belonged to the state's Public School Fund. The governor, who was responsible for it by law, and was unwilling to trust it in the hands of a Union-appointed administrator, took it with him when he left office. Despite all his privations for all those years, Harris never touched a penny of it, and when he came home he immediately returned it to the State of Tennessee.

The Kwakiutl Indians of the Pacific Northwest used to have a unique way of according status within their tribes. Whoever could destroy the greatest amount of wealth and property was the "best man," and accorded the respect of a leader. Although human sacrifices had at one time been common, when sociologist Franz Boaz visited the region in the 1890s they had become a thing of the past and a deliberate destruction of wealth had taken their place. Boaz tells of a cẽremony he witnessed in which gallons of valuable oils were tossed into a fire, followed by seven canoes and four hundred blankets, all to demonstrate to his fellow tribesmen that the party giver was a worthy gentleman.

Although any number of things qualified as destructable, elaborately engraved copper plaques were considered to be the most valuable items and conferred the most status. One of these, which was named the "Causing Destruction" plaque, was of greater worth than twenty canoes, twenty slaves, ten smaller copper plaques, twenty lynx hides, twenty marmot hides, and twenty mink blankets.

Chief Tlatilitla was one Kwakiutl who knew how to use the system to his best advantage. Ostensibly to ally himself through gift-giving with two of his rivals, Tlatilitla insured his own supremacy by breaking an enormously valuable plaque in two and handing a piece to each of his competitors. One was so overcome by the amount represented by Tlatilitla's gift, which by custom he had to match, that he dropped dead on the spot. The second suffered terribly and withdrew from all tribal activities, before dying "of shame" six months later.

If all else fails, you've got to support the home team, right? The folks in Arizona think so. They've made it a crime for any visiting team to score against the University of Arizona football team in their Tuscon stadium. Violators are subject to a $300 fine or imprisonment of at least three months upon conviction.

Answers: Because when you put it in your pocket you double it, and when you take it out you find it in-creases.

Because it is not current.

OCTOBER 16

Question: Can you define these ancient words?

pingle
spuddle
squeck
farture

Notable Births

1758	Noah Webster	1898	William O. Douglas
1886	David Ben-Gurion	1923	Linda Darnell
1888	Eugene O'Neill	1927	Gunter Grass

Notable Events

1793 Marie Antoinette beheaded
1941 House voted to arm U.S. merchant ships
1946 Goering committed suicide shortly before execution
1948 First school for cantors opened, New York City
1951 Premier Ali Khan of Pakistan assassinated
1964 China exploded first A-bomb
1964 Breznhev replaced Khrushchev

On October 16, 1906, William Voigt, an aging cobbler with a long prison record, became Captain von Köpenick, one of the greatest peacetime embarrassments the German Army has ever suffered.

On that date, a group of grenadiers in Berlin was suddenly commandeered by an old gentleman wearing an out-of-date Prussian captain's uniform. He told them they were all going to Köpenick, on the outskirts of the city, and then he hijacked a bus to take them there. The soldiers hesitated to follow the man's orders at first, but he was so correct, firm, and forceful that they were soon doing whatever he directed. Once in Köpenick, the captain marched to them the town hall, where he proceeded to arrest the burgomaster and to examine various official documents. He then took about $2,000 from the town safe and ordered the burgomaster to be sent under custody to Berlin military headquarters. Once outside the town hall, Voigt ordered the soldiers to stand guard for a half an hour and then return to Berlin and Captain von Köpenick then went on his way.

It was nine days before Voigt was apprehended. He offered no resistance, but asked that he be allowed to finish his breakfast before being taken away. He was subsequently sentenced to four years for his impersonation and the robbery. However, publicity about Voigt soon brought world wide attention to the atrocious conditions in German prisons, and this threatened to make the whole episode doubly embarrassing to the already red-faced German government. Despite the fact that Voigt had spent twenty-seven years of his life in jail for a variety of offenses, Kaiser Wilhelm was forced to pardon him.

Curious officials asked him how he was able to take over the troops despite his seventy-odd years and his moth-eaten uniform. Voigt explained he had learned to mimic the peculiar speech and mannerisms of Prussian officers as an entertainment when, as an apprentice cobbler, he used to repair their boots nearly sixty years before.

If I had not been born Peron, I would have liked to be Peron.
Juan Peron

In the fall of 1951, William Munch, aged sixty-eight, of Queens, New York, was arrested for growing marijuana. He explained to police that he grew it and fed it to his pet canaries — all 280 of them — because it improved their singing. Since then, scientists have shown that many birds' songs are improved when their feed includes marijuana seeds.

Weed — a plant whose virtues have not yet been discovered.
Ralph Waldo Emerson

Here is another true nursery rhyme: Little Jack Horner.

John "Little Jack" Horner was a kitchen boy in the household of the abbot of Glastonbury. In 1725, when Henry VIII was in the midst of his fight with the Catholic Church over his divorce, he decided to appropriate all the holdings of the monasteries in England. Hoping to keep some of his own property, the abbot of Glastonbury sent thirteen title deeds to the church's holdings he controlled as a propitiatory offering to the king. Both for security and for a pleasant effect, he had them baked in a pie and selected Little Jack to deliver them. En route, Jack managed to filch one, the deed to the Mells park estate. In the course of events, the lowly scullery boy was allowed to keep the property, and he was eventually knighted. His descendents own the estate and the mansion he constructed ("The House That Jack Built") to the present day.

Answer: To eat when not hungry; to make mountains of molehills; a disease of chickens; stuffing.

OCTOBER 17

Question: Can you arrange these cities from largest to smallest in terms of population?

Mexico City
Moscow
New York
São Paulo

Notable Births

1864	Elinor Glyn	1917	Marsha Hunt
1893	Spring Byington	1918	Rita Hayworth
1900	Ivor Winters	1920	Montgomery Clift
1902	Nathanael West	1927	Tom Poston
1905	Jean Arthur	1930	Jimmy Breslin
1915	Arthur Miller	1946	Bob Seagren

Notable Events

1777	General Burgoyne surrendered at Saratoga
1829	Delaware-Chesapeake Canal opened
1863	Lincoln asked for call-up of 300,000 men
1888	Keel of battleship *Maine* laid, Brooklyn
1933	Einstein arrived in United States as a political refugee
1941	Tojo became Japanese premier
1941	American destroyer *Kearny* torpedoed off Iceland
1977	Supreme Court allowed *Concorde* SST flights to New York

In France during the early Middle Ages, habitual thieves facing execution could be fully pardoned if a maiden would step forward and make an offer of marriage. Usually a criminal would accept this bargain gratefully, but not always. One Jean Poqueron was proffered salvation in Rhiems in 1234 by a particularly homely orphan girl. The condemned man took one look at the woman and said, "I'd rather marry the gallows! Hangman, do your duty."

When the candles are out all women are fair.

Plutarch

If some people got their rights they would complain about having been deprived of their wrongs.

Oliver Herford

President Lincoln once visited a Civil War battlefront, where he was escorted by a young Union captain. With his unusual height and his stovepipe hat, the Commander-in-Chief made a wonderful target. Suddenly there was a volley of rifle fire in their direction and the quick-thinking captain tackled Lincoln, shouting, "Get down, you damn fool!" Once they were in relative safety, the officer realized what he'd said to the president, but Lincoln didn't mention a word of it. Shortly before he returned to Washington, though, Lincoln sought out Captain Oliver Wendell Holmes, Jr., and said, "I'm glad to see you know how to talk to a civilian."

To celebrate his newly granted United States citizenship, Turkish-born Haroutious A. Aprahamian changed his name to Haroutious A. Abrahamian.

Answer: New York; Mexico City; Moscow; São Paulo.

OCTOBER 18

Notable Births

1631	Michael Wigglesworth	1906	Sidney Kingsley
1785	Thomas Love Peacock	1919	Pierre Trudeau
1859	Henri Bergson	1925	Melina Mercouri
1902	Miriam Hopkins	1927	George C. Scott

Notable Events

1622 Treaty of Montpelier reaffirmed Edict of Nantes
1867 Ownership of Alaska formally transferred to United States
1870 Sand blaster patented
1873 Ecuador became a theocracy
1891 First international six-day bicycle race held, New York City
1943 First "Perry Mason" radio show
1944 Hitler ordered mobilization of all men aged 16 to 60
1954 French Indian Ocean settlements voted for union with India

If someone were to ask you to name the original Seven Seas, how many would you get? Try it. The answer follows later on the page.

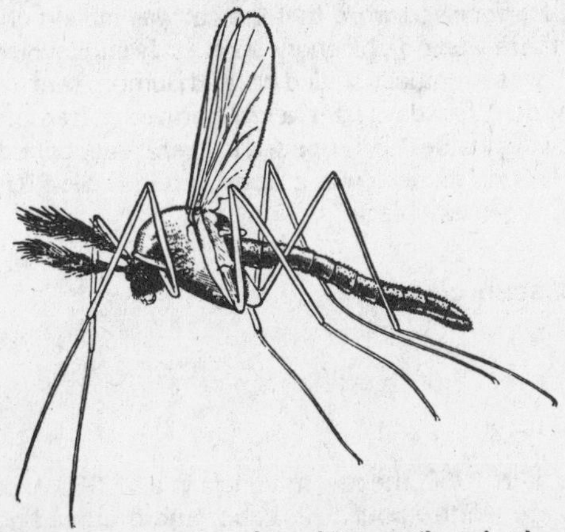

You've never seen a swarm of anything until you've been on the Arctic tundra in summer and suffered its mosquitoes. In Alaska people say that if there were any more of the insects, they'd have to be smaller.

The Atlantic, Pacific, and Indian Oceans, the Mediterranean, the Caribbean — stop right there! Those are all wrong.

The Seven Seas originated in the folklore of the ancient Hindu and Chinese cultures. Loosely translated and placed geographically, they are:

The Sea of Salt Water, surrounding India
The Sea of Sugar Cane, surrounding Burma
The Sea of Wind, surrounding the Malay Peninsula
The Sea of Clarified Butter, surrounding the Sunda Archipelago
The Sea of Milk, surrounding Cambodia and Thailand
The Sea of Curds and Whey, surrounding southern China
The Sea of Fresh Water, surrounding northern China

Questions: When is it hard to get a pocket watch out of your pocket?

Why is a wristwatch like a thing-a-ma-bob?

In October 1946, in San Francisco, veterinarians performing an autopsy on Oscar, a trained seal, found $7.54 in his stomach — 514 pennies, twenty-seven nickels, eight dimes, and a quarter. He'd also swallowed two subway tokens, although he was not in the habit of using public transportation.

In the Martham Churchyard, Norfolk, England, there is a strange stone bearing an Oedipal epitaph:

Here Lyeth the body of Christ[r]. Burroway, who departed this
Life ye 18 day October, Anno Domini 1730.
Aged 59 years.

And there Lyes
Alice who by his Life
Was my Sister, my mistress
My mother and my wife.
Dyed Feb ye 12, 1729
Aged 76 years.

The stone tells a true tale. Here's one account of the story:

That Ch[r]. B. was the fruit of incestuous connexion between a father and daughter, and was early placed in the foundling Hospital, whence, when he came of age, he was apprenticed to a farmer. Coming in after years by chance to Martham, he was hired unwittingly by his own mother, as farm steward, her father, (or rather, the father of both) being dead. His conduct proving satisfactory to his mistress, she married him, who thus became successively, mother, sister, mistress and wife, to this modern Oedipus. Being discovered by his wife to be her son, by a peculiar mark on his shoulder, she was so horror stricken that she soon after died, he surviving her scarcely four months.

Answers: When it' s-ticking there.
It's a watch-ya-ma-call-it.

OCTOBER 19

Question: This looks hard, but only a dumb person can't get the right answer in less than five seconds. How about you?

$1 \times 2 \times 3 \times 4 \times 5 \times 6 \times 7 \times 8 \times 9 \times 0 = ?$

A burglar named Oscar Shelton was almost smarter than the police, but not quite. So as not to leave fingerprints at the scenes of his crimes, he used to wear a pair of socks on his hands. The law caught up with him in 1959, when police matched a footprint they found at a burglarized house with Shelton's.

In Goldalming, England, in 1726, a girl named Mary Toft gave birth to a dozen rabbits — or said she did. She at least managed to convince a local doctor, and if the doctor believed it, it was good enough for most of the rest of the community. Educated people were generally doubtful, but many of the simpler folk bought the story outright. Their faith was further strengthened when it was announced that one of the girl's deliveries had been witnessed by some reliable people, and that the girl herself had volunteered to be examined by doctors in London during her next confinement.

That soon came to pass, and she was taken to a London hospital several weeks before she said the litter would be due. But the physicians in the city were a little more sophisticated than she had expected, and they made sure that the security around Mary's room was so tight that no outsider could smuggle a rabbit into her. Mary's hoax was exposed.

Shortly afterward, however, she revealed the secret of "giving birth" to a magician, and he managed to incorporate the trick into his act, albeit in a slightly different fashion. The next year he pulled the first rabbit out of a hat.

Ancient Chinese proverb — "Do not challenge supernatural unless armed with sword of truth."

Charlie Chan

A fanatic is one who sticks to his guns whether they're loaded or not.

Franklin P. Jones

Notable Births

1784	Leigh Hunt	1922	Jack Anderson
1876	Mordecai Brown	1931	John Le Carré
1889	Fannie Hurst	1967	Amy Carter

Notable Events

1774	*Peggy Stewart* Tea Party, Annapolis
1781	Cornwallis surrendered to Washington at Yorktown
1874	First wedding in a balloon held, Cincinnati
1936	Watertown, South Dakota, high school began to fingerprint its students
1950	First illegal TV station began operations, Johnstown, Pennsylvania
1973	OPEC announced export ban on oil

P.T. Barnum was always on the lookout for genuine oddities that he could exhibit. One fellow from Vermont wrote him that he was in possession of a cat that was completely cherry colored, and asked if Mr. Barnum would like to make an offer for the animal. Barnum was skeptical, and wrote the man for confirmation. He received word that the cat was indeed cherry colored, and there was no chicanery such as dyeing involved. A price of $600 was eventually settled on, and Barnum sent a check for that amount. A few days later, a crate arrived at Barnum's with a cat meowing inside it. P.T. opened it up and out popped a coal-black cat. Around its neck was a note from the seller: "Up in Vermont our cherries are black."

Be obscure clearly.

E.B. White

Back in 1960, the raw materials in a $2,000 American-made car were worth about $22. Labor and overhead accounted for roughly $1,200, and taxes of various sorts took a $500 chunk. Profits for the producers of the raw materials and the parts manufacturers totaled $136, the local dealer took $77, and the auto maker's profit was $65.

❦

This advertisement ran in the classified section of the *Times* of London in 1958:

> . . . sports car, preferably foreign, wanted for weekend by respectable middle-aged civil servant to raise son's status at preparatory school where most fathers have Jaguars.

Answer: 0.

OCTOBER 20

Notable Births

1632	Christopher Wren	1882	Bela Lugosi
1735	James Beattie	1891	Fanny Brice
1854	Arthur Rimbaud	1911	Will Rogers, Jr.
1859	John Dewey	1925	Art Buchwald
1869	Clark Griffith	1927	Joyce Brothers
1874	Charles Ives	1931	Mickey Mantle

Notable Events

1820 Florida became U.S. territory
1910 First cork center baseball used in World Series
1926 Hurricane killed 600 people in Cuba
1944 U.S. forces landed in Philippines
1952 Typhoon in Philippines left 440 dead
1968 Jackie Kennedy and Ari Onassis wed
1973 Saturday Night Massacre; Richardson resigned, Ruckelshaus and Cox fired by Nixon

Question: Can you guess the average elevations of these states?

Hawaii
Iowa
Rhode Island
Idaho

In Arcadia, Missouri, shortly before the 1936 elections, the Republican National Committee hired six cows and had them photographed on a WPA sidewalk, to give the impression that the program was constructing bovine walkways as public works projects.

Roosevelt won anyway.

Lincoln was right about not fooling all the people all the time. But the Republicans haven't given up trying.

Lyndon Johnson

If the Republicans will stop telling lies about the Democrats, we will stop telling the truth about them.

Adlai Stevenson

The koala bear of Australia feeds almost exclusively on eucalyptus leaves, which happen to be a narcotic to him, so he's "out of it" all the time. Despite his cuddly appearance, the koala has a miserable temper; moreover, because of all the eucalyptus, up close the koala smells like a disagreeable coughdrop.

On October 20, 1842, Thomas C. Jones, a navy commander, received a communiqué that the United States was at war with Mexico. Immediately he ordered his squadron of five ships to Monterey. In short order he'd seized the Mexican fort there and declared California to be United Staes territory, a marvelous feat of military efficiency.

Except that he'd misunderstood the message, and the two countries were not at war. The United States government had to issue a very shame-faced apology for the incident.

The fascination that the Dyaks of Borneo felt for the severed heads of their enemies (carrying them at their sides, talking to them, feeding them, etc.) has already been mentioned. Sir Walter Raleigh's head was likewise preserved. After he was decapitated on this day in 1618, his wife, Elizabeth Throgmorton, had his head embalmed. She carried it with her in a pouch at her side for the next twenty-nine years, until she herself died.

Answer: 3030, 1100, 200, 5000.

OCTOBER 21

Questions: Why can't the owner of a forest fell his own trees?

Why is a gardener the finest kind of man?

Notable Births

1772	Samuel Coleridge	1917	Dizzy Gillespie
1790	Alphonse de Lamartine	1928	Whitey Ford
1833	Alfred Nobel	1929	Ursula LeGuin

Notable Events

1097 Siege of Antioch on First Crusade began
1805 Admiral Nelson defeated Spanish armada at Trafalgar
1849 First tattoed man displayed, New York City
1944 LNG tanker exploded in Cleveland, killed 135 sailors
1950 Chinese occupied Tibet
1960 Fourth Nixon-Kennedy debate
1961 Nasser confiscated property of wealthy Egyptians

Although "Spanish" has been tied irreversibly to "Inquisition" for all time and the Inquisition did begin in Spain, it must be said on behalf of Spanish history that many of the punishments administered by the Inquisition were mild. Also, only about one-third of the people "eligible" for torture under the rules of the Inquisition were actually tortured, a much lower figure than many other European versions of the Inquisition.

Three methods of torture were used in Spain over the years (burning at the stake, incidentally, falls into the category of execution, not torture). First was *garrucha*, in which the victim was hung from his wrists, and had heavy weights tied to his feet. He or she would then be raised up slowly, and suddenly dropped. The action of the weights would eventually dislocate the joints.

Second was the *toca*. In this procedure the heretic was tied on a rack, and then the *toca*, a linen cloth, was rolled up and stuffed down his throat. That alone made breathing difficult, but when liquid was poured slowly and conducted down his throat by the *toca* it was practically impossible.

The third, *potro*, was the most common after 1600. It was a constricting torture, in which heavy ropes were wound around the victim's body to be tightened according to the whim of the Inquisitor. It has been recorded that several women over the age of ninety were subjected to the *potro* and made to confess all kinds of crimes of which they were innocent.

Confessions made under torture were, of course, inadmissable, so the accused person was always made to ratify his statements the next day. If he or she would not, and since torture, according to the rules, could only be used once, official records stating that the previous days' torture had been completed had to be changed to read "suspended," and it was back to the rack, or whatever, for the unfortunate victims.

At the end of the Middle Ages the two greatest weapons of war were the catapult and the trebuchet, which was a catapult with a sling. Huge boulders were not the only missiles hurled by these machines during sieges. Dead opponents or live prisoners were often heaved into an enemy's camp or city to lower morale; and dead, rotting animals were sent flying with the hope that they would spread disease and pestilence. At the siege of Carolstein in 1422, some 200 cartloads of manure were rocketed into town.

Would be greatest blessing if all war fought with machinery instead of human beings.

Charlie Chan

Answers: Because no one is allowed to cut when it's his own deal.

Because he has more business on earth than anyone else, he always has good grounds for his actions, he's master of the mint, sets his own thyme, and can raise his celery each year.

OCTOBER 22

Notable Births

1811	Franz Liszt	1907	Jimmie Foxx
1870	Alfred Douglas	1919	Doris Lessing
1882	N.C. Wyeth	1929	Dory Previn
1887	John Reed	1929	Robert Rauschenberg
1905	Constance Bennett	1943	Catherine Deneuve

Notable Events

1685	Revocation of the Edict of Nantes
1721	Peter I proclaimed emperor of all the Russias
1746	Charter for Princeton College granted
1883	First horse show of national importance held, New York City
1913	Mining accident at Dawson, New Mexico, claimed 263 lives
1962	Kennedy ordered Cuban blockade

Question: What is the state shown here?

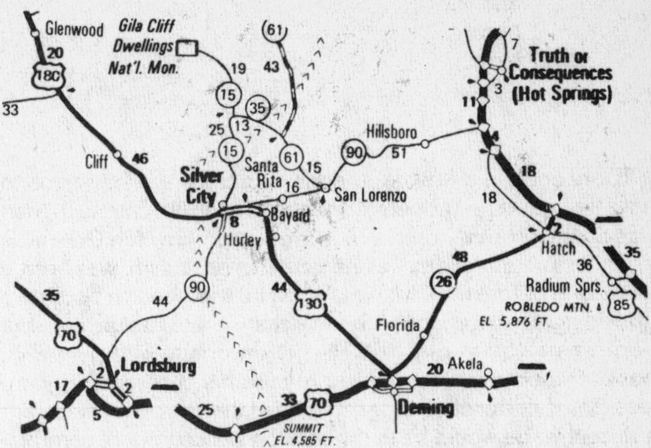

On this date in 1812, John Capen (better known as "Grizzly") Adams was born in Medway, Massachusetts. In 1860, when he came back East after a decade out West during which he accumulated his ursine menagerie, he arranged with P.T. Barnum for the exhibition of his trained bears. Barnum recalled that in their initial meeting, Adams doffed his hat to show him where "General Fremont," one of his bears, had recently slashed him. "His skull was literally broken in ... the fearful paws ... had opened his brain so the workings were visible!" wrote the showman.

But not for long. Poor Grizzly died on October 25, 1860.

Answer: New Mexico.

OCTOBER 23

Question: Can you think of a word to rhyme with?
circular
linoleum
hoax
length

Notable Births

1817	Pierre Larousse	1931	Diana Dors
1845	Sarah Bernhardt	1931	Jim Bunning
1880	Una O'Connor	1940	Pele
1925	Johnny Carson	1942	Michael Crichton

Notable Events

1247	Bethlehem (Bedlam) Hospital founded as a priory
1915	First national horseshoe pitching tournament held, Kellerton, Iowa
1930	Chiang Kai-shek baptized a Methodist
1935	Dutch Schultz shot in Newark
1936	First old-age colony dedicated, Millville, New Jersey
1939	Earl Browder indicted for passport fraud
1940	Hitler and Franco held talks
1942	Rommel stopped by Montgomery at El Alamein
1945	Truman called for universal military training in peacetime
1945	Quisling, Norwegian traitor, executed by firing squad
1956	Hungarian Revolt began

Every once in a while, someone comes along who seems to have a remarkable propensity for cheating death. One such man was Sam Dombey, ironically a gravedigger from New Orleans.

"Indestructable Sam," as he came to be known, was born a slave long before the Civil War. When he was freed he became a gravedigger, a strenuous job for a man in late middle age, but Sam was a tough old bird. He got on poorly with his peers, however, because Sam refused to raise his prices to the going rate. Some of the other diggers decided that the only way to earn a decent wage would be to put the competition out of commission, permanently. They collected $50 and invested it with a voodoo witch doctor called Beauregard, who possessed an all-powerful curse (guaranteed). He performed a special dance with an owl's head at the spot where Sam was to be working the next day, and promised his rivals that Sam would be dead by evening.

The next morning Sam had just started to work when there was a terrific explosion from some bushes near the grave site. He looked up to see a man running away, clutching his face and arm. The breach of the old rifle had blown up in the would-be assassin's face. The powerful medicine man Dr. Beauregard did not divulge how the sling on his arm or the bandages on his head got there.

After that, the diggers' cartel planted a keg of powder beneath a cot in the toolshed where Sam took his daily siesta. When it blew up Sam was cushioned by the mattress and blown straight out the door. The shed was demolished, but Sam, landing twenty feet away, was unhurt.

One would think these two experiences were warning enough for most men, but Sam was a man of principle. He kept on digging graves for the same low rate as ever. But neither would his enemies be deterred. Next they captured him, tied him up, and rowed him out to the middle of Lake Ponchartrain where they dumped him over the side of the boat and quickly pulled away. Sam stood up in two feet of water, unfettered himself, and walked and swam back to shore.

Then Sam's house was set on fire, and as he fled through the front door, he was nailed with a couple of volleys of buckshot square in the chest. The doctors thought he'd had it, but, as ever, Indestructable Sam pulled through.

Soon after this incident, the diggers got a union together, and everyone worked for the same money. There was no further trouble for Sam, and he was old enough to want to retire in a short time, anyway. He lived into the twentieth century, surviving most of the younger men who'd tried to kill him so many times over the years. He was ninety-eight when he died.

If at first you don't succeed, try, try again. Then quit. There's no use being a damn fool about it.

W.C. Fields

Nearly two-thirds of the florist industry's business every year comes from orders for funerals. In 1960, the cost of flowers provided for a typical funeral was $246. In today's dollars (*sic*) that translates to well over $600.

A man's dying is more the survivors' affair than his own.

Thomas Mann

Here lies the body of Susan Lowder
Who burst while drinking a *Sedlit* powder.
Called from this world to her heavenly rest
She should have waited til it effervesced.

Answer: Examples are — tubercular; petroleum; coax or oaks; strength.

Notable Births

1788	Anthony van Leeuwenhoek	1923	Denise Levertov
1788	Sarah Hale	1926	Y.A. Tittle
1882	Sybil Thorndike	1936	David Nelson
1904	Moss Hart	1937	Juan Marichal

Notable Events

1601 Death of Tycho Brahe
1795 Third partition of Poland
1812 American Antiquarian Society founded
1836 Safety match patented
1901 Annie Taylor became first person to go over Niagara Falls in a barrel
1931 Capone got 10 years, $50,000 fine for tax evasion
1973 Betty Fiedan met with Pope Paul VI

Questions: Why do people laugh up their sleeves?

I know something that will tickle you. Do you know what it is?

On October 24, 1901, a widowed, childless, 160-pound, forty-three-year-old schoolteacher named Annie Taylor became the first person to go over Niagara Falls in a barrel. She did it in a specially constructed 4 by 4½-foot barrel, which had been carefully padded and weighted. Only after she had been plucked from the water did she admit to anyone that she could not swim. She had decided on the stunt, she said, because she felt her life was going nowhere, and she would either be killed or the feat would bring her fame and fortune.

She was only partly right. Her fame was fleeting, and she made very little money out of it. She died poor and forgotten.

She used to be a schoolteacher, but she has no class now.
Fred Allen

Incidentally, the survival rate for people who go over Niagara Falls in a barrel or some similar container is about 56%.

Answers: That's where their funnybones are.
It's a feather.

OCTOBER 25

Question: Can you match the country with its capital?

a Tanzania	*1* Riyadh
b Nigeria	*2* Abu Dhabi
c United Arab Emirates	*3* Dar es Salaam
d Saudi Arabia	*4* Lagos

Notable Births

1800	Thomas B. Macaulay	1902	Henry Commager
1825	Johann Strauss	1912	Minnie Pearl
1881	Pablo Picasso	1914	John Berryman
1888	Richard E. Byrd	1941	Helen Reddy
1890	Floyd Bennett	1958	Kornelia Ender

Notable Events

1415	Battle of Agincourt
1854	Charge of the Light Brigade at Balaclava
1874	Britain annexed Fiji Islands
1881	Shootout at the OK Corral, Tombstone, Arizona
1909	Prince Ito of Japan assassinated
1931	George Washington Bridge opened
1935	Hurricane in Haiti killed 2,000 people
1950	Tibet surrendered to China
1960	First electronic wristwatch produced
1971	Red China admitted to United Nations

One day in 1924, Paul Jordan Smith came into his house after a round of golf and found his wife working on a painting that smacked of Dadaistic influences. Smith was no artist or art critic, but he had absolutely no liking for what Picasso, the Distortionists, or the other modern artists were doing to what he considered art. He told his wife that a child could paint as well as these modern geniuses, and set down to prove his point by painting a picture himself. He took a ripped canvas, the oldest paints he could find, a worn brush, and, as he put it, "splashed out the crude outlines of a savage holding up what was intended to be a starfish, but turned out a banana." Having purged his contempt for modern art, he went in to dinner.

Several days later, Smith's son brought home the art critic of the local paper, who expressed his interest in the painting. Smith did not admit that he had painted it, but he did tell the young man he thought it was a rotten work of art. The critic upbraided him, praised the work highly and cited reasons why the canvas was, if not a great picture, certainly an exceptionally good one. At that point, said Smith, "I made up my mind that critics would praise anything unintelligible."

He changed his name for the picture from, *Yes, We Have No Bananas* to *Exaltation,* made up the name Pavel Jerdanowitch for himself ("knowing that critics have a weakness for things foreign"), chose something he called the Disumbrationist School as his mentor, and sent the painting off to a major exhibition in the spring of 1925. Nothing much happened for a time, but then a Paris art magazine requested photos of his other work. Smith was silent, but they wrote again. This time Smith-Jerdanowitch replied that he was too poor to be able to afford photos of his paintings, but sent a biographical sketch instead. The biography described his birth in Moscow and his immigration to Chicago. Then, he said, he contracted tuberculosis, which forced him to go to the South Seas for several years. Based on this phony information and one picture, the French art review soon published a full appreciation of Jerdanowitch's works.

After this, his reputation spread, and Jerdanowitch was to exhibit at the next year's prestigious Marshall Field's show in Chicago. He quickly completed his second masterpiece, entitled it *Aspiration*, and sent it off. It depicted a native woman doing washing over a barrel, watched by what looked like flying fox above one end of a clothesline. Out of the 400 paintings in the show, which reflected the best modern art had to offer, Jerdanowitch's second hour-long experiment in the genre was selected to appear on the cover of the brochure.

Two of his other later paintings were shown the next year in New York City, where they also attracted wide attention. Jerdanowitch's name began to appear regularly in art reviews and in new art books. His works were consistently applauded, and he himself was given great praise as an innovator in a 1926 book *Livre d'Or*, which also featured a full-page reproduction of *Aspiration*.

But for the fact that he knew he was deceiving people, Paul Jordan Smith might have had a great career as an artist. He finally tired of the ruse, however, and told his story to the *Los Angeles Times* the following year. Even this disclaimer didn't stem the tide of his fame.

In 1928, all four of the Jerdanowitch paintings were shown by Boston's Vose Galleries in what the gallery owner termed "the most widely noticed exhibition I have ever heard of." Some critics still insisted that, hoax or not, Jerdanowitch's paintings were those of a primitive genius, and should be taken seriously as art.

Today, there are a few lucky people who took the paintings seriously as investments — each one is worth thousands of dollars.

Most artists are sincere and most art is bad, and some insincere art (sincerely insincere) can be quite good.

Igor Stravinsky

If that's art, I'm a Hottentot!

Harry S Truman

Anyone who sees and paints a sky green and pastures blue ought to be sterilized.

Adolf Hitler

Answer: a-3, b-4, c-2, d-1.

Notable Births

1791	Charles Sprague	1914	Jackie Coogan
1894	John Knight	1919	Edward Brooke

Notable Events

312	Emperor Constantine saw 2-mile-long cross in sky
1785	First mule imported in United States, Boston
1825	Erie Canal opened
1905	Battleship *Potemkin* mutiny; first soviet formed
1910	Hawley and Port landed in Quebec after 1,350 miles in balloon; new record
1911	Chinese republic proclaimed
1951	Rocky Marciano defeated Joe Louis for heavyweight crown

Questions: If a man were to destroy a clock, could he be accused of killing time?

What time is it when the clock strikes thirteen?

Helen, the mother of Constantine the Great, was a Christian convert who undertook a pilgrimage to the Holy Land when she was nearly eighty. On the way she had a vision of the Holy Sepulchre and the True Cross, and was told exactly where in Jerusalem each was located. On arriving in Jerusalem, she and her entourage sought out the location of the Cross. Amazing as it may seem, they found three crosses there, one of which had the power to heal wounds and raise the dead. They consecrated the place, and dubbed it New Jerusalem. That Constantine's mother had found the Cross was more than coincidence, of course; "prophecies" made two or three centuries after the event predicted the circumstances of its discovery with remarkable accuracy.

Most of the cross was left in Jerusalem and stored there in a silver case; some of it went to Rome and some to Constantinople. Wherever the True Cross went, pilgrims followed it, and took splinters from it when they returned home. Saint Cyril, commenting on this phenomenon, happily said that the "whole earth is filled with sacred wood." When skeptics pointed out that there were enough True Cross splinters to build a large ship, the good old Saint Cyril simply attributed it to the miracle of the loaves and fishes all over again.

In any event, the part of the True Cross that was left in Jerusalem by Constantine's mother was captured by the Persians when they took Jerusalem in 614. Heraclius captured it back a dozen years later and returned it to Calvary; though in 636 he had to remove it to Constantinople when his army was routed by the Arabs.

In 1078, a wealthy man of Amalfi secured it after the downfall of Michael VII, and gave it to the shrine of Saint Benedict at Casinum. Later on, parts of it were carried to the Holy Land once more on various crusades, and about half of it ended up in Saladin's hands. What remained by 1238 was sold by Baldwin II, who was heavily in debt to Louis IX of France.

The Cross was reported stolen on May 20, 1575, although there was speculation that a French king had long before sold it to the Venetians. A replacement cross was ordered. It was later claimed that, through some divine process, the copy was given powers only slightly inferior to those of the original. That was quite good enough for the French.

Christ cannot possibly have been a Jew. I don't have to prove that scientifically. It is a fact!

Joseph Goebbels

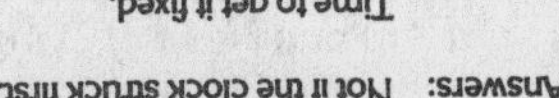

OCTOBER 27

Question: Can you name their vice presidents?
Hayes
Cleveland (1st term)
Benjamin Harrison
Cleveland (2nd term)
McKinley (1st term)

Notable Births

1728	James Cook	1914	Dylan Thomas
1736	James MacPherson	1923	Roy Lichtenstein
1782	Nicol Paganini	1928	Kyle Rote
1859	Teddy Roosevelt	1932	Sylvia Plath
1910	Jack Carson	1945	Melba Moore

Notable Events

1765 Stamp Act Congress met in New York City
1798 French attempt to invade Ireland failed
1889 First Lithuanian Church in America founded, Plymouth, Pennsylvania
1918 Austria-Hungary offered to make separate peace
1954 Marilyn Monroe, Joe DiMaggio divorced
1959 Hurricane claimed 2,000 lives in Mexico
1961 Monsanto Chemical company announced it had halted aging in mice and chickens

There were few people who could surpass Teddy Roosevelt in anything, and there was certainly no one who had a bigger ego. This story circulated when the Rough Rider was president.

After TR had died and gone to Heaven, he made a nuisance of himself with the officials of Paradise. It seemed he was not happy with his state of eternal bliss, and insisted on being given a position of greater responsibility. Finally, to get him out of their hair, the heavenly fathers instructed Saint Peter to have Roosevelt organize and direct a new celestial choir. Roosevelt was pleased with the assignment, but remained annoying. His vision of the chorus was far greater than Heaven had intended. "I must have ten thousand sopranos, ten thousand contraltos, and ten thousand tenors, and I must have them immediately!" he demanded.

Patiently, Saint Peter said, "Yes, of course, of course. But what about the basses?'

TR was indignant. "*I'll* sing bass!"

I don't know why it is that the religious never ascribe common sense to God.

Somerset Maugham

A typical funeral bill during the 1890s was itemized, and was far cheaper than its non-itemized cousin of today. A representative set of charges went something like this:

Services at the deceased's house	$ 1.25
Preserving the remains on ice	$ 10.00
Burial permit	$ 1.50
Embalming	$ 10.00
Washing and dressing	$ 5.00
Hearse rental	$ 8.00

By 1960, the average cost of a funeral had risen to $1,200. It is almost impossible today to be buried commercially for much less than $2,500.

A few days before he was to embark on a steamer to the Orient, the British novelist John Galsworthy was having lunch with his publisher in a London restaurant. The publisher bemoaned the fact that there was no *good* new talent to be found anywhere, and said he was worried about the whole future of book publishing. Galsworthy assured him that new writers were bound to turn up, if only he would be patient. The publisher asked him to keep his eyes open.

Two weeks later, as Galsworthy's vessel was steaming down the west coast of Africa, a young ship's officer approached him with great reverence and a manuscript under his arm. He explained that, although English wasn't his native tongue, he had just completed an English novel. Would Mr. Galsworthy, if it were not too much trouble, look over the book and tell him if the writing was any good? If it was not, the man said, he wanted to know, so that he would not waste his time trying to be a writer, and he could turn his attentions to something more profitable.

Galsworthy agreed to review the manuscript, which was entitled *Almayer's Folly*. Its author was Joseph Conrad, later to become famous as the author of *Lord Jim* and *Heart of Darkness*.

Answer: William Wheeler; Thomas Hendricks; Levi Morton; Adlai Stevenson; Garret Hobart.

Notable Births

1466	Desiderius Erasmus	1914	Jonas Salk
1902	Elsa Lanchester	1926	Bowie Kuhn
1903	Evelyn Waugh	1933	Suzy Parker
1907	Edith Head	1949	Bruce Jenner

Notable Events

1636	Harvard College founded
1886	Statue of Liberty formally dedicated
1893	Carter Harrison, Mayor of Chicago, assassinated
1922	Mussolini marched on Rome
1929	First child born in an airplane, over Miami, Florida
1940	Italy invaded Greece
1958	Accession of Pope John XXIII
1962	Khrushchev offered to withdraw Cuban missiles if United States wouldn't invade

A Quick Lesson in Do-It-Yourself Embalming

To begin, you'll need three to six gallons of embalming fluid. If you can't find a brand name fluid you can mix your own, using dyed and perfumed formaldehydes, glycerine, borax, phenol, alcohol, and water. The proportions aren't too important to the finished product, as Dr. Jesse Carr will explain later.

First of all, the mouth must be sewn together at the inside of the lips. (The needle is brought out through the nostril, usually the left one.) Then you take a trocar, a long hollow needle attached to a tube. Drain the contents of the abdominal and chest cavities, and replace the removed matter with cavity fluid. Pump out the circulatory system, replace the blood and plasma with the embalming solution, and that's about it. In eight to ten hours the tissues will be firm and dry, and ready for "cosmetic restoration."

Careful, though! Regular embalming fluid works differently on various bodies according to the cause of death. While it will give a pleasant pink glow to the flesh of a victim of carbon monoxide poisoning, when it is used on someone who died of jaundice it imparts a green tinge that requires a lot of make-up to conceal.

Although it is widely believed to preserve a buried body, embalming in fact does no such thing. If it has any worthwhile purpose at all, it is to make the open casket at a funeral a little more palatable. Dr. Jesse Carr is no friend of the mortuary industry, but he is a former Chief of Pathology at San Francisco General Hospital and Professor of Pathology at the University of California Medical School, and here's what he has to say about it:

> An exhumed body is a repugnant, moldy, foul-looking object. It's not the image of one who has been loved ... The body itself may be intact, as far as contours and so on; but the silk lining of the casket is all stained with body fluids, the wood is rotting, and the body is covered with mold ... If you seal up a casket so it is more or less airtight, you seal in the anaerobic bacteria — the kind that thrive in an airless atmosphere, you see. These are the putrefactive bacteria, and the results of their growth are pretty horrible ... you're better off with a shroud, and no casket at all.

A rut is a grave with the ends knocked out.

Laurence J. Peter

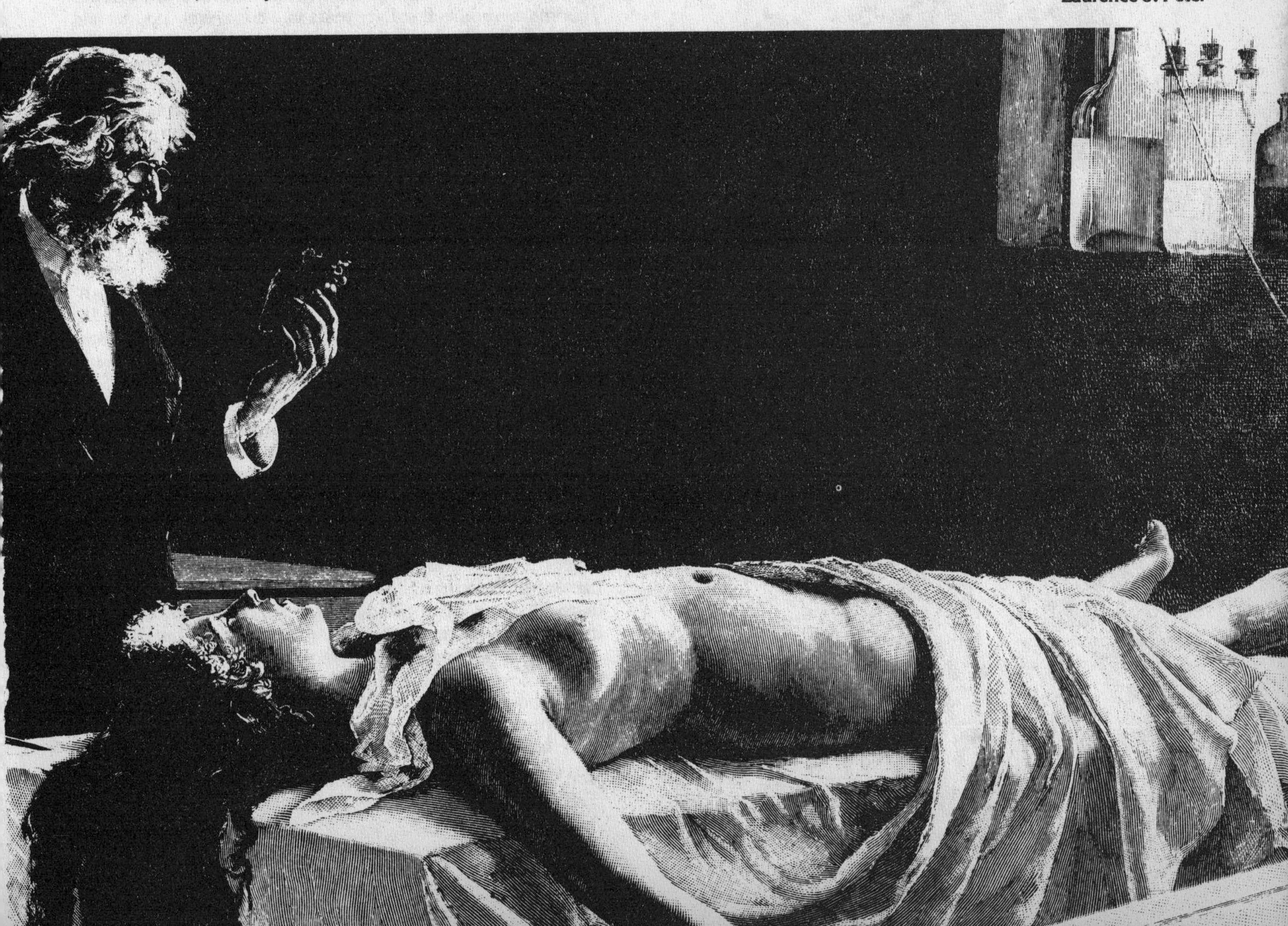

OCTOBER 29

Question: Within ten years, when were the following invented?
adding machine (early)
bulldozer
color photography
cash register

Notable Births

1656	Edmund Halley	1921	Bill Mauldin
1740	James Boswell	1947	Richard Dreyfuss
1899	Akim Tamiroff	1953	Jean Ratelle

Notable Events

1618	Sir Walter Raleigh beheaded
1929	Stock Market crashed
1940	First draft numbers in peacetime chosen
1942	Alaska Highway completed
1947	First forest fire drenched by manmade rain, Concord, New Hampshire
1956	Israel invaded the Sinai Peninsula
1957	Batista suspended Cuban constitution

Until the work done by the astronomer Edmund Halley and his contemporaries provided some reassuring scientific data about the nature of comets, the appearance of one of these "bearded stars" was often believed to presage awful and cataclysmic events. This superstition was not wholly without rationale. Comets were sighted shortly before the war that led to the downfall of Jerusalem in 66 A.D.; the devastation of Italy by the Huns in 373; the victory of the Turks over the Christians in 1456; and the Great Plague of 1664-66. Sneezing fits in Germany, large flocks of pigeons in America, a plague of cats in Westphalia, and countless earthquakes have also been attributed to this heavenly phenomenon.

Although nineteenth-century astronomers determined that even a direct hit with a comet would be harmless to the earth (within its whole head and millions of miles of tail a comet has only a few pounds of solid matter), superstitions and fears die hard. When Halley's Comet returned in 1910, anticomet pills sold for as much as a dollar apiece, and some shamans made tens of thousands of dollars selling them.

Advertising is the art of making whole lies out of half-truths.
Edgar A. Shoaff

Perhaps England's most reclusive inhabitant was a gentleman named Henry Welby, better known as the Hermit of Grub Street. This man lived his first forty years in a completely normal and more than respectable fashion. He served as a member of Parliament and also as sheriff for his county district, and was known throughout his neighborhood as an intelligent, honest, and Christian man. But in 1592, Welby was involved in a quarrel with his younger brother, and his sibling drew a firearm on him. Fortunately, the gun misfired, but Welby was so shaken by the experience that he resolved to remove himself entirely from the company of mankind.

He moved to London and took a house on Grub Street in the Cripplegate section of the city. It was a large place, but Welby himself used only three rooms of it, one for eating, one for sleeping, and one for reading and prayer. He employed a number of servants, but only one old maidservant was ever allowed to see him, and then infrequently. If visitors called, they were confined to an anteroom, and corresponded with by notepaper and pen.

Welby also maintained a severe diet in his hermitage. Usually he only ate bread (he never touched the crust) and oatmeal gruel, although he would occasionally have a salad when certain herbs were in season. On special occasions he would drink milk if it were still warm from the cow, and on holidays he allowed himself an egg yolk, without the white. Water and small beer were his liquid staples. Despite his own diet, and the fact that he had never met any of his neighbors face to face, on Christmas and Easter he would have large feasts sent into his dining room, and there, all alone, he would cut up generous portions of different meats and prepare the rest of the fare for a number of festive dinners. His servants would then convey the meals to families nearby.

He died on October 29, 1636, having seen and been seen by only one person in forty-four years.

His trusted maid died six days later.

Man's soul is lost that does not grieve at the loss of a faithful servant.
Charlie Chan

Answer: 1642, 1923, 1881, 1879.

Notable Births

1735	John Adams	1886	Zoe Atkins
1751	Richard Sheridan	1896	Ruth Gordon
1871	Paul Valery	1927	Joe Adcock
1885	Ezra Pound	1945	Henry Winkler

Notable Events

1759 Earthquake in Syria killed more than 20,000 people
1888 Ballpoint pen patented
1905 Czar capitulated to October Manifesto, gave Duma more power
1912 Vice President candidate Sherman died before Electoral College met
1938 Welles' *War of the Worlds* broadcast; nation panicked
1956 Russians invaded Hungary
1958 Storms in Bangladesh killed 500 people
1964 $380,000 gem robbery at Museum of Natural History

Questions: What has the head of a cat, the body of a cat, and the tail of a cat, but isn't a cat?

What's black and white and very dangerous?

A "Spoonerism" is a quirk of speech in which two or more consonant or vowel sounds are transposed. The name comes from a real person, William A. Spooner, a near-albino Anglican minister who died in 1930. Through some natural dyslexic process, he was constantly getting his phrases mixed up, much to the enjoyment of his students and parishioners. Below is a selection of Spooner's best isms (or at least those which have been reliably attributed to him), some of which have been put into contexts not his own, so that the original intent of the remark is clear.

To a woman who had taken a private pew at church: "I'm sorry, Madam, but that pie is occupewed. May I sew you to another sheet?"

On the mechanical condition of a velocipede: "It's a well-boiled icicle."

Inquiring for one of the masters of Christ Church College: "Excuse me, but is the Bean dizzy?"

When offered a plate containing pink blancmange and figs: "I don't like the stink puff; I'll take pigs, fleas."

On a small cottage: "It's a nosy little cook."

Toasting Her Royal Majesty: "Three cheers for our queer old dean!"

About the successes of the British Navy: "Our cattleships and bruisers have dealt a blushing crow!"

Referring to the kindness of a fellow minister: "He is a shoving leopard to his flock."

From sermons:

"It is easier for a camel to go through the knee of an idol . . .

"Jonah in the Bale's Whelly . . .

"There's no peace in a home where a dinner swells . . .

"Running with the muddly guiltatude . . .

"God will call the fosen chew . . ."

On a lost button: "A glutton dropped from a-bove . . ."

On renewed dedication: "We must undertake this with fresh veal and new zigor."

On the formation of some rocks: "Look at those erotic blacks on the shore!"

About a falling cat: "She just popped on her drawers and away she went."

On his dropped hat: "Will nobody pat my hiccup?"

To a student who had flunked out of school: "You have hissed all my mystery lectures. In fact, you have tasted two whole worms, and you must leave Oxford this afternoon by the town drain."

Got any others?

It is better to speak wisdom foolishly, like the saints, than to speak folly wisely, like the dons.

G. K. Chesterton

Communication of all kinds is like a painting — a compromise with impossibilities.

Samuel Butler

The extraordinary criminal lawyer, Samuel Leibowitz, saved seventy-eight men from the electric chair, but he had no strong liking for the murderers for whom he'd won reprieve. He used to relate that as a group they were not a particularly courteous lot — not one of them had ever sent him a card during the holiday season.

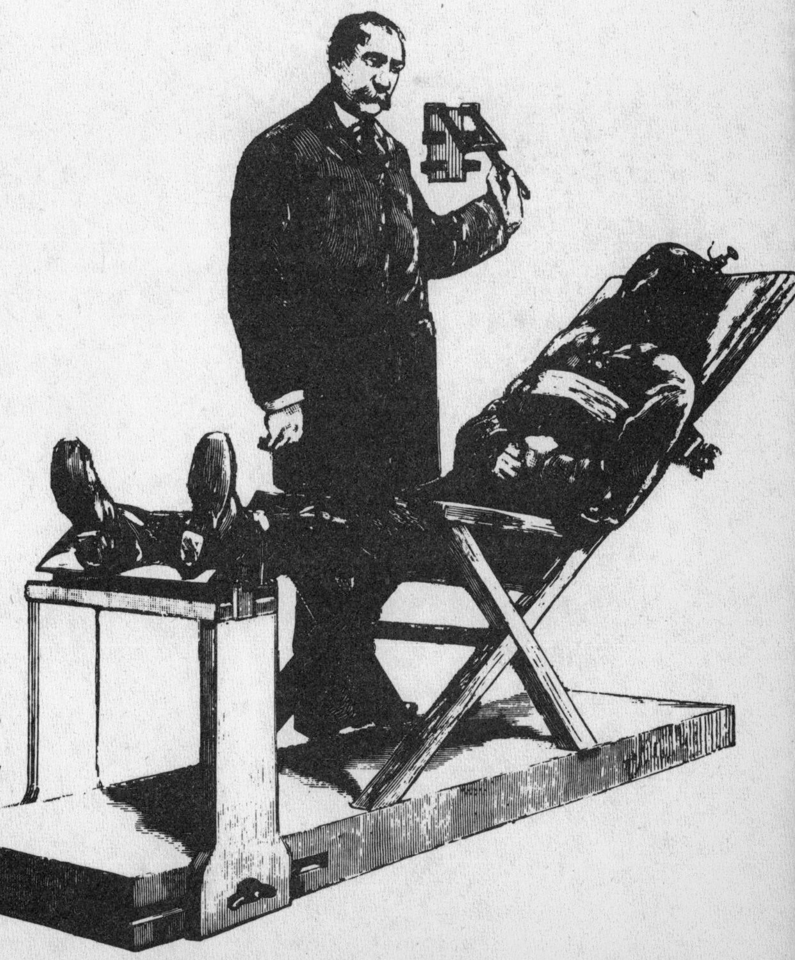

Answers: A kitten.

A skunk with a machine gun.

Sagittarius (The Archer)
November 23 through December 21

NOVEMBER

NOVEMBER 1

Questions: What travels but never moves?

How many balls of string would it take to reach the moon?

In 1971, in an effort to bring his colleagues' attention to the haphazard way in which they sometimes passed odd pieces of legislation and special resolutions, Texas State Representative Thomas Moore, Jr., introduced a statement on behalf of the people of Texas honoring a man from Massachusetts. The resolution before that noble assembly stated: "This compassionate gentleman's dedication and devotion to his work has enabled the weak and lonely throughout the nation to achieve and maintain a new degree of concern for their future," and went on to say that he was not without recognition in his own state: "He has been officially recognized by the state of Massachusetts for his noted activities and unconventional techniques involving population control and applied psychology."

The resolution passed without debate or a dissenting vote.

The man in question was named Albert de Salvo, better known to Americans as the "Boston Strangler."

Time wounds all heels.

Jane Ace

Elmer Frey, aged eighty-one, of Kansas City, Missouri, had to be rushed to the hospital in November 1947, to be treated for injuries he received in a highway accident.

It seems Mr. Frey fell off his tricycle.

You should have thought of all this before you were born.

N.F. Simpson

Notable Births

1500	Benvenuto Cellini	1896	Edmund Blunden
1871	Stephen Crane	1935	Gary Player

Notable Events

1478	Papal Bull began Spanish Inquisition
1618	Thirty Years War began
1755	Earthquake in Portugal killed 60,000 people
1835	Texas declared independence from Mexico
1853	Water cure introduced by R.T. Trall, New York City
1873	Manufacture of barbed wire began
1873	First artificially impregnated rabbit exhibited, New York City
1944	First quadruplets delivered by Caesarian section, Philadelphia
1951	First A-bomb explosion to be witnessed by troops, New Mexico
1963	Diem assassinated in army coup, South Vietnam
1970	Dance hall fire in Grenoble, France, claimed 145 lives
1975	Assassination attempt on President Ford by two Puerto-Rican nationalists, one White House guard killed

Although people almost automatically associate the rickshaw with the Orient and think it has been around for centuries, the vehicle was invented by an American, and is barely a hundred years old. The fellow was named Jonathan Scobie, who was a Baptist missionary serving in Japan when he invented it to help his invalid wife in 1869.

Ability is the art of getting credit for all the home runs somebody else hits.

Casey Stengel

THE BURGLAR COULDN'T FRIGHTEN HIM.

"No, my burglarious friend, I shall throw up nothing at all! I am under the protection of the United States Mutual Accident Association, 320 Broadway, New York. If you wound me I get $50 a week. If disabled permanently I get $2500. If you hit me in the eye I get $1300; for both eyes I get $5000; for hand or foot $5000; for both $10,000. And if you should kill me my family get $10,000, and could live in opulence for the rest of their lives. Blaze away!"

Answers: A road.

One big one.

NOVEMBER 2

Notable Births

1734	Daniel Boone	1913	Burt Lancaster
1744	Marie Antoinette	1917	Ann Rutherford
1795	James K. Polk	1934	Ken Rosewall
1865	Warren G. Harding	1945	Don McLean

Notable Events

1664	First outbreak of the Great Plague in London
1772	Committees of Correspondence formed
1789	Property of Catholic Church in France confiscated
1841	Second Afghan War began
1886	First brothers vied in gubernatorial election, Tennessee
1927	Floods in Vermont killed 120 people
1948	Russell Long elected to Senate seat once held by both his father and mother

Questions: If you can buy eight eggs for twenty-six cents, how many can you get for a cent and a quarter?

If butter is a dollar a pound in Chicago, what are windows in Detroit?

What sort of thing would make a frontiersman like Daniel Boone trade in his buckskins and rifle for a pair of overalls and a shovel? A good woman? Maybe. A plant?

Definitely! Although few people realize it, Daniel Boone made a fortune harvesting ginseng, the medicinal plant that Asian peoples have loved for centuries. In 1778, Daniel showed up on the books of a Philadelphia firm recouping about $30,000 for fifteen tons of ginseng root. For a hardworking man like Daniel, that would work out to about four months' labor. Not bad, considering a skilled craftsman of that era might have made $300 in the same period.

Although ginseng was plentiful in colonial America, it had long been scarce in China, where its popularity stemmed from its medicinal value, its reputation (it was valued highly for its supposed benefit to male sexual performance), and the so-called Doctrine of Signatures. This doctrine, developed over the course of many centuries, was an elaborate pseudo-pharmacopoeia founded on the anthropomorphization of medicinal plants; that is, if a portion of a plant resembled a man's elbow, it was good for treating ailments of the elbow. The ginseng root often resembled a whole man in miniature, and was therefore thought to be a panacea of all the human diseases. Thus, it was the most valuable medicine in the Asian world. Wars were continually fought over ginseng territory, and one Tartar province actually walled itself off from the rest of China to protect its precious resource. So elevated a station did the plant hold that for centuries only the emperor himself was allowed to harvest it. Anyone caught stealing or exporting it was summarily executed.

The first Western ginseng to be exported to Asia was dug by a group of Jesuits near Montreal in 1716. It brought them a phenomenal five dollars a pound. Word spread about easy pickings and high prices, and hundreds of trappers and farmers took up the spade. Many men set to work with their families and became itinerant "'seng" diggers, traveling the Northeast searching for the scattered plots of the golden (in more ways than one) roots. As late as 1773, a fifty-five ton load brought three dollars a pound when it was unloaded in China. One one occasion, a single, perfectly formed root was sold for $25,000. A number of American fortunes were made in the trade, but until recently, Americans hardly touched ginseng themselves.

"Decimate" is one of the most frequently misused words in our language. When something has been decimated, most people think it has been almost entirely destroyed. In fact, decimate means "reduce by a tenth."

During Lord Curzon's term as the English foreign secretary, it was reported that the monks of the Greek monstery at Mount Athos were violating their holy vows. However, the English lord saw a transcribed version of the original complaint, in which "vows" had been miscopied as "cows."

Naturally, Curzon instructed that they be sent a Papal Bull.

The fellow who never makes a mistake takes his orders from one who does.

Herbert V. Prochnow

The horn of a rhinoceros is not made from "horn" at all, as a cow's or a goat's is. It's solid, matted hair which continues to grow throughout the rhino's lifetime. Some of these "horns" have reached lengths of over five feet.

Although there have been over eight hundred thousand species of insects classified, scientists estimate that that number represents only from one-half to one-tenth of all the insect species in the world.

Answers: Eight.
Glass.

NOVEMBER 3

Question: Can you arrange these cities according to the cost of living from the most expensive to the cheapest?

Amman, Jordan
Kinshasha, Zaire
London
New York
Paris

Before Sandy Koufax and Nolan Ryan came along, baseball's fastest pitcher was Bob (Rapid Robert) Feller, born on November 3, 1918, who pitched for eighteen years with the Cleveland Indians. Using a United States Army timing device, his fastball was clocked at 98.6 mph. Feller totalled 2,581 strikeouts during his career.

Although few people are aware of it, Mark Koenig, who played for the New York Yankees during six years of the Ruthian era, once sped a ball at 127 mph, measured by the *same* machine. And yet, in his twelve-year career, Koenig struck out only nine batters! To do him justice, though, Koenig played 1,156 of his major league games as an infielder, and only appeared in five games as a pitcher.

Koenig's lifetime batting average was .279; Feller's a meager .151.

Since we cannot know all there is to know about anything, we ought to know a little bit about everything.

Blaise Pascal

Jim, an English setter owned by a Missouri hotel owner named Sam Van Arsdale, was a pretty smart dog. While he was walking around his property one day, Sam inspected an elm tree and found it had blight. When he speculated out loud as to whether any of his other trees had the disease, Jim barked and ran to another elm. The tree he chose was also blighted. Sam, now intrigued, selected another and another, and each one had Dutch elm disease. Sam thought this was mighty interesting. "Go find a birch tree, Jim," he commanded. Jim did, and subsequently found a locust, an oak, a beech, and any other tree his master directed him to.

Sam began to experiment with Jim. He found that the dog understood everything he said and could count and do simple arithmetic as well. Jim could also pick the winners of horse races. When his master read the field for a race out to him, Jim would bark when he heard the name of the horse he thought would win. The dog was invariably correct.

As Jim's reputation spread, he attracted the attention of two professors at the University of Missouri. In carefully controlled experiments, without Van Arsdale present, Jim performed all his previous feats and demonstrated he could understand orders given in German, Italian, and Spanish, although previously he had heard no more than a few words in any of those languages. Some time after these tests, the Missouri legislature suspended its session for a day so it could witness the remarkable dog's performance. Jim showed them he could even figure out instructions given in Morse Code. When Jim's show was over, the legislators rose as one and gave the dog a thundering ovation.

What explains Jim's amazing abilities? The best guess is that the dog was just plain psychic, and could simply read people's minds, regardless of what they said.

All animals are equal, but some are more equal than others.

George Orwell

Notable Births

1793	Stephen Austin	1901	André Malraux
1794	William Cullen Bryant	1909	James Reston
1831	Ignatius Donnelly	1922	Charles Bronson
1884	Joe Martin, Jr.	1945	Ken Holtzman

Notable Events

1706 Earthquake in Abruzzo, Italy, claimed 15,000 lives
1900 First American auto show held, New York City
1952 First frozen bread marketed
1957 Sputnik II launched, carrying Laika, the first space dog
1958 Volcanic eruption on moon viewed by Russian astronomer
1966 Flooding in Florence and Venice killed 113 people, destroyed millions in art work
1970 Allende took office in Chile

In Colorado in 1875, an entire train sank in a mire of quicksand. The pool was later probed to a depth of fifty feet, but no trace of the train was found.

Visually, they are a nightmare: tight, dandified Edwardian-Beatnik suits and great pudding bowls of hair. Musically they are a near-disaster: guitars and drums slamming out a merciless beat that does away with secondary rhythms, harmony, and melody. Their lyrics (punctuated by nutty shouts of "yeah, yeah, yeah!") are a catastrophe, a preposterous farrago of Valentine-card romantic sentiments. "We're rather crummy musicians," says George, the one who looks like a poet. "We can't sing; we can't do anything," adds Paul, the cherub.

Newsweek, on the arrival of the Beatles in America, February 24, 1964

Answer: Paris, Kinshasha, Amman, London, New York.

NOVEMBER 4

Notable Births

1740	A.M. Toplady	1916	Walter Cronkite
1840	Auguste Rodin	1917	Gig Young
1879	Will Rogers	1918	Art Carney
1907	Paul Douglas	1919	Martin Balsam

Notable Events

1605 Discovery of the Gunpowder Plot; Guy Fawkes arrested
1782 Captain Wilmot of Maryland killed, last American soldier to die in Revolutionary War
1846 Artificial leg patented
1921 Japanese prime minister, Takashi Hara, assassinated
1924 First woman governor elected in United States, Nan T. Ross, Wyoming
1931 League of Nations condemned Japan for trespassing in Manchuria
1939 Roosevelt forbade U.S. ships in western European waters
1947 Man o' War buried, Lexington, Kentucky

Indestructable Sam's (October 23) victories over death may have been more remarkable, but one well-known American patriot also experienced an extraordinary number of deadly situations and came through them all with hardly a scratch.

Before he was even thirty years old, this man had staved off the potentially mortal diseases of smallpox, malaria, dysentery, and pleurisy. While he was in the military during the French and Indian War, he had two horses shot out from under him and his coat was pierced by bullets in four places in one battle alone — yet he emerged unscathed. Returning from an expedition to Fort Le Boeuf, he toppled from a raft into the river's icy waters and was nearly drowned. Almost immediately after that, he was shot at by an Indian from a distance of less than fifty feet. The musket ball missed, but just barely.

The fellow's name was George Washington.

In 1948, Levi Morin of Auburn, Maine, stumbled and fell across a railroad track just ahead of an oncoming train. After the train had passed, Levi looked down and discovered that his leg had been severed from his body by the train's wheels. He hadn't felt a thing.

It was his wooden leg that Morin lost.

Even if you are on the right track, you will get run over if you just sit there.

Will Rogers

Can you name the animal that looks like a big earthworm and has only a front pair of legs? It's a native of Baja California.

(the mole lizard)

Armadillo babies are born in sets of four — all identical "quadruplets," the product of a single egg.

Thirty percent of all shotgun ammunition used in the United States is aimed at rabbits.

Question: Can you match the capital and the country?

a	Port Moresby	*1*	New Zealand
b	Georgetown	*2*	Papua New Guinea
c	Wellington	*3*	Jamaica
d	Kingston	*4*	Guyana

Man o' War's guest book, kept while he was a stud in retirement, totalled over two million names. His funeral was attended by over 2,500 people.

Abraham Lincoln was the only president to be granted a patent. He invented a device for floating barges and other vessels over shallow river shoals, but it was never produced commercially.

Perhaps the only president to write a movie script was Franklin D. Roosevelt. While he was recovering from the attack of polio that crippled him in the early 1920s, he worked on a story chronicling the history of the United States frigate *Constitution*, "Old Ironsides." It was never produced, perhaps because Roosevelt's attempts to market it to the movies were halfhearted.

During his recuperation FDR also mapped out plans for an intercity freight system using dirigibles. This didn't get off the ground, either.

Thomas Jefferson founded the Democratic Party; Franklin Roosevelt dumbfounded it.

Dewey Short

There's a difference between a strain and a sprain. A sprain occurs in a ligament, while a strain is in a muscle.

Answer: a-2, b-4, c-1, d-3.

NOVEMBER 5

Questions: Why is bread like the sun?

If William Penn's mother's sisters had a bakery, what would be the price of pies?

Notable Births

1850	Ella Wheeler Wilcox	1912	Roy Rogers
1855	Eugene Field	1913	Vivien Leigh
1885	Will Durant	1941	Elke Sommer
1906	Joel McCrea	1952	Bill Walton

Notable Events

1733	John Peter Zenger began publishing *New York Weekly Journal*
1793	Duke of Orleans beheaded in France
1813	7,000 Americans invaded Canada on march to Montreal
1911	First transcontinental airplane flight completed
1914	France and Britain declared war on Turkey
1956	France and Britain invaded Egypt at Port Said
1977	Carter vetoed $80 million Clinch River breeder reactor

General Jean Baptiste Jules Bernadotte, a forty-six-year-old, peasant-born Frenchman of Jewish ancestry, was legally adopted by and made the heir to King Charles VIII of Sweden on November 5, 1810. General Bernadotte had treated Swedish prisoners-of-war in an extremely kind and civil manner, and the king was so impressed by his humanity that he made this unique gesture. Eight years later, Bernadotte succeeded to the throne, and the present ruling family of Sweden is descended from him.

Depending on one's status and bank account, there were three basic ways to be mummified in the Egypt of the pharoahs. The first method, which was the most expensive and the most complicated, took forty to seventy days from start to finish. Astringent drugs and spices were injected into the body to embalm it, and then the remains were anointed with oils of cedar, myrrh, and cinnamon. The whole body was then saturated in a niter bath before being washed. Linen bandages soaked in myrrh and gum, sometimes as much as a thousand yards in length, were wrapped around the body to complete the process of mummification. This method cost the equivalent of many thousands of dollars.

The second procedure involved injecting the corpse with a cedar oil extract, washing it, and then wrapping it in bandages that had been soaked in a niter or in some different salt solution. While the most costly process usually involved burial in a sarcophagus, bodies preserved in this fashion were usually laid to rest in sycamore coffins in small tombs. It hurt the Egyptian pocketbook about as much as a thousand-dollar expense would hurt the average American family today.

The vast majority of Egyptians whose bodies were preserved went through a relatively inexpensive and not always effective preservation. Their bodies were soaked or boiled in a resin bath, somewhat haphazardly wrapped in saturated linens, and then placed in simple wood coffins and stored in sepulchres by the hundreds.

Generally, the mummies that have endured the test of time were prepared by the most expensive method. Some mummies of the second kind have endured very well, but very few of the third type have lasted the 2,500 years since they were buried.

Incidentally, one mummy that has come down to us is the body of a king who was usually called "Ahuz." According to the Book of Jashur, this monarch was only twenty-four inches tall. Loosely translated from the ancient Egyptian tongue, "Ahuz" means "Shorty."

Answers: It rises in the yeast and sets in the vest.
The Pie-Rates of Penn's-Aunts (Pirates of Penzance).

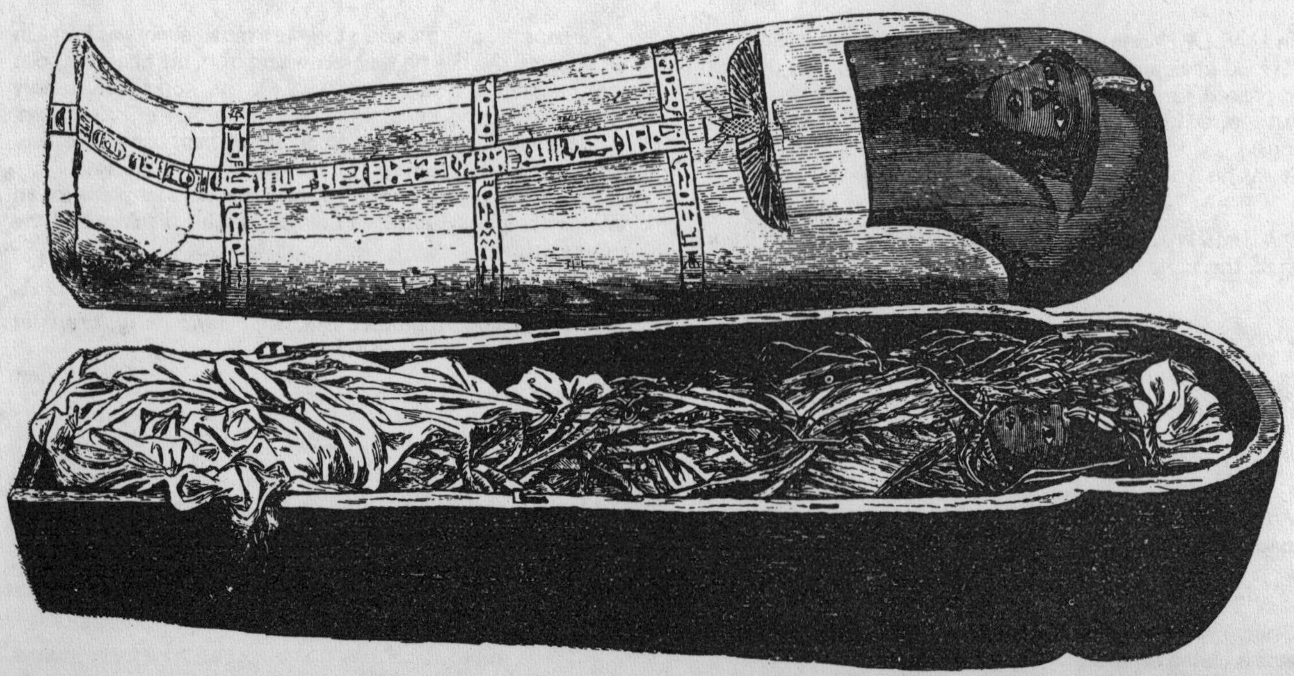

NOVEMBER 6

Notable Births

1558	Thomas Kyd	1887	Walter Johnson
1854	John Philip Sousa	1921	James Jones
1860	Ignace Paderewski	1931	Mike Nichols
1861	James Naismith	1946	Sally Field

Notable Events

1792 Dumouriez conquered Austrian Netherlands
1869 First intercollegiate football game played, New Brunswick, New Jersey
1883 First intercollegiate cross-country championships, New York City
1932 Supreme Court called for a new Scottsboro Boys trial
1942 10,000 perished in tidal wave; Bengal, India
1956 Ike reelected
1961 Knesset passed resolution for resettlement of refugees in Arab states
1961 Hollywood Hills fire began, claimed houses of Joe E. Brown, Zsa Zsa Gabor, Burt Lancaster, Richard Nixon

On one occasion, Ignace Paderewski was traveling through Germany and stayed at an inn in the Black Forest. He noticed a piano there, and asked the innkeeper if he might try it. He stopped after only a few notes, and told the innkeeper that the instrument was not only badly out of tune but had a number of keys that did not make any sound at all.

The man was quite indignant. "If you were a good pianist, you could skip over those keys so it wouldn't matter," he told the distinguished concert artist.

The Michigan State football team had a so-so November in 1931. They lost to Syracuse, 15 to 10, and to the University of Detroit, 20 to 13. They also played to a scoreless tie with the University of Michigan. The only thing that really salvaged the month for them was a victory over Ripon by a score of 100 to 0.

Question: About how long do these animals live?
pig
rabbit
gray squirrel
tiger

Blue whales, for all their mammoth size and mass, can travel faster than twenty knots over long distances, and they are capable of surges of six hundred horsepower.

A little town in Ecuador elected a foot powder as its mayor several years ago. None of the regular candidates was attracting much attention, it seems, and about the same time as the election, a foot powder manufacturer came out with an advertising campaign that fitted right into the political process. "Vote for any candidate," it announced, "but if you want well-being and hygiene, vote Pulvapies."

Shortly before election day, a prankster distributed leaflets which read, simply, "For Mayor: Honorable Pulvapies."

Pulvapies won in a write-in landslide, and reportedly did well outside of town, too.

A Los Angeles District Court judge was removed from the bench in 1975 after the State Supreme Court found her conduct unbecoming to the bar. Among the woman's transgressions were: she wore short skirts to court; kept a poodle in her lap; and serendipitously imprisoned lawyers who made her mad. But the capper to the case was that she'd threatened a police officer when he'd tried to calm her while whe was leaning on her horn in the middle of a traffic jam. She told him to lay off or risk "a .38 caliber vasectomy."

A century ago, a Frenchwoman named de. la Bresse left a fortune of 125,000 francs to be used expressly for clothing snowmen. In 1876, the court upheld the validity of the bequest.

Answer: 10, 5, 10, 16 years, respectively.

NOVEMBER 7

Questions: What do you call a son who is always wiring for money?

What rose is the highest in the public's esteem?

Notable Births

1867	Marie Curie	1926	Joan Sutherland
1903	Dean Jagger	1937	Dick Stuart
1913	Albert Camus	1937	Jim Kaat
1918	Billy Graham	1943	Joni Mitchell

Notable Events

1781 Last woman burned by Spanish Inquisition
1811 William Henry Harrison defeated Indians at Tippecanoe
1861 Ex-president Tyler began serving as Confederate legislator
1877 First state prison for women opened, Sherburne, Massachusetts
1913 Crew coach James Rice called Wellesley College's women's crew better than any male crew in world
1915 40,000 people marched in Chicago to protest Sunday closing of bars
1917 Winter Palace stormed; Russian Revolution underway
1922 First radio broadcast of a wedding
1933 LaGuardia elected mayor of New York City
1940 World's 3rd longest suspension bridge collapsed, Tacoma, Washington

Celebrants at winter carnivals often produce dazzling snow and ice creations, but perhaps the most spectacular was the Ice Palace, which was created in Moscow during the winter of 1740-1. Its purpose, too, was unique.

Late in 1740, Empress Anna Ivanova commissioned the architect, Peter Eropkin, to build a temple of solid ice. Designed on classical Greek lines, the building was eighty feet long, thirty-three feet high, and twenty-three feet wide, and was constructed of ice blocks, which were carefully measured, cut, and finished. The grounds around it were decorated with ice trees, ice statues, and ice birds and animals. There was even a lifesized elephant, whose trunk spouted a twenty-four-foot-long stream of water by day, and a flame by night. Six cannon and two mortars were also fashioned out of ice, and stood outside the palace. They were so well made that they were fired daily for several months.

Many pieces of furniture stood within the temple, each piece meticulously crafted. The most beautiful piece was a four-poster bed, complete with ice pillows and bedclothes. It was the real reason why the empress had built the castle.

Prince Michael Golitsyn had some time before run off and married an Italian Catholic, without the permission of the empress. His wife died soon after the wedding, but the empress was not a forgiving woman. She had the prince arrested, made him court jester, and ordered him to marry a particularly ugly servant woman. Then, she declared, they would spend their honeymoon in the ice house, for all to see.

On the big day, the couple was paraded in a cage which sat atop a real elephant, with scores of misshapen dwarves, imbeciles, bears, and pigs in their wedding train. The ceremony was conducted in due course, and the couple did indeed spend their postnuptial days in the ice house.

There aren't too many details about what happened next, but Empress Anna died later in the year. All that is really known is that her plan backfired: Prince Golitsyn and his wife lived happily ever after.

A husband is always a sensible man; he never thinks of marrying.

Alexander Dumas

If it were not for the presents, an elopement would be preferable.

George Ade

In John Gardner's book *October Light* there is a second book interspersed throughout the text, which Gardner uses on occasions to get his point across. The title of this ersatz novel is *The Smugglers of Lost Souls Rock*, and one of the events in it concerns the attempted electrocution of several competing dope smugglers, using eels as a power source. This may seem farfetched, but it's not. Electric eels can discharge over 600 volts forty times a second — a steady stream of power substantially stronger than any in general domestic or industrial use. A single eel could conceivably kill a man, and hooked up in a series (as they are in the novel), they would be a lethal weapon.

Answers: An electrician.
He-roes.

NOVEMBER 8

Notable Births

1900 Margaret Mitchell
1916 Peter Weiss

Notable Events

1793 French revolutionaries beheaded Madame Roland
1858 Inauguration of first Brazilian railroad
1910 Insect electrocutor patented
1923 Munich beer hall *putsch*, Hitler arrested
1939 *Life with Father* opened
1942 Allies landed in North Africa
1954 American League voted to move Philadelphia Athletics to Kansas City
1976 Park Chung Hee accused of Washington influence peddling

Although Joseph Guillotine didn't invent the machine that bears his name, and he was not, contrary to popular belief, the first person to lose his head beneath it (he wasn't executed), stocks as a punitive device have a somewhat different history. Contraptions similar to stocks existed in Europe before a man named Palmer was commissioned to build a set by the elders of Boston in 1634, but it is almost certain he built the first set in America, and may very well have improved on the design.

In any event, he was the first victim of the punishment in the New World. When he submitted a bill for one pound thirteen shillings to the town for materials and labor, the councilmen found him guilty of price-gouging, fined him a pound, and ordered him to undergo a half hour of public humiliation in the stocks he'd just built.

Wise men learn from other men's mistakes, fools by their own.

H.G. Bohn

In 1958, a gourmet food store in Philadelphia suffered a unique burglary. The only items taken were seventy-two assorted cans of such delicacies as fried ants, roasted caterpillars, baby bees, fried butterflies, smoked frogs' legs, fried worms, and smoked octopus.

Question: What's the state shown here?

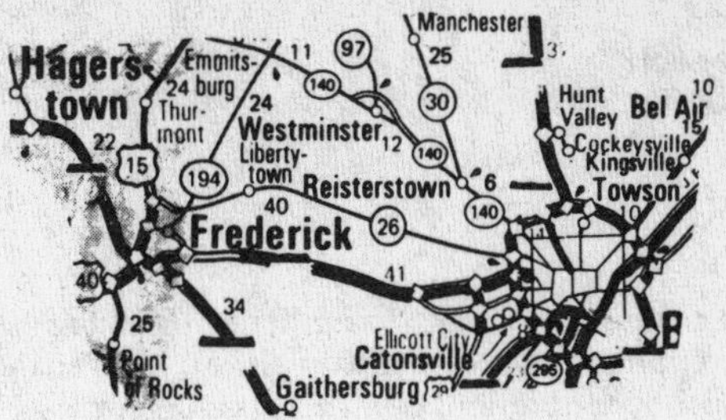

There's a fish native to Brazil called the Hiccup. It sometimes reaches a length of twelve feet, and is able to swallow so much air (it gulps it) and then expel it with such force that the sound can be heard a mile away.

A team of biologists who make studies of such things found that in the top inch of a square foot of soil in a forest there were 1,356 living creatures — including 865 mites, 265 springtails, twenty-two millipedes, nineteen adult beetles, and various numbers of twelve other insect species.

When you swat a fly, swat behind it. Slow motion movies show that flies invariably take off with a backward leap.

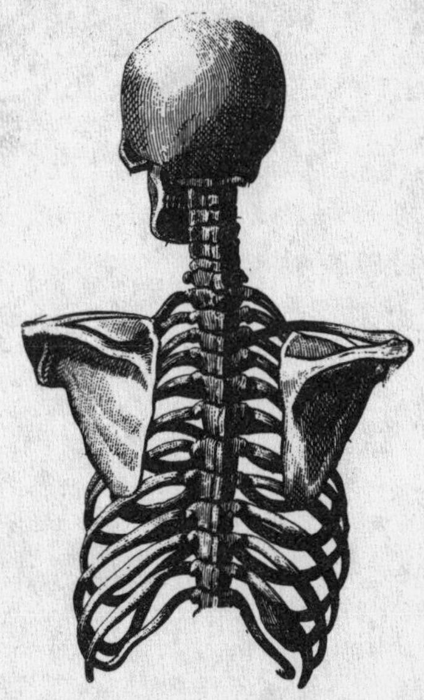

One human being in twenty has an extra rib. The condition is three times as common in men as it is in women, although normally both sexes have twelve pairs each. It is this irregularity that almost certainly gave birth to the story of Adam's rib giving birth to Eve — first told thousands of years ago.

A woman is a woman until the day she dies, but a man's a man only as long as he can.

Moms Mabley

Answer: Maryland.

NOVEMBER 9

Question: About how long do these animals live?

zebra
wolf
sea lion
puma

Notable Births

1818	Ivan Turgenev	1918	Florence Chadwick
1886	Ed Wynn	1928	Anne Sexton
1909	Katharine Hepburn	1934	Carl Sagan
1915	Sargent Shriver	1935	Bob Gibson
1918	Spiro Agnew	1942	Tom Weiskopf

Notable Events

1620	Puritans reached Cape Cod, began to explore coast
1837	Moses Montefiore became England's first Jewish knight
1888	Marie Kelly killed, last victim of Jack the Ripper
1918	Kaiser Wilhelm abdicated
1939	Hitler escaped Munich beer hall assassination attempt
1964	Eisaku Sato elected premier of Japan
1965	Lights out on East Coast; 800,000 people trapped in New York City subways

On its front page for Monday, November 9, 1874, the *New York Tribune* reported that scores of animals had escaped from the Central Park Zoo the previous day. There had been at least 49 people killed and 200 injured, 60 of them seriously, in the melee that followed. The *Tribune* reported that prominent New Yorkers such as Chester Alan Arthur and Samuel Tilden had helped in the hunt for the animals throughout the streets and into Sunday church services, but there were still a dozen dangerous beasts at large.

Various New Yorkers reacted predictably to the story. James Gordon Bennett, the owner of the *Tribune*, was so shocked when he read the story that he collapsed and had to spend the whole day in bed. Dr. George Hosmer, who would later become Joseph Pulitzer's personal secretary and doctor, stormed into the newspaper's offices with a pair of revolvers drawn, and shouted, "Well, here I am!" Major George Williams, city editor of the *New York Times*, went immediately to police headquarters to berate officials for giving the rival *Tribune* a scoop on the animal story. Some citizens formed vigilante groups and went out looking for the renegade beasts, while others simply barricaded themselves in their apartments.

None of the these people had read the last paragraph of the story, which explained that the report of the escape was just a ruse to bring the public's attention to the dilapidated and often dangerous conditions of the zoo in Central Park, which exposed the public to real danger if the animals there decided to revolt against their miserable habitat.

A good scare is worth more to a man than good advice.

Ed Howe

If fifty million people say a foolish thing, it is still a foolish thing.

Anatole France

Answer: 15, 5, 12, 12 years respectively.

Notable Births

570	Mohammed	1879	Vachel Lindsay
1484	Martin Luther	1887	Arnold Zweig
1493	Theophrastus Paracelsus	1889	Claude Rains
1697	William Hogarth	1893	J.P. Marquand
1728	Oliver Goldsmith	1913	Karl Shapiro
1759	Johann von Schiller	1925	Richard Burton

Notable Events

1620 Mayflower Compact signed
1775 U.S. Marine Corps established
1871 Stanley found Livingstone at Lake Ujiji, Tanganyika
1886 Prince Waldemar of Denmark elected King of Bulgaria; refused to serve
1918 Kaiser Wilhelm fled to Netherlands
1942 Assassination of German envoy to Paris by a Jew led to German Jews being herded into concentration camps, and fined $400,000,000
1964 Last Japanese Zero presented to Tokyo by United States government

Not too long ago, the United States Fish and Game Department embarked on a program to introduce a new sport fish into the waters of Lake Michigan. The native fighting fish had been practically exterminated by overfishing and industrial pollution, and so the department selected the Coho salmon to replenish the lake, because it thought the species would be sufficiently hardy to adapt to the lake's environment. There were some problems, however. The female Coho had trouble during the spawning season, because the depth of her body caused her to lose most of her roe on the bottom of Lake Michigan's feeder streams. If she succeeded in spawning, she very often didn't make it back to the mother lake because the water level had dropped during the dry early-summer spawning period, stranding her up in the creeks. In fact, in some tributaries, upward of 90 percent of the initial stock were dying in the spawning streams, which, apart from anything else, caused an odor problem that did not sit well with communities in the area.

Government scientists then decided to cross the Coho with the native walleyed pike, a much slimmer fish which would have little trouble negotiating the shallow riffles of the feeder streams. The crossbreeding was only moderately successful: the new fish, nicknamed the "Cowal," managed the shallows well, but too much of the sluggish nature of the pike came out in the hybrid, and it could not really be considered a fighting fish.

The ichthyologists then tried another combination, which they expected would compensate for the shortcomings of the Cowal and the Coho. They bred the Cowal with the nation's fiercest fighter, the Muskellunge, commonly known as the Muskie.

In theory, and appearance, everything was right with this second-generation crossbreed — which was called the "Cowalski" — except they couldn't teach the damn thing how to swim!

I question whether we can afford to teach mother macramé when Johnny still can't read.

Jerry Brown

You can have your Smiths, your Aldens, and your Standishes. Among the "first families" of Virginia and Massachusetts were the Lumpheads, the Bunnyduckes, the Foulfoots, the Whacktachers, the Klinkhearts, the Inchbalds, the Gunniesackes, the Clutterbuckes, the Narrowcarts, and the Styffchins.

Questions: Why is a crossword puzzle like an argument?

Which is more valuable, a new five dollar bill or an old one?

Chief Monguba of the Bapende tribe of Zaire wore two arrows as a symbol of his office, which stuck through his cheeks and emerged from his mouth. He had a total of fourteen different holes in his face so he could change the arrangement or number of arrows as he chose, according to the occasion.

When Charles M. Schwab worked for steel magnate Andrew Carnegie, he had what he thought was the pleasure of wiring his boss the following message: "All records broken yesterday."

Carnegie telegraphed back, "What have you done today?"

The provost of Paris in 1493 ordered all of the inhabitants of the city who were sick with smallpox to leave Paris within twenty-four hours, or else! Or else — what? Or else suffer the ancient Roman punishment for parricide. That's where they take you, a chicken, a monkey, and a poisonous snake, throw you all in a burlap bag, and then toss you in the river.

When you prevent me from doing something I want to do, that is persecution; but when I prevent you from doing anything that you want to do, that is law and order.

George Bernard Shaw

Answers: Because one word leads to another.

Any five is better than one.

NOVEMBER 11

Question: What is the state shown here?

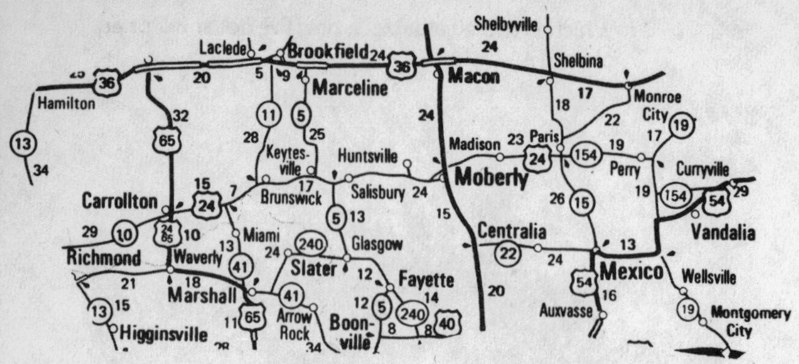

Notable Births			
1815	Elizabeth Cady Stanton	1900	Hugh Scott
1821	Feodor Dostoevsky	1904	Alger Hiss
1836	Thomas Bailey Aldrich	1904	Sam Spiegel
1872	Maude Adams	1909	Robert Ryan
1882	Gustavus VI (Sweden)	1922	Kurt Vonnegut, Jr.
1885	George Patton	1925	Jonathan Winters
1899	Pat O'Brien	1944	Jesse Colin Young

Notable Events

1606	Peace of Zsvitva-Torok
1794	Jacobin Club in Paris closed
1817	Senaa Samma gave first sword-swallowing exhibition, New York City
1918	Armistice signed, ending World War I
1921	Unknown Soldier buried, Arlington, Virginia
1930	Soviets accused Lawrence of Arabia of plotting to overthrow USSR
1933	France barred concessions to Hitler in British dealings
1942	Nazis began occupation of all France
1951	Peron reelected in Argentina

The case of the giraffe who was fed to death by overkind Japanese zoo visitors (April 29) is not unique in the annals of animal parks. A few days after a holiday some years back in which the London Zoo had been mobbed by visitors, one of the park's ostriches died. Veterinarians performing the autopsy found certain inedible substaces in the stomach of the bird which were apparently supplied by people who had heard that ostriches would eat just about anything. The sum total was two handkerchieves, three gloves, a pencil, a Kodak film spool, a piece of a comb, a bicycle tire valve, a penny, four halfpennies, two farthings, a Belgian franc, two collar studs, part of a rolled-gold necklace, an alarm clock winding key, a glove fastener, a five-inch-long piece of wood, and three feet of thick string.

Man — a creature made at the end of a week's work when God was tired.

Mark Twain

The Unknown Soldier of World War I, buried at the Arlington National Cemetery, is actually one of seventy men all of whose names are known. It is, however, not known which of the men is the one buried there.

I gave my life for freedom — This I know;
For those who bade me fight had told me so.

W.N. Ewer

On one occasion during the First World War, General Pershing was out inspecting the situation on the Western Front. The unit he was visiting had suffered a particularly bad time in a recent engagement, and had received many casualties. Pershing noticed an exhausted soldier sitting outside a tent. The man's arm was in a sling, and his head was heavily bandaged. As "Blackjack" approached, he heard the man mutter, "I love my country. I'd fight for my country. I'd starve and go thirsty for my country. But if ever this damned war is over, I'll never love another country again!"

Patriotism is your conviction that your country is superior to all other countries because you were born in it.

George Bernard Shaw

Answer: Missouri.

NOVEMBER 12

Notable Births

1615	Richard Baxter	1903	Jack Oakie
1770	Joseph Hopkinson	1928	Grace Kelly
1834	Alexander Borodin	1961	Nadia Comaneci

Notable Events

1614 Treaty of Xanten realigned German states
1727 France and Bavaria renewed secret treaty of 1714
1920 Keneshaw Mountain Landis elected commissioner of baseball
1927 Holland Tunnel formally opened
1928 First intercollegiate skeet tournament held, Princeton, New Jersey
1931 Hoover ordered $59 million cut from navy budget
1933 Nazi party received 92 percent of vote in German elections
1964 Grand Duke Pierre became leader of Luxembourg
1964 Floods killed 7,000 people in Vietnam

Just after World War I, debate on the floor of Congress centered for a time around the bodies of American soldiers who had been killed in France. The question was whether they should remain in French soil or be brought back to the States and reinterred. As it turned out, there were strong lobbying interests involved: an American undertakers' association wanted the return, and a French wine makers' organization was against it. Frenchmen apparently thought it would be a great boost to their country's nearly destroyed tourist industry if the parents of the dead men had to journey to France to visit the graves of their fallen sons.

Seeing ourselves as others see us would probably confirm our worst suspicions about them.

Franklin P. Jones

The British at various times have had their troubles when it comes to bartering geography. Remember the drunken British surveyor who let a thousand square miles of Maine slip into American hands in the 1840s? Back in 1878, the British ambassador to Turkey had been instructed by his government to make an offer to the vizier for the Mediterranean island of Crete. The English ended up with Cyprus.

What happened? Well, when the ambassador met with the Turkish leader, he forgot which island he'd been told to bid for. All he knew was that is started with a *C*, and he told the vizier as much. The Turk, aware he'd hooked a foolish fish, suggested it was Cyprus the British wanted (the Turks needed the money, and Cyprus was expendable). Saving face, the delegate agreed that was indeed the place, and its purchase was effected.

Although the male ostrich usually has a harem of three or four lady ostriches, he is a conscientious father who wiles away his nights sitting on their eggs. The average ostrich egg is about eighteen times larger by volume than a chicken egg. At one time the world trade in ostrich feathers totalled over ten million dollars a year.

Answer: Nest; muster; nest or nide; watch.

Question: What's the special name for a group of these animals?

vipers
peacocks
pheasants
nightingales

Here's one the average ophthalmologist doesn't see every day. The eyeball pain experienced for 2½ months by a South African youngster was diagnosed in 1979 as the result of a chrysanthemum growing out of the child's eye.

The national debt of the United States today amounts to close to a trillion dollars. Once upon a time the nation didn't owe any money — the entire debt was paid off. And paid off by one unfortunate man, at that.

James Swan was an immigrant from Scotland who settled in Massachusetts as a child. He became a prosperous Boston merchant while he was still a young man, and amassed a huge fortune by the time he was thirty.

After the Revolutionary War he moved to France. That country had been the United States' biggest creditor during the war, and we owed it something over two million dollars; a small figure today, but an enormous sum then.

In 1975, solely out of unselfish generosity, Swan paid the whole debt to the French, principal and interest.

Ironically, thirteen years later the French imprisoned Swan as a debtor himself. A German firm had successfully prosecuted Swan for $150,000 it said he owed them, but he refused to pay the debt and steadfastly denied he owed the Germans anything. He spent the next twenty-two years of his life in prison at Sainte Pélagie.

Swan was freed at the outbreak of the Revolution of 1830, but his was a short liberation. He died three days after his release, at the age of seventy-six.

NOVEMBER 13

Question: Which of the following movie listings is wrong?

Ingrid Bergman in *Gaslight*
Claudette Colbert in *It Happened One Night*
Bette Davis in *A Streetcar Named Desire*
Joan Fontaine in *Suspicion*

Notable Births

354	Saint Augustine	1915	Nathaniel Benchley
1833	Edwin Booth	1922	Oskar Werner
1850	Robert Louis Stevenson	1930	Fred Harris
1856	Louis Brandeis	1934	Linda Christian

Notable Events

1775	Montreal captured by Montgomery
1909	Mining disaster at Cherry, Illinois, claimed 259 lives
1918	Russia canceled Treaty of Brest-Litovsk
1938	Mother Cabrini beatified
1942	Sullivan brothers killed on USS *Juneau*
1946	First artificial snow made for skiing, Mount Greylock, Massachusetts
1960	Norman Mailer received suspended sentence for stabbing wife
1964	Mohammad Ali had hernia operation
1970	Cyclone in Bangladesh killed 300,000 people

Robert Louis Stevenson once took a friend to a restaurant in San Francisco, which had a reputation for a large menu but limited fare — a waiter would invariably take an order only to return and explain that he was sorry, but they were "just out."

To amuse his friend, Stevenson asked for a "double order of boiled behemoth."

Moments later the waiter returned. "I'm terribly sorry, sir," he began, but Stevenson cut him off. "What! Don't tell me you've just run out of behemoth!" he said in a tone of mock annoyance.

"Oh, no, sir," said the waiter. Then he lowered his voice and said confidentially, 'We have plenty, but the truth is that I would not bring it to you, as it is not quite fresh."

A big lie is more plausible than truth.

Ernest Hemingway

Around 1700, a very strange religious sect was formed in the area of Kargopol, Russia. It came to be known as the Brothers and Sisters of the Red Death. Although nominally Christian, it added a few twists to basic Christian beliefs. Marriage was prohibited, but sex was allowed — once. A couple could make love only with the understanding that each would be suffocated beneath a large red pillow immediately afterward.

Whether or not this encouraged membership is hard to determine, as believers were allowed this odd privilege of suicide only after they had recruited twelve new lambs into the fold of the sect.

By 1900, the Brothers and Sisters numbered some 862 people. One of the leaders then predicted that the Millennium would come on November 13 of that year. Subsequently, the believers decided they could earn God's good graces if they were to kill themselves before that date. Accordingly, several weeks before the end of the world was at hand, they locked themselves up in their own homes and then set fire to them. Before the authorities arrived, a hundred sect members had burned to death. When November 13, 1900, did not prove to be the day of Armageddon, the 762-member sect dissolved.

A faith that cannot survive collision with the truth is not worth many regrets.

Arthur C. Clarke

Epitaph of Mr. Strange, Esquire:

Here lies an *honest* lawyer
And that is Strange.

There was a musical movement afoot some seventy years ago called the Futurist movement. It never caught on, and that was probably just as well: these avant-garde composers specialized in the machinery noises. Cars, trolleys, factories, what have you, all were fair game.

The Futurists tried to build a following, though without much success. They knew it, too. Before one big concert in Paris in 1914 the conductor, Luigi Russolo, had all the members of his orchestra take a crash course in self-defense.

It was a wise move. Midway through the performance the audience arose *en masse* and attacked the stage. While half of the musicians continued the piece, the other half defended themselves and their fellows from the patrons of the arts.

By the time the concert was over, eleven music lovers were in the hospital with broken bones and concussions.

Answer: Vivien Leigh appeared in *A Streetcar Named Desire.*

NOVEMBER 14

Notable Births

1765	Robert Fulton	1904	Marya Mannes
1840	Claude Monet	1907	Edward Steig
1861	Frederick Jackson Turner	1908	Harrison Salisbury
1889	Jawaharlal Nehru	1912	Barbara Hutton
1896	Robert Sherwood	1914	Rosemary de Camp
1896	Mamie Eisenhower	1919	Veronica Lake
1900	Aaron Copland	1935	King Hussein

Notable Events

1732 Louis Timothee hired as nation's first librarian, Philadelphia
1832 First street car in use, New York City
1889 Nellie Bly began first solo circumnavigation by a woman
1940 Nazis bombed Coventry, England
1942 Eddie Rickenbacker rescued after 24 days on raft
1976 Plains, Georgia, Baptist Church dropped ban on blacks

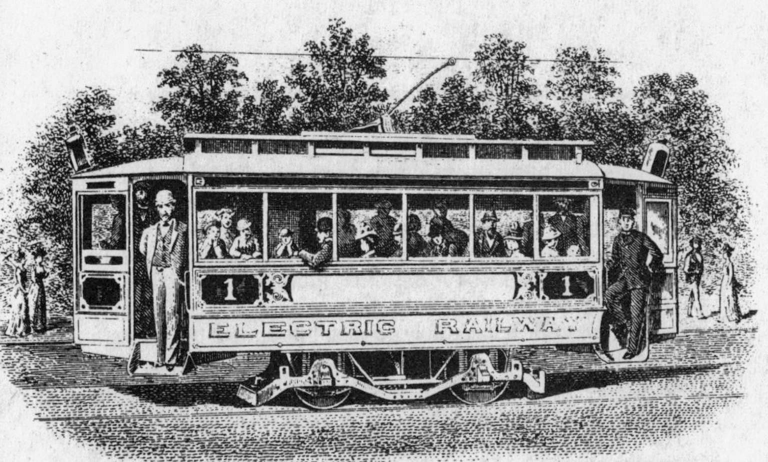

Shortly before Thanksgiving Day in 1946, a man named Patrick Rogers tried to get a ride on a Chicago streetcar. As one, two, and then three bulging cars passed him by, Rogers became increasingly incensed. When he spotted a fourth on its way down the tracks, he strode to the middle of the right of way and began to wave his arms frantically to get the driver's attention.

You guessed it.

A conclusion is the place where you got tired of thinking.
Martin Fischer

To die for an idea is to place a pretty high price upon conjecture.
Anatole France

The playwright Robert Sherwood, who once won three Pulitzer Prizes for Drama in six years, flunked Freshman English at Harvard.

Answers: One steals from the people, the other peals from the steeple. One has its claws at the end of its paws, the other its pause at the end of its clause.

Questions: What is the difference between a thief and a church bell?

What is the difference between a cat and a comma?

Epitaph from Litford Churchyard, England

Here lies in Horizontal position
The outside *case* of
George Routleigh, Watchmaker,
Whose abilities in that line were an honour
To his profession:
Integrity was the *main-spring*,
and Prudence the Regulator
of all the *actions* of his life:
Humane, generous, and liberal,
His *hand* never *stopped*
Till he had relieved distress;
So nicely *regulated* were all his *movements*
That he never *went wrong*
Except when set-a-going
By People
Who did not know
His Key
Even then, he was easily
Set right again:
He had the art of disposing of his *Time*
So well,
That his *Hours* glided away
In one continual *round*
Of Pleasure and Delight,
Till an unlucky *Moment* put a *period* to
His existence;
He departed this Life
November 14, 1802,
Aged 57,
Wound up,
In hopes of being taken in *Hand*
By his *Maker*,
And of being
Throughly *cleaned, repaired,* and *set-a-going*
In the World to come.

Several regions of northwestern Europe during the Middle Ages had an interesting punishment for criminals convicted of knife attacks. The weapon used in the assault was driven hard through the back of the offender's hand and into a block of wood. The man then had to remove his hand from the knife — without moving the knife. He could elect either to slice his hand through to the web of his fingers, or mutilate the middle of it by drawing it vertically up through the blade and over the handle of the knife.

The first settlers of what is now Portland, Oregon, came mostly from Maine and Massachusetts, and were equally divided as to whether their village should be called Portland or Boston. Portland won as the result of a coin toss.

NOVEMBER 15

Question: What is the state shown here?

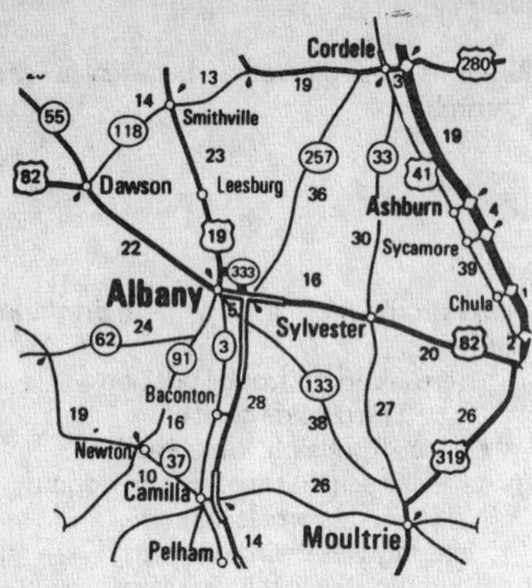

Notable Births

1620	Andrew Marvel	1887	Georgia O'Keeffe
1708	William Pitt the Elder	1891	Averill Harriman
1862	Gerhart Hauptmann	1906	Curtis LeMay
1879	Lewis Stone	1925	Howard Baker
1885	Felix Frankfurter	1929	Edward Asner
1887	Marianne Moore	1934	Petula Clark

Notable Events

1763	Mason and Dixon began their famous survey
1806	Pike's Peak discovered
1849	First American poultry show, Boston
1897	Esterhazy's role in Dreyfus frame-up revealed
1935	Unemployment compensation approved for United States
1937	First air-conditioning of House and Senate
1950	Arthur Dorrington became first black hockey player to sign pro contract

Ornithologists estimate that seventy million years ago there may have been as many as one and a half million species of birds on the earth. Today there are only about ten thousand.

A Philadelphian minister, the Reverend Isaac Bobst, was granted a divorce from his wife in November 1946. Our best guess is that this was on the grounds of cruelty: Bobst testified that his wife had coughed, made faces, and thumbed her nose at him whenever he was in the pulpit.

A man may be a fool and not know it, but not if he is married.

H.L. Mencken

Julian Huxley used to tell the story of the philosopher and the theologian who were at odds over the existence of God. The theologian said the philosopher was like the blind man in a dark room looking for a black cat that wasn't there.

"That may be true," retorted the philosopher, "but a theologian would have found it."

I go to seek a vast perhaps.

Francois Rabelais

Answer: Georgia.

And now for a few highlights in the history of the brassiere.

The bra, *per se*, was invented in 1912 by an American named Otto Titzling (which rivals Thomas Crapper's invention of the flush toilet). A chesty opera singer complained that her corsets were uncomfortable and didn't provide sufficient support for her bosom. Hearing of this, Titzling devised the first modern bra.

The garment itself gets its name from a former World War I fighter pilot turned fashion designer, Philippe de Brassiere. In about 1929, he glamorized the bra as an article of feminine lingerie, and made it incredibly popular throughout the Western world. He also became enormously wealthy in the process, while Titzling, who had never patented his design, had to settle for only a small profit from the boom.

The padded bra was supposedly developed shortly after an Olympics competition in which a Swedish athlete apparently lost a 400-meter hurdle race because she inadvertantly kneed herself in the breast going over a hurdle, which was of course extremely painful. D.J. Kennedy, an Englishman, heard of the mishap, and developed a set of cones made of a rubber tube formed into two spirals, filled with air, and encased in leather. Later innovations to the design were more (or less) sophisticated.

I never loved another person the way I loved myself.

Mae West

NOVEMBER 16

Notable Births

1873	W.C. Handy	1896	Fibber McGee
1886	Arthur Krock	1899	Mary Margaret McBride
1889	George S. Kaufman	1908	Burgess Meredith
1895	Michael Arlen	1920	Gene Littler

Notable Events

1724	John Sheppard hanged for breaking and entering, Tyburn, England
1770	Bruce discovered source of Nile
1796	Catherine the Great of Russia died—under a horse
1869	Suez Canal opened
1894	6,000 Armenian Christians murdered by Turks in Kurdistan
1901	First auto traveled 60 mph
1925	American Association for Advancement of Atheism incorporated,New York City
1934	Death of Alice Liddell Hargreaves, model for "Alice in Wonderland"
1955	First dugong exhibited in America, San Francisco

Hey, diddle diddle!
The Cat and the Fiddle!
The Cow jumped over the Moon!
The little Dog laughed to see such craft,
And the Dish ran away with the Spoon!

Believe it or not (and there is *some* room for speculation), this popular nursery rhyme is a summary of some of the goings-on at the court of Queen Elizabeth I.

The English in the sixteenth century commonly gave their monarchs animal nicknames, which were derived from their physical appearance or their particular qualities. Queen Elizabeth was called the Cat because of the way she played cat-and-mouse games with her ministers and advisors. The Fiddle appears in the rhyme because it was her favorite instrument. Until she was at least fifty years old, she was often known to dance in her chambers to the sixteenth-century equivalent of bluegrass music. The little Dog who laughs is clearly Robert Dudley, Earl of Leicester, a favorite of Elizabeth's who may even have been her lover for a time. Of him she wrote, "He is like my little lap-dog."

"The Dish" was the informal title given in that day to the courtier whose responsibility it was to carry certain golden plates into the dining room for state dinners. "The Spoon" was a similar nickname given to one of the ladies-in-waiting at the court who acted as a taster for the queen to protect her from being poisoned. Elizabeth's "Dish" was Edward, Earl of Hertford and her "Spoon" was Lady Katherine Grey, sister of Lady Jane Grey, the woman who was the unwilling queen of England for nine days in 1553.

This particular Dish and Spoon did in fact run away together and were secretly married. When Elizabeth found them out, she had them confined to the Tower of London. They were in the Tower for seven years, and two children were born to them during that time.

England is the paradise of individuality, eccentricity, heresy, anomalies, hobbies, and humors.

George Santayana

Answers: One irons the linen, the other steals it.
One whacks and loves it, the other vaccinates it.

Questions: What's the difference between an honest laundress and a dishonest one?

What's the difference between the treatment of a child by an adoring mother and a German doctor?

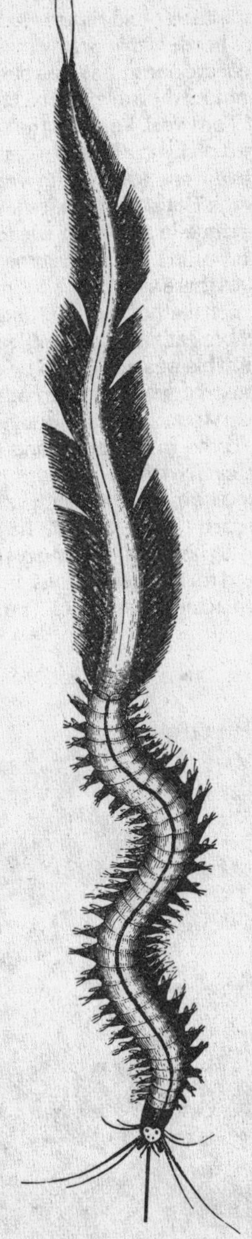

The penis of a planarium, or flatworm, is located in its mouth, almost like a tongue. In addition to its regular functions, it is equipped with spikes and a poison for catching prey, including other planaria.

The European stock dove makes its nest in a rabbit burrow. Big deal.

NOVEMBER 17

Question: How's your movie memory? In what years were these films Academy Award winners?

The Deer Hunter
Oliver!
Gigi
The Life of Emile Zola

Notable Births

1901	Lee Strasberg	1930	Bob Mathias
1905	Mischa Auer	1944	Tom Seaver
1925	Rock Hudson	1945	Elvin Hayes

Notable Events

1790	Congress began first session in Washington, D.C.
1913	First vessel passed through Panama Canal
1940	Italians driven from Greece
1959	First synthetic diamond manufactured
1961	Rockefellers announced impending divorce
1964	United States and Brazil signed extradition treaty
1968	"Heidi" football game

In about 1850, a spiritualist told Hiram Marble that he would find a pirate's treasure horde within twenty miles of Boston. The horde, he said, was near the ocean, and was buried with the pirate himself. The notion intrigued Marble, but he didn't act on it until he heard the story of Tom Veal. Veal was the skipper of a pirate ship that had anchored off Lynn, Massachusetts, in 1658. Three crewmembers who had gone ashore with Veal were later captured and hanged by the British Navy, but the captain escaped. Veal reportedly took refuge in a cave on a ledge now known as Dungeon Rock, which was in Lynn. At the time there was speculation that his booty was there with him.

Then came the Boston earthquake! Veal and whatever he had with him were buried beneath hundreds of feet of solid rock in the massive upheaval. This was attested to by one Joel Dunn, a man known for his integrity, who had been with Veal just before the quake. He had been found unconscious near the cave by a woodcutter. Dunn told the man that he had left the cave just moments before the cataclysm and he was positive that Veal could not have escaped from the collapsing cave.

The prophecy intrigued Marble. In 1852 he bought the Dungeon Rock land and with his family began an exploration for the Veal treasure that lasted for two generations. For extra guidance in this search, he contacted the spirit of Tom Veal through a medium, and for years directed his quest according to the messages he received from the ghost. The digging was laborious work — Marble had to work by hand through the hard porphyry and they seldom progressed beyond a foot a month. When Marble died in 1868, his son Edwin took over and worked the site alone for eighteen more years.

Then — in 1886 — Edwin died. In thirty-four years, the Marbles didn't find a thing.

The ultimate result of shielding men from the effects of folly is to fill the world with fools.

Herbert Spencer

My day's work has been useless as life preserver for fish.

Charlie Chan

You can be sincere and still be stupid.

Charles F. Kettering

If you had money during the time of England's King Ethelbert (860-66) you could really get away with mayhem. The following is a schedule of fines in effect for various offenses during Ethelbert's reign:

For breaking a man's front tooth	6 shillings
For breaking a canine tooth	6 shillings
For breaking a molar (this was later raised to 15 shillings on the reasoning that a molar was a double tooth)	1 shilling
For striking out an eye	50 shillings
For breaking a rib	3 shillings
For breaking a shoulder	20 shillings
For crushing a fingernail	1 shilling
For crushing a thumbnail	3 shillings
For pulling a man's nose	3 shillings
For pulling a man's nose until it bled	6 shillings

Flying fish have been reliably reported to soar distances of up to one thousand feet in a single one of their leaps.

Answer: 1978, 1968, 1958, 1937.

NOVEMBER 18

Question: What does everyone have that he can always count on?

Notable Births

1789	Louis Daguerre	1899	Eugene Ormandy
1831	James Garfield	1901	George Gallup
1836	W.S. Gilbert	1906	Klaus Mann
1861	Edward MacDowell	1909	Johnny Mercer
1874	Clarence Day	1923	Alan Shepard

Notable Events

1805	First women's club organized, Female Charitable Society, Wiscasset, Maine
1820	Palmer reached Antarctica
1877	Russians stormed Kars in Turkish war
1936	Germany and Italy recognized Fascist government in Spain
1940	Lewis quit as CIO head
1941	British began offensive in Libya
1948	Vice-president Albin Barkley married
1952	Government began antitrust proceedings against DuPont Chemical
1964	Hoover called Martin Luther King the "most notorious liar in the country"
1974	Second heart transplant performed on the same patient by Christian Barnard

On November 18, 1307 (or so the story goes), William Tell shot the apple off his son's head. This tale is often associated with Switzerland, but it is not Swiss by origin. A Norwegian version of it dates from the eleventh century, and similar Danish, Icelandic, and Persian stories can all be traced to the twelfth century.

People who believe that the earth is hollow are sometimes among the most brilliant minds of their times. The colonial philosopher and theologian, Cotton Mather, believed there was a universe inside the earth, and the German mathematician, Euler, felt sure there was a small planet within our own, which sheltered an advanced civilization. The astronomer Edmund Halley went further. He believed that beneath the earth's crust (which, he estimated, was 500 miles thick) were three planets spinning in orbit, the size of Mercury, Venus, and Mars.

The most popular theory, and the one that came closest to inspiring an expedition funded on its behalf, was that of John Cleve Symmes. A native of Ohio and a veteran of the War of 1812, Symmes proposed that not only was the earth hollow, but it was also open at both ends. He posited a four-thousand-mile hole at the North Pole, and a six-thousand-mile hole at the South, through which, he said, the interior of the earth could be reached. He believed that once the expedition reached the inside, explorers would find five identical concentric spheres with civilized life on them. He noted the migrations of birds, the existence of warm air and water currents in the polar regions, and the bright twilight of the arctic regions as evidence of the passageways at the two poles. The latter phenomenon he attributed to the sun shining through the hole on the opposite end of the earth at night, its light reflecting off the walls of the hollow planet. When Symmes was asked whether gravity would not simply pull a person from the edge of the hole to the surface of the next sphere, he denied there was any such thing as gravity at all. Scientists had it all wrong. What kept us on the surface of the earth was not a gravitational force, but an "aerial, elastic fluid," which pushed us down and kept us from being thrown off into space. This elastic fluid would also be found within the earth, and would press the explorers to the inside of the shell.

It became Symmes's passion to lead the first expedition. Through his congressional representatives, he petitioned the government in 1822 to outfit a voyage of exploration, but this request was turned down. He tried again the next year with the same result. Then he heard of a Russian exploration that was being organized to explore Antarctica (the Russians had discovered land there in 1822, and Palmer had found the ice cap in 1820), and wrote to see if he could join it. He was invited to come along, but he was too poor to afford the passage to Saint Petersburg, its port of embarkation.

Finally, after six years of hounding Congress, Symmes got a measure through funding a polar expedition. Although it was not specifically designed to investigate his ideas, Symmes was to be a part of it. He was sure this theories would be proven correct. Everything looked hopeful until Andrew Jackson succeeded John Quincy Adams as president. Jackson thought the idea was hogwash and canceled the whole appropriation. (Incidentally, Jackson was unconvinced the world was round, let alone hollow, so that may have had something to do with it.)

Symmes was wrong, but he did pass on his ideas to at least two of the finest writers of the nineteenth century. Edgar Allen Poe's "MS. Found in a Bottle" and "The Narrative of A. Gordon Pym" were both inspired by Symmes's ideas, as was Jules Verne's *A Journey to the Center of the Earth.*

A footnote: Symmes's son, Americus Vespucius Symmes, collected and annotated his father's writings in 1878. He felt sure that, when the inner spheres were explored, they would be found to be populated by the descendents of the Ten Lost Tribes of Israel.

A man who is a genius and doesn't know it probably isn't.
Robert E. Lee

The juice of all grapes is nearly colorless, so the color of wine is determined by the manner in which the juice is fermented. If the juice is fermented with the skins, seeds, and stalks of dark grapes, it will receive a red or maroon color from them.

Answer: His fingers.

NOVEMBER 19

Question: What is the state shown here?

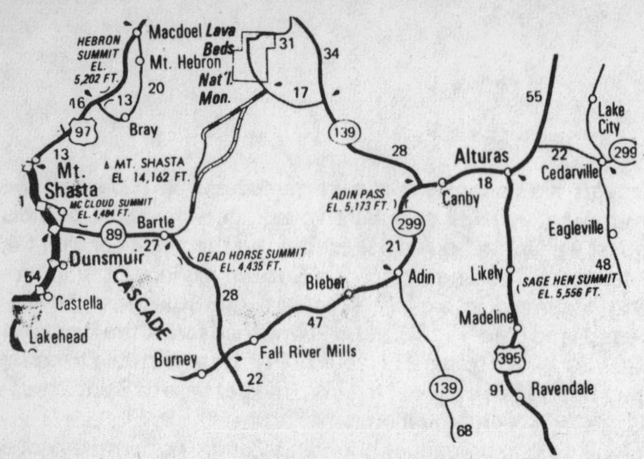

Lincoln's Gettysburg Address, delivered on this day in 1863, did not open to rave reviews. That Lincoln was even invited to speak at Gettysburg was "an afterthought," according to one member of the Board of Commissioners who arranged the ceremony.

Two months before the battlefield was consecrated, Edward Everett, the former secretary of State, a senator and the president of Harvard College, had been invited to deliver the keynote address. It finally occurred to someone in charge that — at least as a courtesy — the president should be asked to say a few words on the occasion. Lincoln was contacted unofficially in October and agreed, perhaps reluctantly, to attend. The only formal correspondence he received concerning his presence came on November 2 — a printed announcement of the ceremony that listed Everett as the principal speaker.

The story that Lincoln scribbled the speech on an envelope while he was riding on the train to Gettysburg is patently false. He began working on the speech on November 8, and there are two draft copies extant in Lincoln's handwriting. He may have made a quick revision here and there, but he definitely did not write the whole speech on the train.

Despite the praise the speech was soon accorded, the audience's reaction at Gettysburg seems to have been relatively cool. Although some Associated Press papers carried a transcript of the speech and indicated where it had been interrupted by applause, Lincoln had given the press agency a copy of the address beforehand. The speculation now is that the AP either prepared the speech for publication early and inserted applause where they expected it to occur, or the pauses were manufactured by the media out of respect for the president's office. John Russell Young, a reporter who covered the event for AP, recalled that he didn't notice any applause at all as he took the words of the speech down in shorthand as Lincoln delivered them.

Other newspapers were less kind: The *Chicago Times* said, "The cheek of every American must tingle with shame as he reads the silly, flat, and dish-watery utterances of a man who has to be pointed out to intelligent foreigners as President of the United States." The Harrisburg *Patriot and Union* commented: "We pass over the silly remarks of the President; for the credit of the nation we are willing that the veil of oblivion shall be dropped over them and that they shall no more be repeated or thought of."

In the Liberian presidential election in 1928, incumbent Charles King beat his challenger Thomas Faulkner by 600,000 votes. The margin of victory was 585,000 more than the number of registered voters in the whole country at the time.

Notable Births

1752	George Rogers Clark	1917	Indira Gandhi
1893	Clifton Webb	1919	Alan Young
1899	Allen Tate	1921	Roy Campanella
1905	Tommy Dorsey	1936	Dick Cavett

Notable Events

1755 Earthquake in Morocco killed 25,000 people
1788 English public told of George III's "mental indisposition"
1863 Lincoln delivered Gettysburg Address
1924 Sir Lee Stack murdered in Cairo
1930 First telephone installed in Vatican
1954 First automatic toll collectors installed, Garden State Parkway, New Jersey (where else?)
1961 Michael Rockefeller reported missing in New Guinea

A 5 by 5 magic square can be made that adds up to 65. Can you make it? Incidentally, the world's largest magic square was put together in 1975 by a thirteen year old. It totalled 578,865!

23	12	1	20	9
4	18	7	21	15
10	24	13	2	16
11	5	19	8	22
17	6	25	14	3

In an average teaspoonful of soil there are two billion bacteria, and many millions of fungi, protozoa, and algae.

Billy Sunday is best known as the major league ballplayer who became an evangelist. But did you know he holds the record for the most consecutive strikeouts by a batter? Yep. The first fourteen times he came up in the majors, he whiffed.

Answer: California.

Notable Births

1752	Thomas Chatterton	1916	Judy Canova
1858	Selma Lagerlöf	1920	Gene Tierney
1884	Norman Thomas	1925	Robert Kennedy
1891	Reginald Denny	1926	Kaye Ballard
1908	Alistair Cooke	1927	Estelle Parsons
1914	Emilio Pucci	1939	Dick Smothers

Notable Events

1780 England declared war on Holland
1914 Passport photos first required
1917 Hindenberg Line broken
1940 Hungary joined the Axis
1945 Nuremburg War Crimes Trial began
1947 Princess Elizabeth married Prince Philip of Greece
1975 Death of Franco

Questions: What has teeth but no face?

Who goes to sleep with his shoes on?

It sounds incredible, but the tulips for which Holland is so famous once ruined that country's economy and created a depression far worse than the one the United States suffered during the 1930s.

Tulips (the name comes from the Turkish word for turban) were first imported from Turkey into Austria and Germany in about 1559. The flowers soon spread to Holland, and reached England by 1600. Europeans quickly developed a mania for them. By 1634, a wealthy individual was considered (if you'll pardon the expression) uncultivated if he didn't have a large and varied collection of tulips. Many of the rich devoted themselves entirely to their gardens, caring for the fragile plants and trying to effect novel crossbreeding among different tulip species.

Because of the craze, speculation in tulip bulbs was rampant. A single root of the *Semper Augustus* variety once sold for 4,600 florins (about 430 pounds sterling), a new carriage, and a team of horses complete with harness. The record price was for a Viceroy bulb. It brought the exchange of eight thousand tons of wheat, sixteen thousand pounds of rye, four oxen, eight sheep, two hogsheads (126 gallons) of wine, over one thousand gallons of beer, 500 gallons of butter, one thousand pounds of cheese, a bed, a suit of clothes, and a costly silver drinking cup.

As the market price and the demand for tulips continued to climb, tens of thousands of Dutch citizens sold their property and possessions for far less than they were worth, just to get into the tulip commodities market. Soon, there were far too many bulb vendors for the bulb buyers to support, and increased supplies from the Middle East created cutthroat competition among them. A few people managed to escape with a change of clothes, but the great majority who had expected to become rich overnight on the sale of a single bulb were completely ruined. Bulbs that had brought the equivalent of 100 English pounds were in a year's time selling for a pound or two.

The Netherlands entered on a generation-long period of economic and social anomie, the Great Tulip Depression. It wasn't until 1700 that the country was back to normal, and all because of a mania for a single flower and the get-rich-quick promise it seemed to offer.

The course of true anything never does run smooth.

Samuel Butler

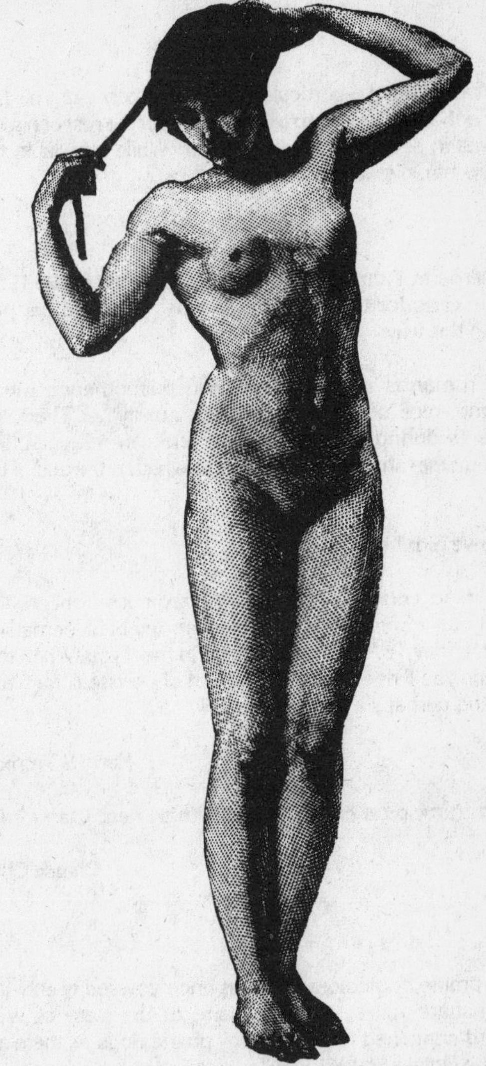

Reacting to the gaudy jewelery and dress of the period, lawgivers in France in the sixteenth century declared that a woman's whole wardrobe, including her shoes and ornaments, could weigh no more than eight ounces.

The word "quintessence" is usually used as a superlative, but its literal meaning is only "fifth essence." This comes from the beliefs of the Pythagoreans 2,500 years ago. To the four known essences of matter, earth, air, fire, and water, these ancients added a fifth, the quintessence, an element so pure and subtle that at the time of creation it flew from the earth and created the stars.

Elizabeth Scott lies buried here.
She was born Nov 20th 1785,
according to the best of her recollection.

Answers: A comb
A horse.

NOVEMBER 21

Question: Can you define these ancient words?

fonkin
scribbet
pash
trantles
ug

Notable Births

1495	John Bale	1920	Ralph Meeker
1694	Voltaire	1921	Vivian Blaine
1893	Harpo Marx	1938	Marlo Thomas
1912	Eleanor Russell	1945	Goldie Hawn

Notable Events

1620	Puritans put ashore at Plymouth
1783	First manned flight in free balloon
1877	Edison announced invention of phonograph
1946	Truman first president to travel on German submarine
1947	Omar Bradley named to succeed Ike as chief of staff of the Armed Forces

Harpo Marx was not a particularly religious man. After his Bar Mitzvah he only once went into a synagogue for the rest of his life, and that was in search of his bootlegger. While he was in the temple, Marx had his wallet lifted.

When Margaret Truman made her singing debut in late 1950, Paul Hume, critic for the *Washington Post*, reviewed her performance in this way:

> Miss Truman is a unique American phenomenon with a pleasant voice of little size and fair quality.... There are moments during her recital when one can relax and feel confident that she will make her goal, which is the end of the song.

Poppa gave him hell:

> I have read your lousy review of Margaret's concert. I've come to the conclusion that you are an "eight ulcer man on four ulcer pay." ... Some day I hope to meet you. When that happens you'll need a new nose, a lot of beefsteak for black eyes, and perhaps a supporter below.

Harry S Truman

Each man think own cuckoos better than next man nightingales.

Charlie Chan

A single prairie dog colony in Texas once covered twenty-five thousand square miles, about the size of the state of West Virginia, and contained twice as many prairie dogs as there are people in the United States today.

Except for some nefarious dealings, the Plymouth Puritans would have landed in New Jersey, and there would have been a dozen more of them. It is well known that the *Mayflower's* tiny sister ship the *Speedwell* had to put back to port twice because she was leaking so badly, and never did make it to the New World. Eighteen of her passengers squeezed on board the *Mayflower*, but twelve stayed behind.

What is less widely known is that the *Speedwell* was, initially, a very seaworthy vessel. However, her crew was required by their contracts to stay with the colonists once they reached America. After spending only one month with the zealous Puritans, the sailors wanted out. They sabotaged the ship by prying cracks in the boards of an otherwise watertight hull.

What kept them from landing in what is now New Jersey involved chicanery among some so-called respectable men. Sir Fernando Gorges and his associates didn't want these extremists anywhere near their Virginia colony (of which New Jersey was a part), and so they bribed the *Mayflower's* captain, a former pirate named Thomas Jones, to land them far north of the region. He and his crew did so, were amply rewarded, and then returned to their piratical pursuits.

Had the Puritans established their Calvinistic traditions in New Jersey instead of in Massachusetts, the famous catch phrase might very well have become, "Banned in Bayonne."

Several years ago, a man named D.L. Rosenhan and eight other people were incarcerated in mental institutions in the western United States. They all told their doctors prior to admittance that they heard voices; sounds like "thud"; words like "empty."

Miraculously, as soon as they had entered an institution, the voices stopped. Great! They were cured! Now they could go home, sane and sound!

Or could they? No, many couldn't. Certainly not right away. Even though all of them had entered the hospitals voluntarily, and had been tested and declared sane by other physicians before they were admitted, it took between seven and fifty-two days for all these people to be released. Although the whole thing had been an investigation of mental health care in the subject hospitals (both public and private), and though each of Professor Rosenhan's patients had been carefully screened, and though all of their symptoms had been fake, not one of the "patients" was released from the respective hospitals as "sane." The final diagnosis of the majority of them was "schizophrenia in remission."

In a follow-up experiment a short time later, one mental health facility was told to expect this same kind of undercover placement of one or two sane persons sometime during the next three months. At the end of the quarter, 193 patients had been admitted to the facility, and 41 of them were suspected by some member of the staff as being the "plant."

Not a single one was.

You won't ever find a pigeon which isn't sick closing its eyes, or napping.

Answer: Small fool; drawing charcoal; the forehead; trifling items, bric-a-brac; fear.

NOVEMBER 22

Notable Births

1819	George Gissing	1899	Hoagy Carmichael
1857	George Eliot	1913	Benjamin Britten
1869	André Gide	1924	Geraldine Page
1874	Elizabeth Patterson	1932	Robert Vaughn
1890	Charles de Gaulle	1943	Billie Jean King

Notable Events

1493 Columbus arrived at Hispaniola on second voyage
1842 First recorded eruption of volcano in United States, Mount Lassen, California
1916 Death of Jack London
1933 Chautemps ministry in France began
1943 Cairo Conference opened
1961 W.E.B. DuBois membership in CPUSA revealed
1963 John F. Kennedy assassinated

A No. 1

Along the nation's railroad lines, scribbled on the walls of stations and stores, carved into fenceposts and trees, there were once thousands of these "calling cards." Now they are rare finds. Predating Kilroy's famous mark by a half a century, they were left by one of America's most famous and most puzzling hobos, "A No. 1."

Born in San Francisco sometime in the late 1860s, this unknown man ran away from home in 1883 and took refuge on the rails. By 1912, he'd been around the world three separate times, taught himself three languages, and written three books about the hobo's life. He even carried endorsements of his position as the country's most notable hobo from Presidents Roosevelt and Taft, and from Thomas Edison. He proudly recorded that for a total of $7.61 in train fares in thirty years he'd logged 505,000 miles.

Yet strangely enough, A No. 1 was, if anything, antihobo. He had none of the conventional hobo vices, and when he rolled into town he'd make a point of shaving and changing his traveling overalls for an impeccable suit. Once he settled into a town for a few days, he'd renew old acquaintances and perhaps give a talk about his vagabond life to some local organization, earning some pocket money this way.

But his chief objective, whether on the rails or off, was to deter youngsters from following the life he'd led. He'd point out that of the runaways who hit the rails every year, 7,000 ended up crippled and 3,500 ended up dead. There was no romance, no rest, no home on the road for anyone. He only hoboed because there was something bigger than himself that made him do it, and Lord, how he wished he could stop. If he found a kid on a train he'd talk to him and try to make him give his family another shot. If his counselling was effective, and it usually was, he'd buy the boy a train ticket home — financed, ironically, by the royalties from his hobo books. One of the youthful fugitives he returned to the straight life, if only for a time, was a fellow named Jack London.

Though A No. 1 lived a transient existence by a combination of design and psychological necessity, he wasn't above planning for his future. Long before his vagabond days were over, he entered a *Police Gazette* magazine competition to find the country's fastest transcontinental tramp. Naturally enough, he won, and he spent the major portion of the one-thousand-dollar prize on a little plot of land in Cambridge Springs, Pennsylvania. He's there now, beneath a stone he had carved decades before his death:

A No. 1
The Rambler
At Rest at Last

Answer: Texas.

Question: What is the state shown here?

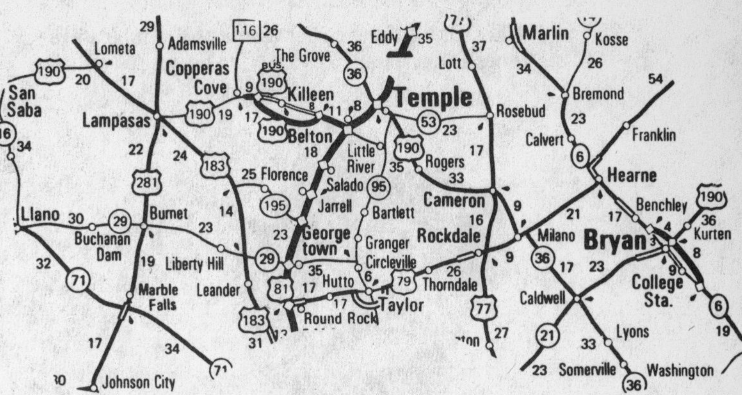

Man who sits by side of road sees world pass by.
Charlie Chan

A fellow named Andrew Freedman once owned the New York Giants baseball club. His exploits as an owner would make some of the more notorious modern-day team czars look like saints. He barred umpires whose calls he didn't like, and once he even attacked a fellow owner so viciously that the man ended up in the hospital.

When Freedman died in 1924 he left his fortune of over five million dollars to be used to establish a home for aging millionaires who had lost all their money. He did this so they could live out their lives in the fashion to which they had become accustomed.

Did you know that, until middle age, George Washington was an inveterate gambler and horse racing aficionado? It's true. He lost a number of small fortunes betting the ponies; monies which he recouped through his amazing success as a horse breeder and trader. He once traded a mediocre horse for 5,000 acres of prime land.

When he gave up gambling and breeding horses, Washington started breeding mules.

NOVEMBER 23

Questions: What's the difference between a photographer and the measles?

What's the difference between a hollow tube and a foolish Dutchman?

Notable Births

1744	Abigail Adams	1887	Boris Karloff
1804	Franklin Pierce	1903	Victor Jory
1859	Billy the Kid	1940	Luis Tiant

Notable Events

1835	Horseshoe-manufacturing machine patented
1890	Luxembourg separated from the Netherlands
1938	German Jews fined 20 percent of all property
1942	Coast Guard Women's Reserve authorized
1948	Zoom lens patented
1978	Earthquakes throughout South America claimed hundreds of lives

William H. Bonney, aka Billy the Kid, has had major cosmetic surgery performed on his image by the entertainment media since his death a century ago. No Robert Redford he: he was once described as "a non-descript, weasel-eyed, narrow-chested, stoop-shouldered, repulsive-looking creature, with all the outward appearances of a cretin." Nor was he an honorable villain in any way. His first murder happened when he was twelve years old, in Silver City, New Mexico. He shot down a defenseless man who, he said, had insulted his mother. In the next nine years he killed twenty more times "not including Mexicans and Indians," according to one source. Also, in every instance recorded, Billy the Kid never killed a man in a fair fight. Unless he had the drop on his opponent, he'd back down.

When he was twenty, he and Pat Garrett were hired by a cattle rancher to protect his herd from rustlers. Soon, Billy and the rancher had a falling out, and the Kid began to rustle the cattle himself. Now Billy's enemy, Garrett was sent out to look for him. As he expected he would, Garrett found him in the arms of a young Mexican woman. Even if Garrett had intended to bring him in alive, Billy didn't give him the chance. When William Bonney died in bed, a .41 Colt and a butcher knife were clutched in his hands.

The most intolerable people are provincial celebrities.

Anton Chekhov

To have a good enemy, choose a friend: he knows where to strike.

Diane de Poitiers

On this date in 1942 began the extraordinary odyssey of Poon Lim, ship's cook. His vessel, the English S.S. *Lomond*, was torpedoed in the South Atlantic. Poon was hurled from the ship, and eventually managed to climb aboard a life raft which floated near him. He spent the next four months and ten days drifting in the open ocean, exposed to the elements, catching fish and sea birds for food. When he was picked up on April 4, 1943, he'd survived adrift at sea for a longer time than any other sailor ever known.

Back in 1949, an East Camden, New Jersey, man named Howard Unruh, aged twenty-seven, one day walked out of his home and for no clear reason shot and killed a druggist, a cobbler, a barber, a six-year-old boy in the barber's chair, a two-year-old child who was watching at the shop window, and eight of his neighbors — a total of thirteen people. When the police apprehended him and asked him his motive for perpetrating such a bloodbath, Uhrug stated, "They were making derogatory remarks about my character." In retrospect, it seems with good reason.

Today, Unruh remains incarcerated in a state mental institution. He is reportedly a withdrawn man who spends most of his time reading.

'Tis healthy to be sick sometimes.

Henry David Thoreau

First Ladies of the United States in the nineteenth century didn't command the attention of the public eye as they do today, and as far as Mrs. Franklin Pierce was concerned, it was probably just as well. Jane Appleton Pierce was a religious fanatic who delivered three sons, all of whom died before reaching maturity. This caused Jane Pierce's already shaky psyche and shaky marriage to fall apart irretrievably. While she lived in the White House, Mrs. Pierce sequestered herself from the other inhabitants and their hangers-on, invariably wore black, and spent a good part of each day writing letters to her dead children.

Now, can you imagine what the *National Enquirer* would do with that?

A man named William Kiele was arrested in Burbank, California, in 1948, on suspicion of assault with a deadly weapon. He had a slingshot and a large supply of staples when he was taken into custody at a burlesque house.

Answers: One makes facsimiles, the other sick families.

One is a hollow cylinder, the other a silly Hollander.

NOVEMBER 24

Notable Births

1632	Benedict Spinoza	1888	Dale Carnegie
1713	Laurence Sterne	1912	Garson Kanin
1784	Zachary Taylor	1921	John Lindsay
1826	Collodi	1925	William F. Buckley, Jr.
1868	Scott Joplin	1938	Oscar Robertson

Notable Events

1793 Revolutionary calendar adopted in France
1848 Pope Pius IX fled to Gaeta after insurrection in Rome
1871 National Rifle Association incorporated
1874 Barbed wire patented by J.F. Glidden, DeKalb, Illinois
1950 United States launched general offensive in Korea
1963 Lee Harvey Oswald killed by Jack Ruby
1976 Earthquake in Turkey left 250,000 people homeless

Question: What's the special name for a group of these animals?
greyhounds
elk
kangaroos
crows

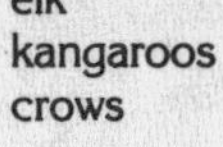

The only public office that Zachary Taylor ever held was president of the United States, a job he never wanted. Taylor himself never voted in a presidential election.

The letter informing Zachary Taylor of his presidential nomination by the Whigs arrived with postage due. He refused to pay, and therefore did not learn about his selection for several days. While he was in office, Old Rough and Ready pastured his horse on the White House lawn. Also, Taylor was the father-in-law of Jefferson Davis, the president of the Confederacy, and he himself served as a Confederate legislator after leaving office.

According to the United States Environmental Protection Agency, enough natural gas is released by the burps of ten cows in the course of a year to provide for the total heating needs of a small family in a modest-sized house. One drawback to cow belches, however, is that they also release some fifty million tons of hydrocarbons into the atmosphere annually.

Everything is worth precisely as much as a belch, the difference being that the belch is more satisfying.

Ingmar Bergman

Talk will not cook rice.

Charlie Chan

Almost 80 percent of the members of the Screen Actors Guild earn less than $2,000 a year acting.

Calendar (or calender) is a more mixed-up word than most people think. Meaning a "chart of the days of the year," it comes from the Latin *calendarium*, which was an account book kept by money lenders to keep track of debts due to them on the *calends*, or the first of each month. This word in turn came from *calare*, "to call," which was what the usurers did to proclaim the due date.

A calender, whose business it is to smooth out fabrics with rollers, should actually have his name spelled calend*rer*, although the term itself is a corruption of cylinder, which is what's used in the calendring process.

A capital C Calendar has no connection with the other two either in meaning or in origin. It comes from the Hindi word *galendar*, and denotes a member of a certain sect of Moslem dervishes.

Look in a dictionary and you'll find the word "canard" defined as a "false story," a "rumor," and a "hoax." These are odd meanings for the French word for a duck. Here's how it came about:

A French journalist about two centuries ago decided to ridicule the growing fashion for extravagant stories he had recently heard, and created the "hungry duck hoax." As he told it, an experiment had recently been completed, which proved beyond doubt the extraordinary voraciousness of ducks.

Twenty ducks had been placed in a pen. One was removed, killed, chopped up in little pieces, and then fed to the other nineteen. In short order these hungry ducks gobbled up their erstwhile companion. Then a second duck was taken, killed, and served to the remaining birds. The ducks ate him as well. This went on until there was only one duck left, who had in effect eaten nineteen ducks in an afternoon. Voracious!

As with any successful hoax, many of the people who heard the *canard* story believed it. It soon spread throughout Europe and to America. In time, any fabrication or hoax of this type came to be called a "canard" in English and several other languages.

Answer: Leash; gang; mob; murder.

NOVEMBER 25

Questions: What's the difference between a cashier and a teacher?

What's the difference between a fish dinner and a race track?

Horatio Alger, Jr., author of the famous series of books in which an all-American boy achieves respect and wealth through hard work and honest dealing, was once a Unitarian minister. In 1866, his Brewster, Massachusetts, congregation sent him packing because of his predeliction for pederasty. Alger was unable to deny charges brought against him by two boys, and he was soon off to New York City to create role models for millions of youngsters.

There's always a temptation to diddle around in the contemplative life, making itsy-bitsy statues.

Thomas Merton

It may be hard to believe, but between 1927 and 1930 there were forty thousand miniature golf courses constructed in the United States. Writing in some of America's more scholarly journals, various intellectuals called it a fad, others said it was a step backward to the croquet of Victorian England, and still others labeled it a waste of time, energy, and money which could be better put to use getting the nation out of the Great Depression.

It was a fad.

It all started on Lookout Mountain, Tennessee, in 1927. A man named Garnet Carter had a hotel on the summit of the mountain, and he had the idea that a toy golf course might be good entertainment for his more sedentary guests. He put up an unpretentious layout for about a thousand dollars, which proved to be an enormous success. Aware of its possibilities, Carter proceeded to register the trademark "Tom Thumb" for his courses, and sell the rights to its use for fifty dollars a year. For two years he sat back and counted as the money rolled in, before selling out to a Pennsylvanian pipe manufacturer for a tidy sum just before the Stock Market crash in 1929.

Still, there are few things as good for the first few years of a depression as an inexpensive diversion, and for a time miniature golf course operators did fairly well. An estimated four million people played daily in 1930, and waiting lines to get on popular courses were often hours long. Al Capone and Queen Elizabeth of Belgium were both avid players.

Miniature golf courses did more than keep people who were out of work off the streets, however. Their 150 million dollars' worth of business with steel, concrete, and pipe manufacturers in 1929 and 1930 was a substantial boon to those hard hit industries, and they directly employed about two hundred thousand people who might not otherwise have had jobs at all. Professional golfers benefited, too. Gene Sarazen, Tommy Armour, and a number of other well-known pros earned some prize money in the first annual miniature golf national championship, which was held at the Lookout Mountain course in 1930. Its total purse of $7,500 compared very favorably with a number of PGA tournament banks at the time. Even the underworld managed to get into the act. There were so many courses in the New York area that two extortion rings sprang up, which preyed exclusively on the little links. Disputes over the two groups' respective territories led to a small gang war in which at least one person was murdered.

But as the Depression deepened and continued, miniature golf courses went the way of tens of thousands of other small enterprises. By 1935, the majority of them had gone out of business. There was a brief revival of interest in them in the late 1940s, and a smaller boom towards the end of the 1950s, but nothing like the glory of the first years. Since the fifties, miniature golf as a recreation has steadily fallen off as "big golf" has become both accessible to and popular with most Americans.

Notable Births

1562	Lopé de Vega	1893	Robert Ripley
1835	Andrew Carnegie	1893	Joseph Wood Krutch
1846	Carrie Nation	1914	Joe DiMaggio
1881	Pope John XXIII	1920	Ricardo Montalban

Notable Events

1034	Malcolm II murdered; succeeded by Duncan
1783	British troops evacuated New York City
1863	Battle of Lookout Mountain began
1884	Evaporated milk patented
1944	Cordell Hull resigned as secretary of State
1952	George Meany elected president of AF of L
1964	Martial law declared in South Vietnam

There is nothing more dreadful than imagination without taste.

Goethe

The term "yokel" for a country bumpkin comes from the Anglo-Saxon *geacol*, meaning "cuckoolike."

Answers: One minds the till, the other tills the mind.

At one there are sauces for your table, and at the other horses for your stable.

NOVEMBER 26

Notable Births

1607	John Harvard	1912	Eugene Ionesco
1731	William Cowper	1919	Frederick Pohl
1901	Melville Bell Grosvenor	1922	Charles Schulz
1909	Lefty Gomez	1933	Robert Goulet
1912	Eric Severeid	1938	Rich Little

Notable Events

1716 First lion exhibited in America, Boston
1741 French, Saxons, and Bavarians captured Prague
1764 Suppression of Jesuits in France began
1832 First streetcar in United States began operation, New York City
1892 France annexed Savoy and Nice
1950 China entered Korean War
1965 First French satellite launched

Question: What is the state shown here?

Al McGoogle was a Yale man at the turn of the century, a real Frank Merriwell type. He broke a number of track records while he was in school and, although no genius, he did manage to earn a degree in English Literature in just four years. What he lacked in intelligence, he made up for in sheer determination.

After he graduated he decided to seek his fortune out West. He landed in Happy Valley, Arizona, which was then still a territory, where he was hired by a fellow named Reed, a sheepman. Reed needed a shepherd, and figured a man with a Yale degree would be equal to the task.

On his first day, Reed took McGoogle out to what was to be his herd, a flock of two thousand head of sheep. He told him to move the sheep slowly towards a landmark several miles away, letting them feed as they meandered, and then to bring them home before dark. Lots of coyotes, he said. As Al headed off with his charges, Reed hollered to him to make sure none of the lambs got away. He meant it as a joke, as he knew there were no lambs in the herd, and that none of the ewes was due for several weeks.

Come nightfall there was no sign of McGoogle or the herd, and Reed began to worry. He decided to give them an hour, during which he grew increasingly more anxious. He was just getting ready to go out and look for them when he heard a string of educated curses and the din of thousands of trampling hooves coming his way through the brush. He watched in the moonlight as McGoogle moved them into a large corral below the chuck tent. To Reed he appeared to be doing a pretty good job, though even at a distance it was obvious that the young man was exhausted.

Finally, McGoogle made his way to Reed and stood before him, haggard, dusty, and drenched in sweat.

"Boss, I quit!" the plucky jock exclaimed. "I used to be a pretty fair track man, or at least I thought so, but any man you've got as a sheepherder could beat me any day. I tell you, I didn't lose one today, but those lambs gave me the darnedest time! Just as soon as I'd run one back into the herd, another would spring out, sometimes two and three of them at once. They're all down there in the corral; you can count them to make sure, then just give me my pay and I'll be off."

Reed hadn't the vaguest idea what McGoogle was talking about. He'd been sure there weren't any lambs in the herd. He moved down to the corral to check things out.

There, huddled in a corner and scared to death, were forty jackrabbits!

The brain is as strong as its weakest think.

Eleanor Doan

John D. Rockefeller used to give the groundskeepers at his estate a five-dollar bonus at Christmas, and then dock them for not working on Christmas Day.

The rights and interests of the laboring man will be protected and cared for, not by the labor agitators but by the Christian men to whom God in His infinite wisdom has given the control of the property interest in this country.

George Baer

These capitalists generally act harmoniously, and in concert, to fleece the people.

Abraham Lincoln

Cincinnati policeman Louis A. Schmidt was fired from his job in December 1952, because he admitted that while he was on duty he'd "downed two drinks — both fifths."

Answer: Oklahoma.

NOVEMBER 27

Question: Which of the following movie listings is wrong?
Gary Cooper in *High Noon*
Spencer Tracy in *Captains Courageous*
Bing Crosby in *The Philadelphia Story*
José Ferrer in *Cyrano de Bergerac*

Notable Births
1874 Charles Beard
1912 David Merrick

Notable Events
1790 Oath of Civil Allegiance refused by French clergy
1873 Hoosac Tunnel completed
1879 Amnesty offered to French Communists after 2,000 of them were massacred
1941 Last Italian troops surrendered in Ethiopia
1942 French navy scuttled at Toulon

Other aspects of everyday life went on in England during the middle of the Second World War, including scientific research not entirely related to the war effort.

One group of naturalists reported in November 1943 that it had analyzed an acre of pasture soil and estimated it contained 666,300,000 mites; 248,375,000 springtails; 71,850,000 root aphids and other sucking bugs; 26,775,000 bristle-tails; 22,475,000 centi- and millipedes; 17,825,000 beetles; and 15,200,000 various arthropods.

We do not know one millionth of one percent about anything.

Thomas Edison

Ethiopian peasants, it is said, never understood multiplication. They could, however, halve and double numbers with counting-pebbles (dividing a number of pebbles into two equal parts to find half of a number, duplicating a pile of pebbles to double the number). From this primitive beginning, they developed an ingenious "multiplication system" that baffles most western observers.

Suppose a merchant wanted to buy 15 goats at, say, $13 apiece. We would calculate the cost by simple multiplication ($195), but to see how the Ethiopian would find it, set the numbers 13 and 15 in two columns, labeled Half and Double. Either number can go in either column, but for the sake of this illustration set them up like this:

HALF	DOUBLE
13	15

Now halve the 13 to get 6½. Ignore the ½; Ethiopians don't understand fractions. Then double the 15.

Continue doubling and halving pairs of numbers, discarding all fractions, until the Half column reaches 1:

HALF	DOUBLE
13	15
6~~½~~	30
3	60
1~~½~~	120

At this point Ethiopians invoked an ancient superstition. They considered that any pair of numbers with an even number in the Half column was evil and had to be destroyed. In this example, scratch out the 6 and 30.

Finally, add the remaining numbers in the Double column and there's your answer:

HALF	DOUBLE
13	15
6	30
3	60
1	120
	195

It works!

Try the system with any pair of numbers, large or small. It will always work.

Scot Morris, *The Book of Strange Facts and Useless Information,* (New York: Doubleday, 1979)

It seems many of Oliver Cromwell's beliefs in good old restrained, down-home Puritanism were mere pretensions. He managed to "elect" his unable son Richard to a number of public offices, including that of chancellor at Oxford. On one occasion as a young man at a Christmas celebration at his uncle's estate, Cromwell rubbed manure all over his gloves and leggings and went around befouling everyone he could. At the wedding of his daughter Frances in November 1657, he threw sack-posset and sweetmeats at the ladies to soil their clothes, and rubbed greasy food all over the guests' chairs. He also stole the groom's wig and tried to throw it into the fire, but some one stopped him, so he sat on it instead.

For all this, Cromwell was a God-fearing man, however. Whenever he sat down to dinner, he said this solemn grace: "Some men have food but no appetite. Some have appetite but no food. I have both. The Lord be praised."

It seldom pays to be rude. It never pays to be half rude.

Douglas

The English instinctively admire any man who has no talent and is modest about it.

James Agee

There are no true muskrats in the Eastern Hemisphere.

A half century ago, a pair of bank swallows habitually made their nest on a transfer steamer on the Tennessee River. The boat made a daily run between Guntersville and Hobbs Island, a distance of twenty-four miles, and every spring the swallows were "run" ragged from trying to keep up with the steamer to feed their nest-bound young.

In Hampton Court, England, in June of 1955, eight-year-old Neil Dronfield fell into the Thames River. A fellow named Frank Willingdale jumped in to save the child, but it was soon apparent he would be unable to prevent him drowning. Mrs. Willingdale leapt to their rescue, followed eventually by the four Willingdale children, aged two to seven.

A stranger finally pulled all seven people from the water, and left without saying so much as who he was.

Answer: Bing Crosby starred in *High Society* (the musical adaptation).

NOVEMBER 28

Notable Births

1628	John Bunyan	1904	Nancy Mitford
1757	William Blake	1908	Claude Levi-Strauss
1829	Anton Rubenstein	1932	Midge Costanza
1894	Brooks Atkinson	1933	Hope Lange
1895	Jose Iturbi	1952	Francie Larrieu

Notable Events

1801 U.S. bought peace from Algiers and Tunis for $800,000, a frigate, and $25,000 a year
1806 Bedford Asylum founded in Dublin
1908 Marianna, Pennsylvania, mine disaster claimed 154 lives
1919 Latvia declared war on Germany
1922 First skywriting demonstration, New York City
1933 Actions of lynch mob at San Jose, California jail, approved by Governor Rolfe
1942 Cocoanut Grove fire in Boston killed 491
1951 31 dismissed in IRS Bureau scandal

Questions: What's the difference between a boxer and a lapdog?

What's the difference between attempted murder and killing a pig?

This handbill was distributed in the Norwich, England, region in August 1826:

St. James's Hill, back of the Horse Barracks.

The Public are respectfully informed that Signor CARLO GRAM VILLECROP, the celebrated Swiss Mountain Flyer, from Geneva and Mont Blanc, is just arrived in this City, and will exhibit with a Tyrolese Pole, fifty feet long, his most astonishing Gymnastic Flights, never before witnessed in this country. Signor Villecrop had had the great honour of exhibiting his most extraordinary Feats on the Continent before the King of Prussia, Emperor of Austria, the Grand Duke of Tuscany, and all the resident Nobility in Switzerland. He begs to inform the Ladies and Gentlemen of this City that he has selected St. James's Hill and the adjoining hills for his performances, and will first display his remarkable strength in running up the hill with his Tyrolese Pole between his teeth. He will next lay on his back, and balance the same Pole on his nose, chin, and different parts of his body. He will climb upon it with the astonishing swiftness of a cat, and stand on his head at the top; on a sudden he will leap three feet from the Pole without falling, suspending himself by a shenese cord only. He will also walk on his head up and down the hill, balancing the Pole on one foot. Many other feats will be exhibited, in which Signor Villecrop will display to the audience the much-admired art of toppling, peculiar only to the Peasantry of Switzerland. He will conclude his performance by repeated flights in the air, up and down the hill, with a velocity almost imperceptible, assisted only by his Pole, with which he will frequently jump the astonishing distance of Forty and Fifty Yards at a time. Signor Villecrop begs to assure the ladies and gentlemen who honour him with their company that no money will be collected till after the exhibition, feeling convinced that his exertions will be liberally rewarded by their generosity. The Exhibition to commence on Monday, the 28th of August 1826, precisely at half-past five o'clock in the evening.

More than 20,000 people came to the hill on the evening of the twenty-eighth — practically the whole population of the town. Needless to say, Signer Villecrop did not show up, and the multitude soon realized it was a hoax. The majority took it good naturedly, of course, as they hadn't been charged any admission — until they returned home and many of them discovered they'd been robbed. A large cadre of thieves had concocted the whole affair to get the richer folks out of their homes — all the better to rob you by, m'dears.

Maurizio Pesce was fined 400 lire in Acqui, Italy, in 1958 for creating a disturbance by constantly honking a car horn. The car in question belonged to the young man's father. Maurizio was eighteen months old at the time.

In moments of crisis my nerves act in the most extraordinary way. I size up the situation in a flash, set my teeth, contract my muscles, take a firm grip on myself, and without a tremor, always do the wrong thing.

George Bernard Shaw

Answers: One faces the licks, the other licks the face.
One is assault with intent to kill, the other a killing with intent to salt.

NOVEMBER 29

Question: What is the state shown here?

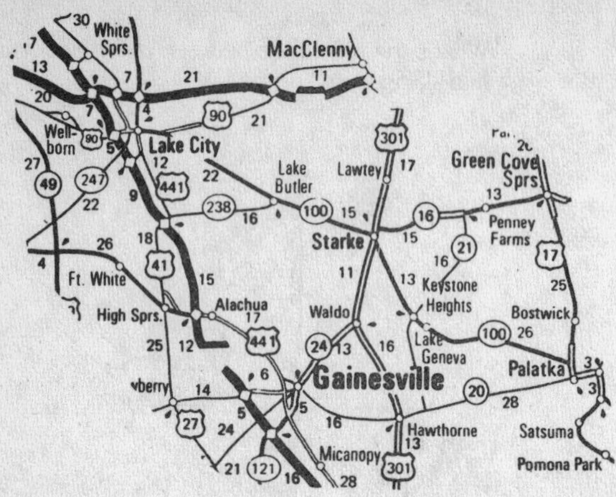

Notable Births

1799	Bronson Alcott	1920	Elmo Zumwalt
1832	Louisa May Alcott	1929	Don January
1876	Nellie Taylor Ross	1933	John Mayall
1898	C.S. Lewis	1933	David Reuben

Notable Events

1732 Earthquake took 2,000 lives in Naples, Italy
1864 Sand Creek Massacre
1890 First army-navy football game played
1923 Allied Reparation Committee began investigation of German economic conditions
1932 Electric bridge table patented
1963 DC-8F crashed on take-off from Montreal, 118 dead
1973 Fire in Kumamoto, Japan, store killed 107 people

One of the more (or less) interesting depositories of medical memorabilia in the United States is the Mütter Museum, which is known as the Museum of the College of Physicians of Philadelphia. It contains such wonderful things as the skulls of hundreds of American Indians who died from syphilis, chests full of items taken from the stomachs of compulsive swallowers, the straw-stuffed colon of a man who was constipated for over a decade, and collections of freaks of nature too numerous and/or too odd to mention.

One other item of note is the tumor that was removed from the mouth of Grover Cleveland while he was president. Cleveland had to have most of his upper jaw removed in the operation, and was fitted with an artificial jaw of vulcanized rubber in its stead. The surgery was kept secret for fear of the effects it might have on his presidency and on the economic health of the nation, which was already poor at the time. The public did not learn of the operation until 1917.

In a museum in Havana there are two skulls of Christopher Columbus, "one when he was a boy and one when he was a man."

Mark Twain

It is against navy regulations for an officer to cheer at a football game. The regulations do seem to encourage the occasional use of toilet paper streamers by midshipmen, however.

Lord Robert Baden-Powell, who founded the Boy Scouts in the first decade of this century, was much better known to his generation as one of England's most famous spies. In the 1890s, he worked undercover for the British Army in Germany, Algeria, and Tunisia, often posing as an eccentric lepidopterist with some very odd habits. While others saw Baden-Powell as a funny old coot with a butterfly net who delighted in sketching his specimens, to British intelligence he was a genius whose drawings of butterflies conveyed the size, layouts, and armaments in military installations belonging to half a dozen countries of which Britain was wary.

Pretend you're the detective investigating these peculiar circumstances:

A man was found in a third-floor bathroom, dead of a stab wound to the heart. The door had been locked from the inside, and it was obvious the window had not been opened, since it was painted shut. But there was no murder weapon to be found, and it would have been impossible to flush a knife down the toilet or a drain. The coroner had ruled that it was definitely not suicide.

This was an actual case in New York City several years ago. What happened?

(The man had been stabbed outside, struggled home and locked himself in the bathroom, where he died.)

Teodora L. Herrerra had just about completed a successful bank robbery in 1959 when, as an afterthought, the cashier who'd just handed him thousands of dollars asked if he'd please sign for the money. Herrerra singed his own name and was picked up by the police a short time later.

Theories like fingerprints — everybody have them.

Charlie Chan

Answer: Florida.

NOVEMBER 30

Notable Births

1554	Philip Sidney	1920	Virginia Mayo
1667	Jonathan Swift	1923	Efrem Zimbalist, Jr.
1817	Theodor Mommsen	1924	Shirley Chisolm
1835	Mark Twain	1924	Allan Sherman
1874	Winston Churchill	1927	Richard Crenna
1912	Gordon Parks	1929	Dick Clark

Notable Events

1710 Turkey declared war on Russia
1731 Earthquake in China killed 100,000 people in Peking alone
1774 16-string Jack (John Rann) executed for highway robbery
1887 First indoor softball game played
1954 Metorite struck woman, Sylacauga, Alabama

Mark Twain was a courteous and generous man, but he would only turn his other cheek so far. Once he went to one of his neighbors and asked if he could borrow a particular book. The man agreed graciously, providing that Twain used it right there and then. "I make it a rule," he explained.

A few days later, the same gentleman came over to Twain's house and asked if he could borrow his lawnmower.

"Of course, of course, my friend," Twain told him, "but I must ask you to use it here. You know, I make it a rule."

The Frenchman Paul Bourget was needling Mark Twain about the peculiar interest many Americans have in their ancestry. "Life can never be entirely dull to an American," he said, "When he has nothing else to do he can always spend a few years trying to discover who his grandfather was."

Twain told him he was exactly right, and added, "But I reckon a Frenchman's got a little standby for a dull time too; he can turn in and see if he can find out who his *father* was."

Answer: 48, 40, 30, 35 mph.

Question: About how fast can these animals go?

quarterhorse
zebra
grizzly bear
jackal

Twain had an extreme dislike of uncomfortable clothing, and often went about in a very informal fashion. This bothered his wife Libby a great deal. One day she discovered him returning from a short visit to a neighbor's without a collar or tie on. She reprimanded him soundly for this breach of etiquette, and he pretended to be greatly chastised. He immediately wrote this note to his friend as an apology for the manner in which he had called:

> A little while ago I visited you without my collar and tie for about a half an hour. The missing articles are enclosed. Will you kindly gaze at them for thirty minutes and then return them to me?

Political nepotism ain't what it was, and that's too bad. The second secretary of the United States Navy, Robert Smith, didn't get his job through patronage — he got it through the "Help Wanted" ads. When Jefferson became president in 1801, the entire United States fleet consisted of three ships, and there was no one the president wanted to embarrass by the naval appointment once the first secretary resigned. So an advertisement was placed in the local papers. Smith was selected as the most qualified individual, and he served until 1805. This is the only time a Cabinet level government position has been filled in this fashion.

Do you know how army "tanks" got their name? It goes like this:

The caterpillar-tracked war vehicle, which we called a tank, is only about sixty-five years old. It was developed as the secret weapon that would enable the British and their allies to overcome the stalemate of trench warfare — which the First World War had become by 1915. To throw possible spies off track, when the first tanks were being built, the workmen were told to refer to them as "cisterns." The story was that they were designed to carry water to the troops in the deserts of North Africa. "Cisterns" apparently confused too many people, and the vehicles ended up simply as "tanks."

Baltaji Mohammad Pasha was the Turkish head of state and commander-in-chief of its army in 1711. In that year, a superbly trained and equipped Turkish force of 270,000 men surrounded Czar Peter the Great and the Russian forces in Moldavia, Romania. The Russians were out of food and water, had no horses, and were completely at the mercy of the Turkish grand vizier.

Pasha did some hard thinking, then let them go.

When King Charles XII of Sweden questioned the strategy behind letting Turkey's greatest enemy escape, the vizier said simply, "But if I were to take the Czar prisoner, who would rule Russia?"

After a lost war, one should write only comedies.

Novalis, Baron von Hardenberg

It would seem that chemical poisonings may have some occasional plusses as well as minuses. Scientists have speculated that Isaac Newton's strange paranoia, spasms, and general decline while he was only in his fifties is attributable to the mercury poisoning he might have received in the course of his many experiments. That's a minus. Here are two odd plusses: Experts have speculated that Goya's brilliantly nightmarish paintings towards the end of his life could have been occasioned by lead poisoning, the result of his mixing his own heavily leaded paint throughout his lifetime. And quite recently, Vincent van Gogh has received the scrutiny of medical researchers, who contend that his insanity may very well have been chemically induced. The last few years of his life were characterized by bizarre psychotic episodes, among which was the famous incident in which he cut off his ear. His paintings of those years are also heavily yellow in tone. At the time, van Gogh's doctor, a man named Gachet, was treating him with digitalis, a heart stimulant prepared from the flower called the purple foxglove. One of its side effects is called xanthopsia, a condition in which everything takes on a yellow tinge, and the subject sees halos, somewhat like the sun's corona. Take a look at van Gogh's 1890 painting *Portrait of Dr. Gachet*, done shortly before the artist's death. That's a purple foxglove the doctor is holding. Dr. Gachet was treating himself with digitalis at the same time, and was suffering from the same side effects, although he attributed them to his general melancholia, not to the drug. Gachet died just a few months after van Gogh. Van Gogh committed suicide because of the effects of the digitalis; Gachet was simply killed by it.

A fellow named Jean Gai, of Bordeaux, France, may hold the all-time record for the number of stepchildren to one man. During his long life, Gai married sixteen times, acquiring a total of 121 stepchildren. He never fathered one of his own.

There was once a queen of the island of Madagascar named Ranavalona who issued a curious edict: she forbade anyone she knew to appear in her dreams. Those who disobeyed this order were immediately executed.

One of the world's most unusual legal filibusters occurred in France in March 1816. Army General Jean Travot was being tried for treason by a court martial in Rennes. His lawyer was a twenty-seven-year-old man named Louis Bernard. Although Bernard presented a masterful defense, and the case against the general was a flimsy one, the judges were determined to find him guilty. They did, and sentenced him to be executed immediately. The lawyer requested that the execution be delayed at least until the general's wife presented his petition to the king at Versailles, which would only take five days. The motion was denied. Bernard then asked the court if he could explain his reasons for the request to the military panel. The judges assented, whereupon he launched into his argument. He spoke nonstop, around the clock, for almost 120 hours — until Travot's wife arrived with the royal pardon.

In August 1925, a twenty-year-old woman named Mary Vickery disappeared from her home town of Coston, Kentucky. That winter a body was discovered inside an abandoned mine shaft and identified as hers. A thirty-one-year-old cab driver named Condy Dabney was arrested, mostly on the strength of statements made by one Marie Jackson. Jackson testified that the three of them had gone off together on the night in question and that, in the course of the evening's events, Mary and Condy had gone off into the bushes together. She said further that she had seen Mary resist the cabbie's advances, and that he had subsequently beat her unconscious, raped, and killed her. At his trial Dabney denied even knowing Mary Vickery, although he admitted knowing Ms. Jackson, and there was no love lost between them. He was eventually convicted and sentenced to life imprisonment.

A year later, an alert policeman in another Kentucky town noticed Mary Vickery's name in a hotel register. She was alive and well. As the puzzle unraveled, it was revealed that Vickery didn't know either Jackson or Dabney, and Marie Jackson ended up in prison for perjury. She said that her motive had been her dislike of Dabney.

It turned out that Mary Vickery had been aware for a long time of the fact that Dabney had been convicted of her murder. When asked why she hadn't stepped forward to stop the miscarriage of justice she said succinctly that she "couldn't be bothered."

In 1938, the New York Board of Censors banned all movies *mentioning* divorce, pregnancy, birth control, illegitimacy, and a host of other similarly heinous things.

The word "lozenge" (as in throat) has nothing to do etymologically with medicine in any way. A lozenge is simply a parallelogram with its corners cut off. Pills or cough drops were originally called lozenges because of their shape, and later because of their association with medicinal use. Often, medieval tombstones were cut like lozenges for decoration. The word originally came from the Old French *losange*, meaning "flattery."

A couple of years ago, the Connecticut Legislature proclaimed the praying mantis as the state insect, after a ninety-minute debate. At the time, Connecticut boasted the nation's only female governor, Ella Grasso. (See January 2.)

Capricorn (The Goat)
December 22 through January 20

DECEMBER

DECEMBER 1

Questions: What's the difference between an ear trumpet and a tunnel?

What's the difference between the land and the oceans?

Arthur Conan Doyle named his supersleuth Sherlock after the American poet whose works he most admired, Oliver Wendell Holmes. When Oliver Wendell Holmes, Jr., retired from the Supreme Court in 1932 at the age of ninety he could still recite by heart all the plots of the Sherlock Holmes mysteries.

Male cobras have two penises. Copulation can take as long as two days, with half of the time taken up by the male and female cobras pretending to kill each other in an elaborate mating ritual.

There is no fury like a woman searching for a new lover.

Cyril Connolly

The following are tendencies only, and represent in most instances a slight difference from the rest of the population; but the results of a number of scientific researches into intelligence indicate that a disproportionate number of intelligent people:

Are the only or eldest child of a family—

Were breast-fed as infants, either solely or in combination with a baby bottle—

Sleep fewer hours than the rest of us—

Are apt to be slightly more masculine in their characteristics if female, or slightly more feminine if male.

Heredity is what sets the parents of a teenager wondering about each other.

Laurence J. Peter

Notable Births

1886	Rex Stout	1913	Mary Martin
1893	Ernst Tolher	1935	Woody Allen
1898	Cyril Richard	1935	Lou Rawls
1910	Alicia Markova	1939	Lee Trevino

Notable Events

1842	First navy officer convicted of mutiny, hanged
1881	Golden Spike driven on Southern Pacific Railroad, near El Paso
1909	First Christmas Club payment made, Carlisle, Pennsylvania
1913	First drive-in gas station opened, Pittsburgh, Pennsylvania
1924	First national corn-husking championship held, Alleman, Iowa
1955	Rosa Parks refused to give up a bus seat; Montgomery bus boycott began
1955	International treaty signed making Antarctica scientific preserve
1961	CPUSA indicted for failure to register as subversive group

The telephone preceded widespread literacy among the Kaguyak Indians of the Alaskan Archipelago. To overcome the natives' inability to read the phone book and the numbers on the dials themselves, Ma Bell provided pictures of familiar animals on Kaguyaks' phones: seals, bears, foxes, etc. A similar system has been used at international exhibitions in recent years to denote areas of the fairgrounds.

Henry IV, England's king at the beginning of the fifteenth century, was a man of simple tastes who was offended by pretension and ostentation. He once passed a law prohibiitng any of his subjects from wearing jewelry and other personal ornaments. Nobody paid much attention to it until Henry tacked on an amendment that excluded prostitutes and thieves from having to abide by the statute. Almost overnight, England became an unbejeweled country, and stayed that way until Henry's French wife appeared at a state function bedecked like a whore. It was the end of the effectiveness of that law, at least.

Integrity has no need of rules.

Albert Camus

In 1949, Lloyd's of London began to issue a hole-in-one insurance, which allowed for a payment of up to ten pounds for those unfortunate players who aced a golf hole and were expected to buy a round of drinks for everyone on the course.

The manufacture of corncob pipes in the United States requires over fifteen million corncobs a year.

Answers: One is hollered in, the other hollowed out.

One is dirty, the other tide-y.

DECEMBER 2

Notable Births

1838	Queen Liliuokalani	1924	Alexander Haig
1885	Nikos Kazantzakis	1925	Julie Harris
1915	Adolph Green	1962	Tracy Austin

Notable Events

1805 Battle of Austerlitz
1823 Monroe Doctrine declared
1848 Ferdinand I of Austria abdicated
1859 John Brown hanged
1933 First transatlantic telephone wedding
1942 First successful nuclear fission experiment
1954 Senate condemned Joe McCarthy
1959 Fire in Frejus, France, killed 323

Question: A man in an orange suit rushed into a department store just before closing time and selected an orange hat that cost $67 (with tax). "I want the hat," he told the cashier, "but doggone, the smallest bill I have is a hundred. Can you change it?" Without using dollar bills or coins, the cashier made change with six bills. How did the cashier manage?

One of the permanent results of the Norman Conquest of England in 1066 was the changes it affected in the language, particularly in the naming of food. Needless to say, the Norman lords ate far better than the subjugated Anglo-Saxons once their feudal domains had been established, and because of this our present-day English words for meats are almost all of Norman origin. The words beef, veal, mutton, pork, venison, and poultry are all derived from Old French, and so is the word "butcher" itself. In contrast, the words for the plainer foods the English ate, such as bread, beans, peas, and eggs, are almost all Anglo-Saxon. Most of the names for the animals the farmers tended are also of Anglo-Saxon origin, including ox, pig, sheep, deer, and fowl. But when an animal was slaughtered for food, that was the last the natives had to do with it or its name. It disappeared as a carcass (the Anglo-Saxon term for flesh) to reappear on a Norman's table as a dish of veal, beef, or other delicacy. Bacon was about the only meat most rural English had before the two cultures gradually blended, and even its name is of French ancestry.

Answer: He gave him one $20, one $5, and four $2s.

DECEMBER 3

Question: What is the state pictured here?

Notable Births

1755	Gilbert Stuart	1930	Jean-Luc Goddard
1857	Joseph Conrad	1930	Andy Williams
1923	Maria Callas	1937	Bobby Allison

Notable Events

1800	French defeated Austrians at Hohenlinden
1922	First successful technicolor movie released
1934	France and Germany signed Saar Treaty
1948	Stribling revealed existence of pumpkin microfilm to Congress (Alger Hiss case)
1952	General Perez seized power in Venezuela
1964	786 Berkeley students arrested in free speech sit-in
1967	First successful heart transplant performed
1972	Typhoon Therese killed 169 in Philippines

Milwaukee policemen Frank Smith and Frank Berg took a rookie cop named Leo Markowski out on patrol with them one night in 1955, hoping to show the young man the finer points of the art of questioning suspicious individuals. Simply to demonstrate their information-gathering methods further, they hailed a pair of gentlemen who just happened to be passing by at the time.

Markowski couldn't have had finer teachers. By the time Smith and Berg were satisfied with the strangers' story, the two had admitted they were AWOL from the army, had committed burglaries in Nevada, Colorado, and Nebraska, and had a gun hidden in a nearby alley, which they planned to use to hold up a local gas station later that night!

What right have you to think? Haven't you been in the police force long enough to know that?

J.C. Snaith

Today there are nine times as many scientists on earth as there have ever been throughout the history of man. In a generation from now (we should live so long) that will still be true, even including this present generation of scientists. It has been estimated that 90 percent of our present-day scientific knowledge was unknown before 1920.

In 1535, the folks in Corcuetos, Spain, started work on a cathedral in their city. Ninety years later, on the day that it was officially considered completed, it collapsed.

In the middle of the seventeenth century, Bishop Dom Bernard de Salazar was the prelate for the region of Chiapa, Mexico, a thriving little Spanish colonial settlement. The only thing the invaders really liked outside of the wealth that the vanquished Indians of Mexico had given the Spanish was chocolate. The Spanish women of the town used it for cosmetic purposes, believing it imparted a healthy glow to their complexions. (They were probably right, since these were the days of cocaine chocolate.) They used a good deal of it, often as a cocoa drink, and became — if not physically — at least psychologically addicted to it.

When the addiction to chocolate overflowed into church services, and the clink of cups and saucers interrupted the sermons of Dom Bernard, he vowed to wage an all-out holy war on the immoderate use of chocolate.

For weeks he preached against it, finally even stationing guards at the church doors to relieve the women of their cocoa and its accoutrements as they entered, but the determined women managed to circumvent these measures with impunity. As a last resort, Dom Bernard told they he would excommunicate any transgressors of his anticocoa pronouncements. Soon, the majority of the women had been thrown out of the church. Disagreements in the streets over the situation led to squabbles, squabbles to fights, and fights to small riots, but Bernard would not modify his position one iota. He vowed to fight it out on that line even if it took all summer for the women to give in to God's and his will.

After several weeks, the women made the first move towards reconciliation. They presented Dom Bernard with a large gift of the finest chocolate money could buy: a gesture that they wished once again to be friends. Dom Bernard was extremely pleased — *and dead within a week from poisoned chocolate!*

Egotism is the anesthetic that dulls the pain of stupidity.

Frank Leahy

Answer: Kentucky.

DECEMBER 4

Notable Births

1795	Thomas Carlyle	1922	Deanna Durbin
1835	Samuel Butler	1930	Harvey Kuenn
1875	Rainer Maria Rilke	1933	Horst Bucholz
1892	Francisco Franco	1941	Marty Reissen

Notable Events

963	Rome Synod deposed Pope John XII
1897	Peace treaty between Greece and Turkey ratified
1932	Von Schleicher's ministry began in Germany
1935	Saint Joseph's College began anti-Communist courses
1972	Airplane crash in Canary Islands took 155 lives
1974	DC-8 crashed in Sri Lanka, claimed 191 victims

It took the English historian Thomas Carlyle three years to write the first volume of his history of the French Revolution. Upon its completion, he sent it to his friend John Stuart Mill for his approval. Mill's housekeeper mistook it for wastepaper and used it to kindle a fire.

Needless to say, it was Carlyle's only copy.

One day in April 1955, a fellow named John Cartwright was convicted of drunkenness in Wilmington, North Carolina, and ordered to leave town. The Wilmington cops picked him up the next day, drunk again. He explained to the judge that he had a very good reason for disobeying the original order: "Everytime I raised my good leg off the ground, the wind would come up and spin me around; and I had to take a drink to steady myself."

Answer: Louisiana, Nebraska, Rhode Island, New Hampshire, Delaware.

Question: Can you name the states with these mottos?

Union, Justice, Confidence
Equality before the law
Hope
Live free or die
Liberty and Independence

Moles are prodigious workers. A single mole has been observed to dig a tunnel a hundred yards long in one evening. In proportion to his size, a man would have to dig a tunnel over fifty miles in length and large enough for him to crawl through to match the mole.

WALL STREET

1. Never go a-clamming at high water, or never, as a rule, go into Wall Street when Stocks and Bonds are on the topmost round of the financial ladder. Go in once to buy and once to sell; for the man who goes there and holds on and gets tangled up in the tape, is like a fly in a spider's web.

2. Buy only after a great decline, when the last little lamb has fled, and when the press and every friend you have are generously volunteering the opinion that the market is going all to pieces. In fact, before buying, you ought to begin to feel yourself that the bottom has dropped out.

3. Beware of advisers who are forever seeing disaster ahead. Never let any one persuade you to trade on the short side. It is a bad plan at best to sell another man's property. He probably knows better what it is worth than you do.

4. Never be in haste to buy. Take your time. Stocks are not going to leave town. And never buy without ample margin. But being once in, "stay!" Never run; but always remember that it is the man who tents on the battlefield who gets the spoils. And also remember, in every combat you have in this life, that if you don't run the other fellow must.

Never consent to take a loss.

Much nonsense has been written about the first loss being the least, etc. But you do not go in to take any loss at all. If you go in on the conditions I have named, stay and take your profit. It is only a question of time.

5. Buy nothing without first making yourself acquainted with what you propose to purchase. Property that is not open to the ready inspection of all is the best property in the world to let alone.

6. Beware of impecunious gentlemen who are full of "points." Your mental answer to such should always be, "Physician, heal thyself."

7. Never, under any circumstances, permit yourself to be set astraddle of the market. It is said to be a pretty safe position, but to my mind it is the position of a coward or a fool. It is hardly possible for you to make, and you will surely lose your commissions and your interest.

8. Never talk about stocks. As a rule the world over, no man who talks much ever thinks much. And then there are nobler things for a gentleman to talk about than stocks, if talk he must. So keep your stock opinions to yourself and pool the opinions of others.

9. And, finally, believe largely in your own convictions. Have your own opinions and follow them. Have your rules and follow them as a general follows the tactics of war. And then if you make money you make it yourself, and can do it again; and if you lose it, why, you at least lose it scientifically.

DECEMBER 5

Questions: Why are jewelers and jailers opposites?

What is the difference between a bad pianist and sixteen ounces of butter?

Notable Births

1782	Martin Van Buren	1901	Walt Disney
1830	Christina Rossetti	1902	Strom Thurmond
1839	George Armstrong Custer	1906	Otto Preminger
1890	Fritz Lang	1934	Joan Didion

Notable Events

1456	Earthquake near Naples killed 60,000 people
1492	Columbus discovered Haiti
1786	Shays's Rebellion, Massachusetts
1792	Trial of Louis XVI began
1868	First bicycle school opened, New York City
1908	First numbers used on football uniforms, University of Pittsburgh
1927	First king born on American soil, Rama IX of Thailand
1929	First national nudist association formed
1932	Repeal of Prohibition lost by 6 votes in House
1934	Stalin purged 66 German sympathizers

Even a quick narrative of the trials, tribulations, and beliefs of the 300-year-old pacifist Doukhobor sect would take a month's worth of space in this book, but if you liked Father Riker and his Holy City (see September 27) you'll fully appreciate the Doukhobors. In just this past century, significant aspects of their history have included incest, illegitimacy, wife-swapping, enforced illiteracy, and burial alive; winter marches half the length of Canada undertaken without food, water, or clothing; ritual arson of their own homes; bombings of schools, churches, municipal property, railroad lines, and power plants; secret orders concealed in hymns broadcast over the radio; extortion by a half a dozen Anti-Christs; and a link-up with a Soviet spy network. Things got so out of hand at one point twenty years ago that British Columbian policemen and Canadian Mounties had to use itching powder as a deterrent to naked Doukhobor women who sat on the officers' faces to prevent them from carrying out their orders.

If people demonstrate in a manner to interfere with others, they should be rounded up and put in a detention camp.

Richard Kleindienst

Answers: One sells watches, the other watches cells.

One pounds away, the other weighs a pound.

On December 5, 1664, a ship with eighty-one people on board sank in the Menai Strait, off north Wales. A man named Hugh Williams was the sole survivor. Sixty people lost their lives on December 5, 1785, when another ship went down. The sole survivor of that disaster was named Hugh Williams. On the same date in 1860, another shipwreck claimed twenty-five lives. A man named Hugh Williams was the only one who survived.

DECEMBER 6

Notable Births

1886	Joyce Kilmer	1906	Agnes Moorehead
1887	Lynn Fontaine	1920	Dave Brubeck
1896	Ira Gershwin	1921	Otto Graham
1898	Gunnar Myrdal	1924	Wally Cox
1904	Eve Curie	1953	Dwight Stones

Notable Events

1884 Aluminum tip set on Washington Monument
1907 Mining accident in Monongah, West Virginia, took 361 lives
1917 Explosion in Halifax, Nova Scotia, killed 1,654 people
1917 Finnish Republic proclaimed
1922 Irish Free State proclaimed
1973 Gerald Ford sworn in as vice president

Question: What is the state shown here?

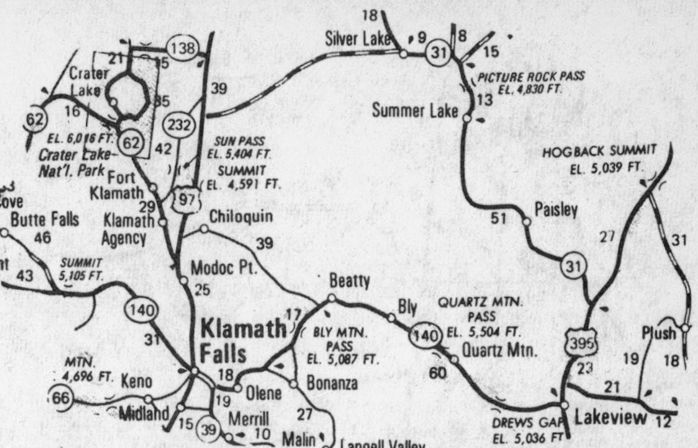

Among its many definitions, the word "bull" means a linguistic blunder. For some reason, the Irish have become well known for their habit of giving the English language a carnival ride at times, and an "Irish Bull" has come to mean a particular kind of linguistic confusion. Read the piece below and you'll get the idea. It was written during the time of the Rebellion by an Irish member of Parliament to a friend in London, and is his attempt to write the ultimate Irish Bull.

My dear Sir: — Having now a little peace and quietness, I sit down to inform you of the dreadul bustle and confusion we are in from these blood-thirsty rebels, most of whom are (Thank God!) killed and dispersed. We are in a pretty mess; can get nothing to eat, nor wine to drink, except whiskey; and when we sit down to dinner, we are obliged to keep both hands armed. Whilst I write this, I hold a pistol in each hand, and a sword in the other. I concluded in the beginning that this would be the end of it; and I see I was right, for it is not half over yet. At present there are such goings on that everything is at a standstill. I should have answered your letter a fortnight ago, but I did not receive it till this morning. Indeed, hardly a mail arrives safe, without being robbed. No longer ago than yesterday a coach with the mails from Dublin was robbed near this town: the bags had been judiciously left behind for fear of accident, and by good luck there was nothing in it but two outside passengers who had nothing for the thieves to take. Last Thursday, notice was given that a gang of rebels were advancing here under the French standard; but they had no colors, nor any drums except bagpipes. Immediately every man in the place, including women and children, ran out to meet them. We soon found our force much too little; and we were far too near to think of retreating. Death was in every face; but to it we went, and by the time half our little party were killed we began to be all alive again. Fortunately, the rebels had no guns, except pistols, cutlasses, and pikes; and as we had plenty of guns and ammunition, we put them all to the sword. Not a soul of them escaped, except some that were drowned in an adjacent bog; and in a very short time, nothing was to be heard except silence. Their uniforms were all different colors, but mostly green. After the action, we went to rummage a sort of camp which they had left behind them. All we found was a few pikes without heads, a parcel of empty bottles full of water, and a bundle of French commissions filled up with Irish names. Troops are now stationed all around the country, which exactly squares with my ideas. I have only time to add that I am in great haste.

Yours truly,

P.S. If you do not receive this, of course it must have miscarried; therefore I beg you will write and let me know.

In 1659, the Massachusetts Bay Colony made it illegal and punishable by a fine of five shillings to observe Christmas in any way.

⚜

On one day in 1896, practically the entire British Indian Ocean fleet sailed into the main harbor of the island of Zanzibar. Outraged at this presumably unwarranted display of force, the Sultan of Zanzibar sent out his *entire* navy, the *Glascow*, to engage the Limeys. When the war ended, thirty-seven minutes later, the *Glascow* was on the bottom, the sultan's palace had been flattened, and 500 citizens of Zanzibar were dead.

It was just a misunderstanding. A cricket match was being held on the island, in which several British Navy teams had been invited to play, and the rest of the fleet had come along to cheer their men to victory.

I see no reason in saving up indignation for a rainy day.

Heywood Broun

Answer: Oregon.

DECEMBER 7

Question: What is the state shown here?

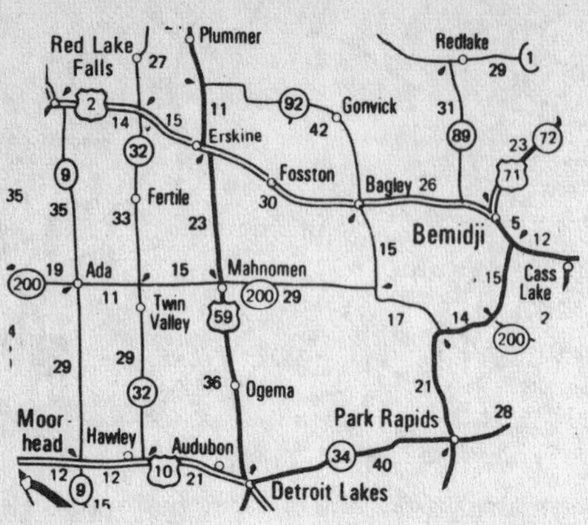

The English Parliament once passed a law calling for the construction of a new jail in Chelmsford, using the materials of the old jail. The bill also directed that the prisoners be kept in the old jail until the new one was completed.

Life must be lived forwards; but can only be understood backwards.

Soren Kierkegaard

Herbert and Bonnie Jackson, who met through a Lonely Hearts Club advertisement, were divorced in Baltimore in 1954. Herbert said that her ad had stated she was five feet, four inches tall, and 118 pounds, while actually she was over six feet and weighed 450 pounds. They'd got married anyway, but he went on to say that it had become "too much for me when she grabbed the kettle and scalded me, and then shot at me, and then left me, saying I didn't appreciate a fat woman."

Although castration was finally outlawed by the Catholic Church in 1878, it has yet to disappear completely in many parts of the world. Today there are more castrati in India than there are Jews in Poland, and there are about ten thousand Jews in Poland.

Give him an inch and he'll take a mile.

Anonymous

Notable Births

1542	Mary, Queen of Scots	1912	Rod Cameron
1876	Willa Cather	1915	Eli Wallach
1888	Heywood Broun	1932	Ellen Burstyn
1888	Joyce Cary	1947	Johnny Bench

Notable Events

1917	United States declared war on Austria-Hungary
1941	Pearl Harbor bombed
1941	I.C. Kidd became first admiral killed in World War II
1946	Fire in Atlanta hotel killed 119 people
1949	Chiang Kai-shek fled to Formosa

Of course the Irish bull has many ethnic imitators. Here's a recent French-Canadian one:

My dear male son Claude,

Jus a few line to let you know dat hi ham still alive. Hi ham writing dis letter slowly because hi know dat you can not read fas. You won't know de house when you get home — we move.

Dere was a washing machine in de new house when we move in, but hit ain't working too good. Last week hi put 14 shirt into hit, pulled de chain, an hi ain't seen de shirt since.

About your Papa, he has nice new job, 624 men under him, cutting de grass in de cemetery. Your sister Pauline had a baby dis morning. He haven't foun out whedder it's a boy or a girl, so hi don't know whedder you are haunt or honcle. Your honcle Pierre, he drown las week in de vat of whiskey up at Tree River. Some of his workmate dive hinto help him, but he fight dem off bravely. We cremate his body, an it take tree days to put out de fire.

Your Papa he did not have too much to drink hat Christmas. Hi put a bottle hot castor oil in his mug of beer. Hit keep him going till New Year's Day. Hi went to de doctor on Tursday an your Papa he come with me. De doctor put a small tube in my mout an tol me not to hopen hit for ten minute. Your Pape he hoffer to buy de tube from de doctor.

Hit honly rain twice dis week. Firs for tree day, den for four day. Monday she was so windy dat one of our chicken he lay de same egg tree time.

We got a letter from de undertaker. He say we make de las payment on your grandmama or hup she come.

Your loving Mama

P.S. Hi was going to sen you ten dollar, but hi had already seal de envelope.

Plover-Clover

The Plover and the Clover can be
told apart with ease,
By paying close attention to the
habits of the Bees,
For En-to-molo-gists aver the Bee
can be in clover
While Ety-molo-gists concur
there is no B in plover.

Robert Williams Wood

Answer: Minnesota.

DECEMBER 8

Notable Births

65 B.C.	Horace	1913	Delmore Schwartz
1765	Eli Whitney	1925	Sammy Davis, Jr.
1865	Jean Sibelius	1930	Maximilian Schell
1868	Norman Douglas	1936	David Carradine
1894	James Thurber	1937	James MacArthur

Notable Events

1792 First cremation in United States
1854 Immaculate conception proclaimed Catholic dogma
1863 Lincoln issued amnesty declaration
1881 Ring Theater fire, Vienna, took 850 lives
1941 Britain declared war on Spain
1959 First scented movie shown
1964 Notre Dame got injunction against movie, *John Goldfarb Won't You Please Come Home?*, objected to depiction of students as "gluttons and drunks"
1973 Nixon's tax returns made public, revealed questionable $500,000 deduction for papers

Question: Can you rank these states according to the number of divorces (most to fewest)?

California
Nevada
New Jersey
Texas

Glass eyes are not solid, and never have been. They are actually shells of glass. In fact, since about 1920, most "glass" eyes have been made of celluloid, because it is not as affected as glass is by the chemicals in the secretions that lubricate the eye. These substances etched the surface of glass eyes, which eventually led to the irritation of the ocular membrances and required the replacement of a glass eye about every other year.

Artificial eyes are very, very old. The Egyptians were making glass eyes three thousand years ago.

Little Known Laws

If the world seems frustrating at times, it may be due to one or more laws you didn't know about. For example:

MURPHY'S LAW: If something can go wrong it will.

WEILER'S LAW: Nothing is impossible for the guy who doesn't have to do it himself.

CHISOLM'S LAW: Anytime things seem to be going along too well, you've probably overlooked something.

FINAGLE'S LAW: Once a job or a situation is really fouled up, anything you do to improve it will only make it worse.

HARDIN'S LAW (Frank Hardin): Every time you come up with a terrific idea, you find someone else has thought of it first.

WEAVER'S LAW (Jackson Weaver): Every time you buy something, the manufacturer comes out the next week with a new improved model at lower cost.

ROSS'S LAW (Al Ross): Bare feet magnetize sharp metal objects so that they always point upward from the floor — especially in the dark.

BUXBAUM'S LAW: Anytime you back out of your driveway or parking lot, day or night, there will always be a car coming, or a pedestrian walking by.

GINSBURG'S LAW (Uncle Dave): At the precise moment you take off your shoe in a shoestore, your big toe will pop out of your sock to see what's going on.

GOLD'S LAW (Bill Gold): Everyone knows what Gold's Law is — it's shredded cabbage.

From *Urban Folklore from the Paperwork Empire.*

In the little town of Taree, Australia, in 1959, a man named Charles Peters was bitten by a poisonous snake. He immediately shot himself in the arm above the place where he'd been bitten, hoping thereby to bleed out the toxin.

He survived, and was arrested for carrying a gun on Sunday.

The hearing of an elephant is about as acute as that of a cat. Both animals can hear something as soft as the footsteps of a mouse.

Answer: California; Texas; New Jersey; Nevada.

DECEMBER 9

Questions: What kind of coat should you put on a house?

Why does time fly so fast?

Notable Births

1608	John Milton	1911	Lee J. Cobb
1848	Joel Chandler Harris	1912	Tip O'Neill
1897	Hermione Gingold	1916	Kirk Douglas
1898	Emmett Kelly	1922	Redd Foxx
1902	Margaret Hamilton	1929	John Cassavetes
1909	Douglas Fairbanks, Jr.	1941	Beau Bridges
1911	Broderick Crawford	1942	Dick Butkus

Notable Events

1798	Charles Emmanuel of Sardinia forced to abidicate
1884	Ball-bearing roller skates patented
1907	First tuberculosis Christmas Seals
1909	First American monoplane flown
1931	Zamora elected in Spain
1935	Supreme Court rejected Hauptmann's appeal
1959	United States began removal of troops from Iceland
1965	Kosygin announced half-billion military budget cut

Although many of his records have long since been surpassed, Edward Weston remains the modern world's most accomplished walker.

It all began in 1860, when he was twenty-one years old. He'd wagered a walk to Washington, D.C., against a bag of peanuts that Abraham Lincoln would lose the election that year. Abe didn't. His pay-off on the wager was to walk the 478 miles from Boston to Washington the next spring in less than ten days, and to attend Lincoln's inauguration. It turned out that he was a few hours late to witness the actual swearing-in ceremony, though he did reach the capital in time for the evening's inaugural ball, sore feet and all.

But his feat brought more than a personal memory of that momentous occasion — it brought him fame, which eventually brought him fortune. Edward Weston was off and *walking*!

The Civil War necessitated putting his career aside for a time, but at its conclusion, Weston took up where he'd left off. In 1867, he took on a challenge that he could not walk from Portland, Maine, to Chicago in twenty-six days. He did so, and earned $10,000. For the next forty years, he entertained similar proposals in the States, and traveled to Europe several times as well, where he consistently defeated the best walkers on the Continent.

To celebrate his sixty-eighth birthday he repeated his Portland-to-Chicago trek four decades later, and beat his time as a young man by twenty-nine hours, even with the longer course involved. Two years later, he journeyed from New York to San Francisco over a 3,895-mile route in 104 days, and repeated the feat the next year over a 3,600-mile course in less than seventy-seven days.

As fate would have it, while he was perambulating around in Brooklyn in 1927 at the age of eighty-eight, he was struck by a car and severely injured. Edward Weston died in a wheelchair two years later.

No man who is in a hurry is quite civilized.

Will and Ariel Durant

The English name for the walrus came from Iceland via Scandinavia. In Icelandic, he is known as the *hross-hvalr*, or "horse-whale," from his equine-sounding vocalizations. In the Scandinavian tongues, the name was inverted to whale-horse, and the English word "walrus" comes from that.

In 1946, the navy listed Watertender James Telfer as a deserter, and set out to look for him. When Telfer was apprehended in 1948 it was discovered he'd been living in a barracks at the navy installation at Treasure Island, California, almost the whole time, and had been a regular player on a navy baseball team.

Did you know that for thirty-one years, George Washington operated a ferry on the Potomac River, and for some time was a fishmonger along the Atlantic seaboard? It's true. At various times in his life, he was also what is known as "land-poor" (lots of holdings, but no cash), and he had to borrow money to attend his own inauguration.

Grover Cleveland took his duties seriously. As sheriff of the Erie County Jail in Buffalo, New York, it was his responsibility to see that condemned men were put to death. Instead of delegating this chore to a subordinate, in 1872 and 1873 Cleveland personally pulled the trap on two men.

Moths don't eat clothes. The *larvae* of moths eat clothes, but not moths as moths.

The Penguin — The Swordfish

We have for many years been bored
By that old saw about the sword
And pen, and now we all rejoice,
To see how Nature made her choice:
She made, regardless of offendin'
The Sword-fish mightier than the Pen-guin.

Robert Williams Wood

Answers: A coat of paint.

So many people are trying to kill it.

Notable Births

1787 Thomas Gallaudet
1805 William Lloyd Garrison
1822 Cesar Franck
1830 Emily Dickinson
1851 Melville Dewey
1911 Chet Huntley

Notable Events

1790 Austria renounced scheme to trade Bavaria for Netherlands
1896 First intercollegiate basketball game
1936 Edward VIII abdicated to marry Wallis Simpson
1941 Japan invaded Philippines
1958 First domestic jet airliner service began
1964 Charges against 21 defendants dismissed in Schwerner, Goodman, Chaney case

A South Carolinian named Will Queen a while back was convicted of "highway robbery," as it was officially termed in that state. He received eight months in jail for having held up and robbed a man of $136. The interesting thing about this incident was that Queen had lost both arms above the elbow in an accident a few years before.

You can't keep a good man down.

Charles H. Hardin was elected governor of Missouri in 1874 by the smallest margin in history — less than a vote. At the time, Missouri's governor was officially chosen through a system similar to that of the Electoral College. Counties went for or against a candidate, and votes were apportioned according to their populations. But some of the counties were very sparsely populated, and a county of fewer than 500 residents received only portions of one vote. When the final tally was made, Hardin had defeated his challenger, General Francis Cockrell, by one-sixth of a vote.

In Micklehurst, England, this epitaph depicting life as a tavern is to be found:

Life is an Inn, where all men bait,
The waiter Time, the landlord Fate;
Death is the score by all men due,
I've paid my shot — and so must you.

This epitaph is from Eyrie, Aberdeenshire:

Erected to the memory of Alexander Gray, some time farmer in Mill of Burns, who died in the 96th year of his age, having had 32 legitimate children by two wives.

Here lies Johnny Cole
Who died, on my soul,
After eating a plentiful dinner;
While chewing his crust,
He was turn'd into dust
With his crimes *undigested* — poor sinner!

Answers: One is a stunted hag, the other a hunted stag.
One is hard to get down, the other hard to get up.

Questions: What's the difference between a small witch and a deer during hunting season?

Why are a pill and a hill different?

A century ago a fellow named Behanzin was the chief of a tribe living in the French colony of Dahomey, which is located between Togo and Nigeria. He was a remarkable man. Among his special privileges as the tribe's leader was his practice of polygamy, and he took full advantage of it. Although no reliable record exists of the number of wives Behanzin had, it is known he fathered 902 children. Depending on the status of the mother, the chief's children had many doors opened or closed to them as royal offspring. Sixty sons became chiefs in their own right, but over 200 ended up as ordinary laborers. Behanzin also commanded an army of over five thousand members — all women.

One of his most jealously guarded privileges as king was the wearing of sandals or shoes. Of the many thousands of people he ruled, no one beside himself was allowed to wear shoes. Everyone else went barefoot. The penalty for transgression of this rule was death.

Behanzin was eventually ousted by the French, and he died in exile in 1906.

Some of the new-fangled fancy batteries have warning labels on them cautioning against the improper disposal of the spent cells. They're not kidding. In 1980 a Danish man was seriously injured when a crematorium wall exploded. The culprit: a silver oxide battery that had been used to power the dead woman's pacemaker.

There's a saying in the navy that goes "There's a right way, a wrong way, and the Navy way." The guided missile destroyer *Farragut* recently had the unhappy responsibility of conducting a burial at sea. At the end of the ceremony the coffin was dispatched to the ocean, as usual — but it would not sink. The honor guard who were present to fire the traditional salute used up over 200 rounds of ammunition before they managed to blast enough holes in the box to sink it.

DECEMBER 11

Question: The new prisoner asked his cellmate, "How long have you been in?" "Well," his cellmate said, "if I had been in twice as long as I have been, it would be another three years until I was three-fourths of the way through a twenty-year sentence." How long had the cellmate been in prison?

Notable Births

1801	Christian Grabbe	1922	Marie Windsor
1803	Hector Berlioz	1931	Rita Moreno
1843	Robert Koch	1938	Connie Francis
1905	Gilbert Roland	1939	Thomas McGuane
1918	Alexander Solzhenitsyn	1950	Christina Onassis

Notable Events

1719	First Aurora Borealis recorded in America
1919	First monument to an insect in United States dedicated, Alabama
1930	Bank of the United States declared insolvent, 400,000 depositors affected
1931	Japan abolished gold standard
1937	Italy quit League of Nations over Ethiopian chastisement
1941	Japan captured Guam
1941	Germany and Japan declared war on United States
1964	Cuban freedom fighters attacked United Nations with bazooka

The United States Department of Agriculture once did a survey of the insect population over Tallulah, Alabama. Taking samples from 50 to 14,000 feet above the ground, it reported an estimated twenty-five million insects per cubic mile of air. The insect found at the highest altitude was, surprisingly, a spider, carried aloft by the wind.

Despite the notoriety that the bank-robbing team of Bonnie and Clyde derived from Hollywood a decade ago, they were, in truth, only small fry among the criminals of their time. Their biggest heist by far was $3,500. They did manage to kill a fair number of people, though — at least thirteen — murdering several of them without any provocation.

However, after their career ended in an ambush, with the police, their "popularity" with the common folk became immediately apparent. Hundreds of people descended on the scene of their deaths practically before the shootout was over. Clyde lost his shirt, T-shirt, and nearly an ear to souvenir hunters, and Bonnie almost had her dress stripped from her before police could stop the throng. Every piece of glass from the car was picked up from the road, and nearby trees were felled so that bullets could be dug from their trunks. The separate funeral homes in Dallas to which the bodies were taken a few days later were each besieged by twenty thousand curiosity seekers and/or well-wishers, and the mobs that followed the bodies to the cemetery were so thick that Clyde's own sister was unable to get closer than forty feet from his grave for burial service.

About 5 percent of all identical twins have identical handwriting.

Epitaph from Stoke Newington, England:

This tomb was erected by William Picket, of the city of London, Goldsmith, on the melancholy death of his Daughter Elizabeth.
A testimony of respect
From greatly afflicted parent;
In memory of Elizabeth Picket, *Spinster,*
Who died Dec 11, 1781.
Aged 23 years.
This much lamented
Young person expired in consequence
of her clothes taking fire
the preceeding evening.
Reader if ever you should witness such an affecting scene; recollect that the only method to extinguish the flame is to stifle it by an immediate covering.

From a tombstone in Wethersfield, Connecticut:

Here lie interred Mrs. Lydia
Beadle Aged 32 Years
Ansell Lothrop Elizabeth Lydia & Mary
Beadle her Children: the eldest aged
11 and the youngest 6 years Who
on the morning of the 11th day of Decr AD 1782
Fell by the hands of William Beadle
an infatuated man who closed the
horrid sacrifice of his Wife
& Children with his own destruction.

Parker Brothers, the board game company, each year prints more than $18,500,000,000,000 worth of Monopoly money. In United States dollars, this is more money than is printed by all the nations in the world.

Answer: Six years.

DECEMBER 12

Notable Births

1745	John Jay	1914	Morey Amsterdam
1821	Gustave Flaubert	1915	Frank Sinatra
1863	Edvard Munch	1924	Edward Koch
1893	Edward G. Robinson	1929	John Osborne
1897	Margaret Chase Smith	1933	Flip Wilson

Notable Events

1804	Spain declared war on England
1842	French evacuated Prague
1877	Diaz became President of Mexico
1899	Golf tee patented
1913	Mona Lisa discovered in Florence, returned to Louvre
1936	Chiang Kai-shek declared war on Japan
1975	Fire in Saudi-Arabian tent city took 138 lives

Parrot-Carrot

The Parrot and the Carrot one may easily confound,
They're very much alike in looks and similar in sound,
We recognize the parrot by his clear articulation,
For carrots are unable to engage in conversation.

Robert Williams Wood

In 1924, a real-life Jack Sprat took a wife. His name was Pete Robinson, and he weighed only 58 pounds. He married Bunny Smith, a woman who weighed 467 pounds. Both were circus sideshow attractions.

Answers: Your lap.
Horseradish or pepper.

Questions: What do you lose when you stand up?

What food stays hot longest in the refrigerator?

Back in the 'teens there was a New Jersey man who barnstormed the East as a lightweight fighter under the name of Matty O'Brien. O'Brien wasn't a great fighter, but he was a kind and personable fellow, and he'd go out of his way to help his friends. One person he helped along was talented but barely known singer named Bing Crosby.

Years later, O'Brien got in touch with Crosby and asked him for a favor. It seemed in the meantime he'd had a son who was more inclined to follow music than pugilistics, and promised to be a pretty good singer. He wondered if Bing could help the boy get the music education he wanted so badly, but which his father could not afford. Bing graciously returned the favors O'Brien had done him in the past by seeing to it that boy did get that training.

The youngster's real name was Frank Sinatra.

Occasionally you a hear a story about an individual who amasses an enormous fortune in a few minutes, simply by calling a roulette wheel correctly eight or ten times in a row. It doesn't happen too often, though, so be careful. If you had a 100 men, each guessing red or black on five separate wheel spins a minute, for forty hours a week, a dozen correct calls in a row *might* occur on any one wheel once every few weeks. Under the same arrangements, a total of fifty correct calls in a row could be expected to occur once every nine million years.

Two men were playing golf with another man whom neither trusted. On the first few holes, they noticed that he'd only tried to shave one stroke, and they quickly corrected him. Then, on the fifth, the man put his ball into a narrow ravine. Rather than incur a shot for coming out, he decided to take his chances playing away. He disappeared for several minutes into the gully, and there was much thrashing and cursing. Finally the ball flew out.

"How many strokes?" asked one of the men.

"Three," replied the cheater, disgustedly.

"But we heard six," said the other.

"Echoes."

Golf is a good walk spoiled.

Mark Twain

Here's another Herrerra (November 29) story. A fellow named Charles Merriweather broke into the home of a Baltimore woman, raped her, and then demanded all her money. When she produced less than twelve dollars, he forced her to write a check, warning her that if it bounced, he'd be back. The woman wrote the check out to Charles A. Merriweather, and police had an easy time apprehending the criminal.

Trout are among the most voracious fish in the piscene world, and will eat almost anything, in large quantities. Interestingly enough, the trout gets its name from the Latin *trocta*, meaning "greedy fish."

DECEMBER 13

Question: What country or countries were ruled by each of the following?

Egbert
Ethelbald
Edwy the Fair
Ethelred II the Unready

Notable Births

1797	Heinrich Heine	1916	Archie Moore
1818	Mary Todd Lincoln	1925	Dick Van Dyke
1835	Phillips Brooks	1929	Christopher Plummer
1897	Drew Pearson	1935	Lindy McDaniel
1903	Carlos Montoya	1943	Ferguson Jenkins

Notable Events

1294 Peter the Hermit abdicated the papacy
1545 Council of Trent met to condemn Luther and Calvin
1789 Austrian Netherlands declared independence
1862 Battle of Fredericksburg
1920 Michelson measured size of fixed star
1937 U.S. gunboat *Panay* sunk by Japanese planes
1957 Earthquake in Outer Mongolia left 1,200 dead

During the last twenty-five years of his life, one talented and famous man, a former Cabinet member in fact, was invited on many occasions to meet with presidents of the United States. Politely, he declined every such request. It was not that he was eccentric or a hermit, or a political or personal enemy of any of the officials — he simply believed that he was a Jonah of the first order.

In 1901, President McKinley had asked him to join his party at the Pan-American Exposition in Buffalo. He reluctantly accepted, and was with the president when Leon Czolgosz fired the two shots which claimed McKinley's life eight days later.

Two decades earlier, while he was the secretary of War in Garfield's Cabinet, he had been summoned by the president a few days before Garfield was to leave on a tour of New England. For some reason, the Chief Executive asked him to recount all he knew about the events surrounding Lincoln's assassination sixteen years before and he obliged. Garfield was shot two days later.

It was understandable that Garfield had asked him about Lincoln's murder because he had been present at Ford's Theater on that tragic might. Quite a young man at the time, he had returned to his parents' home that evening and been given a message that they had gone to see the play *Our American Cousin*, and wished him to meet them there. He reached the theater just as Lincoln's body was being carried out to a house across the street, where the president died the next morning. He had been at his bedside when Lincoln expired.

The man's name was Robert Todd Lincoln: the president's son.

I don't care what's written about me so long as it isn't true.
Katharine Hepburn

Answer: All of them were early kings of England.

An Episcopal minister on vacation hired a guide to take him fishing in Maine. In the course of their conversation, the guide told the minister how he had once had Philips Brooks, author of the hymn "O Little Town of Bethlehem," as a customer. The minister immediately fell to talking about Brooks and what a great man he was.

"Yes," agreed the guide, "if it hadn't been for his awful language."

The minister was astonished, but the guide insisted that he'd heard Brooks swear. The minister still refused to believe it, and asked what the bishop had said.

The guide explained tht Brooks had hooked a fine big bass, fought the fish valiantly for several minutes, and then got him next to the boat. "I went to gaff the fish and darned if he didn't just then slip off the hook and swim away. I looked up at Mr. Brooks and said, 'Now, that's a damned shame,' and he replied, 'Yes, it is.' But that was the only time I heard him use such language."

The men who can be charged with the fewest failings are generally the most ready to allow them.
Samuel Johnson

"Tip," the word for a gratuity, is an acronym from the coffee houses of London of over two centuries ago. Customers who wished special attention be paid to them would drop a few pence into a collection box for the help, which was marked "To Insure Promptness." Later this was abbreviated to the initials T.I.P., and the bread of life of many service people was born.

Talk about Jonahs!

On February 28, 1844, President John Tyler and a number of Washington notables visited the U.S.S. *Princeton*, the first American propeller-driven warship. On its return up the Potomac river, a salute was fired from the vessel's biggest gun, the "Peacemaker." Though this cannon had been tested with a forty-nine-pound charge, it breeched the twenty-five-pound charge, and the secretary of the Navy, the secretary of State, the commanding officer of the *Princeton*, a former senator, a former ambassador, and the president's servant were all killed. Seventeen other passengers were injured. Tyler was below decks at the time.

DECEMBER 14

Notable Births

1503	Nostradamus	1919	Shirley Jackson
1546	Tycho Brahe	1935	Lee Remick
1896	Jimmy Doolittle	1946	Patty Duke
1917	Dan Dailey	1946	Stan Smith

Notable Events

1861	Prince Albert died
1890	First battle of Sioux Indian War
1894	Eugene Debs jailed for his part in railroad strikes
1911	357-foot Bromo Seltzer tower completed, Baltimore
1911	Amundsen reached South Pole
1937	Political parties banned in Brazil
1941	Japan attacked Hong Kong
1964	"Hurricane" Carter outpointed for middleweight crown

Question: What is the state pictured here?

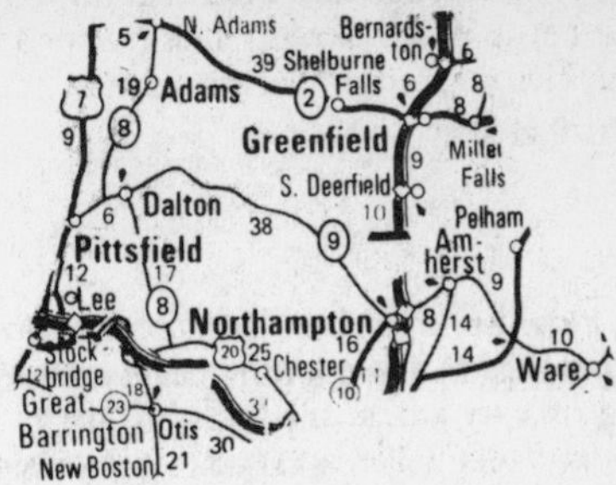

A Joplin, Missouri, man named Robert Kelley had a sore throat for over eight years. Finally he decided in December 1946, to have an X-ray taken. The film revealed that Kelley had a 3½-inch-long fishhook lodged in his throat, although he could not remember ever having swallowed it.

George Grant, an American living in London, made a fortune gambling that Prince Albert would die. In the autumn of 1861, the London papers reported that the Prince Consort's health was failing. Grant immediately bought up all the black crepe in the city and its environs, and waited. Sure enough, Albert died on this day in 1861, and Grant had all the mourning crepe cornered. He made a quarter of a million dollars on the deal.

The superior man understands what is right; the inferior man understands what will sell.

Confucius

Here lies the bones of David Jones,
Laid both dead and dumb.
He read a law and plead a cause
But died from drinking rum.

Over the grave of a brave engineer.

Until the brakes are turned on time,
Life's throttle-valve shut down,
He works to pilot in the crew
That wears the martyr's crown.
On schedule time, on upper grade
Along the homeward section,
He lands his train in God's roundhouse
The morn of resurrection.
His time is full, no wages docked,
His name on God's pay roll,
And transportation through to Heaven
A free pass for his soul.

You can't keep a good man down on the farm.

In May 1955, Thomas Gilmore escaped from Florida Prison Camp #8515 with the camp's car, the superintendent's pistol, shirt, and pants, and the camp's two bloodhounds.

The equipment used by astronomers must be extremely precise, and so must their calibrations be. An error of a 1/5,000 of an inch in a space of ten feet in the positioning of certain equipment will result in a mistake of over sixty-five million miles in calculating the distance to the *nearest* star.

Had I been present at the Creation, I would have given some useful hints for the better ordering of the universe.

Alfonso X of Spain

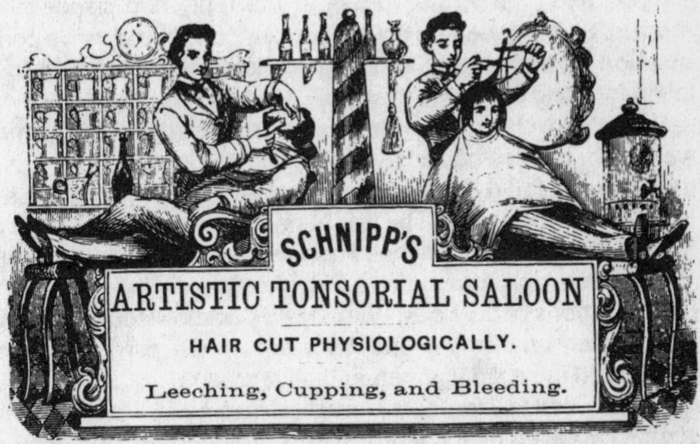

The barber pole originated at a time when barbers were as much bloodletters and surgeons as they were practitioners of the tonsorial art. The first poles were simply lengths of wood with strips of cloth wrapped around them, and they were used in the bloodletting procedure. When a patient was being blooded (the most popular time of the year was the spring) the barber-surgeon would have him grasp the pole to immobilize his arm and bring his veins closer to the surface. The cloth strips would be used as tourniquets and bandages. When the operation was over, the bloody strips would be wrapped around the pole again and the pole would be put outside the shop to dry. Gradually, the pole developed by association into the barber's sign, and a painted red-and-white pole later replaced the real one used for the operation. By the middle of the eighteenth century in England, it was mandatory for all barbers and surgeons to use a barber pole as their business sign. Those who didn't could legally be fined and their licenses were suspended or revoked.

Answer: Massachusetts.

DECEMBER 15

Question: *Sputnik*, the first satellite to orbit the earth, has become a household word. But do you remember the name of the Soviets' first manned space capsule? Do you remember the name of the first American in space?

Notable Births

1613	La Rouchfoucauld	1904	Kermit Bloomgarden
1888	Maxwell Anderson	1913	Muriel Rukeyser

Notable Events

1745	Frederick II victorious at Kesseldorf
1791	Bill of Rights adopted
1840	Napoleon's remains brought to Les Invalides
1854	First street-cleaning machine used
1930	Martial law declared in Spain
1936	21 American nations signed neutrality pact
1943	First Marine officer of Chinese descent commissioned
1943	Senate refused to promote Patton to full general
1945	Former Japanese prime minister Konoye committed suicide
1964	First quintuplet arrested; Marie Dionne, for assault
1965	Windstorm in Bangladesh killed 10,000 people

In Bangalore, India, in November, 1815, a private in the British Army named John Wilson was courtmartialed and sentenced to death for what a military judge ruled was an "act of rebellion." Wilson was a lifelong teetotaller, and had refused his daily ration of rum.

He was summarily shot.

The rights given you are the rights given you by this committee (HUAC). We will determine what rights you have and what rights you have not got.

J. Parnell Thomas

One night in 1921, two policemen on foot spotted a man carrying two bundles near India Wharf in Brooklyn. Before they could stop him, he tossed one of the burlap-wrapped packages into the water. The other proved to contain the dismembered parts of a woman. The cops took the man, a fellow by the name of Travia, into custody.

When he was quesitoned by detectives, Travia gave a candid account of the previous night's proceedings. He'd picked up a woman in a bar and had taken her to his apartment for a little romance. Once she was there, the woman, already drunk, demanded more liquor and started talking money. An argument ensued and Travia, also drunk at the time, had slapped her around. She'd ended up on the floor, unconscious from a combination of the beating and the alcohol. Travia said he'd then fallen into bed and gone to sleep.

When he woke in the morning he discovered that the woman was dead. He also had a terrible headache. He told police that at the time he could think of nothing else to do but chop up the body and dispose of it. The two bundles had only been a part of the corpse; the torso and head remained at his lodgings.

When the police went there with him they did indeed find the other portions of the body. With Travia's acknowledgment of his guilt (albeit unknowing and unmeant on his part) the police concluded they had an open-and-shut case.

Then Charles Norris, the medical examiner, came on the scene. He called their attention to the strange vermilion color of the decapitated head, which lay near the coal burning stove. No, he told the officers, Travia hadn't killed the woman. Her death had resulted from carbon monoxide poisoning. The fumes from the stove were responsible, just as they were for his headache. Had Travia been closer to the stove, or as drunk as the woman was, he too would have been dead. An autopsy confirmed the doctor's diagnosis, and at the hearing Travia was exonerated of all culpability and set free.

Well, almost free. Immediately after his release, Travia was served a summons for transporting a body on a public thoroughfare without a city permit.

Like a struggling spiritualist slipping her card into a passing coffin.

Derek Marlowe

It's been estimated that the Empress Josephine spent the equivalent of $200,000 a year on cosmetics.

Answer: Vostok; Alan B. Shepard, Jr.

DECEMBER 16

Notable Births

1770	Ludwig von Beethoven	1900	V.S. Pritchard
1775	Jane Austen	1901	Margaret Mead
1863	George Santayana	1917	Arthur C. Clarke
1899	Noel Coward	1939	Liv Ullmann

Notable Events

1740 Frederick II entered Silesia
1773 Boston Tea Party
1809 Napoleon and Josephine divorced
1835 Fire in New York city did $18 million damage
1857 Earthquake in Calabria left 10,000 dead
1879 Transvaal Republic proclaimed
1907 Great White Fleet embarked on circumnavigation
1916 Rasputin killed
1920 Earthquake in China left 180,000 dead
1931 Borah called for diplomatic relations with Russia
1960 Aircraft collision over New York city killed 134 people
1964 Ted Kennedy left hospital after 6 months with broken back

Beethoven was such a messy dresser that he was once arrested for vagrancy. He died of cirrhosis of the liver, a common ailment of alcoholics.

If the average man is made in God's image, then such a man as Beethoven or Aristotle is plainly superior to God.

H.L. Mencken

Grant Wood's best known painting, *American Gothic, 1930*, features two gaunt figures standing before what appears to be a farmhouse in the Midwest. The model for the woman was Grant Wood's sister; the man was the family's dentist. Wood later discovered that the model for the farmhouse was, in fact, a brothel.

The phrase, "by the skin of your teeth" comes from the Book of Job (19:20) and, because Job is known to be one of the oldest books in the Bible, this cliché is perhaps older than any other one in use today.

According to Sylvester Graham, excessive sex, even between married couples, can lead to:

> . . . langour, lassitude, muscular relaxation, general debility and heaviness, depression of spirits, loss of appetite, indigestion, faintness and sinking at the pit of the stomach, increased susceptibilities of the skin and lungs to all atmospheric changes, feebleness of circulation, chilliness, headache, melancholy, hypochondria, hysterics, feebleness of all the senses, impaired vision, loss of sight, weakness of the lungs, nervous cough, pulmonary consumption, disorders of the liver and kidneys, urinary difficulties, disorders of the genital organs, spinal diseases, weakness of the brain, loss of memory, epilepsy, insanity, apoplexy, abortions, premature births, and extreme feebleness, morbid predispositions, and an early death of offspring.

Questions: What is it that a man can use for shaving, brushing his teeth, and sleeping in?

What are the hardest things in the world to deal with?

The foregoing extract appears in a book entitled *A Lecture to Young Men on Chastity, Intended Also for the Serious Consideration of Parents and Guardians.* It was published in 1834.

Among Graham's other notable accomplishments was the invention of the graham cracker, which he believed was the healthiest food possible and a panacea for the world's ills, among which he numbered tobacco, coffee, tea, meat, corsets, and featherbeds. Specifically, it was claimed that graham crackers would quell the libidinous urgings of young women.

Do you know that, early in the 1970s, peanut butter was removed from the menus of Catholic school lunch programs in South Africa because a group of nuns found it to be an aphrodisiac?

How it got in my pajamas I'll never know.

Groucho Marx

The more I think you over the more it comes to me what an unmitigated Middle Victorian ass you are.

H.G. Wells

Answers: A razor, a toothbrush, and pajamas.

Old cards.

DECEMBER 17

Question: If people lived forever, which of these people would be the oldest and the youngest?
Giuseppe Garibaldi
Sam Houston
Davy Crockett

Notable Births

1778	Humphrey Davy	1886	Ty Cobb
1807	John Greenleaf Whittier	1894	Arthur Fiedler
1830	Jules Goncourt	1903	Erskine Caldwell
1873	Ford Madox Ford	1929	William Safire

Notable Events

875	Charles II crowned Holy Roman Emperor
1791	One-way traffic initiated in New York City
1819	New Granada and Caracas joined to create Columbia
1903	Wright Brother flight at Kitty Hawk
1939	*Graf Spee* scuttled off Uruguay
1940	FDR proposed lend-lease plan
1961	323 died in Brazilian circus fire
1969	Marriage of Tiny Tim

Sarah Jacob, a young girl from Lletherrnnoryadd-ucha, Wales, gained some notoriety in 1869 because, it seemed, she got along very well without having to eat. Her parents, an uneducated farm couple, said that when their daughter was ten years old she had suffered a convulsion, and from that time had required no nourishment whatsoever. Word of Sarah's remarkable fast spread, and she soon became a popular attraction.

The vicar of the parish, the Reverend Evans Jones, doubted the story, and so asked to be allowed to observe her. Permission was granted, and he watched Sarah for a week. At the end of that time, he had not seen her take anything to eat or drink, and so was convinced she needed no nourishment. Rabid as only a convert can be, the clergyman took it upon himself to put the child in the public eye as a miracle of God. He published an account of her life in February 1869, and curiousity seekers from all over Britain began to flock to the tiny Welsh village. Jones acted as the host for the visitors, and was often rewarded with donations for his parish from the pious who were convinced that God was caring for the child.

But a doctor named Robert Fowler would not believe that she never ate. When he first visited the young woman he heard her stomach rumbling, as if she were digesting food, and he also learned that Sarah, despite not eating in two years, still had normal bodily excretions. He asked if he might observe her. The Reverend Jones, truly believing his charge was genuine, immediately agreed. Sarah's parents did so more reluctantly.

Fowler proceeded to conduct the first secure vigil of Sarah Jacob, using several teams of assistants who watched her around the clock. Soon Sarah grew pale and very weak. She begged for food. The Reverend Jones realized then that her parents had deceived him, and pleaded with them to let her eat. The Jacobs would not admit the hoax (they'd made a good deal of money off their daughter), and prohibited anyone from feeding her.

On December 17, 1869, supposedly two years, two months, and a day after her last meal, Sarah Jacobs died of starvation. She had actually been without food for less than three weeks.

Useless to sprinkle salt on tail of time.

Charlie Chan

Warner Brothers Studios picked up the movie rights to an obscure play about forty years ago, called *Everybody Comes to Rick's.* None of the top brass at the studio was especially enthusiastic about its possibilities, but the feeling was that it might make a nice little "B" vehicle for Ronald Reagan and Ann Sheridan. Apparently, neither of them wanted it. Then the two leads were offered to George Raft and Hedy Lamarr. That, too, fell through. At last the studio found two actors who would agree to appear in the film, and production finally got underway.

But problems with the film didn't stop there. No one, including the scriptwriters, was especially happy with the screenplay, and the writers and several of the actors would occasionally retire from the set to do some improvising over a few bottles of whiskey. The final script for the next scene was often in the actor's hands only a few minutes after the previous scene had finished shooting.

The two actors who ended up in the movie weren't exactly unknown at the time — Humphrey Bogart and Ingrid Bergman — but no one expected that the Academy Awards for that year for Best Director, Best Screenplay, and Best Picture would be won by the picture *Casablanca.*

For what it's worth: Not only did George Raft decline the role of Rick in *Casablanca,* he also turned down the parts Bogart eventually played in *High Sierra* and *The Maltese Falcon.*

Back in 1877, a fellow in Arizona named George Warren made a fair amount of money and a large reputation as a sprinter. He'd take on all comers in the 100-yard dash, either for a flat prize or a percentage of the gambling action these challenges always engendered among the spectators. Despite staking most of his opponents to substantial head starts, Warren almost always won. Soon there were no people left to race against.

That's when Warren got careless and began boasting he could take a horse and rider on over a 100-yard long course, down and back. Soon enough the dare was accepted, and the prize money agreed upon: Warren's share in the Copper Queen mine against a purse of $5,000.

Warren did, in fact, beat the horse and rider to the halfway point, but he was no match for them down the stretch, and he lost his share of the Copper Queen.

Too bad: that portion of the mine that he lost that day would have eventually made him over $20,000,000!

Statistics produced by the National Safety Council some years back (before the fifty-five mph speed limit) revealed that for every ten mph above forty-five mph that a car involved in an accident was traveling, the chances of a passenger in the car being killed increased by 250 percent. At forty-five mph there was one chance in 125 of a fatality; at fifty-five mph one in fifty; at sixty-five one in twenty; and at seventy-five mph, one in eight.

People who insist on drinking before driving are putting the quart before the hearse.

Laurence J. Peter

Answer: Davy Crockett; Giuseppe Garibaldi.

Notable Births

1707	Charles Wesley	1888	Robert Moses
1779	Joseph Grimaldi	1910	Abe Burrows
1835	Lyman Abbott	1913	Willy Brandt
1863	Oliver Herford	1916	Betty Grable
1870	Saki	1918	Ossie Davis

Notable Events

1398 Delhi taken by Tamerlane, 100,000 prisoners slaughtered
1717 Prussian colonies in Africa sold to Dutch
1839 First celestial photograph taken
1865 Slavery officially abolished in United States
1903 Treaty gave United States Panama Canal rights
1931 Jack "Legs" Diamond murdered
1933 Chaco Truce ended border dispute between Bolivia and Paraguay
1936 First giant panda arrived in United States
1961 India seized Portuguese enclaves
1964 LBJ announced United States would build sea-level canal in central America

While she is in estrus, the female chimpanzee may engage in copulation as often as twenty times a day.

The gentleman who has come down to us as Tamerlane (from Timur-i-leng, meaning Timur the Lame) was not a merciful fellow, although he did have an appreciation of what frightened people the most. He used this gift to instill in the minds of his enemies just what kind of treatment they could expect to receive if they chose to stand against his advances. At Isfahan, Baghdad, and Delhi, he left pyramids of the skulls of thousands of his victims. Once, he simply walled up two thousand men alive in a tomb at Sebsewar, Persia.

A gentleman is someone who is never unintentionally rude.
Oscar Wilde

Answer: Virginia.

Question: What is the state shown here?

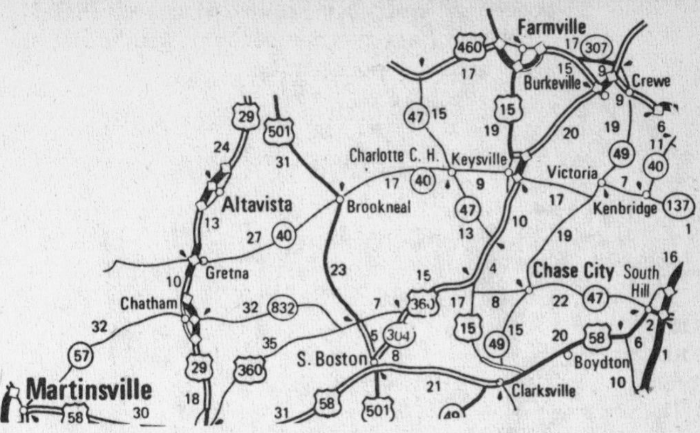

The phrase "to run the gauntlet" comes from a British corruption of a Swedish punishment dating from the time of the Thirty Years War. It has nothing to do with gauntlets (gloves) except by derivation. The Swedish word for it is *gatlopp*, or gate-run, used to describe a particular ordeal in which a man must run a certain length while other men are placed with switches or other weapons alongside it, beating him as he runs.

The court jester and the court fool were entirely different offices. The fool was a kind of village idiot, who was often physically misshapen and was kept because the courtiers found his stupid antics amusing. The court jester was physically normal and had a superior mind. His office was to amuse the court with his intelligence and sarcastic wit.

Truth is the nursing mother of genius.
Margaret Fuller

DECEMBER 19

Question: A man put his license plates on upside down. The police read a number that way, which was 78,633 more than the correct number. What was the man's plate number supposed to be?

Notable Births

1852	Albert Michelson	1907	H. Allen Smith
1894	Ford Frick	1910	Jean Genet
1901	Oliver LaFarge	1920	David Susskind
1902	Ralph Richardson	1934	Al Kaline
1906	Leonid Breznhev	1939	Cicely Tyson

Notable Events

1154 Coronation of Henry II, House of Plantagenet began
1777 Washington encamped at Valley Forge
1842 United States recognized Hawaiian independence
1871 Corrugated paper patented
1907 Mining disaster at Jacob's Creek, Pennsylvania, killed 154 men
1920 First indoor curling rink opened, Brookline, Massachusetts
1974 Rockefeller sworn in as vice-president

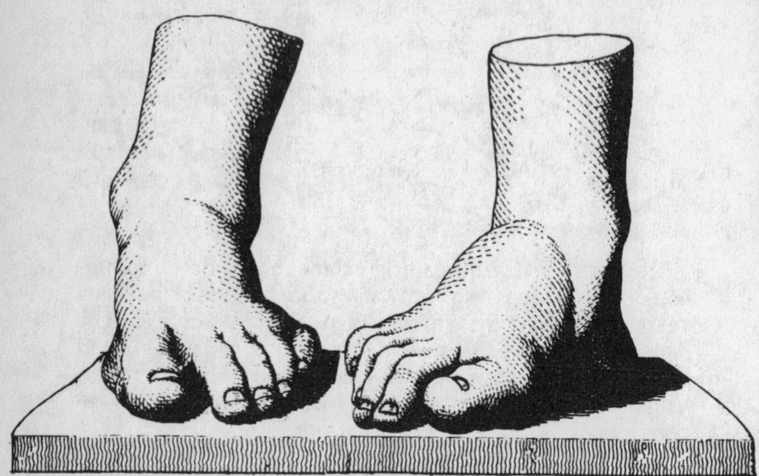

Shoes that were differently designed to fit the left and right feet did not catch on in the United States until after the Civil War.

The mausoleum which houses the remains of Mr. and Mrs. Warren G. Harding cost $800,000 when it was constructed in 1927.

Peter Hurkos is a world-renowned psychic whose reputation has led to him being brought into everything from treasure hunts to police investigations. He was hired to hunt treasure by a wealthy gentleman of Roubaix, France, in 1951. The man had hidden a tin box full of gold in his garden when the private ownership of gold was illegal in France. Now that it had been legalized, he wanted to cash in his horde, but he could not find it. He offered Hurkos a quarter of the approximately $30,000-worth of gold the box contained if Hurkos could find it for him.

Hurkos surveyed the garden, and paced back and forth across it several times. No clues. More of the same — still nothing came into his mind. Then he was suddenly "drawn" to the greenhouse, where he began overturning all the flower boxes. The gardener tried to make him stop, but Hurkos wouldn't be deterred. Soon he'd found the chest. The gardener subsequently confessed that he'd found it in the course of his work and had been planning to remove it from the property. The case was solved.

Hurkos, however wonderful his powers may be, isn't perfect. If he were, he'd have been able to read his employer's mind. The man refused to pay the amount he'd promised, pointing out that there was nothing in writing to effect their purported agreement.

A verbal contract isn't worth the paper it's written on.

Samuel Goldwyn

The biggest liar in the world is They Say.

Robert Louis Stevenson

Much has been made of Governor Jerry Brown of California taking an impromptu jaunt to Japan, which really was undertaken on the spur of the moment. Well, former President Richard Nixon also boasts not one but two similar treks — into Russia. When he was in Finland on business in 1965, Nixon hopped on a train to Moscow without warning. Twenty hours later, at 11 P.M., he strode up to the residence of Premier Khrushchev, wanting to talk. The Soviet leader was not in, so Nixon had to content himself with debating the deputy director of the Moscow State University and a policeman.

Two years later, he again made an unannounced and apparently unplanned trip to Moscow, once more to see Khrushchev. As usual, the Russian was not to be found, and Nixon ended up at the site of his famous Kitchen Debate, Sokolniki Park, where he reportedly tried to harangue passersby into discussing politics with him.

A man should keep his friendships in constant repair.

Samuel Johnson

During one of the big blizzards which hit the Northeast during the winter of 1977, the firm of Cartelli Pontiac in Massachusetts jokingly offered a discount of one dollar off the sticker price of any used car for each snowball a buyer brought in. Mrs. Martha Paquette of South Hadley gathered her family and friends together for four hours of snowball making, then trekked off to Cartelli's. She brought 1,834 snowballs with her, and got a 1969 Catalina for $61.

I've realized, after fourteen months in this country, the value of money, whether it is clean or dirty.

Nguyen Cao Ky

The first roll of commercially produced toilet paper was marketed in 1857. For fifty cents the consumer received 500 sheets of a specially treated paper, each watermarked "Gayetty," after the manufacturer. In addition to being hygienic, the product also claimed to cure piles.

Answer: 10968.

Notable Births

1853	René Bazin	1902	Max Lerner
1868	Henry Firestone	1904	Irene Dunne
1900	Gabby Hartnett	1911	Hortense Callisher

Notable Events

1780 Conscientious objectors to Revolutionary War released from prison
1803 United States took title to Louisiana Purchase
1820 Missouri levied bachelor tax
1860 South Carolina seceded
1893 Georgia enacted first antilynch law
1924 Hitler released from prison after beer hall *putsch*
1928 First international dog sled mail run began
1976 Death of Chicago mayor Richard Daley

Adolf Hitler believed a lot of strange things, including the idea that the earth was hollow, with holes at the poles. He believed this strongly enough to have a set of variables calculated on this premise, and ordered various branches of his military communications and espionage networks to use the figures instead of the commonly accepted "fudge-factors" for gravity, and so forth. Of course, this screwed up their work royally, but orders *were* orders!

This notion of Hitler's probably wasn't directly responsible for Germany losing World War II, but it definitely didn't help the Nazis win it.

Logic is the art of going wrong with confidence.

Joseph Wood Krutch

A journey of a thousand miles . . .

In the autumn of 1956, in Brixham, England, Rhoda Clark refused to pay the fee of one pound for her dog license. She said she did it as a protest against "H-bomb tests, German rearmament, the flouting of the Magna Carta and the Declaration of Human Rights, and British Government policy."

The way of the world is to praise dead saints and to persecute living ones.

Nathaniel Howe

Question: About how fast can these animals go?
white-tailed deer
rabbit
gray fox
wild turkey

At the end of the eighteenth century, the government of the Pontine region of Italy discovered that a strain of wild rice, which had accidentally developed there, was far superior in taste and nutritional value to any other in the Western world. Aware that a rice monopoly would be the best of all investments for the future, a total embargo against its exportation was enacted and rigidly enforced.

Several years later, an American gentleman who knew of the rice's reputation was being given a tour of the region. As he and his escorts strolled the marshes, the man casually plucked the heads off some of the plants and surreptitiously put them in his pocket. When he returned to the United States, he selected the marshy areas of the eastern Carolinas for the seeds' cultivation. The rice thrived there.

That's how Thomas Jefferson brought Carolina wild rice to America.

Practical politics consists in ignoring facts.

Henry Adams

I've never known a country to be starved into democracy.

George Aiken

Only about two percent of American women can stand on their heads without help.

The world's first international dogsled mail, which started on this day in 1928, ran from Lewiston, Maine, to Montreal. Of the 600 miles in the journey, 540 were run over bare ground.

Answer: 30, 35, 42, 15 mph.

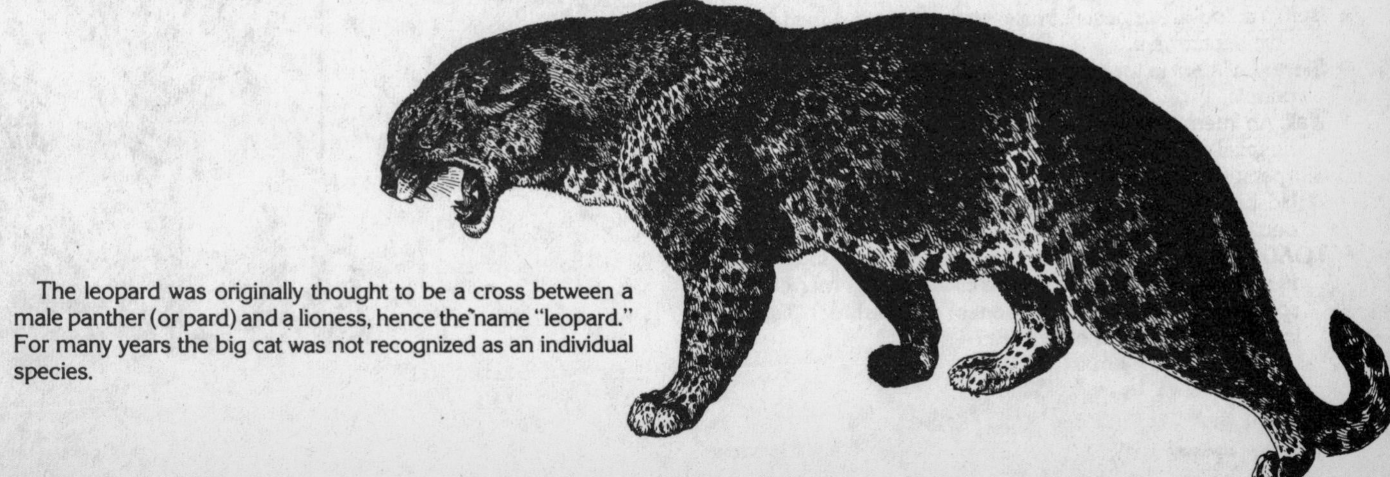

The leopard was originally thought to be a cross between a male panther (or pard) and a lioness, hence the name "leopard." For many years the big cat was not recognized as an individual species.

DECEMBER 21

Question: What is the state shown here?

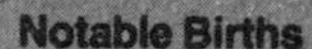

Notable Births

1117	Thomas à Becket	1917	Heinrich Böll
1804	Benjamin Disraeli	1918	Kurt Waldheim
1842	Peter Kropotkin	1937	Jane Fonda
1879	Josef Stalin	1940	Frank Zappa
1892	Walter Hagen	1944	Michael Tilson-Thomas

Notable Events

1192	Richard the Lionheart taken prisoner in Austria
1849	First ice-skating club formed, Philadelphia
1913	First crossword puzzle published
1931	Winston Churchill hit by car in New York City; said accident was his own fault
1932	House approved 3.2-proof beer
1945	Ezra Pound declared insane
1954	British High Court of Chivalry met for the first time in 223 years
1964	House of Commons voted to abolish death penalty
1974	Charges brought against CIA for domestic spying

All occupations tend to develop their own slang terms, jargon which is mostly understood only by people in the particular industry. This slang abounds in the military, in sports, and in advertising ("Let's put it on the train and see if it gets off at Westport").

Doctors have their own private language, too, a code that often serves to relieve the tensions of life and death around the hospital, as well as to mask from the public some of the less sophisticated happenings associated with the profession.

Black Crow: The award given annually to the physician who has succeeded in performing the most postmortems.

Blue Blazers: The term applied to blond, blue-eyed, fraternity-type hospital administrators — Young Turks whose function is either unknown, or is liaison with the public.

BMS: Best Medical School, or Best Medical Student, somewhat derisively applied to overachievers who succeed in increasing a doctor's workload in the interest of proper medical care.

Bounce: To get rid of a patient to another department of the hospital, and thus unload whatever responsibility the patient may engender.

Boxed: What happens to a player who strikes out for the last time. The box, needless to say, is a coffin.

GOMER: Get Out of My Emergency Room, used when an admittee is beyond medical help.

LOL in NAD: Little Old Lady in No Apparent Distress. Said when the patient is diagnosed as not in serious condition, contrary to said patient's belief.

M & M: Mortality and Morbidity, a regular rap session devoted to the discussion of mistakes and lessons learned.

MOR, ROR: Marriage On Rocks, Relationship On Rocks — a condition common to internship and its long hours, which often strains two people beyond their breaking point.

Pipes: Large veins, easily punctured by needles. Interns love patients with good pipes.

Buff: To "polish" a patient, make him or her look good for the next department.

Sieve: An intern in the emergency room who lets in far too many people.

Wall: An intern in the emergency room who does not let into the hospital patients who should be admitted.

Slurpers: Doctors devoted to the quest of becoming the chief of Hospital Administration; applies sometimes to non-medical personnel as well who are excessively upwardly mobile.

TOAD: Because of its basically negative connotations, this is seldom used in places where civilians (non-medical personnel like families and loved ones) can overhear it. It stands for "Trashy Old Alcoholic Derelict."

⚜

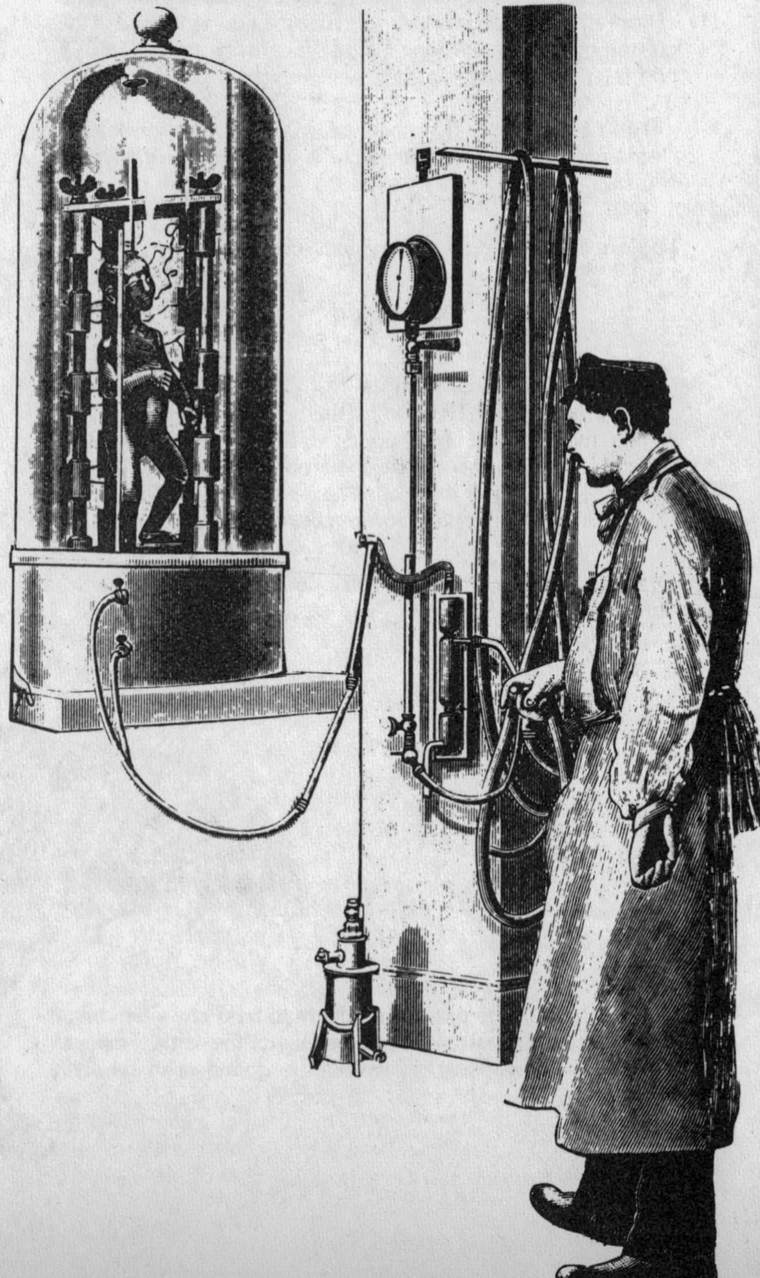

Answer: New York.

DECEMBER 22

Notable Births

1639	Jean Racine	1901	Andre Kostelanetz
1696	James Oglethorpe	1905	Kenneth Rexroth
1856	Frank Kellogg	1912	Lady Bird Johnson
1858	Giacomo Puccini	1917	Gene Rayburn
1869	Edward Arlington Robinson	1924	Ruth Roman
1882	Deems Taylor	1944	Steve Carlton

Notable Events

1440 Execution of Bluebeard
1894 Dreyfus found guilty in treason frame-up
1928 Commission appointed to investigate German reparation payments
1956 First gorilla born in captivity, Ohio
1976 *Argo Merchant* oil spill

Question: How's your movie memory? In what years were these films Academy Award winners?

You Can't Take It with You
Casablanca
Lawrence of Arabia
The Lost Weekend

Mass murders and murderers, whether political, religious, sexual, or insane, have always been around. Like Bram Stoker's *Dracula* (January 11), there was a real man on whom the story of Bluebeard is based. He was the Frenchman Giles de Laval, the Marshall de Retz, who was born about 1396. Upon the death of his father in 1416, de Laval took a commission in the king's army, and steadily rose in rank. In 1429 he was one of Joan of Arc's captains at Rouen, and the next year he was made counselor and chamberlain to the king. Throughout his first thirty-five years he gave no indication of his future depravity.

In 1432, he left the army and settled down to a life of leisure—his marriage and two subsequent inheritances had left him the richest man in France. Although he had earlier been a conservative and highly respectable gentleman, he now began to live in an outrageously expensive and debauched manner. He kept his personal cavalry of 200 horses in the finest of uniforms, maintained a retinue of fifty personal servants, and had enormous staffs to run his many estates. He built new chapels for his priests, and clothed them in expensive vestments.

Soon he began to have to sell his properties to support his costly lifestyle. His family eventually filed suit against him for his spendthrift habits. De Laval then sought out alchemists and sorcerers for help, and even made a pact with the devil in an attempt to continue his life in the way he'd grown accustomed.

It appears that the devil took him up on the contract. At about this time, de Laval began his vicious tortures of children. He or his servants would either trick a child into one of his castles or he would talk a peasant child's parents into giving him the boy or girl into his care. In either case, the children would never be heard from again. Once inside the castle's walls, they would be humiliated, tortured, and then killed in every way imaginable. They were then dismembered, and their blood, hearts, and entrails used in satanic ceremonies. Suspicions against de Laval grew until finally in 1440 he was arrested. He then confessed to his appalling degradations.

Although he was tried only on the evidence of the remains of 126 young people found on two of his properties, in eight years he was probably responsible for hundreds of ruthless murders.

Just before Christmas in 1946, The Cordelia Hosiery Shop in Atlanta put 300 pairs of sheer black nylon stockings on display in its front windows to lure customers. The store was sold out of the then rare commodity within half an hour, when the nylons were seen by a group of girls in town for a Salvation Army convention.

Good fisherman, like clever merchant, knows lures of bright colors.

Charlie Chan

Just before Jimmy Carter took office, a black minister named King applied for membership in the all-white Plains Baptist Church, which Carter attended. It was as much a publicity ploy for King as it was an action to bring attention to the segregated nature of the church.

Many years ago, another story was told of a deeply religious black man who tried to join a white, upper-crust church. The church's pastor put the man off with gentle arguments, and sensing the real reason for the church's position, the black man said he'd just go away for a few days and ask the Lord what He thought he should do.

Meeting on the street a week later, the two men stopped and exchanged greetings. Then the minister asked the old man if he'd talked with God about his application.

"Yes, sir, I sure did, and the Lord told me it wasn't any use. He said He Himself had been trying to get into your church for years, and He's never made it yet, either!"

I sometimes think that God in creating man somewhat overestimated his ability.

Oscar Wilde

Answer: 1938; 1941; 1962; 1945.

DECEMBER 23

Questions: What's the difference between a crown prince and the water in a fountain?

What's the difference between an auction and seasickness?

Notable Births

1805	Joseph Smith	1925	Harry Guardino
1862	Connie Mack	1926	Robert Bly
1872	John Marin	1935	Paul Hornung
1888	J. Arthur Rank	1941	Elizabeth Hartman
1900	Otto Soglow	1942	Jerry Koosman
1918	José Greco	1945	Rick Wohlhuter

Notable Events

1728 Treaty of Berlin signed between Russia and Germany
1783 George Washington resigned his commission
1876 Turkish constitution approved
1933 Train wreck near Paris killed 200 people
1972 5,000 died in Nicaraguan earthquake
1973 French Caravel crashed in Morocco, killing 106

Baseball magnate Connie Mack was out hunting in North Carolina once when he came upon a young man with a bagful of squirrels. Mr. Mack, observing that the boy carried no weapon, asked how he'd taken the animals. The teenager explained he'd thrown rocks at them. Mack couldn't believe it, and asked for a demonstration. The boy found a rock, spotted a squirrel some seventy-five feet away, and let fly.

Right between the eyes.

Mack was astonished, and was ready to sign him on the spot for the Athletics. "Son, you'll be the greatest southpaw the world has ever seen," he told him.

The boy disagreed. "No, I won't, sir, begging your pardon."

"What do you mean?" asked Mack.

"I ain't a lefty. It's just if I use my right arm I mangles 'em too badly."

On December 23, 1854, an earthquake in Japan created a tidal wave which was recorded 4,800 miles away in San Francisco, twelve hours, sixteen minutes later. The swell there was eight inches high, and lasted for a half an hour. It was followed at one-hour intervals by seven other waves, each gradually smaller than the previous one. The average speed of the initial wave across the Pacific was 390 miles an hour.

Answers: One is heir to the throne, the other thrown in the air.

One is a sale of effects, the other the effects of a sail.

DECEMBER 24

Notable Births

1745	Benjamin Rush	1822	Matthew Arnold
1754	George Crabbe	1907	I.F. Stone
1809	Kit Carson	1907	Cab Calloway
1818	J.P. Joulé	1922	Ava Gardner

Notable Events

1618 Peace made among Turkey, Sweden, and Poland
1784 Methodist Episcopal Church in America founded
1814 Treaty of Ghent ended War of 1812
1851 Library of Congress destroyed by fire
1889 Bicycle backpedal brake patented
1933 Armenian archbishop assassinated in New York City
1941 Japanese took Wake Island
1943 Ike named to command invasion of Europe
1948 First completely solar-heated house occupied, Dover, Massachusetts
1966 U.S. CL-44 crashed into Vietnamese village, 129 killed

Washington Crossing the Delaware is one of America's most famous paintings, but in the interests of drama and composition, the artist, Emanuel Leutze, made several blunders. Of course, Washington should never have stood up in such a small boat, that much is evident to anyone. But had Washington stood up during the real crossing, there wouldn't have been too much to worry about: the boats the troops used were Durham boats, forty- to sixty-feet long. The flag shown is wrong, too. The event took place on Christmans Eve in 1776; but the ensign shown in the painting wasn't adopted by the Continental Congress until the following year. It's also doubtful whether the soldiers would have been holding their muskets barrel-up in a sleet storm.

Kit Carson ran away from the saddlemaker to whom he was apprenticed in 1826. His master missed him so much that he posted a reward of one cent.

Question: What is the state shown here?

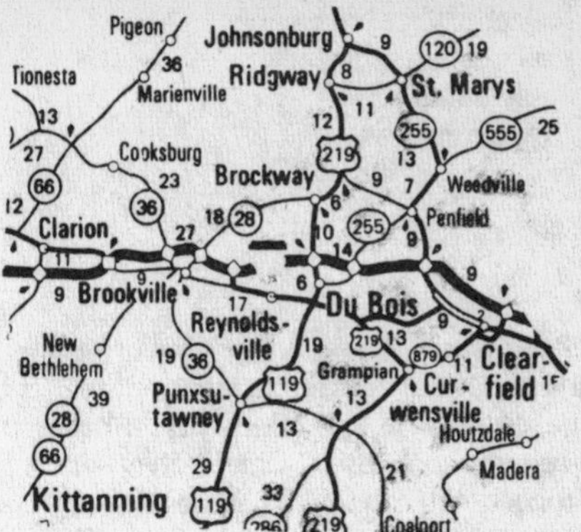

Christmas 1835 was supposed to be "Rebellion Day" in America. An ambitious Arkansas criminal named John Murrel had recruited an army of five thousand lawbreakers through his nationwide contacts, who were ready to descend on banks, jewelry stores, and other depositories of wealth. Another part of his plan involved torching all the major cities of the South as well as scores of smaller metropolises nationally. It was his belief that this enormous episode of crime would hopelessly befuddle law enforcement agencies and permit him and his accomplices all to make clean getaways.

One person usually can't keep a secret, and five thousand people certainly could not. Local, state, and federal authorities got wind of the plan early on, and most of the would-be lawbreakers were taken into custody before the day set for the crime wave.

Today's rebel is tomorrow's tyrant.

Will and Ariel Durant

Answer: Pennsylvania.

DECEMBER 25

Question: Within ten years, when were the following invented?
electric vacuum cleaner
air cushioned vehicle
rifle bullet
gyrocompass

In Saint Petersburg, during a Christmas masquerade ball in 1804, a party of several celebrants arrived at mid-evening dressed in Chinese costume and bearing on a palanquin an individual they referred to as their "Chief." They set the litter on the floor and proceeded to do their "national dance" around it. The stoic Chief was unaffected, inscrutable even. Then the bearers drank, mingled with the crowd, and made merry. Although the Chief was unsociable, the other guests thought it was part of his act, or perhaps the result of a drunken stupor.

In the course of the next hour, the attendants took their leave, apparently on their way to other festivals that night. For some reason their leader remained behind. Finally, after almost all the guests had gone, the party's host pulled down the Chinese Chief's mask — and discovered a corpse. The body was never identified, and the murderers were never caught.

Life is not a festival or a feast, it is a predicament.
George Santayana

Notable Births

1821	Clara Barton	1914	Tony Martin
1883	Maurice Utrillo	1918	Anwar Sadat
1892	Rebecca West	1924	Rod Serling
1904	Gladys Swarthout	1934	Carlos Castaneda
1906	Clark Clifford	1946	Larry Csonka

Notable Events

800	Charlemagne crowned Holy Roman Emperor
967	Otho II Crowned Holy Roman Emperor
1066	William the Conqueror crowned king of England
1620	Puritans at Plymouth started first common house
1776	Washington crossed the Delaware and attacked Trenton
1884	1,000 people died in Spanish earthquake
1930	Lake Placid bobsled run opened to public
1941	Hong Kong surrendered to Japan
1950	Stone of Scone stolen from Westminster Abbey
1971	Fire in Seoul, South Korea hotel left 162 dead

When the Puritans landed in Massachusetts, they were very surprised to hear an Indian addressing them in broken English. This was Squanto, whose help probably was responsible for the survival of Plymouth in its first two years. He astonished them further with his fluent Spanish; he'd lived in Spain for several years, and had made the round trip from America with two groups of Spanish explorers. Yes, he knew some French, too.

Answer: 1907; 1877; 1849; 1911.

DECEMBER 26

Notable Births

1716	Thomas Gray	1893	Mao Tse-tung
1837	George Dewey	1921	Steve Allen
1891	Henry Miller	1927	Alan King

Notable Events

1785 Religious tests abolished in Virginia
1793 Allies defeated French at Weissenburg
1805 Pennsylvania Academy of Fine Arts established
1865 Coffee percolator patented
1877 Socialist Labor Party held first convention, Newark
1890 Britain occupied Sikkim, Uganda, and Mashonaland
1932 Earthquake in China killed 70,000 people
1943 U.S. government seized railroads
1972 Death of Harry Truman

It so incloseth the oriface of the stomach, and fortifies the heart within, that it is very good to help digestion; and therefore of great use to be taken about three or four o'clock in the afternoon, as well as in the morning. It much quickens the spirits, and makes the heart lightsome; it is good against sore eyes, and the better if you hold your head over it and take in the steam that way. It supresseth fumes exceedingly, and therefore is good against the headache, and will very much stop any defluxion of rheums, that distill from the head upon the stomach, and so prevent and help consumptions and the cough of the lungs. It is excellent to prevent and cure the dropsy, gout, and scurvy. It is known by experience to be better than any other drying drink for people in years, or children that have any running humours upon them, as the king's evil, etc. It is a most excellent remedy against the spleen, hypochondriac winds, and the like. It will prevent drowsiness, and make one fit for business, if one have occasion to watch, and therefore you are not to drink of it after supper unless you intend to be watchful, for it will hinder sleep for three or four hours.

It is observed that in Turkey, where this is generally drunk, that they are not troubled with the stone, gout, dropsy, or scurvy, and that their skins are exceedingly clear and white. It is neither laxative nor restringent.

What's this? Another liquor advertisement from the days of Queen Elizabeth? Not quite, but close. It comes from an advertising handbill for England's first coffeehouse, *circa* 1652.

The S in Harry S Truman is not an initial — it's the former president's full middle "name." When Truman was born his parents couldn't decide whether to name him after his paternal grandfather Anderson Shippe Truman, or his maternal one, Solomon Young. They compromised on S.

One Matthew Hopkins was the official witchfinder for Essex, England, at about the time of the reign of James I. In his most productive year, he found sixty witches, all of whom were hanged. Hopkins attributed his success to his knowledge of witch marks — warts, moles, scorbutic spots, and wens — which, he claimed, were used as teats to suckle imps and familiars.

Of course, not everyone with a wart was a soldier of Satan, so many accused witches were forced to undergo trial by water. Suspects were tied with one hand fastened to the opposite foot and then thrown into a pond or a river. If they floated they were witches; if they sank they were only drowned, and therefore quite innocent of witchcraft. King James himself justified this process by reasoning that an individual who floated had renounced his baptism to ally himself with the devil, and therefore the water would not receive him.

Question: How's your movie memory? In what years were these films Academy Award winners?
An American in Paris
The Greatest Show on Earth
Midnight Cowboy
Tom Jones

The worst men often give the best advice.

Nathan Bailey

Answer: 1951, 1952, 1969, 1963.

DECEMBER 27

Question: What is the state shown here?

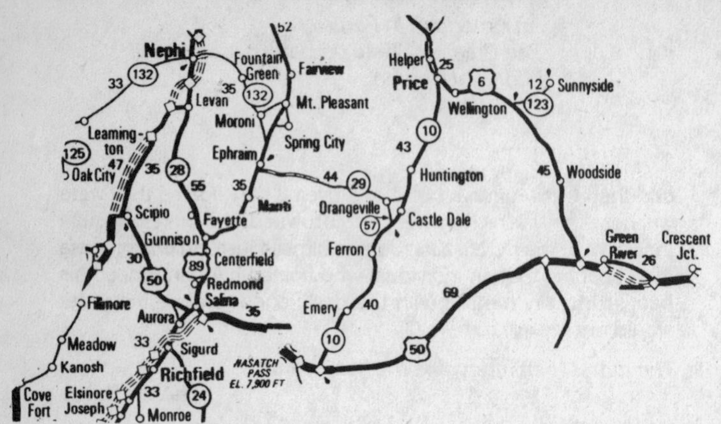

Notable Births

1571	Johann Kepler	1901	Marlene Dietrich
1822	Louis Pasteur	1906	Oscar Levant
1879	Sydney Greenstreet	1910	Charles Olson

Notable Events

1794 France invaded Holland
1845 First anesthesia administered during childbirth
1902 Britain broke off German alliance negotiations
1938 First skimobile began operation, North Conway, New Hampshire
1939 Earthquake in Turkey took 23,000 lives
1975 Mine explosion in Chasnala, India, killed 431 people

The first riot in United States history (that is, after the Declaration of Independence) was, surprisingly enough, against the doctors of New York City. It wasn't the result of malpractice or high fees though, as we in these days might reasonably expect. A medical student's ghoulish sense of humor occasioned the riot in 1788, which left at least eight people dead and injured scores of others.

Young John Hicks, Jr., was dissecting a corpse one day in the course of his studies when he happened to notice a crowd of small boys observing him. Deciding he'd like to be rid of this annoying audience, he took a severed arm and waved it at the children, exclaiming, "This is your mother's arm! I just dug it out of her grave! If you don't get out of here I'll slap you with it!" That dispersed the boys all right, and set in motion a very strange set of events.

At the time, there were next to no legal ways for a doctor to acquire a body for medical research or teaching purposes. Graverobbers, or "resurrectionists" as they were known, did a thriving business. One of their most common methods was to loot a new grave on Long Island, which was then sparsely populated, buy a ticket on the ferry for their "drunken friend," and smuggle the body into one of Manhattan's hospitals or medical schools under cover of darkness. It may well have been through this procedure that New York Hospital procured the body that Hicks was working on at the time of the incident.

As it happened, one of the children he threatened had lost his mother recently. The boy told the story to his father, who then went to the cemetery to check up on his wife's grave. He found it dug up, the coffin battered in, and the remains gone. The news spread quickly through lower Manhattan, and a mob of several thousand people soon formed.

The rioters marched to the hospital intent on lynching every medical man in the place. The doctors there had no idea why they were being besieged, but most of them reasoned with their feet and fled through the rear windows of the building before it was completely surrounded. One doctor and three students who'd remained to try to protect the equipment were fortunately saved by the police who had arrived by that time, but the authorities were far too few to keep the rioters from destroying all the equipment and medical specimens they could find.

Governor Clinton assumed that the rioters had spent their rage on the first day, and so did not take the precautions he should have. The events of the next day taught him never to trust that assumption again. One Sir John Temple had his house ransacked, some of the mob having equated "Sir John" with "surgeon." John Jay, soon to become the first chief justice of the Supreme Court, was knocked unconscious by a rock when he strayed too close to the fray, and Baron von Steuben, the German officer who'd become a hero during the Revolution, was knocked on the head with a brick as he pleaded with Clinton not to give the militiamen orders to fire. Since the governor was sensitive to the fact that his failure to act decisively the day before had led to further injury and property damage, he did finally give the order. By the time the episode was over, property damage ran well into the tens of thousands of dollars, dozens of people had been severely injured, and eight were dead.

Answer: Utah.

DECEMBER 28

Notable Births

1721	Madame de Pompadour	1911	Sam Levenson
1856	Woodrow Wilson	1913	Lou Jacobi
1905	Earl "Fatha" Hines	1925	Hildegarde Neff
1908	Lew Ayres	1934	Maggie Smith

Notable Events

1828	Earthquake in Japan killed 30,000 people
1835	Seminole War began
1850	Rangoon, Burma, destroyed by fire
1869	Chewing gum patented
1948	Egyptian premier Pasha assassinated
1974	Earthquake in Pakistan killed 5,200 people

Question: How's your movie memory? In what years were these films Academy Award winners?
Gentlemen's Agreement
Rebecca
The Apartment
Around the World in 80 Days

A few quick notes about John Chapman, better known as Johnny Appleseed:

The legend of Johnny Appleseed is very close to the truth. He did spend most of his life wandering around what in his time was the Western frontier, planting and cultivating orchards, but he didn't travel as far as most people believe. Althouth he was responsible for introducing edible apples to about one-hundred-thousand square miles of territory, about three-quarters of his professional life was spent within the borders of Ohio. And although apples were his specialty, he was dead set against the practices of grafting and pruning, much to the detriment of the trees he planted and cared for.

Apples weren't his only interest in life. His days were spent in horticulture, true; but he devoted his evenings to preaching his own brand of fervent but peculiar Swedenborgianism. In terms of actual religious practice, Appleseed's convictions were closer to Jainism than to anything else; for instance, if he saw that his fire was burning the mosquitoes who ventured too close to the flames, he'd dowse it to save them. He was also merciful to the wasps that stung him while he was tending his trees, although he did once kill a rattlesnake that had bitten him, before he control himself.

Although he specialized in apples, he also sowed thousands of acres with a malodorous weed called dog fennel, wrongly believing that it helped to prevent malaria. The plant thrived and spread rapidly, and for many decades was one of the greatest trials of the farmers in the Midwest. Hay fever sufferers curse it to this day.

A life spent in making mistakes is not only more honorable but more useful than a life spent in doing nothing.

George Bernard Shaw

This is tough: What do you get when you add together (correctly) a macaroni box, several meat skewers, some elastic bands, a few dozen staples, a jackknife, and the imagination of a man named Door Felt? Hint: there's a clue in the question. The answer appears below.

The Shan language, which is spoken in parts of Burma, is a tonal language like many other Asian tongues. If intonated properly, the sentence "ma ma ma ma ma" in Shan can mean "Help the horse! A mad dog is coming!"

Language — a form of organized stutter.

Marshall McLuhan

In southern France during the thirteenth century, anyone convicted of lying had his nose and upper lip cut off.

A guy who twitches his lips is just another guy with a lip twitch — unless he's Humphrey Bogart.

Sammy Davis, Jr.

The prototype of the first modern adding machine.

Answers: 1947, 1940, 1960, 1956.

DECEMBER 29

Question: Can you guess the average elevations of these states?
Kentucky
Maryland
Delaware
California

Notable Births

1800	Charles Goodyear	1917	Thomas Bradley
1808	Andrew Johnson	1920	Viveca Lindfors
1809	William Gladstone	1937	Mary Tyler Moore
1876	Pablo Casals	1938	Jon Voight
1915	Robert Ruark	1952	Gelsey Kirkland

Notable Events

1170	Thomas à Becket assassinated
1782	First nautical almanac published
1851	First YMCA organized, Boston
1931	Discovery of heavy water announced
1933	Premier Duca of Romania assassinated
1934	Japan renounced Washington Naval Treaty of 1922
1972	*Life* magazine ceased publication
1977	Carter "abandoned" Washington, much "lust," said Polish translator, in error

Charles E. Bolton was a dapper, middle-aged man with silver hair and a silver mustache, who carried a gold-topped cane. He was also an occasional poet, who left most of his writings in strongboxes — of the stagecoaches he robbed.

Bolton was not at all your average Western outlaw. His victims unanimously agreed that he was a gentleman bandit who never used his gun except to flourish it in the driver's face. Bolton also claimed that he robbed only the stages, never the passengers themselves, although that's debatable. He was not a prolific criminal — perhaps half a dozen hold-ups at most can be attributed to him before his capture in 1883 (a laundry mark on a handkerchief eventually led to his identification). Most of his hauls netted him less than $1,000.

After his trial he was sentenced to serve a long term at San Quentin, but he was such an exceptionally well-behaved prisoner that he was paroled after only four years. He went straight after that, or, at least, was never again apprehended, and lived the remainder of his life in such obscurity that no one is really sure when he died, although 1899 is a good guess.

As a matter of fact, he wouldn't be remembered today if it weren't for the colorful pen name he used to sign his poetry. Charles E. Bolton in his heyday was better known as "Black Bart."

Many of our presidents have had other interests beyond government in which they have excelled, sometimes performing better work pursuing their avocations than they did as Chief Executive. Warren G. Harding was an expert and inveterate poker player, Woodrow Wilson a scholar and college president, Ike a fair golfer, Kennedy an historian, and Teddy Roosevelt a naturalist.

Our two leaders who've come closest to being removed from office had talents that few of their contemporaries appreciated. Andrew Johnson was an expert tailor who throughout his life, even while in the White House, made most of his own clothes. As a gesture of friendship when he was governor of Tennessee he made a full suit of clothes for the governor of neighboring Kentucky.

And Richard Nixon, though more renowned for his prowess as a bench warmer for Whittier College's football team, was an accomplished actor who once received the accolade of no less a judge than Darryl F. Zanuck. The mogul once told Nixon that a recent rendition of his was, "The most tremendous performance I've ever seen."

He called right after the "Checkers" speech.

He is as good as his word — and his word is no good.

Seamus McManus

Voters quickly forget what a man says.

Richard Nixon

Answer: 750; 350; 60; 2900.

DECEMBER 30

Notable Births

1865	Rudyard Kipling	1914	Bert Parks
1867	Simon Guggenheim	1919	Jo Van Fleet
1869	Stephen Leacock	1930	Jack Lord
1873	Al Smith	1935	Sandy Koufax

Notable Events

1853 Gadsden Purchase ratified
1862 Battle of Murfeesboro, Tennessee
1903 Iroquois Theater fire in Chicago killed 602 people
1913 Ductile tungsten patented, led to modern electric light
1949 France granted Vietnamese independence
1959 *George Washington*, first ballistic missile submarine, commissioned

Question: Can you define these ancient words?
brool
backstress
blackguard
mung

One of the best ideas the United States government has ever backed was — don't laugh — the United States Army Camel Corps. Unfortunately, it was the right idea at the wrong time.

Although the use of camels as beasts of burden for the army had been suggested sometime after the Louisiana Purchase was made, at that time it was considered sheer folly. When Army Lieutenant Edward Beale broached it again after the Mexican War had left the United States with tens of thousands of square miles of additional desert, it was once more regarded as a pipe dream. But Beale was confident that camels were much better suited to the rigors of the dry Southwestern lands than the army's traditional pack animals, the horse and the mule, and he continued to petition Washington to at least give the camels a trial. Finally he won the support of Jefferson Davis, and later convinced the Illinois senator, Shields, who managed to get $30,000 appropriated for an experimental program.

Two men were sent to Europe and the Middle East to observe camels in action. There they witnessed camels performing four times the workload of a horse, and doing it for days without food or water. They returned to the states with thirty-three beasts.

Initial trials were conducted in central Texas during the summer of 1856. At first, the citizenry acted derisively towards the unusual beasts, but when they saw camels loaded with over 1,200 pounds of gear moving about effortlessly, the sarcasm quickly changed to affection. A good number of Texans realized the camel could be the key to the rapid development of the nation's new area. Even more remarkable was the fact that over 75 percent of the money that had been originally appropriated for the program was returned to the government, unused.

The Camel Corps still had its critics, however, and so Lieutenant Beale, now in charge of the CC, decided he'd stifle public disdain once and for all. The supply roads to California were miserable byways at that time, and yet they were pivotal to the development of the territories of New Mexico and Arizona as well as to the southern part of the state of California. With his troop of camels and a handful of men, Beale built a road of far better quality, far more cheaply, and three times as quickly as anyone had estimated it could be done. Barring unforeseen circumstances, camels were there to stay, and rightly so.

As fate would have it, circumstances rapidly changed. The Civil War halted the development of the West, while railroad technology advanced rapidly in the North. After the war, the camel stood not a chance against the Iron Horse. Though several dozen animals had been imported from Asia during the conflict, the USACC was through. Some of the camels were given away, others auctioned off. Two freight companies eventually accounted for fifty-eight of the total of the seventy-five camels in the United States, with the others going to circuses, prospectors, homesteaders, and the like. The last-known survivor of this great experiment died in the Los Angeles Griffith Park Zoo in 1934.

A footnote to the Camel Corps is in order here. With the original thirty-three camels, the United States also acquired the services of three camel trainers. Elias Calles, one of these men, eventually settled in Mexico. One of his sons, Plutarco by name, later became minister of War, prime minister, and president of Mexico (1924-8). He is considered to be one of that nation's strongest chief executives.

As late as 1929, according to *Time* magazine, better than half the population of the York, Pennsylvania, region believed in witchcraft.

Answer: A guttural hum; a lady baker; one in charge of pots; a madding crowd.

DECEMBER 31

Question: Can you rank these countries according to the number of telephones in use per 100 people (from the greatest to fewest)?

Czechoslovakia
Greece
Iceland
Norway

Notable Births

1591	Jacques Cartier	1930	Odetta
1738	Lord Cornwallis	1943	Sarah Miles
1869	Henri Matisse	1943	John Denver
1880	George Marshall	1946	Cliff Richey

Notable Events

1600	British East India Company chartered
1775	Arnold repulsed at Quebec
1830	First parade by an occult society in America, Mobile, Alabama
1877	R.B. Hayes celebrated silver wedding anniversary
1917	Prohibition began in Canada
1955	General Motors became first corporation to make $1,000,000,000 profit in a year

Today is the last day this year to earn enough money to pay your taxes. Did you know that in 1974 and 1975 the following corporations paid no United States corporate income tax whatsoever, though each one was profitable in the year under which it is listed?

1974	1975
Ford	Ford
Lockheed	Delta Airlines
Honeywell	Northwest Airlines
U.S. Industries	Manufacturers Hanover
American Airlines	Western Electric
Eastern Airlines	Bethlehem Steel
American Electric Power	Lockheed
Allstate Insurance	National Steel
	Phelps Dodge
	Freeport Minerals

These corporations were able to get away tax free through investment tax credits and provisions in the United States corporate tax laws, which in some cases allow corporations to deduct tax payments made to foreign governments from their United States taxes. In fact, in 1975 the nation's 148 largest corporations paid about $20,000,000,000 to foreign countries in taxes, and only half that amount to the United States Treasury. Ford Motor Company reported its earnings in such a way that it actually got a $189,000,000 rebate on its taxes from 1973.

Every child born in America can hope to grow up to enjoy tax loopholes.

Richard Strout

Governments last as long as the under-taxed can defend themselves against the overtaxed.

Richard Berenson

During their periodic population explosions, the density of field mice can reach 12,000 per acre — so don't begrudge your cat his fun.

What passes for history today is often only an imaginative label given to an era by "historians" writing in a later time. Socrates, Plato, and Aristotle never made a claim for the "Greatness that was Greece" — the appelation comes from Plutarch. The Roman historian Tacitus did not know that his Empire was declining and falling — Edward Gibbon gave us those terms. The importance of the Magna Carta in history is mostly the invention of the English historian Coke. Although Gibbon lived in its midst, he was not aware that there was an Industrial Revolution going on. That term comes from Arnold Toynbee. Thomas Babington Macauley at his most chauvinistic never appreciated that there was a concept of the "English People"; and the great nineteenth-century American historian Bancroft was ignorant of the importance of the contemporary "Frontier" in U.S. history — that was defined by Frederick Jackson Turner in 1890.

. . . a historical fact is at bottom always arbitrary, always selective, always a fictionalized reconstruction secreted by the imagination of the historian who makes the "synthesis."

C.E. Ayres

If you've ever had the oriental delicacy called "birds' nest soup," you may have wondered what it really is. Well, it's a real bird's nest, made by one of the members of the swift family — and constructed from their spit.

And a final thought, for a Happy New Year:

Although you can't love every man,
Love a few as best as you can;
And though you cannot change the world,
Try.

I wonder if what we are publishing now is worth cutting down trees to make paper for the stuff.

Richard Brautigan

End of journey bring sadness.

Charlie Chan

I hate quotations. Tell me what you know.

Ralph Waldo Emerson

Answer: Iceland, Norway, Greece, Czechoslovakia (based on 1979 data).